OXFORD MONOGRAPHS IN INTERNATIONAL LAW

GENERAL EDITOR: PROFESSOR IAN BROWNLIE CBE, QC, FBA
Chichele Professor of Public International Law in the University of
Oxford and Fellow of All Souls College, Oxford.

HUMAN RIGHTS IN THE PRIVATE SPHERE

OXFORD MONOGRAPHS IN
INTERNATIONAL LAW

The aim of this series of monographs is to publish important
and original pieces of research on all aspects of public international law. Topics which are given particular prominence
are those which, while of interest to the academic lawyer, also
have important bearing on issues which touch the actual conduct
of international relations. None the less the series is wide in
scope and includes monographs on the history and philosophical
foundations of international law.

Human Rights in the Private Sphere

ANDREW CLAPHAM

CLARENDON PRESS · OXFORD

1993

Oxford University Press, Walton Street, Oxford OX2 6DP
Oxford New York Toronto
Delhi Bombay Calcutta Madras Karachi
Kuala Lumpur Singapore Hong Kong Tokyo
Nairobi Dar es Salaam Cape Town
Melbourne Auckland Madrid
and associated companies in
Berlin Ibadan

Oxford is a trade mark of Oxford University Press

Published in the United States
by Oxford University Press Inc., New York

British Library Cataloguing in Publication Data
Data available

Library of Congress Cataloging in Publication Data
Clapham, Andrew.
Human rights in the private sphere / Andrew Clapham.
p. cm. — (Oxford monographs in international law)
Includes bibliographical references and index.
1. Civil rights—Europe. 2. Civil law—Europe. 3. Civil rights.
4. Civil law. I. Title. II. Series.
KJC5132.C58 1993 341.4'81'094—dc20 93-7542
ISBN 0-19-825799-6

1 3 5 7 9 10 8 6 4 2

Typeset by Best-set Typesetter Ltd., Hong Kong
Printed in Great Britain
on acid-free paper by
Bookcraft Ltd., Midsomer Norton, Avon

Editor's Preface

THE third monograph concerned with the subject-matter of human rights to appear in this series is a thesis produced by a British lawyer working at the European University Institute in Florence under the supervision of my old friend Antonio Cassese. Andrew Clapham's substantial study focuses principally upon the relatively neglected area of relations between non-State bodies. This involves the important and yet complex area of putative obligations of the State to ensure or to encourage the observance of human rights standards in the sphere of private relations: for example, racial discrimination practised by clubs and exclusive clauses in wills.

The problems touch upon the fundamental question of identifying the content of human rights standards and the role of the State in enjoining good behaviour. The quality and utility of Dr Clapham's work is enhanced by the sections on the relevance of the European Convention on Human Rights in the Courts of the United Kingdom and the strong comparative element.

All Souls College,
Oxford

IAN BROWNLIE

20 July 1993

Acknowledgements

I SHOULD like to thank everyone at the European University Institute, Florence, who helped me during my time there. This book is a revised and updated version of my doctoral thesis, which I defended at the Institute in June 1991. I should like to thank my supervisor Professor Antonio Cassese for his inspiration, generosity, and enthusiasm. The Institute provides a unique environment in which to carry out research and I greatly profited from the encouragement and assistance of researchers, academic staff, and members of the administration.

As the recipient of a Human Rights Fellowship from the Council of Europe I am also indebted to many people who work in the Human Rights Directorate there. In particular I was lucky to meet Dr Andrew Drzemczewski when my thesis was in its early stages. His tireless enthusiasm and endless patience have contributed enormously to the final product. I should like to thank him and the other members of my jury: Sir Vincent Evans, Professor Juan Antonio Carrillo Salcedo, and Professor Luis María Díez-Picazo Giménez. I am lucky to have other friends who were also kind enough to listen and react when I explained the substance of my work. Special thanks go to Nomi Bar-Yaacov, Reiner Grundmann, Maggie Nicholson, Margo Picken, and Sean Smith.

Many others at the Institute, the Council of Europe, and elsewhere have helped me considerably and I should like to thank in particular Laura Biagiotti, Sandra Brière, Annick Bulckaen, Roberto Confaloneri, Lindsay Farmer, Eric Gallo, Meg Henry, Angelika Lanfranchi, Emir Lawless, James Lawson, Mark Neville, and Evie Zaccardelli.

The original thesis was awarded the Premio Obiettivo Europa by the Rotary Clubs of Florence, Colombes, and Valencia. I am very grateful for their generous support and for their interest in this study. Lastly, I must thank my parents, whose support has been unfailing.

A.B.C.

New York
31 August 1992

Contents

Abbreviations

AC	Appeal Cases (Law Reports, UK)
AFDI	*Annuaire français de droit international*
AJCL	*American Journal of Comparative Law*
AJIL	*American Journal of International Law*
All ER	*All England Law Reports*
Applic.	Application (European Commission of Human Rights)
ASDI	*Annuaire suisse de droit international*
ATF	*Recueil officiel des arrêts du Tribunal Fédéral Suisse*
B. Verf. GE	Entscheidungen des Bundesverfassungsgerichts (Decisions of the federal Constitutional Court)
BBC	British Broadcasting Corporation
BEUC	Bureau Européen de l'Union des Consommateurs
BG Bl.	*Bundesgesetzblatt* (Federal Law Gazette, Austria)
BGH	*Entscheidungen des Bundesgerichtshofes* (Decisions of Federal Supreme Court, FRG)
Bull. EC	*Bulletin of the European Communities*
BYIL	*British Year Book of International Law*
CDE	*Cahiers de droit européen*
Ch. D.	Chancery Division (Law Reports)
CLJ	*Cambridge Law Journal*
CLP	*Current Legal Problems*
CLR	Cyprus Law Reports
CMLR	Common Market Law Reports
CML Rev.	*Common Market Law Review*
Collection	*Collection of Decisions of the European Commission of Human Rights*
Corte Cost.	Corte Costituzionale
CRR	Canadian Rights Reporter
CSCE	Conference on Security and Cooperation in Europe
D. & R.	Decisions and Reports of the European Commission of Human Rights
EC	European Community
ECHR	European Convention on Human Rights
ECJ	European Court of Justice
ECR	European Court Reports (Reports of the Court of Justice of the European Communities, Luxembourg)
ECSC	European Coal and Steel Community
EEC	European Economic Community (Treaty)
EHRR	European Human Rights Reports
EIRR	*European Industrial Relations Review*
ELR	*European Law Review*
EPC	European Political Cooperation

EP Debs.	European Parliament Debates
EP Doc.	European Parliament Document
Eu. GRZ	*Europäische Grundrechte Zeitschrift*
EUI	European University Institute
FIDE	Fédération Internationale pour le Droit Européen
GAOR	General Assembly Official Records
GYIL	*German Yearbook of International Law*
Harv. CR-CLL Rev.	*Harvard Civil Rights-Civil Liberties Law Review*
HMSO	Her Majesty's Stationery Office
HRLJ	*Human Rights Law Journal*
HRQ	*Human Rights Quarterly*
HRR	*Human Rights Review*
IACHR	Inter-American Commission of Human Rights
ICJ Rep.	International Court of Justice Reports
ICLQ	*International and Comparative Law Quarterly*
ICR	Industrial Cases Reports
ILC	International Law Commission
ILJ	Industrial Law Journal
ILM	International Legal Materials
ILR	International Law Reports
ILRM	Irish Law Reports Monthly
Imm. AR	Immigration Appeal Reports
IR	Irish Reports (Republic of Ireland)
IRA	Irish Republican Army
IRLR	Industrial Relations Law Reports
ITU	International Telecommunications Union
LGR	Local Government Reports
LIEI	*Legal Issues of European Integration*
LQR	*Law Quarterly Review*
LS	*Legal Studies*
Mich. LR	*Michigan Law Review*
MLR	*Modern Law Review*
NILQ	*Northern Ireland Law Quarterly*
NILR	*Netherlands International Law Review*
NJ	*Nederlandse Jurisprudentie*
NJW	*Neue Juristische Wochenschrift*
NLJ	*New Law Journal*
NQHR	*Netherlands Quarterly of Human Rights*
NYIL	*Netherlands Yearbook of International Law*
OAS	Organization of American States
OJ	Official Journal of the European Community
PL	*Public Law*
PQ	*Parliamentary Quarterly*
QB	Queen's Bench (UK Law Reports)
RCDI	*Recueil des cours de l'Académie de Droit International de La Haye*

RDH/HRJ	*Revue des droits de l'homme/Human Rights Journal*
RDPSP	*Revue de droit public et de science politique en France et à l'étranger*
René Cassin	*René Cassin: Amicorum discipulorumque liber* (4 vols., Paris: International Institute of Human Rights, 1969–72)
Res. DH	Resolution of the Committee of Ministers of the Council of Europe
Rev.	*Revue*
RMC	*Revue du Marché Commun*
RTDE	*Revue trimestrielle de droit européen*
RUDH	*Revue universelle des droits de l'homme*
Series A	Reports of the European Court of Human Rights
Series B	Reports of the pleadings before the European Court of Human Rights
SLT	*Scottish Law Times*
SP & P.	*Social Philosophy and Policy*
UNTS	United Nations Treaty Series
UNY	*United Nations Yearbook*
WLR	Weekly Law Reports
Yearbook	*Yearbook of the European Convention on Human Rights*
YEL	*Yearbook of European Law*
Za. ÖRV	*Zeitschrift für ausländisches öffentliches Recht und Völkerrecht*

Table of Cases, Applications and Communications

EUROPEAN COMMISSION AND COURT OF HUMAN RIGHTS

EUROPEAN COURT OF JUSTICE

UNITED NATIONS COMMITTEE ON THE ELIMINATION OF RACIAL DISCRIMINATION

UNITED NATIONS HUMAN RIGHTS COMMITTEE

UNITED STATES

Table of National Legislation

Table of Treaties, Declarations, European Community Legislation and Draft International Instruments

Introduction

This book challenges several traditional assumptions concerning human rights. In particular it challenges the presumption that the fundamental rights and freedoms contained in the European Convention on Human Rights are irrelevant for cases which concern the sphere of relations between individuals. It asks whether victims should be protected from non-state actors, and attempts to develop a coherent approach to 'human rights in the private sphere'. It is the application of human rights law to the actions of private bodies which I label 'human rights in the private sphere' or 'the privatization of human rights'. The book concentrates on the rights contained in the European Convention on Human Rights, and their enforcement in the courts of the United Kingdom and at the European level: at the European Commission and Court of Human Rights in Strasbourg, and at the European Court of Justice in Luxembourg.[1]

WHY EXAMINE CASE-LAW?

The decisions of judges are clearly not the only aspect of the question of human rights in the private sphere. Issues such as sex discrimination, racial discrimination, and privacy are also determined by prejudice, politics, and power. Moreover, by concentrating on case-law one risks emphasizing the attention which the legal system gives to protecting the private affairs of men in the public eye; and one risks missing the inequality and violence suffered by women in the private sphere. By starting with reported cases one forgets the violations which never posed a problem for a judge;

---

[1] In this study the term 'human rights' is used to refer to the rights contained in the European Convention on Human Rights and other international human rights treaties. The term 'civil rights' has a technical meaning under the Convention and the scope of this term is covered in Ch. 7. 'Fundamental Community rights' are defined in Ch. 8. The term 'civil liberties' is usually associated with certain rights granted under national law in the United Kingdom. Cf. S. D. Bailey (ed.), *Human Rights and Responsibilities in Britain and Ireland: A Christian Perspective* (Basingstoke: Macmillan, 1988), 7. The present study does not attempt to define the term 'civil liberties'. The meaning to be given to this term would seem to be an ideological choice rather than a legal exercise. See the House of Lords 'Debate to call attention to the state of civil liberties under this Administration', 23 May 1990, HL Debs., cols. 904–35; see also 'On Liberties', *New Statesman and Society* editorial (27 Jan. 1988), 5; Gostin (1988).

and one avoids cases of hardship which are more pressing than the hard cases faced by higher courts.

But this study is not an abstract proposal for a blueprint with which to solve all the injustices of the private sphere. It is, in part, addressed to a particular community; this is the community of lawyers and decision-makers who already deal with the human rights law covered in this book. The arguments and policy put forward therefore remain more or less within the normative framework of the European Convention on Human Rights and the decisions which are influenced by it. Where appropriate, suggestions have been made about how to promote a wider dialogue between the courts and society.

In fact, the hidden effect of this case-law on public attitudes and perceptions surrounding the problems should not be underestimated. At least in the United Kingdom, many of the judgments covered in this book have already entered into the 'folklore' of the civil liberties debate and the popular appreciation of human rights law. More generally, conflicts and power struggles are now, more than ever, expressed in the language of rights. By concentrating on the responses of judges it is hoped that we may make sense of the rights debate and reveal some of the fundamental values we are trying to promote. Often the best way to understand the appeal and potential of rights is through an examination of the combat in the courtroom rather than by dissecting the power of politicians.

Two features of the research deserve explanation. First, this study is both descriptive and prescriptive. This is or should be inevitable when tackling the subject of human rights. Human rights are often the claims of the oppressed for better treatment; they represent ever-evolving standards and cannot be treated as static rules. Second, there is often detailed examination of the cases; this has been undertaken to challenge and confront those who criticize the 'vague' and 'impractical' nature of human rights. The detail is designed to show that human rights law can be used in practice as a 'higher law' against which other law can be judged.

WHY FOCUS ON THE EUROPEAN CONVENTION ON HUMAN RIGHTS?

At the national level the way judges use the Convention as an aid to interpretation suggests that this treaty, or indeed other international treaties such as the International Covenant on Civil and Political Rights, can play an important role even in domestic courts. These treaties need not be perceived as exotic foreign norms; they can be the basis for legitimate inspiration for judges faced with competing claims. This book concentrates on the interaction between the United Kingdom and the

Convention but the principles enunciated may be of relevance in other Common Law countries such as Nigeria, New Zealand, and Australia.[2] This is a particularly fertile area following the adoption in the Commonwealth context of the Bangalore Principles, the Harare Declaration on Human Rights, the Banjul Affirmation, and the Abuja Confirmation of the Domestic Application of International Human Rights Norms.[3] Essentially these documents stress the importance of developing 'a culture of respect for internationally stated human rights norms which sees these norms applied in the domestic laws of all nations and given full effect' (Harare). They stress the legitimate use that national judges may make of such international human rights: 'Obviously the judiciary cannot make an illegitimate intrusion into purely legislative functions; but the use of international human rights norms as an aid to construction and as a source of accepted moral standards involves no such intrusion' (Abuja).

The European Convention itself operates as a judicially enforceable code of human rights. Although it may be relied on at the rhetorical level, there are reasoned decisions as to its operation in practice which have an important influence on the legal orders of the Contracting Parties as well as on other legal orders.[4] The methods and case-law of the Convention's enforcement machinery in Strasbourg have influenced the supervision of the American Convention on Human Rights (1969), and some of the concepts and procedures are present in various ways in the African Charter of Human and Peoples' Rights (1981), the Draft Charter on Human and Peoples' Rights in the Arab World (Syracuse, 1986), and the Draft Pacific Charter of Human Rights (Apia, 1989). The Inter-American Court of Human Rights has already referred to the case-law of the European Court of Human Rights (although the European organs have not reciprocated with a reference to the less-developed American

[2] For the situation in Australia and some of the developments regarding the Commonwealth generally see M. Kirby, 'Implications for Australia of the Continuing Internationalization of Human Rights', paper presented to the conference 'Australia and Human Rights: Where to from here?' (Australian National University, 15–17 July 1992), to be published in P. Alston (ed.), *Australia and Human Rights* (Oxford: Oxford University Press).

[3] The Bangalore Principles are published in 14 *Commonwealth Law Bulletin* (1988), 1194; for the Harare Declaration see Commonwealth Secretariat, 'Developing Human Rights Jurisprudence', ii. 9; for the Banjul Affirmation see Commonwealth Secretariat, iii. 3; for the Abuja Confirmation see iv. 15; all these documents are available from Interights, London; see also Advisory Group, *Put our World to Rights: Towards a Commonwealth Human Rights Policy* (London: Commonwealth Human Rights Initiative, 1991). Most recently see the Balliol Statement, Oxford, 21–3 Sept. 1992 (not yet published), available from Commonwealth Secretariat and Interights, London.

[4] The most important of these other legal orders are the Inter-American system for the protection of human rights under the American Convention on Human Rights (1969), the European Community legal order, and the Canadian legal order following the adoption of the Charter of Rights and Freedoms in 1982. In addition it is worth noting that the European Convention on Human Rights was incorporated into the constitutions of twenty-four Commonwealth countries on independence.

case-law). Much of the analysis contained in this book is relevant for the application of the International Covenant on Civil and Political Rights.

To a limited extent the rules of interpretation for the Convention are neither those of constitutional law, nor those of international law. The Commission and Court repeatedly refer back to their own decisions and methods of interpretation, and in this way the Strasbourg system has found a sort of autonomy. The particularly 'European' flavour and tradition found in the judgments means that the Convention system can be analysed in relative isolation from other international human rights treaties. However, perspectives from the United States, Canada, and the European Community legal order have been included, together with several references to humanitarian law as well as public international law.

WHY FOCUS ON CIVIL AND POLITICAL RIGHTS?

Much of the thrust of the application of civil and political rights in the private sphere demands social, economic, and cultural action to make those rights effective. Where the state has positive obligations to ensure human rights in the private sphere there may be duties to tackle inequality in social, economic, and cultural structures. In fact, as will be seen, the Convention covers topics such as legal aid, trade union rights, education, and pollution. The ideological advantages of refusing to countenance the protection of civil and political rights unless social and economic rights are first recognized have now faded.

Much of the theory examined in this study will apply to international instruments on economic and social rights and their application at the international and national levels. But to cover those instruments properly deserves another book.

WHY FOCUS ON THE UNITED KINGDOM?

First, the Convention has a unique status in the United Kingdom. Of the twenty-four States which are bound by the Convention, eighteen have the Convention as part of their domestic law.[5] This arises either constitutionally or by legislative enactment.[6] Of the six States which do not have the

---

[5] Austria, Belgium, Cyprus, the Czech and Slovak Federal Republic, Finland, France, Germany, Greece, Italy, Liechtenstein, Luxembourg, Malta, The Netherlands, Portugal, San Marino, Spain, Switzerland, Turkey.

[6] For some of the policy implications of this method of incorporating international law into domestic law see Jackson (1992: 310–40).

Convention as part of domestic law,[7] only the United Kingdom has no written constitution.[8]

Second, in the twenty-three States which have the Convention as part of domestic law or have a written constitution, the rights and values found in the Convention are often reproduced in their constitutions. This means that when questions of civil or human rights arise at the national level, they are decided not on the basis and case-law of the Convention, but usually by reference to the States' own constitutional and legal values. The debates concerning the applicability of constitutional rights to the behaviour of private bodies are relevant but not identical to the questions surrounding the application of the European Convention to private bodies. This is partly because these constitutions often contain relevant values not found in the European Convention, such as freedom of contract, or the right to develop, or other commercial freedoms; such constitutional values have often been seen as conflicting with human rights such as the right not to be discriminated against, or the right to belong to a trade union. Because the same conflicts do not really arise in the same way under the Convention a detailed consideration of the approach taken under different European constitutions has not been included in this book.

Third, the role of the European Convention on Human Rights in the United Kingdom is in a state of flux. Different judges have different ideas as to its usefulness. This book was written over a period which saw fairly intense debate on the subject. However, the debate has rarely moved past the question: do we trust the judges? Parts of this book attempt to show the real relevance of the Convention. This is attempted not by reference to abstract theories of legitimization, but by occasional speculations as to whether a different result might have been achieved had the Convention had a different status in the internal law of the United Kingdom.

Fourth, the legal culture in the United Kingdom is very different from that of the vast majority of its European neighbours. Not only do the judges have a very different career structure and training,[9] but also in the United Kingdom there is no tradition of written constitutional values or fundamental human rights with which the legislator may not interfere.[10]

---

[7] Denmark, Iceland, Ireland, Norway, Sweden, United Kingdom.

[8] Although San Marino could be said to have no written constitution.

[9] See Prof. G. F. Mancini, 'Politics and the Judges: The European Perspective', *MLR* (1980), 1, where he states that he is forced to leave out of his discussion the English judges due to their special characteristics, individually and as a group.

[10] Note this dismissal of 'fundamental' rights: 'In particular, the description of those familial rights and privileges enjoyed by parents in relation to their children as "fundamental" or "basic" does nothing, in my judgment, to clarify either the nature or the extent of the concept which it sought to describe' (Lord Oliver in *Re K.D. (a Minor) (Ward: Termination of Access)* [1988] 1 All ER 577 at 588). Lord Oliver was referring specifically to the

Fifth, the United Kingdom has a relatively underdeveloped system of public/administrative law. The debate relating to the appropriateness of such a system illuminates the main concern of this research: should human rights apply in the private sphere? Indeed it may be that the very absence of an autonomous public law system in England has led to some of the general confusion over the applicability of the Convention in the private sphere.

Sixth, privatization was a political priority of the United Kingdom's Government throughout the 1980s. Not only were former state bodies privatized but a number of state activities were tendered out to private firms. By 1992 the United Kingdom had its first 'private' prison.[11] In addition, some sectors were deregulated so that control became vested in private self-regulatory bodies. In the context of an examination of the European Convention this meant that some applications in Strasbourg started life as complaints about the activities of nationalized/public companies and finished after the said company had been privatized.[12] The privatization phenomena will be of increasing relevance across Europe: while 'Human Rights Now' may have been the slogan of the 1980s, the graffiti on the walls of Bucharest and Sofia at the beginning of the 1990s call for 'Privatization Now'.

Seventh, interest groups in the United Kingdom have played an important role both in supporting applications before the Convention organs and in submitting 'third-party' interventions before the Court. Both these roles are crucial in the context of the operation of human rights in the private sphere (see Chapter 9).

Lastly, one might note that an examination of the reception which the United Kingdom judges already accord an international treaty such as the Convention may be pertinent for actors in other jurisdictions similarly grappling with the national application of international human rights treaties.

Different chapters in this book may appeal to different audiences and may even be read in isolation. Some are more or less descriptive accounts of the status of the Convention in the United Kingdom legal order

Convention and its interpretation by the European Court of Human Rights, in *R. v. UK* (1987), Series A, vol. 121.

[11] See A. Sampson, 'Crime and Furbishment', *Guardian* (1 Apr. 1992), 15.

[12] e.g. during the *Malone* case (judgment of 2 Aug. 1984, Series A, vol. 82) the relevant sector of the Post Office became British Telecom; during *Baggs* v. *UK* (Applic. 9310/81, friendly settlement approved by the Commission, 8 July 1987) British Airports Authority became Heathrow Airport Ltd.; see also *Case of Powell and Rayner*, judgment of 21 Feb. 1990, Series A, vol. 172. (The issue is also pertinent in Community law, where the European Court of Justice had to decide whether to apply duties under a directive to the British Gas Corporation: the Corporation was privatized by the time of the case. See Ch. 8.)

(Chapters 1 and 2); others, such as Chapter 5, are purely philosophical. Some are addressed to international lawyers (Chapter 4) while others may be of interest to specialists in European law (Chapters 7 and 8). One chapter is of purely comparative interest and has been included for illustrative rather than analytical purposes (Chapter 6, dealing with the United States and Canada).

Part I has two functions: to show the variety of ways in which the Convention is used in the United Kingdom courts and to construct the framework which will enable us to examine the specific question of the Convention's use against private bodies in the United Kingdom. Part I does not specifically examine the Convention's use against private parties, as this has to be done in the light of the developments in the case-law of Strasbourg and Luxembourg which are dealt with in detail in Part II.

Part II starts with two chapters which deal with 'the theory'. The first of these, Chapter 4, begins with references to the way the issue has been dealt with in various fields of international law, and then outlines two approaches to the question of the application of human rights in the private sphere. The first approach suggests that a dynamic, evolutive interpretation of the European Convention implies that it is applicable in the private sphere; the second suggests that denying such an application, for whatever reason, creates a 'dangerous' distinction between 'public' and 'private' which, apart from the practical difficulties, not only hinders progressive change but also leaves many victims unprotected.

Having suggested why the Convention should apply in the private sphere, Part II continues (in Chapter 5) by analysing theoretical arguments as to *why* human rights merit protection, and so suggests *how* the Convention might apply in the private sphere.

Next come three chapters which deal with 'the practice'. Chapter 6 involves a brief exposition of the problems encountered by the United States Supreme Court when faced with questions of fundamental rights and 'state action'. These are similar to some of the problems faced by the European Commission and Court of Human Rights. A central supra-national or federal court will not only have to be continually aware of straining its own legitimacy, but also has to reconcile protection of cultural pluralism with minimum standards. Moreover, similar tensions exist—the tension between white racists and various black or Asian groups; the tension between corporate power and organized labour; the tension between private property and its public use. Further comparisons are made with the Canadian Charter of Rights and Freedoms and its judicial interpretation.

Chapter 7 examines in detail the case-law of the European Commission and Court of Human Rights, Article by Article. In this way it is hoped to illuminate some of the outstanding problems which still surround the third-party effect of the European Convention on Human Rights. Chapter 8 deals with the Community legal order and the case-law of the European Court of Justice in Luxembourg. In particular this last Court has had to address the issue of protecting fundamental rights in the private sector when deciding whether directives (such as the equal treatment directive) apply 'horizontally', that is, against non-state organs.

The last two chapters address the implications of these theoretical suggestions and practical developments. Chapter 9 looks at the procedural implications of the application of human rights in the private sphere. In particular it highlights the importance of third-party briefs in Strasbourg or at the national level where the case affects the interests of individuals and groups not party to the proceedings. Finally, Chapter 10 revisits the terrain covered in Part I but considers the implications which the European developments have for the courts in the United Kingdom. Chapter 10 synthesizes the developments concerning the 'privatization of human rights' at the European level with the study of the relevance of the Convention in the United Kingdom legal order. The United Kingdom legal order has been examined in detail because a reference to the Convention will have a different significance depending on the context in which it is raised at the national level. For instance, the use of the Convention as part of Community law in the national courts involves mandatory reference to the decisions of the European Court of Justice, and so it is the inter-pretation of that Court which will be considered; whereas if the British courts are considering a case concerning judicial review of administrative action, the Convention's use against private bodies may depend on whether the court considers that this is a body over which the courts should have the power of judicial review.[13] Part I operates to define these contexts clearly. It may be that where the Common Law is under consideration the public or private nature of the defendant will be irrelevant, but in the context of judicial review or European Community law this will be of paramount importance. Not only do the different contexts involve different substantive legal questions, but they will involve different background considerations. Judges may have very different intuitive reactions to rein-terpreting the most recent legislation enacted as a result of a European Community directive, and abolishing or rewriting elements of ancient Common Law offences such as are found in the laws of libel. Because so much depends in English law on the remedy being sought, it is vital to distinguish the different contexts in which the Convention may arise.[14]

---

[13] See R. v. *Panel on Take-Overs and Mergers, ex p. Prudential Bache Inc.* [1987] 2 WLR 699.

[14] '[F]or typically English law fastens, not upon principles but upon remedies' (per Lord Wilberforce in *Davey* v. *Spelthorne BC* [1984] AC 262 at 276).

The dichotomy between the national and international dimensions has had to be exaggerated, as this study is concerned with standards of respect for European human rights and private bodies, and at the European Court of Human Rights only state behaviour is justiciable. However, at the national level, in some circumstances, no such restrictions apply, so private bodies may have a duty to behave in conformity with European norms as developed through the decisions of the European supranational organs. The very strength of the Convention is its ability to straddle the national and international dimensions, synthesizing the international standards with national enforcement procedures.

The conclusions draw together some of the threads which run through this study and addresses the general question of the application of human rights in the sphere of relations between non-state actors. It offers a new approach to the question based on the comparative material covered in Parts I and II. This approach is presented as the application of 'human rights in the private sphere' or the 'privatization of human rights'. By calling for the recognition of the privatization of human rights it is not suggested that the State should divest itself of responsibility for ensuring respect for human rights; instead it is suggested that the State should not be considered to have a monopoly over the abuse of power.

PART I

The Different Ways in which the European
Convention on Human Rights is Relevant,
or may become Relevant, in the United
Kingdom Courts

I

The Relevance of the Convention in the United Kingdom Courts

The United Kingdom was one of the key actors in the drafting of the European Convention on Human Rights, was one of the original signatories on 5 November 1950, and on 8 March 1951 was the first State to ratify the Convention. Although the Convention has not been incorporated into domestic law it is surprisingly relevant in the domestic courts of the United Kingdom. Chapters 1 and 2 deal with some of the case-law of the British courts and these decisions have been analysed under a number of headings. The Convention may be relevant in the following situations:

1. as an aid to statutory interpretation (see Section 1.1);
2. as part of the Common Law (Section 1.2);
3. as part of European Community law (Section 1.3);
4. as a factor to be taken into consideration by administrative bodies when exercising their discretion (Section 1.4);
5. due to a pending application in Strasbourg (Section 2.1);
6. due to the case-law of the European Court of Human Rights (Section 2.2);
7. due to a 'friendly settlement' under the Convention (Section 2.3).

1.1 THE CONVENTION AS AN AID TO STATUTORY INTERPRETATION

In 1974 the House of Lords first used the Convention as an aid to statutory interpretation. In *R.* v. *Miah* Lord Reid, who delivered the only opinion, relied on Article 11(2) of the Universal Declaration of Human Rights and Article 7 of the European Convention on Human Rights to demonstrate that it was 'hardly credible that any government department would promote, or that Parliament would pass, retrospective criminal legislation'.[1]

This conclusion stemmed from the general principle that, so far as the language permits, Parliament is presumed to legislate in accordance

---

[1] [1974] 1 WLR 683 at 698.

with international law.[2] Where the rule of international law is straight-forward, as it was in this case—States may not create criminal offences retroactively—then the solution is relatively easy.[3] But other human rights are more problematic; their ambit depends largely on how much recognition is given to the individual right by any one court or judge.

A second case illustrates how different judges are prepared to give different emphases to the right in question. Article 9(1) of the Convention states that everyone has the right to freedom of religion, and this right can be restricted in order to protect the rights and freedoms of others (Article 9(2)). When the Court of Appeal in *Ahmed* v. *Inner London Education Authority*[4] was asked to consider Section 30 of the Education Act 1944 in the light of Article 9, it was divided as to the weight which should be given to freedom of religion.

The case concerned a Muslim schoolteacher with a contract to teach five days a week. The contract provided for a lunch break from 12.30 to 1.30 p.m. Mr Ahmed, as a devout Muslim, had a duty to attend Friday prayers, unless he had an excuse, as defined in the Koran. The prayers at the nearest mosque were from 1 p.m. to 2 p.m. This meant he missed about forty-five minutes of teaching each Friday. The Inner London Education Authority proposed to vary his contract to a $4\frac{1}{2}$-day week and Mr Ahmed resigned. The case arose out of a claim for unfair dismissal. It turned on an interpretation of Article 30 of the Education Act 1944, the relevant part of which reads as follows: 'no teacher . . . shall . . . receive any less emolument or be deprived of or disqualified for any promotion or any other advantage by reason of . . . his religious opinions or his attending or omitting to attend religious worship.'

Lord Denning read this as subject to the implied phrase 'so long as the school timetable allows'. He dismissed the European Convention as 'drawn in such vague terms that it can be used for all sorts of unreasonable claims and provoke all sorts of litigation'.[5] He continued, 'as so often happens with high-sounding principles, they have to be brought down to earth. They have to be applied in a work-a-day world.'[6] Lord Denning determined that Mr Ahmed's right to manifest his religion was subject to the rights of

---

[2] *Bloxham* v. *Favre* [1883] 8 PD 101 Sir James Hannen, P. It is not necessary here to explain the effect of international law in the internal legal order of the UK. As will be seen, the Convention has a rather special role.

[3] Similarly, in *R.* v. *Deery* [1977] 20 Yearbook 827, Art. 7 was used to decide that the Firearms Regulations Amendment Order (NI) 1976, which increased the maximum term of imprisonment from five to ten years in Northern Ireland, did not operate retroactively. So a sentence of six years passed on Deery for an offence committed before the order was an error. However, it was stated that should a statute clearly suggest retroactive penalties then the court must follow the statute and the presumption of adherence to treaty obligations would be rebutted.

[4] *Ahmed* v. *ILEA* [1978] 1 All ER 574.

[5] At 577.   [6] Ibid.

others, namely, the education authority and 'the children whom he is paid
to teach', and concluded: 'I see nothing in the European Convention to
give Mr Ahmed any right to manifest his religion on Friday afternoons in
derogation of his contract of employment, and certainly not on full pay.'[7]
The Court of Appeal found against Mr Ahmed.

Scarman, LJ (as he then was), dissented. He took a rather different
approach to the interpretation of Section 30:

> there were until recently no substantial religious groupings in our country which
> fell outside the broad categories of Christian and Jew. So long as there was no
> discrimination between them no problem was likely to arise. The five day school
> week, of course, takes care of the Sabbath and of Sunday as days of special
> religious observance. But with the advent of new religious groups in our society
> s. 30 assumes a new importance . . . society has changed since 1944; so also has
> the legal background. Religions such as Islam and Buddhism, have substantial
> followings among our people. Room has to be found for teachers and pupils of
> the new religions in the educational system, if discrimination is to be avoided.
> This calls not for a policy of the blind eye but one of understanding. The system
> must be made sufficiently flexible to accommodate their beliefs and their observ-
> ances, otherwise they will suffer discrimination, a consequence contrary to the
> spirit of s. 30, whatever the letter of that law.[8]

Scarman, LJ, then listed the legal changes which had occurred since
1944, including the United Kingdom's international obligations under the
European Convention and the Charter of the United Nations. He continued: 'Today therefore, we have to construe and apply s. 30 not against
a background of the law and society of 1944 but in a multi-racial society
which has accepted international obligations and enacted statutes designed
to eliminate discrimination on grounds of race, religion, colour or sex.'[9]

A number of points arise out of these two very different approaches.
First, the use of the Convention in the Court of Appeal, which for most
practical purposes is the final court of appeal,[10] depended not so much on
its precise legal status as an aid to interpretation but on the willingness of
the individual judges to take the Convention into account—not only its
provisions but also the philosophy and practice behind it.

Second, the rule which is generally supposed to legitimize the use of
the Convention as an aid to statutory interpretation—that the legislature
is presumed to legislate in accordance with international obligations—is
not relied on as such. Clearly 'Parliament in 1944 never addressed its
mind to the problems of this case.'[11] Indeed in most cases of statutory

---

[7] At 578.   [8] At 583.   [9] Ibid.
[10] See the comment of Donaldson, MR: 'So in practical terms of the everyday life of this
country this Court is the final court of appeal and must always be the final court of appeal in
circumstances of real urgency' (*C. v. S.* [1987] 2 WLR 1123).
[11] Scarman, LJ, at 585.

interpretation in accordance with international human rights obligations, it is unlikely that the facts of the case will have been foreseen when Parliament debated the Act. One could go further and say that even if they were foreseen, the Act was probably deliberately left ambiguous due to compromises and amendments incorporated during the legislative process. The strength of a judicially enforceable human rights instrument, such as the European Convention on Human Rights, lies in the fact that unforeseen situations can be resolved without the necessity of implementing new legislation. Problems can be resolved by virtue of the dynamic nature of the Convention, according to changing perceptions of morals and society.

The European Court of Human Rights itself, in a case concerning laws on homosexuality in Northern Ireland, stated in *Dudgeon* v. *United Kingdom*:

> As compared with the era when that legislation was enacted, there is now a better understanding, and in consequence an increased tolerance, of homosexual behaviour to the extent that in the great majority of the Member States of the Council of Europe it is no longer considered to be necessary or appropriate to treat homosexual practices of the kind now in question as in themselves a matter to which the sanctions of the criminal law should be applied.[12]

But, theoretically, the question of Parliament's intention remains. In 1977 the Northern Ireland Standing Advisory Commission on Human Rights felt it was not clear whether the presumption of conformity with the Convention applies only to legislation enacted *after* ratification of the Convention.[13]

The case which is generally relied on as a precedent that it is legitimate to refer to a treaty in order to construe legislation is *Salomon* v. *Commissioners for Customs and Excise*.[14] In that case Diplock, LJ, stated that there was 'a *prima facie* presumption that Parliament does not intend to act in breach of international law, including therein treaty obligations'. But he was in that case construing an Act which, although it did not say so, was deliberately intended to carry out the terms of a Treaty[15]—a Treaty, incidentally, which was ratified *after* the Royal Assent of the Act which had implemented its terms into domestic law! Diplock, LJ, suggested that courts may refer to treaties where 'extrinsic evidence' makes it plain that the legislation 'was intended to fulfil Her Majesty's Government's

---

[12] (1981), Series A, vol. 45, at 24.

[13] *The Protection of Human Rights by Law in Northern Ireland*, Northern Ireland Standing Advisory Commission on Human Rights, Cmnd. 7009 (London: HMSO, 1977), para. 5.25.

[14] [1967] 2 QB 116 at 143.

[15] Convention on the Valuation of Goods for Customs Purposes 1950 (Cmnd. 9233), and Customs and Excise Act 1952.

obligations under a particular convention',[16] even if the statute does not expressly refer to the Convention. The judgment of Diplock, LJ, would seem to suggest that only legislation which was passed with the intention of fulfilling obligations under the European Convention on Human Rights can be interpreted with respect to the Convention. He even warns: 'Of course the court must not merely guess that the statute was intended to give effect to a particular Convention. The intrinsic evidence of the connection must be cogent.'[17] However, future references to this passage by Diplock, LJ, seem to have ignored the need for such 'linkage' and the rule of construction now seems to be that 'in the absence of very clear words indicating the contrary . . . [there is] a presumption that Parliament has legislated in a manner consistent, rather than inconsistent, with the United Kingdom's treaty obligations'.[18]

For the reasons already given, it is suggested that the concept of giving effect to the intentions of Parliament is an unhelpful one. A better justification for using the Convention as an aid to statutory interpretation is that all statutes ought to be interpreted 'so as to be in conformity with international law'.[19] This is not, however, the attitude which was taken by the House of Lords Select Committee on a Bill of Rights in 1978;[20] yet there is some evidence that judges are prepared to take this broad brush approach.

Lord Scarman, after stating that neither the European Convention nor the decision of the European Court of Human Rights in The *Sunday Times* case was part of the law of the United Kingdom, went on to justify his reference to the Convention:

I do not doubt that, in considering how far we should extend the application of Contempt of Court, we must bear mind the impact of whatever decision we may be minded to make on the international obligations assumed by the United Kingdom under the European Convention. If the issue should ultimately be, as I

---

[16] At 143.

[17] Ibid.

[18] Donaldson, MR, in *R. v. Sec. of State for the Home Department, ex p. Brind* [1990] 1 All ER 469 at 477; and see the judgment of the House of Lords in this case, [1991] 1 All ER 720, where Lord Ackner affirmed this view.

[19] Diplock, LJ, *Salomon v. Commissioners for Customs and Excise* [1967] 2 QB 116 at 141: 'I think we are entitled to look at it, because it is an instrument which is binding in international law: and we ought always to interpret our statutes so as to be in conformity with international law. Our Statute does not in terms incorporate the Convention nor refer to it. But that does not matter. We can look at it.' He is of course referring to the Convention on the Valuation of Goods for Customs Purposes.

[20] *Report of the Select Committee on a Bill of Rights*, House of Lords paper 176 (London: HMSO, 1978): 'Furthermore there is a case for saying that even the tenuous influence the Convention does have on the construction of Acts of Parliament is confined to Acts passed since we ratified the Convention. . . . The justification for invoking the terms of a Treaty to construe an Act seems to be that Parliament must be taken to be aware of our international obligations when it passed the Act' (at 28).

think in this case it is, a question of legal policy, we must have regard to the Country's international obligation to observe the European Convention as interpreted by the European Court of Human Rights.[21]

This seems to be a more 'honest' approach to the use of the Convention, as no reference is made to the implied intention of the framers of the secondary legislation under consideration.[22] It could, however, be challenged on the grounds that it denies the 'transformation' tradition of English law. This states that treaties ratified by the executive are not part of the law until transformed by Parliament through legislation into domestic laws.[23] It is suggested that this challenge fails. It fails due to the special nature of the European Convention on Human Rights and other relevant human rights instruments. The Convention declares principles; these principles can be legitimately used to interpret statutes where there is evidence of an intention by the legislature to give effect to those principles, either in the statute under consideration or in another statute. So, in this way, when Scarman (in *Ahmed* v. *Inner London Education Authority*) referred to the Convention he referred to it in the context of other legislation dealing with discrimination: the sex discrimination and race relations Acts and also the Trade Union and Labour Relations Act 1974.[24]

It remains to be seen to what extent the Convention will be used in cases involving statutes passed before the United Kingdom's ratification of the Convention. But the approach of the House of Lords Select

---

[21] *A.-G.* v. *BBC* [1980] 3 WLR 109 at 130.

[22] The court here had to decide if a Local Valuation Court was a 'court' for the purposes of RSC Order 52 r. 1(2) relating to contempt of court.

[23] See *The Parlement Belge* (1879) 4 PD, 129. D. H. Ott has noted that in this case the judge, Sir Robert Phillimore, was concerned not to deprive British subjects of their rights of action under Common Law without their consent. Phillimore held that private rights could not be removed without an Act of Parliament. The judgment can therefore be seen as an incidence of the court's protecting the citizen from the executive and insisting on the necessity of parliamentary legislation. The precedent need not prevent the courts from interpreting enactments so that they conform to the international protection which the executive has decided to guarantee citizens under its jurisdiction. See Ott (1987: 39). For a number of suggestions relating to policy reasons for not automatically applying international law see Jackson (1992: 310–40).

[24] This is not dissimilar to Ronald Dworkin's account of Judge Earl's theory of legislation: 'He said that statutes should be constructed from texts not in historical isolation but against a background of what he called general principles of law: he meant that judges should construct a statute so as to make it conform as closely as possible to principles of justice assumed elsewhere in the law. He offered two reasons. First, it is sensible to assume that legislators have a general and diffuse intention to respect traditional principles of justice unless they clearly indicate the contrary. Second, since a statute is part of a larger intellectual system, the law as a whole, it should be constructed so as to make that larger system coherent in principle' (Dworkin 1986: 19–20).

Committee on a Bill of Rights is difficult to justify, resting as it does on an implied intent at a particular point in time.[25]

The above analysis has dealt only with statutes but the general interpretative rule has been held to apply to subordinate legislation as well.[26]

1.1.1 The special case of statutory interpretation, where the statute is similar to the Convention

At the time of writing this situation has arisen in the case of six statutes:

Magna Carta 1297;
the Bill of Rights 1688;
the Emergency Provision Act (Northern Ireland) 1973;
the Police and Criminal Evidence Act 1984;
the Interception of Communications Act 1985;
the Criminal Justice Act 1988.

So far, the European Convention has only been really relied on in the case of the Emergency Provisions Act, Section 6(2) of which limits the grounds on which a confession can be excluded: where 'the accused was

---

[25] It has been suggested that the use of the Convention as an aid to interpretation for statutes passed before the Convention's ratification can still be rationalized in terms of 'Parliament's intention', 'if one regards the parliamentary intention on which the presumption is based as being that the courts will interpret legislation in accordance with the developing international obligations of the United Kingdom' (Duffy 1980: 585). The problem with this approach is that often the developing international obligations are strongly resisted by the UK Government, as evidenced by the numerous failures to achieve 'friendly settlements' in Strasbourg in cases involving the UK. So it has to be admitted that it is unlikely that the legislature intended the courts to interpret legislation in accordance with the evolving obligations imposed on the UK; but rather in accordance with how the Government perceived those obligations. Another argument against such an approach is that international obligations may oblige States to take positive measures to ease discrimination. This is apparent not only from the Court's decision in the *Marckx* case (1980), Series A, vol. 31, but also from the comments of the Commission when considering Mr Ahmed's application to them: 'the Commission further observes that the object of Article 9 is essentially that of protecting the individual against unjustified interference by the State, but that there may also be positive obligations inherent in the effective "respect" for the individual's freedom of religion.' *X* v. *UK* 22 D. & R. 27 at 33. Therefore on the intention theory we have to conclude that if Parliament intends to comply with the obligation to take positive measures, then it will have already taken these measures to a sufficient degree, and so there can be no justification for judicial interference.

[26] See *Brind* v. *Sec. of State* [1991] 1 All ER 720 at 734 per Lord Ackner: 'It is well settled that the convention may be deployed for the purpose of the resolution of an ambiguity in English primary or subordinate legislation.' In this case there was no perceived ambiguity and the issue was therefore whether there was a presumption that administrative discretion conferred by Parliament had to be exercised within Convention limits. The House of Lords held there was no such presumption. To make such a presumption 'would be to go far beyond the resolution of an ambiguity' (per Lord Bridge at 723). See also below s. 1.4, and the discussion of the *Brind* case.

subjected to *torture* or to *inhuman* or *degrading treatment* in order to induce him to make the statement'.

McGonigal, LJ, in the Northern Ireland Court of Appeal found that the terms 'torture', 'inhuman', and 'degrading treatment' were taken from Article 3 of the European Convention and that Parliament was accepting as guidelines the standards laid down in the Convention.[27] He went on to examine some of the Commission's case-law on Article 3. This use of the Convention's case-law is legitimized by a clear parliamentary intention.

An interesting question arises out of the Bill of Rights 1688, where it is provided 'that excessive baile ought not to be required nor excessive fines imposed nor cruell and unusuall punishments inflicted'.[28] In *Williams* v. *Home Office (No. 2)*,[29] although the judge was referred to the European Convention on Human Rights and to the Standard Minimum Rules for the Treatment of Prisoners (1973),[30] he decided to read the Bill of Rights 1688 as only prohibiting punishment which was both cruel *and* unusual. Therefore as the punishment (solitary confinement) was not unusual, it was not prohibited by the Bill of Rights 1688. Clearly a prohibition on 'cruell and unusuall punishments' can be interpreted so that either cruel or unusual punishments are prohibited. If a rationale is needed for taking such a step then reference to Rule 31 of the Standard Minimum Rules for the Treatment of Prisoners would seem to be sufficient: 'Rule 31:— Corporal punishment, punishment by placing in a dark cell, and all cruel, inhuman or degrading punishment shall be completely prohibited as punishments for disciplinary offences.' Taken together with the Bill of Rights 1688 this is enough to suggest that cruel punishment is prohibited by law. The lack of weight which was given to the Rules and the Convention where an ambiguity arose does not suggest that the new European Prison Rules[31] will be readily referred to.[32]

The weakest statutory link to the Convention is Magna Carta 1297,

---

[27] *R.* v. *McCormick* (1978) 21 Yearbook 789; for a decision on the same point see *R.* v. *McGrath* (1980) NILQ 288 (Court of Appeal).

[28] *Halsbury's Statutes of England*, vi (3rd edn.), 490.

[29] [1981] 1 All ER 1211.

[30] Resolution of the Committee of Ministers of the Council of Europe, 73(5) *European Yearbook* (1973), 323, Rule 31.

[31] Rec. R(87)3 of the Committee of Ministers. These rules substantially modernize the old Standard Minimum Rules and are intended to improve the practical application of the rules and contain 'new moral standards'.

[32] See *R.* v. *Sec. of State for the Home Department and Another, ex p. Herbage (No. 2)* [1987] 1 All ER 324, Court of Appeal interlocutory proceedings. In this case the applicant relied on the Bill of Rights 1688 and the European Convention together. The Court of Appeal found that the right under the Bill of Rights 1688, not to have 'cruell and unusuall punishments' inflicted, was a fundamental right going beyond the Prison Rules 1964 and may be grounds for relief under RSC Order 53. On the question of interim relief see the decision of the House of Lords in the same case, [1987] QB 872.

which was referred to by the Court of Appeal in 1975.[33] In *R.* v. *Secretary of State for the Home Department, ex parte Phansopkar*,[34] Scarman, LJ (as he then was), referred to the delay involved with applications for immigration and stated:

Delay of this order appears to me to infringe at least two human rights recognized, and therefore protected by, English law. Justice delayed is justice denied: 'We will not deny or defer to any man either justice or right:' Magna Carta. This hallowed principle of our law is now reinforced by the European Convention for the Protection of Human Rights 1950.[35]

Scarman later refers to the combination of Magna Carta 1297 and the Convention to show that the law would not permit the Secretary of State to maintain his position, and that the Immigration Act 1971 would be interpreted accordingly. It is unlikely that such a link between Magna Carta and the Convention will be relied on in the courts in the future. But what is probable is that statutes passed as a result of decisions against the United Kingdom (or other States) in Strasbourg will be interpreted with reference to the Convention and its case-law.[36]

The Police and Criminal Evidence Act 1984 states in Section 76(2) that confessions obtained by 'oppression' are inadmissible. 'Oppression' is defined in Section 76(8) as including 'torture, inhuman or degrading treatment and the use or threat of violence whether or not amounting to torture'. This is based in part on Article 3 of the Convention. So far, the extent to which the Convention or its case-law will come to be relevant in this field remains to be seen.

It is worth mentioning that Section 2 of the Interception of Telecom-

---

[33] Most of Magna Carta's provisions have been repealed; it is Clause 29 of the 1297 text which the Court of Appeal referred to (see below). This is one of the few remaining clauses. For further detail on the history of Magna Carta see Pallister (1971).

[34] [1975] 3 All ER 487 at 510.

[35] At 510; the second human right is referred to later on as being the right to respect for privacy and family life as defined by Art. 8 of the Convention.

[36] For example, the Contempt of Court Act 1981 (although none of the provisions is directly modelled on the Convention) was passed as a result of the *Sunday Times* case (1979) Series A, vol. 30. In *A.-G.* v. *English* [1982] 3 WLR 278, which was decided subsequent to the enactment of the new Act, the references to the Convention are rather oblique and perhaps deliberately avoid taking into account the European Court of Human Rights' decision which effectively 'overruled' the House of Lords decision in *A.-G.* v. *Times Newspapers* [1974] AC 273. For a detailed examination of the Act in this context see Lowe (1983). In his dissenting speech in *Guardian Newspapers* v. *Sec. of State for Defence* [1985] AC 339 Lord Scarman, when examining the Contempt of Court Act 1981, found a 'striking structural resemblance to the way in which many of the Articles of the European Convention . . . are framed: namely, a general rule subject to carefully drawn and limited exceptions'. In argument it was suggested that the word 'necessary' in S. 10 of the Contempt of Court Act 1981 should be construed in the way the European Court of Human Rights construes it; this was so because the Act had been passed in order to comply with the Convention. This point was not taken up by their Lordships.

munications Act 1985 authorizes the Home Secretary to issue warrants for the purpose of interception *inter alia* in the interests of national security. This reference to a phrase also found in the Convention would be irrelevant but for the fact that the legislation was passed as a direct result of the condemnation of the United Kingdom in the *Malone* case. In the parliamentary debates on the appropriateness of including national security as a ground for issuing a warrant the phrase was considered 'especially appropriate' because of the parallel with the Convention.[37]

Section 134 of the Criminal Justice Act 1988 creates the offence of torture. The statutory provisions aim to implement the United Kingdom's international obligations under the Convention against Torture and Other Cruel, Inhuman or Degrading Treatment or Punishment.[38] The definitions of torture and who may be indicted for this offence are limited to the definitions found in the United Nations Convention, so the offence is limited to public officials, persons acting in an official capacity, or persons acting at the instigation or with the consent or acquiescence of a public official or person acting in an official capacity. Torture is defined as intentionally inflicting severe pain or suffering on another in the performance or purported performance of official duties. Nevertheless the case-law and standards established by the Strasbourg organs concerning torture under Article 3 of the European Convention on Human Rights may come to be considered should the British courts have to apply the relevant provisions of the Criminal Justice Act to the facts of a case.[39]

1.1.2 A direct clash between a statute and the European Convention

Before leaving the area of statutory interpretation mention should be made of the situation where there is a perceived clash between a statute and the Convention. Of course it is not clear at what point it is no longer possible to interpret a statute so as to be in conformity with the Convention, so that a judge is obliged to find the two in irreconcilable opposition. In the United Kingdom, when a statute is in opposition to a treaty, the statute must prevail.[40] However, in the context of the European Convention on Human Rights Lord Denning felt able to depart from this

---

[37] See Ewing and Gearty (1990: 68).

[38] Adopted by the UN General Assembly, 10 Dec. 1984, entered into force 26 June 1987, ratified by the UK on 8 Dec. 1988.

[39] As will be seen in Ch. 7 the scope of Art. 3 ECHR is considerably wider than the definition of torture contained in the Criminal Justice Act 1988. It is worth noting that the Criminal Justice Act amends Schedule 1 to the Suppression of Terrorism Act 1978 by inserting a new para. 9A adding the offence of torture to the Schedule, and the Extradition Act 1870 is amended so that torture is included in Schedule 1; Criminal Justice Act 1988 ss. 22 and 136 respectively.

[40] *Mortenson* v. *Peters* [1906] 14 Scots LTR 227; *The Parlement Belge* (1879) 4 PD 129.

orthodoxy. In *Birdie* v. *Secretary of State for Home Affairs*[41] Lord Denning, MR, stated that 'if an Act of Parliament did not conform to the Convention I might be inclined to hold it invalid';[42] this surprising statement was repudiated in a later case in the same year, when Lord Denning returned to the orthodox view: that treaties do not become part of the law until made so by Parliament, and that 'if an Act of Parliament contained any provisions contrary to the Convention, the Act of Parliament must prevail'.[43] He continued, 'But I hope that no Act ever will be contrary to the Convention. So the problem should not arise.'

The point did arise for Lord Denning in *Taylor* v. *Co-Op. Retail Services*.[44] After examining the *Case of Young, James and Webster*,[45] decided by the European Court of Human Rights in Strasbourg, he concluded:

Mr Taylor was subjected to a degree of compulsion which was contrary to the freedom guaranteed by the European Convention on Human Rights. He was dismissed by his employers because he refused to join a 'closed shop'. He cannot recover any compensation from his employers under English law because under the Acts of 1974 and 1976, his dismissal is to be regarded as fair. But those Acts themselves are inconsistent with the freedom guaranteed by the European Convention. The United Kingdom Government is responsible for passing those Acts and should pay him compensation. He can recover it by applying to the European Commission, and thence to the European Court of Human Rights.

Similarly Fox, LJ, found that the 'Convention is not part of the law of England and it cannot be used in the English Courts to displace the provisions of an English Statute'. More recently, in *Re M. and H.*, Lord Brandon affirmed that in the event of a conflict between an unambiguous statute and the Convention the courts are bound to give effect to the statute.[46]

---

[41] [1975] 119 SJ 322.
[42] See 359 of BYIL (1975).
[43] *R.* v. *Sec. of State for Home Affairs ex p. Bahjan Singh* [1976] 1 QB 198 at 207.
[44] [1982] ICR 600.
[45] Series A, vol. 44.
[46] House of Lords, [1988] 3 WLR 485 at 498. 'I am, however, willing to assume, for the purposes of dealing with the contention of counsel for the father, that the denial to him of the right referred to above constitutes a breach of articles 6 and 8 of the Convention. Even on that assumption it seems to me that counsel's contention is founded on a misapprehension as to the status of the Convention in relation to English law. Although the United Kingdom is a party to the Convention, Parliament has not so far seen fit to make it a part of our country's domestic law. This means that English courts are under no duty to apply its provisions directly, Further, while English courts will strive when they can to interpret statutes as conforming with the obligations of the United Kingdom under the Convention, they are nevertheless bound to give effect to statutes which are free from ambiguity in accordance with their terms, even if those statutes may be in conflict with the Convention.'

1.1.3 Summary of the Convention's use in the context of statutory interpretation

1. In a direct clash between a statute and the Convention, the statute (if unambiguous) must prevail.[47]

2. If a statute or secondary legislation is 'ambiguous' then it is legitimate for the courts to use the Convention, as Parliament is presumed not to legislate contrary to its international obligations. It may be that the only reason that the statute seems 'ambiguous'[48] is due to the existence of the Convention or its aims. In this sense the Convention has a greater role than merely solving ambiguities.

3. It is suggested that the interpretation of Acts passed before the ratification of the Convention should be carried out in such a way that the decision conforms with the principles and minimum standards established under the Convention.

4. More and more statutes are likely to be construed in the light of the Convention and its case-law, especially where the statute takes a phrase directly from the Convention.

1.2 THE CONVENTION AS PART OF THE COMMON LAW

The Convention has been used mostly to buttress the principles already contained in the Common Law. Thus, in one of the first references to it, Lord Kilbrandon, in the House of Lords, stated (in the context of a libel action): 'one must be watchful against holding the profit motive to be sufficient to justify punitive damages: to do so would be seriously to hamper what must be regarded, at least since the European Convention was ratified, as a constitutional right to free speech.'[49] Similarly, the right to public assembly, a Common Law right, is, according to Forbes, J., 'in fact, specifically mentioned in Article 11 of the European Convention on

---

[47] *Taylor* v. *Co-Op. Retail Services* [1982] ICR 600; and *R.* v. *Greater London Council, ex p. Burgess* [1978] ICR 991 Lord Widgery, CJ, at 995 (also on the 'closed shop'). See more recently *Maclaine Watson* v. *Dept. of Trade* [1989] 3 All ER 523 at 530 (Lord Templeman) and R. Higgins 'The Relationship between International and Regional Human Rights Norms and Domestic Law', Judicial Colloquium, Balliol College, Oxford, 21–3 Sept. 1992.

[48] On the subjective nature of a finding of ambiguity and the relevance of values and principles see Dworkin (1986: 350–4): 'When is the Language Clear . . . Does it become unclear whether Nazis may inherit if we think the original authors of the statute [governing inheritance] would not have wanted Nazis to inherit if they had anticipated them? It is only because *we* think the case for excluding murderers from a general statute of wills is a strong one, sanctioned by principles elsewhere respected in the law, that we find the statute unclear on that issue.'

[49] *Broome* v. *Cassell & Co. Ltd.* [1972] AC 1027 at 1133.

Human Rights'.[50] Despite such deference to the Convention's norms, the Convention had no real bearing on the outcome of these or other cases where it was referred to in the same way.[51]

These references have made little impact and are no cause for surprise. Two cases which are more startling in relation to the Convention are *Cheall* v. *APEX* and *UKAPE* v. *ACAS*. In these cases Lord Denning found two 'Common Law rights' which had been confirmed by the European Court of Human Rights, and therefore it was the duty of the Court of Appeal to give effect to these rights. The rights were (1) The right to be a member of a trade union of one's choice; (2) The right to have one's union recognized for collective bargaining. Lord Denning had recourse to the first right in *Cheall* v. *APEX*.[52] He relied on the *Young, James and Webster* v. *United Kingdom*[53] judgment of the European Court of Human Rights. Without going into a detailed examination of this judgment of the European Court of Human Rights we might still comment on Lord Denning's use of this case-law. His interpretation of the Convention in this context can be criticized on a number of grounds.

First, the European Court specifically limited this decision to the facts of the case and to employees who are employed before the implementation of the 'closed shop' agreement; the facts of *Cheall* were completely different. Second, Mr Cheall wanted to move from one union (ACTSS) to another (APEX). Article 11 guarantees the right to join a union for the protection of one's interests. Mr Cheall's interests would also have been served by membership of the original union.

Third, Mr Cheall had been expelled from APEX in accordance with the Bridlington Principles (which are the rules which the Trade Union Disputes Committee employs when regulating inter-union disputes). It was put to Lord Denning that these rules were necessary to keep order in industrial relations, and that an invalidation of the rules would lead to industrial chaos. In the language of the Convention: Article 11(2) allows for restrictions on Article 11(1) where they are necessary in a democratic society, for the protection of the rights and freedoms of others (here the employers and union members). Lord Denning construed Article 11 as a right without limitations, and ignored the collective rights of the individuals already in the collective:

---

[50] Forbes, J., in *Hubbard* v. *Pitt* [1976] QB 143 at 156, although he later found justifications for limiting this right.

[51] See the House of Lords case *Gleaves* v. *Deakin* [1979] 2 All ER 497, where Lord Diplock referred to the Convention when making the suggestion that, in future, private actions for criminal libel should be brought only with the consent of the Attorney-General. The Libel Act 1843 creates an offence even where the 'libellous' statement is true, unless the defendant can show it was for the public interest.

[52] *Cheall* v. *APEX* [1982] 3 All ER 855.

[53] (1981) Series A, vol. 44.

I take my stand on something more fundamental. It is the freedom of the individual to join a trade union of his choice. . . . Even though it should result in industrial chaos, nevertheless the freedom of each man should prevail over it. There comes a time in peace as in war, as recent events show,[54] when a stand must be made on principle, whatever the consequences. Such a stand should be made here today.[55]

Fourth, Lord Denning may have overestimated Mr Cheall's chances of success in Strasbourg. As a justification for the decision Lord Denning stated that he wanted to save Mr Cheall the time and expense of a trip to Strasbourg. But only States can be respondents in Strasbourg. This was a case involving the rules of a union and their relation to an individual; it was not apparent that the United Kingdom would be held to have violated the Convention, nor indeed was it so decided.[56]

The decision of the Court of Appeal (with Lord Denning in the majority) was overruled by the House of Lords.[57] Lord Diplock (who gave the only opinion) dismissed the 'supposed rule of public policy'[58] reinforced by Article 11 in the following terms: 'Freedom of association can only be mutual; there can be no right of an individual to associate with other individuals who are not willing to associate with him.'

Lord Denning's second 'Common Law right', supposedly reinforced by the Convention, arose in the case of *UKAPE* v. *ACAS*.[59] Although less weight was given to the Convention in this case than in *Cheall*, the case is interesting as no reference is made to the judgments of the European Court of Human Rights.[60] For instance in the *National Union of Belgian Police* case the Court held *inter alia* that Article 11 contained no implied right to consultation, for the purposes of collective bargaining.[61]

The Court of Appeal was again overruled by the House of Lords.[62] Lord Scarman referred to the point on the European Convention and rejected the idea that Article 11 included a right for every trade union

---

[54] Lord Denning was speaking just after the Falklands War.

[55] [1982] ICR 557.

[56] To what extent States are responsible for private action will be dealt with in detail in Part II. It should be explained that Mr Cheall's application to the European Commission of Human Rights was dismissed as inadmissible *ratione personae* as the 'expulsion was . . . the act of a private body in the exercise of its Convention rights under Article 11. As such it can not engage the responsibility of the respondent government.' *Cheall* v. *UK* [1986] 8 EHRR 76. Compare the Employment Act 1990.

[57] *Cheall* v. *APEX* [1983] 2 WLR 679.

[58] That an individual has a right to join and remain a member of the union of his or her choice.

[59] [1979] ICR 303.

[60] *National Union of Belgian Police* case (1976) Series A, vol. 19; *Swedish Engine Drivers' Union* case (1976) vol. 20; *Schmidt and Dahlstrom* case (1976) vol. 21.

[61] (1976) Series A, vol. 19.

[62] [1981] AC 424, where there was no argument on the Convention, nor was there reference to the pertinent Strasbourg cases.

to recognition for the purposes of collective bargaining. He continued: 'Until such time as the statute is amended or the Convention both becomes part of our law and is interpreted in the way proposed by Lord Denning M.R., the point is a bad one.'[63]

These last two cases lead to the conclusion that the use of the Convention as part of the Common Law may depend entirely on the enthusiasm with which any one judge is prepared to embrace it.[64] It does not really follow the developments in Strasbourg and is in danger of polarizing opinion as to the validity of the Convention. The blame for this could be laid:

- on the shoulders of practising barristers[65] for failing to bring to the attention of the Bench the relevant case-law;
- on Parliament and the Government for failing to give the Convention a defined status and priority.[66]

Other factors which have led to this situation are:

- the absence of a suitable body such as a 'Human Rights Commission' to co-ordinate and assist complaints in the United Kingdom courts based on the Convention;
- the lack of familiarity of a good proportion of the legal profession with the European dimension in United Kingdom law;[67]
- a mistrust of 'the chaps at Strasbourg',[68] and 'those people over there'.[69]

---

[63] At 446.

[64] See Lord Denning's comments on the Convention when interviewed on the radio. 'Asked whether he approved of the Convention he said "yes". Asked whether he wanted it introduced into our law he said "No, I prefer it as it is. I can look at it when I like and I don't have to look at it when I don't like."' Quoted by Lord Scarman in *The European Convention on Human Rights: Two New Directions, EEC:UK* British Institute of Human Rights, conference held at King's College, London, 15 Feb. 1980. Also note the lack of reference to the Convention when Lord Denning was faced with a large militant union demanding recognition from the Post Office, *R.* v. *Post Office, ex p. ASTMS* [1981] ICR 76.

[65] See Warbrick (1980: 852–3); and also in *The ECHR: Two New Directions EEC:UK* (above n. 64), at 43. It is worth mentioning that the British Institute of Human Rights opened a data base containing case-law of the Convention organs on 10 Dec. 1990 and that this data base can be consulted by practising lawyers.

[66] In particular see Lester (1985: 273–96; 1984: 56), and comments at 33 in *The ECHR: Two New Directions, EEC:UK* (above n. 64).

[67] The extent to which judges rely on the work of a few specialists is clearly evidenced by the comment made by Donaldson, MR, in *Duke* v. *Reliance Systems* [1987] 2 WLR 1225 in the context of construing a statute so as to be in conformity with an EEC directive: 'I come back to the question, "what is the meaning of section 6(4)?" It is submitted by Mr Lester, who is perhaps more knowledgeable about this sort of legislation than any other member of the Bar.'

[68] Lord Hailsham (former Lord Chancellor) in a radio interview on the question of incorporation of the European Convention (*Listener* (12 Feb. 1987): 'Would a Bill of Rights Politicise British Judges?', 16).

[69] Lord Denning in the debate on the Human Rights and Fundamental Freedoms Bill in

1.2.1 The use of the Convention to create or 'discover' the Common Law

In contrast to the cases discussed in the previous section there are a number of recent cases which carefully follow the Convention's juris-prudence. *Malone* v. *Commissioner of Police for the Metropolis (No. 2)*,[70] is decisive authority for the rule that the courts have no authority to make a declaration solely on the grounds that a Convention right has been violated. The case is important as it reveals to some extent the very English conception of a 'right'. Included in Mr Malone's claim was a request for a declaration that the interception and monitoring of his telephone lines violated Article 8 of the Convention (respect for private and family life, home, and correspondence).

Order 15 r. 16 of the Rules of the Supreme Court states that 'No action or other proceedings shall be open to objection on the ground that a merely declaratory judgment or order is sought thereby, and the court may make binding declarations of right whether or not any consequential relief is or could be claimed.' According to the argument of Mr Malone, this meant the Court could give a declaration not only as regards legal rights but also as to moral and international obligations. After very careful consideration by Sir Robert Megarry, VC, this argument was rejected:

I can see nothing in Order 15 r. 16 to open the doors to the making of declarations on a wide range of extra-legal issues. . . . declarations will only be made in respect of matters justiciable in the courts; treaties are not justiciable in this way; the Convention is a treaty with nothing in it that takes it out of that category for this purpose; and I therefore have no power to make the declaration claimed.

A declaration, then, can only be claimed in respect of a legally justiciable 'right' in the United Kingdom. The nature of this 'right' is far removed from the tradition of civil or human rights but contains the notion of a remedy or relief. The relationship between the individual and the State or law-making body is in the following terms: 'England is not a country where everything is forbidden except that which is expressly permitted.'[71]

Put another way this means that anyone can do anything unless it is expressly prohibited. So, when it was put to Sir Robert Megarry, VC, that the power to tap telephones had to be given, either by statute or by the Common Law, he replied that no positive authority was given by the law to permit people to smoke. Both telephone tapping and smoking were an invasion of other people's privacy. This comparison is only valid due to the English tradition that no difference should be made regarding

the House of Lords, 9 Apr. 1986, HL Debs., col. 268. (Lord Denning had moved an amendment to the Bill which was intended to end the right of individual petition to Strasbourg.)

[70] [1979] 2 All ER 620.   [71] Megarry, VC, [1979] Ch. D. 366.

the standards that are imposed on individuals and on public servants. With no theoretical 'public law' structure, this means that the police or any other public authority are free to do anything, unless it has been previously expressly outlawed.

Sir Robert Megarry, VC, was certain that this situation was not in conformity with the Convention as interpreted by the European Court of Human Rights in the *Klass* case,[72] and pointed out that 'telephone tapping is a subject which cries out for legislation'.[73] Thus, although the Convention was admittedly violated, no Common Law 'right' existed.[74] And, although the Convention was extensively examined, it was felt that, even if it had been a legitimate source of a right, it would not have been used in this context to find for the plaintiff, as its terms were too general to be appropriate to regulate a matter as complex as telephone tapping. This case may have decided that Articles of the Convention, on their own, are incapable of creating rights in the United Kingdom Courts, but some judges have since relied on the Convention when deciding which direction the Common Law should take.

In *Harman* v. *Home Office*[75] it was argued that when English law was unclear it should be interpreted in accordance with international obligations and that this was so even when it was the Common Law which was unclear.[76] The case involved an appeal against a finding for contempt of court against Ms Harman, a solicitor and then a legal officer for the National Council for Civil Liberties. Ms Harman had been acting for a prisoner who had alleged *inter alia* 'cruel and unusual punishments' contrary to the Bill of Rights 1688, arising out of his treatment in an experimental 'control unit' in prison.[77]

After an order for discovery had been granted in relation to certain documents,[78] these documents were read out in open court. A few days later Ms Harman allowed a journalist who had been absent from part of

[72] (1978) Series A, vol. 28.

[73] [1980] Ch. D. at 380. Since this decision the European Court of Human Rights has found in favour of Mr Malone *Malone* v. *UK* (1985) Series A, vol. 95, and Parliament has passed the Interception of Telecommunications Act 1985.

[74] Note, Megarry, VC, refused to 'discover' that the Common Law (buttressed by Art. 8) had always protected the home and family life: 'It seems to me that where Parliament has abstained from legislating on a point that is plainly suitable for legislation, it is indeed difficult for the court to lay down new rules of common law or equity that will carry out the Crown's treaty obligations, or discover for the first time that such rules have always existed' ([1979] 2 All ER at 647).

[75] [1983] AC 280.

[76] See also *R.* v. *Lemon* [1979] AC 617 at 655 (House of Lords), *Broome* v. *Cassell & Co. Ltd.* [1972] AC 1027 at 1135 (House of Lords), *Blathwayt* v. *Baron Cawley* [1976] AC 397 at 426 (House of Lords).

[77] *Williams* v. *Home Office (No. 2)* [1981] 1 All ER 1151 (High Court), 1211 (Court of Appeal). This is the case examined in the previous section, 'Statutory Interpretation'.

[78] Which contained details of the nature of the control units regime and the method by which prisoners were selected for it.

the hearing to have access to the documents which had been read out. The journalist wrote an article critical of the Home Office Ministers and civil servants, and the Home Office brought an action against Ms Harman alleging contempt of court, on the grounds that she was in breach of her obligation only to use the discovered documents for the purposes of the case.

It was undisputed that had this, or any other, journalist taken a shorthand note of the proceedings or ordered a transcript of the case, and then written an article based on such information, there could have been no action for contempt of court. The sole issue was whether the circumstances of the 'short cut' taken by the journalist constituted a contempt of court by the solicitor Ms Harman.

Lord Diplock stated at the beginning of his opinion that the case was '*not* about freedom of speech, [or] freedom of the press', and that it did not 'call for consideration of any of those human rights and fundamental freedoms which in the European Convention on Human Rights are contained in separate articles each starting with a statement in absolute terms but followed immediately by very broadly stated exceptions'.[79] The majority dismissed the appeal and found Ms Harman to be in contempt of court.[80]

Lords Scarman and Simon, in a joint dissenting opinion, referred to the case-law of the European Court of Human Rights,[81] and pointed out that the exceptions to Article 10 (of the Convention) 'must be narrowly interpreted' in the words of the Strasbourg Court, and that according to that Court the exceptions were limited to those situations which demonstrated a 'real pressing need', and no such need existed here.

Clearly the use of the Convention was not outlawed in this situation, but different perceptions of its purpose led to opposite conclusions. Lord Diplock saw the exceptions to the right to free speech as 'broadly stated'. Lords Scarman and Simon referred to the Strasbourg interpretation of the right to free speech and found that the exceptions had to be 'narrowly interpreted'.

In 1987 the House of Lords made reference to the Convention in three separate cases.[82] This has clearly established its legitimacy as a source of

---

[79] [1983] AC at 299, cf. Lord Oliver in a case involving the sterilization of a mentally handicapped girl of 17: 'this case is not about eugenics; it is not about the convenience of those whose task it is to care for the ward or the anxieties of her family; and it involves no general principle of public policy,' in *Re B. (a Minor)* [1987] 2 WLR 1213 at 1224.

[80] Ms Harman took her case to Strasbourg, where it ended in a 'friendly settlement' and an undertaking by the UK Government to change the Rules of the Supreme Court (Applic. 10038/82 [1984] 7 EHRR 146). See s. 2.3 on 'friendly settlements'.

[81] *Handyside* case (1976) Series A, vol. 24, *Sunday Times* case (1979) Series A, vol. 30.

[82] *Hone* v. *Maze Prison Board of Visitors* [1988] 1 All ER 321; *Re K.D. (a Minor) (Ward: Termination of Access)* [1988] 1 All ER 577; *A.-G.* v. *Guardian Newspapers Ltd.* [1987] 3 All ER 316.

principle when interpreting the Common Law. By 1988 the general logic of the Convention had infiltrated a number of judgments concerning confidentiality; yet the approach of the Convention was still held to do no more than mirror the Common Law method. Lord Donaldson, MR, stated this in the second *Spycatcher* case in the following way:

The starting point of our domestic law is that every citizen has a right to do what he likes, unless restrained by the common law, including the law of contract, or by statute. If therefore, someone wishes to assert a right to confidentiality, the initial burden of establishing circumstances giving rise to this right lies on him. The substantive right to freedom of expression contained in art. 10 is subsumed in our domestic law in this universal freedom of action. Thereafter, both under our domestic law and under the convention, the courts have the power and the duty to assess the 'pressing social need' for the maintenance of confidentiality 'proportionate to the legitimate aim pursued' against the basic right to freedom of expression and all other relevant factors. In so doing they are free to apply 'a margin of appreciation' based on local knowledge of the needs of the society to which they belong: see *Sunday Times v UK* (1979) 2 EHRR 245 and *Lingens v Austria* (1986) 8 EHRR 407. For my part I detect no inconsistency between our domestic law and the convention. Neither adopts an absolute attitude for or against the maintenance of confidentiality. Both contemplate a balancing of private and public attitudes.[83]

The impact of the incorporation of phrases such as 'pressing social need', 'proportionality', and 'margin of appreciation' should not be under-estimated, as they evoke the case-law of the Strasbourg organs. It is interesting that Lord Donaldson accepts the proportionality test in this context while it was expressly ruled out as unworkable when invoked as a ground for judicial review of administrative action (see below Section 1.4). Nowhere is the logic of the Convention more evident than in the judgment of Scott, J., in the Divisional Court: 'I can see no "pressing social need" that is offended by these articles. The claim for an injunction against these two newspapers in June 1986 was not, in my opinion, "proportionate to the legitimate aim pursued".'[84] Nevertheless Lord Donaldson, although he accepted the method, found himself in 'profound disagreement with the judge' on this particular point. He found that the public interest in the due administration of justice outweighed the public interest in publication.[85]

---

[83] *A.-G. v. Guardian (No. 2)* [1988] 3 All ER 594 at 596, and see also Dillon, LJ, at 615, and Brightman, LJ, at 627–8 and 637 (reference to 'duties and responsibilities' in Art. 10(2)). Similarly see the opinions of Lord Griffiths at 652 and Lord Goff at 660 and 666 in the House of Lords.

[84] [1988] 3 All ER 545 at 587.

[85] Perhaps it is worth very briefly outlining some of the background to this case. The *Guardian* and the *Observer* had published reports of the forthcoming trial in Australia concerning the Attorney-General's attempts to obtain injunctions to restrain publication of

In a later related case concerning the *Sunday Times* Lord Oliver similarly found that the balance weighed in favour of the necessity of 'maintaining the authority of the judiciary, if for nothing else'.[86] However, the last word in this section has to be from the most recent case of *Derbyshire County Council* v. *Times Newspapers Ltd. and Others*.[87] In this case the Court of Appeal had to define the extent of the Common Law tort of libel. The *Sunday Times* had published two articles questioning the propriety of certain investments made by the Council. The articles had headings such as 'Bizarre Deals of a Council Leader and Media Tycoon' and 'Revealed: Socialist Tycoon's Deals with a Labour Chief'. The judgment concedes that full use should be made of Article 10 to resolve an uncertainty in municipal law. The court found that to allow a local authority to sue for libel was not necessary in a democratic society. It was an unjustifiable restriction on freedom of expression. The case really turns on proportionality, as the court considered that the other options open to the local authority—actions for criminal libel or malicious falsehood— might be legitimate restrictions on freedom of expression where the reputation of the local authority might be damaged so as to impair its function for the public good. It was the existence of alternative less intrusive measures which made the possibility of a civil libel action disproportionate and unnecessary.

The case is important because instead of the court using the Convention to bolster conclusions arrived at by other means the Convention was the starting-point for the judicial reasoning. After referring to the established case-law on confidentiality which was said to be consistent with the Convention in the *Spycatcher* cases cited above, Balcombe, LJ, continued: 'So art. 10 does not establish any novel proposition under English law. Nevertheless, since it states the right to freedom of expression and the qualifications to that right in precise terms, it will be convenient to consider the question by reference to art. 10 alone.'[88]

---

the book *Spycatcher*. The Attorney-General obtained interlocutory injunctions against these newspapers and it was these injunctions which Scott, J., was referring to when he invoked the Convention's logic. Scott, J., took into consideration two allegations in the newspaper reports which were of particular public interest. The first concerned a plot by the British Secret Service to assassinate President Nasser of Egypt, the second related to a plot by MI5 officers to destabilize the Wilson Government.

In the end, the European Court of Human Rights found that the UK had violated the Convention: *Case of the Sunday Times* v. *UK (No. 2)* (1991) Series A, vol. 217; *Case of the Observer and Guardian* v. *UK* (1991) Series A, vol. 216.

[86] *A.-G.* v. *Times Newspapers Ltd. and Another* [1991] 2 All ER 398 at 421.

[87] *Derbyshire CC* v. *Times Newspapers Ltd.* [1992] 3 All ER 65.

[88] At 77, and see Balcombe, LJ: 'This court is in a position to define the extent of this common law tort in such a way as not to require a positive amendment of the law by Parliament. In my judgment we both can and should consider the effect of art 10. This I now proceed to do' (at 79).

Moreover the Court made extensive use of the Strasbourg case-law to accommodate the stress which the European Court and Commission of Human Rights have placed on freedom of the press and the legitimate discussion of persons with public functions in the public domain. This case probably represents the high point in the judicial consideration of the Convention as a tool for resolving uncertainty in the Common Law. Butler-Sloss, LJ, went so far as to say: 'But where there is an ambiguity, or the law is otherwise unclear or so far undeclared by an appellate court, the English court is not only entitled but, in my judgment, obliged to consider the implications of art. 10.'[89]

1.2.2 *Summary of the Convention's use as regards the Common Law*

1. The 'rights' contained in the Convention, when considered on their own, are not 'rights' for the purposes of a declaration or other relief in the United Kingdom courts.[90]

2. The Convention has often been cited as 'evidence' of certain Common Law rights. Sometimes the existence or ambit of these rights is not beyond dispute.[91]

3. The Convention can be legitimately used to determine in which direction the Common Law should develop, but the result of such an exercise depends very much on how much attention is given to the interpretation of the Convention as developed by the Strasbourg organs.[92] Most recently the weight of the Convention has been decisive in determining not only an ambiguity but also the non-existence of a remedy.[93]

1.3 THE CONVENTION AS PART OF COMMUNITY LAW

The interaction between Community law and the European Convention on Human Rights is very complex and will be dealt with in Chapter 8, when the case-law of the European Court of Justice in Luxembourg is considered. It is sufficient now to make two points before examining the situation as it arises before the United Kingdom courts.

1. At the moment, no case can be brought against the European Community (either as an entity or as a collection of Member States) before

---

[89] At 93. Cf. Lord Keith [1993] 1 All ER 1011 at 1021.

[90] *Malone* v. *Commissioner of Police for the Metropolis (No. 2)* [1979] 2 All ER 620.

[91] *Cheall* v. *APEX* [1982] 3 WLR 685; *UKAPE* v. *ACAS* [1979] 1 WLR 570.

[92] *Harman* v. *Home Office* [1983] AC 280; and see the criticism by Lord Scarman of the *Spycatcher* decision, 'Wright: How the Law Lords Got it Wrong', *The Times* (19 Aug. 1987), 10.

[93] *Derbyshire CC* v. *Times Newspapers Ltd. and Others* [1992] 3 All ER 65. Cf. [1993] 1 All ER 1011 (House of Lords).

the Strasbourg organs.[94] Therefore the use of the Convention at the national level, in this context, is important as the route to Strasbourg may be barred.[95]

2. The European Court of Justice (the Court of the European Communities) has declared that the Convention can supply guidelines to be followed when the Court is ensuring the protection of fundamental rights within the framework of European Community law. Member States and their courts are obliged to ensure compatibility with fundamental rights when implementing Community law,[96] and general principles such as freedom of expression will have to be taken into account by national courts when weighing the legitimacy of derogating from Community freedoms.[97] So, for example, any measures which allowed Governments to restrict the free flow of information around the Community on the grounds outlined in Article 56 EEC (public policy, public security, or public health) have to be considered against the background of the fundamental importance of freedom of expression 'consecrated' in Article 10 ECHR.[98]

Unlike the case-law of the European Court of Human Rights, the case-law of the European Court of Justice is directly incorporated in the law of the United Kingdom by statute, and judges are bound to make their judgments in conformity with it. Section 3 of the European Communities Act 1972 reads:

Decisions on, and proof of, Treaties and Community instruments, etc.

(1) For the purposes of all legal proceedings any question as to the meaning or effect of any of the Treaties, or as to the validity, meaning or effect of any Community instrument, shall be treated as a question of law (and, if not referred to the European Court, be for determination as such in accordance with the principles laid down by and any relevant decision of the European Court).

(2) Judicial notice shall be taken of the Treaties, of the Official Journal of the Communities and of any decision of, or expression or opinion by, the European Court on any such question aforesaid; and the Official Journal shall be admissible as evidence of any instrument or other act thereby communicated of any of the Communities or of any Community institution.

---

[94] See generally House of Lords Select Committee on the European Communities, *Human Rights Re-examined*, HL paper 10, (London: HMSO, 1992). And see *Confédération Française Démocratique du Travail* v. *The European Communities*, Applic. 8030/77, [1979] 2 CMLR 229, for an early application to the European Commission on Human Rights.

[95] To what extent accession by the Community to the ECHR is desirable or necessary is a question which will be addressed in Pt. II, in Ch. 8. The effect that such accession may have on the UK's legal order will be dealt with in Ch. 10.

[96] *Wachauf* v. *FRG* [1989] ECR 2609, para. 18.

[97] *ERT* case, C-260/89, judgment of 18 June 1991, para. 41.

[98] Ibid.

Clearly, judges in the United Kingdom are obliged to consider the arguments and judgments relating to the European Convention on Human Rights, as interpreted by the European Court of Justice at Luxembourg, but only when deciding 'a Community Law question'. For the present purposes 'a Community Law question' may arise in one of three ways:

1. Is a national measure, taken in order to comply with Community obligations, contrary to the Convention?[99]
2. Is a Community obligation under secondary legislation with 'dircet effect' contrary to the Convention?[100]
3. Has a 'primary Community fundamental right',[101] meaning a right contained in the Treaty of Rome and declared to have 'direct effect', been violated?

The judgment of the High Court in *Allgemeine Gold- und Silberscheideanstalt* v. *The Commissioners of Customs and Excise* provides a useful example of a situation on the fringes of the interaction of Community law and the Convention. Two men, Mr Thompson and Mr Johnson, fraudulently induced the AGOSI Company (a German company situated in Germany) to part with 1,500 gold krugerrands. Payment had been accepted in the form of an unguaranteed cheque drawn on an English bank, which

---

[99] For delegated legislation this happens through s. 2(2) of the European Communities Act 1972, which empowers Ministers or departments to make provisions or regulations. In Ch. 8.1.2.2 it is suggested that only these national measures are reviewable for conformity with the Convention according to the case-law of the ECJ. Arguably also reviewable are any national measures taken in a field occupied by Community law, or where national action is 'influenced or restricted by Community rules'; see Crossick and Karpenstein, (1981: 90–1); J. H. H. Weiler suggests that in 'areas of Community jurisdiction', i.e. 'an area of positive Community policy', Member State action is reviewable for conformity with the human rights protected by Community law. Such an area includes 'pre-emptible areas such as Agriculture, Competition, and Foreign Commerce' as well as areas where the Court has held that 'Community competences are exclusive'—'Fisheries and Common Commercial Policy'. See Weiler (1991: 555–642) and see Ch. 8.1.2.1.

[100] See s. 2(1) of the European Communities Act 1972, which incorporates directly applicable Community law into UK law without future enactment.

[101] This relates mainly to Art. 7 (prohibition on discrimination on the grounds of nationality), Art. 48 (free movement of workers), Arts. 52 and 59 (freedom of establishment and services), and Art. 119 (principle of equal pay). For the decisions of the ECJ which accord these Articles of the Treaty of Rome direct effect (either individually or in combination), see: L. Collins, *European Community Law in the United Kingdom* (3rd edn. London: Butterworths, 1984), 89–92. So far, the English courts have been unwilling to hold that the Treaty includes by implication the rights found in the Convention; see *Allgemeine Gold- und Silberscheideanstalt* v. *The Commissioners of Customs and Excise* [1978] 2 CMLR 292 (discussed below). In Scotland the courts had not only held that the Convention does not form part of Community law, but also doubted that it has a part to play in statutory interpretation: *Kaur* v. *Lord Advocate* [1980] 3 CMLR 79. However, according to N. Walker, the recent Scottish case of *Lord Advocate* v. *The Scotsman Publications Ltd. (Inside Intelligence)* [1988] SLT 705 is House of Lords authority for the proposition that the Convention now has the same status in Scottish law as it does in English law; see 'Spycatcher's Scottish Sequel', *PL* (1990), 354–71 at 367.

was subsequently dishonoured. It was clear from the contract that the Company retained ownership of the krugerrands. The two men tried to smuggle the krugerrands into England, but a customs officer discovered the coins concealed in a spare tyre.

The action in the High Court arose from a request by the AGOSI Company for the return of the krugerrands on the grounds that they were innocent, and that EEC provisions on the free movement of goods imposed on Member States a human rights obligation not to confiscate property of a Community national without compensation. No particular Article of the Treaty of Rome was relied on, but the submission made by the plaintiffs was that the Treaty governs all matters concerning the free movement of goods and within the Treaty there is an implied guarantee for the respect of fundamental human rights.

This was rejected by Donaldson, J. (as he then was), who refused to find any implied Articles in the Treaty of Rome. The argument was rejected in the following way:

The Solicitor-General submits that the Treaty of Rome takes effect according to its express terms and that there are no implied *Articles*. He asks, forensically, why so many distinguished people are wasting so much time debating the need for a new Bill of Rights incorporating the provisions of the European Convention on Human Rights if we already have one in the Treaty of Rome and the relevant legislation giving effect to that Treaty. It is a good question. In his submission section 44 of the 1952 Act is quite unaffected by the Treaty of Rome. If the Plaintiffs think that British domestic legislation infringes the European Convention their remedy lies in a complaint to the European Court of Human Rights . . .[102]
I accept the Solicitor-General's submissions.[103]

In order to use the Convention as part of Community law it is necessary to find specific provisions in the Treaty of Rome. In this situation the Convention will be considered: 'they [the human rights enshrined in the

---

[102] Their complaint was held admissible by the European Commission of Human Rights, who later found by nine votes to two that there had been a breach of Art. 1 of the First Protocol (no one to be deprived of their possessions except in the public interest) (Applic. 9118/80; the report of the Commission is annexed to the Court's judgment of 24 Oct. 1986, Series A, vol. 108 at 31). However, the Court found no violation of this Article by six votes to one, and allowed a wide margin of appreciation to States in this situation. Note that in the English courts the Convention right in isolation from Community law was given very little weight: 'Lest there be any misunderstanding, let me make it clear that the fundamental right upon which he relies is not that ancient right so dear to every Englishman, namely the right to smuggle. It is the right not to be deprived of property without compensation, save as a penalty for the commission of a criminal offence' (at 294). And in the Court of Appeal per Bridge, LJ: 'If I were satisfied, which I am not, that there is a principle in international law as that for which the [German company's counsel] contends, I should still be wholly unconvinced that it would be open to us to write into the Customs and Excise Act 1952 the extensive amendments which it would be necessary to introduce in order to give effect to that principle' ([1978] 2 CMLR 292 at 295).
[103] Donaldson, J., [1978] 2 CMLR 292 at 295.

Convention] may be part of the background against which the express provisions of the Treaty have to be interpreted.'[104] The second area where it was admitted (*obiter*) that the Convention would be taken into account was where the rights and duties of Community institutions are under consideration. As the customs officers in this case were not 'in this category' this avenue was closed.

It is submitted that the most relevant area of overlap between the Convention and Community law will be where secondary legislation has been enacted to comply with Community obligations.[105] When interpreting this legislation it may be that one party will refer the court to a decision of the European Court of Justice, which the court will be obliged to take into account through Section 3(1) of the European Communities Act 1972. The fact that in the European Court of Justice the Convention is referred to as part of the general principles of Community law means that in this indirect way the courts will be forced to familiarize themselves with the substance of the Convention. The European Court of Justice has clearly stated that Member States are to have regard to the principles found in the ECHR when implementing Community obligations through domestic legislation, or when implementing secondary Community legislation.[106]

As we shall see in Chapter 8, judgments from Luxembourg are more likely to use the principles and jurisprudence of the Convention as an aid to interpretation than to formulate concrete rulings on the scope of the Convention or the priority it should be given in national law. This approach will probably be mirrored in the United Kingdom courts, but the difference between a Community law situation and a case involving interpretation of a United Kingdom statute (such as those dealt with in Section 1.1) is that, in theory, Community law may be superior to domestic legislation.[107] Thus it may be legitimate to depart from the words of a statute or regulation, or even the precedents of the Common Law, in order to give effect to rights and obligations under the Treaties. To the extent that the Convention is used as an aid to the interpretation of Community law it may well be that it already functions as a Bill of Rights which can be used for judicial review of legislation.[108]

---

[104] Ibid.

[105] Under s. 2(2) European Communities Act 1972, the type (1) situation referred to above.

[106] See *Rutili*, Case 36/75 [1975] ECR 1219, and *Wachauf*, Case 5/88, 13 July 1989 [1989] ECR 2609.

[107] By virtue of s. 2(1) of the European Communities Act 1972, but see *Duke* v. *Reliance Ltd.* [1988] 2 WLR 359, where it was decided that s. 2(4) of the European Communities Act 1972 could not be read so as to distort the meaning of a British statute in order to enforce the Sex Discrimination Act 1975 in conformity with an unimplemented Community directive.

[108] Of course under English law there is the possibility of a direct clash between a statute passed subsequent to the European Communities Act 1972 and accession to the Treaty of Rome, and the Treaty itself. The likely outcome of such a clash will not be speculated on

1.3.1 Summary of the uses of the Convention as part of European Community law

1. The Convention is not an implied Article of the EEC Treaty (Treaty of Rome); it has been dismissed in both the English and the Scottish courts where the Community law factor is incidental and not based on a specific Article of the EEC Treaty.[109]

2. Where an Article of the EEC Treaty is under consideration, the case-law of the European Court of Justice may well be of paramount importance: to the extent that that Court has referred to the Convention, the United Kingdom courts will be bound to take the European Convention on Human Rights and its case-law into account. This is particularly so when the issue turns on the proportionality of the national derogation from the Article of the EEC Treaty.[110]

3. Where a national court has to determine the legitimacy of a measure which derogates from a fundamental freedom this has to be approached with regard to respect for fundamental rights such as freedom of expression.[111]

4. Where the Community institutions and personnel are involved, their behaviour will have to conform to the European Convention on Human Rights and the United Kingdom courts will interpret the relevant law in this way (so long as they have the jurisdiction to do so).

5. More and more domestic legislation is likely to be passed as a result of Community obligations, whether this is apparent or not.[112] It is

---

here. Indeed Lord Bridge, speaking extrajudicially, has refused to express any opinion on the matter; see Bridge (1984: 115–20 at 119). Lord Bridge comes out in favour of incorporation of the Convention in domestic law, and is reported as saying that 'if any judges wanted to say that by way of Community law the European Convention could be directly applied there was nothing to stop them doing so' (125: 'Summary of the Discussion'). Unless the statute has been passed with an expressed intention that it should supersede Community law the Supremacy of Community law is now much more settled: *R. v. Sec. of State for Transport, ex p. Factortame* [1990] 2 AC 85, *Factortame (No. 2)* [1990] 3 WLR 818 (ECJ), 856 (HL). See D. Oliver, 'Fishing on the Incoming Tide', 54 *MLR* (1991), 442–56.

[109] *AGOSI* case (in the High Court), above. See also *Kaur* v. *Lord Advocate* [1980] 3 CMLR 79 (Court of Session, Outer House), no link to Community law found.

[110] See Ch. 8.1.2.1 and the *Rutili* case. This situation is the type (3) case referred to at the beginning of this section.

[111] *ERT* case (above). Presumably other fundamental rights and freedoms would also enjoy such a status.

[112] For difficulties in this area see *Duke* v. *Reliance Systems* [1988] 1 All ER 626, where the question arose: was the Sex Discrimination Act 1975 passed with EEC Directive 76/207/EEC in consideration? The House of Lords concluded that the 'Proposals for the equal treatment directive date 9 February 1976 were in circulation when the Bill for the Sex Discrimination Act 1975 was in discussion but it does not appear that these proposals were understood by the British Government or the Parliament of the United Kingdom to involve the prohibition of different retirement ages linked to different pensionable ages' (at 635). See also G. G. Howells, 'European Directives: The Emerging Dilemmas', 54 *MLR* (1991), 456–63.

legitimate[113] to use the Convention to interpret this legislation, where ambiguities arise.

1.4 THE CONVENTION AS A FACTOR TO BE TAKEN INTO ACCOUNT BY ADMINISTRATIVE BODIES WHEN EXERCISING THEIR DISCRETION

In an early case of judicial review, *R. v. Secretary of State for Home Affairs ex parte Bhajan Singh*,[114] Lord Denning held that 'immigration officers and the Secretary of State in exercising their duties ought to bear in mind the principles stated in the Convention. They ought, consciously or subconsciously, to have regard to the principles in it—because after all, the principles in the Convention are only a statement of the principles of fair dealing; and it is their duty to act fairly.'[115]

However, in a later case, *R. v. Chief Immigration Officer, ex parte Salamat Bibi*,[116] he significantly changed his position, and the status of the Convention in this context, finding the Convention to be 'indigestible':

I desire, however, to amend one of the statements I made in *R v Secretary of State for Home Affairs, ex parte Bhajan Singh*. I said then that the immigration officers ought to bear in mind the principles stated in the convention. I think that would be asking too much of the immigration officers. They cannot be expected to know or apply the convention. They must go simply by the immigration rules laid down by the Secretary of State and not by the convention. I may also add this. The convention is drafted in a style very different from the way which we are used to in legislation. It contains wide general statements of principle. They are apt to lead to much difficulty in application; because they give rise to much uncertainty. They are not the sort of thing which we can easily digest. Article 8 is an example. It is so wide as to be incapable of practical application . So it is much better for us to stick to our own statutes and principles, and only look to the convention for guidance in case of doubt.[117]

Lord Denning was not alone in taking this stance. Roskill, LJ (as he then was), in his concurring judgment stated: 'there are no grounds for imposing on those who have the difficult task, which immigration officers have, to perform the additional burden of considering, on every occasion, the application of the convention.'[118] Similarly Geoffrey Lane, LJ, stated:

---

[113] Not only because the Convention is part of the background against which Community law must be interpreted, but also due to the rule of statutory interpretation, that legislation ought to be interpreted so as to conform with international law or international obligations.

[114] [1975] 2 All ER 1081.   [115] At 1083.

[116] [1976] 3 All ER 843.   [117] At 847.

[118] At 849, he also felt that the dictum of Scarman, LJ (as he then was), in *R. v. Sec. of State for the Home Department, ex p. Phansopkar* [1975] 3 WLR 225, to the effect that it was the duty of public authorities in administering the law to have regard to the Convention, was too wide.

'One only has to read the Article in question, article 8(2), to realize that it would be an impossibility for any immigration officer to apply a discretion based on terms as wide and as vague as those in article 8(2).'

It is important to note that these judgments are based on the practicality of asking immigration officers to consider Article 8 (the right to respect for family life, etc.) when deciding individual immigration cases. If the rationale for the irrelevance of the Convention in this area is the intolerable burden it would place on busy immigration officers, who are ill equipped to apply 'general statements of principle', then the question arises: is it relevant for other public bodies such as Ministers, local authorities, or other bodies acting in a judicial way? And may other Articles be distinguished as less difficult? For example, Article 3 (prohibition of torture, inhuman, or degrading treatment) has no limitation clause and is arguably more capable of 'practical application'.

In *R. v. Secretary of State for the Home Department, ex parte Fernandes*[119] the Court of Appeal, relying on the *Bibi* case, held that the Secretary of State was under no obligation to consider whether his actions were in contravention of the Convention. Again this was in the context of deportation of immigrants and the interpretation of Article 8. However, it is suggested that this was an unfortunate extension of the rule in *Bibi* which was based on the impracticability of immigration officers balancing the various factors involved in Article 8. The same argument cannot be applied to decisions of the Secretary of State, who should be able to consider and evaluate the provisions of the Convention and even its case-law. Although the Convention does not give rise to enforceable rights as it is not part of the law, the Treaty was entered into by the Executive and as such produces international obligations on the Crown. As a member of the Executive and a Crown employee it is surely not illogical that the Secretary of State should at least take into account these obligations when making decisions, even if technically not bound by them in national law.

The facts of *R. v. Secretary of State for the Home Department, ex parte Kirkwood*[120] provided an opportunity for the courts to hold that the Secretary of State was obliged to consider the Convention when Article 3 was alleged. This they declined to do. Earl Kirwood was wanted in the State of California on a murder charge. He was arrested in England, and after a request by the United States Government for his extradition, he was committed to prison. As his return to California could mean many years on 'death row' should he be convicted, he applied to the European Commission of Human Rights, claiming that his extradition would lead to inhuman or/and degrading treatment as prohibited under Article 3.

---

[119] [1981] Imm. AR 1.　　[120] [1984] 2 All ER 390.

The 'death row' phenomenon can be stated as follows: once the death penalty has been passed, there is a complex and lengthy system of appeals, the litigation usually goes on for several years, and the constant anxiety of not knowing whether the death penalty is to be commuted or not can be extremely distressing.[121]

Earl Kirkwood had filed an application against the United Kingdom with the European Commission of Human Rights. The Commission indicated to the United Kingdom Government that the hearing on admissibility would take place in March 1984, but in February 1984 the Secretary of State issued a warrant ordering Mr Kirkwood to be surrendered to the United States authorities. Mr Kirkwood applied for judicial review of the Secretary of State's decision, claiming it was unreasonable on the following three grounds:

1. that the Secretary of State had failed to consider the legal obligations on the United Kingdom to provide him with an effective remedy in the event of a breach of Article 3 of the Convention;
2. that he had failed to consider the fact that, if Mr Kirkwood was extradited before his hearing with the Commission, he would be deprived of that remedy;
3. that he had prejudiced the Commission's findings or had decided that Mr Kirkwood should be returned irrespective of the findings of either the Commission or the Court of Human Rights.

Mann, J., relying on the *Fernandes* case, held that the Secretary of State was not bound by obligations under the Treaty as it was not part of the law of the United Kingdom, and therefore it was not unreasonable to continue with the extradition in isolation from the provisions of the Convention or the pending proceedings in Strasbourg.

This reasoning does not stray outside the autonomous concept of a 'reasonable' decision. For a decision to be unreasonable the test is that laid down by Lord Greene, MR, in the *Wednesbury* case,[122] whereby a decision is considered unreasonable if relevant factors have been ignored, irrelevant factors have been taken into account, or the decision is one which no reasonable decision-maker could have made. Ostensibly an

---

[121] Note, the inhuman or/and degrading treatment would be directly imposed by the State of California, which is not a Party to the Convention; however, it is now clear that the responsibility of the extraditing State may be incurred by the actions of non-contracting Parties or even private bodies. See *Altun* v. *FRG*, Applic. 10308/83, 36 D. & R. 203, and the rejection of the Government's argument in the *Kirkwood* case before the European Commission of Human Rights (*Applic. 10479/83* v. *UK* [1984] 6 EHRR 373) that the application should be declared inadmissible *ratione loci*. This important development is discussed in full in Pt. II, when the *Soering* case is considered.

[122] *Associated Provincial Picture Houses* v. *Wednesbury Corporation* [1947] 2 All ER 680.

objective test, there is here plenty of scope for judicial abstinence or interference. According to the decision in *Kirkwood*, the Convention is not a factor to be taken into account.

At this point we might draw the interim conclusion that judicial resistance to the use of the Convention as a factor involved in administrative decision-making is particularly strong. This is so despite the early dicta of Lord Widgery, CJ: 'There is no doubt that the terms of the Convention . . . are properly to be regarded in this country where an issue in this country makes them relevant, and if authority were necessary for that, it is to be found in *Birdie* v. *Secretary of State for Home Affairs*.'[123]

Although the courts have now refused to hold that the Secretary of State is obliged to decide in conformity with the Convention, it should be noted that the House of Lords has stated (*obiter*) that 'The most fundamental of all human rights is the individual's right to life and, when an administrative decision under challenge is said to be one which may put the applicant's life at risk, the basis of the decision must surely call for the most anxious scrutiny', per Lord Bridge in *R.* v. *Home Secretary, ex parte Bugdaycay*.[124] This passage was relied on in the *Soering* case[125] by the European Court of Human Rights in dismissing the applicant's contention that there had been a breach of Article 13 of the Convention, as he had not been able to argue his right under Article 3 in the proceedings for judicial review of the Secretary of State's decision to extradite him. The Court found that he had not presented the details of the conditions which would amount to inhuman or degrading treatment should he be extradited, and that if he had done so 'such a claim would have been given "the most anxious scrutiny" '.[126] It is suggested that it was unfortunate that the European Court did not agree with the Commission's conclusion[127] that, in these circumstances, the United Kingdom's law as developed by the courts was in violation of the Convention, as there is no real possibility of an effective remedy when one complains that an administrative decision violates one's rights under the Convention. The passage from the House of Lords judgment actually refers to the right to life, whereas the applicant would have been claiming the right not to be subjected to inhuman or

---

[123] *R.* v. *Sec. of State for Home Affairs, ex p. Bhajan Singh* in the Divisional Court [1976] 1 QB 198 at 202.

[124] [1987] 1 All ER 840 at 952, and see Templeman at 956.

[125] Judgment of 7 July 1989, Series A, vol. 161.

[126] At para. 122 of the judgment.

[127] The Commission concluded by seven votes to four that there had been a violation of Art. 13 by the UK, having noted that it was not contested by the UK that the 'courts limit their examination to the question of whether the Secretary of State has acted illegally, irrationally or improperly and do not examine the applicant's fear that he might be exposed to inhuman or degrading treatment or punishment'. At para. 166 of the Commission's report of 19 Jan. 1989, annex to judgment of 7 July 1989, Series A, vol. 161.

degrading treatment (he too was likely to face 'death row'). The European Court of Human Rights merely left the issue open, concluding: 'in any event it is not for this Court to speculate as to what would have been the decision of the English courts.'[128]

The inability of the courts to examine the Secretary of State's actions for conformity with human rights is highlighted by several recent cases concerning deportations. Mr Cheblak was a Lebanese citizen who worked as an academic and was employed by the Arab League in London as a senior research officer. Shortly after the beginning of the war against Iraq in 1991 he was arrested and informed of the Home Secretary's intention to deport him 'for reasons of national security'.[129] The Court of Appeal reaffirmed that the nature of national security meant that they would not, and could not, demand further details regarding the necessity of this decision. They also reaffirmed that, as long as the decision could not be said to be 'irrational', it would not be reviewed. Lord Donaldson even offered a rationale for the 'surprising' decision of the Secretary of State: 'Those who are able most effectively to undermine national security are those who least appear to constitute any risk to it.'[130]

The European Commission of Human Rights has now held in several cases that judicial review of the Secretary of State's deportation decisions for 'Wednesbury unreasonableness' does not afford an effective remedy as demanded by Article 13 of the Convention.[131] However, the European Court of Human Rights has, so far, preferred to afford States a 'margin of discretion in conforming to their obligations under this provision'.[132]

There may still be scope left for the argument that, where the decision is made due to authority given by statute or in consequence of an interpretation of a statute, then the Convention is a relevant factor to be taken into account by the body taking the decision. This would be so due to the principle that, wherever possible, statutes have to be interpreted in accordance with the Convention.

Although judicial review of administrative action will often be a case of interpreting the empowering statute to find out if the decision was *ultra*

---

[128] At para. 122 of the judgment.

[129] *R. v. Sec. of State for the Home Department, ex p. Cheblek* [1991] 2 All ER 319. For the non-judicial safeguards surrounding such a decision see 329–33.

[130] At 333.

[131] *Soering* v. *UK*, report of the Commission of 19 Jan. 1989, and *Vilvarajah and Others* v. *UK*, report of the Commission of 8 May 1990.

[132] *Case of Vilvarajah and Others* v. *UK*, Series A, vol. 215, para. 122. See also *Soering* v. *UK*, Series A, vol. 161. For a resolution of the Committee of Ministers which held that the absence of effective judicial review of the Secretary of State's decision concerning telephone tapping was a breach of Art. 13 of the Convention, see Res. DH (90)36 of 13 Dec. 1990, Applics. 12175/86 and 12327/86, *Hewitt, Harman and N.* v. *UK*. However, this sector is now regulated by the Security Service Act 1989. For a critical review of the new framework see Robertson (1989: 128–76) and Ewing and Gearty (1990: 175–89).

vires or not, some of the most important cases of judicial review will now involve administrative decisions where no empowering statute falls to be considered. In *Council of Civil Service Unions* v. *Minister for the Civil Service*[133] the Prime Minister had issued an instruction that the staff at Government Communications Headquarters (GCHQ) would no longer be permitted to belong to national trade unions. The House of Lords found that even though this instruction was issued under a Prerogative power it was still reviewable as if it had been empowered by statute.

Similarly, in *R.* v. *Panel for Take-Overs and Mergers, ex parte Prudential Bache Inc.*[134] the self-regulating panel was set up neither by statute nor by the Prerogative, but the supervisory jurisdiction of the High Court extended to cover the decisions of this body due to their public law nature. The decision is cited here to emphasize the fact that judicial review cannot really be considered as one aspect of statutory interpretation. To some extent the judges may feel they are justified in ignoring the Convention when deciding on the reasonableness[135] of administrative

---

[133] [1985] AC 374.

[134] [1987] 2 WLR 699. The implications of this decision will be dealt with in Ch. 10, when the nature of the public/private divide in British administrative law is examined.

[135] Lord Diplock in the *CCSU* v. *Minister for Civil Service* case took the opportunity to redefine the heads of judicial review as (1) illegality, (2) irrationality, and (3) procedural impropriety, which includes failure to observe the basic rules of natural justice. Should the rules of natural justice come to include, say, Art. 6 of the Convention, then it may be that the Convention could be given more attention. Lord Diplock also suggested that a further head might be adopted in the future, that of 'proportionality'; and he specifically referred to the fact that this is 'recognised in the administrative law of several of our fellow members of the EEC'. It should be noted that the concept of proportionality has also gained favour with the European Commission and Court of Human Rights. If these new heads of judicial review are embraced by the courts then it may be that elucidation of terms such as 'natural justice' and 'proportionality' will require reference to the Convention or even to the case-law of the ECJ in Luxembourg. For the way that this Court has developed this field see Schwarze (1986b: 401). In an article (1987: 368 at 374–81) advocating new heads of judicial review rather than the *Wednesbury* reasonable tests, J. Jowell and A. Lester suggest that the following principles be applied: proportionality, legal certainty, consistency, and fundamental human rights. All these principles emerge from Community or Convention law. Most recently the Court of Appeal has clearly stated that proportionality cannot be considered a separate head of review but is one aspect of reasonableness: *R.* v. *Sec. of State for the Home Department, ex p. Brind* [1990] 1 All ER 469; see also *Colman* v. *General Medical Council* [1989] 1 Medical Law Reports 23 QBD, and [1990] 1 All ER 489 (Court of Appeal). It should be noted that one cannot conclude that proportionality (as understood in Community law and in several other Member States) is therefore established in English law; the reason that the courts did not accept proportionality is exactly because it was not considered part of English law and its inclusion could 'create a monster that could quickly get out of control and cause widespread disruption of many administrative processes that might attract its application' (Auld, J., at [1989] 1 Medical Law Reports 30). Also, 'In our opinion the application of such a concept of proportionality would result in the courts substituting their own decisions for that of the minister and that is something which the courts of this country have consistently declined to do. The courts will not abrogate to themselves executive or administrative decisions which should be taken by executive or administrative bodies' (Watkins, LJ, cited by Donaldson, MR, in *Brind* at 479). For the extent that these cases deal with the Convention see below.

action, as the rules of statutory interpretation may be irrelevant due to the absence of any sort of ambiguity contained in a statute.

This was deemed to be the situation in *R.* v. *Secretary of State for the Home Department, ex parte Brind*.[136] This case concerned directives issued by the Home Secretary to the BBC and IBA prohibiting the broadcasting of direct statements by representatives of proscribed organizations in Northern Ireland. A number of journalists together with a union official from the National Union of Journalists applied for judicial review of the Minister's decision on the grounds *inter alia* that the directives were unlawful, in that they were in breach of Article 10 of the Convention.

The Convention was 'at the forefront' of the applicant's argument and Lord Donaldson, MR, dealt with the status of the Convention in some detail. His judgment clarifies a number of issues dealt with so far in this study. Having recalled that the principles in the Convention are difficult to distinguish from the English Common Law ('at least if the Convention is viewed through English judicial eyes'[137]), and that the Convention is an international treaty which has not been incorporated into English law, even though there are 'well informed supporters of this course', he confirmed that the 'duty of the English courts is to decide disputes in accordance with English domestic law as it is, and not as it would be if full effect were given to this country's obligations under the treaty, assuming that there is a difference between the two'.[138] He continued:

It follows from this that in most cases the English courts will be wholly unconcerned with the terms of the convention. The sole exception is when the terms of primary legislation are fairly capable of bearing two or more meanings and the court, in pursuance of its duty to apply domestic law, is concerned to divine and define its true and only meaning. In that situation various prima facie rules of construction have to be applied, such as that, in the absence of very clear words indicating the contrary, legislation is not retrospective or penal in effect. To these can be added, in appropriate cases, a presumption that Parliament has legislated in a manner consistent, rather than inconsistent, with the United Kingdom's treaty obligations . . . .[139]

Thus far I have referred only to primary legislation, but it is also necessary to consider subordinate legislation and executive action, whether it be under the

---

[136] [1990] 1 All ER 469 (Court of Appeal), [1991] 1 All ER 720 (House of Lords). For a comment on the Court of Appeal judgment see J. Jowell, 'Broadcasting and Terrorism, Human Rights and Proportionality', *PL* (1990), 149–56. See also *R.* v. *General Medical Council, ex p. Colman* [1990] 1 All ER 489, examined in Ch. 10.

[137] At 477.

[138] Ibid.

[139] Lord Donaldson refers to Diplock, LJ's, judgment in *Salomon* v. *Customs and Excise Commissioners* [1966] 3 All ER 871 at 875 (se s. 1.1 above), the passage in *Chundawadra* v. *Immigration Appeal Tribunal* [1988] Imm. AR 161 at 173 (which repeats the Diplock judgment verbatim), and the passage by Lord Diplock in *Garland* v. *British Rail Engineering Ltd.* [1982] 2 All ER 402 at 415.

authority of primary or secondary legislation. Counsel for the applicants submits that, where there is any ambiguity in primary legislation and it may accordingly be appropriate to consider the terms of the convention, the ambiguity may sometimes be resolved by imputing an intention to Parliament that the delegated power to legislate or, as the case may be, the authority to take executive action, shall be subject to the limitation that it be consistent with the terms of the convention. This I unhesitatingly and unreservedly reject, because it imputes to Parliament an intention to import the convention into domestic law by the back door, when it has quite clearly refrained from doing so by the front door.[140]

Donaldson then asserted that the empowering legislation was in no way ambiguous and:

It follows that whilst the Home Secretary, in deciding whether or not to issue a directive and the terms of that directive, is free to take into account the terms of the convention, as at some stage he undoubtedly did, he was under no obligation to do so. It also follows that the terms of the convention are quite irrelevant to our decision and that the Divisional Court erred in considering them, even though in the end it concluded that it derived no assistance from this consideration.[141]

Gibson, LJ, also considered Articles 10, 1, and 13 of the Convention and the argument that the Convention had not been incorporated precisely because successive governments considered that there already existed the necessary arrangements within the domestic order for compliance. He considered that the principle of interpretation existing in the Common Law meant that the Convention was relevant when construing legislation, when declaring and applying the Common Law, and when reviewing the exercise of administrative discretion. Nevertheless he confirmed that, although it was correct to use the Convention to construe an Act of Parliament passed after the Treaty had been signed, the Convention could not be used to review the substantial validity of the action of the Minister.[142]

---

[140] [1990] 1 All ER 469 at 477–8.

[141] Ibid.

[142] Professor Eric Barendt has criticized the Court of Appeal's reasoning in this case. He relies on the broad terms of the opinion of Lord Diplock in *Garland* v. *British Rail Engineering Ltd.* [1983] 2 AC 751 at 771: 'It is a principle of construction of United Kingdom statutes, now too well established to call for citation of authority, that the words of a statute passed after the Treaty has been signed and dealing with the subject matter of the international obligation of the United Kingdom, are to be construed, if they are reasonably capable of bearing such a meaning, as intended to carry out the obligation and not to be inconsistent with it.' Barendt suggests that it is clear that this applies equally to the Convention and therefore the Convention should be used to construe the legislation which delegates the relevant power 'as only conferring authority to issue directives in conformity with the Convention, at least where the text of the statute makes that interpretation possible' ('Broadcasting Censorship', 106 *LQR* (1990), 354–61 at 357). For discussion as to the possible necessity of some sort of 'linkage' between the statute 'dealing with the same subject matter' and the Treaty see s. 1.1. above. The question does not really seem to be whether the Court accepts that Parliament intended power to be exercised in conformity

Watkins, LJ, in the Divisional Court had come to the opposite conclusion: 'where Parliament has created for a minister a statutory power in terms which place no limitation on that power, then reference must be made to Article 10 by a court when deciding what are the limitations to be placed on the use of that power.'[143] However, this was expressly overruled in the Court of Appeal.

The appeal to the House of Lords concerned two points: the relevance of the Convention and the proportionality principle. Most of the opinions affirm that the Secretary of State's action cannot be reviewed by the courts for conformity with the Convention.[144] It was affirmed that because Parliament has not incorporated the Convention and because Parliament

has been content for so long to leave those who complain that their Convention rights have been infringed to seek their remedy in Strasbourg, it would be surprising suddenly to find that the judiciary had, without Parliament's aid, the means to incorporate the Convention into such an important area of domestic law and I cannot escape the conclusion that this would be a judicial usurpation of the legislative function.[145]

The judgment does not represent an anti-human rights, or even an anti-European, stance. What the majority of the House of Lords reaffirmed was that the courts have no authority to review ministerial decisions unless they are 'unreasonable' in the narrow sense defined in *Wednesbury*. According to their Lordships the judgment would have to be 'perverse' or 'irrational'. They referred to passages of Lord Diplock's opinion in the *Council of Civil Service Unions* v. *Minister for the Civil Service* case, where he likened an irrational decision to 'a decision which is so outrageous in its defiance of logic or of accepted moral standards that no sensible person who had applied his mind to the question to be decided could have arrived at it'.[146]

---

with Art. 10 or any other international obligation, but rather whether Parliament could be said to have intended that the courts should be able to review the Minister's actions for conformity with the international norms. It is presumably a reluctance to impute this last intention which led the Court of Appeal and the House of Lords to reject the relevance of the Convention as well as the doctrine of proportionality.

[143] Cited at 485 by McCowan, LJ, who disagreed on this aspect.

[144] Lord Templeman was prepared to go beyond the *Wednesbury* principles of unreasonableness, which he thought were inappropriate due to their subject-matter and date. He embraced the language of the European Court of Human Rights and asked whether the interference with freedom of expression was justifiable as necessary and proportionate to the damage which the restriction is designed to prevent. He acknowledged that the Secretary of State must be afforded a margin of appreciation and concluded that there had been no abuse of power.

[145] Lord Bridge at 723; see also Lord Ackner, 'If the Secretary of State was obliged to have proper regard to the Convention, i.e. to conform to Article 10, this inevitably would result in incorporating the Convention into English law by the back door' (at 734–5).

[146] [1985] AC 374, 410.

It is worth noting in parentheses that, if the judges had had the benefit of a Bill of Rights, in the form of the Convention, it would seem that they would nevertheless have found that the ministerial directives were not in breach of Article 10. All the speeches suggest that the object of the Minister's action was legitimate and the action taken proportionate to the aim to be achieved.

The proportionality test was also rejected by most of their Lordships.[147] Lord Ackner said that the doctrine could not be followed until the Convention was incorporated by Parliament. Lord Lowry found the idea impractical, likely to give rise to uncertainty and prolonged decisions, as well as taking up the courts' time 'which could otherwise be devoted to other matters'.[148] Lord Roskill was not prepared to apply the principle in the present case but did not 'exclude the possible future development of the law in this respect, a possibility which has been canvassed in some academic writings'.[149] It is difficult to see why this result is not a violation of Article 13 of the Convention. Clearly there is no access to a national tribunal for the determination of whether there has been a violation under Article 10.[150]

This case is important not only because it gives the clearest statement so far by the House of Lords concerning the applicability of the Convention in the English courts, but also because it deals with exactly the sort of subject-matter which some people argue should be decided by judges using the Convention and which others argue is a matter of policy and executive discretion better left to elected politicians. The latter group are unwilling to see the courts engage in balancing acts weighing the public interest or national security against individual rights as defined by a European Court. These questions are dealt with more fully in Chapter 3.

A similar approach was also taken in the case of *R. v. Secretary of State for the Home Office, ex parte Weeks*.[151] This case is worth examining in detail as it illustrates perfectly the hiatus between the Convention and the internal law of the United Kingdom. It is also evidence of the fact that cases relating to the Convention are not really concerned with big debates such as abortion or euthanasia, but more often revolve around individual claims. In 1966 when Robert Weeks was 17 years old he entered a pet

---

[147] Although Lord Templeman seems to have applied the proportionality doctrine to the case (see above).

[148] At 739.

[149] At 725, and see Jowell and Lester (1987).

[150] The decision of the House of Lords has also been applied in the context of judicial review of the Secretary of State's discretion on whether to surrender an applicant to the USA under Art. V(2) of the United States of America (Extradition) Order 1976. See *R. v. Sec. of State for the Home Department, ex p. Chinoy*, 14 Apr. 1991, *The Times*, 28 (judgment of 10 Apr. 1991).

[151] *The Times* law reports 15 Mar. 1988.

shop brandishing a starting pistol loaded with blank cartridges, pointed the pistol at the owner, and told her to hand over the till. He stole 35p, which he dropped on the floor on leaving the shop. Later that day, he telephoned the police to say he would give himself up. He was apprehended on the street by two police officers. He took the starting pistol from his pocket and it went off. In the ensuing struggle two more blanks were fired, one of which resulted in a powder burn on the wrist of one of the police officers. It emerged that he had committed the robbery because he wanted to pay back £3 which he owed his mother, who had told him that morning to find lodgings elsewhere.[152]

At his trial there was no evidence of mental instability, 'however a probation report . . . prepared by a probation officer, who had supervised Robert Weeks for two years, characterized him as being susceptible to fluctuation of mood and emotionally immature, and as having a morbid interest in the literature of violence and a fascination for guns. The report also stated that he had taken to drinking heavily from time to time and that he had a high potential for aggression.'[153] Robert Weeks pleaded guilty to armed robbery, assaulting a police officer, and being in the unlawful possession of a firearm. 'In respect of the first offence, he was sentenced to life imprisonment; for the second and third offences he received 2 and 3 years' imprisonment respectively, all sentences to run concurrently.'

The imposition of an indeterminate life sentence was justified by the trial court judge, as he was satisfied that Robert Weeks was 'a very dangerous young man' and that a life sentence meant that he could be released 'if and when those who have been watching him and examining him believe that with the passage of years he has become responsible'.

Ten years later in March 1976 Mr Weeks was released on licence. However, following a number of incidents[154] over the next year his licence was revoked after consideration by the Parole Board, and in 1977 he was again imprisoned indefinitely.

In 1982 Mr Weeks applied to the European Commission of Human Rights complaining of breaches of Articles 5(1) and (4) ECHR concerning the right not to be deprived of one's liberty. In brief, in 1987 the European Court of Human Rights eventually found a breach of Article 5(4). This was due to the fact that, when the Parole Board took the decision to recall Mr Weeks to prison, there was no facility for the individual to have full disclosure of the adverse material in the Board's possession; further-

---

[152] Facts taken from *Weeks* case (1987) Series A, vol. 114, p. 10, para. 12.

[153] At para. 13 of the Series A judgment.

[154] Breaking into a beach hut and stealing a pullover, driving while uninsured, taking a dumper truck for his own use, possession of an air pistol as a prohibited person, theft of alcohol, and damaging a police blanket.

more the periodic review carried out by the Parole Board did not satisfy the guarantees contained in Article 5(4) as the final decision lay with the Home Secretary. Interestingly, the Court also decided that although judicial review was available this only enabled the applicant to challenge the illegality, irrationality, or procedural impropriety[155] of a decision, and that there was no provision which allowed the 'lawfulness' to be challenged, 'lawfulness' being expressed to include lawfulness under Article 5(1) of the Convention.

For present purposes it is this last point which is important. The new heads of judicial review were considered inadequate. According to the European Court of Human Rights, administrative discretion in such cases must be challengeable with respect to its lawfulness. It would seem that this is not yet the case under English law, where the challenge is with respect to the decision's reasonableness. In the *Malone* case the European Court of Human Rights found that although the interference with the applicant's telephone calls was legal under English law it could not be said to be 'in accordance with the law'; this phrase 'does not merely refer back to domestic law but also relates to the quality of the law, requiring it to be compatible with the rule of law, which is expressly mentioned in the preamble to the Convention'.[156] This reference to the rule of law is probably not that helpful,[157] but the essence of the Court's test is that the law must be accessible, clear, and precise, so that one has a clear indication as to the way in which such activity may be carried out.

Unless the scope of judicial review is developed so as to include the possibility of a challenge for unlawfulness (with respect not only to domestic law but also to Convention law), judicial review cases will continue to be decided in a way which ignores the Convention, and applicants will be forced to seek their remedy in Strasbourg.

The *Weeks* case has revealed another rupture between internal law and the Convention. Mr Weeks applied to the Home Secretary for compensation, following an announcement that such compensation was payable

---

[155] These categories are the new ones suggested by Lord Diplock in *CCSU* v. *Minister for Civil Service* [1985] AC 374.

[156] Judgment of 2 Aug. 1984, Series A, vol. 82, para. 67.

[157] A. V. Dicey's influential expostion of the rule of law demands: (1) no punishment without a breach of the law, (2) no one to be above the law and everyone to be subject to the jurisdiction of the ordinary courts, and (3) constitutional principles to be the result of judicial decisions relating to cases brought by private individuals before the courts; this conception of the rule of law is dealt with in more detail in Ch. 4.3.2, but its emphasis on negative freedom rather than positive rights means that the activity complained about and the lack of legal authorization in the *Malone* case is not actually a breach of the rule of law according to Dicey. Perhaps it is covered by Professor Wade's definition, which includes the imperative that 'Every act of governmental power, i.e. every act which affects the rights, duties or liberties of any person, must be shown to have a strictly legal pedigree' (*Administrative Law* (Oxford: Clarendon Press, 1977), 23). However, here the action is not by the Government and privacy is not recognized as a legally enforceable right or liberty.

to ex-prisoners who had been wrongly convicted. It was accepted by Mr Weeks and reiterated by the High Court that Article 5(5) of the Convention could not be relied on as it is not part of the United Kingdom's legislation. Article 5(5) reads as follows: 'Everyone who has been the victim of arrest or detention in contravention of the provisions of this Article shall have an enforceable right to compensation.'

The High Court stated that whether the 'United Kingdom was in breach of her obligations under Article 5(5) . . . was not a matter the Court could rely on or decide. The matter might fall for consideration in Strasbourg.'[158] Again we have to conclude that an Article of the Convention cannot be relied on on its own to ground an action. This is so even in an uncontentious case where it is unquestionable that there has been a breach of the Convention.

The *Weeks* cases illustrate two important emerging themes: first, the application and evolution of the Convention is most relevant in the United Kingdom context when evaluating administrative practices, such as the use of the Prerogative, the operation of the Parole Board, and the discretion of the Secretary of State. None of these can be controlled for compliance with the Convention at the domestic level. These cases can only be illustrated by detailed examination of the provisions. To a large extent, the spectre of a Convention couched in 'wide' and 'vague' terms is unjustified. The Strasbourg organs over the last thirty-five years have managed to develop a code of minimum standards in the same circumstances. Secondly, there do exist real gaps where the judges would have been prepared to apply the Convention in favour of the applicant, but they are prevented from so doing due to the Convention's lack of domestic status in internal law.

1.4.1 The special area of prisoners' rights

The United Kingdom Government has lost a significant number of cases concerning practices in United Kingdom prisons.[159] One of the members of the European Commission of Human Rights, Professor Henry G. Schermers, writing in his professorial capacity, has made interesting suggestions as to why the rules regarding United Kingdom prisons are out of step with European Standards:

Why has the treatment of prisoners in Britain given so much more reason for complaint than treatment of prisoners on the continent? One reason could be that

---

[158] For the European Court of Human Rights' eventual award of just satisfaction under Art. 50 see *Weeks* v. *UK*, Series A, vol. 145, 5 Oct. 1988. The Court unanimously held that the UK was to pay Mr Weeks £8,000 damages and £1,793.33 costs and expenses.

[159] See n. 171 below.

during the war many leading personalities on the continent had been put in prison by the Nazis. The reforms of prison rules which took place after the war were therefore influenced by people who knew prison from the inside. This is why most prison regulations on the continent are rather humane. The same development did not take place in Britain. Another reason may be that at one time a part of the personnel of British prisons was recruited from the former colonial army and consisted of people who were more used to tough discipline than the social workers used in many prisons on the continent.[160]

The particular circumstances in which prisoners find themselves make recourse to the Strasbourg machinery especially inappropriate. Complaints about torture or inhuman treatment, interference with correspondence, or lack of legal representation before loss of remission are urgent, and rulings of the European Court of Human Rights several years after the original events will be of little use to the original complainants.[161] Indeed, the cases of *Silver* v. *United Kingdom*[162] and *Golder* v. *United Kingdom*[163] illustrate the absurdity of relying on the Court alone to protect prisoners' rights. Mr Silver had been dead for four years when the Court gave its judgment in his favour, and Mr Golder was already out on parole by the time of the Court's judgment in his case.

The United Kingdom courts have often taken the case-law of the European Court of Human Rights into account in this area and it has been referred to to justify a liberal interpretation of the Prison Rules[164] or the Common Law[165] or even to hold a standing order *ultra vires* and hence invalid.[166]

It is clear that there will be future changes in the prison rules and practice in order to conform to European standards.[167] The courts will be obliged to refer to the Strasbourg case-law in this area with increasing frequency. It may well be that this development will permeate into the allied area of immigration control. So far it seems that the Strasbourg organs have felt less inhibited when dealing with the prison regime in the

---

[160] 'Human Rights in Europe', *LS* (1986), 170 at 177.

[161] The coming into force on 1 Feb. 1990 of the European Convention for the Prevention of Torture or other Inhuman or Degrading Treatment should go some way to supplementing the protection offered under the ECHR. For the operation of this Convention see Cassese (1989: 128) and A. Cassese (ed.), *The International Fight against Torture* (Baden-Baden: Nomos, 1991).

[162] (1983) Series A, vol. 61.

[163] (1975) Series A, vol. 18.

[164] *R.* v. *Home Sec., ex p. McAvoy* [1984] 1 WLR 1408; for a restrictive interpretation of the Prison Rules and the right to legal representation see *Hone* v. *Maze Prison Board of Visitors* [1988] 1 All ER 321, discussed in Ch. 2.2.

[165] *Raymond* v. *Honey* [1982] 1 All ER 756.

[166] *R.* v. *Sec. of State for the Home Department, ex p. Anderson* [1984] 1 All ER 920 (reference to *Silver* and *Golder*).

[167] Note the new European Prison Rules 1987 Rec. R(87)3 (Council of Europe).

United Kingdom than in the area of immigration and extradition. It may be that it is easier to attempt to construct minimum standards for prisons in Europe than continually to review the discretionary decisions of immigration officers and Ministers of the Government. However, the European dimension should not be underestimated, and findings in Strasbourg have recently led to changes in the immigration rules and a greater awareness of the interaction between immigration practices and the Convention.[168] On the other hand the courts are still generally prepared to give a large amount of autonomous discretion to immigration officers[169] and the Secretary of State.[170]

1.4.2 Summary of the Convention's use in administrative decision-making

1. Should an administrative decision ignore the provisions of the Convention, there will be no intervention by the United Kingdom courts; the decision is not considered 'unreasonable' as such. It is suggested that judicial review should include review for the lawfulness of the decision. Lawfulness includes compliance with European Convention law.

2. It is suggested that the Secretary of State as an officer of the Crown should have to have regard to the Crown's international obligations, that is, the Convention and its case-law.

3. Where no ambiguity exists in the primary legislation, the secondary legislation will not be judged against the Convention as such a step would 'introduce the Convention by the back door'.

4. The increasing number of findings against the United Kingdom in the area of prisoners' rights[171] means that the Convention will become

---

[168] *Case of Abdulaziz, Cabales and Balkandali* (1985) Series A, vol. 94; also note the older case of *The East African Asians* (1970) 13 Yearbook 928 and the first admissible petition against the UK *Alam and Khan* v. *UK*, Applic. 2991/66 [1967] 10 Yearbook 478; and note the extended treatment of the Convention procedure in I. Macdonald, *Immigration Law and Practice* (London: Butterworths, 1983), 252–68.

[169] Perhaps Lord Denning was extreme in the confidence which he had for immigration officers: 'It seems to me that the immigration officers do their work efficiently and honestly and fairly. I have never known a case where they have been unfair' (1980: 155).

[170] See *R.* v. *Governor of Brixton Prison, ex p. Soblen* [1963] 2 QB 243 and *R.* v. *Sec. of State for the Home Department, ex p. Hosenball* [1977] 3 All ER 452.

[171] *Ireland* v. *UK* (1978) Series A, vol. 25: ill treatment of republican prisoners in Northern Ireland. Interrogation methods including wall-standing, hooding, subjection to noise, deprivation of sleep, and reduction of diet. Breach of Art. 3. *Case of X* v. *UK* (1981) Series A, vol. 46: no sufficient system of review for the continuing confinement of prisoners of unsound mind in mental hospitals. *Golder* v. *UK* (1975) Series A, vol. 18: access to the courts; *Silver* v. *UK* (1983) Series A, vol. 61, *McCallum* v. *UK* (1990) Series A, vol. 183: interference with prisoners' correspondence and access to the courts. *Case of Campbell and Fell* v. *UK* (1984) Series A, vol. 80: lack of legal representation when charged with a disciplinary offence which could result in the loss of more than three years' remission. *Weeks* v. *UK* (1987) Series A, vol. 114: return to gaol for a recidivist serving a life sentence, as a result of a minor offence committed on parole, with no hearing; *Thyne, Wilson and*

more and more relevant in this area. The decisions of prison authorities are 'reviewable' in Strasbourg for their compliance with the Convention. The special circumstances in which prisoners find themselves require urgent decisions concerning their human rights, so it is to be hoped that the domestic courts will become more willing to examine the merits of these cases. Although the House of Lords shut the door in the face of proportionality in the case concerning review of ministerial discretion, it may have left it ajar for cases such as prisoners' rights.

Gunnell v. *UK* (1990) Series A, vol. 190: no judicial review of discretionary life sentences for sex offenders. All the above were findings of a violation by the Court of Human Rights, and there are also several instances of 'friendly settlements' being achieved before the case arrived before the Court. See *Knechtl* v. *UK* (1969) 13 Yearbook 730, which resulted in changes in the prison rules. Also important are 'voluntary' changes made by the Government once it has seen the Commission's report; see e.g. *Hamer* v. *UK*, Res. DH (81)5 and *Byrne* v. *UK* Res. DH (87)6.

2

The Relevance of the Strasbourg Proceedings for the United Kingdom Courts

2.1 THE RELEVANCE OF THE CONVENTION DUE TO A PENDING APPLICATION IN STRASBOURG

The same question may arise simultaneously in the United Kingdom courts and before the European Commission of Human Rights. For example, in the *Kirkwood* case,[1] Earl Kirkwood had complained to the Commission that his extradition to California (where he was wanted for murder) would constitute inhuman or degrading treatment. The warrant for his extradition was issued before this application was heard. When the application for judicial review of this decision came before the High Court, Kirkwood's other application was still pending before the Commission. The High Court decided not only that the Secretary of State was not bound to consider the substantive provisions of the Convention, but also that the Secretary of State is not obliged to consider the actual fact of a pending application before the European Commission of Human Rights concerning the same circumstances.[2]

In practice the Commission can issue an 'indication' to a Contracting State as to which interim measures it would like to see whilst an application to Strasbourg is pending. In *Kirkwood's* case an indication was given that Earl Kirkwood should not be extradited. Although this 'indication' was renewed twice, it lapsed and further renewal was refused.[3] It was after this lapse that the warrant for the extradition was issued. Although these 'indications' do not create obligations in international law it seems that

---

[1] *R. v. Sec. of State for the Home Department, ex p. Kirkwood* [1984] 2 All ER 390 (discussed in Ch. 1.4).

[2] In *Uppal* v. *Home Office* 21 Oct. 1978 *The Times*, Sir Robert Megarry, VC, examined Art. 25 of the Convention, which concerns the right to submit individual petitions to the Commission and the declarations by States that they will allow such petitions; Art. 25 reads in part: 'Those of the High Contracting Parties who have made such a declaration undertake not to hinder in any way the effective exercise of this right.' Megarry, VC, held that this did not mean that the applicants had a right to stay the Secretary of State's deportation order, pending the hearing of the petition at the European Commission of Human Rights.

[3] Indication given 14 July 1983, renewed until 17 Oct. 1983 and again until 14 Nov. 1983, lapsed 15 Dec. 1983; there is no explanation from the Commission why a further request on 7 Feb. 1984 was refused.

in practice they are respected.[4] A recent application against Sweden concerned an applicant's expulsion from Sweden despite an indication from the Commission under Rule 36. Although the Commission concluded that there had been a violation of Article 25, which obliges States not to hinder the effective exercise of the right to petition the Commission, the Court concluded by ten votes to nine that the failure to comply with the Commission's indication did not amount to a violation of Article 25.[5] It is hoped that this case will not weaken the persuasive value of indications from the Commission. On the other hand, this still leaves the situation where indications lapse or are never issued;[6] in these situations the British courts do not consider a pending application a relevant factor to be taken into account by the Secretary of State (nor does it seem to be a factor for other decision-making bodies). The reasons for the irrelevance of the Convention in this context not only revolve around the Convention's lack of status in national law, but must also be attributed to the particular features of the Strasbourg procedure.

The time-span between a decision on admissibility by the Commission, and the judgment of the Court, which creates the international legal obligation, will be several years. Also, the case may well end in a 'friendly settlement' (Article 28) before the final report of the Commission and the eventual decision of the Court. This means that at the time of a pending application before the Commission, the actual legal obligations which may result from the Strasbourg proceedings will always be fairly contingent and unlikely to arise in the near future.

In some circumstances it may therefore be justifiable for national courts to ignore the fact of a pending application; but in the cases referred to above the situation is rather special. If the applicant is extradited by the national authorities to a country which is not a party to the Convention, the applicant will have lost the chance of a remedy completely. Where an applicant is alleging that he or she will be subject to torture or the death penalty that chance may be especially significant.

A case which did result in the person deported being executed was *Amekrene* v. *United Kingdom*.[7] Mr Amekrene (the deportee) was shot by

---

[4] *Kirkwood* at 395.

[5] *Case of Cruz Varas and Others*, Series A, vol. 201.

[6] As in the cases of *Uppal* v. *Home Office* (1978) 21 Yearbook 979; *R.* v. *Sec. of State for the Home Department, ex p. Fernandes* 20 Nov. 1980 The Times, and most recently in the *Case of Vilvarajah and Others* v. *UK*, Series A, vol. 215. In this case the Commission decided not to make a Rule 36 indication and the applicants were subsequently deported by the UK Government to Sri Lanka. When the Commission adopted its opinion on 8 May 1990 they were split seven votes to seven on whether there had been a violation of Art. 3. The casting vote of the President resulted in an opinion of no violation. The Court eventually found by a vote of eight to one that there had been no violation of Art. 3.

[7] Applic. 5961/72, (1973) 16 Yearbook 356.

firing squad on his return to Morocco, and his widow succeeded in obtaining a friendly settlement (compensation of £37,000) from the United Kingdom Government, on the grounds that the conditions surrounding his deportation might have breached certain Articles of the Convention.

One of the latest provisions of the Convention to come into force is Article 1 of the Sixth Protocol: 'The death penalty shall be abolished. No one shall be condemned to such penalty or executed.'[8] Article 2 allows for the death penalty in respect of acts committed in time of war. It will now be difficult for the Strasbourg organs to give only cursory consideration to an extradition or deportation involving a possible death penalty.[9] As more States ratify the Fourth Protocol (no expulsion of nationals or collective expulsion of aliens) and the Sixth Protocol (prohibition of the death penalty) the Strasbourg organs will eventually become more confident in developing limitations concerning extradition and deportation. It is to be hoped that pending applications will not be seen by the relevant government departments as a mere delaying tactic, and that national authorities and courts will take into consideration not only the fact of a pending application before the European Commission on Human Rights, but also the 'Strasbourg' interpretation of the relevant substantive provisions as that interpretation evolves.[10]

2.1.1 *Pending applications and prisoners' right to correspondence*

In *Guilfoyle* v. *Home Office*[11] the applicant had been arrested on charges connected with the Birmingham pub bombings by the IRA. He wished to correspond with his solicitor about assaults on him and others by prison officers, whilst he was in prison on remand awaiting trial. When the prison governor stopped a letter from his solicitor, an application was lodged by the latter, on his behalf, alleging breaches of the Convention due to the interference with the applicant's correspondence and hindrance of 'effective exercise of' his right to petition the Commission.[12] Under Rule 37A(1) of the Prison Rules, once a prisoner is party to legal proceedings his or her correspondence 'shall not be read or stopped'. Mr

---

[8] In force from 1 Mar. 1985 (though not yet ratified by the UK).

[9] For such a case see Ch. 7.3.1.1 and the discussion of the *Soering* case.

[10] Note, in other countries judicial proceedings have been suspended pending an application to the European Commission: Dutch Hague District Court decision of 2 Sept. 1980, Case 80/591 (deportation); Belgian Council of State decision of 20 Jan. 1978 (extradition); cited in Drzemczewski (1987: 561). Another approach which can be taken is for the extraditing State to agree to extradition on condition that the receiving State accords the prisoner certain guarantees (see Swiss Federal Tribunal decision ATF 107 (1981) 1(*b*) 68, again cited by Drzemczewski).

[11] [1981] 2 WLR 223.

[12] Under Art. 25 of the Convention.

Guilfoyle sought a declaration that his future correspondence should not be read or stopped, as he was now a party to legal proceedings.

The Court of Appeal unanimously held that he was not a party to legal proceedings. It held that proceedings at the Commission were not legal proceedings because the Commission does not exercise a judicial function, 'they only make a report on the facts and state their opinion. They make no order at all—nothing which can be enforced by anyone.'[13] And it added that even if the Commission's proceedings could be considered legal proceedings, the applicant could not be considered 'a party' to those proceedings. This was because he could never be a party to proceedings before the Court, as only the Commission or Member States appear before the Court.[14] This rather restrictive decision may be departed from in the light of the new rules of the European Court of Human Rights, but it is noteworthy that, again, proceedings at Strasbourg are given no recognition even in a procedural context.[15]

Although this decision does not prevent applications to Strasbourg it does represent a willingness to place obstacles between prisoners and their advisers. This is particularly unfortunate as prisoners are a group in special circumstances: first, they are one of the groups most likely to suffer a severe physical violation of their rights,[16] and secondly, in the

[13] Per Lord Denning, MR, at 227.

[14] Now that the Rules of Procedure of the European Court of Human Rights have been amended (1982) officially to permit applicants to take part in proceedings before the Court (if represented by an advocate) (Rule 27(2)), the decision in *Guilfoyle* may have to be reconsidered should the same complaint arise again in the UK courts. Should the UK sign and ratify the Ninth Protocol, and should ten States ratify that Protocol, there could be no doubt that an individual was party to proceedings as that Protocol grants a right, after leave by the Court, for the individual to seise the Court. Note, Lord Denning, MR, suggested that the applicant would become a party to legal proceedings once the complaint had been ruled admissible; as decisions on admissibility are more than just a question of leave to continue, it is proposed that this suggestion should not be followed, and that an applicant is a party to legal proceedings from the time when the application is lodged at the Commission.

[15] This should be compared to Lord Denning's references to decisions of the Commission as relevant when denying a plaintiff rights claimed under the Convention. In *R. v. Sec. of State for the Home Department, ex p. Hosenball* [1977] 3 All ER 452 he referred to the inadmissible application of *Agee* v. *UK*, Applic. 7729/76, 7 D. & R. 164, and in *R. v. Home Sec., ex p. Singh* [1975] 3 WLR 225 he referred to a German application when restricting the right to marry. Reference to the Commission's 'decision' on admissibility by national courts when denying a violation of human rights can be criticized on several grounds. First, the Convention's organs in Strasbourg operate to uphold a minimum standard of human rights in Europe; second, decisions on admissibility often involve no investigation of the facts or issues; and third, these decisions are taken by a majority of the Commissioners present and voting, so it may be that had all the Commissioners heard the application they might have found it admissible.

In France, where litigants can rely on the substantive provisions of the Convention, due to Art. 55 of the Constitution of 1958, magistrates and lower courts have often referred to decisions on admissibility of the Commission, but nearly always as justification for a finding of no violation of the Convention. See Cohen-Jonathan and Eissen (1985).

[16] As prisons run on a system of privileges, when all those privileges have been lost a

words of the Commission, there exists a 'basic human need to express thoughts and feelings including complaints about real or imagined hardships. This need is particularly acute in prison, as prisoners have little choice of social contacts, hence the importance of having access to the outside world by correspondence.'[17]

2.1.2 Similar cases in Strasbourg and at the national level

Another area where a pending application in Strasbourg may be relevant to a case under consideration by a national court is where the application in Strasbourg turns on a similar factual situation. An opinion of the Commission contained in a report or even a declaration on admissibility may be taken into consideration, overtly or tacitly.

In *R. v. Secretary of State for the Home Department, ex parte Tarrant*[18] the Divisional Court were referred to the pending *Campbell and Fell* case.[19] They specifically mentioned that the Commission's report had no authority, but nevertheless noted that their own conclusion—that there was a right to legal representation before the Board of Visitors for prisoners facing serious disciplinary charges—was the same as that of the Commission (although reached by a different route). In situations such as this it has to be admitted that the opinions of the Commission and the consequent pending case before the Court may have a significant influence.

When there is no express reference to a relevant pending application, it is more difficult to speculate as to its influence. It has been suggested[20] that, when the House of Lords in the *Khawaja* case[21] reversed its earlier decision in *Zamir*,[22] the fact that Zamir had already applied to the Commission and had had his application declared admissible[23] was not extrinsic to their Lordships' decision to construe a more lenient rule concerning deportation of immigrants, and depart from their own decision in *Zamir*.

'difficult' prisoner may find himself or herself subject to particularly severe punishment. Of course, the assaults on Guilfoyle were not part of a system of punishment, and took place before his trial; according to Lord Denning: 'Guilty as he was of serious offences, he makes complaint of his treatment *after* he was arrested and before he was tried. He says that he and others in prison on remand were assaulted by prison officers while he was at Winston Green prison in Birmingham in 1974. It looks as if they did get a little bit of rough handling by someone or other. They were bruised and received black eyes: but nothing more' [1981] 2 WLR 223 at 225.

[17] In *Silver* v. *UK*, report of the Commission, para. 322, reproduced in Series B, vol. 51, p. 81.
[18] [1984] 1 All ER 799.
[19] [1984] 5 EHRR 207.
[20] By Griffith (1985b: 110).
[21] *R. v. Sec. of State for the Home Department, ex p. Khawaja* [1983] 2 WLR 321.
[22] *Zamir v. Sec. of State for the Home Department* [1980] 2 All ER 768.
[23] *Zamir* v. *UK*, Applic. 9174/80, 29 D. & R. 153.

Because the time from a decision on admissibility to final determination by the Court or the Committee of Ministers may be several years, it is likely that, as long as the provisions of the Convention cannot be relied on in the English courts, there will be parallel applications in Strasbourg, concerning the same or similar facts. It may be that, as the reports of the Commission become more accessible and awareness of, and enthusiasm for, the Strasbourg machinery increases, the decisions of the Commission or the fact of a similar pending application will have more and more influence.

2.1.3 Summary of the relevance of a pending application in Strasbourg

1. A United Kingdom court will not automatically order a deportation order to be stayed due to the mere fact of a pending application in Strasbourg.[24]

2. It has not been considered unreasonable for the Home Secretary to disregard the fact of a pending application in Strasbourg when ordering an extradition[25] or deportation,[26] although, in practice, if 'indications' are issued by the Commission they are usually complied with.

3. A prisoner whose application is being considered by the Commission, is not 'a party to legal proceedings' for the purposes of Rule 37(1)A of the Prison Rules, and so his or her correspondence is not protected under that rule.[27]

4. A decision of the Commission declaring a complaint admissible may have some persuasive effect on the United Kingdom courts,[28] even if the relevance of these decisions is sometimes denied by the courts.[29]

2.2 THE RELEVANCE OF THE CONVENTION DUE TO THE CASE-LAW OF THE EUROPEAN COURT OF HUMAN RIGHTS IN STRASBOURG

In several other countries legislation has been passed to give effect to the case-law of the Commission and Court of Human Rights.[30] Nevertheless

---

[24] *Uppal and Others* v. *Home Office* 21 Oct. 1978 The Times.

[25] *R.* v. *Sec. of State for the Home Department, ex p. Kirkwood* [1984] 2 All ER 390.

[26] *R.* v. *Sec. of State for the Home Department, ex p. Fernandes* 21 Nov. 1980 The Times.

[27] *Guilfoyle* v. *Home Office* [1981] 2 WLR 223.

[28] Note, it is not only the courts that take the decisions and opinions of the Commission into consideration; for example the Commission's reports in *Hamer* v. *UK*, Applic. 7114/75, and *X* v. *UK*, Applic. 8186/78, that Art. 12 had been violated by denying prisoners the right to marry were accepted by the Government and the marriage laws were later amended. For a detailed discussion of the influence of the Convention outside the courts see Symmons (1983: 387–428).

[29] *R.* v. *Sec. of State for the Home Department, ex p. Tarrant* [1984] 2 WLR 613.

[30] See Drzemczewski (1988: 149).

the House of Lords has stated in the United Kingdom that: 'neither the Convention nor the European Court's decision in the *Sunday Times* case is part of our law. This House's decision, even though the European Court has held the rule it declares to be an infringement of the Convention, is the law.'[31]

However, the existence of the European Court of Human Rights and even its jurisprudence has had considerable effect on some judgments. Lord Denning's judgment in *Cheall* v. *APEX* is a striking example:

Nor did the repeal [of the legislation] affect the fact that our government had adhered to the Convention for the Protection of Human Rights and Fundamental Freedoms. Every man could, by going to the European Court of Human Rights at Strasbourg, vindicate his rights under the Convention. Just as the three railwaymen did when they were dismissed for refusing to join a trade union. The European Court of Human Rights directed that the United Kingdom Government should pay compensation to the three railwaymen. That was on August 13, 1981, in *Young v United Kingdom* (1981) IRLR 408. By being vindicated in this way, we reach the conclusion that article 11(1) of the Convention is part of the law of England or at any rate the same as the law of England. The Courts of England should themselves give effect to it rather than put a citizen to all the trouble and expense of going to the European Court of Human Rights at Strasbourg. Our Courts should themselves uphold the right of every man to join a trade union of his choice for the protection of his interests.[32]

More recently, the House of Lords examined in detail the case-law of the European Court of Human Rights on legal representation in disciplinary proceedings. In *Hone* v. *Maze Prison Board of Visitors*[33] the appellants claimed as a matter of natural justice to be entitled to legal representation before the prison Board of Governors on a disciplinary charge. They relied on the judgment of the European Court of Human Rights in the *Campbell and Fell* case[34] and Article 6(3)(c) of the Convention.[35] The House of Lords stated that a 'strict interpretation' of this provision would lead to a right to legal representation in 'all disciplinary proceedings where the facts charged constituted a crime',[36] and this would apply to proceedings both before the governor and before a Board of Visitors. The practical difficulties which would follow from such a 'strict inter-

---

[31] Lord Scarman in *A.-G.* v. *BBC* [1980] 3 WLR 109 at 130.

[32] [1982] 3 WLR 685. This reasoning was criticized in the section on the Common Law in Ch. 1.2.

[33] [1988] 1 All ER 321. The consolidated appeal of Mr McCartan is dealt with in the same judgment. For a comment see G. Richardson, 'The House of Lords and Prison Discipline', *PL* (1988), 183–7.

[34] Judgment of 28 June 1984, Series A, vol. 80.

[35] Art. 6(3) reads: 'Everyone charged with a criminal offence has the following minimum rights . . . (c) to defend himself in person or through legal assistance of his own choosing.'

[36] At 328.

pretation' seem to have suggested to their Lordships that such an interpretation has to be circumscribed as the judgment continues: 'It is not
surprising, therefore, to discover that the provision has been the subject
of interpretation by the European Court of Human Rights to ensure that
its application does not exceed the bounds of common sense.'[37]

The judgment then cites at length a passage from the *Engel* case,[38]
where the European Court of Human Rights dealt with a case concerning
military discipline, and the *Campbell and Fell* case, which concerned the
applicability of Article 6(3) to disciplinary offences heard by the prison
Board of Visitors in the United Kingdom. The House of Lords lists
the principles developed by the European Court of Human Rights for
distinguishing between disciplinary offences outside the scope of Article 6
and criminal matters which are afforded the guarantees contained in
Article 6.

Of these principles the third was the most relevant in the instant case: it
is necessary to have regard to the nature and degree of severity of the
penalty which might be incurred. In Campbell's case there was a risk of a
complete loss of remission and the consequent loss of 570 days' remission
was considered by the European Court of Human Rights to be a sanction
which 'came close to, even if it did not technically constitute, deprivation
of liberty'.[39] They therefore found that Article 6 was applicable.

In one of the instant cases before the House of Lords the appellant was
awarded a total of 130 days' loss of remission.[40] However, the House of
Lords found that both the European Court's approach and that of the
English law have the same objective, that is, to allow flexibility in deciding
whether a person appearing before a disciplinary tribunal should be
legally represented, and that the Convention did not require an absolute
right to representation as claimed by the appellants. The House of Lords
offers no concrete reasons as to why Mr McCartan's situation should be
treated differently from Mr Campbell's, but presumably differences are
permitted due to the necessity of procedures which allow for a certain
amount of discretion. Even if the differences in the loss of remission had
been mentioned this could not really justify the difference in treatment.
The right to legal representation cannot be judged *ex post facto* according
to the penalty imposed. The existence of the right depends on the *risk* of
a severe penalty. The case of *Hone and McCartan* is interesting as it
shows both the United Kingdom courts' willingness to refer to the case-
law of the Convention organs, and their insistence that English law has

---

[37] At 328.

[38] Judgment of 8 June 1976, Series A, vol. 22.

[39] At paras. 70–3.

[40] According to the case-law of the Commission the cumulative penalty is irrelevant; for
Art. 6 to be applicable each penalty must be considered by itself.

the same objectives even if 'the technique is different'.[41] What is remarkable is that, despite the House of Lords' acceptance that 'in this respect the European Convention and the common law are harmonious',[42] there is no attempt to offer the same protection as that offered in Strasbourg. Bearing in mind that judgments in Strasbourg represent a minimum level of protection, and that the Strasbourg Court is faced with the need to allow a 'margin of appreciation' to Contracting States, as well as the necessity of formulating judgments which consider 'the traditions of the contracting states'[43] in this area, it is surprising that the House of Lords ignored the Strasbourg Court's judgment on the facts which contained a violation of the Convention. It seems that in some cases the margin of appreciation offered by the House of Lords towards the national authorities which have to make discretionary decisions will be greater than that afforded to national authorities by the European Court of Human Rights.[44]

Even if some of these cases suggest that the courts have been unwilling really to examine the case-law of the Commission and Court of Human Rights this looks set to change. At least in the recent *Derbyshire County Council* case considered in Chapter 1.2 the logic and dynamic of the Convention's case-law was fully considered and cited at length by the Court of Appeal. The court weighed whether allowing the Council the right to bring libel proceedings would respond to a 'pressing social need' and was 'necessary in a democratic society' to the extent that was 'proportionate' to the goal: the protection of the 'reputation' of the Council.

Another case concerns the Isle of Man Court of Appeal. In *Teary (Sergeant of Police)* v. *O'Callaghan*[45] this court recognized the significance of the *Tyrer* case,[46] which found that birching as a judicial punishment was degrading punishment contrary to Article 3 of the Convention. O'Callaghan (16 years old) had been sentenced by magistrates to be whipped with the birch (four strokes). Despite the willingness of O'Callaghan to be birched,[47] the Court of Appeal annulled the sentence,

---

[41] At 328.

[42] At 328.

[43] *Engel* case, para. 82.

[44] Note the House of Lords' concern that granting a right to legal representation would be 'a wholly unnecessary waste of time and money, contrary to the public interest', per Lord Goff in *Hone* [1988] 1 All ER 327, and Lord Lowrey in *Brind* feared that if the threshold of reasonableness were lowered to include a proportionality test this would lead to an increase in applications for judicial review and 'the expenditure of time and money by litigants, not to speak of the prolongation of uncertainty for all concerned with the decision in question, and the taking up of court time which could otherwise be devoted to other matters. The losers in this respect would be members of the public, for whom the courts provide a service'([1991] 1 All ER 720 at 739).

[45] [1981] 4 EHRR 232.

[46] European Court of Human Rights, judgment of 25 Apr. 1978, Series A, vol. 26.

[47] Note, at the time of the appeal O'Callaghan had instructed his lawyer to drop the appeal and had surrendered himself to the police station and was demanding to be whipped;

but pointed out that the court would take no consideration of the political consequences which might follow from allowing the sentence to stand, such as the United Kingdom being expelled from the Council of Europe, and that the sentence was nevertheless lawful. The decision to annul the sentence was based on the grounds that the courts should have regard to international obligations.

This case shows that the courts, even when faced with a popular legitimate law, such as the law of the Isle of Man on birching, may prefer to follow the Strasbourg lead. A parallel can be drawn between this case and the situation concerning homosexuality in Northern Ireland, where the Court of Human Rights, faced with another popular[48] law (which prohibited sexual relations between men), found a breach of human rights: *Dudgeon* v. *United Kingdom*.[49] It is in these types of situation involving unpopular minority interests that human rights theory is really tested. Both laws were relatively popular in the Isle of Man and Northern Ireland respectively and it was the European Court of Human Rights in Strasbourg that held the laws to violate human rights. It may well be that such a court can bring a detachment to bear on domestic laws that national courts may find hard. It is for this reason that even if the United Kingdom were to adopt the European Convention in the form of a Bill of Rights, the right of individual petition to Strasbourg should still be kept open, so that the European Court of Human Rights has the chance to examine cases arising in the United Kingdom context and give authoritative judgments on the scope of the rights guaranteed by the Convention.

Also, it may be that the existence of the Strasbourg Court together with its past case-law has a significant effect. Particularly pertinent are Lord Bridge's remarks in the House of Lords judgment in the interlocutory proceedings concerning publication of the *Spycatcher* book by certain newspapers.[50] In his dissenting opinion he stated that his confidence in the 'capacity of the common law to safeguard the fundamental freedoms essential to a free society, including the right to freedom of speech, which is specifically safeguarded by Article 10 of the Convention', had been 'seriously undermined' by the opinions of the three judges in the majority. And he later stated that if the Government continued in its fight to suppress details about the book being published 'they will face inevitable condemnation and humiliation by the European Court of Human Rights

however, it was decided that the case raised important constitutional questions and the request to drop the appeal was not granted. The case was sent back to the magistrates, who imposed a sentence of three months' detention.

[48] Note the 'Save our Sons from Sodomy' campaign by Ian Paisley and others. Polls seem to have revealed that the Province was evenly split on the issue of repealing the laws on homosexuality. See Thorold (1982).

[49] (1981) Series A, vol. 45.

[50] *A.-G.* v. *Guardian Newspapers* [1987] 3 All ER 316.

in Strasbourg'. This prediction was subsequently borne out when the European Court of Human Rights found that the United Kingdom had violated the right to freedom of expression.[51]

2.3 THE RELEVANCE OF THE CONVENTION DUE TO A 'FRIENDLY SETTLEMENT' IN STRASBOURG

According to Article 28 of the Convention, once the petition has been accepted, the Commission has a duty to try to ensure a friendly settlement 'on the basis of respect for Human Rights'. If such a settlement is achieved the case can no longer pass on to the Court of Human Rights, but the applicant is given some sort of relief and the State Party usually undertakes to change the practice in question. Friendly settlements may have a significant influence on changes in domestic law. For example, the friendly settlement in *Hodgson and Others* v. *United Kingdom*[52] resulted in the drafting of Section 159 of the Criminal Justice Act 1988. The press now have a right to appeal to the Court of Appeal against an order excluding the press or public from any part of a trial.[53] Similarly the application *X* v. *United Kingdom*[54] resulted in an official circular to all English educational authorities warning that the use of corporal punishment in schools can amount to inhuman or degrading punishment contrary to Article 3. Other changes have been made in areas concerning immigration practices, prisoners' correspondence, solitary confinement, and the law of contempt of court.[55] Better publicity concerning the terms of such friendly

---

[51] *Case of the Observer and Guardian* v. *UK*, Series A, vol. 216; and see *Case of the Sunday Times (No. 2)*, Series A, vol. 217. The judgments are complex due to the decision to split the period under consideration into two separate periods. Note also the discussion in Ch. 1.2.1 concerning the Court of Appeal and House of Lords' decisions on the merits (second *Spycatcher* case), which lifted the injunctions. By the time of the conclusion of these decisions both applications had been lodged with the Commission. These applications, of course, referred to the interim injunctions. One might also note that the *Sunday Times* claimed £224,340.60 in legal costs and expenses. The European Court of Human Rights eventually awarded it £100,000. The *Guardian* and *Observer* claimed £211,530.28 and were awarded £100,000. If one considers the cost to the Government of their own expenses, the road to Strasbourg clearly leads to more that international condemnation.

[52] Applic. 11553/85 and *Channel 4* v. *UK*, Applic. 11658/85, decision on admissibility 9 Mar. 1987.

[53] For the details of this application see Robertson and Nicol (1990: 6–7, 264).

[54] Applic. 7907/77, 14 D. & R. 205.

[55] Other examples of domestic changes following friendly settlements include *Alam* v. *UK*, Applic. 2991/66 (immigration), and *Knechtl* v. *UK*, Applic. 4115/69 (prisoners' correspondence); *A.* v. *UK*, Applic. 6840/74, 20 D. & R. 5 (solitary confinement in Broadmoor Hospital), and *Harman* v. *UK*, Applic. 10038/82, 38 D. & R. 53, 46 D. & R. 57 (contempt of court regarding documents already read out in open court), although in some of these settlements (as well as in others) the changes represent only a minimal revision of the situation. Occasionally a case may be struck off the Commission's list where the case is

settlements would assist courts and others with their task of ensuring the conformity of their actions with the Convention. However, it is exactly in order to avoid embarrassment and adverse publicity that governments opt for a friendly settlement. Perhaps a system of internal circulars could ensure judicial familiarity with the latest developments concerning the United Kingdom's approach under the European Convention, whilst allowing the Government quietly to award *ex gratia* sums to applicants.

settled and the law changed; see *Applic. 15397/87* v. *UK*, concerning distinctions in the age at which male and female young offenders were liable to custodial sentences.

3

Incorporation of the European Convention on Human Rights in the United Kingdom?

So much has been written about the desirability and feasibility of a written constitution for the United Kingdom that no attempt will be made to summarize the various difficulties involved,[1] or the political stances taken.[2] This chapter imagines a future legal order with the more recent proposals that have reached Parliament for a Bill of Rights which incorporates the Convention already in place,[3] and seeks to show that such a Bill of Rights would not transfer vital political questions to an unelected body of judges, but could operate to prevent some violations of civil liberties, and at the same time perform an important educative function.

3.1 INCORPORATION OF THE EUROPEAN CONVENTION INTO DOMESTIC LAW, EITHER AS A BILL OF RIGHTS OR AS AN INTERPRETATION ACT

In 1986 and 1987 there were two separate attempts to incorporate the European Convention on Human Rights into the law of the United

---

[1] See Jaconelli (1981); Abernathy (1983: 431). The perceived constitutional difficulties are best appreciated by consulting the various official reports: *Report of the Select Committee of the House of Lords on a Bill of Rights*, HL paper 176 (London: HMSO, 1978); *The Protection of Human Rights by Law in Northern Ireland* Northern Ireland Standing Advisory Commission on Human Rights, Cmnd. 7009 (London: HMSO, 1977); Home Office (1976).

[2] A useful analysis of political attitudes is Oliver (1986: 131); see also Wright (1986: 414); Graham and Prosser (1988: 184); compare Ewing and Gearty (1990: 275); and Norton (1982: esp. 244–94). For the particular policies of the various political parties in Northern Ireland see Committee on the Administration of Justice (1984). For some of the more philosophical questions see Finnis (1985); Milne (1977: 389). For a more pragmatic approach to the subject see Kerridge (1983); Gifford (1986: 113–22); J. McBride, 'The European Convention on Human Rights and the Protection of Civil Liberties in the UK', in Wallington (1984: 201–25); Lester (1985: 273–96); McCluskey (1987).

[3] The proposals put forward by the Institute for Public Policy Research, *A British Bill of Rights* (London, 1990), and Liberty, *A People's Charter* (London, 1991), go beyond the rights in the Convention and Liberty's proposal includes a sophisticated mechanism for parliamentary review of legislation and judicial decisions. Although it is not possible to outline these proposals here, it is worth noting that both stress the importance of a human rights commission to accompany any future Bill of Rights (see Ch. 9).

Kingdom.[4] The first attempt was the Human Rights and Fundamental Freedoms Bill, introduced as a private Member's Bill in the House of Lords. This Bill passed through all its stages in the House of Lords, but was given no time by the Government in the House of Commons.

The second attempt was the Human Rights Bill, another private Member's Bill, with support from all parties, but not backed by the Government. On 6 February 1987, at the second reading of the Bill, ninety-six Members of Parliament voted in favour of it and sixteen voted against. However, due to a procedural rule requiring at least 100 votes in favour, the Bill proceeded no further.

Although there have been several similar attempts in the past to incorporate the European Convention,[5] it seems that the form that such a Bill may take is becoming more settled. In 1990 this issue was debated twice in the House of Lords.[6] The latest clause on entrenchment means that the old arguments on the sovereignty of Parliament do not arise in the same way. As Parliament retains the power to pass any Act even after an adverse judgment by the courts, accusations of 'government by the judges' or 'the spectre of a judicial super-legislative' do not have the same relevance.

The exact proposals as regards entrenchment can be briefly explained as follows. When the Bill last went through the House of Lords, the original proposal was for a 'Bill of Rights' which would entrench the Convention,[7] to the extent that a future Act of Parliament would have to state expressly that it was to operate notwithstanding the Bill of Rights/ Human Rights Act.[8] However, at the Second Reading in the House of Lords this clause was amended after objections that it 'flies in the teeth of a well established constitutional doctrine that one Parliament can not bind a subsequent Parliament. That principle is intrinsic to the doctrine of the sovereignty of Parliament in this country and has prevailed for many centuries.'[9]

---

[4] For the background see R. Blackburn, 'Legal and Political Arguments for a United Kingdom Bill of Rights', in Blackburn and Taylor (1991: 109–20); and R. Blackburn, 'Parliamentary Opinion on a New Bill of Rights', *PQ* (1989), 469.

[5] For the details of these attempts see Zander (1985).

[6] Motion entitled 'Debate to call attention to the state of civil liberties under this Administration', 23 May 1990, HL Debs., cols. 904–35; Early Day Motion on incorporation of the European Convention on Human Rights, introduced by Lord Holme of Cheltenham, 5 Dec. 1990; see R. Hudson, 'ECHR and a Bill of Rights', *NLJ* (1990), 1757.

[7] Arts. 2–12, 14, and the First Protocol including the UK's reservation.

[8] 'Save in so far as such enactment is an Act which expressly directs that this subsection shall not apply to the doing of the act in question, or is made pursuant to a power which expressly so directs', part of Clause 4(2) of the Human Rights and Fundamental Freedoms Bill (HL) No. 21 1985.

[9] Lord Lloyd of Hampstead, Debate on the Human Rights and Fundamental Freedoms Bill, 9 Apr. 1986, HL Debs., vol. 109, no. 47, col. 269.

The amended clause provided that no provisions of future Acts are to be construed as authorizing acts contrary to the Convention, unless such a construction is unavoidable in order to give effect to the Act.[10] This amendment changes what could be described as a Bill of Rights (with an express derogation clause) into an Interpretation Act. In other words, under the first version, should a court be faced with a statute passed by Parliament[11] which contravened the Convention (as interpreted by the national court), then that court would give the Convention priority and hold the Act invalid. Under the second version, if the effectiveness of the Act requires an interpretation which contravenes the Convention, the Court has to give priority to the Act of Parliament.

There is therefore a big difference between the two in terms of constitutional theory; however, one should not be considered a 'stronger' version than the other. It is quite possible that the legislature would choose, in some circumstances, to include a 'notwithstanding clause'. If evidence is needed for this proposition, it can be found in the latest clauses used to oust the jurisdiction of the courts; for example, the Interception of Communications Act 1985[12] creates a new Tribunal and then specifically disallows any review of the Tribunal's decision by the courts,[13] and the Local Government Finance Act 1987 reads in part, 'This section shall have effect notwithstanding any decision of a court purporting to have contrary effect.'

Similarly in Canada, where the new Charter for Fundamental Rights and Freedoms 1982 (which supplants the Canadian Bill of Rights) has been enacted, the Quebec legislature quickly passed legislation ensuring that all Acts passed before the Charter are 'to operate notwithstanding the *Canadian Charter of Rights and Freedoms*'.[14] Although the motives for such action are primarily linked to this Province's political objections to the manner of adoption of the Charter, the 'notwithstanding' formula has been used by the Quebec legislature in new legislation passed since

[10] In full the clause, Clause 4(2), reads: 'No provision of an Act passed after the passing of this Act shall be construed as authorising or requiring the doing of an act that infringes any of the fundamental rights and freedoms, or as conferring power to make any subordinate instrument authorising or requiring the doing of any such act, unless such a construction is unavoidable if effect is to be given to that provision and to the other provisions of the Act.' This formula was adopted in the Human Rights Bill (House of Commons), no. 19, 10 Dec. 1986.

[11] Passed after the Human Rights Act and not expressly stating that it was to take effect notwithstanding the Human Rights Act.

[12] Enacted as a result of the judgment of the European Court of Human Rights in the *Malone* case (telephone tapping). For an appraisal and criticism of this Act, and its failure really to comply with the spirit of the *Malone* judgment, see Fitzgerald and Leopold (1987: 133–54).

[13] s. 7(8) reads: 'The decisions of the Tribunal (including any decisions as to their jurisdiction) shall not be subject to appeal or liable to be questioned in any court.'

[14] An Act Respecting the Constitution Act 1982 SQ 1982 s. 1 (Quebec).

the Charter was adopted.[15] In the past, even the federal legislature had recourse to the formula when it passed an Act wherein 'it is hereby declared that this Act shall operate notwithstanding the Canadian Bill of Rights'.[16]

Moreover, under the Bill of Rights version the implication is that judges can be asked to hold a whole Act of Parliament invalid. This they will clearly be reluctant to do, and in a borderline case may choose to uphold the whole Act. Under the Interpretation Act variant, the emphasis is on interpreting provisions of Acts so as to be in conformity with the Convention.

This issue of future Acts of Parliament and their validity is not so important in practice. As has been seen in the previous two chapters, the vast majority of human rights cases coming before the courts concern administrative practices and rules, together with old statutory and Common Law offences. The proposals for incorporation of the European Convention include not only methods of judicial review of legislation, but also that 'no person shall do any act . . . which infringes any of the fundamental rights and freedoms of any other person'.[17] The judicial review which is proposed can usefully be described using the terminology developed by Professor Cappelletti in *Judicial Review in the Contemporary World* (1971).

The review would be 'decentralized'. This means that any court could apply the 'higher law' of the European Convention, to construe provisions or decisions so as to be in conformity with the Convention. Also any court could prohibit or declare invalid action which contravened the rights set out in the Convention. The Convention would not only be used by the highest court when contemplating the validity of Acts of Parliament, but also by the lower courts when deciding questions as diverse as the legality of a street protester's obstruction of the highway, whether to grant an injunction to prevent publication, and different questions of discrimination. In this way the vocabulary of the Convention would become part of the legal culture at all levels and not only relevant to decide major constitutional issues.[18]

The review would be *incidenter*. This means that the Convention would normally be raised as an additional argument in the context of a legal conflict, rather than relied on to initiate an action. This would mean that knowledge of the Convention and its practice would be dispersed through the widest community possible. In countries where constitutional matters

---

[15] See Tarnopolski (1983: 227–74).

[16] Canadian Public Order Act 1970 s. 12(1).

[17] Clause 3(1) Human Rights Bill 1986.

[18] It might be added that there would be an element of centralization as the Strasbourg organs would usually deliver the authoritative interpretation of the Convention.

can only be raised in a special context and only in a central court or council, only a few specialists are familiar with the constitution's provisions and philosophy; not only does this mean that there is restricted access to arguments based on constitutional-type rights, but it considerably diminishes the educative effect of such a codification of fundamental rights and duties. For the Convention to become a living code, rather than a dead letter, it must be debated and considered in different contexts in every court and tribunal, and not just by the 'great and the good' sitting in judgment. It is suggested that this decentralized/incidenter version is the most appropriate in the context of incorporation of the Convention into United Kingdom law.[19]

At this point it is submitted that the Convention could have an enormous impact on administrative practices and the decisions of the lower courts, should it be incorporated. Whether or not the decisions of the Court of Appeal or the House of Lords would be radically different is difficult to guess. It may be worth returning briefly to some of the decisions which we examined earlier.

In *Re the Council of Civil Service Unions*[20] all the judges in the House of Lords accepted the argument that the 'national security issue' meant they had no authority to review the Prime Minister's decision to ban trade union membership at GCHQ. It might therefore be suggested that the incorporation of the Convention, allowing as it does for restrictions in the interests of national security, would have made no difference to the result achieved under the present law. This may be so, but the case-law of the European Court of Human Rights requires that the rights take effect with limited restrictions. This means that it would be for the Crown to show evidence of the restriction being necessary in the interests of national security. It is debatable whether this shift in the burden of proof would make any difference to the outcome, but what is clear is that the job which the Court is doing would be exposed: the judges would be faced with a clear choice between the right to join and form trade unions, as found in Article 11(1), and the Minister's objection that it was necessary to restrict this right on the grounds of national security.

---

[19] When A. Lester (1968) suggested a sort of constitutional council this may have been meant as a preliminary step or compromise. His more recent suggestions refer to incorporation along the lines outlined above (Lester 1984, 1985; Jowell and Lester 1987); similarly the proposals of Sir Leslie Scarman (as he then was) for a Supreme Court (1974: 77–82) have been dropped in favour of the Bill described above, which he helped to draft. For Lord Scarman's later proposals see Scarman (1984: 5). However, the issue of a separate constitutional council has been revived by S. Lee; see 'Arguments against a Bill of Rights', in Neuberger (1987). Most recently see *A British Bill of Rights* (London: Institute for Public Policy Research 1990), which stresses the role of the High Court and the judicial review process.

[20] [1984] 3 All ER 935.

After failing in the House of Lords the unions took the case to Strasbourg, where the Commission declared the application inadmissible.[21] From the perspective of the disappointed applicants there are two relevant reactions to such an outcome:

1. The restrictions which are allowed are so wide that the core of the right becomes meaningless—incorporation of the Convention would have made no difference in this particular case.[22]
2. Despite many progressive decisions by the Commission in the past, its make-up now reflects an increasingly 'Conservative Europe', and having considerably expanded the scope of the Convention, the Commissioners are now treading much more carefully. It is perhaps possible that an English Bench might have been less wary of finding a violation of Article 11. In any case the Commissioners' decision shows the necessity of 'repatriating' this Bill of Rights.[23]

There is no way of accurately stating what would have happened if the Convention had been part of domestic law. A realistic approach must consider the long-term effects of incorporation; even if different decisions cannot be foreseen in the immediate future, the educative impact of the rights discourse would eventually have some influence.

It is sometimes suggested that such a rights discourse would only exacerbate attempts by collectivities to assert their rights. As we saw above, judges sometimes naturally gravitate to awarding individuals rights over their colleagues in the collective. This can undermine the effectiveness of the collective and weaken its power to organize. So far, the collective right to associate has not been given much priority at either the national or international level.

Nevertheless, the Convention, while stressing a rights approach, need not give rise to a culture based around individualistic rights holders. The framework of the Convention is capable of supporting a reasoned approach to the clash of interests between individuals and collective organizations. On balance, it is suggested that using the Convention would be more likely to stimulate a democratic debate about the nature and purpose of

---

[21] *Council of Civil Service Unions and Others* v. *UK*, Applic. 11603/85, 50 D. & R. 228; the Commission found that the workers at GCHQ could be considered as 'members . . . of the administration of the State' under Art. 11(2) and that the restrictions were 'lawful' in the narrow sense (in accordance with the law) and in the wider sense (proportionate to the aim to be achieved).

[22] For an example of this approach see Mr N. Brown, Labour Party spokesman in the debate on the Human Rights Bill, 6 Feb. 1987, HC Debs., col. 1278.

[23] Both these reactions were variously expressed at the conference 'A Bill of Rights for the U. K.?' (conference on the incorporation of the ECHR, organized by the NCCL and the Cobden Trust and held in London, 29 Jan. 1987) by some of those who had been involved in this application to the Commission. At the time of writing the conference is unpublished.

the rights being claimed. Ignoring the Convention leaves the debate exclusively in the hands of lawyers, who are the only ones entitled to 'devine and define' ancient Common Law rights.

In fact, the current situation, whereby the Convention is only debated in Strasbourg, means that the clash of rights is not debated at all in the domestic arena. When the issue arises at the international level, the conflict is handed over to an even more select set of lawyers, debated in a foreign land, and possibly eventually determined by twenty-six judges, most of whom will be unfamiliar with the balance of industrial relations in the United Kingdom.

It is also worth returning to *Attorney-General* v. *Guardian Newspapers Ltd.*[24] (the interim injunctions in the *Spycatcher* case, discussed in Chapters 1 and 2). In this case the restrictions in the Convention were relied on by one of the majority judges, Lord Templeman, to uphold an injunction against the newspapers. Such a restriction on the 'fundamental principle of freedom of the press' was legitimized by reference to the restrictions permitted in the Convention by Article 10(2). In *Lord Advocate* v. *Scotsman Publications Ltd. and Others* Lord Templeman developed his approach to paragraph 2 of Article 10 and stated: 'In my opinion it is for Parliament to determine the restraints on freedom of expression which are necessary in a democratic society.'[25] However, it may be that, had the Convention had the effect of law rather than its present rather confused status, the majority of their Lordships would have chosen freedom of expression over the Common Law concepts of 'confidentiality' and 'breach of contract'. Most pertinent is the fact that, if the case had really revolved around an interpretation of the European Convention, the Court would have had to consider in depth the case-law of the European Commission and Court of Human Rights.[26]

This case-law includes two decisions of the European Court of Human Rights, where paramountcy was given to the freedom of the press, and where it was stated that 'freedom of expression constitutes one of the

---

[24] [1987] 3 All ER 316.

[25] [1989] 2 All ER 852 at 859; see N. Walker, 'Spycatcher's Scottish Sequel', *PL* (1990), 354–71 at 368. Walker warns that: 'Viewed in the context of the debate over reception of the Convention in our domestic courts, this novel doctrine might, in the face of appropriately crafted legislative initiatives, accord government such extensive control over its own 'margin of appreciation' as to empty the Convention of effective content in respect of the development of cognate areas of common law' (at 370).

[26] Note, Clause 6 of the proposed Human Rights Bill reads: 'For the purpose of this Act judicial notice shall be taken of the Convention and the Protocols thereto to which the United Kingdom is signatory and of all published judgments of the European Court of Human Rights and of all published reports and decisions of the European Commission of Human Rights established by the Convention.' In fact the case-law of the Court was referred to in the proceedings of the main action: see Lord Donaldson, MR, *A.-G.* v. *Guardian (No. 2)* [1988] 3 All ER 595 at 596.

essential foundations of a democratic society'.[27] It also includes the decision of the Commission in the *Harman* v. *United Kingdom* case,[28] which ended in a friendly settlement, but arose out of a finding of contempt of court concerning publication of documents read out in open court. As the House of Lords in the interim proceedings in the *Spycatcher* case imposed a ban on reporting proceedings in open court in Australia, the spirit of the *Harman* v. *United Kingdom* settlement could have been of particular relevance, especially as it came after a House of Lords decision in which the majority had eschewed the Convention as irrelevant.[29]

It seems clear that incorporation of the Convention will not automatically lead the judges to different conclusions,[30] indeed the judge at first instance, all three judges in the Court of Appeal, and two members of the House of Lords in the trial of the substantive issues in the *Spycatcher* case referred to Article 10 of the Convention and occasionally used its language in their judgments and speeches[31]—despite the fact that the Convention is not at present incorporated into the law. However, it must be stated that the Convention, and more importantly the case-law of the Strasbourg bodies, would have an educative effect in cases which touch on issues raised by the Convention.

The potential educative effect of the Convention is already clear from the way that critics of government action now frequently phrase their attacks on the Administration in terms of the rights contained in the Convention. Some critics have gone on to speculate on what would have

---

[27] *Sunday Times* case (1979) Series A, vol. 30, p. 40, para. 65, and *Lingens* case (1986) Series A, vol. 103, p. 26, para. 41; of course the case-law also includes the *Handyside* case, Series A, vol. 24, where the Court allowed a 'margin of appreciation' to the UK and upheld the ban on *The Little Red Schoolbook*, but this case was distinguished in the *Sunday Times* case as one which turned on a question of morals and thus merited less interference from a supranational court than cases where the restriction is justified in order to protect the authority of the judiciary.

[28] Applic. 10038/82, 38 D. & R. 53, 11 May 1984 (admissibility); report of the Commission, adopted 15 May 1986, see *Information Sheet No. 20* (Strasbourg: Council of Europe, 1987), 42; the friendly settlement contained an undertaking by the UK Government to amend the rules concerning disclosure of documents, and compensation for Ms Harman (legal expenses) of £36,360, 46 D. & R. 57.

[29] *Harman* v. *Home Office* [1983] AC 280 (see Ch. 1.2.1).

[30] Note that in *Malone* Megarry, VC, commented that, even if he had felt that he could 'incorporate' the Convention into the Common Law, he would not have attempted to 'legislate' judicially in such a complex field. Similarly in *AGOSI* Bridge, LJ, stated that even if he were satisfied that the principle of international law existed and had been violated, he would not be prepared to rewrite the legislation in 'order to give effect to that principle'. In *Harman* the majority of the House of Lords found that the Convention was not relevant to the main issue, which they felt was a construction of the rules of discovery of documents. It was only the minority who thought the case raised questions concerning freedom of expression.

[31] *A.-G.* v. *Guardian (No. 2)* [1988] 3 All ER 545 (Chancery Division), 594 (Court of Appeal), 638 (House of Lords). See Ch. 1.2.2 for more details.

happened if the Convention had been law, and then call for its enactment.[32] For example, in January 1987 the Special Branch carried out a raid on the offices of the *New Statesman*. This raid lasted for four days without a break; other raids took place at the offices of the BBC, and at the houses of the journalist Duncan Campbell and the television producer Brian Barr. This prompted considerable criticism of the Government, but most interesting for present purposes is the fact that opponents of the Government phrased their attacks in terms of the Convention: David Owen stated that this raid 'shows the need for a bill of rights',[33] and Peter Kelner in the *New Statesman* constructed a scenario where the Interpretation Act (referred to above) was already part of the law:

Let us imagine that Sir Edward's bill was already on the statute book. The Special Branch arrive at the BBC's Scottish headquarters in Glasgow. They produce their warrant in conformity with the Official Secrets Act and the Police and Criminal Evidence Act. Under the Human Rights Act the BBC's lawyers would be able to test the warrant in a far more fundamental way than they were able to do last Saturday.

Article Ten of the Convention states that:

Everyone has the right to freedom of expression. This right shall include freedom to hold opinions and to receive and impart information and ideas without interference by public authority and regardless of frontiers ...

Last weekend's raid on the BBC violated its right both to receive and impart information. By removing the transmission copies of *all* of Duncan Campbell's films (and not just the one on the Zircon Project), it violated the BBC's right to impart information.

Suppose the BBC's lawyers had armed themselves with this article of the convention and sought an injunction to restrain the Special Branch from proceeding with their search. The lawyers working for the security services would presumably have based their claim to continue the search on paragraph two of Article Ten:

The exercise of these freedoms, since it carries with it duties and responsibilities, may be subject to such formalities, conditions, restrictions or penalties as are prescribed by law and are necessary in a democratic society, in the interests of national security, territorial integrity or public safety ...

'The interests of national security': upon those five words would the state seek to uphold its right to raid offices at weekends, wake up film technicians in the middle of the night and take away boxloads of films and papers. Doubtless the security

---

[32] *Observer*: 'The Real Case for a Bill of Rights' (1 Feb. 1987), 11; *Guardian*: 'Win One for Civil Liberties' (3 Feb. 1987), 12, 'Relentless Hounds in the Pursuit of Freedom' (3 Feb. 1987), 25, 'How to Take the Wrong Attitude to Citizen's Rights' (5 Feb. 1987), 19; *Financial Times*: 'Writing Civil Liberties into Law' (2 Feb. 1987); *The Economist*: 'Spycatcher Shambles' (8 Aug. 1987), 14, 'Out of the Bag' (8 Aug. 1987), 21–2; *New Statesman*: 'Civil Liberties: Overcoming the SEJ Factor' (Peter Kelner) (6 Feb. 1987), 3, 'Human Rights under the Law' (Lord Gifford) (6 Feb. 1987), 12.
[33] *Guardian* (2 Feb. 1987), 6.

services' lawyers would argue that the mere statement that 'the interests of national security were at stake' should be sufficient: it would be unnecessary to *prove* that national security were in jeopardy.

But wait. Article Ten does not leave the concept of 'national security' unqualified. It refers to 'formalities, conditions, restrictions or penalties as are prescribed by law *and are necessary in a democratic society*' (emphasis added). In other words, it is not enough for the state to say 'national security is at stake', or even 'national security is at stake and we've got the Official Secrets Act to back us up m'lud'. A judge, hearing the BBC's application for an injunction against the Special Branch, would have to be satisfied that the violation of human rights indicated by the warrant was based on rules that were 'necessary in a democratic society'.

If the BBC were to have fought last Saturday's warrant on those grounds under a Human Rights Act, a judge would have had three options. He could have held an immediate hearing and found for the Special Branch; or held an immediate hearing and held for the BBC; or stopped the search, ordered the BBC not to move or destroy any of the material relating to Campbell's programmes, and ordered a full scale hearing of the issue of whether the search was lawful.[34]

This passage is important as it shows two things: first, the Convention has entered into the vocabulary and imagination of those who want to hold the Government accountable; secondly, it is not the result of the scenario which is of immediate significance, but the possibility of it taking place. In this way some alleged violations (whether or not they might actually be justified in the courts later on) might be prevented; this is because their perpetrators may fear having their action scrutinized in the light of the Convention.

Another call for the incorporation of provisions of the Convention has come from G. McCormack after the shooting of three IRA members in Gibraltar.[35] McCormack compares the Criminal Law Act 1967, which provides that 'a person may use such force as is reasonable in the circumstances in the prevention of crime or in effecting or assisting in the lawful arrest of offenders or suspected offenders or of persons unlawfully at large' (Section 3), with Article 2 of the Convention, which states in paragraph 2 that the Article is not violated if the use of force was no more than absolutely necessary:

1. in defence of any person from unlawful violence;
2. in order to effect a lawful arrest or to prevent the escape of a person lawfully detained;
3. in action lawfully taken for the purposes of quelling a riot or insurrection.

---

[34] *New Statesman* (6 Feb. 1987), 3.
[35] *Independent*: 'Lack of Clarity on Lethal Force' (25 Mar. 1988), 18.

He suggests that Article 2 presents a clearer test. In effect this would mean that a killing by a member of the security or police force would contravene Article 2 unless it could be shown that the death was absolutely necessary; this is in effect just a question of a higher burden of proof, since under the criminal law now in force it is for the prosecution to show 'beyond reasonable doubt that the [soldier's] act of shooting constituted, in the circumstances, unreasonable force',[36] this being a question of fact.

Such a change could also make a difference in a claim based on civil law. In *Farrell* v. *Secretary of State for Defence* the widow of a man who was shot dead by soldiers while he was robbing a bank sued the Government for compensation.[37] However, the jury found that the soldiers had reasonable cause to suspect a bomb, and that it was reasonable to shoot to kill, and that such shooting was not out of proportion to the occasion. So the widow lost her case. She made an application to the European Commission of Human Rights which was declared admissible, as the Commission felt that the case raised the issue as to whether 'the use of force was no more than absolutely necessary to effect a lawful arrest'[38] (Article 2(2)(b)). However, the case ended in a friendly settlement,[39] with Mrs Farrell accepting the £37,000 offered to her by the Government. We cannot infer from this that the test under the Convention is more favourable to the widow than the test under the Criminal Law Act (Northern Ireland) 1967. We can only conclude that the Government was prepared to act on 'compassionate grounds and in order to terminate' the proceedings before the Commission;[40] whereas a jury in Northern Ireland were satisfied that the shooting was reasonable.[41]

These detailed comparisons of the different laws applicable in the United Kingdom courts and in the bodies of the Council of Europe in Strasbourg show some of the differences that incorporation of the Convention would make, yet they also demonstrate the usefulness of an international forum for challenging various state practices.[42] We should

---

[36] *A.-G. for Northern Ireland's Reference (No. 1 of 1975)* [1977] AC 105 at 139.
[37] [1980] 1 All ER 166.
[38] *Farrell* v. *UK*, Applic. 9013/80, 30 D. & R. 96, 11 Dec. 1982 at 102.
[39] *Farrell* v. *UK*, Applic. 9013/80, 38 D. & R. 44, 2 Oct. 1984.
[40] Extract from a letter of the UK Government quoted in 38 D. & R. 47.
[41] In another case, *Stewart* v. *UK*, Applic. 10044/82, 39 D. & R. 162, 10 July 1984, which involved an application by the mother of a 13-year-old boy killed by a plastic bullet fired by a British soldier, the Commission found that the use of force had been proportionate to the aim pursued—preventing serious injury in a 'riot' situation.
[42] Of course it could be argued that incorporation of the Convention would make it more difficult to obtain relief in Strasbourg, as it would take longer and be more expensive to exhaust domestic remedies as required by Art. 26. Also it might be argued that the scope allowed for claims under Art. 13 (complaints of no effective national remedy) would be reduced; similarly it could be said that incorporation would mean that the Commission would allow a larger margin of appreciation, as it would be unwilling to act as a 'fourth

be wary of those who argue that all questions of human rights should be decided at home.[43] It is not always a case of plaintiffs having to take the long and costly road to Strasbourg, but sometimes more a question of airing a difficult issue in an international forum.[44] Indeed the most often repeated argument in favour of incorporation of the Convention refers to the existing situation where the United Kingdom's 'dirty laundry is washed in public' and argues that these issues should be decided privately at home in the United Kingdom. However, an essential part of laundering dirty washing is airing it. Often a case in Strasbourg creates the opportunity to air grievances which might otherwise receive less attention.

3.2 JURY TRIALS

The rights contained in the Convention could have a significant effect on the outcome of jury trials where the provisions of the Convention would have superior status to domestic laws. This means that someone arrested for offences under the Public Order Act 1986 could plead in their defence the right to freedom of peaceful assembly and freedom of association. This could make a considerable impression on a jury. Similarly, in trials concerning Official Secrets, the defendant could rely on the right to freedom of expression, including the right to hold opinions and to receive and impart ideas. Of course all these rights are subject to restrictions in the interests of national security, public safety, and the prevention of disorder and crime, but the important point is that the right would be part of the law and therefore could be argued. It is not enough that the restriction exists in law, it has to be implemened 'in proportion' to the aim to be achieved.

---

instance'. None of these arguments is borne out in practice (Kerridge 1983: 272); for example in none of the countries where the Convention has been incorporated has there been a significant drop in the number of applications declared admissible by the Commission. Further evidence is provided by the the *Sunday Times* case (1979), where the European Court of Human Rights effectively reviewed the way that the House of Lords had balanced the right to free speech against the right to a fair trial and, in a way, 'overruled' them. Although it might be true that some cases would take longer to complete their domestic stage, this might be offset by the case subsequently being better prepared by the time it arrived at Strasbourg and therefore likely to pass more quickly through the various stages there (Kerridge 1983: 271–3).

[43] For example, Lord Hailsham: 'What we have done is put ourselves in the hands of judges at Strasbourg, instead of putting ourselves in the hands of judges in Westminster or Edinburgh' (*Listener* (12 Feb. 1987), 16: 'Would a Bill of Rights Politicise British Judges?').

[44] See esp. *Tyrer* v. *UK* (1978) (judicial birching in the Isle of Man) and *Dudgeon* v. *UK* (1981) (prohibition on homosexual sex in N. Ireland); in both these cases local opinion was in favour of laws which were eventually found to be incompatible with the Convention.

3.3 DISCRETIONARY DECISIONS

It is further suggested that the provisions of the Convention would have their greatest significance where discretionary decisions are taken. If the Convention were part of domestic law, its provisions would have to be considered not only in the courts but also when a discretionary power is exercised. Some of the most important cases which reach the Strasbourg Court and Commission, having originated in the United Kingdom, involve discretionary decisions in prisons and mental hospitals. To these can be added the cases which involve the decisions of the Secretary of State as well as decisions taken by the police and immigration officers. Should the Convention come to be considered in this way, so that violations of human rights are prevented rather than compensated, the effective protection of human rights could be greatly enhanced.

For example, the Public Order Act 1986 Section 14 concerns public assemblies of twenty or more people in a public place. It grants the police the power to impose restrictions on the size, location, or duration of the assembly, if the police reasonably believe that the assembly may result in 'serious disruption to the life of the community'. Should the police use this power unreasonably the decisions could be challenged by means of judicial review after the event, and the European Convention would be relevant. But even if the judiciary were to find against the police, the right of assembly would still have been seriously violated. The real strength of the Convention in this context lies in the fact that there would be an overriding right to assembly, and this would have to be taken into account by the police *before* exercising their discretion to impose restrictions. It would not only be the threat of judicial review which would ensure consideration of the Convention but also the fact that those who were arrested in defiance of the restrictions would be able to rely on the right to assembly at their criminal trial in front of a jury.

That the provisions of the Convention have a part to play in situations such as these is quite clear, and it is worth noting that the Government has sent a circular to the Chief Officer of Police and various Clerks to the Magistrates and Crown Courts pointing out that the provisions in the Public Order Act 1986 should be implemented in such a way that the provisions of the European Convention on Human Rights are not contravened.[45]

---

[45] See Home Office Circular No. 11/1987 ref. QPE/86 5/19/2 of 23 Feb. 1987, para. 11: 'The right to assemble, demonstrate and protest peacefully within the law is fundamental to our democratic way of life. Senior police officers responsible for the policing of assemblies and demonstrations will no doubt continue to have regard to the need to protect these rights within the framework provided by the law, including Part II of this Act. Under Articles 10 and 11 of the European Convention on Human Rights (to which the United Kingdom is a

3.4 THE JUDGES

The arguments against incorporation have usually revolved around the question of who should have the final word in such cases: the judges or the elected legislature? Opponents to incorporation in the past have pointed to the fact that judges cannot be voted out of office nor are they particularly representative of the community in terms of their education, class, sex, colour, age, and social interests.[46] Also it is often said that a Bill of Rights would politicize the judges, in that their appointment would become a matter of great political importance to the Government of the day.[47] All these arguments lose some of their force when the proposals involve an Interpretation Act, rather than a Bill of Rights, as in this case the Government still has the final say, and the risks of a head-on clash between the Government and the judges are considerably reduced.

From the previous chapters it is clear that the judiciary already decide cases which raise issues under the Convention.[48] Incorporation of the Convention would expose many of the choices which judges make as 'judgments' between competing claims; in this sense they would be more political, but it is suggested that little would change as regards their appointment. Indeed, if the presence of the European Convention as part of the law of the United Kingdom acted as a catalyst for instigating a considered system of judicial appointment and retirement, the 'legitimacy' of judicial review would be slightly enhanced. The importance of judicial representativeness is underlined by D. Pannick in his book *Judges*:

If it would not result in an unacceptable diminution in the quality of our judges, basic principles of representative government suggest that the judiciary should cease to reflect the values, background, and interests of so narrow a slice of society. One important way to encourage respect for the law is to show those whose behaviour it regulates that the law is made by those whom it binds, not by a remote group whose attitudes and ideals are foreign to those of ordinary people. The judiciary can claim many virtues. But it can not pretend to be representative of the populace. A broadening of the judicial base would do much to strengthen the rule of law. (1987: 53)

---

signatory) everyone has the right to freedom of expression and to assemble peacefully and associate with others.'

[46] See Griffith (1979: 17; 1985*b*). For a survey of the background of the judiciary see 'Judges on Trial', *Labour Research* (Jan. 1987), 9.

[47] See Lloyd (1976: 121).

[48] Note also the numerous cases raising questions of 'fundamental human rights' where the Convention was not referred to, and which were therefore not reported in the previous chapters: *Re B. (a Minor) (Wardship Sterilisation)* [1987] 2 All ER 206 (House of Lords decision granting authority to Sunderland Council to carry out a sterilization operation on a 17-year-old mentally handicapped girl); *Re Adoption (Surrogacy)* [1987] 2 All ER 826; *C. v. S.* [1987] 2 WLR 1108 (father's attempt to obtain an injunction to prevent an abortion).

Having called for a more representative judiciary Pannick is forced to conclude that there are few representative judges waiting in the wings:

The English judiciary includes few women, even fewer blacks, and nobody under the age of 40. English judges tend to be elderly gentlemen most of whom have had a public school education. It is disturbing that our judges come from so narrow a range of the community.

To adjudicate cases is to exercise discretion in fact finding, sentencing, applying the law and awarding costs. Such powers should be exercised by judges of disparate backgrounds, ages, races, and sexes. This is for two main reasons. First, it is inequitable in a democratic society that one set of values should so predominate on the Bench. Secondly, there is a danger that minority groups and women faced by a Bench where they see few, if any of their number will lose respect for the law. A more diverse judiciary is unlikely to be attained while appointment is confined to practising barristers. There are few blacks, women, and Labour Party supporters among the ranks of senior barristers. (1987: 59)

Although historically it would have been nearly impossible for ordinary people to become lawyers, some barriers have been removed; yet in many ways the profession, and particularly the Bar, remains unattractive to representatives of those groups most oppressed under the law. At this point perhaps we should take a different perspective, and ask whether, if the law came to include the European Convention, so that questions of dignity, discrimination, and democracy were openly debated in the courts by lawyers, in the vocabulary of human rights—would practitioners from a wider base be attracted to the law?[49] We could go further and say that concentrating on the lack of representativeness among the senior barristers and the judiciary misses the point—there are already many lawyers who both represent, and are representative of, disadvantaged groups. These lawyers may be 'legal aid solicitors; barristers servicing legal aid solicitors; lawyers working in Community law centres and Citizen's Advice Bureaux'[50] or legal activists working for pressure groups such as CPAG (Child Poverty Action Group) or JCWI (Joint Council for the Welfare of Immigrants).[51] It is incoherent to expect those who are lobbying for radical changes in the law simultaneously to take on the role of the judge and upholder of the present order. Of course the judiciary should be more representative than it is at present: not only would this make the system seem fairer, but it would also allow a much wider range of

---

[49] This is not to say that there are no representative barristers in the UK; see the recent research by S. A. Scheingold, 'Radical Lawyers and Socialist Ideas', *Journal of Law and Society* (1988), 122–38. It is worth noting the emphasis which is placed on a rights strategy (125, 135). Ronald Dworkin argues that the legal profession changed in the USA due to a 'rights conception of the rule of law'. See 'Political Judges and the Rule of Law' in Dworkin (1985*a*: 9–32 at 31).

[50] This group is discussed by Cooper (1986: 161).

[51] See Dhavan and Partington (1986: 236).

experiences to be brought into the decision-making process; but the real question to be addressed is, should the judges, whatever their composition, be allowed to review the acts of the legislature in this way?

3.5 THE LEGITIMACY OF JUDICIAL REVIEW

At the theoretical level it is hard to make a case for giving the judges the power to annul provisions contained in legislation or even subordinate legislation. But if we examine this power in the context of the United Kingdom and the European Convention on Human Rights, then it emerges that, so far, the major beneficiaries of the judicial decisions in Strasbourg based on the Convention have been prisoners,[52] mental patients,[53] immigrants,[54] and children.[55] In most cases these beneficiaries do not have the right to vote,[56] so it can be argued that, as they have no power through the ballot box, it is legitimate to protect their 'interests' (rights) with a supra-legislative norm or Convention. To legitimize generally the institution of judicial review of legislation is more problematical.[57]

For example, Article 1 of Protocol 1 concerns respect for possessions. So it would seem that the Convention is a potential tool, in the hands of those with property, against a government trying to redistribute wealth. But Article 1 of the First Protocol contains paragraph (2), which allows for deprivation of possessions in the 'public interest'. It is important to note that the European Court of Human Rights has held (in a case which was brought by shareholders complaining about the Labour Government's nationalization legislation of 1977) that they will allow a large 'margin of appreciation' as regards nationalization, and that the Court would respect the legislature's judgment for future legislation.[58]

---

[52] *Ireland* v. *UK* (1978); *Golder* v. *UK* (1975); *Silver* v. *UK* (1983); *Weeks* v. *UK* (1987); and also the numerous findings and settlements of the Commission.

[53] *X* v. *UK* (1981), and also note the changes made in the UK in the light of findings against other countries by the Strasbourg organs.

[54] *Abdulaziz, Cabales and Balkandali*, judgment of 28 May 1985, Series A, vol. 94; *Alam and Kahn* v. *UK* [1967] 10 Yearbook 788; this friendly settlement stimulated changes in the UK appeals legislation in the field of immigration.

[55] *Campbell and Cosans* v. *UK* (1982) Series A, vol. 48; *Tyrer* v. *UK* (1979).

[56] See Representation of the People Act 1983: prisoners: s. 3(1); mental patients: s. 7(1); and children (under 18): s. 1(1)(c).

[57] For one suggestion see M. Cappelletti, in Favoreu and Jolowicz (1986: 314), where he concludes that: 'As long as constitutional judges act with this very purpose in mind—to reinforce fundamental freedoms—the democratic legitimacy of judicial review can hardly be denied.' See also 'The Futile Search for Legitimacy', ch. 1 of Tribe (1985, esp. 6–7). For a philosophical approach to this question see O'Hagan (1984), who, having dealt with aspects of Hegel, Marx, Tönnies, and Habermas, argues for a philosophy of law which gives a central place to judicial review, and in particular to the civil rights found in the Convention.

[58] *Case of Lithgow and Others*, 8 July 1986, Series A, vol. 102.

Similarly in the *Case of James and Others*,[59] where the Duke of West-minster complained of a breach of Article 1 of the First Protocol, due to the operation of the Leasehold Reform Act 1967 (as amended), which grants, in certain circumstances, to a tenant (under a long lease) the right to buy the freehold of the property, the Strasbourg Court held that the national legislature was to enjoy a wide margin of appreciation in inter-preting social and economic policies. If the Court had held that the Convention protected the wealth of landlords and shareholders against the reforms of an elected legislature, it would have suggested to many that the rhetoric of 'human rights' was another device to entrench the values of liberal individualism against periodic tides of 'reformist' socialism.

Although it is quite possible that a British court could have interpreted the same Article and come to the opposite result—and found in favour of the shareholders/landlords—under the present doctrine of parliamentary sovereignty, Parliament (or in reality the Government) would be able to pass legislation which reversed the court's decision. There are several examples of government legislation with this effect. For example, after the Secretary of State's direction concerning the take-over of Lambeth Council by commissioners was held invalid by the courts,[60] the Govern-ment passed the National Health Service (Invalid Direction) Act 1980 which declares the 'invalid' direction to take effect as if it had been valid.

Obviously a judicial ruling that nationalization legislation was invalid could prove embarrassing for a government committed to the 'rule of law', but it must be emphasized that the possibility of such a ruling has been much diminished by the *Lithgow* judgment in Strasbourg, and in any event such a ruling would hardly deter any government committed to radical change.

3.6 CONCLUSION ON THE DESIRABILITY OF A BILL OF RIGHTS

If the 'big cases' in the House of Lords are unlikely to be decided differently (especially where the issue of 'national security' is raised by the Government), and judicial decisions are liable to be reversed by retrospective legislation, it might be said that the present proposals for a Bill of Rights (Interpretation Act) would change very little. While in no way suggesting that a Bill of Rights would solve all the inequalities and injustices which exist, it is suggested that its introduction could have at least an important educative impact. It could have an impact in different spheres in the following ways:

[59] *Case of James and Others*, 21 Feb. 1986, Series A, vol. 98.
[60] *Lambeth Council* v. *Sec. of State for Social Services* (1980) 79 LGR 61.

1. It could have an effect on the judges and legal profession who would be called on to examine both the Convention and the case-law of the European Commission and Court of Human Rights.

2. It would provide some sort of accessible code for ordinary people as to some of their principal rights on arrest[61] and after detention,[62] and could be particularly important for groups such as prisoners and refugees; not only are minimum 'European standards' emerging in relation to such people, but they are already becoming increasingly familiar to groups such as the prisoners themselves. The Convention has sometimes formed a focal point for certain pressure groups in the United Kingdom,[63] including MIND (National Association for Mental Health); STOPP (Society of Teachers Opposed to Physical Punishment); NIGRA (Northern Ireland Gay Rights Association); NCCL (National Council for Civil Liberties), now renamed 'Liberty'; JUSTICE (British Section of International Commission of Jurists); CAJ (Committee on the Administration of Justice); PROP (Preservation of the Rights of Prisoners); JCWI (Joint Council for the Welfare of Immigrants). This is a phenomenon particular to the United Kingdom,[64] but is of increasing relevance at the European level in Strasbourg now that there are greater rights of audience before the Court, and that the procedure for intervention by interested 'third parties' is more familiar. What is most relevant to the present discussion is the fact that there exists a certain amount of expertise and experience of the Convention which is to some extent accessible to the groups who stand to benefit most from incorporation of the European Convention into United Kingdom law.

3. Public authorities, or rather their officers, would be obliged to consider the Convention and its jurisprudence when exercising their discretion. In this way not only would there be remedies for failure to consider the Convention, but it may also be that, in some circumstances, violations would be avoided.

4. It may be that the principles contained in the Convention will become persuasive generally. For example, Article 14 states that the rights in the Convention 'shall be secured without discrimination on any ground such as sex, race, colour, language, religion, political or other opinion, national or social origin, association with a national minority, property, birth or other status'.[65] The strength of such wide Articles lies

---

[61] Art. 6(3).

[62] Art. 5.

[63] For the tactics involved in these campaigns see Grosz and Hulton (1986: 138–57).

[64] The late Judge Wiarda, former President and one of the longest-serving judges at the European Court of Human Rights, suggested that this in some part explains the disproportionate number of cases against the UK which end in hearings before the Court of Human Rights. See *Forum* (Council of Europe), 1/85 at 2.

[65] Although the Article refers to the other Articles in the Convention, it is not necessary

in their capacity to fill gaps where legislation has not been enacted, through lack of either foresight or enthusiasm.

Since the appearance of the AIDS virus, gay men have been increasingly discriminated against.[66] Gay men are clearly covered by Article 14, and it would seem that the practice of denying life assurance policies or endowment mortgages to those whose life-style suggests homosexuality[67] is a violation of the spirit of Article 14.[68] However, it is clear that only States can be held responsible before the Court of Human Rights in Strasbourg. (Whether or not this Court is ready to extend state responsibility so as to encompass failure to legislate in a situation such as the one outlined above is a question which will be examined in Part II.)

It is worth noting a declaration of the Commission des Droits de la Personne du Québec to the effect that Article 10 of the Quebec Charter of Human Rights and Freedoms prohibits a refusal to rent accommodation to someone affected by or suspected of carrying AIDS, and prohibits a refusal of access to a hotel or restaurant, or a refusal by an employer to hire, or a dismissal on the grounds of being an AIDS sufferer, and that the Commission will accept complaints along these lines.[69] Clearly human rights charters can have a real role to play in such cases.[70]

---

to show that one of the other Articles has been violated; it is enough that the matter is covered by one of the other Articles. See *Belgian Linguistics* case (1967) Series A, vol. 6.

[66] This mainly occurs in four spheres: employment, education, the Church, and insurance. See also Wacks (1988: 254–5), who points out that the ELISA-Western blot (WB) series of tests does not test for AIDS, but only 'indicates previous viral exposure and an increased *risk* of developing the disease. There is a real danger of discrimination against homosexuals and bisexuals if this fact is overlooked' (254).

[67] For research involving twelve insurance companies see *Labour Research* (Sept. 1987), 11–12, where comments from Royal Life Insurance suggest that a 'promiscuous homosexual, even with a negative HIV test' would not be offered terms. For the American experience see Shatz (1987: 1782); and Clifford and Inculano (1987: 1806).

[68] Probably coupled with either Art. 3 or Art. 8; arguably the reference in Art. 14 to 'other status' covers the status of AIDS sufferers, so that discrimination in certain fields would be prohibited; doubtless there might be some cases where it would be legitimate to exclude an AIDS sufferer from certain types of work, and the situation is one which calls for concrete legislation, but this example shows how rights to privacy, association, and non-discrimination may be instrumental in filling a legislative vacuum. The philosophical force of the right to dignity and autonomy ought to 'trump' background justifications based on prejudice. (Some of the philosophical justifications for rights are dealt with in Ch. 5.) Of course this is only one point of view; another approach views majoritarian communal prejudice against AIDS sufferers as capable of 'trumping' the rights of those with AIDS, and suggests that the use of a rights thesis to protect AIDS sufferers is antidemocratic: the 'public prefer such decisions [concerning the rights of AIDS sufferers] to be taken by elected bodies which are answerable directly to the public; not by courts which are not' (McCluskey 1987: 39).

[69] *Droits et libertés forum (Bulletin de la Commission des Droits de la Personne du Québec)*: 'La Charte protège les sidatiques contre la discrimination' (4 (June 1988), 1–2).

[70] Note that the federal Canadian Charter of Rights and Freedoms has now been interpreted as prohibiting discrimination on grounds of sexual orientation: *Veysey* v. *Canadian Correctional Service* [1989] 44 CRR 364 (FTD).

Whether or not insurance companies would be obliged to conform with the norms of the Convention under a new Bill of Rights depends on the exact wording of that Bill.[71] It would have been most significant if the norms of the Convention had had an educative force, so that a policy of discriminating against those with a certain life-style had never been implemented.[72] Of course, such a change in attitude would not follow immediately in the wake of a Bill of Rights, but the above example of the insurance companies raises several questions. If the Bill of Rights is to operate as an educative force, should it create not only rights for groups and individuals but also duties to respect those rights? If the Bill of Rights were to operate only as a guarantee of protection for the individual when threatened by the State, would it not abandon those threatened by big business? Are we more interested in the breach of the rules by the perpetrator, or the harm to the victim? To what extent the European Convention on Human Rights has already been used against private bodies in the case-law of the European Commission and Court of Human Rights in Strasbourg is an issue which needs further examination. Although the question is often posed as one of 'state responsibility', these European bodies have had occasion to consider the applicability of the European Convention on Human Rights to the actions of 'private bodies', and the lead of Strasbourg may well be most decisive in determining the extent to which the Convention will be used against private bodies and institutions, both at the international level and in the United Kingdom. It is to this supranational dimension that we now turn.

[71] Under the present proposals it is quite feasible that the insurance companies could be held to be violators of the Convention, as the Act would apply to any 'public body'—defined as 'a body of persons, whether corporate or unincorporate, carrying on a service or undertaking of a public nature and includes public authorities of all descriptions'. The question of the applicability of the Convention to 'public bodies' is covered in detail in Part II.

[72] On the subject of the rights of lesbians and gay men in European law see generally *Homosexuality: A European Community Issue*, K. Waaldijk and A. Clapham (eds.) (Dordrecht, Nijhoff, 1993).

PART II

The Application of Human Rights in the Sphere of Relations between Non-State Bodies

4

International Human Rights and Private Bodies: Two Approaches

4.1 INTRODUCTION

Part II deals primarily with the case-law of international or 'supranational' organs: the European Commission of Human Rights (Strasbourg), the European Court of Human Rights (Strasbourg), and the European Court of Justice of the European Communities in Luxembourg. This part also contains a brief excursus through the case-law of the Supreme Court of the United States and the Supreme Court of Canada. The approach of these last two courts is interesting for present purposes due to the influence of the Common Law dimension as well as the presence of similar centripetal tensions to those found at the supranational level in Europe.

One particular aspect of this case-law is analysed: the protection of human rights when the immediate violation is by private individuals or bodies (as opposed to officials or States). This question has already commanded considerable attention as regards the European Convention on Human Rights;[1] however, most of these commentators stick with the questions: was the European Convention *meant* to create duties for private bodies? or does textual analysis lead to the conclusion that the Convention can be interpreted as creating rights against private bodies?[2] Since these commentaries were written, the European Court of Human Rights has clearly stated that the rights in the Convention create obligations for States which involve 'the adoption of measures designed to secure respect for private life *even in the sphere of the relations of individuals between themselves'.*[3] This has also been affirmed by the Court in the context of the right to counter-demonstrate: 'Like Article 8, Article 11 sometimes requires positive measures to be taken, even in the sphere of relations between individuals, if need be.'[4]

---

[1] Eissen (1961); *Les Droits de l'homme et les personnes morales* (colloquium) (Brussels: Bruylant, 1970); *René Cassin*, iii; Jeammaud (1981: 71); Drzemczewski (1983: ch. 8); Daes (1983); Barsotti (1984); Forde (1985: 253); Niset (1987: 123).

[2] See esp. de Meyer (1973: 255), and the counter-arguments put by K. J. Partsch at 275 of the same volume.

[3] *Case of X and Y v. The Netherlands* (1985) Series A, vol. 91, para. 23 (emphasis added).

[4] *Case of Plattform 'Ärzte für das Leben'* (1988) Series A, vol. 139, para. 32.

These two judgments, *X and Y* and *Plattform Ärzte*, suggest that the question is no longer: do the Convention rights apply in the private sphere? Now it is: which rights apply? and to what extent?[5] This study takes up the challenge laid down by Professor Rivero after he had concluded that there can be little justification for differentiating between the private and the public abuse of power: 'Il resterait à analyser les indications de ces conclusions, non plus au niveau des États, mais au niveau de la société internationale. Ce serait un nouveau et vaste problème.'[6] A. G. Toth has pointed to the following passage in the first edition of the manual on the Convention written by van Dijk and van Hoof: 'Precisely on account of the fundamental character of these rights it can not be understood why they should deserve protection in relation to the public authorities, but not in relation to private individuals.'[7] He then states: 'Such a general statement does not seem justified: the question of *Drittwirkung*[8] must be raised and examined *in relation to each of the rights protected.*'[9]

---

[5] The Steering Committee on Human Rights in Strasbourg has set itself the subject 'Implications of human rights in relations between the State and Individuals and violations of human rights by individuals or groups' in its *Third Medium Term Plan for 1987–1991: 'Democratic Europe: Humanism, Dignity, Universality'* (Strasbourg, Dec. 1986), 18–19 (this Plan was adopted by the Committee of Ministers on 26 Nov. 1986 in Res. 86(21)). The question has already been raised once before at the Council of Europe; see *Parliamentary Conference on Human Rights* (Vienna, 18–20 Oct. 1971) (Strasbourg: Council of Europe, 1972), 71–2, and the subsequent Rec. 683 (1972), which called on a Committee of Experts to 'Study the possibility of preparing a charter to protect human rights against private persons and agencies' (C8). However, the Committee felt that 'the extension of the concept of human rights to include also the relations between private persons would have major consequences in several member countries, in various fields of domestic law, particularly in regard to civil and labour law', although some experts thought the question of 'considerable importance, since essential human rights in the social and economic field are threatened particularly by private persons and agencies' (DH/Exp(73)44 of 16 Nov. 1973 at 9). The question now seems to have been settled for the government experts, at least in the Committee of Experts for the Improvement of Procedures for the Protection of Human Rights (DH-PR). See 'The European Convention on Human Rights: Institution of review proceedings at the national level to facilitate compliance with Strasbourg decisions', paras. 9, 61–8, which specifically refer to different types of civil cases based on the Convention in domestic law (13 *HRLJ* 1992), 71–8.

[6] ('The question now has to be analysed not at the national but at the international level. This presents a new and vast problem.') (Rivero 1971: 322). Similarly Barsotti points out that conflicts have to be resolved 'nella stessa sede' ('from where they originated') i.e. the inter-state legal system (Barsotti 1985: 431).

[7] van Dijk and van Hoof (1984: 15–16). The note by Toth was a book review in *YEL* (1986), 461.

[8] This is a reference to the developed German theory of the application of fundamental rights to the legal relations between individuals, i.e. to the private sphere. At this point it would not be helpful to describe this theory in all its variants. (*Drittwirkung* is more accurately *Drittwirkung der Grundrechte* or the third-party effect of fundamental rights/'effets quant aux tiers des droits fondamentaux'.) The best account (in English) is Lewan (1968: 571–601); for a more recent analysis see Rigaux (1990: 674–85), who clearly demonstrates the inappropriateness of notions of *Drittwirkung* in this field. See also the discussion in Ch. 7.1.

[9] A. G. Toth *YEL* (1986), 461 (book reviews) (emphasis added); Niset makes a similar

These are exactly the approaches which will be followed: the problem will be examined at the international level and in the context of various Articles of the European Convention: Articles 2, 3, 6, 8, 10, 11, 13, and 17. These are the Articles in relation to which this question has already been touched on by the European Commission and Court of Human Rights.

4.2 BUT ONLY STATES CAN BE ACCUSED OF VIOLATING INTERNATIONAL HUMAN RIGHTS!

The proposition that the European Convention on Human Rights covers the protection of human rights against the actions of private bodies and individuals not only challenges traditional assumptions[10] and conceptions[11] of human rights, but is hard to reconcile with the fact that only States Parties to the European Convention on Human Rights can be accused before the Convention organs.[12] However, it will be shown that this proposition is relevant to both the present situation and the future of the European Convention on Human Rights. The question of the private abuse of human rights can and does arise in the following ways:

1. When applicants are told that their applications are inadmissible, as they themselves have to respect the Articles contained in the Convention.

plea: 'La question de la *Drittwirkung*, évoquée par la doctrine, n'a cependant, à ce jour, pas encore fait l'objet de recherches systématiques de la part des experts' (1987: 128), and later: 'L'obligation qui s'impose aux bénéficiaires des droits garantis de respecter différents intérêts jugés prioritaires ou équivalents (cas des articles 8, 9, 10, 11 de la Convention et 2 du protocole no. 4) pourrait être étudiée, de même que la question de la *Drittwirkung*. Celle-ci ferait avantageusement l'objet d'un exposé descriptif de la situation actuelle' (1987: 137).

[10] 'A tacit assumption underlying much discussion of human rights seems to be that, although all persons have these rights, the obligations corresponding to a person's rights lie only on his or her own government. I shall refer to this as "the standard assumption"' (Nelson 1981: 281). Nelson then searches for philosophical considerations to justify such an assumption—he suggests that ethical relativism, and the fact that rights require interpretation, leads to the conclusion that 'these rights are, in effect rights against institutions' (294).

[11] e.g. 'Human Rights, I stress, are rights against society as represented by government and its officials' (Henkin 1979: 2); and 'human rights are held or at least exercised, primarily in relation to the State' (Donnelly 1985: 6). But more recently Henkin seems to have modified his stance: 'But a state party is obligated also "to ensure" the recognized rights. That seems to imply that rights recognized are not merely rights against government (as are rights under the U.S. Constitution for example), but also against other persons' (Henkin 1987: 10).

[12] See Art. 25 and a passage in an early commentary by Goslong, *Das Rechtsschutzsystem der Europäischen Menschenrechtskonvention* (1958), which is quoted by Eissen (1962: 232) and translated (247) as 'Individuals are not Parties to the Convention and therefore assume no obligations under it. This is quite clear from Article 1 and Article 25, which authorises applications against States only.' See Eissen (1962: 230–53), who rejects such an interpretation, stating: 'the absence of international sanctions does not necessarily exclude the existence of obligations' (233).

2. When the State is held responsible for a private violation, due to its failure to legislate or take other preventive action.

3. Where the European Commission or Court of Human Rights decides whether a particular body is an organ of the State or a private body.

4. Where the State is held responsible due to a domestic court sanctioning or failing to compensate a private violation.

5. Where Council of Europe human rights treaties are relevant. The European Convention on Transfrontier Television will highlight the existence and scope of the 'duties and responsibilities' (Article 10(2)) which accompany the right to freedom of expression and the right to receive and impart information. In the context of the written press the European Court of Human Rights has already referred to this phrase when denying a journalist protection under Article 10(1).[13] The Court has likewise had to decide to what extent broadcasters are under a duty to respect other people's rights to freedom of expression and pluralism in broadcasting.[14] The new possibilities for transnational broadcasting may well provide the Strasbourg organs with plenty of cases in which they may be 'forced' indirectly to impose duties and responsibilities on broadcasters and journalists.

Similarly the Council of Europe Convention for the Protection of Individuals with Regard to Automatic Processing of Personal Data (1981) does not give jurisdiction to the Court but to a Consultative Assembly (Articles 18–20). But it is worth noting that Article 3(1) reads as follows: 'The Parties undertake to apply this Convention to automated processing of personal data in the public and private sectors.'[15] This inter-governmental recognition of the importance of providing guarantees to individuals faced with threats from non-state actors may come to reinforce the application of the European Convention on Human Rights in the private sphere.

6. Where a private violation is alleged at the national level. In this situation the restrictions of Article 25 do not apply. For example, an employee or tenant may wish to complain that his or her employer or landlord has discriminated on the grounds of religion. The Convention has been deemed relevant in such cases.[16] It is not even necessary that

---

[13] *Case of Markt Intern*, judgment of 20 Nov. 1989, Series A, vol. 165, at para. 37.

[14] *Groppera* case, judgment of 28 Mar. 1990, Series A, vol. 173 at paras. 69 and 70. The Court accepted that the legislation in question had the aim of protecting the rights of others 'as it was designed to ensure pluralism, in particular in information, by allowing a fair allocation of frequencies' (at para. 69).

[15] In force since 15 Oct. 1985; for text see *European Yearbook* (1981), 329–43.

[16] See Evans (1979: 109–98, esp. 125, 137, 153, 169, 185); for some more recent examples see Velu (1990: 138, paras. 89–96, 280, 302, 578, 644, 649, 680, 702, 713, 738, 794). See also a decision of the Tribunal Civil de Bruxelles, 21 Nov. 1990, concerning the duties of the press under Arts. 8 and 10 of the Convention: *Forrest et SPRL, Malta-Forrest* v. *Braekman et SA Rossel* [1991] Jurisprudence de Liège, Mons et Bruxelles 24–8.

the Convention should have the status of internal law,[17] as its provisions may be considered as elements of 'public policy', 'ordre public', 'Treu und Glauben' ('good faith'), or the 'Wertordung' ('value order').[18] A further way in which a private violation may be relevant at the national level would be where someone brings a case against the State claiming that the authorities did not sufficiently protect their rights against violation by private bodies.[19]

7. If the present plans[20] to create a preliminary ruling procedure for the Strasbourg Court were ever to be implemented, then the Strasbourg organs might have to consider on a regular basis questions of private violations of rights. The purpose of such a procedure would be to elucidate, for the benefit of national courts, the best interpretation of the Convention. As some national courts already consider the Convention relevant to disputes between private parties, the Court would be thwarting the purpose of the procedure if it refused to rule on questions concerning private violations.

4.3 TWO APPROACHES

The intention here, however, is not merely to challenge the traditional conceptions concerning international human rights law. It is suggested that two different approaches actually justify the contention that it is no longer viable to cling to the traditional view that the Convention only covers human rights violations by States:

1. International law recognizes that individuals or private bodies are capable of committing violations of human rights and there

---

[17] In the countries covered by Evans (1979), the Convention did have the status of internal law (Austria, Belgium, Federal Republic of Germany, The Netherlands, Switzerland). Malta has recently enacted the European Convention Act 1987, and there is no limitation in this Act restricting claims against private individuals (see Art. 4(1)).

[18] See Drzemczewski (1983: 204–18) and Rigaux (1990: 674) for examples. For the use of the Convention in the UK see Chs. 1 and 2.

[19] See Evans (1979: 169).

[20] See Rec. 1020 (1985) adopted 2 Oct. 1985 and the Study prepared by A. H. Robertson —app. 1 to doc. 5459 of 17 Sept. 1985. Advocates of such a procedure include Drzemczewski (1983: 339–41) and Arnull (1985: 376). For arguments against such a procedure see Muchlinski (1984: 240–8) (book review). A full bibliography concerning the question of preliminary rulings for the Strasbourg Court is given by Betten and Korte (1987: 76). The Steering Committee for Human Rights, at its meeting 22–6 May 1989, endorsed the conclusions of the Committee of Experts for the Improvement of Procedures for the Protection of Human Rights (DH-PR) that it would not be appropriate at the present time to pursue examination of the possibility of preliminary rulings by the European Court of Human Rights (*Information Sheet No. 25* (Strasbourg: Council of Europe), 61). For an introduction to the work of the DH-PR and other inter-governmental committees in the field of human rights at the Council of Europe see Drzemczewski (1990: 89–117).

are various jurisdictions to prevent, punish, or compensate these violations; therefore a contextual[21] interpretation of the European Convention on Human Rights requires that it include such violations.

2. In practice it is impossible to differentiate the private from the public sphere. Even if we feel we can distinguish between the two, such difficult distinctions leave a lacuna in the protection of human rights, and can in themselves be particularly dangerous.

4.3.1 Approach 1: The evolution of human rights and duties

This first approach leads us straight into the doctrinal debate surrounding the issue of whether the individual is a subject of international law.[22] It is not intended to rehearse this debate in the context of the entire field of public international law. But it is worth stressing that, in the context of human rights law, private bodies and individuals do have 'rights' and 'duties' and must be considered to some extent subjects of international law.

Evidence of the existence of *rights* is present in particular in the machinery of the European Commission and Court of Human Rights in Strasbourg. Not only can an individual or non-governmental body petition the Commission,[23] but since 1982 applicants have had certain rights to take part in proceedings before the Court of Human Rights,[24] and following the tenth ratification of the Ninth Protocol individuals will have the

---

[21] That treaties should be interpreted in such a way rather than according to their literal meaning is clear from the advisory opinion of the ICJ in *The Legal Consequences for States of the Continued Presence of South Africa in Namibia (South West Africa) Notwithstanding Security Council 271 (1970)* [1971] ICJ Rep. p. 31, para. 53; in the case-law of the European Court of Human Rights there are several passages which refer to the necessity of an evolutive and contextual approach to the interpretation of the Convention: *Tyrer* v. *UK* (1978) pp. 15–16, para. 31; *Marckx* v. *Belgium* (1979) p. 19, para. 41; *Dudgeon* v. *UK* (1981) p. 24, para. 60 (further reference is made to these paragraphs below).

[22] See A. Cassese, 'Individuo (diritto internazionale)' in *Enciclopedia di diritto* (Milan: Giuffrè, 1971), xxi. 223, for an extensive bibliography. More recently the doctrine is reviewed by G. Fourlanos, 'Subjectivity in International Law and the Position of the Individual', *Nordisk Tidsskrift for International Ret* (1984), 9; and Barboza (1984: 375–91).

[23] Art. 25; there is an analogous procedure under the Optional Protocol to the International Covenant on Civil and Political Rights, whereby individuals may petition the Human Rights Committee of the UN as regards a violation of that Covenant. Henkin points to the Optional Protocol and concludes: 'so even if a "conservative" view is taken that State parties have only undertaken obligations to other State parties it has to be admitted that "the individual can claim an international right to this particular remedy"' (Henkin 1987: 11). (The Optional Protocol was adopted by the General Assembly on 16 Dec. 1966 and has been in force since 23 Mar. 1976.)

[24] Formalized in the revised Rules of Court (adopted 24 Nov. 1982), Rule 33(3)(*d*) in connection with Rule 30. It seems that this has become the norm rather than the exception, so now the judges are faced with three sets of lawyers: those of the respondent Government, the Commission's delegates, and those of the applicant.

possibility of seising the Court.[25] Moreover, not only is the judgment of the Court addressed to the respondent State, but the Court has the power to award compensation to individual applicants. (So for example in the *Bozano* case,[26] where France was found to have violated Mr Bozano's right to security of the person by unlawfully deporting him to Switzerland in order to 'ease' his extradition to Italy, Mr Bozano was awarded 100,000 French francs.[27])

A counter-argument would run as follows: individuals can petition the Commission, but this is only an investigative/conciliatory body whose main aim is to achieve a friendly settlement[28] or provide a legal opinion.[29] Individuals have no right at present to seise the Court; this can only be done by a Contracting Party or by the Commission.[30] Any procedural rights of audience which applicants may actually have do not in fact alter their substantive *rights*: an award of compensation is not enforceable, and so these judicial awards are irrelevant as regards legal subjectivity. A third possibility is to suggest that the regional protection of human rights, as found in the European and American Conventions, represents a 'third order of law, which is neither national nor international'.[31]

Nevertheless what is clear is that individuals do have *duties* under international law. This was established with the introduction of legal instruments outlawing slavery and piracy,[32] and with the regulation of the high seas and outer space.[33] In the context of human rights, the Charter of the International Military Tribunal (at Nuremberg) clearly fixes duties on individuals for 'crimes against humanity'.

On 1 October 1946 the Nuremberg Tribunal delivered a judgment in which the concept of individual responsibility was clearly recognized. It stated that individuals had duties to obey international law: 'that international law imposes duties and liabilities upon individuals as well as

---

[25] See Council of Europe docs., H(90)9 and H(90)10; the Ninth Protocol was signed by fifteen States in Rome on 6 Nov. 1990. On the possibility of merger of the Commission and Court see H(92)14.

[26] *Bozano* case, 18 Dec. 1986, Series A, vol. 111.

[27] *Bozano* case (Art. 50) 2 Dec. 1987, Series A, vol. 124.

[28] Art. 28 ECHR.

[29] Art. 31 ECHR.

[30] Art. 44 ECHR, but see the new Ninth Protocol (above), not yet in force. Art. 5 provides the procedure which enables the individual to put his or her case before the Court. The case will still go first to the Commission in the normal way.

[31] Muchlinski (1985: 381); Muchlinski rejects the 'third order' approach. Cf. Drzemczewski (1980: 54).

[32] A modern example is Art. 15 of the Geneva Convention on the High Seas 1958, defining the crime of piracy in international law. (This Article is substantially the same as Art. 103 of the UN Convention on the Law of the Sea (Montego Bay), which is not yet in force).

[33] See Condorelli (1988: 149–56), s. 8, 'Droits de l'homme et imputation: Quelques réflexions sur les questions de la *Drittwirkung* et de la responsabilité de l'État pour faits de particuliers'.

upon States has long been recognized . . . Crimes against international law are committed by men, not by abstract entities, and only by punishing individuals who commit such crimes can the provisions of international law be enforced.'[34]

The principles of international law recognized by the Nuremberg Tribunal were affirmed in a Resolution of the General Assembly of the UN on 11 December 1946.[35] On the same day the Assembly passed a Resolution on the crime of genocide[36] which states in part that 'Genocide is a crime under international law which the civilized world condemns, and for the commission of which principals and accomplices—*whether private individuals*, public officials or statesmen, and whether the crime is committed on religious, racial, political or any other grounds are punishable' (emphasis added).

The subsequent Convention on the Prevention and Punishment of the Crime of Genocide (signed on 9 December 1948)[37] states in Article IV that private individuals will be punished for the crime of genocide. Genocide is a crime under international law and can be tried in any court; the fact that private individuals can be held responsible must colour interpretations of the Universal Declaration of Human Rights signed the next day, on 10 December 1948. The first few lines after the preamble to the Declaration run as follows:

The General Assembly proclaims this Universal Declaration of Human Rights as a common standard of achievement for all peoples of all nations, to the end that *every individual* and every organ of society, keeping this Declaration constantly in mind, shall strive by teaching and education to promote respect for these rights and freedoms and by progressive measures, national and international, to secure their universal recognition and observance. (emphasis added)

The Declaration then specifically states in Article 29(1)[38] that 'everyone has duties to the community'.

This Declaration is referred to in several human rights treaties,[39] including the two UN Covenants: the Covenant on Economic, Social and Cultural Rights,[40] and the Covenant on Civil and Political Rights.[41] Both

---

[34] Transcript of Proceedings (1 Oct. 1946), 16, quoted in Daes (1983: 42). See also Röling (1979: 199), where the question of 'superior orders' is discussed. The rejection of this possible defence by the Tribunal is another indication that the individual is responsible as a private individual and not as a state agent.

[35] Res. 95(1).

[36] Res. 96(1).

[37] In force since 12 Jan. 1951.

[38] For a detailed history of the drafting of this Article see Daes (1983: 17–21).

[39] e.g. the ECHR (1950), the American Convention on Human Rights (1969), and the African Charter on Human and Peoples' Rights (1981), as well as the UN Conventions on various forms of discrimination referred to below.

[40] Signed 16 Dec. 1966, entered into force 3 Jan. 1976.

[41] Signed 16 Dec. 1966, entered into force 23 Mar. 1976.

Covenants contain a fifth preambular paragraph that reads as follows: '*Realizing* that the individual, *having duties to other individuals and to the Community* to which he belongs, is under a responsibility to strive for the promotion and observance of the rights recognized in the present Covenant' (emphasis added). Forde suggests that such statements 'seem merely to acknowledge that States are permitted to regulate specific rights enjoyed by individuals, a power which is expressly granted by a number of those instruments' articles' (1986: 264). But examination of the *travaux préparatoires* suggests that individuals are obliged to respect the human rights contained in the Civil and Political Rights Covenant.

It is suggested that the following passages are indicative of a certain consensus regarding the importance of threats from individuals or private bodies:

Although a suggestion was made that freedom of assembly should be protected only against 'governmental interference', it was generally understood that the individual should be protected against all kinds of interference in the exercise of this right.[42]

As was the case during the debates concerning the right of peaceful assembly, a proposal that the right of association, including trade union rights, should be protected only against 'governmental interference' was rejected.[43]

In discussing paragraph 2[44] it was pointed out that slavery, which implied the destruction of the judicial personality, was a relatively limited and technical notion, whereas servitude was a more general idea conveying all possible forms of man's domination over man. While slavery was the best known and the worst form of bondage, other forms existed in modern society which tended to reduce the dignity of man. A suggestion to substitute the words 'peonage and serfdom' for servitude was rejected as those words were too limited in scope and had no precise meaning. A proposal was also made to insert the word 'involuntary' before 'servitude' in order to make it clear that the clause dealt with compulsory servitude and did not apply to contractual obligations between persons competent to enter into such obligations . . . The proposal was opposed on the ground that servitude in any form, whether involuntary or not, should be prohibited. It should be prohibited. It should not be made possible for any person to contract himself into bondage.[45]

On the other hand, in the area of discrimination, the opponents of such an extension of human rights into the private sphere seemed to win at the time of the drafting of the Covenant:

[42] A/2929 ch. vi para. 139 and Bossuyt (1987: 414).
[43] A/2929 ch. vi para. 148 and Bossuyt (1987: 426).
[44] Art. 8(2).
[45] A/2929 ch. vi para. 18 and Bossuyt (1987: 167).

In connection with the amendment of Greece and the United Kingdom . . . to insert the words 'in this respect', it was maintained by the supporters of the amendment that the law should prohibit any discrimination in respect of the principle of 'equal protection of the law', if the latter clause were adopted; but that the law could not prohibit all types of discrimination, particularly discrimination in private relations.[46]

This amendment was actually accepted, so it seems that Article 26 in the Civil and Political Rights Covenant was originally intended to prohibit discrimination only where it leads to unequal protection by the law, and not generally when it is perpetrated by private persons.

However, as already claimed, it is neither a literal nor a teleological interpretation but a contextual/evolutive/dynamic one that is most appropriate to examination of the theory and practice of the European Convention on Human Rights. This was clearly stated by the European Court of Human Rights in the *Tyrer* v. *United Kingdom* case in 1978: 'The Court must also recall that the Convention is a living instrument which, as the Commission rightly stressed, must be interpreted in the light of present day conditions. In the case now before it the Court can not but be influenced by the developments and commonly accepted standards in the penal policy of the member States of the Council of Europe in this field.'[47] (The Court went on to find that birching, as a form of judicial punishment, was no longer an acceptable practice, and constituted degrading punishment under Article 3.) A year later in the *Marckx* v. *Belgium* case the Court stated:

It is true that, at the time when the Convention of 4 November 1950 was drafted, it was regarded as permissible and normal in many European Countries to draw a distinction in this area between the illegitimate and the legitimate family. However the Court recalls that this convention must be interpreted in the light of present day conditions . . . In the instant case, the Court cannot but be struck by the fact that the domestic law of the great majority of the member States of the Council of Europe has evolved and is continuing to evolve, in company with the relevant international instruments[48] towards full judicial recognition of the maxim '*mater semper certa est*'.[49]

---

[46] A/5000 para. 111, 3rd Committee, 16th Session (1961) and Bossuyt (1987: 489).

[47] Series A, vol. 26, pp. 15–16, para. 31.

[48] The instruments referred to were the Brussels Convention of 22 Sept. 1962 on the Establishment of Maternal Affiliation of Natural Children, and the European Convention of 15 Oct. 1975 on the Legal Status of Children Born out of Wedlock; it is important to note that these Treaties had both been adopted since the Convention and that although each had at the time only been ratified by four members of the Council of Europe, the Court was prepared to give considerable weight to their contents: 'In fact, the existence of these two treaties denotes that there is a clear measure of common ground in this area amongst modern societies' (para. 41). This latter Convention was given considerable attention by the Court of Human Rights in the *Inze* case (1987) Series A, vol. 126, where great reliance was placed on its provisions as evidence of the importance which States now attach to the principle of non-discrimination between legitimate and illegitimate children.

[49] (1979) Series A, vol. 31, p. 19, para. 41; a similar dynamic is employed in *Dudgeon* v.

It is not just the European Court of Human Rights that considers it legitimate to take such an evolutive approach to the interpretation of the Convention. The International Court of Justice (ICJ) has taken just such an approach in certain analogous situations in the wider sphere of public international law: 'Moreover, an international instrument has to be interpreted and applied within the framework of the entire legal system prevailing at the time of the interpretation.'[50] The International Court of Justice stated that it 'must take into consideration the changes which have occurred in the supervening half century, and its interpretation can not remain unaffected by the subsequent development of law, through the Charter of the United Nations and by way of customary law.'[51] Although the half-century they refer to is 1919–71 it must be just as legitimate to consider the European Convention of 1950 in the light of human rights law at the beginning of the 1990s.

Human rights law at the beginning of the 1990s includes the various UN Conventions on discrimination: the Unesco Convention against Discrimination in Education (1960);[52] the International Convention on the Elimination of All Forms of Racial Discrimination (1965);[53] the Convention on the Elimination of All Forms of Discrimination against Women (1979);[54] and the UN Declaration on the Elimination of All Forms of Intolerance and of Discrimination Based on Religion or Belief.[55]

UK (1981) Series A, vol. 45, p. 24, para. 60: 'as compared with the era when that legislation was enacted, there is now a better understanding, and in consequence an increased tolerance, of homosexual behaviour . . . in the great majority of the member States of the Council of Europe.'

[50] Advisory opinion of the ICJ on the *Legal Consequences for States of the Continued Presence of South Africa in Namibia (South West Africa)* [1971] ICJ Rep. p. 31, para. 53.

[51] [1971] ICJ Rep. p. 31, para. 53. The ICJ legitimizes its approach by referring to Art. 22 of the Covenant of the League of Nations 1919, which contains the phrases 'the strenuous conditions of the modern world' and 'the well-being and development' of the people concerned, and suggests that these are evolving rather than static concepts, so 'the parties to the Covenant must consequently be deemed to have accepted them as such'. Similarly the third preambular paragraph of the European Convention contains the phrase 'the maintenance and *further realisation* of Human Rights'. So the States Parties to the Convention can be presumed to agree to an evolving interpretation.

[52] Adopted by the General Assembly 14 Dec. 1960 and in force 22 May 1962, this Convention defines 'discrimination' as including 'any distinction, exclusion, limitation or preference which, being based on race, colour, sex, language, religion, political or other opinion, national or social origin, economic condition or birth, has the purpose or effect of nullifying or impairing equality of treatment in education' (Art. 1(1)). And '"education" refers to all types and levels of education' (Art. 1(2)): as the Member States agree in Art. 3(*b*) 'to ensure, by legislation where necessary that there is no discrimination in the admission of pupils to educational institutions', the clear conclusion is that the Convention covers discrimination by private schools as well as by state schools.

[53] Adopted by the General Assembly on 21 Dec. 1965 and in force since 4 Jan. 1969.

[54] Adopted by the General Assembly on 18 Dec. 1979 and in force since 3 Sept. 1981.

[55] Res. 36/55 adopted by the General Assembly 25 Nov. 1981; for text see 21 *ILM* (1982), 205; no Convention text has been adopted by the General Assembly, but see below for details of the draft Convention.

In these instruments it is repeatedly emphasized that to eliminate these types of unfair discrimination it is essential for States to prohibit 'private' discrimination. Article 2(*d*) of the racial discrimination Convention calls on States to bring to an end by all possible means racial discrimination by any persons, group, or organization, and Article 5(*f*) of the same Convention requires a right of access to 'transport, hotels, restaurants, cafés, theatres and parks'.

The oblique and contradictory mention of 'public life' in the Racial Discrimination Convention[56] is not repeated in the Convention concerning discrimination against women, Article 1(1) of which is almost identical to Article 1(1) of the other Convention but for the omission of the word 'public'.[57] In 1992 the expert Committee responsible for this Convention made an important 'General recommendation on violence against women'.[58] The recommendation starts by stating that 'Gender based violence is a form of discrimination which seriously inhibits women's ability to enjoy rights and freedom on a basis of equality with men.' It then links gender-based violence to discrimination and violations of human rights, explicitly stating that the Convention covers public and private acts.[59] The recommendation also examines 'private' activity such as family violence and abuse, forced marriage, dowry deaths, acid attacks, and female circumcision. Other areas of violence in the private sphere covered by the recommendation are sexual harassment at work and family violence. In addition, the propagation of pornography is stated to contribute to gender-based violence. This recommendation represents a giant leap forward in the conceptual thinking surrounding human rights theories and illustrates the crucial importance of collapsing the public/private boundary in the human rights field.[60]

---

[56] It has been suggested that in conflicts between the reference to 'public life' in Art. 1(1) and the operative provisions of Art. 5 the latter should prevail. Schwelb (1966: 1005–6); cf. Forde (1985: 262): 'the fact that certain of the rights . . . 5(*b*) and (*f*)—are expressly stated as applying to private action, lends support to the argument that the other entitlements were not intended to be protected against nongovernmental infringements outside the public domain.' See also Meron (1985: 293–5).

[57] T. Meron has stated that this Convention 'clearly extends the prohibition of discrimination to private life', *Human Rights Law-Making in the United Nations* (Oxford: Clarendon Press, 1986), 60.

[58] Committee on the Elimination of Discrimination against Women, General Rec. 19, CEDAW/C/1992/L.1/Add.15, 29 Jan. 1992.

[59] The Recommendation states: 'Under general international law and specific human rights Covenants, States may also be responsible for private acts if they fail to act with due diligence to prevent violations of rights, or to investigate and punish acts of violence, and to provide compensation.' The Recommendation then adds that 'States parties should take appropriate and effective measures to overcome all forms of gender based violence, whether by public or private acts' (paras. 10 and 11).

[60] For a thought-provoking examination of the structure of violence and discrimination against women see MacKinnon (1989).

Similarly in the 1981 Declaration on Discrimination Based on Religion or Belief there is no longer any reference to 'public life',[61] and now there are duties[62] on those who bring up children to inculcate a 'spirit of understanding, tolerance, friendship among peoples, peace and universal brotherhood, respect for freedom of religion or belief of others'. Of course these are not duties which correspond to Hohfeldian claim-rights, but from their inclusion we infer that the Declaration is aimed at discrimination by anyone and not just state bodies.

Still within the general sphere of discrimination is the practice of apartheid. Reference must be made to the International Convention on the Suppression and Punishment of the Crime of Apartheid (1973).[63] This Convention makes it a crime under international law for any individual to commit any of a number of specified acts. Criminal responsibility applies specifically to individuals as well as to representatives of the State (Article III), and those accused can be tried by any competent tribunal of a State Party to the Convention.

Recent developments at the UN now specifically attempt to cover the 'private sector'. For example Article 3(1) of the Convention on the Rights of the Child[64] reads: 'In all actions concerning children, whether undertaken by public or private social welfare institutions, courts of law or administrative authorities or legislative bodies, the best interests of the child shall be a primary consideration.' And if one examines the discussions concerning this text there are revealing passages: 'The view was expressed that, if parents should be protected from States, the child should be protected from parents;'[65] this resulted in Article 7 *quarter* (later Article 16) being inserted.[66]

Some evidence of the future direction of international law can be found

---

[61] Although the 1967 draft International Convention on the Elimination of All Forms of Religious Intolerance contains the phrase 'public life' in Art. 1(*b*) this project has not been considered by the General Assembly and has been temporarily dropped by the UN (see Res. 3027 of 18 Dec. 1972) in favour of the Declaration, which was adopted in 1981. Besides, as the draft Convention in Art. VII calls on States to enact law to prohibit such discrimination by 'any person, group, or organization' it could be claimed that in the case of contradiction Art. 1 gives way to Art. VII.

[62] The actual word 'duty' appears only in the draft International Convention on the Elimination of All Forms of Religious Intolerance (1967).

[63] Signed 30 Nov. 1973, in force since 18 July 1967; for text see 13 *ILM* (1974), 50.

[64] For the final text see 28 *ILM* (1989), 1448, adopted by the UN General Assembly on 20 Nov. 1989, A/RES/44/25 of 5 Dec. 1989. In force 2 Sept. 1990 following ratification by twenty States.

[65] E/CN.4/1988/28 para. 38.

[66] This Article reads: '1. No child shall be subjected to arbitrary or unlawful interference with his or her privacy, family, home or correspondence, nor to unlawful attacks on his or her honour and reputation. 2. The child has the right to the protection of the law against such interference or attacks.' Note the absence of any reference to public authority in the Article.

in the work of the International Law Commission (ILC) in its Draft Code of Crimes against the Peace and Security of Mankind.[67] The Commentary to draft Article 21 on human rights states:

It is important to point out that the draft article does not confine possible perpetrations of the crimes to public officials or representatives alone. Admittedly, they would, in view of their official position, have far-reaching factual opportunity to commit the crimes covered by the draft article; yet the article does not rule out the possibility that private individuals with de facto power or organized in criminal gangs or groups might also commit the kind of systematic or mass violations of human rights covered by the article; in that case their acts would come under the draft code.[68]

Similarly, the draft provisions before the ILC concerning complaints before the proposed international criminal court state: 'It shall be immaterial whether the person against whom a complaint is directed acted as a private individual or in an official capacity.'[69]

We might also note the importance of the Resolutions of the Parliamentary Assembly of the Council of Europe. This Assembly is comprised of representatives from the twenty-six national parliaments of the twenty-six Member States of the Council of Europe. An interesting paragraph is found in Resolution 428 (1970):[70]

> C7 The right to privacy afforded by Article 8 of the Convention of Human Rights should not only protect an individual against interference by public authorities, but also against interference by private persons including the mass media. National legislations should comprise provisions guaranteeing this protection.

The effect of such Resolutions is uncertain. It is suggested that they represent an important source of evolving standards from which the European Court of Human Rights may draw inspiration.[71] It would

---

[67] See report of the ILC, 29 Apr.–19 July 1991. GAOR 46th Session, Supplement no. 10 (A/46/10), 238; GAOR 47th Session, Supplement no. 10 (A/47/10), 9.

[68] Art. 21 covers: murder, torture, slavery and forced labour, persecution on social, political, racial, religious, or cultural grounds; in a systematic manner or on a mass scale; or deprivation or forceable transfer of population.

[69] A/CN.4/442 para. 45.

[70] Text adopted 23 Jan. 1970.

[71] The paragraph cited above is part of a declaration on mass communication media and human rights; other relevant paragraphs include A2, A6, A7, A8, B(*b*) (media to respect Art. 6 ECHR), C1, and C3. It is worth noting that this is a Resolution rather than a Recommendation, and as such does not require action by the Committee of Ministers nor is its implementation expressed to be within the province of governments. It is quite plausible that such Resolutions have a somewhat similar status to UN Resolutions, and hence are at least evidence of emerging European Convention law, at least in cases (such as this one) where the Resolution includes a declaration and where the contents are specific enough to become operational as law. (See Cassese (1986: 192–5) for the different historical attitudes to the status of UN Resolutions.) More generally, when the Court of Human Rights seeks to enforce a common European standard, such Resolutions could be said to be evidence

however be unfortunate if the Court relied too heavily on these Resolutions or on draft Resolutions which failed to get the necessary consensus in order to justify restrictive interpretations of the Convention.[72]

Important references by the Court to a Recommendation of the Parliamentary Assembly were made recently in the *Cossey* and *B. v. France* cases in the context of the refusal by the United Kingdom and French authorities to issue the applicants (who were both post-operative male to female transsexuals) with a birth certificate showing their sex as female.[73] In *Cossey* the Court was split ten votes to eight and found in favour of the Government. The majority judgment refers to the relevant Resolution of the Parliamentary Assembly and states that the report which accompanies it reveals the same diversity of practice as obtained at the time of the Court's previous *Rees* judgment. The Court states that this Recommendation and a similar Resolution adopted by the European Community's Parliament 'seek to encourage the harmonisation of laws and practices in this field'.[74] Nevertheless, although the European Community Parliamentary Resolution calls for harmonizing measures in the context of asylum requests and sex discrimination at the workplace, the Council of Europe Recommendation is a straightforward appeal for national changes in legislation, in particular concerning rectification of birth and identity papers.[75] The fact that there had been few changes in

---

of 'common ground . . . amongst modern societies' (*Marckx* case para. 41). Occasionally representatives and delegates have referred to a Resolution in order to urge a restrictive interpretation of an Article. For example it was argued in the *Belgian Linguistics* case that the use of the word 'desirable' in Res. 136 (1957) and Rec. 285 (1961) meant there was a gap in the international practice which had not yet been filled (pleadings (1967) Series B, vol. 3, pp. 353, 414, also vol. 4, pp. 127–8).

It is suggested that recommendations, resolutions, and opinions of the Parliamentary Assembly of the Council of Europe may represent a vast untapped mine of relevant evidence as to evolving European standards. Further relevant Recommendations and Resolutions include: Rec. 528 (1970) (mass communication media and human rights); Rec. 747 (1975) (press concentration); Rec. 748 (1975) management of national broadcasting); Rec. 834 (1978) (threats to freedom of the press and television), esp. paras. 3, 5, 8, 9 (threats from monopolies, trade unions, sponsors, and advertisers); Rec. 952 (1982) (on international means to protect freedom of expression by regulating commercial advertising). Van Dijk and van Hoof refer to Res. 428 (1970) in the context of freedom of expression and state that it is 'a document which in itself is not legally binding, but may indicate a trend in the legal opinion within the Contracting States or some of them' (1990: 388).

[72] See the examples in n. 71.

[73] *Cossey* case, judgment of 27 Sept. 1990, Series A, vol. 184; *B. v. France*, judgment of 25 Mar. 1992, Series A, vol. 232-C.

[74] At para. 41 of the judgment. The Parliamentary Assembly's Recommendation is Rec. 1117 (1989), adopted on 29 Sept. 1989, reproduced in *Information Sheet No. 25* at 114. The Recommendation is the result of the report of the Legal Affairs Committee, rapporteur S. Rodotà; see doc. 6100. The European Parliament's Resolution is of 12 Sept. 1989, *OJ* (1989), no. C 256, 9 Oct. 1989, p. 33, also reproduced in *Information Sheet No. 25* at 143.

[75] A Recommendation is addressed to the Committee of Ministers; it is a request for action and requires a two-thirds majority rather than the simple majority which is necessary for a Resolution.

the legal orders of the Contracting States does not necessarily negate the conclusion that an evolving European standard has emerged which points to a violation of the right to privacy where the authorities deny the right to change one's birth certificate following a sex change operation. This is the position taken by three of the dissenting judges, who relied on the above-mentioned Resolution and Recommendation, stating that: 'the decisions of these representative organs clearly indicate that, according to prevailing public opinion, transsexuals should have the right to have their new sexual identity fully recognized by the law.'[76] The dissenting opinion of Judge Martens similarly gives the parliamentary texts more importance and considers that they constitute evidence of 'societal development'.[77] In *B.* v. *France* the applicant again referred to the above-mentioned Resolutions and Recommendations and the Court found by fifteen votes to six that there had been a violation of Article 8. They distinguished the situation in the United Kingdom as involving a more complex system with major obstacles linked to changing the current system. The Court referred to the fact that attitudes are changing and increased importance is being attached to the problem of transsexualism. For the moment, there is only sparse evidence of the Court following texts of the Parliamentary Assembly as evidence of an evolution in European standards.

4.3.1.1 Some examples from public international law

4.3.1.1.1 An inter-state claim

The ILC's draft Articles on state responsibility do not seem to go as far as the European Commission of Human Rights' case-law. If we take, for example, terrorist activity, the emphasis is on attribution of actions to the State. The ILC draft Articles demand an '"act of the state" under international law'.

Two judgments of the ICJ have discussed international responsibility for 'private' acts, and in both cases the judgment turned on the proximity which these groups had to the respondent State. Only after it was concluded that the groups in question had actually come to act on behalf of the State was Iran held to be responsible for the militants who held the American diplomats hostage in the Embassy in Tehran,[78] where the State had financed, trained, equipped, armed, and organized the *contra* forces, they had breached their obligation under customary international law not to intervene in the affairs of Nicaragua.[79]

---

[76] Joint dissenting opinion of Judges Palm, Foighel, and Pekkanen, at para. 3.

[77] Jouge Martens at paras. 5.5, 5.6.1, 5.6.2, of his dissenting opinion.

[78] *Case Concerning United States Diplomatic and Consular Staff in Tehran*, judgment of 24 May 1980 [1980] ICJ Rep. esp. paras. 56, 61, 63, 67, 73, 74, 76, 79.

[79] *Case Concerning Military and Paramilitary Activities in and against Nicaragua*, judgment of 27 June 1986 [1986] ICJ Rep. esp. para. 292(3) cf. paras. 107, 108, 109.

In addition to the fact that the ICJ and the ILC's draft Articles on state responsibility concentrate on action which can be attributed to the State, we have to consider the fact that international law and the ILC draft demand an international wrongful act (draft Articles 1–5: for example, where attacks on the lives or property of foreigners are at issue), whereas the Convention protects everyone regardless of nationality. Whilst in the *United States* v. *Iran* case there was a breach of the provisions of the Vienna Conventions of 1961 and 1963 on international diplomatic law, and in the *Nicaragua* v. *United States* case the question concerned intervential and breaches of international humanitarian law, the jurisdiction of the Commission and Court of Human Rights stems from a simple breach of a right protected by the Convention. This need not involve any international element at all. So, rape in violation of Article 8, killing in violation of Article 2, or denial of rights to associate under Article 11 can all involve the responsibility of the State. No transfrontier element, or failure to take due diligence with regard to the care of aliens, is required.

For completeness we should mention that it may be hypothetically possible that a State could be held responsible in an inter-state claim under general public international law for a failure to legislate to control human rights abuses by its own nationals with respect to its own nationals. In a detailed study of *Inter-State Accountability for Violations of Human Rights* Dr Kamminga concludes that it is actually possible for a State to bring an international law claim against another State for a breach of the latter State's international obligations in the field of human rights 'even though the interceding state's own material interests or those of its nationals had not been affected'.[80] His conclusion is based on a combination of Article 5(2)(*e*)(iii) of part 2 of the ILC's draft Articles on state responsibility,[81] as well as on the American Law Institute's Restatement (Third) of Foreign Relations Law.[82]

---

[80] M.T. Kamminga, 'Inter-State Accountability for Violations of Human Rights' (doctoral thesis, Erasmus University, Amsterdam, 1990), at 187.

[81] Art. 5(2) identifies what constitutes an 'injured State' under general international law, and catalogues the circumstances under which breach of a right gives rise to responsibility to the injured States. Art. 5(2)(*e*) includes the relevant right for our purposes: 'If the right infringed by the act of a State arises from a multilateral treaty or from a rule of customary international law, any other State party to the multilateral treaty or bound by the relevant rule of customary international law, if it is established that: (iii) the right has been created or is established for the protection of human rights and fundamental freedoms.'

[82] 'A state violates international law if, as a matter of state policy, it practices, encourages or condones: (a) genocide (b) slavery or slave trade (c) the murder or causing the disappearance of individuals (d) torture or other cruel, inhuman or degrading treatment or punishment (e) prolonged arbitrary detention (f) systematic racial discrimination (g) a consistent pattern of gross violations of internationally recognized human rights' (at s. 702 of the *Restatement (Third) of the Foreign Relations Law of the United States* (1987).

In this context Kamminga suggests that the category 'human rights and fundamental freedoms'[83] is wider than the international obligations 'of essential importance for the safeguarding of the human being',[84] and wider than the concept of the 'basic rights of the human person'.[85] Kamminga suggests that the current state of international law means that even a single breach of an international human rights obligation is sufficient to create an internationally wrongful act.[86] Applying his thesis to the operation of international human rights in the private sphere we can deduce that, in theory, state responsibility could arise in extreme cases of private killings or private racial discrimination against a State's own nationals, even where there is no evidence that the private actors are acting on behalf of the State. Of course it would have to be shown that the State had omitted to act to curtail, prevent, or punish such action, but the possibility remains.[87]

The lack of state practice does not deprive Kamminga's thesis of its theoretical value. Not only does it prevent States from hiding behind a legal shield when faced with mounting demands that the State take steps against another State concerning purely domestic human rights abuses in that other State (be they committed by public or private authorities), but it also goes to show that it can be argued that the European Court of Human Rights should apply the Convention to the acts of private bodies without suggesting anything that is fundamentally inconsistent with the current international law of state responsibility.[88] The real difference is

[83] See Art. 5(2)(*e*)(iii) above.

[84] From the ILC's definition of international crimes, see draft Art. 19(3)(*c*).

[85] The right defined as giving rise to *erga omnes* obligations by the ICJ in the *Barcelona Traction* case, judgment of 5 Feb. 1970 [1970] ICJ Rep. para. 34.

[86] At 170.

[87] Of course, for several reasons this possibility has to be seen as more theoretical than practical. Most importantly, States will obviously be reluctant to police other States over their internal human rights record and embarrass them before the International Court of Justice; even if they were so willing, everything is still conditional on the States' acceptance of jurisdiction under Art. 36(2) of the Statute of the ICJ and under the actual treaty or customary rights in question. In the case of most human rights treaties, alternative settlement or control mechanisms will exist. For example, the International Covenant on Civil and Political Rights provides for an inter-state complaint procedure under Art. 41, which is essentially nothing more than a conciliation process rather than a judicial remedy. For details see Robertson (1982: 50–4).

[88] D. Shelton suggests that the recent decisions of the Inter-American Court of Human Rights in a number of Honduran cases (see below s. 4.3.1.3) 'have led to the convergence of the traditional law of state responsibility for injury to aliens and the more recently established state obligations to respect and ensure fundamental human rights' Shelton (1990: 1–34). Although abductors and death squads can be compared to the danger posed to aliens under the traditional international law regarding state responsibility for aliens, this analogy is inappropriate in the European context, where, it will be suggested, the rights in the Convention are sometimes binding on the private persons themselves at the national level and hence the State may be responsible for failing to facilitate this. The standard at the international level will therefore be something less demanding than the traditional due diligence test. A finding that a State has failed to provide a procedure cannot be compared to a finding that the State had failed to take due care to protect aliens from a violent attack.

that human rights abuses would probably have to reach a higher level of seriousness under international law, and that the Convention deals mostly with individual applications rather than inter-state cases.

4.3.1.1.2 The United Nations Human Rights Committee

As soon as we move away from inter-state responsibility under international law towards international procedures granting individuals the right to complain under the various universal human rights instruments, it is clear that the international monitoring bodies may be prepared to accept complaints which concern a State's inability to control violations of human rights by private individuals.

A detailed analysis of the practice of the Human Rights Committee on this question is outside the scope of the present work.[89] Nevertheless it may be worth considering some of the Committee's 'General Comments' made under Article 40(4) of the International Covenant of Civil and Political Rights as, for the most part, they cover the same rights as those protected under the Convention. It would be inappropriate to deal with these Comments under the sections dealing with the Convention rights as the Committee, in issuing these Comments, is acting as a monitoring rather than quasi-judicial body. The Committee's Comments relate to the supervision of States' reports, whilst the case-law of the Commission and Court relates to actual cases and controversies. The Comments are not responses to applications directed essentially against a private human rights violation; they are a reminder to States Parties that steps should be taken to protect human rights in the private sphere, and that the States' reports should also deal with state action taken to limit abuses of human rights in the private sphere. On the other hand they are ultimately relevant for cases and controversies at the national and international level.

The Comments are relevant at the national level because they authoritatively determine the scope of protection offered by the specified Article in the Covenant. They are relevant at the international level as the Committee may refer to its own Comments when deciding cases under the Optional Protocol to the Covenant. For example, in a case concerning torture and disappearances in Colombia there was apparently insufficient evidence to link the plain-clothed perpetrators to the State. The Human Rights Committee referred to its own General Comment on Article 6 (see

---

[89] A cursory perusal of the views of the Human Rights Committee suggests that this question has yet to be considered. In Communication 14/61, *Seta* v. *Finland*, the Committee simply states that it started 'from the premise that the State Party is responsible for the actions of the Finnish Broadcasting Company (FBC), in which the State holds a dominant stake (90%) and which is placed under specific government control' (GAOR 37th Session, Supplement no. 40 (A/37/40), 161–7). Cited by Cohen-Jonathan (1991: 111). On the work of the Human Rights Committee see generally D. McGoldrick, *The Human Rights Committee* (Oxford: Clarendon Press, 1991).

below) and held that Colombia had violated Article 6 because it had 'failed to take appropriate measures to prevent the disappearance and subsequent killings of José Harneva and Emma Rubio de Herrera and to investigate the responsibility for their murders'.[90]

4.3.1.1.3 Selected General Comments of the United Nations Human Rights Committee

Since 1981 the Committee has published 'General Comments' on the Articles of the International Covenant on Civil and Political Rights. Their purpose is 'to draw attention to insufficiencies disclosed by a large number of reports; to suggest improvements in the reporting procedure and to stimulate the activities of these states and international organizations in the promotion and protection of human rights'.[91] Nevertheless these comments have a 'special juridical status',[92] and certain relevant passages will be briefly mentioned here.

Article 6 (right to life):[93] The Committee refers to a number of private actions threatening human rights and the State's duty to deter such activity: the duty to prevent propaganda for war and incitement to violence (referring to the connection with Article 20), the duty to prevent and investigate disappearances, and the desirability of taking all possible measures to reduce infant mortality and increase life expectancy through the adoption of measures which eliminate malnutrition and epidemics.[94]

Article 7 (prohibition on torture, or cruel, inhuman, or degrading treatment or punishment):[95] In the Committee's view the article extends to corporal punishment and patients in medical institutions. According to the Committee's Comment adopted in 1982 it 'is also the duty of public authorities to ensure protection against such treatment even when committed by persons acting outside or without any official authority'.[96] But the Committee's 1992 General Comment on the same Article goes even further and clarifies that the scope of the protection to be undertaken by the State extends to cover torture or other cruel, inhuman, or degrading treatment or punishment by people acting in their *'private capacity'*.[97]

---

[90] Communication 161/1983, *Herrera Rubio* v. *Colombia*, views adopted on 2 Nov. 1987 or 31st Session of the Committee, GAOR 43rd Session, Supplement no. 40 (A/43/40), 190–8 at 198. Cited by Cohen-Jonathan (1991: 114).

[91] GAOR 36th Session, Supplement no. 40 (A/36/40), annex VII, at 107.

[92] Elkind and Shaw (1986: 29 n. 32); they cite *inter alia* Tomuschat, who states that the Comments constitute 'juridically the most important interpretation of the Covenant, more important than the opinion of a State,' (UN doc. CCPR/C/SR 371, para. 1).

[93] GAOR 36th Session, Supplement no. 40 (A/37/40), annex V, 93.

[94] Quaere, could Art. 2 ECHR be relied on against a State which refused to distribute condoms in response to AIDS? Art. 2 allows no derogation on grounds of public morality.

[95] (A/37/40), 94, later revised by General Comment no. 20(44) Art. 7, CCPR/C/21/ Rev.1/Add.3.

[96] At 95 of (A/37/40).

[97] Para. 2 of the General Comment reads in part: 'It is the duty of the State party to

The Committee's Comment also declares that States should indicate the provisions of their criminal law which prohibit and specify the penalties applicable 'whether committed by public officials or other persons acting on behalf of the State, or by private persons' (para. 13). The references to 'private capacity' and 'private persons' leave no doubt that Article 7 of the Covenant has now been interpreted as covering the private sphere.

Article 9 (right to liberty and security of the person): 'The Committee points out that Paragraph 1 is applicable to all deprivations of liberty, whether in criminal cases or in other cases such as, for example, mental illness, vagrancy, drug addiction, educational purposes, immigration control, etc.'[98] This broad definition seems to include most situations and suggests that Article 5(1) of the Convention, which is almost identical, can be given a similarly wide interpretation where 'private' incarceration is concerned.[99]

Article 10 (treatment of persons deprived of their liberty): The 1982 General Comment on this Article referred to 'all institutions where persons are lawfully held against their will, not only in prisons but also, for example, hospitals, detention camps or correction institutions'. But the 1992 General Comment which replaces it was deliberately intended to cover private institutions.[100] The new comment adds 'or elsewhere' to the list of institutions and declares that States Parties should ensure observation of humane treatment 'in all institutions and establishments within their jurisdiction where persons are being held'. The wording 'under their jurisdiction' was specifically rejected by the Chairman as it would have excluded private institutions. 'Within their jurisdiction' was held to cover the private sphere.

Article 19 (the right to hold opinions without interference): The Committee communicates to States that 'little attention has so far been

afford everyone protection through legislative and other measures as may be necessary against acts prohibited by article 7, whether inflicted by people acting in their official capacity, outside their official capacity or in a private capacity.'

[98] At 95 of (A/37/40); see also the General Comment on Art. 10(1) (all persons deprived of their liberty to be treated with respect for the inherent dignity of the human person), at 96 of (A/37/40).

[99] The approach in the General Comment seems closer to the minority rather than majority opinion in the *Nielson* case, judgment of 28 Nov. 1988, Series A, vol. 144. The case concerned the placement of a child in a child psychiatric ward. The majority thought that the case raised the exercise of parental rights and that it was not covered by Art. 5(1). The minority joint dissenting opinion of Judges Thòr Vilhjalmsson, Pettiti, Russo, Spielmann, de Meyer, Carrillo Salcedo, and Valticos held the view that the conditions in the ward constituted a deprivation of liberty within the meaning of Art. 5 and they stated: 'The respondent State is accountable for this deprivation. It not only tolerated it, but also associated itself with it through the action and assistance of its organs and officials' (provisional translation, p. 24 of the report of the judgment).

[100] The author was present during the open session of the Committee on this Comment during its forty-fourth session.

given to the fact that, because of the development of modern mass media, effective measures are necessary to prevent such control of the media as would interfere with the right of everyone to freedom of expression in a way that is not provided for in paragraph 3'.[101]

Article 17 (protection against unlawful interference with privacy, family, home, or correspondence as well as unlawful attacks on honour or reputation): 'In the view of the Committee, this right is required to be guaranteed against all such interferences and attacks whether they emanate from State authorities or from natural or legal persons.'[102]

Lastly, in order to give as complete a picture as possible, we should mention two other General Comments which are of less relevance to the interpretation of the Convention by the Strasbourg organs. These General Comments do, however, indicate that the international law of human rights is coming to cover the private sphere more and more.

Article 24(1) (rights of children): 'Every possible measure should be taken to reduce infant mortality and to eradicate malnutrition among children and to prevent them from being exploited by means of forced labour or prostitution, or by their use in the illicit trafficking of narcotic drugs, or by other means.'[103] 'In cases where the parents and the family seriously fail in their duties, ill treat or neglect the child, the State should intervene to restrict parental authority and the child may be separated from his family when circumstances so require.'[104]

Non-discrimination: 'When reporting on Articles 2(1), 3 and 36 of the Covenant, States Parties usually cite provisions of their constitution or equal opportunity laws with respect to equality of persons. While such information is of course useful, the Committee wishes to know if there remain any problems of discrimination in fact, which may be practised either by public authorities, by the community, or by *private persons or bodies*. The Committee wishes to be informed about legal provisions

---

[101] (A/38/40), annex VI, 109.

[102] (A/43/40), annex VI, 181; the Comment continues: 'The gathering and holding of personal information on computers, data banks and other devices, whether by public authorities or private individuals or bodies, must be regulated by law. Effective measures have to be taken by States to ensure that information concerning a person's private life does not reach the hands of persons who are not authorized by law to receive, process and use it, and it is never used for purposes incompatible with the Covenant. In order to have the most effective protection of his private life, every individual should have the right to ascertain, in an intelligible form, whether and if so, what personal data is stored in automatic data files and for what purposes. Every individual should also be able to ascertain which public authorities or private individuals or bodies control or may control their files. If such files contain incorrect personal data or have been collected or processed contrary to the provisions of the law, every individual should have the right to request rectification or elimination' (at 182 of (A/43/40)).

[103] (A/44/40), annex VI, at 173.

[104] (A/44/40), at 174.

and administrative measures directed at diminishing or eliminating such discrimination.'[105]

4.3.1.1.4 Conclusions on the General Comments of the Human Rights Committee

These Comments of the Committee cannot be compared to judgments of the European Court of Human Rights. It is not suggested that if the Committee were faced with communications under the Optional Protocol which essentially complained about private violations and the State's failure to prevent or rectify them, the Committee would easily find the State had violated the Covenant. What is important about the passages quoted above is that they remove one possible line of legal defence from the armoury of States. States may not argue that international human rights treaties have no relevance for the activities of private actors. States cannot argue that civil and political rights instruments do not oblige them to take positive action to curtail breaches of the international standards by private individuals. States are obliged to accept the 'privatization' of human rights as a juridical fact.

According to J. B. Elkind and A. Shaw the 'third party applicability' of the Covenant and the obligations of the States Parties under the Covenant is 'even clearer than under the Convention'.[106] They cite observations by members of the Committee, such as those of Professors Graefrath and Opsahl,[107] which confirm the 'third-party applicability' of the Covenant. The use of the phrase 'third-party applicability' goes beyond the application of the Covenant to positive obligations on the State in the private sphere and confirms that the Covenant can be used directly against private bodies in the national legal order where that order recognizes the direct effect and self-executing nature of the right in the Covenant.

4.3.1.1.5 Complaints to the United Nations Committee on the Elimination of Racial Discrimination

It is worth detailing one other procedure under the UN machinery. From the report of a communication filed under Article 14 of the International

---

[105] UN doc. CCPR/C/Rev.1/Add.1 p. 3, emphasis added.

[106] Elkind and Shaw (1986: 28); see also the acceptance by Buergenthal (1981: 77): 'the provision implies an affirmative obligation by the state to take whatever measures are necessary to enable individuals to enjoy or exercise the rights guaranteed in the Covenant, including the removal of governmental and possibly also some private obstacles to the enjoyment of these rights. The obligation to "ensure" rights creates affirmative obligations on the state . . . as regards some rights in some circumstances, it may perhaps require the state to adopt laws and other measures against private interferences with enjoyment of the rights.' See also Schachter (1981: 326).

[107] UN doc. CCPR/C/SR 321 para. 34 (Opsahl): '[The Covenant] by its substance was capable of extending rights to all persons. . . . [It] should be considered to have third party applicability;' and UN doc. CCPR/C/SR 321 para. 46 (Graefrath).

Convention on the Elimination of All Forms of Racial Discrimination it is clear that the Committee had no difficulty dealing with a complaint which arose out of a dismissal by a private employer on racist grounds. The Committee found that The Netherlands had failed to ensure protection in respect of the complainant's right to work under Article 5(e)(i).[108] Of course, the applicability of other Articles of this Convention to the private sphere remain disputed;[109] nevertheless the decision is worth noting as another instance of the international application of human rights in the private sphere.

4.3.1.2 Duties for non-governmental forces under the law of internal armed conflict

4.3.1.2.1 Non-international armed conflict

The humanitarian law which applies during internal armed conflict gives rise to certain duties for private bodies. The applicable law is complicated and need not be detailed here.[110] The minimum protection offered by Common Article 3 to the four Geneva Conventions of 1949 contains obligations for 'each Party to the conflict'. These obligations are to 'Persons taking no active part in the hostilities' as well as to the 'wounded and sick'. Briefly, the actual prohibitions include: attacks or cruel treatment, the taking of hostages, humiliating and degrading treatment, and sentences or executions without judicial safeguards. Lastly, the Article includes a positive obligation to collect and care for the sick and wounded.

The designation of a situation as 'an armed conflict not of an international character' so as to trigger the application of Common Article 3 to the Geneva Conventions of 1949 is obviously an act of considerable political importance for all sides to the conflict. The insurgents will often welcome the designation of their attacks as constituting armed conflict as this confers a curious sort of international recognition on them;[111] the applicability of Common Article 3 reinforces the special role of the International Committee of the Red Cross (ICRC).[112] On the other hand

---

[108] GAOR 43rd Session, Supplement no. 18 (A/43/18), Report of the Committee on the Elimination of Racial Discrimination, annex IV, Communication 1/1984, *Yilmaz-Dogan* v. *The Netherlands*, opinion adopted on 10 Aug. 1988 at the thirty-sixth session of the Committee.

[109] See Schwelb (1966); Forde (1985); Meron (1985).

[110] See Cassese (1979, 1980); Meron (1989); Y. C. Sandoz, C. Swinarski, and B. Zimmerman (eds.), *Commentary on the Additional Protocols of 8 June 1977 to the Geneva Conventions of 12 August 1949* (Geneva: Martinus Nijhoff, 1987); Swinarski (1984); T. Meron, *Human Rights in Internal Strife: Their International Protection* (Cambridge: Grotius, 1987).

[111] This is despite the fact that Common Art. 3 ends with the sentence: 'The application of the preceding provisions shall not affect the legal status of the Parties to the conflict.'

[112] Common Art. 3 includes the paragraph: 'An impartial humanitarian body, such as the International Committee of the Red Cross, may offer its services to the Parties to the conflict.'

the Government may be less willing to acknowledge the situation as one of armed conflict, preferring instead to portray it as a fight against criminals and terrorists.[113] Despite fairly concrete conditions suggested by the ICRC *Commentary* on the Conventions there is no authoritative body which can affirm the applicability of Common Article 3,[114] although Resolutions of the General Assembly and UN Commission on Human Rights may occasionally state that the humanitarian rules contained in Common Article 3 are to be respected by both sides in a particular conflict.[115]

Even if governments deny the applicability of Common Article 3 and violate its provisions in practice, the fact remains that it represents a standard with which to hold accountable both governmental and private non-governmental forces. In some cases Special Rapporteurs and Representatives appointed by the UN Commission on Human Rights have flirted in their reports with recording abuses of the provisions of Common Article 3 by non-governmental forces.[116] Moreover human rights organizations such as Human Rights Watch and Amnesty International have been guided by these standards when reporting on abuses of human rights by 'armed opposition groups'.[117]

---

[113] It was only towards the end of the fighting in Algeria that the French Government recognized the applicability of Common Art. 3. Its applicability has been denied on many occasions including during the Greek civil war and by the UK in relation to Northern Ireland.

[114] Briefly, the 1950 ICRC *Commentary* suggested that the party in revolt against the *de jure* Government possesses an organized military force and has the means of ensuring respect for the Convention, and that the *de jure* Government has recognized the insurgents as belligerents, or claimed these rights itself, or the dispute has been admitted to the agenda of the UN Security Council or General Assembly as being a threat to international peace, a breach of the peace, or an act of aggression.

[115] See e.g. the UN Commission on Human Rights Resolution on El Salvador, 1991/71, preambular para. 6 and operative para. 9. See also General Assembly Resolutions 45/172 and 46/133 on El Salvador.

[116] See e.g. the report on the human rights situation in El Salvador by the Special Representative of the Commission on Human Rights, E/CN.4/1992/32, 16 Jan. 1992.

[117] The oral intervention of Amnesty International at the 48th Session of the UN Commission on Human Rights under agenda item 12 explained their latest policy as follows: 'In times of internal armed conflict not only do governments remain bound by international human rights law: both governments and their opponents should observe minimum standards laid down by humanitarian law. Amnesty International has long condemned the torture and killing of prisoners by armed opposition groups; as part of the continuing development of our work we will now oppose a wider range of abuses by such groups, guided by the protection of the individual enshrined in Common Article 3 of the Geneva Conventions. We will oppose other deliberate and arbitrary killings in addition to the execution of prisoners. Deliberate killings of people not taking part in the conflict are in this sense always arbitrary whether the victim was targeted individually or the object of an indiscriminate attack. We will also oppose the taking or holding of hostages, condemning absolutely the arbitrary threat to life, liberty and security implicit in the condition of a hostage. We will document patterns of such abuses, and seek opportunities to bring pressure to bear on the perpetrators.' The introduction to the *Amnesty International Report: 1992* (London: AI Publications, 1992) mentions some of the groups who are alleged to have carried out such abuses in 1991 including: the Mozambique National Resistance, the Sudan People's Liberation Army,

4.3.1.2.2 Protocol I of 1977 and wars of national liberation

Article 1(4) of Protocol I to the Geneva Conventions classifies three types of war of national liberation as international armed conflict so that all the applicable rules to those conflicts apply. It covers 'armed conflicts in which peoples are fighting against colonial domination and alien occupation and against racist régimes in the exercise of their right to self-determination'.

When this norm was formulated it was specifically aimed at two States: Israel and South Africa. Israel cast the only negative vote against the adoption of the provision whilst South Africa persistently objected to the rule and did not participate in the final session. Although Israel is unlikely to become a Party to the Protocol, and the situation in South Africa is now less pertinent, the provision is not without relevance. Professor Cassese has categorized the Afghanistan conflict (during the 1980s) and the Indonesian occupation of East Timor as within the scope of Article 1(4) (1986: 279). To determine the Article's strict applicability to these or other conflicts where the party is not yet a Party to the Protocol one would have to examine the binding nature of that rule as a norm of customary international law. This has been examined in the doctrine and need not detain us here.[118] Suffice it to say that no government has yet been prepared to characterize itself as colonial, racist, or in alien occupation.

Nevertheless the attempt to assimilate wars of national liberation to international armed conflicts has had some persuasive effects even if the legal obligation has not been recognized. Under Article 96(3) of Protocol I the authority representing the people struggling against the colonial, alien, or racist Party to the Protocol can undertake to apply the Conventions and the Protocol by making a declaration to the depository (the Swiss Federal Council). A number of declarations of this kind have been deposited with the ICRC by groups such as the ANC, SWAPO, the PLO,

---

Revolutionary Armed Forces of Colombia and the National Liberation Army in Colombia, Shining Path in Peru, Afghanistan's Mujahidin opposition groups, Sikh separatist groups in Punjab, the Tamil Tigers in Sri Lanka, the IRA, the Ulster Volunteer Force (UVF), the Ulster Freedom Fighters (UFF), the Basque separatist organization Basque Homeland and Liberty (ETA), the Kurdish Workers' Party in Turkey, and Palestinian armed groups in the Israeli-Occupied Territories.

See also _Human Rights Watch: World Report 1992_ (New York: Human Rights Watch, 1991), 22–3, 218–20, 309; Asia Watch, _The Sri Lankan Conflict and Standards of Humanitarian Law: An Appeal to the Government of Sri Lanka and the LTTE Leadership_ (23 Apr. 1992).

[118] A. Cassese, 'Wars of National Liberation', in Swinarski (1984: 314–24); L. R. Penna, 'Customary International Law and Protocol I: An Analysis of Some Provisions', in Swinarski (1984: 201–25); G. Abi-Saab, 'Wars of National Liberation in the Geneva Conventions and Protocols', 165 _RCDI_ (1979), 357–455; J. Salmon, 'Les Guerres de libération nationale', in Cassese (1979: 54–112).

and the Eritrean People's Liberation Front.[119] In the end, no one can really measure to what extent the potential existence of humanitarian obligations for national liberation armies actually mitigates the violence and procedures used by these groups. Similarly, as explained above, governments will rarely openly admit applying and enforcing the laws of war in relation to national liberation armies. Nevertheless there are occasional glimmers which indicate that the international recognition of certain struggles as wars of national liberation does have concrete mitigating effects on the behaviour of the Parties and their organs.[120]

4.3.1.2.3 Protocol II of 1977 and civil war

The protection offered by Protocol II to the Geneva Conventions goes beyond the minimum standards contained in Common Article 3. However, in order to trigger the application of Protocol II the intensity of fighting has to be greater than that traditionally required for the application of Common Article 3. According to Article 1(2) of the Protocol the Protocol does not apply to situations of internal disturbances, riots, and sporadic acts of violence. In addition Article 1(1) of the Protocol demands that the dissident armed groups are under responsible command and exercise such control over part of the territory that they are in a position to carry out military operations and implement the guarantees in the Protocol.

The minimum standards contained in Common Article 3 remain in effect even when Protocol II is applicable. The Protocol supplements these standards with extra protection for civilians, children, and medical and religious personnel. It also details the procedural guarantees that have to be afforded to people interned or detained. The important fact for our purposes is that it applies this wide range of duties to both sides. Therefore, rights and duties similar to the non-derogable provisions contained in treaties such as the European Convention on Human Rights and the International Covenant on Civil and Political Rights become legally binding on the dissident non-governmental forces. However as with the situations outlined in the previous two sections, few governments ever admit the application of this Protocol and there is little evidence of the provisions being enforced after an abuse.

One case where the Protocol was applicable was El Salvador. Reference

---

[119] See also the other examples given by M. Veuthey, *Guérilla et droit humanitaire* (Geneva: ICRC, 1983), p. xxvi. Of course, even if the respective States were Parties to the Protocol, the declaration would be of dubious legal effect because the ICRC is not the designated depository.

[120] In a case concerning the sentencing of SWAPO fighters the judge would seem to have considered the evolving acceptance of Art. 1(4) as relevant to sentencing, so that relatively light sentences were imposed. See C. Murray, 'The Status of the ANC and SWAPO in International Humanitarian Law', 100 *South African Law Journal* (1983), 402; *S.* v. *Sagarius* [1983] 1 SA 833 (SWA).

is made to Protocol II in Resolutions of the UN Commission on Human Rights and the General Assembly whilst the FMLN declared that they were willing to abide by the guarantees contained in the Protocol. Nevertheless, both sides continued to breach humanitarian law. Interestingly, in this particular situation the San José Agreement, signed by both sides on 26 July 1990, lists those human rights by which both sides agree to be bound and outlines the role of the United Nations in monitoring breaches of these and other international human rights. The subsequent reports of ONUSAL (the UN monitoring operation in El Salvador) are divided into different sections detailing violations by the Government as well as violations by the FMLN.[121] The recommendations contained in these reports and of the UN Special Representative on El Salvador are similarly addressed to both sides of the conflict.

4.3.1.2.4 Final remarks on the humanitarian law of internal armed conflict

To detail all the rights and duties applicable in the private sphere during different classes of internal armed conflict would require another book. In any event, enforcement is left primarily in the hands of States who have little interest in declaring that the internal armed conflict has reached the intensity which triggers the applicable humanitarian law. Because this decision has to be a political one, international organizations are precluded from applying the standards of humanitarian law without implicitly passing judgment on the type of armed conflict concerned and conferring a sort of 'recognition' on the armed opposition group. We are left with the conclusion that international humanitarian law is theoretical rather than practical and that its application is riddled with pitfalls.[122] Even if the one organization entrusted with guardianship of the Conventions, the ICRC, is able to seek to enforce the relevant provisions of humanitarian law, such action is usually limited to private exhortations and quiet diplomacy, due to that organization's operational dependency on the consent of the parties and its general commitment to confidentiality.

Nevertheless, governments and armed opposition groups do occasionally proclaim that they are abiding by these standards, and the specificity of these standards to the circumstances of armed conflict make them useful. It is now up to the international community to find imaginative ways

---

[121] See esp. the third report of ONUSAL, which consists of the report of the Director of the Mission's Human Rights Division for Nov.–Dec. 1991 (A/46/876—S/23580, 15 Feb. 1992).

[122] F. Kalshoven and Y. Sandoz (eds.), *Implementation of International Humanitarian Law* (Dordrecht: Martinus Nijhoff, 1989); for some examples of the 'grey zone' between human rights law and humanitarian law see generally 'I. Human Rights and Humanitarian Law', 91(1)*Bulletin of Human Rights* (Geneva: United Nations), 1–61.

around the political minefields which are scattered throughout this branch of law.[123] One recent initiative had been the 'Declaration of Minimum Humanitarian Standards'. This is a declaration compiled by a number of independent experts; it seeks to bind 'all persons, groups and authorities', and is to be applicable in 'all situations, including internal violence, disturbances, tensions, and public emergency'. The authors hope that non-governmental organizations 'will refer to the declaration as to accepted normative standards'. The declaration seeks to avoid the difficulties which surround this area of law by stating that it is to apply in all situations (peacetime and wartime). In this way using the declaration involves crossing no threshold of applicability. In addition the declaration is to be applied to everyone and it specifically states that 'the observance of these standards shall not affect the legal status of any authorities, groups, or persons involved in situations of internal violence, disturbances, tensions or public emergency'.[124]

Internal armed conflict is unlikely to disappear in the near future. More and more insurgents now have relatively easy access to modern weaponry, and the end of the Cold War coupled with the disintegration of the Soviet Union has meant that nationalists and ethnic groups now have more to gain through force than in recent times. Conflicts such as those in Yugoslavia and Somalia have been violent and brutal with scant regard for the norms of humanitarian law.

On 22 February 1993 the Security Council passed Resolution 808 with regard to the former Yugoslavia. The Council decided 'that an international tribunal shall be established for the prosecution of persons responsible for serious violations of international humanitarian law in the territory of the former Yugoslavia since 1991.[125] The Resolution went

---

[123] See D. Weissbrodt, 'The Role of International Organizations in the Impementation of Human Rights and Humanitarian Law in Situations of Armed Conflict', 21 *Vanderbilt Journal of Transnational Law* (1988), 313. International human rights organizations are faced with a particularly complex task. They are criticized by governments for failing to detail and publicize abuses by 'terrorists', yet, when they do address these groups, they are accused by the same governments of encouraging the international recognition of insurgents. See H. Burkhalter, 'Fujimori Attacks Human Rights Groups, while the Killing Continues in Peru', *Human Rights Watch Quarterly Newsletter* (Winter 1992), 10. Furthermore, there are a plethora of practical problems related to investigating, publicizing, and addressing abuses committed by armed opposition groups.

[124] See T. Meron and A. Rosas, 'Declaration of Minimum Humanitarian Standards', 85 *AJIL* (1991), 377–81. This declaration has been circulated as a document of the Sub-Commission on Prevention of Discrimination and Protection of Minorities (E/CN.4/Sub.2/1991/55) and during the first special session of the UN Commission on Human Rights on 13 Aug. 1992, which dealt with the human rights situation in the former Yugoslavia. See also T. Meron, 'The Protection of the Human Person under Human Rights Law and Humanitarian Law', 91(1) *Bulletin of Human Rights* (Geneva: United Nations), 33–45.

[125] The Conventions and Protocol I contain a list of 'grave breaches' which the parties and the High Contracting Parties are required to repress. See most recently the report of

on to request the Secretary-General to collate information relating to violations of humanitarian law, including grave breaches of the Conventions, and recommend additional measures that might be taken. This international action suggests the creation of a possible war crimes tribunal and may herald a new way of dealing with individuals (acting in any capacity) who violate the humanitarian law of armed conflict.

4.3.1.3 Regional developments and the Inter-American system

Turning from universal human rights protection to regional Conventions other than the European Convention on Human Rights, both the American Convention on Human Rights[126] and the African Charter of Human and Peoples' Rights[127] specifically refer to private threats to human rights. And there are chapters on the duties of the individual in the American Declaration of the Rights and Duties of Man (1948),[128] and in the African Charter of Human and Peoples' Rights.[129] Although the Permanent Arab Regional Commission on Human Rights has been in existence since 1968, as yet there is no conclusion to the proposed Arab Charter of Human Rights.[130] In the Inter-American Convention to Prevent and Punish Torture,[131] Article 3(*b*) covers non-state actors acting at the instigation of a public servant, and similarly the European Convention for the Prevention of Torture and Inhuman or Degrading Treatment or Punishment[132] covers

the Secretary-General, S/25704 of 3 May 1993. The report suggests prosecution of: grave breaches of the Geneva Conventions of 1949, violations of the laws or customs of war. genocide and crimes against humanity.

[126] Signed 22 Nov. 1969, entered into force 18 July 1978.

[127] Approved by the Organization of African Unity 26 June 1981, in force since 21 Oct. 1986; for text see 21 *ILM* (1982), 58–68, though in this Charter there is only provision for a Commission to 'promote' and 'ensure' the rights contained in the Charter, and no facility to adjudicate on complaints by individuals. It may be that the role of the Commission will be extended: Art. 45(4).

[128] Adopted 2 May 1948 (Arts. XXIX–XXXVIII, 'Duties').

[129] Arts. 27–9. Art. 27, 'exercise of rights with due regard to the rights of others'; Art. 28, 'duty to respect and consider his fellow beings without discrimination'; Art. 29(1) duty concerning development of the family, (2) duty to serve national community, (3) duty to respect the security of the State, (4) duty to preserve social and national solidarity, (5) duty to defend national independence, (6) duty to work and pay taxes, (7) duty to strengthen positive African cultural values, (8) duty to promote African unity.

[130] For details see Robertson (1982: 161–5). For 'The Draft Charter on Human and Peoples' Rights in the Arab World' see *Information Sheet No. 21* (Council of Europe: Strasbourg, 1988), App. xxxx, 243. This is an unofficial draft after a meeting in Syracuse, 5–12 Dec. 1986. There are clear passages which recognize the operation of rights in the private sphere, e.g. Art. 29 (the State is to ensure the right to strike).

[131] Signed 9 Dec. 1985, OAS Treaty Series no. 67, in force 28 Feb. 1987; for text see *Information Sheet No. 20* (Council of Europe: Strasbourg, 1987), 139.

[132] In force 1 Feb. 1989; for text see *Information Sheet No. 21* (Strasbourg: Council of Europe, 1988), 130; or 27 *ILM* (1988), 1152.

people detained in private as well as public institutions.[133] A special example of such recognition of the threat to human rights from private bodies can be found in Article 13(3) of the American Convention on Human Rights.[134]

13(3). The right of expression may not be restricted by indirect methods or means, such as the abuse of government or private controls over newsprint, radio broadcasting frequencies, or equipment used in the dissemination of information, or by any other means tending to impede the communication and circulation of ideas and opinions.[135]

And the Inter-American Commission on Human Rights has clearly stated, in the context of violent attacks, that 'the governments must prevent and suppress acts of violence, even forcefully, whether committed by public officials or *private individuals*, whether their motives are political or otherwise'.[136]

One communication to the Commission against Guatemala related to the Coca-Cola bottling plant. The communication described murders that the company had paid for and, in addition, it alleged that the company had organized an advertising campaign in the newspapers to defame and denigrate the union leader so that there would be no outcry when he was murdered.[137] As the Government of Guatemala did not reply to the Commission's requests for information, the Commission presumed the facts to be true[138] and declared that the Government had violated Articles 4

---

[133] See Explanatory Report paras. 28–32 and Cassese (1989: 139–40). Although the UN Convention against Torture and Other Cruel, Inhuman or Degrading Treatment or Punishment (1984) defines torture in Arts. 1(1) and 16 by reference to a public official's instigation, consent, or acquiescence, this restriction is not reproduced in the European Convention for the Prevention of Torture, which covers even people detained in private institutions, where those persons are deprived of their liberty by a public authority (Art. 2).

[134] It is perhaps worth noting that Art. 13, which specifically mentions 'private controls', has been held to be definitive as to the operation of Art. IV of the American Declaration of the Rights and Duties of Man, so that this prohibition on private interference with the right of expression is applicable even where Member States of the OAS are not parties to the American Convention, as was the situation in the case *Rubin* v. *Paraguay*, IACHR Case 9642, Res. No. 14/87, decision of 28 Mar. 1987, p. 111 (see p. 113 for the reference to Art. 13). It is worth noting that in this case concerning interference with a radio station the Commission held the Government had violated Art. IV by its omission and inaction concerning those who were responsible for the attacks.

[135] And see also Art. 14, 'The right to reply', where 'every newspaper, motion picture, radio and television company, shall have a person responsible, who is not protected by immunities or special privileges'; Art. 25, 'Right to judicial protection'; Art. 32, 'Relationship betweem duties and rights'.

[136] IACHR, 'Report on the Situation of Human Rights in the Republic of Guatemala', OAS doc. OEA/Ser.L/V/II.53, doc. 21, rev. 2, 13 Oct. 1981, para. 10 (emphasis added).

[137] Res. 38/81, Case 4425 (Guatemala) 25 June 1981, para. 1 (IACHR, *Annual Report, 1980–1981*, OAS doc. OEA Ser.L/V/II. 54, doc. 9, rev. 1, 16 Oct. 1981, 81–6).

[138] Under Art. 39 of the American Convention on Human Rights.

(right to life), 5 (right to humane treatment), 7 (right to personal liberty), 8 (right to a fair trial), 15 (right of assembly), 16 (freedom of association), and 25 (right to judicial protection) of the American Convention.

More recently in *Velásquez Rodríguez* v. *Honduras*[139] the Inter-American Court of Human Rights was concerned with a 'disappearance' and certain difficulties surrounding the proof of a link to the State's forces. The Court offered a very wide interpretation of Article 1(1) of the American Convention, stating that this Article implies an obligation to organize the governmental apparatus so that everyone is ensured a free and full enjoyment of their human rights.[140] It specifically confirmed that private individuals can violate human rights and that this can be imputable to the State:

An illegal act which violates human rights and which is initially not directly imputable to a State (for example, because it is the act of a private person or because the person responsible has not been identified) can lead to international responsibility of the State, not because of the act itself, but because of the lack of due diligence to prevent the violation or to respond to it as required by the Convention.
. . . [T]he violation can be established even if the identity of the individual perpetrator is unknown.[141]

Two duties for the State emerge. First, where due diligence by the State could have *prevented* the abuse of human rights then the State is internationally responsible. Second, where the State fails to *respond* it is similarly responsible because 'those [private] parties are aided in a sense by the government, thereby making the State responsible on the international plane'.[142]

4.3.1.3.1 The Inter-American Commission and acts of violence by 'irregular armed groups'

The Inter-American Commission on Human Rights differs from the European Commission of Human Rights in that it has a role outside the action it takes upon receipt of communications under the relevant regional

---

[139] Judgment 29 July 1988; for the text of the judgment see 28 *ILM* (1989), 291.

[140] Para. 166. For an examination of this and similar cases see Shelton (1990: 1–34). Shelton notes that the approach of the Inter-American Court differs from the European Court of Human Rights in that the latter Court does not recognize that Art. 1 ECHR can be violated independently. Not too much emphasis should be placed on this distinction, as the European Court has nevertheless shown its willingness to find the Contracting States responsible for similar failures to prevent and remedy violations by private persons (see Ch. 7.6).

[141] Para. 172–3.

[142] Para. 177.

human rights Convention.[143] It has promotional and reporting functions with regard to all the Member States of the Organization of American States (OAS). Since the entry into force of the Protocol of Buenos Aires the Commission is also a formal Charter organ of the OAS with an extra consultative role to the Organization.

One particular aspect of the Commission's work is the production of country reports. Reports have been produced on Chile, Cuba, Nicaragua, Argentina, Bolivia, Colombia, El Salvador, Guatemala, Haiti, Paraguay, Surinam, and Uruguay. These countries saw many victims of terrorism, and as early as 23 April 1970 the Commission adopted a Resolution wherein it condemned 'acts of political terrorism and urban or rural guerrilla terrorism, as they cause serious violations of the rights to life, personal security and physical freedom, freedom of thought, opinion and expression, and the rights to protection, upheld in the American Declaration and other international instruments'. Over the years the Commission took into account the atmosphere of violence as part of the general background to human rights violations addressed in its reports on countries such as El Salvador (1978), Argentina (1980), Colombia (1981), Guatemala (1981 and 1983), and with regard to the Miskito Indians in Nicaragua (1983). The Commission also considers this sort of private violence when analysing the suspension of guarantees in times of emergency.

But certain governments argued that their actions were necessary to deal with terrorist attacks and called on the Commission to condemn and concern itself with 'the human rights of the victims of terrorism'.[144] This issue has been given careful consideration and the Commission's position is explained in the Commission's *Annual Report 1990–1991*. The Commission states that two phenomena induced it to review its early position adopted in 1970. The first related to the fact that the OAS had produced a number of studies and draft instruments on terrorism but no agreement was reached concerning definitions of terrorism or its links with human rights. Second, the Commission felt that its duty was to stress that unqualified respect for human rights had to be a fundamental part of anti-subversive strategies. The Commission could not lend credence to

---

[143] See Art. 41 of the American Convention on Human Rights (ACHR) for the functions of the Commission with regard to States Parties to the Convention, Art. 18 of the Statute of the Commission with respect to all Member States of the OAS, Art. 19 of the Commission's Statute for States Parties to the Convention, and Art. 20 of the Commission's Statute for OAS Member States that are not parties to the Convention. See generally T. Buergenthal, R. Norris, and D. Shelton, *Protecting Human Rights in the Americas* (3rd edn.) (Kehl am Rhein: Engel, 1990).

[144] See the *Annual Report of the Inter-American Commission on Human Rights 1990–1991*, 504–14. My comments draw heavily on the Commission's own account of this issue as detailed in the relevant pages of its annual report.

the claims of governments that human rights violations were inevitable due to the 'war' being waged against terrorists. The Commission would present information concerning terrorist violence to explain governmental violence but never to justify it. However, the issue remains a controversial one.

In 1990 the OAS General Assembly adopted a Resolution on irregular armed groups and recommended to the Inter-American Commission that it should include references to the actions of such groups in reporting on the status of human rights in the American States. In addition, the Working Group on the Strengthening of the OAS has agreed to study the idea of a special legal regime to cover human rights violations by irregular armed groups. The Commission's *Annual Report 1990–1991* addresses this issue and the implications it has for the inter-American system.

The Commission's report starts by recalling the legal background. It stresses that the traditional concept of human rights materialized into international laws and that these laws were the same laws that instituted the organizations charged with the international protection of human rights. They warn that if the concept of human rights is used to refer to any act that adversely affects the attributes of a person then the idea becomes so sweeping that the element of specificity is lost. The report later states:

The situation that arose in Europe between the two world wars dramatically demonstrated the need to develop a system that contemplates those situations in which the State, whose function it is to protect the individual, becomes his assailant. When it comes to the State, the individual is defenseless because he lacks the means to protect himself. This is where the rights of the individual acquire an added dimension that puts them above the rights of States and makes the individual a subject under international law. Thus, his individual rights can be protected by the international community, organized and juridically regulated by means of treaties. This is the substance of the legal contract between the individual and the State that is formalized in the concept of human rights.[145]

The perspective taken here is one of a treaty body charged with quasi-judicial functions regarding human rights granted by the State to individuals. The Commission has jurisdiction only over the acts and omissions of States. In this way it has the same role as the European Commission and Court of Human Rights. But, as was explained above, the Inter-American Commission has other more wide-ranging functions. Its concern is not only to safeguard a neat, specific concept of human rights as part of the international legal order but also to preserve its own effectiveness as an actor for the protection of human rights in the Americas.

The Commission's report pointed to the over-broad notion of 'irregular

---

[145] At 507.

armed groups' and how this could include the actions of drug traffickers as well as criminal urban violence. The Commission warns that, should it become involved in any 'act of violence perpetrated by an armed group', this 'would have an adverse effect on the American system for protecting human rights and do nothing to enhance its operation'.

It is not merely that the Commission cannot take on more work but that the investigation of terrorist or other violent acts by non-state actors poses a special set of difficulties. First, in order to assess the veracity of the information given to them by governments the Commission would have to hear the version of the illegal/terrorist group. But the Commission's report points out that many believe that it should essentially be the function of the State to investigate and punish violence and there is no role for an international organization here. Second, the Commission is concerned about the repercussions of its involvement where the irregular armed group is a party to an internal armed conflict. Because many of the terrorist acts take place in the context of armed conflict, actions by an organ of an inter-governmental organization could contribute to the standing and eventual international recognition of the armed groups as belligerents. Third, the Commission has to consider whether its actions will contribute at all to the correction of problems associated with terrorism and the enjoyment of individual rights.

These problems are similar to some of those faced by non-governmental human rights organizations which were alluded to in the above section on internal armed conflict. Not only is conceptual clarity at stake but expanding activities to cover terrorist acts disproportionately stretches resources towards an area where reporting can have little effect; the personal safety of the human rights workers is put more at risk than ever; and governments are unlikely ever to be satisfied that the organization has achieved the correct 'balance'.

What relevance do these considerations have for the application of the European Convention on Human Rights? It is suggested that the same problems do not arise in the context of the Strasbourg organs. The European Commission of Human Rights has few extrajudicial functions equivalent to those of the Inter-American Commission. It does not prepare country reports. It cannot be requested to report on the activities of the IRA or the organization Basque Homeland and Liberty (ETA). There is no risk that the Council of Europe would be indirectly recognizing the conditions of armed conflict nor that it would confer 'international' recognition on one or another group. In fact, as we shall see, the Commission and Court have addressed acts of violence by non-state actors and have found the State responsible under the Convention for failing to prevent or remedy them. This must be the role of such international bodies: to hold States accountable for failing to prevent and remedy private abuses. It has been argued that if they are forced to address private violations directly they would fail in their responsibility as they would in turn be relieving States of their international responsibility.[146] This is the perceived danger which often leads to reticence on the part of human rights specialists when attempts are made to apply the language of human rights to the private sphere.

We should not confuse the practical difficulties of confronting armed groups directly over reports of human rights abuses in countries such as Peru and Cambodia with the danger of refusing to admit that human rights violations ever occur in the private sphere at all. This leads into the next justification: that it is dangerous to exclude private violators of rights from the theory and practice of human rights. Dangerous because it could leave victims unprotected and dangerous because it reinforces a deceptive separation of the public and private spheres.

4.3.2 Approach 2: Difficult and dangerous distinctions

The concept of international human rights applying to the actions of private bodies cuts across the 'traditional' understanding of the international law of human rights. Most authors list rights which they consider only apply against the State: 'the traditional view of what personal liberty and security in these contexts means is freedom of restraint by the State; and the structure of Article 5 (ECHR) would indicate that this is its meaning there. Other examples could be given.'[147] Three tendencies work against such an interpretation: (1) the Diceyan view that the State and private individuals should be judged by the same standards and the same judges; (2) the development of human rights law so as to include private violators; (3) societal developments such as private prisons, mental hospitals, and private police forces.

If we remain within the area of Article 5 and the right to liberty we can see how each of these tendencies affects the 'traditional view':

1. Over one hundred years ago Dicey gave the following example in his lecture on 'The Right to Personal Freedom':

Suppose that in 1725 Voltaire had at the instigation of an English lord been treated in London as he was treated in Paris. He would not have needed to depend for redress upon the goodwill of his friends or upon the favour of the Ministry. He could have pursued one of two courses. He could by taking the proper steps have caused all his assailants to be brought to trial as criminals. He

---

[146] The ILC's draft Art. 5 of the draft Code of Crimes against the Peace and Security of Mankind clearly states: 'Prosecution of an individual for a crime against the peace and security of mankind does not relieve a state of any responsibility under international law for an act or omission attributable to it.'

[147] Forde (1985: 263).

could, if he had preferred it, have brought an action against each and all of them: he could have sued the nobleman who caused him to be thrashed, the footman who thrashed him, the policeman who threw him into gaol, and the gaoler or lieutenant who kept him there. Notice particularly that the action for trespass, to which Voltaire would have recourse, can be brought, or as the technical expression goes, 'lies' against every person throughout the realm. It can and has been brought against governors of colonies, against secretaries of state, against officers who have tried by Court-martial persons not subject to military law, against every kind of official high or low. Here then we come across another aspect of the 'rule of law.' No one of Voltaire's enemies would, if he had been injured in England, have been able to escape from responsibility on the plea of acting in an official character or in obedience to his official superiors. Nor would any of them have been able to say that because he was a government officer he must be tried by an official. Voltaire, to keep to our example, would have been able in England to have brought each and all of his assailants, including the officials who kept him in prison, before judges and jurymen who were not at all likely to think that official zeal or the orders of official superiors were either a legal or a moral excuse for breaking the law. (1889: 200)

Of course Dicey was concerned that state officials should not evade responsibility, he was not concerned with inculpating private actors, but it seems that the ensuing Anglo-Saxon emphasis on state actors has led to the conception that only state actors can violate the right to liberty. It might have been this sort of concern which led to the wording of Article 13 ECHR[148] and Article 2(3)(a) of the International Covenant on Civil and Political Rights.[149] Although both Marc-André Eissen and Jean Raymond have argued that Article 13 ECHR implies that the Convention covers breaches committed by private individuals,[150] the matter has never been adjudicated by the Court or Commission.

The best conclusion would seem to be that the inclusion of the phrase 'notwithstanding that the violation has been committed by persons acting in an official capacity' was intended to exclude any possibility of government agents claiming they were 'acting under orders'.[151] One cannot conclude that Article 13 implies that violations by private persons are outside the scope of the Convention.

2. Article 9 of the 1966 Covenant on Civil and Political Rights deals with 'personal liberty and security' and is very similar to Article 5 of the

---

[148] Art. 13 reads: 'Everyone whose rights and freedoms as set forth in this Convention are violated shall have an effective remedy before a national authority notwithstanding that the violation has been committed by persons acting in an official capacity.'

[149] Art. 2(3)(a) reads: 'Each State Party to the present Covenant undertakes: a. To ensure that any person whose rights or freedoms as herein recognized are violated shall have an effective remedy, notwithstanding that the violation has been committed by persons acting in an official capacity.'

[150] Eissen (1962: 237); Raymond (1980: 170).

[151] See Schachter (1981: 326).

European Convention. However, by the 1960s there was already an awareness of the real threats posed by private bodies. Article 9(5), which is the same as Article 5(5) of the European Convention on Human Rights, deals with compensation for violations of the rights contained in the Article, and was referred to in the following way in the *travaux préparatoires*: 'The right to compensation set forth in general terms, would seem likely to be invoked against individuals as well as against the State as a legal person.'[152]

3. It is clear that the current trend in Europe for privatization, private enterprise, and self-regulation will mean that more and more services will be tendered out or privatized. A traditional reading of human rights law as only applicable to state officials would leave many 'private' actors outside the human rights dialogue. For example, in 1987 the United Kingdom Government hired the ship MV *Earl William* from the Sealink company, which had been recently privatized. The ship was moored at Harwich and was used to hold Tamils and other asylum seekers. Operations on board the ship were handled by the private security firm Securicor. Should we consider that the alleged[153] abuse and maltreatment by the guards do not come within the sphere of international human rights protection, as the perpetrators are not 'real' policemen but a private security firm? Of course, all the normal criminal and tort laws apply in such a situation. But the success of the international supervision of human rights is due to its ability to highlight an abnormal situation where human dignity is threatened through the inability of the law to guarantee basic human rights.

In Part I the point was made that the strength of the European Convention on Human Rights lies in its educative force: clearly it is no longer satisfactory that only 'public' officials should be exposed to its provisions and jurisprudence. For the Convention to be really educative it must also bind those who are not normally considered organs of the State. So 'private' police, gaols, hospitals, schools, and housing associations would have to consider international human rights standards in addition to any other statutory obligations.

4.3.3 Difficult distinction

Over fifty years ago it was already being argued: 'Those who wield [State] power we have subjected to some sort of responsibility to a democratic electorate, and to various constitutional limitations. Yet much of this

---

[152] A/2929 ch. vi para. 36 and Bossuyt (1987: 217).
[153] See 'UK's Immigration Laws: Are they Fair?', *Labour Research* (Nov. 1987), 15–17 at 16. Consider also the death of Earnest Hogg who was in the care of a private security firm, The *Sunday Times*, 9 May, 1993, 1.3.

recognized political power is not different in kind or degree, from much of the power that some individuals and private groups can lawfully exercise against other individuals.'[154] This passage is quoted by Brian Bercusson at the beginning of a paper on 'Economic Policy: State and Private Ordering' (1988: 361). In the context of law as an instrument of economic policy, Bercusson examines the functional equivalents in the private sector of state instruments, measures, and implementation of economic policy; at the end of the study he concludes in part:

I am not concerned here to distinguish private and public law. On the contrary, my argument is that the study of the legal implementation of economic policy by the State cannot be separated from the study of the law governing the economic relations between private actors. Illustrations are legion: State regulation through the imposition of duties may rely on private enforcement mechanisms; State taxation may be defeated by private financial arrangements, State benefits will have a differential impact on different private actors' ability to apply successfully, and so on. (1988: 418)

The difficulties arising from an attempt to disentangle the public from the private in an analysis of economic policy are just as prevalent in the field of human rights. So, assuming the traditional view that only state organs are capable of violating human rights, and assuming that what constitutes a state organ is to be determined with reference to national law (which is an approach the Commission has taken in the past,[155] and still sometimes appears to take[156]), a hypothetical example might run as follows: a small

---

[154] H. L. Hale, 'Force and the State: A Comparison of "Political" and "Economic" Compulsion', *Columbia Law Review* (1935), 149.

[155] Applic. 1706/62, *X* v. *Austria*, decision 4 Oct. 1966, 9 Yearbook 112–66, esp. 156–8 (official receiver incurs state responsibility) and 162–4 (Board of Creditors/ *Gläubigerausschuß* does not trigger state responsibility); and again in Applic. 10259/83, *S.P.R.L. ANCA and Others* v. *Belgium* (10 Dec. 1984) 40 D. & R. 170 at 178, para. 3 (state responsibility for official receiver/*curateur de faillite*); note also the evidence of the British Government in Applic. 3059/67, *X* v. *UK*, 28 *Collection* 89–93, suggesting the independence of the BBC and denying state responsibility; this issue was not decided either in this case or in a similar one, Applic. 4545/70, *X and the Assoc. of Z* v. *UK*, decision 12 July 1971, (1971) 14 Yearbook 538. Both these cases concerned Sir Oswald Moseley and the British Union of Fascists and their attempts to broadcast on television.

[156] See the attitude of the Commission in *Nielson* v. *Denmark*, Applic. 10929/84 (30 June 1987), where the claim was on Art. 5 and the Commission took account of the fact that the hospital was a state hospital. The Commission's report fixes state responsibility through the decision of the Chief Physician of the child psychiatric ward of the state hospital. The Court took a different approach and found that the decision to hospitalize was essentially the mother's exercise of her rights of parental authority. In this case the Court did not find it necessary to go further into the question of 'the possible application of Article 5 to situations in which there is a deprivation of liberty resulting from the action of a private person' (judgment of 28 Nov. 1988, Series A, vol. 144, para. 73). Reading the dissenting opinions of Judges Thòr Vilhjalmsson, Pettiti, Russo, Spielmann, de Meyer, Carrillo Salcedo, and Valticos it would seem that the Court is likely to construe Art. 5(1) as covering all deprivations of liberty. In *Applic. 9444/81* v. *UK*, decision of 9 July 1983, the Commission

(state) cottage hospital where the patients are mostly covered by private insurance, and where most jobs are tendered out to private firms, might still be classified as 'public', and a vast (private) corporation patronized[157] almost exclusively by the State would almost certainly fail to be termed an organ of the State. Thus complaints about abuses of human rights (say discrimination or anti-union practices) would be justiciable in the case of the cottage hospital but not in the case of the vast corporation. It is suggested that such a contradiction is unjustifiable. Although it may be within the letter of the law, it flies in the face of a conception of law as coherent.[158]

Supporters of a private/public distinction might argue that examples such as this merely point to a weakness concerning definitions in English legal theory, and that the developed Continental legal notions of 'public' and 'private' could be adopted. But we are examining the question at the supranational level. Even if the United Kingdom could develop definitions so that 'public' and 'private' could be defined without contradiction, there would still remain discrepancies between the twenty-six Member States of the Council of Europe. Would it not be contradictory for the Commission to have jurisdiction to hear a complaint against the United

states: 'A trade union clearly no State organ whose acts or omissions could as such entail any responsibility under the Convention for the High Contracting Party concerned' (at 5 of the unpublished transcript). Compare *Cheall* v. *UK*, Applic. 10550/83, decision of 13 May 1985, 42 D. & R. 178–86 at 186, where the Commission considers the reasonableness of the union's rules (this case is discussed in detail in Ch. 7). See also *Van der Heijden* v. *The Netherlands*, decision of 8 Mar. 1985, Applic. 11002/84, 41 D. & R. 264 at 270: '[The Commission] may not receive applications directed against individuals—in this case, the Foundation, which is a private law corporation' ('qui est une personne morale de droit privé').

[157] That the State has the potential to use and abuse its power not only through force but also by selective manipulation of its wealth, and that this creates new risks for democracy, is clearly shown by Daintith (1985: 174–97). We might also consider the status of public interest groups regularly consulted by Government and corporations in which the State has a holding (often 51% or 49%). The explanation of the term 'quago'—quasi-autonomous governmental organization—leaves us no wiser as to its 'publicness' (the acronym 'quango' is just as mystifying—quasi-autonomous non-governmental organization). For the detail of the UK Government's involvement in these and other bodies see Lewis (1985: 198–228); for examples of government incentives and patronage in the 'private sector' see I. Harden and N. Lewis, 'Delegalisation in Britain in the 1980's', EUI Working Paper no. 84/125 (1984) esp. 14–16. The emergence of 'next steps' agencies, as a stage on the way to privatization of functions such as education and control of accountability, has given rise to the term 'pingos' (partly independent government organizations).

[158] Ronald Dworkin advocates such a conception in ch. 6 of *Law's Empire*, where he suggests that integrity should be the ideal central to law, and that concepts such as fairness and justice are necessarily subordinate. Dworkin argues that a solution (which ignored integrity) to the abortion debate could involve a statute which stated that women born in even years would be allowed an abortion, whereas women born in odd years would be denied the possibility of an abortion. This 'chequerboard' solution contains an 'internal compromise' which would be unacceptable to most people. This is because the solution treats 'people differently when no principle can justify the distinction' (Dworkin 1986: 180).

Kingdom involving the Independent Broadcasting Association, but not one against the Federal Republic of Germany, where German television companies[159] are involved? Similarly, the Commission has already held that the Lutheran Church is a public law corporation exercising powers delegated by the State (Federal Republic of Germany), in particular with regard to the regulation of cemeteries.[160] On the other hand, with respect to the levying of contributions by the Roman Catholic Church in Austria, the Commission considered that the member's duty to pay these contributions is an obligation of civil law enforceable in the civil courts. This part of the application was therefore dismissed *ratione personae*.[161]

Bearing in mind that one of the aims[162] of the Council of Europe is greater unity between its Members, and that this is to be achieved through the 'further realisation of human rights', then the solution which results in the best 'fit' is one which disregards public and private law distinctions at the national level, and examines all violations whosoever commits them, and then decides whether the Member State will be held responsible[163] for failing to prevent (or grant redress for) such a violation.

It is suggested that even if harmonization of the public/private legal boundaries were desirable, at the European level this would be nearly impossible. Carol Harlow has colourfully illustrated this:

I believe myself that the 'public/private' classification is part of another, more insular, tradition. It is nothing more than an attempt by the judiciary to conceal political issues behind a formalist façade and to shield from public criticism some highly executive-minded decisions. Nevil Johnson has rightly called our legal theory 'very thin gruel indeed'. The 'public/private' distinction is not thick enough for gruel. To continue his culinary metaphor, our judges can be linked to crafty restaurateurs, seeking to pass off unpalatable common law left-overs as delicacies from classic French cuisine. But Brown Windsor Soup is not easily disguised as *Crème Vichyssoise*. (1980: 265)

---

[159] See *X* v. *FRG*, Applic. 2413/65, 16 Dec. 1966, 23 Collection at 7.

[160] '[T]he Federal Republic of Germany is, from the point of view of the Convention, answerable for the acts of which the applicant is complaining' (Applic. 8363/78, decision of 12 May 1980, *X* v. *FRG*, 20 D. & R. 163–7 at 166.

[161] '[C]ollection is an autonomous activity of the churches, and the State's activity in this field is limited to the exercise of the power of control' (*Applic. 9781/82* v. *Austria*, decision of 14 May 1984, at 5 of the unpublished report, now published in 37 D. & R. 42.

[162] Art. 1 of the Statute of the Council of Europe (for text see 1 *European Yearbook* (1955), 378) and also the third preambular paragraph of the ECHR.

[163] This 'wide' use of the word 'responsible' implies responsibility for failing to prevent the human rights violation, and should not be confused with 'liability for the acts of State organs'. For the former see Brownlie (1983*b*: 159–79). For the latter see Brownlie (1983*b*: 132–58). The ILC's draft concerning the responsibility of States for acting illegally contains the following Article: '11(1) The conduct of a person or a group of persons not acting on behalf of the State shall not be considered as an act of the State under international law.' Brownlie's criticism is relevant here: 'The issue of classifying "acts of State" is esoteric, irrelevant, and confusing' (1983*b*: 164). This warning should be borne in mind when considering the enforcement of the ECHR.

4.3.4 Dangerous distinction: Critical conceptions of the concept

Peter Cane has termed the approach taken so far to the public/private distinction 'integrationist' (1987: 57). That is to say the influence of Dicey leads

modern scholars . . . [to] stress the similarities and analogies between governmental and private activity and play down the public–private distinction; what
matters for questions of legal liability is the nature of the activity not the identity
of the person or body conducting it; and since activities are not by their nature
either public or private, the distinction is irrelevant to the regulation and control
of human activity. (Cane 1987: 61)

He is here referring to British attitudes to administrative law and, after a
revealing analysis of the use of the public/private concept in this context,
suggests that 'different attitudes to the public–private distinction can be
related, at a very abstract level, to different accounts of the role of the
individual in political life and hence to different accounts of the nature of
democracy and the state'. If this is true in the context of English administrative law, it is also true in a wider context. If we explore some of the
theories on the division between the public and the private spheres we
find several 'schools' who condemn the use of the public/private distinction as dangerous.

According to Carole Pateman the 'dichotomy between the private and
the public is central to almost two centuries of feminist writing and
political struggle' (1983: 281). This is because the dichotomy 'obscures the
subjection of women to men within an apparently universal, egalitarian
and individualist order' (1983: 283). And, due to the fact that 'liberalism
conceptualizes civil society in abstraction from ascriptive domestic life',
'the latter remains "forgotten" in theoretical discussion. The separation
between private and public is thus re-established as a division *within* civil
society itself, within the world of men' (1983: 285). Pateman is here
distinguishing between the private sphere and a forgotten domestic sphere.
It is exactly this domestic sphere which feminists and others urge should
be considered and regulated rather than shielded by law.[164] A striking

---

[164] For some examples of how international law obscures and ignores women as individuals
and goups see H. Charlesworth, C. Chinkin, and S. Wright, 'Feminist Approaches to
International Law', 85 *AJIL* (1991), 613–45. More generally see Taub and Schneider (1982:
117–39); MacKinnon (1989: 190–4). Note also the point made by N. Rose: 'By the start of
the twentieth century, the family is administered and policed by practices and agencies
which are neither private—in that their powers are constructed legally, they are the recipients
of public funds and their agents are publicly accredited by some form of licensing—nor
organs of political power in that their operations and objectives are not specified by the
decrees and programmes of political forces but operate under the aegis of moral principles,
and increasingly, by professional expertise underpinned by the power of a claim to truth. To
claim that the content of family relations is either unregulated or delegated to husbands is to
fundamentally mistake the nature of the modern family and its political role, it is to fall
victim to the public/private dichotomy not to transcend it' (1987: 61).

example of the law's reticence with regard to entering this sphere is the fact that in some legal systems a man cannot be convicted of raping his wife.[165]

Such forgetfulness is present not only in liberal theories of society but also in various labour theories which

assume that it is possible to understand economic activity in abstraction from domestic life. It is 'forgotten' that the worker, invariably taken to be a man, can appear ready for work and concentrate on his work free from the everyday demands of providing food, washing and cleaning, and care of children, only because these tasks are performed unpaid by his wife. And if she is also a paid worker she works a further shift at these 'natural' activities.[166]

If we do indeed turn to the field of labour law, we again find vehement criticism of the operation of a public/private dichotomy. One critique is not only 'integrationist', arguing that 'public' and 'private' are used to 'characterize the same phenomena' (Klare 1982: 1360), and that judges are capable of arriving at opposite conclusions regarding identical premisses, but it also argues that 'the core ideological function served by the public/private distinction is to deny that the practices comprising the public sphere of life—the worlds of business, education and culture, the community and the family—are inextricably linked to and at least partially constituted by politics and law'. As a result, 'The primary effect of the public/private distinction is thus to inhibit the perception that the institutions in which we live are the product of human design and can therefore be changed.'[167] Although Professor Klare is here writing from the perspective of American law, where links to the State (state action) are needed if constitutional protection is to be invoked, similar ideological sentiments are also prevalent in European scholarship.

The distinction between public and private law has been rejected by sociologists as inappropriate. For Durkheim: 'All law is private in the

---

[165] For other examples of the law's refusal to interfere see Taub and Schneider (1982: 121–4). The most recent English case-law on marital rape is cited in Ch. 7 n. 198.

[166] Pateman (1983: 296); in the European context the survey carried out in ten countries of the European Community at the request of the Directorate for Information of the Community concludes that, for almost a third of Community citizens, the ideal family is one where the wife has a job less demanding than her husband's, and plays a bigger role than he does in the home and caring for the children; and when men were asked their own preference, 52% stated that they would prefer their wife not to work; this has to be contrasted with the 63% of women who (if they already had enough money to live comfortably) would work. (Supplement no. 16 to *Women of Europe, Women and Men of Europe* (1983), 55–7.

[167] Klare (1982: 1417); Duncan Kennedy makes a similar plea in the context of legal education: 'Rights discourse, moreover, simply presupposes or takes for granted that the world is and should be divided between a state sector that enforces rights and a private world of "civil society" in which atomized individuals pursue their diverse goals. This framework is *in itself*, a part of the problem rather than of the solution. It makes it difficult even to conceptualize radical proposals such as, for example, decentralized democratic worker control of factories' (1982a: 48–9).

sense that it is always about individuals who are present and acting; but more importantly, all law is public, in the sense that it is a social function and that all individuals are, whatever their various titles, functionaries of society.'[168] More recently (and sometimes inspired by Durkheim (Supiot 1987: 177–200)) sociologists, political scientists, and lawyers have been rediscovering what has been described as neo-corporatism, and have sometimes doubted its democratic legitimacy. It is precisely because such neo-corporatist institutions seem to fall into the chasm which runs along the public/private divide that their accountability and representativeness have not been questioned in the past. Those concerned to further participatory democracy as a legitimate form of rational decision-making point to such institutions or associations and argue that a division between the public and the private spheres means that such decision-making processes are not subject to the scrutiny that is applied to clearly 'public' processes: 'a revised concept of law and constitutionality should inform a public, reasoned decision-making process, so that barriers which define the spheres of influence of law, administration and politics are broken down in order to foster the deployment of resources necessary for collective learning and hence for rational and efficient policy-making' (Harden and Lewis 1986: 54).

All the above arguments have been taken out of context, and from various diverse traditions and disciplines, and none of them is really addressed to the question of human rights; but the question of human rights in Europe does arise in each of the contexts referred to above—family life,[169] sexual life,[170] work life,[171] administrative life,[172] and economic life.[173] If some commentators in these areas are pleading that the

---

[168] Durkheim (1964: 68) (amended translation A.B.C.). Durkheim continues: 'Les fonctions maritales, paternelles, etc. ne sont ni délimitées, ni organisées d'une autre manière que les fonctions ministérielles et législatives, et ce n'est pas sans raison que le droit romain qualifiait la tutelle de *manus publicum*. Qu'est-ce d'ailleurs que l'État? On sait combien la question est controversée; il n'est pas scientifique de faire reposer une classification fondamentale sur une notion aussi obscure et mal analysée' (E. Durkheim, *De la division du travail social* (1902; 9th edn. Paris: Presses Universitaires de France, 1973), 33). Durkheim goes on to define two sorts of law: repressive and restitutive; however, this classification does not really help us in the field of human rights.

[169] *Marckx* case (1979) Series A, vol. 31; *Airey* case (1979) vol. 32; *Case of Abdulaziz, Cabales and Balkandali* (1985) vol. 94; *Case of Johnstone and Others* (1986) vol. 112; *Cases of O. and H.* (1987) vol. 120; *Cases of W., B., and R.* (1987) vol. 136.

[170] *Handyside* case (1976) vol. 24; *Dudgeon* case (1981) vol. 45; *Norris* case (1988) vol. 142; *Rees* case (1986) vol. 106; *Cossey* case (1990) vol. 184; *B.* v. *France* (1992) vol. 232-C.

[171] *National Union of Belgian Police* case (1976) vol. 19; *Swedish Engine Drivers' Union* case (1976) vol. 20; *Case of Young, James and Webster* (1981) vol. 44; *Leander* case (1987) vol. 116.

[172] *Case of X* v. *UK* (1981) vol. 46; *Feldebrugge* case (1986) vol. 99; *Deumland* case (1986) vol. 100; *Case of Van Marle and Others* (1986) vol. 101; *Rees* case (1986) vol. 106; *Cossey* case (1990) vol. 184; *B.* v. *France* (1992) vol. 232-C.

[173] *Case of Sporring and Lönroth* (1982) vol. 52; *Case of Lithgow and Others* (1986) vol. 102; *Case of Powell and Rayner* (1990) vol. 172.

public/private distinction is dangerous, then those who wish efficiently to protect human rights must at least consider their pleas.

In concluding this chapter we should return to the plea of Marc-André Eissen, the Registrar of the European Court of Human Rights, who must be credited as one of the first (1961: 167) and most convincing advocates of the application of the Convention to the actions of private individuals. Having shown that the text of the Convention can be interpreted so as to create duties on private bodies, he concludes that such an interpretation:

répond en tout cas beaucoup mieux, nous avons la ferme conviction, aux besoins profonds du monde moderne. Elle gagne en outre du terrain auprès des juridictions nationales: n'est-ce point la preuve qu'elle offre un intérêt pratique appréciable et qu'elle n'a rien d'artificiel? Si l'on voit dans la convention une réalité vivante appelée à se développer sans cesse, si l'on préfère aux délices stériles de l'exégèse la recherche de solutions à la fois respectueuses du droit et conformes au bien commun, pourquoi écarter une possibilité de progrès, pourquoi repousser une idée féconde et généreuse? (1971: 162).

5

Limits to the Application of Human Rights in the Private Sphere

The main conclusion of the last chapter was that there should be protection from all violations of human rights, and not only when the violator can be directly identified as an agent of the State. It was suggested that, in the case of the European Convention on Human Rights, this could be legally justified by a dynamic interpretation which considered the general evolution of international law, and in particular the international law of human rights.

This is not the same as advocating the abolition of the notions of public and private. Indeed the Convention itself guarantees respect for private life in Article 8. This Article clearly demonstrates a significant difference between rights in the private sphere and rights in the public sphere. Anyone wishing to rely on their 'right to information' (Article 10) may come up against private individuals relying on their 'right to respect for private life' (Article 8); this conflict does not arise where it is the State which is withholding information. The State has no right to privacy; it has a claim to *secrecy*.

Furthermore, the considerations which justify the protection of privacy are not the same as those which justify secrecy.[1] The border between privacy and freedom of expression may indeed shift depending on whether the content of the speech relates to a private person or a public official.[2] Indeed there may sometimes be arguments based on the 'general *public* interest' of certain information, even where it originates from a private individual. In such cases it may be that freedom of information 'trumps' the right to privacy. What will be argued here is that it is not the fact that the allegations relate to an official but the fact that they relate to public

---

[1] See generally Pennock and Chapman (1971); Neuberger (1987).

[2] See the different attitudes of the US Supreme Court in three libel cases: *New York Times* v. *Sullivan* 376 US 254 (1964) (public official), *Time Inc.* v. *Firestone* 424 US 448 (1976) (public figure), and *Gertz* v. *Robert Welch, Inc.* 418 US 323 (1974) (private individual); more recent cases are discussed by Hixson (1987: esp. 157–243), where he explains that the private behaviour of public officials/figures is beyond the reach of legal protection from the media (161); see also the decision of the European Court of Human Rights, *Lingens* case (1986) Series A, vol. 103. (The US Supreme Court cases will be discussed in Ch. 6.)

life which may give the case a special importance. It is not that the violation takes place in a defined institutionalized public sphere where the State has a recognized jurisdiction, but that it relates to the sphere of the public, that is to say the sphere which is in the public domain. It is suggested that the terms 'public' and 'private' should be avoided only as 'dispositive'[3] labels which trigger the jurisdiction of the Strasbourg machinery, but should be kept as 'explanatory' tools in order to establish whether a right has been violated.

Several scholars, while admitting the desirability of the extension of the Convention to cover private relations, foresee problems which are not immediately solved by reference to the text of the Convention. Professor Rolin (at the time President of the European Court of Human Rights), speaking at a colloquium in 1960,[4] saw the following conundrum: under Belgian law, then in force, anyone under the age of 25 needed the consent of their parents in order to get married; any opposition by the parents could be challenged in the national courts. If the courts were to allow parents to refuse their consent on purely racial grounds, then there would be a violation of the Convention; but (he said) it would be unacceptable to interfere in the relationship between the two fiancés should one of them break off the engagement on purely racial grounds. Rolin's example of the limits to the extension of the Convention into the private sphere may now seem a little dated, but an analogous contemporary example might run as follows: the Convention ought to cover the case where a shop owner refuses to serve someone on account of their colour, but it is less clear how it might operate in the case of ethnic choice when choosing sperm from a sperm bank.[5]

The answers to such problems concerning 'private' ordering are not really found in the international conventions and covenants which call for the elimination of all types of discrimination based on sex, race, religion, etc., even though these instruments often specifically refer to discrimination in the private sphere—by outlawing discrimination in cafés, theatres, and other 'private' situations.

Another example may serve to highlight the dilemma we face when human rights norms are extended into the private sphere. Although it is now fairly well accepted that the State should not hinder free speech, especially where the opinions expressed run contrary to the prevailing

---

[3] 'Dispositive' and 'explanatory' are the terms used by Cane (1987: 66–7) in the context of the public/private dichotomy in British administrative law.

[4] At 215 of *La Protection international des droits de l'homme dans le cadre européen* (Paris: Dalloz, 1961).

[5] Already in the UK the Warnock Committee has concluded that the ethnic origin of the donor is a relevant detail which should be made available to prospective parents. Para. 4.21, Warnock Report 1984, published in Warnock (1985).

consensus, it is not clear why a 'private' group, say a religious association, should be obliged to lend its platform to a rival organization of heretics, nor why a union or employer should have to provide facilities for a splinter breakaway union.[6]

If we reject the category of 'organ of the State' as meaningless and dangerous, and complain that its use leads to contradictory and incoherent[7] results, then we need to find a new framework with which to understand the operation of the rights in question. It is suggested that reference to private property is unhelpful. First, as has already been noted, it is often unclear how 'private' private property really is: when the Government reduces the tax payable on petrol, is this a subsidy to the oil companies? Is a state-regulated private monopoly 'private'? When a company relies entirely on tax incentives and government patronage, is it still 'private'? Why should it be different from a company where the State owns 51 per cent of the shares or from a company where the Government has a 'golden share'? Is a self-regulating occupational organization, such as the Law Society, private?[8]

Second, even if we could find completely private bodies, there may still be a case for making them comply with public standards. For example private television companies may be obliged to screen the party political broadcasts of all major parties, and American privately owned corporate towns and private shopping precincts have been forced to allow their premises to be used as a market place not only for goods, but also for the market of ideas.[9] Private data banks are subjected to restrictions as to

---

[6] Cf. s. 43 of the Education (No. 2) Act 1986, which requires universities 'so far as is reasonably practicable' not to deny facilities to persons or bodies on any ground 'connected with their beliefs, views, policies or objectives'. This has been commented on by A. M. Tettenborn: 'It would be, to say the least, remarkable if . . . a college with (say) a strong Catholic bias be bound, if it had the facilities available, to entertain a conference of evangelical activists, Muslim fundamentalists or devil worshippers' (1987: 1022). And see Barendt (1987: 344–50), who highlights the fact that the Section introduces a fundamental duty to secure freedom of speech (348). It seems the Section applies to public and private universities—s. 43(5)*a* refers to 'any university'. Although there is at the moment probably only one really private university in the UK—Buckingham University—there are several campuses of foreign universities which are financed by the State. s. 43 represents an interesting example of human rights application in the private sphere especially as it is concerned with the principle of free speech and a duty not only to refrain from violating rights (negative freedom) but also to ensure the exercise of those rights (positive freedom).

[7] For the importance of a legal system which exhibits coherence and integrity see Dworkin (1986: esp. 176–218), discussed in the previous chapter.

[8] For further examples see Jones (1988).

[9] See *Marsh* v. *Alabama* 326 US 501 (1946) (company town); and *Amalgamated Food Employers Union Local 590* v. *Logan Valley Plaza* 391 US 308 (1968) (Supreme Court ruling that the interest of free speech outweighed the private-property interests of shopping-centre owners). However, subsequent Supreme Court rulings retreat from this position: see *Lloyd* v. *Tanner* 407 US 551 (1972) and *Hudgens* v. *NLRB* 424 US 507 (1976) (these cases are discussed in the next chapter).

who may or may not have access to their files. In short, vital media are controlled by private interests. As the extent of this phenomenon is not insignificant, there have to be inroads into the sanctity of the owner's control over private property.

A final reason why an appeal to the institution of private property is unhelpful in this context is that all ownership over property, and all the mechanisms for enforcing that ownership, are granted by the State. Therefore to draw a line between that which is held in private ownership and that which is held by the State is to some extent incoherent and contradictory.

At this point it is worth identifying and summarizing three trends which have forced us to redefine the parameters of the public and the private spheres. First, the emergence of new fragmented centres of power, such as associations, pressure groups, political parties, trade unions, corporations, multinationals, universities, churches, interest groups, and quasi-official bodies, has meant that the individual now perceives authority, repression, and alienation in a variety of new bodies, whereas once it was only the apparatus of the State which was perceived in the doctrine to exhibit these characteristics. This societal development has meant that the definition of the public sphere has had to be adapted to include these new bodies and activities.

Secondly, we can trace a philosophical trend whereby the classical definition of the private as the domestic sphere, with the head of the household wielding absolute power, has been surpassed. The hierarchy of the private sphere under this definition was based on a 'natural' order, with women, children, and slaves seen as 'naturally' inferior. Because the public sphere was composed of equals (freemen) it was different from the private sphere. Although this classical distinction gave way to one which identifies the public with the nation-state and the private with the free market, even this now has to be re-evaluated with the emergence of the Welfare State and the recognition of state intervention in the economy and the laws of contract. The latest criticisms of the Welfare State do not help to define the parameters of public and private, but merely demonstrate that fixing the boundary is a normative act. Deciding what should belong in the public sphere is an ideological battle. The publicization of the private sphere will benefit some and disadvantage others. Transferring the ideological tension about the roles of the State and the market into legal classifications of private and public only conceals and mystifies the real debate. The public/private distinction can quickly become a weapon utilized in order to deny or claim jurisdiction: the police might refuse to intervene in an incident of domestic violence because it is essentially a 'private affair'; they might demand entry to a private meeting as it could endanger 'public order' or offend 'public decency'; a private act such as kissing on a street corner might become an obstruction of the 'public highway' or a 'public nuisance'. The mistake is to jump from a concern to protect privacy/private life to the belief that society can be divided into two realms: one which is inherently under the jurisdiction of the apparatus of the nation-state, and one where the State is forbidden to enter. Anyone attempting this last categorization is merely prescribing their own political philosophy.

Thirdly, the supranational factor has meant that the individual–State dichotomy is no longer sufficient to explain complex relations in modern society. Not only do supranational organs introduce a new power relationship with potential for abuse of power between the individual and the supranational authority, but there also now exist various groups (national or multinational) which may bypass the state machinery and exercise direct influence on supranational authorities, which, in turn, directly exercise power over the individual. Again we see how a conception which posits the individual and his or her activities in the private sphere, and the State's activities in a public sphere, is inadequate when attempting to analyse certain modern phenomena and construct an appropriate reflexive response to the human rights problems raised.

If the old conceptions of private property and public activity are unhelpful in our quest to find a structure with which to understand the limits of human rights protection in the private sphere, we should perhaps ask much more fundamental questions about the rights to be protected.

5.1 WHY PROTECT HUMAN RIGHTS?

R. J. Vincent has pointed out that 'it would be more appropriate to speak of human rights as the vocabulary of our time rather than the idea of our time: it provides the terms in which the discussion of (individual and other) values in international politics is carried on. It is . . . simultaneously part of a propaganda war and a healing philosophy' (1986: 264). It is clear that the rhetoric of human rights can be used as an instrument of propaganda in the world of international relations. Moreover, concern for human rights is now increasingly used to justify reductions in foreign aid and development assistance to countries tainted as violators of human rights. This may account to some extent for the continuing popularity of the rhetoric of human rights in international politics, but it does not explain the power of the language of rights in the hands of those who perceive their rights to be violated. Everyday campaigns rally around the banner of 'rights': the right to vote, the right to strike, the rights of the mentally ill, the right to free speech, the right to work, the right to food, the right to equal pay for equal work, the right of a woman to control her own body, the rights of the unborn, the rights of animals, the rights of future generations, and the right to peace. Claiming one's rights quickly becomes associated with *being right*. This linguistic trick may to a very limited extent account for the forcefulness of rights discourse in the English language, but in order to discover justifications for the classical liberal rights contained in the European Convention on Human Rights we might examine modern moral and philosophical justifications. If we understand the moral justification for such rights, we may be able to build a framework for understanding human rights in the private sphere.

Although the philosophy of John Locke[10] is of considerable importance, as his conception of rights filtered into the American Declaration of Independence and later into the French Declarations of 1789 and 1793,[11] and these in turn influenced the drafting of the European Convention on Human Rights in 1950, we will start our examination with modern secular justifications;[12] these moral philosophies seem more relevant to the circumstances of today. This is so first, because the impulse to draft the European Convention at the end of the 1940s sprang from revulsion at the atrocities committed by 'democratic' States, and the Convention therefore contains rights such as the right to a fair trial, the right to form trade unions, the right to freedom of religion, and the right to have an interpreter provided free of charge by the State (rights not traditionally associated with the 'natural rights' doctrines); and secondly, because by 1950 there was already widespread acceptance in Western Europe of the role of the Welfare State—a concept which is absent from the early philosophies of rights (Burns 1972: 16–30).

Several attempts have been made to justify the priority to be given to rights. If we examine some of these justifications we notice the implicit assertion that human rights should apply between individuals, and that rights are not confined to claims against the State. This conclusion on its own is of limited relevance, as the arguments for the application of legal rights will have to be legal arguments, but it is hoped that through this examination of moral philosophy we can discover analytical tools which will help us to understand how human rights operate in the private sphere. It may be useful to distinguish duty-based, goal-based, and rights-based theories.[13]

---

[10] Other candidates whose work might lead to the philosophical roots of human rights would be: Aquinas, Hobbes, Grotius, and Tom Paine.

[11] For a history of human rights see Robertson (1968*b*).

[12] The justification of rights which links them to God is still fairly influential: 'Nevertheless I am an enthusiast for democracy. And I take that position, not because I believe majority opinion is invariably right or true, indeed no majority can take away God-Given human rights' (Mrs Thatcher, then Prime Minister, address to the General Assembly of the Church of Scotland, 21 May 1988; for full text see *Observer* (22 May 1988), 1–2).

[13] This classification was introduced by Ronald Dworkin (1977: 171).

5.2 DUTY-BASED, GOAL-BASED, AND RIGHTS-BASED THEORIES

5.2.1 A duty-based theory

In *A Theory of Justice* J. Rawls suggests examples of natural duties: 'the duty to help another when he is in need or jeopardy, provided one can do so without excessive risk or loss to oneself; the duty not to injure another; the duty not to inflict unnecessary suffering' (1971: 115). These duties 'hold *between persons irrespective of their institutional relationship*'.[14] They are binding because justice as fairness allows for such principles, as parties in an original position of equality and ignorance would have agreed to such principles defining natural duties.

As these are duties and not rights, we are concerned here not with the victim's suffering but with a 'deeper concern for the rational integrity of those who are disposed to treat distinctively human characteristics in a purely instrumental way' (Waldron 1984: 13). If we take a case of torture as our paradigm, then it could be said that 'the deliberate infliction of suffering debases and degrades the torturer, derogating from his humanity and undermining his rational integrity' (Waldron 1984: 13). Such an account begs the conclusion that the public/private character of the actor is irrelevant, as it is the nature of the action itself which is destructive to both violator and victim, although the emphasis is here on the violator.

5.2.2 A goal-based theory

A goal-based theory might allow for rights and duties as long as they gave way to goals such as the greatest happiness for the greatest number, or the welfare of the greatest number. Professor Ronald Dworkin has criticized utilitarian goal-based theories in the following way: in calculating the greatest happiness we would have to take account of some citizens' external preferences (say the preference of Nazis for Aryans rather than Jews); additionally we would have to take into account intensity of feeling, so that difficulties might creep in when assessing the happiness and taking account of the preferences of a poet rather than a pin-ball player (1984), or when paying equal respect to the wishes of environment-alists against those of developers when the choice is between more jobs or devastation of a mountainside (1978: 141).

However, although most political theories contain some implicit commitment to utilitarianism it is possible to postulate a goal-based theory with a different goal. The goal could be to ensure a community where rights were respected, or where democracy was preserved. If we return to

---

[14] Rawls (1971: 115), emphasis added.

the torturer's dilemma, a utilitarian might propose that torture would result in greater overall welfare as accomplices would be rounded up, crimes prevented, and potential criminals dissuaded from embarking on a trail of crime. But if we take the goal as the protection of democracy, then torture is incompatible with that goal: 'if torture, even supposing it can be confined to exceptional cases, were permitted by law in a democracy, would not the community be undermining its own values and the State its own legitimacy? . . . There are means that a democratic society must refrain from using simply because it is a democracy: and torture is a case in point' (Marie 1985: 21).

Democracy has to address its long-term interests as well as its immediate concerns (Marie 1985: 22); so collective good can be reconciled with individual rights. From this point of view even where a torturer has to choose between greater utility and individual rights, individual rights remain absolute rather than prima facie.[15] It is worth recalling that although the system of the European Convention on Human Rights has many of the attributes of a goal-based theory—with restrictions on rights being allowed where they are 'necessary in a democratic society' or 'in time of war or other public emergency threatening the life of the nation'[16]—some rights remain absolute with no provision for legitimate derogation.[17].

5.2.3 A rights-based theory

According to Dworkin rights-based political theories suggest that codes of conduct are 'instrumental, perhaps necessary to protect the rights of others, but having no essential value in themselves. The man at their center is the man who benefits from others' compliance' (1977: 173). However, Dworkin's theory is a rights-based *political* theory with a political right as its ground rule: governments must treat those whom they govern with equal concern and respect.[18]

---

[15] Cf. Lukes (1985: 67), who argues that the torturer is morally obliged to torture for the greater good, in the situation where the victim knows the whereabouts of a primed bomb which is about to kill dozens of people.

[16] Art. 15 ECHR.

[17] Arts. 2 (the right to life), 3 (no one to be subjected to torture or to inhuman or degrading treatment or punishment), 4(1) (no one to be held in slavery or servitude), and 7 (no retroactive penal offences).

[18] Dworkin (1978: 125), where he states the principle that the 'government treat all those in its charge *as equals*, that is, as entitled to its equal concern and respect. That is not an empty requirement: most of us do not suppose that we must, as individuals, treat our neighbor's children with the same concern as our own, or treat everyone we meet with the same respect. It is nevertheless plausible to think that any government should treat all its citizens as equals in that way.' And see 'What Rights do we Have?', ch. 4 in Dworkin (1977), where he suggests that for a right to have power in political argument it must be an individual right against the State (269).

For a rights-based *moral* theory we could consider the work of Alan Gewirth, who has attempted an epistemology of human rights.[19] According to Gewirth we are not forced to conclude that 'people are born having rights in the same way as they are born having legs' (1981: 121). Gewirth justifies the basis of human rights by showing that rights are the necessary conditions for action—in order to act each actor requires freedom and well-being. We can justify human rights in the following way: every rational agent regards his or her freedom and well-being as necessary goods—they are the necessary conditions for achieving his or her purposes —as all agents regard their purposes as good. It follows that a rational agent must regard these conditions for acting as necessary goods (1981: 130). This requires that 'other persons at least refrain from interfering with his having freedom and well-being' (1981: 132). Gewirth then concludes that, on pain of self-contradiction, each agent must admit that all other humans have these rights.

This rights theory supports the suggestion that human rights apply between individuals, the question of whether the violator is employed by the State being irrelevant to the reasoning behind the justification. This being said, it is unhelpful to our paradigm of the torturer's dilemma, as it does not explain why we accept that anyone can be legitimately deprived of their liberty at all, whilst there exists a point at which treatment becomes torture and so in violation of human rights.

Gewirth has addressed the torturer's dilemma and concludes that in the following situation there is an absolute right:

Suppose a clandestine group of extremists have obtained an arsenal of nuclear weapons; to prove that they have the weapons and know how to use them, they have kidnapped a leading scientist, shown him the weapons, and then released him to make a public corroborative statement. The terrorists have now announced that they will use the weapons against a designated large distant city unless a certain prominent resident of the city, a young politically active lawyer named Abrams, tortures his mother to death, this torturing to be carried out publicly in a certain way at a specified place and time in that city. Since the gang members have already murdered several other prominent residents of the city, their threat is quite credible. Their declared motive is to advance their cause by showing how powerful they are by unmasking the moralistic pretensions of their political opponents. (1984a: 99)

Gewirth introduces the 'principle of intervening action' to argue that it is 'only through the intervening of lethal actions of the terrorists that the son's refusal eventuates in the many deaths. Since the moral responsibility is

---

[19] Gewirth (1984b: 1–24; 1982; 1981: 119–47). See also Mackie (1984: 168–81); another candidate might be R. Nozick, *Anarchy, State, and Utopia* (Oxford: Basil Blackwell, 1974), but although the book opens with the assertion that every individual has certain inalienable rights, no justification is offered.

not the son's it does not affect his moral duty not to torture his mother to death, so that her correlative right remains absolute' (1984a: 104).

Leaving this extreme example aside Gewirth expresses the moral principle as follows: 'agents and institutions are absolutely prohibited from degrading persons, treating them as if they had no rights or *dignity*.'[20] At this point we seem to have come full circle—as it is difficult to see why this conclusion is any different from a duty-based theory with the violator at the centre. Indeed, it is often suggested that we should focus on duties, as rights are merely generated from duties.[21]

What emerges from this over-simplified excursus into moral philosophy? It seems it is unnecessary to choose one theory to justify morally the rights we have. In the torturer's dilemma our concern seems to be composite:

1. concern for the torturers; as we abhor the monstrous act demanded of them, and we feel this diminishes their dignity;
2. concern for the goal (democracy was suggested earlier); as we feel it is hypocrisy both to condemn and to instigate violence;
3. concern for the victim; as his or her dignity is eroded.

It is suggested that there emerge two justifications which may help us to understand problems of human rights. These are *dignity* and *democracy*. These tools seem particularly appropriate due to their recurrence in the international human rights Declarations, Covenants, Conventions, and Resolutions.[22]

---

[20] Gewirth (1984a: 108) (emphasis added); for development of the human rights–human dignity link see Gewirth (1984b: 22–4).

[21] Bedau (1984: 63); and Arnold (1984: 74–86), who concludes that 'we might make more progress towards understanding our legal concepts and priorities by the language of duty than by the language of rights' (86).

[22] See the second preambular paragraph of the Charter of the UN (26 June 1945) referred to in the fifth preambular paragraph of the Universal Declaration of Human Rights (10 Dec. 1948): 'Whereas the peoples of the United Nations have in the Charter reaffirmed their faith in fundamental human rights, in the *dignity* and worth of the human person and in the equal rights of men and women and have determined to promote social progress and better standards of life in larger freedom', and in Art. 1: 'All human beings are born equal in *dignity* and rights', and Arts. 22 (everyone entitled to the rights indispensable for his dignity and the free development of his personality) and 23 (the right of everyone who works to 'just remuneration ensuring for himself and his family an existence worthy of human *dignity*'); and the second preambular paragraphs of both the International Covenant on Civil and Political Rights and the Covenant on Economic, Social and Cultural Rights (both adopted 16 Dec. 1966) recognize 'that these rights derive from the inherent *dignity* of the human person'. Also the Proclamation of Tehran (23 May 1968) states in para. 5: 'The primary aim of the United Nations in the sphere of human rights is the achievement by each individual of the maximum freedom and *dignity*', and later urges 'all peoples and governments to . . . redouble their efforts to provide for all human beings a life consonant with freedom and *dignity* and conducive to physical, mental, social and spiritual welfare'. Mention should also be made of the Helsinki Final Act (1975), which declares that States 'will promote and encourage the effective exercise of civil, political, economic, social, cultural

It is not suggested that human rights can be categorized into those which are designed to protect dignity and those which protect democracy.[23] If one looks at the debates on the Universal Declaration of Human Rights, it is striking how keen everyone is to protect both dignity and democracy.[24] Even in the case of the terrorists and the torturer, Gewirth (who deduces the basis of human rights from action, necessary goods for action, and dignity) inserts factors into his scenario which are only relevant for the protection of democracy:

1. the terrorists choose a prominent resident of the city—a *politically active lawyer*;

and other rights and freedoms all of which derive from the inherent *dignity* of the human person and are essential for his free and full development' (Principle VII, para. 2). The African Charter on Human and Peoples' Rights (1981) refers to the struggle of the African people for dignity in the eighth preambular paragraph, and guarantees every individual the right to respect for the dignity inherent in a human being (Art. 5). Turning to democracy the fourth preambular paragraph of the European Convention on Human Rights reads: 'Reaffirming their profound belief in those fundamental freedoms which are the foundation of justice and peace in the world and are best maintained on the one hand by an effective political *democracy* and on the other by a common understanding and observance of the human rights upon which they depend'; note also the references to 'democratic society' in Arts. 8(2), 9(2), 10(2), 11(2), Protocol no. 4 Art. 2(3). Similarly see the American Convention on Human Rights (1969), Arts. 16(2) (freedom of association), 22(3) (freedom of movement and residence), 29c ('No provision of this Convention shall be interpreted as: precluding other rights or guarantees that are inherent in the human personality or derived from representative *democracy* as a form of government'), and 32(2); see also the references to a democratic society in the Draft Charter on Human and People's Rights in the Arab World (1986), Arts. 37 (right to peaceful assembly and meeting) and 38 (right to freedom of association). At the universal level reference could be made to Art. 29 of the Universal Declaration, which refers to the 'general welfare in a democratic society', as does Art. 4 of the Economic, Social and Cultural Rights Covenant. Art. 8(1)(c) of this last Covenant (the right of trade unions to function freely), and in the Civil and Political Rights Covenant Arts. 14(1) (exclusion of the press and public from trials in case of national security), 21 (right of peaceful assembly), and 22 (right to freedom of association), all refer to the interests of a democratic society.

[23] This is the traditional approach, e.g. Cassin (1951: 278), where the rights contained in the Universal Declaration of Human Rights are divided into four columns: the first (Arts. 3–11) and fourth (Arts. 22–7) belong to the 'ordre personnel', whereas the second (Arts. 12–17) relates to the individual's relationship with certain groupings and the third (Arts. 18–22) relates to civil/political rights.

[24] See General Assembly 181st plenary meeting, 10 Dec. 1948, at 879. Count Carton de Wiart (the Belgian delegate): 'The essential merit of that declaration was to emphasize the high dignity of the human person after the outrages to which men and women had been exposed during the recent war.' And see also Mr Katz-Suchy (the Polish delegate), who 'noted with regret that except in one article the word "democracy" had carefully been deleted from the draft declaration and that nowhere in the document was there any allusion to the necessity of combating fascism' (182nd plenary meeting 905). And Mr Carrera Anrade (Equador): 'The declaration of human rights contained a number of new rights which were the logical result of the victory of democracy' (193rd meeting at 919); and Mr Vyshinski (USSR), who referred to two opposing tendencies present during the preparation of the draft declaration: 'The first tendency was that of the defence of the principle of democracy and the securing of peace,' the other tended towards reaction and aggression (193rd meeting, 929).

2. the terrorists demand that the torture be carried out *publicly* in a *specified place*;

3. the declared motive of the terrorists is the unmasking of the *moralistic pretensions* of their *political opponents*.

The question arises: would our concerns have been the same had the demand been for one mass-murderer to torture another mass-murderer, in a secret place, without anyone knowing, and that this would save the lives of millions of people?[25]

It is suggested that human rights (more particularly those contained in the European Convention on Human Rights) often have the dual purpose of the protection of both dignity and democracy. Evidence of the relevance of such an approach can be found in the judgment of the European Court of Human Rights in the *Lingens* case.

In this connection the court has to recall that freedom of expression, as secured in paragraph 1 of Article 10, constitutes one of the essential foundations of a *democratic society* and is one of the essential conditions for its progress and for *each individual's self fulfilment.*[26]

These two aims should not be seen as conflicting but as complementary.[27] However, they are not so intertwined as to be inseparable. It is suggested that dignity and democracy are the tools with which to analyse human rights in the private sphere.

5.3 DIGNITY AND DEMOCRACY AS ANALYTICAL TOOLS

It is suggested that, when we confront a situation involving a human rights claim, an appeal to the twin concepts of dignity and democracy will enable us to see the limits of the right in question. For example, if we return to the case of the protesters in the private shopping precinct (this being the only forum in the town), democracy demands that there is full participation and representation of different ideas in the community. Should the courts issue an injunction, it could be contrary to human

---

[25] Ronald Dworkin suggests that in the classic rescue dilemmas the individual is under less constraint than the 'state personified' (1985*a*: 184). He says that in acting arbitrarily the State would have to violate the principle it needs to justify its acts, whereas the individual violates no such principle.

[26] *Lingens* case (1986) Series A, vol. 103, p. 26, para. 41 (emphasis added).

[27] See Raz (1986: 207): 'The provision of many collective goods is constitutive of the very possibility of autonomy and it cannot be relegated to a subordinate role, compared with some alleged right against coercion, in the name of autonomy.' And 'rights are not to be understood as inherently independent of collective goods, nor as essentially opposed to them. On the contrary they both depend on and serve collective goods. Hence there is no general rule giving either rights or collective goods priority in cases of conflict' (255). See also 261. (For 'collective goods' read 'democracy', and for 'autonomy' read 'dignity'.)

rights as it would thwart democracy. But if we turn to the theoretical case of a coven of witches demanding to speak at a Christian prayer meeting, there is no question of democracy being threatened where the witches are free to disseminate their views via alternative means.

Both these situations relate to freedom of speech and democratic participation, yet in one situation banning the speakers results in a breach of human rights and in the other it does not. It is suggested that in the shopping precinct example this is because there is a *public* element, yet in the witches example there is not. (Of course 'public' in this context does not require a nexus with the State, but simply means relevant to the interests of the community or collective goods.) But if the witches were denied the right to meet at all, this would threaten their dignity, as their freedom of conscience, expression, or autonomy would be restricted. Freedom of expression (and several other freedoms) contains these dual goals—dignity and democracy. Once we identify which aim is our foremost concern in any one situation, we can escape from the intractable riddle of conflicting human rights, or endless 'balancing and weighing' exercises.

Where the right involved is justified by the goal of democracy there has to be a public element in order to justify protection of the right. But where the right can be justified by an appeal to dignity, we do not need such a public element and consequently the right must always be protected. This could be formulated as a duty-based theory. Individuals or private bodies have a duty not to subject others to indignities, and have a further public duty not to thwart the collective good of democracy where this is threatened. This is completely consistent with the tenor of Article 29 of the Universal Declaration of Human Rights but denies the role of the State as the guarantor of this state of affairs; for this reason the version which emphasizes rights and goals is preferred as an aid to understanding the situation at the international level.

5.3.1 Interim summary

For the purposes of the European Convention it is unnecessary to prove that we have these moral rights. The legal rights are already in place. However, what I have tried to show is that the best justification for these rights rests on the twin concepts of dignity and democracy, and that, as these terms are used in the various international human rights instruments, they are appropriate tools with which to understand claims about human rights. The proposed thesis is: that if the situation calls for the right to be justified by the goal of democracy then there has to be a public element in the private actors' activities, that is, the private actor is operating in the sphere of the public or the public domain; in a situation where the justification for the right in question concerns dignity, then rights must be protected even in the absence of a public element—inhuman treatment threatens dignity in every circumstance.

5.3.2 Democracy

Of course the terms 'democracy' and 'dignity' have been subject to various definitions and explanations. For present purposes it is enough to state that a wide conception of these concepts is appropriate. Democracy obviously includes more than periodic voting in elections and the fairness of the representation procedure.[28] Nor is democracy solely concerned with state institutions.[29] To discern further facets of the concept of democracy in this context we should first turn to the case-law of the European Court of Human Rights. The Court refers several times to the demands of 'pluralism, tolerance and broadmindedness, without which there is no democratic society'.[30] Other decisions in Strasbourg have emphasized the importance of free public discussion on subjects of general importance,[31] and have affirmed that 'The Court's supervisory functions oblige it to pay the utmost attention to the principles characterizing a "democratic society". Freedom of expression constitutes one of the basic conditions for its progress and for the development of every man.'[32] If we now include 'participation', 'representation', and 'accountability', we approach a wide definition which may be useful when we come to analyse human rights questions.

Relevant 'hallmarks' of a democratic society might include the following:

1. participation;
2. accountability;
3. representativeness;
4. pluralism;
5. tolerance;
6. broadmindedness;
7. freedom of expression which allows for free public discussion;
8. protection of minorities.

These terms are merely designed to point to the scope of democracy in

---

[28] See Ely (1980), who limits the legitimacy of constitutional rights to cases where they are guarantees against malfunction in the 'process of representation'.

[29] See Claus Offe and Urlich K. Preuss, 'Democratic Institutions and Moral Resources', in Held (1991: 143–71, esp. 162–71).

[30] e.g. *Handyside* case (1976) para. 49; *Dudgeon* case (1981) para. 53. Again Raz's philosophy illustrates how such values operate at the collective and individual level simultaneously: 'It is a public good, and inherently so, that this society is a tolerant society, that it is an educated society, that it is infused with a sense of respect for human beings etc. Living in a society with those characteristics is generally of benefit to individuals' (1986: 199).

[31] See Fawcett (1987: 261).

[32] *Handyside* case (1976) para. 49.

the present context. The list is not an attempt exhaustively to define democracy; the terms have been chosen because they reflect, to some extent, the terminology of the European Commission and Court of Human Rights.[33]

5.3.3 Dignity

Turning to dignity we will have to include more than Kant's practical imperative: 'Act in such a way that you always treat humanity, whether in your own person or in the person of any other, never simply as a means, but always at the same time as an end.'[34] This could be said to be the underlying foundation to the various rights/duties solutions to the torturer's dilemma, but the demands of dignity are now expressed in the language of 'each individual's self-fulfilment',[35] and so relate not only to the power of one individual over another but also to the creation of the necessary conditions for each individual to be able to achieve this state.[36] Perhaps we can take a twofold approach to the protection of dignity:

1. everyone's humanity must be respected;
2. the conditions for everyone's self-fulfilment (or autonomy[37] or self-realization[38]) must be created and protected.

---

[33] See Ch. 7; for the concept of 'involvement' in decision-making see *W., B., and R. v. UK*, Series A, vol. 136, pp. 28, 73–4, 119; this has been expressed above as participation and accountability. The proper treatment of minorities is a concept referred to in *Young, James and Webster*, Series A, vol. 44, para. 63; see also Council of Europe, *Démoeratie et droits de l'homme* (Khel: Engel, 1990); Bullinger (1985: 88); on participation and human rights at the universal level see H. J. Steiner, 'Political Participation as a Human Right', *Human Rights Yearbook* (1988), 77–134.

[34] I. Kant, *The Moral Law (Groundwork of the Metaphysic of Morals)*, tr. H. J. Paton (London: Hutchinson, 1965).

[35] *Lingens* case (1986) para. 41.

[36] In the context of human rights in the private sphere Barsotti has pointed to the twofold approach of the Convention on the Protection of Individuals with Regard to Automatic Processing of Data. He suggests that the first group of norms (Arts. 5, 6, 7, 8) represent 'i limiti di tale utilizzione, da osservare nell'interesse della "personne concernée"', whereas the second group (Arts. 9(2)(3), 12(2)) 'fissa le guaranzie per un effecttivo esercizio del diritto all'informazione di essa' (Barsotti 1984: 430).

[37] This is the term used by Raz; see (1986), esp. ch. 7 'The Nature of Rights', ch. 14 'Autonomy and Pluralism', ch. 15 'Freedom and Autonomy'. See also J. Maritain, *The Rights of Man and Natural Law*, tr. D. C. Anson (New York: Charles Scribner's Sons, 1943): 'It [the common good of society] involves, as its chief value, the highest possible attainment (that is the highest compatible with the good of the whole) of persons to their lives as persons, and to their freedom of expression or autonomy—on to the gift of goodness which in their turn flow from it' (9). And 'the most fundamental aspiration of the person is the aspiration towards the *liberty of expansion and autonomy*' (44).

[38] J. Galtung defines violence as 'anything avoidable that impedes human self-realization' and interprets 'human self-realization' as satisfaction of human needs. See *Transarmament and the Cold War: Peace Research and the Peace Movement* (Copenhagen: Christian Ejlers, 1988), 271.

These two approaches can also be understood as relating to direct and indirect attacks on dignity. Direct attacks may involve killing, torture, slavery, traffic in persons, coercion, verbal abuse, discrimination, mal-treatment—these could be categorized as *indignities*.[39] Often international law treaties dealing with these subjects cite 'human dignity' as their goal. Indirect attacks are likely to involve denying the opportunity for self-fulfilment: denying the right to associate, to make love, to take part in social life, to express one's intellectual, artistic, or cultural ideas, to enjoy a decent standard of living and health care. This idea is reflected in Article 22 of the Universal Declaration of Human Rights: 'Everyone, as a member of society, has the right to social security and is entitled to realization, through national effort and international co-operation and in accordance with the organization and resources of each State, of the economic, social and cultural rights indispensable for his dignity and the free development of his personality.'

This framework, which structures the justification for human rights around the protection of democracy and dignity, will be the analytical scheme within which an attempt is made critically to evaluate the judicial decisions which have dealt with the application of human rights in the private sphere.

---

[39] See Cohn (1983: 228), and see 232–40 for references to 'dignity' in national constitutions.

6

Fundamental Rights in the Private Sphere: The United States and Canada

The limited objectives of this chapter deserve some explanation. No attempt will be made to offer an analysis of the case-law of the United States and Canadian courts concerning the application of the relevant constitutional rights to the private sphere. What this chapter seeks to do is to emphasize the differences between these jurisdictions and the jurisdictions which have to apply the European Convention on Human Rights. Our aim is to explain why the case-law from the other side of the Atlantic should not be seen as offering solutions to the interpretation of the Convention's application in the private sphere. The appropriateness and reasons for the evolution of this case-law in its home ground is only covered superficially. Paradoxically, the comparative exercise has been embarked on in order to counsel against making such comparisons.

6.1 THE UNITED STATES

Developments in the United States provide a rich tapestry of public/private questions. At the theoretical level attacks on the public/private dichotomy have a central place in the Critical Legal Studies Movement. As we saw in Chapter 4.3.4 much of this work seeks to demystify the law by dissolving the barriers erected between the 'public world of politics' and the 'private world of law'. Although many of these academics would be sceptical about a 'rights'-based approach to social change, due to their perception of an inherently individualistic component in rights, their analysis of the public/private dichotomy is not inextricable from their rejection of 'rights'. Indeed part of their critique of rights rests on the supposed ineffectiveness of rights due to their inapplicability in the private sphere. The following passage is probably fairly representative: 'Rights discourse, moreover, simply presupposes or takes for granted that the world is or should be divided between a state sector that enforces rights and a private sector world of "civil society" in which atomized individuals pursue their diverse goals.'[1]

[1] Kennedy (1982a: 48–9). See also Kennedy (1982b: 1349–57).

Even those who would support a rights approach focus in their critique on the incoherence of the present approach:

In the public sphere, which includes selection of government officials and political expression, basic concepts of freedom, democracy, and equality are applicable. However, in the private sphere, which encompasses almost all economic activity, we allow no democracy or equality, only the freedom to buy and sell.... Fundamental social issues, such as the use of our resources, investment, the energy problem, the work of our people, and the distribution of our goods and services, are all left to 'private'—mainly corporate—decision makers.[2]

It is suggested that if fundamental rights come to operate in the private sphere, the critique which labels them as vacuous bourgeois tools of legitimization whose function is to deceive citizens into believing in the justness of the system begins to lose some of its force.[3] In this way we can support the critique of the distinction put forward by writers within the Critical Legal Studies tradition, while adhering to a rights-based approach to social change. Still at the theoretical level, the philosophical analysis of the moral basis of 'due process' may be of particular help when defining the limits of human rights in the private sphere.[4]

At the practical level it has often been the Supreme Court which has faced these questions, and its case-by-case approach may illuminate aspects of the European supranational dimension. In several ways the Supreme Court is analogous to the European Court of Human Rights. It often operates to bring States into line with minimum standards of human rights, and this may take place despite fierce opposition at the local level thousands of miles away. Also, both Courts may have to cope with the different substantive and procedural laws of the various States over which the Court has jurisdiction. This produces a similar dilemma for both Courts—whether to allow for local autonomy or concede to the demands for unity and uniformity. Of course the differences are significant. There

---

[2] D. Kairys, 'Freedom of Speech', in Kairys (1982: 163–4); see also the comments on the 'privatization' of the means of communication at 166.

[3] For a full analysis of the rejection of fundamental rights by some members of the Critical Legal Studies Movement, see Sparer (1984: 509–73). For convincing minority criticism of the Critical Legal Studies Movement (CLS) see R. Delgado, 'The Ethereal Scholar: Does Critical Legal Studies Have what Minorities Want?', 22 *Harv. CR-CLL Rev.* (1987), 301–22, esp. 305: 'White CLS members see rights as oppressive, alienating and mystifying. For minorities, they are invigorating cloaks of safety that unite us in a common bond.' See also M. J. Matsuda, 'Looking to the Bottom: Critical Legal Studies and Reparations', 22 *Harv. CR-CLL Rev.* (1987), 323–99, esp. 389–92, and P. J. Williams, 'Alchemical Notes: Reconstructing Ideals from Deconstructed Rights', 22 *Harv. CR-CLL Rev.* (1987), 401–33: 'In discarding rights altogether, one discards a symbol too deeply enmeshed in the psyche of the oppressed to lose without trauma and much resistance' (433).

[4] See T. M. Scanlon, 'Due Process', F. I. Michelman, 'Formal and Associational Aims in Procedural Due Process', and E. L. Pincoffs, 'Due Process, Fraternity, and a Kantian Injunction', all in J. Roland and J. W. Chapman (eds.) *Due Process: Nomos XVIII* (New York: New York University Press, 1977), 93–125, 126–71, 172–81.

is no system of federal courts in Europe, and the Council of Europe cannot be compared to the federal Government of the United States. But in the specific context of human/fundamental rights the similarities are important.

1(*a*) The Supreme Court in dealing with a case based on constitutional rights can only hear allegations against state or federal violations of the Constitution (except for rare complaints under the slavery provision of the Thirteenth Amendment).

(*b*) The Strasbourg Court can only hear allegations against Member States.

2(*a*) Cases concerning the protection of fundamental rights through constitutional control of state action which come before the Supreme Court have often been orchestrated by social action groups such as the American Civil Liberties Union, the International Labor Defense, the American Publishers' Association, and the Industrial Workers of the World,[5] with lawyers targeting test cases.

(*b*) The Strasbourg Court is often petitioned by applicants who represent wide sections of the population. Similarly, non-governmental groups have been active in supporting applications before the European Court of Human Rights.[6]

3(*a*) Some of the concerns and traditions of the Supreme Court arise out of a series of wars—particularly the Civil War, which was primarily concerned with a human rights issue: slavery. The First World War and the Russian Revolution are also relevant, as both raised questions of dissent and freedom of speech in the United States.

(*b*) The European Convention was drafted by the survivors of the Second World War, and again the results should be considered against the background of war. There was a particular commitment to entrench guarantees against totalitarianism. Questions of discrimination, association, and freedom of expression were given a high priority.

---

[5] Most importantly the incorporation of the First Amendment freedoms came about through a number of cases all of which were sponsored by interest groups. See Cortner (1981: 282 and 75–95).

[6] See *Malone* case (1984) Series A, vol. 82, intervention by the Post Office Engineering Union (assisted by Interights and Justice); *Ashingdane* case (1985) vol. 93, intervention by MIND; *Glasenapp and Kosiek* cases (1986) vols. 104–5, attempted intervention by the Prison Officers' Association; *Lingens* case (1986) vol. 103, International Press Institute (assisted by Interights); *Monnell and Morris* v. *UK* (1987) vol. 115, submission by Justice; *Leander* v. *Sweden* (1987), attempted intervention by NCCL on behalf of three civil service trade unions. For further details see Lester (1988: 341–50). See also Ch. 9 below.

There already exists some comparative scholarship on the protection of human rights in America and Europe.[7] This work has provided very useful background material, but does not include a comparison of the jurisprudence on human rights in the private sphere. It is hoped that such a comparison is justifiable for the reasons outlined above. Even if there are more contextual differences than similarities, similar tensions exist: the tension between white racists and various black or Asian groups; the tension between men and women; the tension between corporate power and organized labour; the tension between private property and its public use; and the tension between conceptions of obscenity and pluralism. More contentiously it is suggested that there exists a tension between upholding minimum standards and demands that 'civil/private' law be determined at the state level by the state executives/legislatures/judiciary. All these conflicts are specifically found in the context of the private sphere. It is proposed to examine briefly how the United States Supreme Court has approached these questions.

In order to understand the evolution of the Supreme Court's jurisprudence the decisions have to be seen in their historical context against a changing social background.

6.1.1 The history of the Fourteenth Amendment

The human rights contained in the European Convention find their counterparts in the Amendments to the United States Constitution, more particularly in the Fourteenth Amendment, as most of the other Amendments and Articles of the Constitution only apply to the actions of the *federal* government (in any of its branches: legislative, executive, or judicial).[8] As there is no equivalent to federal action in the Council of Europe system we have to examine how the Fourteenth Amendment came to regulate *state* action.[9]

---

[7] However, in Frowein, Schulhofer, and Shapiro (1986: 231–344), the emphasis is on integration. Note that in the USA those who sought to challenge governmental authority in the period between the wars were concerned with the overthrow of both the state and the federal authorities; no such dual attack has existed in Europe. This is an important difference to be borne in mind when comparing the European Court of Human Rights with the Supreme Court (see 256–7 of the above article).

[8] Art. I paras. 9, 10 as well as the Fifteenth, Nineteenth, Twenty-Fourth, and Twenty-Sixth Amendments all apply to state action, but they are of limited relevance for present purposes.

[9] There exists no real equivalent in the European Convention to the 'colour of law' provisions. These laws prohibit the deprivation of 'rights, privileges and immunities secured or protected by the Constitution' either by private individuals implicated in official action by conspiracy etc. or by officials acting outside their competence or off duty. For the purposes of the comparative exercise the different legal frameworks do not need to be exhaustively explained here. The relevant provisions are s. 20 of the Criminal Code, 18 USC ss. 241, 242; 42 USC ss. 1983, 1985(3). For further explanation see Abernathy (1977: 46–101).

In 1789 James Madison included, in his list of proposed amendments to the Constitution, an article which prohibited States from infringing the right to trial by jury, rights of conscience, and freedom of speech or of the press. Although this amendment was accepted by the House, it was rejected outright by the Senate, and so the federal Bill of Rights which came into effect in 1791 contained no provision limiting the power of States. This was subsequently affirmed by the Supreme Court in *Barron v. Mayor of Baltimore*.[10]

In the pre-Civil War period the States were primarily responsible for the protection of the fundamental rights and freedoms of their citizens; the Supreme Court had no superior jurisdiction over State governmental acts in this area. However, in the wake of the Civil War the further Amendments made it clear that the States were not to enjoy unlimited power. For our purposes the Fourteenth Amendment is the most important:

All persons born or naturalized in the United States, and subject to the juris-diction thereof, are citizens of the United States and of the State wherein they reside. No State shall make or enforce any law which shall make or abridge the privileges or immunities of citizens of the United States; nor shall any State deprive any person of life, liberty, or property, without due process of law; nor deny to any person within its jurisdiction the equal protection of the laws.

The Fourteenth Amendment was enacted in 1868 but the Supreme Court took a very cautious approach to its interpretation for nearly a century. The phrase 'privileges and immunities' was held not to include human rights normally guaranteed at the state level, but only federal privileges.[11] 'Due process of law' was construed to refer only to fundamental fairness, to be assessed in the overall picture, and not referring to particular provisions in the Bill of Rights. Furthermore, there were rulings that grand jury indictment[12] and exemption from self-incrimination[13] (both specifically guaranteed by the federal Bill of Rights) were outside the due process clause of the Fourteenth Amendment, and so citizens could not demand these rights *vis-à-vis* the State.

This cautiousness has to be viewed in the context of a society which gave considerable priority to property rights rather than personal rights, and successful plaintiffs under the Fourteenth Amendment were mainly people seeking to protect corporate finance. We should also remember that this was a time of cautious federalism. Traditionally, it was the States which had both violated and protected personal rights, and a shift in

---

[10] 32 US 7 Pet. 243 (1833).
[11] *Slaughter-House* cases 16 Wallace 36 US (1873).
[12] *Hartado* v. *California* 110 US 516 (1884).
[13] *Twining* v. *New Jersey* 211 US 516 (1908); other restrictive interpretations include *Davidson* v. *New Orleans* 96 US 97 (1878).

protection towards federal constitutional protection would not have been achieved without considerable resistance.

However, by 1938 the Supreme Court was hinting that the provisions of the Bill of Rights were included in the Fourteenth Amendment and so were binding on the States themselves.[14] In 1947 the minority opinion in *Adamson* v. *California* stated that 'due process' incorporated all the rights in the Bill of Rights;[15] but this approach has been ultimately rejected in favour of selective incorporation.

Today, nearly all the provisions of the Bill of Rights have been incorporated into the Fourteenth Amendment by a series of judicial decisions.[16] This process highlights a fundamental difference between the American and Council of Europe systems. In the United States fundamental rights are now mostly debated in terms of the federal Constitution (the trans-state dimension), rather than by reference to state law; in Europe, on the other hand, the transnational dimension (at least at the moment) plays a secondary role.

In order to avoid confusion it should be pointed out that 'state action' is sometimes used by commentators to describe action by all levels of government, both local (state) and national (federal), but in the context of this chapter 'state action' is limited to local (state) behaviour; the federal dimension has no counterpart in the Council of Europe system, and its inclusion would be confusing.[17]

6.1.2 State action and the Supreme Court

As the Constitution specifically covers only governmental action the cases which come before the Supreme Court alleging a breach of the fundamental rights enshrined in the Bill of Rights have to fix responsibility on a governmental actor. When this question was introduced in the context of the Strasbourg Court it was suggested that it could be analysed into various possibilities (Chapter 4.2). We can try to construct an analogous table for the Supreme Court.[18]

---

[14] *US* v. *Carolene Products Co.* 304 US 144 (1938) at 152 n. 4.

[15] 322 US 46 (1947), meaning the first eight Amendments.

[16] See e.g. *Chicago, B. & Q. R. Co.* v. *Chicago* 166 US 226 (1897) (right to just compensation); *Gitlow* v. *New York* 268 US 652 (1925), *Fiske* v. *Kansas* 274 US 380 (1927) (freedom of speech); *Near* v. *Minosota* 283 US 687 (1931) (freedom of the press); *DeJonge* v. *Oregon* 299 US 353 (1937) (freedom of assembly); *Cantwell* v. *Connecticut* 310 US 296 (1940) (free exercise of religion); *Gideon* v. *Wainwright* 372 US 335 (1963) (right to counsel); *Robinson* v. *California* 370 US 660 (1972) (prohibition on cruel and unusual punishments).

[17] When we examine this question at the European Community level we shall see that Community action can be compared to federal action. However to include the Community dimension at this stage could over-complicate matters.

[18] The figures correspond with the labels in Ch. 4. To some extent this tabulation fits with the divisions formulated by Professor L. H. Tribe: (3) and (4) correspond to quadrants (2 &

1(*a*) Failure of application due to the applicant's attempt to use the Convention to threaten rights contained in the Convention, or due to an obligation to ensure respect for the 'rights of others'[19] (Strasbourg system).

1(*b*) Restrictions placed on complainants who may have to respect principles contained in the Constitution[20] (Supreme Court level).

2(*a*) State responsible due to a failure to legislate or take other action in an area of private violations[21] (Strasbourg system).

2(*b*) Apparently there is no equivalent liability under the Constitution. There would seem to be no state action through mere omission or acquiescence in United States law.[22] (But facilitating violations may trigger state responsibility.[23]) (Supreme Court level)

3(*a*) An application is admissible as it is decided that the body accused is an organ of the relevant Member State (Strasbourg system).

3(*b*) Private actor has government resources, or is in a position of monopoly,[24] or there is deemed to be a nexus so that the activity is termed governmental.[25]

---

3) and (1 & 4) respectively. See Tribe (1985: 246–66); nevertheless too much significance should not be attached to these similarities as my table works from the situation in Strasbourg towards an equivalent situation in the Supreme Court rather than vice versa.

[19] e.g. *Kommunistische Partei Deutschland* v. *FRG*, Applic. 250/57 (1955–7), 1 *Yearbook* 223.

[20] Note some state constitutions include responsibilities for individuals, demanding that they respect the rights in the (state) constitution.

[21] e.g. *Airey* case, Series A, vol. 32; *Marckx* case, Series A, vol. 31; *Case of X and Y* v. *The Netherlands*, Series A, vol. 91; in *Mrs W.* v. *UK*, Applic. 9348/81, 32 D. & R. 190, the Commission held that the UK did have a duty to protect people from terrorist attacks, but in this case the Government had complied with that duty. And see generally Art. 13 of the ECHR discussed in Ch. 7. Compare *Bowers* v. *De Vito* 686 F. 2d 616 (1982), an American case where it was held that 'there is no constitutional right to be protected by the State against being murdered by criminals or madmen' (at 618, Posner, J.) (cited by Tribe 1985: 247).

[22] '[T]his Court . . . has never held that a State's mere acquiescence in a private action converts that action into that of the State' (*Flagg Bros.* v. *Brooks* 436 US 149 (1978) at 164). See also *Moose Lodge No. 107* v. *Irvis* 407 US 163 (1972) (no state action where a club refused to serve Blacks).

[23] *Brown* v. *Socialist Workers '74 Campaign Committee* 103 S. Ct. 416 (1982). See also some of the cases in federal Courts of Appeal concerning state responsibility for failure to provide police protection to Jehovah's Witnesses: *Catlette* v. *US* 132 F. 2d 902 (4th Cir. 1943) and *Lynch* v. *US* 189 F. 2d 476 (5th Cir. 1951), where a sheriff allowed his black prisoner to be kidnapped and beaten by a member of the Ku-Klux-Klan and the court found that culpable inaction constituted denial of equal protection. Cases cited by Abernathy (1977).

[24] *Jackson* v. *Metropolitan Edison Company* 419 US 345 (1974).

[25] In *Kerr* v. *Enoch Pratt Free Library*, 149 F. 2d 212 (4th Cir. 1945), 326 US 721 (1945) Kerr sued for damages and an injunction on the grounds that the library had refused her admission to a training class because she was black. The library was partly funded by the City of Baltimore. The Court of Appeals held that control by the State and the extent of the governmental contribution brought the action within the 'state action' concept. On the other hand in *Dorsey* v. *Stuyvesant Town Corporation* 299 NY 512, 87 NE 2d 541 (1941), 399 US 981 (1950) a split Supreme Court held that tax incentives from the City of New York to the

4(*a*) State held responsible due to a national court sanctioning or failing to compensate a private violation[26] (Strasbourg system).

4(*b*) State law invoked and upheld by a state court in a dispute between two private parties, or judicial relief denied in private dispute; this action becomes 'state action' reviewable by the Supreme Court[27] (Supreme Court level).

5. There is no equivalent to the Council of Europe's Convention on Transfrontier Television.

6(*a*) Where a private violation is alleged at the national level, by either the plaintiff or the defence (Council of Europe Member State level).

6(*b*) Where a private violation is alleged at the state level under a state constitution or where constitutional provisions are invoked in order to determine what constitutes public policy[28] (state court level in the United States).

These differentiated categories are complex, but they confirm the multi-faceted nature of the public/private divide in the context of the application of the Bill of Rights by the Supreme Court. It is suggested that lurking behind these procedural categories lies an ideological resistance to state intrusion into a 'private sphere'. This ideology can be variously related to the idea of freedom of contract, a *laissez-faire* economy, the importance of autonomy for state legislators/administrators/judiciary, or continuing racism.

However, we cannot boldly assert that those who fought to protect the private sphere were the capitalists, anti-federalists, and racists; much depends on which private sphere we are talking about. For instance when it comes to regulating sexual practices, such as intercourse *per anum*,[29] group sex, oral sex, and homosexuality,[30] those who fought to defend the

---

Corporation (the Corporation had been granted a twenty-five-year tax exemption) did not mean that Stuyvesant was a state agency for the purposes of the Fourteenth Amendment. Dorsey was refused tenancy because he was black but the requisite state action was held to be absent. See also *Burton* v. *Wilmington Parking Authority* 365 US 715 (1961), where a private restaurant operated under a lease from a state authority as an integral part of a public parking service, and the Supreme Court found that racial discrimination by the restaurant triggered state action and the protection of the Fourteenth Amendment.

[26] See Velu (1986: 77–117).

[27] *Shelley* v. *Kraemer* 334 US 1 (1948).

[28] See Gould (1986: 900–3), where he cites cases where the terminable-at-will doctrine has been circumscribed by 'the public policy exception': 'Traditionally, the guarantees of the Constitution apply to public employees, thus providing them with, for instance, the right of free speech against government interference. Under the public policy exception, some courts have extended this guarantee to private employees' (900; citation omitted).

[29] *Bowers* v. *Hardwick* 106 S. Ct. 2841 (1986).

[30] Although the statute in question in *Bowers* v. *Hardwick* prohibited anal intercourse for everyone, the Supreme Court concentrated on the fact that the plaintiff was homosexual.

('private') world of business and commerce from regulation by the State, may be the first to advocate state intervention in this area of 'private' life. Therefore labels for the different approaches are hard to define. We cannot label some judges 'activist' and others 'conservative', depending on whether they favour intervention in the private sphere or not. They may be activists concerning the law's intervention to protect a certain traditional moral code, yet offer restrictive interpretations on employment matters and the law's role as regards discrimination. A further complication arises from the fact that abstentionism as regards certain spheres may be due to a concern to preserve even more protective Common Law rights which would be overridden by the application of the federal Constitution. We should also avoid trying to formulate a coherent doctrine in this area as the result of the case has often depended on which judges find themselves in the majority.[31]

Furthermore not only does the reasoning vary, depending on different perceptions of the truly private sphere, but we also find different emphases depending on the actual complaint within the right to 'due process'. This led Judge Friendly (speaking extrajudicially) to suggest that 'more state involvement will be required to produce a holding of unconstitutionality when the constitutional claim is lack of procedural due process, or even infringement of asserted First Amendment rights, than when the claim is of racial discrimination. Surely the result in *Jackson* v. *Metropolitan Edison Co.* would have been different if the company had refused to serve blacks.'[32]

It would be fair to conclude that there is no test as to how to draw the public/private dividing line according to the Supreme Court. The case-law suggests that the following questions may help us to understand the state action test:

   1. *Which private sphere* are we dealing with? The sphere of employment; of housing; of sexual life; of domestic life;[33] of administrative life; of

---

[31] Compare *Rendell-Baker* v. *Kohn* 457 US 83 (1982) and *Blum* v. *Yaretski* 457 US 991 (1982), in which the Supreme Court declared that a 'private' school (99% funded from public funds) and a 'private' nursing home (often funded by Medicaid) were not state actors, with *Lugar* v. *Edmondson Oil Co.* 457 US 922 (1982), where the dissenting minority from the previous two judgments found themselves in the majority, so that the state action requirement was triggered when a state clerk issued a writ. For a theoretical analysis of the possibilities open to the court and a list of the inconsistent results achieved up to 1988 see L. Alexander and P. Porton, *Whom Does the Constitution Command?* (New York: Greenwood Press, 1988).

[32] Friendly (1982: 1292; footnote omitted).

[33] *DeShaney* v. *Winnebago County DSS* 109 S. Ct. 998 (1989).

[34] See generally M. M. Burns, 'The Exclusion of Women from Influential Men's Clubs: The Inner Sanctum and the Myth of Full Equality', 18 *Harv. CR-CLL Rev.* (1983), 321–407. For a Supreme Court decision on the public/private nature of such clubs see *New York State* v. *City of New York* 101 L ED 2d 1 (1988), where the court took a functional

all-male clubs;[34] of all-female organizations;[35] of public accommodation; of activities which might be better regulated at the state level than at the federal level.

2. *Which rights* are we dealing with? The right not to have one's electricity cut off without due process of law, or the right not to be discriminated against on the grounds of one's colour, sex, or sexual orientation.[36]

3. *Which judges* are we dealing with? As was seen in Part I, it is fair to say that judges may have different approaches to the relevance of human rights. However, for the reasons given above we cannot label some judges as activist and others as conservative when the area of analysis is human rights in the private sphere.[37] Nor is it of much help to attach the labels 'liberal' and 'conservative', as again the scope of the private sphere is perceived in different ways. We should simply bear in mind that the results of the cases will not be consistent, and will often be contradictory, depending on which judges find themselves in the majority.

6.1.3 From autonomous private sphere to recognition of the Welfare State and back again

Most cases in this area make some reference to the *Civil Rights* cases (1883),[38] where the Supreme Court invalidated the Civil Rights Act 1875. This Act had sought to ensure equal accommodation in all inns, public conveyances, and places of amusement. This was designed to ensure that the vestiges of slavery and racism did not linger on, and that recently liberated Blacks would not be excluded from 'civil society'. This decision of the Supreme Court ingeniously shifts an inquiry into the rights of Blacks on to the question of the 'liberty' of the innkeepers, theatre

approach, upholding a local law forbidding discrimination by certain clubs with more than 400 members. Kansas and Florida have passed laws based on the New York City laws but New York State has yet to outlaw such discrimination. N. G. Blumenfeld, 'Why Do Clubs Still Exclude Women & Blacks', *New York Times* (25 Apr. 1992), A23.

[35] See generally C. R. Feldblum, N. F. Krent, and V. G. Watkin, 'Legal Challenges to All-Female Organizations' 21 *Harv. CR-CLL Rev.* (1986), 171–225.

[36] It seems that the lower federal courts have constructed a sort of hierarchy of rights for the purposes of state action cases, which places racial discrimination at the top and breach of procedural due process at the bottom. For a critique of this differential approach see Jakosa (1984: 193–223), and the references therein, e.g. 'more government involvement would be required to find state action in sex discrimination cases than in race discrimination' (*Spirit* v. *Teachers Insurance and Annuity Association* 475 F. Supp. 1298 (SDNY 1979) at 1312 n. 22). See also The Editors of the Harvard Law Review, *Sexual Orientation and the Law* (Cambridge, Mass.: Harvard University Press, 1989).

[37] Compare Morrisson (1981), who analyses the European human rights system in terms of the activism and self-restraint of the individual Commissioners and judges.

[38] 109 US 3 (1883).

owners, and railroaders. The court held that these businessmen must be left their autonomy to decide such private matters. The court held that Blacks had not had their rights 'impaired'—only 'invaded'—by private action; they could instead bring a civil suit under the Common Law.[39] However, it was not only the right to discriminate against Blacks which was protected, in *Coppage* v. *Kansas*[40] state legislation which prevented employers from discriminating against union members was struck down by the Supreme Court. Again the court suggested that the right to associate remained intact, as trade unionists could apply for other jobs elsewhere.

The legacy of these cases is considerable—it has ensured that the concept of an autonomous private sphere, immune from state intervention, has remained. The clear statement that 'Individual invasion of individual rights is not the subject matter of the Amendment'[41] has dogged the approach in subsequent cases.

Only after the crucial decision in *West Coast Hotel* v. *Parrish*[42] in 1937 was it clear that the court had recognized the idea of a 'positive' or Welfare State. In that case minimum wage laws were upheld. 'Liberty' was held to involve not only the liberty to draw up contracts, but also the protection of the law against attacks on people's welfare. In a historical account of the state action doctrine, Ira Nerken explains that:

With this recognition, simple distinctions between what is public and what is private generally have fallen as the complex relationship between state power and private economic power has been made apparent. Where once private power could boldly claim a right to be free of state control, now the state is seen to have affirmative obligations to protect individuals from the depredations characteristic of unrestrained action in the private sector. (1977: 298)

However, by 1989, the private sphere and the role of the Welfare State were again shut out by the Supreme Court in the case of *DeShaney* v. *Winnebago County Department of Social Services*. The purpose of the Fourteenth Amendment was held to be 'to protect the people from the State', not to ensure that the State protected them from each other'.[43] In 1980 a Wyoming court granted a divorce to the parents of Joshua DeShaney

---

[39] My explanation draws heavily on the in-depth analysis of Nerken (1977: 297–366). And see Goodman (1982: 1335), who reminds us that 'The Court assumed without deciding that the *failure* of the states to vindicate those rights [the essential rights of victims of discrimination] *would have amounted to unconstitutional state action.*'

[40] 236 US 1 (1915).

[41] *Civil Rights* cases (1883) at 11 (Bradly, J.) (although by 1964 the Supreme Court accepted that the Fourteenth Amendment did give Congress the power to legislate outlawing discrimination in certain types of accommodation). See *Heart of Atlanta Motel* v. *US* 379 US 241 (1964), upholding the Civil Rights Act 1964.

[42] 300 US 379 (1937).

[43] *DeShaney* v. *Winnebago County DSS* 109 S. Ct. 998 (1989) at 1003.

and awarded custody to his father. Joshua was 1 year old. His father moved to Winnebego County and remarried. At the time of his second divorce his father's second wife told the Department of Social Services (DSS) that the father had previously 'hit the boy causing marks and [was] a prima facie case for child abuse'. Joshua's father denied this and the DSS took no action.

In June 1983 Joshua was admitted to hospital with multiple bruises and abrasions. The DSS placed Joshua in the temporary custody of the hospital while it determined what steps to take regarding the situation and the suspicion of child abuse. It was decided to take a series of measures[44] to protect Joshua but not to demand that he remain in the custody of the court. Over the next few months Joshua's case worker observed suspicious injuries on Joshua's head and that the recommended measures had not been complied with. When Joshua was 4 years old he was beaten so severely by his father that he fell into a coma and suffered severe brain damage which left him retarded and likely to spend the rest of his life in an institution.

The complaint of Joshua and his mother alleged that the County had deprived Joshua of his liberty by failing to intervene to protect him against a risk of violence at his father's hands, of which they knew, or should have known. They relied on the Due Process Clause of the Fourteenth Amendment. The United States Supreme Court dismissed their complaint. The majority judgment reverts to a literal original intention reading of the Constitution:

But nothing in the language of the Due Process Clause itself requires the State to protect the life, liberty, and property of its citizens against invasion by private actors. The Clause is phrased as a limitation on the State's power to act, not as a guarantee of certain minimal levels of safety and security.[45]

The court's previous recognition of the legitimate role of the Welfare State only extended so far as to refrain from quashing provisions aimed at greater equality in the market-place. An 'affirmative obligation' would be placed on the State. The extent of governmental obligation was said to be left by the framers of the Constitution to 'democratic political processes'.

The court also rejected the argument that there existed a 'special relationship' between Joshua and the State. The Court's opinion stated that state responsibility for an individual's safety and well-being was only triggered 'when a person is institutionalized and wholly dependent on the

---

[44] These measures entailed recommendations that Joshua should enrol in a pre-school programme, that his father be provided with counselling services, and that his father's 'girlfriend' move out of the house.

[45] At paras. 2–5 of the judgment.

State'. With one eye on the implications of holding that the State has positive obligations the opinion denies state action:

The most that can be said of the state functionaries in this case is that they stood by and did nothing when suspicious circumstances dictated a more active role for them. In defense of them it must also be said that had they moved too soon to take custody of the son away from the father, they would likely have been met with charges of improperly intruding into the parent–child relationship, charges based on the same Due Process Clause that forms the basis of the present charge of failure to provide adequate protection.[46]

It is the fear of the publicization of the private which drives the majority of the court at the end of the 1980s. The joint dissenting opinion states: 'Because of the Court's initial fixation on the general principle that the Constitution does not establish positive rights, it is unable to appreciate our recognition in *Estelle* and *Youngberg* that this principle does not hold true in all circumstances.'[47] The opinion continues by illustrating that it is not that the State renders someone unable to care for themselves but that some people are incapable of taking care of themselves long before the State steps into their life. The fact of state or other incarceration should not be the deciding factor. The dissenting opinion argues that the line between action and inaction is not so neat. It points to the existence of the child-welfare system in Wisconsin and the effect that has on the private sphere:

In these circumstances, a private citizen, or even a person working in a government agency other than the DSS, would doubtless feel that her job was done as soon as she had reported her suspicions of child abuse to DSS. If DSS ignores or dismisses these suspicions, no one will step in to fill the gap. Wisconsin's child-protection program thus effectively confined Joshua DeShaney within the walls of Randy DeShaney's violent home until such time as DSS took action to remove him. Conceivably, then, children like Joshua are made worse off by the existence of this program when the persons and entities charged with carrying it out fail to do their jobs.[48]

In this case the test used by the majority has shifted from the public/private one to an action/inaction test. But the effects for the protection of human rights in the private sphere are similar. Failing to recognize the violence within the walls of Joshua's home due to reluctance to judge 'inaction' has a disparate effect, as it fails to protect those who suffer in the domestic rather than public sphere.[49]

---

[46] At para. 11, p. 1007.
[47] At 1008.
[48] At 1011.
[49] See C. MacKinnon, 'Sex Equality', 100 *Yale Law Review* (1991), 1281–328 at 1325.

6.1.4 Conclusions on the stage action doctrine

The question on which the courts in the United States will now concentrate is: how much government involvement is there? But no quantitative or qualitative criteria have emerged with any clarity. It was argued in the last two chapters that this sort of inquiry is *deceptive* (in that it can serve to mask and avoid subjective judgments about the importance of the right involved); it is *dangerous* (in that it reinforces a dichotomy which suggests that the private sphere cannot be altered or changed); and it is *inconsistent* (tax incentives cannot really be seen to be so very different from subsidies, and, in any event, every action which is not specifically ordered by the State is nevertheless tolerated where reasonable preventive or punitive measures remain unimplemented).[50]

However, it is still this governmental involvement test which the courts present as determing the outcome of the case. As we shall see below, this 'state action' doctrine has been rejected by the Canadian courts as inappropriate to defining the limits of the Charter. First, the courts have noted that a test which relies on state funding would bring a whole host of organizations within the purview of the Canadian Charter. And second, the Supreme Court has stated that a test which allows a court order to constitute state action implies that the results of all private litigation can be potentially reviewed for conformity with the scope of the Charter. The Canadian courts are not shackled with the wording of the Fourteenth Amendment, nor with a desire to respect the original intentions of the drafters of the American Bill of Rights, nor with a history of legislative inertia concerning private racism and sexism. Nevertheless they have chosen their own formulation of the public/private divide.

---

[50] Note, this is particularly relevant in a Common Law country: 'The only difference is that in the latter alternative [State allows practice] the state has legitimated the practice through its common law rather than by specific statutory enactment' (R. J. Glennon and J. F. Nowak, 'A Functional Analysis of the Fourteenth Amendment "State" Action Requirement', *Sup. Ct. Rev.* (1976), 221 at 230 (cited by Jakosa 1984: 210)). Note the approach by R. D. Mohr to the discrimination question: 'it is exactly in the area of business dealings that people think that a violation of rights ought to trigger state coercion. Lying in a business deal is considered actionable fraud. Therefore, though not every private insult to an individual that violates his desert for equal respect ought to engage state coercion, such disrespect in the business world, the world of public functions, should. If someone shouts, "hey, nigger" at me from a speeding car, the shout is an insult, yet it is socially mitigated by the publicly received cowardliness of the shouter and ought, in any case, to be protected by free speech rights. But if I, on the same grounds, am turned away with my family from a hotel lobby, the insult hurled at me because I am black is publicly affirmed. In that circumstance, permissible state coercion should be actualized in law and is not trumped by any free speech consideration. Where insult and disrespect socially perpetuate further violations of the right to equal respect, state action is particularly well motivated. And this will almost always be the case in the public world of business, public accommodations, and housing' (*Gays/Justice* (New York: Columbia University Press, 1989), 142–3).

6.2 CANADA

The Canadian experience concerning the Charter of Rights and Freedoms[51] is particularly interesting in the context of the present study as it can be related to nearly all the issues with which we are concerned. Comparisons can be made to the United States Bill of Rights,[52] to the European Convention on Human Rights,[53] to the dynamics of the European Community,[54] to the development of the Common Law, to the question of individual rights in conflict with the individual rights of others in a collective, to the importance of third-party interventions in court proceedings, and to the practical and various ideological objections to erecting a public/private distinction in cases involving human rights.[55]

Having said this, the Charter also contains rights and procedures which are particularly Canadian and reflect the culture and history of that country.[56] For present purposes it is enough to mention the far-reaching guarantees for equality, language rights, collective/community rights, the possibility of a legislative override, and the recognition of the Welfare State as a means of ameliorating conditions of inequality. What follows is an analysis of some of the cases which raise questions as to the scope of the Charter for regulating behaviour in the 'private' sphere. This analysis is necessarily illustrative rather than comprehensive.

6.2.1 Does the Charter apply to the acts of private bodies?

This question generated a welter of academic writing.[57] The approach eventually taken by the courts is unlikely to stem the tide of commentary as new aspects of the same problem seem bound to recur. It is not proposed to rake over the ashes of this debate. I shall examine the interests involved and the difficulties which have faced the courts and then determine to what extent the Canadian approach is instructive

---

[51] Incorporated in the Constitution Act 1982, enacted by the Canada Act 1982 (United Kingdom), in force 17 Apr. 1982 (except for s. 15, which came into force 17 Apr. 1985).

[52] Tarnopolski (1983: 227–74).

[53] Hovius (1985: 213–61); D. Turp and G. A. Beaudois (eds.), *Perspectives canadiennes et européennes des droits de la personne* (Cowansville: Yvon Blais Inc., 1986).

[54] D. Soberman, 'The Canadian Federal Experience: Selected Issues', in Cappelletti, Seccombe, and Weiler (1986: 513–72).

[55] Y. de Montigny, 'Section 32 and Equality Rights', in Bayefski and Eberts (1985: 565–97); Fudge (1987: 485–554).

[56] See D. J. Elkins, 'Facing our Destiny: Rights and Canadian Distinctiveness', *Canadian Journal of Political Science* (1989), 699–717.

[57] Some of the most influential pieces arguing against the application of the Charter to private parties include: Hogg (1985: 674–8); Swinton (1982: 41); for articles which argued in favour of the application of the Charter to the acts of private bodies see de Montigny (1985); Gibson (1982: 213).

for our main concern—the application of the European Convention on Human Rights.

6.2.1.1 The *Dolphin Delivery* case

On 18 December 1986 the Supreme Court of Canada gave its judgment in *Dolphin Delivery Ltd.* v. *Retail, Wholesale and Department Store Union, Local 580.*[58] The case concerned an interlocutory injunction against a trade union to prevent it picketing business premises. The trade union concerned was the bargaining agent for the employees of the company Purolator. This company had locked out its employees in a labour dispute. The trade union threatened to picket the premises of Dolphin Delivery, another courier company which had done business with Purolator before the lock-out, and which was doing business with a third company, Super-courier, following the lock-out. According to the court there was a connection between Supercourier and Purolator. The case therefore concerned the law of secondary picketing.

The trade union applied to the British Columbia Labour Relations Board for a declaration that Dolphin and Supercourier were allies in the dispute with the union. Such a declaration would have rendered the picketing of Dolphin lawful. The Board declined to make the declaration on jurisdictional grounds. The collective bargaining agreement between Purolator and the union was stated to be governed by federal legislation, the Canada Labour Code, and not the Labour Code of British Columbia. The Board therefore had no jurisdiction in the matter as it fell to be decided under federal law. In fact the Canada Labour Code is silent on this question and so the matter falls to be decided under the Common Law.

Dolphin was informed that its premises would be picketed if it did not cease to do business with Supercourier. Dolphin immediately applied for an injunction to restrain the picketing. This application was granted, as the judge at first instance found the purpose of the picketing involved either the Common Law tort of inducing breach of contract or the Common Law tort of civil conspiracy.[59] The union appealed to the Court of Appeal and introduced a new element—the Charter. The union argued that the Common Law principles adopted and applied by the judge had the effect of infringing fundamental freedoms protected by the Charter (in particular, freedom of expression and freedom of association). The Court of Appeal stated that freedom of association could not be invoked to protect this type of activity. As far as freedom of expression was

---

[58] [1986] 2 SCR 573.
[59] [1982] BCWLD 100, order of Sheppard, LJSC.

concerned, two judges concluded that it could not be invoked (and that even if it could the restricitions were reasonable under Section 1 of the Charter). The third judge, Hutcheon, JA, stated that peaceful picketing is a protected form of expression under the Charter. However, he felt that the question of whether Dolphin and Purolator were allies had to be left to the judge at first instance. He added that a finding that they were allies would have excluded Section 1 of the Charter, as picketing an ally would be a legitimate exercise of freedom of expression.

In the Supreme Court the union limited its claim to freedom of expression. One member of the court, Justice Beetz, agreed with the majority of the Court of Appeal that picketing was not expression under the Charter. But the rest of the Supreme Court held that the picketing which Dolphin sought to restrain involved the exercise of the right to freedom of expression. Nevertheless, the appeal was dismissed on the ground that the case involved private litigation under the Common Law. Having clearly stated that the Charter applies to the Common Law due to Article 52 of the Constitution Act 1982,[60] the court stated that the Charter did not apply where an individual attempted to found an action against another individual on the basis of the Charter. According to the Supreme Court, if private litigation is divorced from any connection with Government due to the lack of reliance on a statute, regulation, etc., then the Charter is excluded.

First, we shall examine how the court came to this conclusion, and second, we will look for possible reasons why it decided this way. The Supreme Court examined both sides of the doctrinal divide. It explained that according to one view the Charter, 'like most written constitutions, was set up to regulate the relationship between the individual and the Government. It was intended to restrain governmental action and to protect the individual. It was not intended in the absence of some governmental action to be applied in private litigation.'[61] McIntyre, J., quoted extensively from a number of commentators who had declared that the Charter was not applicable to private disputes.[62] He then made reference to the doctrine which put forward the contrary view,[63] and

---

[60] s. 52(1) reads: 'The Constitution of Canada is the supreme law of Canada, and any law that is inconsistent with the provisions of the Constitution is, to the extent of the inconsistency, of no force or effect.'

[61] McIntyre, J., at 693.

[62] McIntyre, J., goes on to examine some of the literature and its reception by the Canadian Courts; see Hogg (1985: 670); Swinton (1982); Tarnopoliski and Beaudoin (1982: 422); and A. McLellan and B. P. Elman, 'To whom Does the Charter Apply? Some Recent Cases on s. 32', *Alberta L. Rev.* (1986), 361 at 367.

[63] The Court cited Gibson (1982: 213); D. Gibson, 'Distinguishing the Governors from the Governed: The Meaning of "Government" under Section 32(1) of the Charter', 13 *Manitoba LR* (1983), 505; and M. Manning, *Rights, Freedoms and the Courts* (Toronto: Emond-Montgomery Ltd., 1983).

continued, 'I am in agreement with the view that the *Charter* does not apply to private litigation. It is evident from the authorities and articles cited above that that approach has been adopted by most judges and commentators who have dealt with this question.'

The core factor which influenced McIntyre's judgment was the text of Section 32 of the Charter.[64] He held that the position and inclusion of the word 'government' led to the conclusion that it referred to the executive or administrative branch of Government and not to 'government in its generic sense—meaning the whole of the governmental apparatus of the state—but to a branch of government'.[65] He continued that the Charter applies to the action of the legislative, executive, and administrative branches of Government in both public and private litigation. Moreover, he added that the Charter applies whether the action depends on statute or the Common Law.

McIntyre's judgment then tackles the question of 'The element of governmental intervention necessary to make the *Charter* applicable in an otherwise private action'. He refused to follow the approach of Professor Hogg in his book *Constitutional Law of Canada*.[66] Professor Hogg had suggested that where the Common Law had 'crystallized into a form that can be enforced by the courts' then an enforcement order which would infringe a Charter right could be precluded by the Charter and the Charter would 'by necessary implication . . . modify the common law rule'. McIntyre, J., found this approach 'troublesome' and held that, although the courts were bound by the Charter,

To regard a court order as an element of governmental intervention necessary to invoke the *Charter* would, it seems to me, widen the scope of the *Charter* application to virtually all private litigation. All cases must end, if carried to completion, with an enforcement order and if the *Charter* precludes the making of the order, where a *Charter* right would be infringed, it would seem that all private litigation would be subject to the *Charter*.[67]

McIntyre, J., stated that 'A more direct and a more precisely-defined connection between the element of government action and the claim advanced must be present before the *Charter* applies.'[68] Later he stated: 'it is difficult and probably dangerous to attempt to define with narrow

---

[64] Art. 32(1) reads: 'This Charter applies (*a*) to the Parliament and government of Canada in respect of all matters within the authority of Parliament including all matters relating to the Yukon Territory and Northwest Territories; and (*b*) to the legislature and government of each province in respect of all matters within the authority of the legislature of each province.'

[65] At 598.

[66] Hogg (1985: 677); note Hogg's suggestion was partly based on the logic of *Shelley* v. *Kraemer* (see above).

[67] At 598–9.   [68] At 599.

precision that element of governmental intervention which will suffice to permit reliance on the *Charter* by private litigants in private litigation.'[69] What the judgment makes clear is that where one party brings a case against another relying on the Common Law and no act of government is involved, the Charter is inapplicable.

This is not to say the Charter is irrelevant, as the judiciary will apply the principles of the Common Law 'in a manner consistent with the fundamental values enshrined in the Constitution'.[70] However, to challenge the operation of the Common Law the party needed a 'factor which removed the case from the private sphere'. The order of the court was not enough.

6.2.1.1.1 Possible reasons why the Charter was not applied to the private litigants relying solely on the Common Law

The court was faced with some ambiguity in the text of the Charter and no clear legislative intention (de Montigny 1985). A leading textbook had suggested that in this sort of case the Charter was applicable. Yet the Supreme Court excluded the Charter. It is suggested that two factors may have played a role in its reaching this decision. First, McIntyre, J.'s, judgment specifically mentions that the undesirable result of applying the Charter to this type of case would be 'to widen the scope of *Charter* application to virtually all private litigation'. Such a consequence would not only mean a deluge of cases requiring definitive judgments from the Supreme Court, but could also throw the state of the Common Law into confusion. Every precedent and rule would be potentially susceptible to challenge and, furthermore, each application of the Common Law would be open to challenge for conformity with the Charter as being unjustified 'in a free and democratic society' (Section 1 of the Charter). In other words, every Common Law decision would be appealable on grounds of proportionality. We could call this the 'flood-gates' or 'legal certainty' rationale.

Second, the court was faced with the Common Law of British Columbia rather than a complete legal vacuum. Applying the Charter in this field would have been an intrusion into the 'private law' of the Provinces which might have been seen as a federalizing/centralizing act determining the applicable law in an area which had previously been determined at the provincial level. The extension of the scope of the Charter beyond federal action to the government of the Provinces (Section 32) had already resulted in Quebec passing legislation to operate 'notwithstanding the Charter' (Tarnopolski 1983: 271). Applying the Charter to private litigation might have been perceived as a further intrusion on the competence

---

[69] At 560.   [70] Ibid.

of the Provinces. Some of the authors cited with approval by the court stressed that an application of the Charter to private litigation would mean that alternative dispute resolution could be sidestepped or rendered redundant, and that such procedures often had a 'built in mechanism to encourage settlement'. The Charter has to be implemented by the courts, which usually have no such mechanism. We might tentatively suggest that these factors led to 'cautious federalism' from the court.[71]

6.2.1.2 The *Blainey* case

In *Re Blainey and Ontario Hockey Association*[72] the Ontario Court of Appeal used the Charter to decide the issue of girls being allowed to play in boy's hockey teams. Justine Blainey was 12 years old at the start of the proceeding. She wished to play as a full member of a team where all the other members were boys. There were *ad hoc* arrangements for girls who were 12 years old or under to play on boy's teams but for a team to participate in the regular schedule every member of the team had to be a member of the Ontario Hockey Association (OHA) and the regulations of the OHA required that members be male.

Justine's mother complained on behalf of her daughter of sex discrimination to the Ontario Human Rights Commission. Section 1 of the Ontario Human Rights Code reads: 'Every person has a right to equal treatment with respect to services, goods and facilities, without discrimination because of race, ancestry, place of origin, colour, ethnic origin, citizenship, creed, sex, age, marital status, family status or handicap.' The Commission advised Mrs Blainey that the Commission had no jurisdiction to hear the complaint due to Section 19(2) of the Ontario Human Rights Code. Section 19(2) reads: 'The right under section 1 to equal treatment with respect to services and facilities is not infringed where membership in an athletic organization or participation in an athletic activity is restricted to persons of the same sex.' The Code came into force before Section 15 of the Charter and so it was within the jurisdiction of Ontario to enact it. Mrs Blainey sought therefore to challenge the constitutionality of Section 19(2) under the Charter.

Before examining the challenge to Section 19(2) we must consider two other arguments. First, it was argued that the Charter covered private activity and so the OHA regulations could be challenged as contrary to

---

[71] Note, Fudge (1987: 490 n. 18) reports that the Supreme Courts of Saskatchewan and Newfoundland have found Common Law rules concerning husband's rights to sue for loss of consortium contrary to s. 15 without 'worrying about the application of Article 32', *Shwarchuk*, v. *Hansen* (1984) 30 CCLT 121 (Sask. QB); *Power* v. *Moss* (1986) 38 CCLT 31, 185 APR 5 (Nfld. TD).

[72] [1986] 26 DLR (4th) 728, leave to appeal to the Supreme Court of Canada refused.

the Charter. This was rejected, with the court quoting passages by the commentators referred to above.[73] Second, it was submitted that the OHA and its parent the Canadian Amateur Hockey Association (CAHA) were agents of the Government of Canada. It was suggested that the rules of these associations 'could be regarded as acts done pursuant to powers granted by law'. Dubin, JA, for the majority of the court found 'no such nexus'. He stated that the only relationship between these bodies and the Government of Canada was that they received grants. There was no form of 'governmental agency' or exercise of 'governmental function'.[74]

However, the challenge to the constitutionality of Section 19(2) of the Human Rights Code succeeded. This Section was held to deny Justine the protection of the Human Rights Code: *but for* the operation of this Section Justine would have the protection of the Code. The Court had to consider whether Section 19(2) was justifiable pursuant to Section 1 of the Charter. At first instance the judge had held that it was a reasonable limit on the right to equality and was therefore constitutional. The majority of the Court of Appeal did not agree. It was pointed out that the onus of proof was on the party seeking to justify the restriction of freedom; and the restriction has to be shown to be proportionate to the government aim in question. No effort was made by the Commission to justify the Section as they supported the contention that it was unconstitutional.

The dissenting judge, Finlayson, JA, stressed that the Court had not heard arguments to justify Section 19(2), whose 'objects are *bona fide* and are of the most serious'.[75] He was also concerned that the Court had not been provided with 'some factual background' and that counsel for the Canadian Association for the Advancement of Women and Sport had not been able to file information as part of his intervention. Finlayson, JA, found that Section 19(2) satisfied the test in Section 1 of the Charter as 'a reasonable limit prescribed by law that has been demonstrably justified in our society'.[76]

Professor Mandel has described the follow-up to this case in his book *The Charter of Rights and the Legalization of Politics in Canada*:

When the matter finally got back to the Human Rights Commission for a hearing, it turned out that this was not a clash between male and female but between the Human Rights Commission and the Blaineys on the one hand, and the men, and especially the women, responsible for amateur hockey on the other. The sports people were vehement that desegregation of amateur hockey would ruin it, not for men and boys, but for women and girls. Nobody denied that a minority of the girls could play boys'-style hockey on a level good enough to compete with the

[73] Tarnopolski and Beaudoin (1982: 422–3); Swinton (1982: 44–5). These authors rely heavily on the wording of Art. 32 and the existence of the provincial human rights codes which cover discriminatory behaviour.
[74] At 738.   [75] At 759.   [76] At 759.

boys. That was the problem. According to Fran Rider, President of the Ontario Women's Hockey Association (OWHA), though most girls could not compete with the boys, the few top players in her league were as good as any of them. These girls would be gobbled up by the boys' teams as winning assets. The effect would be to deprive the girls' teams of their best players. They would lose role models, and the quality of the play would deteriorate. (1989: 270)

Evidence was produced which showed that desegregation would result in girls' sport being labelled 'second rate', and that desegregation in Quebec had 'ruined' girls' hockey in that Province. The final ruling was that girls and women could not be excluded from the boys' leagues.

Mandel labels this process the legalization of politics. His concern is that relying on individual rights to resolve conflicts denies compromise and excludes the parties most concerned with issues (in this case other women hockey players). Mandel's critique of the legalization of politics can inform our study of the privatization of human rights. The *Blainey* case was essentially an example of the application by one private individual of human rights against another private body—the OHA. However, the interests, rights, and freedoms of that body were not fully considered because the traditional approach to human rights demands that the conflict be formulated in terms of an individual–State conflict. In this case the interests of the public body/State do not coincide with the interests of the other individuals in the collective in question. These 'third parties' are excluded in procedural and substantive terms.

As we shall see, this exclusion is exaggerated at the international level, where the European Convention on Human Rights and its supervisory organs inevitably emphasize the role of the States Parties to the Convention. It may be that the privatization of European human rights demands new procedures at the international level in Strasbourg in order fully to consider all the conflicting interests involved.[77] The approach of the Canadian courts, whereby jurisdiction is determined through a governmental element (such as legislation, etc.), whilst not overtly proclaiming the privatization of human rights, is nevertheless indicative of some of the pitfalls of the judicial application of human rights in the private sphere. (In *Blainey* the Charter was effectively applied to the rules of a private sports association (without real representation of the wider collective interests).

6.2.1.3 The public/private dichotomy and its ideological implications in Canada

At first blush the two decisions discussed above would suggest that unions are outside the scope of the Charter and women may succeed in invoking

---

[77] See Ch. 9.

the Charter in order to counter sex discrimination by private bodies (where they can point to legislation which tolerates discrimination). But the legal route whereby the Charter was excluded or applied means that the public/private test could come to hinder rather than help both organized labour and women.

Unions are not necessarily beyond the reach of the Charter. In the *Lavigne* case[78] an individual challenged the use of union dues for political purposes by invoking the Charter's protection of freedom of association and expression. The union's lawyers argued that the Charter was inapplicable because the collective agreement was private. This argument was rejected, as the union was held to be bargaining with the School of Mines, whose Council of Regents as a Crown Agent had negotiated the eventual contract. The Charter ruling meant that public sector unions had to set up new schemes for the collection and use of political funds in accordance with the judgment.[79] Mandel again describes the follow-up to the judgment at first instance, including the attempt by the union to take its 'revenge' under the Charter. The union attempted to use the Charter to claim that tax-deductible contributions to business and to the right-wing pressure group that had backed the *Lavigne* case violated freedom of expression and association. The failure of the courts to apply the Charter to this sphere leads Mandel to state:

So the Charter logic that requires public sector unions to respect the freedoms of their dissenters cannot be readily applied to either the government, corporations, or right wing lobby groups. *Lavigne* may mean that public sector unions are the only institutions in Canada that have to respect the rules of liberal democracy! . . . *Lavigne* effectively stigmatizes 'political activity' by unions as less legitimate than collective bargaining activity, even if this was not its precise holding. It rigidifies the separation of public and private spheres and, in effect confines the union to the private sphere where they are no match for business. And it does this at the same time as the Charter prohibits government from making business stay out of politics. (1989: 216)

---

[78] *Re Lavigne and Ontario Public Service Employees Union et al.* [1986] 29 DLR (4th) 327; *Re Lavigne and Ontario Public Service Employees Union et al.* [1987] 41 DLR (4th) 86; *Lavigne* v. *Ontario Public Service Employees Union* [1991] 4 CRR (2d) 192; see Mandel (1989: 209). In the Supreme Court Wilson, J., applied his government entity test proposed in *McKinney* v. *University of Guelph* (1990) 2 CRR (2d) 1. This means a combination of a 'control test', a 'traditional government function test', and a 'statutory authority specifically granted to enable it to further a governmental objective to promote the broader public interest'. The conclusion was therefore that the employers in *Lavigne* were a government entity.

[79] The *Lavigne* case was reversed in the Court of Appeal and this result was upheld by the Supreme Court of Canada. The Charter was ultimately held to apply to this situation due to the nexus with Government of the employers. But there was held to be no violation of the Charter, as the governmental action was held to be proportionate to the aims pursued.

It might be tempting to dismiss this analysis as idiosyncratic, but the point has already been taken up by academics in Britain. In the context of constitutional reform in Britain, Professor Ewing concludes his analysis of 'Trade Unions and the Constitution: The Impact of the New Conservatives' by warning: 'Recent experience from jurisdictions such as Canada suggests that institutional reforms, such as a Bill of Rights, will at best give a veneer of legitimacy of government attacks on trade unions, and at worst will be an additional source of weakness giving further ammunition to those concerned to undermine organised labour.'[80]

Turning to the question of sex discrimination, the public/private distinction is perceived by some commentators to have equally damaging concrete and ideological implications. In the same way that the disruption of settled industrial relations procedures through the judicial application of individual freedoms has attracted criticism on grounds of lack of competence, judicial application of the equality guarantees in the Charter have been said to have failed to appreciate 'the socio-historic roots of current inequality'.[81] This critique of the courts' approach to sex discrimination under the Charter again illustrates the unfortunate effects of a public/private split in the application of the Charter. Women are denied the use of the Charter to challenge the behaviour of employers, trade unions, and landlords, yet men may challenge legislation designed to redress socio-economic disadvantages suffered by women. Different legislative provisions concerning state benefits for single mothers, sexual intercourse with a female person under 14, and sexual intercourse with a stepdaughter have all been struck down by the courts as a breach of the equality provisions of the Charter (Fudge 1987). Because the courts do not feel in a position to legislate to extend socio-economic protection across gender lines, women are effectively denied the benefits of such protective legislation until such time as positive legislation is reintroduced.

When we consider the operation of the Charter in the context of the modern Welfare State it emerges that the Charter has opened the way for protective legislation concerning working conditions and women's rights to be successfully challenged in the courts. The result is that the resources of workers' and women's organizations will be considerably strained in the defence of that legislation.[82] In cases where the government of the

---

[80] Ewing (1988: 152); see also Christian and Ewing (1987: 195–7); T. J. Christian and K. D. Ewing 'Sunday Trading in Canada', *CLJ* (1987), 4–6.

[81] Fudge (1987: 497), and see the references therein; Fudge continues: 'the success of this approach depends, to a large extent, upon the court's rejection of the public/private split which is both implicit in the notion of formal legal equality and a cornerstone of liberal democracy and jurisprudence.' Note also Mandel (1989: 271).

[82] See Fudge (1987: 528): 'Cases such as *Seaboyer and Canadian Newspapers* have increasingly demanded the attention and resources of groups like LEAF which were originally formed to use the *Charter* to further feminist struggles for equality. As a result of the

day is unsympathetic to the rights in question this burden will be especially heavy. The result of such challenges may be the immediate deregulation or privatization of some spheres of activity, but the existence of the public/private distinction may deprive workers', women's, and other organizations of the chance to challenge abuses of 'private' power, either in the old 'private' sphere or in the newly privatized spheres. The ideological objection to this split runs deeper. By the labelling as 'private' of issues such as abortion and union activity, the issues are somehow perceived as subordinate to 'public' concerns and therefore less worthy of debate.

I am not suggesting that the Canadian judiciary has conspired to disadvantage workers' and women's organizations through the application of a public/private dichotomy. The public/private split is the legacy of the traditional approach to constitutional rights.[83] What are being questioned are the consequences of using the constitutional precepts which informed the constitutionalists of the eighteenth and nineteenth centuries to answer the 'human-rightists' in the Welfare State of the twentieth century.

6.2.2 The relevance of the Canadian approach for the Strasbourg organs

It is worth emphasizing some of the differences and similarities between the application of the Charter in Canada and the operation of the Convention in Strasbourg. In the *Dolphin Delivery* case we witnessed a

---

Charter, feminist organizations are having to spend precious time, energy and money in the courts defending legislation it took many women many years to achieve. Perhaps this is the ultimate paradox of the *Charter*: whilst feminist organizations are attempting to develop situated and contextual theories of equality which will address women's social and historical subordination, innumerable other litigants, including defendants charged with sexual assault offences and right-to-life organizations, are simultaneously invoking the *Charter* to claim a formal equality which may well erode victories which feminist[s] believed they had already won' (footnotes omitted). See M. Eberts, 'The Canadian Charter of Rights and Freedoms: A Feminist Perspective on the First Ten Years', in P. Alston (ed.), *International Human Rights Law in Comparative Perspective* (Oxford: Oxford University Press, forthcoming). See also Mandel (1989: 294), whose concern is with the political alternatives to litigation: 'What if the Charter had not been available? Then all the devotion, energy and resources that were poured into the litigation would have been available for other forms of political action. And these other forms would have gained in urgency and effectiveness from the lack of the judicial alternative.' See also 207–17: 'Using the Courts to Fight Unions.'

[83] 'The automatic response to a suggestion that the Charter can apply to private activity, without connection to government, will be that a Charter of Rights is designed to bind governments not private actors. That is the nature of a constitutional document: to establish the scope of governmental authority and to set out the terms of the relationship between the citizen and the state and those between the organs of government.' Swinton (1982: 44), cited with approval by McNair, J., in *Cat Productions Ltd.* v. *Macedo et al.* [1985] 1 FC 269, 5 CPR (3d) 71, 5 CIR 207 (TD), at 274; and again by Dubin, JA, in *Blainey* at 737, and cited again by the Supreme Court in *Dolphin Delivery* at 596.

cautious approach to regulating industrial relations through the rights guaranteed in the Charter. The Supreme Court is faced with different jurisdictions and the prospect of ensuing uncertainty should the Charter come to be considered the highest law in this field. Similarly, at the European level, the European Court of Human rights has been warned of the dangers of meddling in this field.

In 1976 Mr Danelius, as agent for the Swedish Government in the *Swedish Engine Drivers' Union* case,[84] argued that the European Court of Human Rights should not apply Article 11 so as to cover relations between trade unions and their members or relations between trade unions and employers, and warned that should the Court of Human Rights use Article 11 in this way the Court could find itself having to lay down a labour relations code which would cover all the different industrial relations systems in the different countries which are Parties to the Convention.[85] As it happened the Court felt it did not have to rule on the question, as the bargaining agency, which had refused to bargain collectively with a minor union, was clearly a state agency. And, as we shall see, the question was again avoided in the *Young, James and Webster* case,[86] where the Court held that it was the legislation which infringed the individual rights concerned and not the fact that British Rail was a nationalized state monopoly.

After an examination of the case-law of the Strasbourg Court on Article 11 and labour law, M. Forde concludes that:

The principal question the experience with these four cases raises is the appropriateness of judges, many of whom possess relatively little industrial relations expertise, laying down common standards for collective bargaining systems of great complexity that often differ fundamentally from each other. Especially at the international level, there is a grave danger of amateurs, no matter how eminent they may be as jurists, tinkering with arrangements they do not fully understand, and tending to impose standards that may work in their own countries upon entirely different labour market systems of other states.[87]

Neither the Supreme Court of Canada nor the European Court of Human Rights can avoid these questions on grounds of jurisdiction where an individual complains that legislation is at the root of the violation of fundamental rights. Although the exclusion of private litigation based on Common Law rights is understandable in the Canadian context it would be inappropriate to import this restriction into the Convention case-law. First, the Strasbourg Court does not have the problem that, if it declared

---

[84] Judgment of 6 Feb. 1976, Series A, vol. 20.
[85] Series B, vol. 18, p. 146.
[86] Series A, vol. 44.
[87] Forde (1984: 332); see also Forde (1985: 253–80).

the Common Law incompatible with human rights, the result would lead to immediate chaos and uncertainty. The judgments of the European Court of Human Rights do not have legal effect in the domestic orders of Common Law countries. Second, the Strasbourg Court is not caught in the same dilemma as the Supreme Court, as it is one step removed from the formulation of the Common Law and so would not in effect be overruling its own case-law. Third, the Strasbourg Court's case-law has already confirmed that the Contracting Parties may have positive obligations flowing from the Convention and that these may 'sometimes require positive measures to be taken even in the sphere of relations between individuals'.[88]

6.2.3 The relevance of the Canadian approach for the British courts

It is suggested that the Supreme Court's approach to the question of human rights in the private sphere should not be imported by the British courts. At the moment, the approach of the British courts has been to acknowledge the relevance of the Convention in determining and developing the Common Law. This is also currently the position of the Supreme Court of Canada.[89] Although the British courts have been ready to assert that the Common Law reflects the Convention and vice versa, no judgment has ever actually explicitly changed the Common Law.[90] If the Convention were to be incorporated into United Kingdom law the British courts could be faced with the same dilemma that faced the Supreme Court in *Dolphin Delivery*. It is suggested that they should not follow the example of the Supreme Court for the following reasons.

First, the Supreme Court took into account the existence of provincial decentralized human rights codes and disputes procedures. These do not exist in the British context. Second, incorporation of the Convention would be designed to repatriate the remedies which exist in Strasbourg. As we shall see, individuals may have a remedy in Strasbourg where the Common Law denies them their human rights even in the sphere of relations with other private individuals. Third, a government keen to

---

[88] *Case of Plattform 'Ärzte für das Leben'*, Series A, vol. 139, para. 32, the paragraph concerned Art. 11.

[89] In *Dolphin Delivery*, after having denied the application of the Charter to litigation between two private parties where one party relies on the Common Law, McIntyre, J., stated: 'I should make it clear, however, that this is a distinct issue from the question whether the judiciary ought to apply and develop the principles of the common law in a manner consistent with the fundamental values enshrined in the Constitution. The answer to this question must be in the affirmative. In this sense, then, the Charter is far from irrelevant to private litigants whose disputes fall to be decided at common law' (at 599).

[90] See Chs. 1.2, 10.2.

avoid the scope of the Convention could start to deregulate certain areas so that they were solely covered by the Common Law.[91]

In Constitution Paper no. 1, A British Bill of Rights, published in 1990 by the Institute for Public Policy Research, the proposed Bill of Rights is said to apply to 'any act or omission by or on behalf of any person or body (including the Crown) in the performance of any public function'. The drafters of the Bill add in the commentary to this clause a reference to Section 32 of the Canadian Charter.[92] For the reasons set out above it is suggested that the Canadian solution took place in a context which is very different from the British one.[93]

---

[91] Although it could be argued that the act of deregulation was itself a governmental act this would not really avail a plaintiff as a court would be unlikely to hold a whole deregulating statute void on the grounds that one individual had had his or her rights disproportionately infringed under the resulting applicable Common Law.

[92] See Lester *et al.* (1990: Clause B and the commentary at p. 19). It is stated that the Bill would not be 'a direct source of rights and obligations as between *private* persons—for example, so as to enable a disaffected worker to sue a trade union, an employee to sue their employer for discrimination, or an individual to sue a peeping Tom neighbour for breach of privacy'. The authors also mention Clause 3 of the draft New Zealand Bill of Rights. This Clause has been vigorously criticized as out of step with New Zealand's obligations under the Civil and Political Rights Covenant as interpreted by the General Comments of the Human Rights Committee; see Elkind and Shaw (1986), whose alternative draft Bill of Rights excludes the Clause in question so as to include the possibility of actions in the private sphere. See Ch. 10.7.6, for more detail concerning the eventual solution chosen in New Zealand.

[93] The British debate is considered more fully in Ch. 10.

7

The Application of the European Convention on Human Rights to the Acts of Non-State Actors: The Case-Law of the European Commission and Court of Human Rights[1]

7.1 'ECOLOGICAL LIABILITY' FOR PRIVATE HUMAN RIGHTS VIOLATIONS

Chapter 4 suggested two approaches to the possible application of the Convention in the private sphere. The first was that the method of interpretation of the European Court of Human Rights was forward-looking and contextual, rather than backward-looking and positivist, and therefore it had to take into account current trends in international and constitutional law which suggest that individuals have to be protected from acts which violate human rights, even when the actors are private bodies. Furthermore, an 'effective' implementation of the Convention means that the changing social context within which it operates has to be considered. The ever-increasing threats from non-state actors mean that the Convention organs now have to offer real increased protection from these developing threats. The second approach suggested that the creation of a private/public distinction in this field is arbitrary, and leads to unfair discrimination and prejudice; accordingly such a dangerous distinction should be avoided.

Nevertheless, it was further suggested that simply to apply the Convention in the private sphere across the whole spectrum of fundamental rights is inappropriate, and that to understand this subject better it is essential to deal with each right separately. According to the explanatory preamble to the Bill on fundamental rights which was eventually to become part of the Dutch Constitution:

---

[1] The Resolutions of the Committee of Ministers under Art. 32 of the European Convention on Human Rights have not been separately analysed as they contain no independent reasons for the decision taken. Although the Committee of Ministers is acting in a quasi-judicial function under Art. 32 it does not depart from the reasoning of the Commission even if it decides differently on the question of the existence of a violation. Where developments concerning a Resolution of the Committee of Ministers have had an impact on the development of the Convention these have been mentioned (e.g. s. 7.3.1.4, concerning corporal punishment, and Ch. 1.4.2, concerning prisoners' rights).

No more consideration should be given to the thought that all fundamental rights in general do not have any effect whatsoever or, on the contrary, that all fundamental rights have the same effect to the same extent on horizontal relations. The question concerning the horizontal effectiveness need not be answered in a similar fashion for every fundamental right. The answers may differ from article to article, or from one part of an article to another, perhaps only in respect to various particular categories found in a single article. This approach has the advantage of liberating the problem of horizontal effectiveness from its dogmatic nature and of bringing it back to normal proportions of constitutional interpretation.[2]

Some lawyers might argue that such an approach, whilst appropriate for constitutional interpretation, has no place at the supranational level, where only States are bound by the relevant treaties. Although the question was not raised in this form it has been directly tackled by the European Court of Human Rights. In a way the germs of the Court's acceptance of the Convention's application to private action at the international level can be traced to the drafting of the new Dutch Constitution referred to above. In the record of the public hearing in the *Case of X and Y* v. *The Netherlands*[3] the following exchange is reproduced.

JUDGE WALSH. I also would like to ask a question of the respondent government . . .
 You introduced the term *Drittwirkung*. Is it basically the contention of your Government that the Convention speaks only to Governments and States but does not regulate rights between fellow citizens?
MR KORTHALS ALTES. That is a difficult question to answer.
JUDGE WALSH. As you are probably aware, this is a matter which arises in German and Austrian constitutional law and I think also in Swiss. You introduced the word and I recall that about four years ago in the Netherlands International Law Review there was an article on this very point in relation to the Convention on Human Rights. I was wondering what is the particular attitude of the Government: does it say that the Convention speaks only to Governments and States or does it also . . . ?
MR KORTHALS ALTES. No, that is certainly not the position of the Dutch Government.[4]

The importance of this concession by the Dutch Government should not be underestimated.[5] The article referred to would seem to be the article by Dr Andrew Drzemczewski 'The European Human Rights Convention

---

[2] Cited according to D. Simons, 'Bestand und Bedeutung der Grundrechte in den Niederlanden', *Eu. GRZ* (1978), 450, at 454, quoted by Starck (1982: 112).
[3] Judgment of 25 Mar. 1985, Series A, vol. 91; the pleadings are reproduced in the Series B publication.
[4] At 95 of the Series B publication.
[5] I am grateful to Professor Alkema for pointing me to this exchange. Professor Alkema was one of the lawyers for the applicant in the case and he has stressed the importance of this concession by the Government in his article 'The Third-Party Applicability or "Drittwirkung" of the European Convention on Human Rights' (1988: 37 n. 19).

and Relations between Private Parties' (1979). This article starts with a summary of the latest *Drittwirkung* developments in the constitutional orders of the Federal Republic of Germany and Belgium and suggests that other countries such as The Netherlands, Austria, and Switzerland may soon start applying the Convention to legal relations between private parties. It is not inconceivable that the position of the Netherlands Government was also influenced by another article also published in the *Netherlands International Law Review*. This second article, written three years after Drzemczewski's article, is entitled 'The Complete Revision of the Dutch Constitution', and was by Professor Burkens (1982). It is important that the origins of *Drittwirkung* are traced by Drzemczewski to different constitutions whilst the second article deals directly with the new Dutch Constitution. Burkens explains that in chapter 1 of the Dutch Constitution 'the possibility is left open that the courts cannot only apply the civil rights in the relationship between the citizens and the government, but also between citizens themselves'.[6] Drzemczewski's comparative research into *Drittwirkung* and the acceptance by the new Dutch constitutional order of third-party applicability may have combined to tease out the concession by the Dutch Government at the level of the international supervision of the European Convention on Human Rights in the *X and Y v. The Netherlands* case.

There is, however, a difference between a constitutional settlement which leaves open the possibility of constitutional values/rights being applied between private parties in the domestic courts, and international supervision of the effectiveness of the practical guarantees which are nationally implemented to ensure that the rights in the European Convention are respected by private persons. One could argue that even if a State is prepared to recognize, through its own constitution or courts, a *Drittwirkung* for constitutional rights, this does not imply that it accepts international supervision of the implementation of the Convention in such a way that it applies directly against private bodies at the national level. Furthermore, there exists in the doctrine a difference between *mittelbare Drittwirkung* and *unmittelbare Drittwirkung*. The former means that the values and principles surrounding constitutional fundamental rights are to

---

[6] At 331–2. Burkens continues: 'One example which springs to mind is the case in which a tenant wishes to display a political poster in his window, despite a clause in the rent agreement prohibiting this during an election campaign.' This example fits with the thesis presented in Ch. 5. The right at issue is aimed at the protection of democracy. The action takes place in the sphere of the public. Therefore the right should be protected even from purely private violations. It is suggested that the right to put up the poster deserves less protection should the tenant wish to put the poster in a corridor which is not open to the public but only accessible by the landlord. At this point putting up the poster does not contribute to public debate or launch the tenant's politics in the market-place of ideas. It becomes an invasion of the rights of others, namely the landlord's right to privacy (Art. 8 ECHR).

be considered by the courts when they are deciding private law cases. The latter means that the rights themselves can be directly applied against private bodies by the courts. What seems to have happened is that the more usual *mittelbare Drittwirkung* application, as developed at the national level,[7] has been adopted at the international level in its *unmittelbare* form. In the *X and Y* case[8] the European Court of Human Rights actually demanded that individuals be protected from other individuals' actions where such actions threaten rights under the Convention. The European Court did not suggest that in their application of private law courts should be inspired by the principles which lie behind their constitutions and the Convention (*mittelbare Drittwirkung*). The Court seems to presume that States are obliged to ensure that national courts protect Convention rights when these rights are directly relied on against other private individuals. An alternative view is that of Judge Spielmann and Mr Dean Spielmann, who suggest that the *X and Y* case is an affirmation of *mittelbare Drittwirkung* at the international level. It is, they say, indirect because the Government has to adopt legislation to give effect to the right.[9]

It is suggested that it is unfortunate that the questions have been cloaked with the mystique of the *Drittwirkung* doctrine. *Drittwirkung* has had to be dealt with here in order to illustrate the rather curious way in which it was accepted by a respondent government before the European Court of Human Rights. Without detailing all the competing theories of *Drittwirkung*, it is suggested that *Drittwirkung* is not helpful at the international level. The European Court of Human Rights is not seeking to harmonize constitutional traditions but to ensure international protection for the rights contained in the Convention. Key questions in *Drittwirkung* doctrine are the weight to be given to different rights such as: the right to free development of the personality, the right to work, the right to strike,

---

[7] See Horan (1976: 848); Lewan (1968: 571); Scheuner (1971: 253); Zanghi (1971: 269); J. J. Arbrantes, 'L'Effet à l'égard des particuliers des droits et libertés fondamentaux' (1981), on file at the Council of Europe.

[8] Discussed in detail below.

[9] 'Abuse of Rights and Equivalent Concepts: The Principle and its Present Day Applications', Council of Europe doc. CJ-DE/XIX(89)6, XIXth Colloquy on European Law, Luxembourg. See also Spielmann (1990), esp. the conclusion, where he outlines two different types of indirect *Drittwirkung* at the international level: 'However the European Court and Commission of Human Rights have accepted the positive obligation theory, thus applying *indirectly* the Convention to non-State entities. The European Court *did not reject* any *direct* third party effect, but refused to decide in general terms on the issue. Is it now nevertheless possible for the Court and Commission to engage State responsibility at the international level in respect of the *direct* third party effect? A possible issue could be that such a responsibility is engaged if the domestic courts and tribunals fail to apply *directly* the provisions of the Convention between non-state persons (Direkte Drittwirkung or direct horizontal effect) [this] would *indirectly* be subject to control on the international level by the European Court and Commission ("Indirekte Drittwirkung" or indirect horizontal effect of the "Direkte Drittwirkung" or direct horizontal effect).'

the right to property, freedom of conscience, the right to equality, the right to free enterprise, and the right to freedom of contract. The way these rights are ordered and protected in the private sphere determines the social and economic priorities which a government wishes to impose. Each constitutional order has inherited or created a finely balanced mixture of such rights, and the national courts' appreciation of the operation of such constitutional rights can effectively determine the balance of power in any one state. *Drittwirkung* theories[10] which are based on the presence of social power or the sanctity of freedom of contract (protected under Article 2 of the German Basic Law) cannot really help to solve the international protection of the rights found in the European Convention on Human Rights.

Having rejected the usefulness of any *Drittwirkung* theory, we will attempt to suggest ways forward for the Commission and Court of Human Rights. It is suggested that one should start from the premiss that all violations of human rights, whether by state or non-state bodies, implicate the State and are justiciable by the Commission and Court of Human Rights. The late Professor Evrigenis, writing when he was still a member of the European Court of Human Rights, comes very close to endorsing such a position.

Having analysed a number of judgments of the Court concerning Articles 8 and 10, he concludes that, first, the Court 'takes account of changes in the legal and social situation and in the legal and social thinking in Europe' (1982: 135), and secondly, the Court is having increasingly to recognize the fact that 'The growing complexity of the social fabric is obliging the state to take positive action to protect rights and freedoms which, in the traditional view, only required protection against interference by the public authorities' (1982: 136). He suggests that this second conclusion has two aspects. The first is that the traditional division between civil and political rights on the one hand, and economic and social rights on the other, has been weakened. His approach to the second aspect is directly relevant with respect to the present analysis:

The other aspect of human rights protection affected by this case-law is interference which is not directly the result of State activity. Human rights are currently exposed to violation by powers other than the State, and the individual must be protected against this danger. We are here concerned with the effects of human rights on third parties, a question covered by the German term, '*Drittwirkung*'.

---

[10] The most accessible account in English of the competing *Drittwirkung* theories is Lewan (1968); see also the other references in n. 7 above. For some of the more recent developments in Austria the reader is referred to R. Nowak, 'Zur Drittwirkung der Grundrechte: Die österreichische Lage aus rechtsvergleichender Sicht', *Eu. GRZ* (1984), 133. Now that much of the doctrinal debate has cooled down one of the most succinct explanations of the current situation is Kommers (1989: 368).

Although not the author of such interference, the state is still regarded as liable and has a duty to intervene and prevent it. It is not merely answerable for violations committed by itself but also, in a more general sense, for all violations committed within its territory. One could say, indeed, that the modern State has a kind of 'ecological liability' in the human rights field. Be that as it may, this extension of the public authorities' role obliges them to go beyond mere abstention and take positive action. (1982: 137)

According to Evrigenis this liability covers Contracting States when brought before the Convention organs:

Is this part of the defences surrounding human rights covered by the Convention? In its recent judgement in the *Young, James and Webster* case, which was concerned with trade union freedoms, the Court indeed seemed to suggest that this was so. If only by implication, it had already adopted a similar attitude in the *Airey* judgment. In the latter judgment, the respondent State was considered responsible for the fact that the applicant was deprived of effective access to justice, although the main, if not the only, reason for this was the high fees charged by members of the Bar. (1982: 137)

In the next few sections the case-law of the Commission and Court of Human Rights will be examined in some detail. The thesis that the State has a kind of 'ecological liability' for every act which violates human rights on its territory will be tested in the context of a number of selected Articles of the Convention.

It was tentatively suggested in Chapter 4 that there are a number of ways in which the question of the Convention's application to the actions of private bodies can generally arise. Only some are relevant in the context of control by the Convention organs:

1. When applicants are told that their applications are inadmissible, as they themselves have to respect the Articles contained in the Convention.[11]

2. When the State is held responsible for a private violation, due to its failure to legislate or take other preventive action.

3. Where the Commission or Court decides whether a particular body is an organ of the State or a private body.[12] For example, it is still not

---

[11] e.g. Art. 17 and *Kommunistische Partei Deutschland* v. *FRG* (1955–7) 1 Yearbook 223, and similarly where the complainant is told that there are limitations on his or her rights which are 'necessary for the protection of the rights and freedoms of others' (Arts. 8(2), 9(2), 10(2), 11(2), and Art. 2 of Protocol 4).

[12] For some of the unpublished decisions of the Commission which have been declared inadmissible due to the complaint being addressed against a private person see Mikaelsen (1980: 87–93). Other more recent decisions include Applic. 8363/78, decision of 12 May 1980, 20 D. & R. 162 (Lutheran Church); Applic. 9781/82, decision of 14 May 1984, unreported (Roman Catholic Church); Applic. 9444/81, decision of 9 July 1983, unreported (trade union); Applic. 11864/85, decision of 24 Jan. 1986, unreported (corporate bank).

clear whether an abuse by a nationalized industry[13] or state broadcasting company directly incurs the responsibility of the State.[14] Special bodies have often been held not to incur the State's responsibility, especially where the bodies are of an international nature. Other cases include the Commission's denial of the responsibility of the United Kingdom for two particular bodies: the Spandau Prison in Berlin due to the joint nature of the United Kingdom's responsibility,[15] and the Judicial Committee of the Privy Council.[16] Borderline cases have included legal counsel[17] and solicitors, who, although they may be technically defined, as in the United Kingdom, as officers of the Supreme Court, are said by the Commission not to count as officials of the State.[18]

4. Where the State is held responsible due to a national court sanctioning or failing to compensate a private violation.[19] In such cases the Strasbourg organs have a clear link to the state apparatus but the approach may be different because the supervision actually concerns the behaviour of a private actor and its conformity with the standards contained in the Convention.

7.2 PRIVATE DUTIES TO RESPECT THE RIGHTS CONTAINED IN THE CONVENTION

7.2.1 Article 17

Article 17 reads:

Nothing in this Convention may be interpreted as implying for any state, group or person any right to engage in any activity or perform any act aimed at the

---

[13] 'Accordingly there is no call to examine whether . . . the State might also be responsible on the ground that it should be regarded as employer or that British Rail was under its control.' *Young, James and Webster* v. *UK* (1981) Series A, vol. 44, para. 49. The question has however been answered by the ECJ, in the context of which nationalized industries are obliged to respect fundamental rights as contained in unimplemented directives under Community law. See below Ch. 8.

[14] *X and the Association of Z* v. *UK*, Applic. 4515/70, 38 Collection 86; Applic. 3059/67, 28 Collection 89.

[15] *Ilse Hesse* v. *UK*, Applic. 6231/73 (1975) 18 Yearbook 146.

[16] *X* v. *UK*, Applic. 3813/68 (1970) 13 Yearbook 586.

[17] e.g. *X* v. *UK*, Applic. 11819/85, decision of 16 Oct. 1986, para. 1.

[18] *X* v. *UK*, Applic. 6956/75, 8 D. & R. 103.

[19] This question has received some attention: *Judicial Power and Public Liability*, Fifteenth Colloquy on European, Law, held in Bordeaux, 17–19 June 1985 (Strasbourg: Council of Europe, 1986); see esp. 77–117, the report by J. Velu 'Essential Elements for a Legal Regime Governing Public Liability for Judicial Acts', which deals specifically with the Convention. For the way in which national courts have special duties to interpret the duties of private bodies in accordance with Community directives under the *Von Colson* principle, see Ch. 8 below.

destruction of any of the rights and freedoms set forth herein or at their limitation to a greater extent than is provided for in the Convention.

On 17 August 1956 the German Bundesverfassungsgericht (Federal Constitutional Court) made the following declarations concerning the Kommunistische Partei Deutschland (German Communist Party):

1) The Communist Party of Germany is anti-constitutional.
2) The Communist Party of Germany shall be dissolved.
3) The creation of organizations to replace the Communist Party of Germany and the continued existence of existing bodies as substitute organizations shall be prohibited.
4) The property of the Communist Party of Germany shall be confiscated by the Federal Republic of Germany and used in the interests of the community.

An application against Germany was brought before the European Commission of Human Rights alleging breaches of Articles 9, 10, and 11 (freedom of thought, expression, and association).[20] The Commission concluded that the aim of the German Communist Party was to establish in society a Communist system through a proletarian revolution and the dictatorship of the proletariat, and that this involved the destruction of a number of the rights or freedoms contained in the European Convention on Human Rights.

It went on to decide that the organization and aims of the German Communist Party constituted an 'activity' as described by Article 17, so that the German Communist Party could not rely on Articles 9, 10, or 11. In this way, according to the Commission, the German Communist Party (a private organization) finds itself obliged to respect the rights contained in the Convention or face dissolution.

In another application[21] brought by the chairman and vice-chairman of a racialist political party (Nederlandse Volks Unie) the Commission again used Article 17. The chairman had suggested in a pamphlet (which was about to be distributed) the removal from The Netherlands of all non-Whites and migrant workers:

The truth is that the major part of our own population since a long time has had enough of the presence in our country of hundreds of thousands of Surinamers, Turks and other so-called guest workers, who moreover are not at all needed here and that the authorities as servants of our people merely have to see to it that those undesired aliens leave our country as soon as possible.

The chairman was sentenced to prison by the Dutch courts for incitement to racial hatred. The chairman and vice-chairman complained of a violation

---

[20] Applic. 250/57, *Kommunistische Partei Deutschland* v. *FRG* (1955–7) 1 Yearbook 223.
[21] Applics. 8348/78 and 8406/78, *Glimmerveen and Hagenbeek* v. *The Netherlands* (1980) 18 D. & R. 187.

of their freedom of expression under Article 10 and also of the invalidation of their list of candidates by the Central Voting Board of Amsterdam and The Hague, which they alleged constituted a breach of Article 3 of the First Protocol. The Commission declared that due to Article 17 the applications were incompatible with the provisions of the Convention. Racial discrimination is prohibited under the Convention through a combination of Articles 14 and 3. Those who attempt to destroy this right not to be discriminated against on grounds of race will not be able to rely on the rights set out in the Convention.

However, it is only when the Convention is used as a tool by someone, to threaten the rights and freedoms set out in the Convention, that Article 17 is used against them. Where the aim of the applicant and the rights claimed are separate, then Article 17 has no relevance. So in *Lawless* v. *Ireland*[22] the alleged IRA activities of the applicant did not deprive him of his right to rely on Articles 5 (security of the person) and 6 (the right to a fair trial).[23]

Lastly, under Article 17, we might mention that Sir James Fawcett, the former President of the Commission, in considering the right to assembly of the Christians against Racism and Fascism in their application before the Commission,[24] differentiated the Christians from the National Front, who had threatened a counter-demonstration. He cites the Commission: 'Whilst it was clear that the applicant association [CARF] had wholly peaceful intentions it is nevertheless true that its statutory purposes were expressly directed against the National Front policies, and it could therefore not be excluded that the proposed procession could also give rise to disorder' (1987: 276). Fawcett continues: 'If the reasoning here is that the National Front might counter-demonstrate, causing disorder, it *alone* should be banned under Article 17' (1987: 276; emphasis added). Therefore Article 17 may be relevant to justify discriminatory treatment in the enjoyment of one's rights.

7.2.2 The rights of others

It is not only under Article 17 that applicants may find the Convention being used against them. Articles 8, 9, 10, 11, and Article 2 of the Fourth Protocol refer to restrictions on the rights contained in the Articles, where such restrictions 'are in accordance with law and are necessary in a

---

[22] (1960–1) Series A, vol. 3.

[23] See also *de Becker* v. *Belgium*, Applic. 214/56, opinion of Commission, 8 Jan. 1960, Series B, vol. 2, where the Commission found that the applicant's pro-Nazi views related to his past and that there was no evidence that he would abuse his freedom of expression so as to come within the prohibited activity outlined in Art. 17.

[24] *Christians against Racism and Fascism* v. *UK*, Applic. 8191/78, 17 D. & R. 93.

democratic society . . . for the protection of the *rights and freedoms of others*' (emphasis added).

In *Groppera Radio AG and Others* v. *Switzerland*[25] the applicants were a Swiss company broadcasting from the Pizzo Groppera, an Italian mountain near the Swiss border. The programmes, which consisted of music, information, and commercials, were retransmitted through cable networks in Switzerland. In 1984 a Swiss federal ordinance prohibited Swiss cable companies from rebroadcasting from transmitters which did not satisfy international telecommunications rules. When the European Court of Human Rights had to rule on the aim of the Government's interference it was accepted *inter alia* that the ordinance pursued a legitimate aim, 'the protection of the rights of others', as it was designed to ensure pluralism (in particular as regards information) by regulating the fair allocation of frequencies. This case confirms that applicants can be denied the protection of the Convention where their action threatens 'the rights of others'.[26]

Even where the phrase 'the rights of others' does not appear in the Article relied on, the Commission has denied a complainant his right on the ground that he was obliged to observe one of the other rights found in the Convention. A German lawyer who had been obliged to work as a legal aid counsel requested an advance on his fee. When this was refused he complained to the European Commission of Human Rights, basing his application on Article 4(2) (no one shall be required to perform forced or compulsory labour). The Commission replied in the following terms:

The Convention itself recognizes the necessity of providing for free legal assistance (see Article 6(3)(c)). It is clear therefore that the obligation of practising lawyers to perform duties as legal aid counsel for which they receive reasonable remuneration can never be considered as constituting forced or compulsory labour in the sense of Article 4(2) of the Convention.[27]

---

[25] Judgment of 28 Mar. 1990, Series A, vol. 173.

[26] The relevant paragraphs of the Court's judgment are paras. 69–70. See also A. Clapham, in Cassese and Clapham (1990: 153–5), where the case *Applic. 8416/79* v. *UK* is cited as evidence for the proposition that an individual's rights can be restricted where they conflict with the rights of others to the same right; in this case a husband was denied an injunction preventing his wife from aborting their child, as his claim under Art. 8 (respect for private and family life) was rejected by the Commission, which stated that the applicant had to respect the 'rights of others' under Art. 8(2), i.e. his wife's own right to privacy. In the case of *Open Door and Dublin Well Woman* v. *Ireland*, Series A, vol. 264, the European Court of Human Rights decided that it was unnecessary to decide whether the term 'others' extends to the unborn (at para. 63). In this case they accepted that the Irish law in question pursued the legitimate aim of the protection of morals, but that the Supreme Court's restriction on information about abortions abroad was disproportionate to this aim.

[27] *Applic. 7641/76, X and Y* v. *FRG* (1978) 10 D. & R. 224 at 230 (quoted in van Dijk and van Hoof (1990: 18–19); see also *Van der Mussele* v. *Belgium* (1983) Series A, vol. 76.

7.2.3 *Private actors 'estopped' in Strasbourg*

The last two sections demonstrate that, in certain circumstances, private individuals may have duties under the Convention and these duties may operate to deny the applicants' rights in Strasbourg when their applications come before the European Commission and Court of Human Rights. These cases show that the right-threatening activities of private individuals do not operate in isolation from the European Convention. If a group's right to freedom of expression is removed by a national court, then that group loses its right to complain at the international level if its conduct was at variance with the values found in the Convention. Of course the private groups are not the respondents in Strasbourg, but the Strasbourg organs do have to consider to what extent private groups have to respect the Convention. This last point is important for two reasons. First, the Commission and Court admit the philosophical possibility that private groups have to respect the rights guaranteed by the Convention; and second, any case-law on this topic may be very relevant for national courts should they have to decide on a case brought directly against a private body.[28]

7.3 POSITIVE OBLIGATIONS AND STATE RESPONSIBILITY

The next two ways in which the Convention is applied in Strasbourg to private behaviour arise out of what can be loosely termed 'state responsibility'; although it should be stated at the outset that there is no intention here to refer to the international law on state responsibility, which is not, and should not be, considered appropriate in the context of the European Convention (see Chapter 4.3.3).[29] One of the main advocates of an extension of state responsibility, in this context, so as to cover the

---

[28] See Ch. 4.2, point (5), and Ch. 10.

[29] Compare Forde (1985: 264–80), and Warbrick (1983: 93–6), who both lean towards using international law concepts of state responsibility, acts of state, and state organs. But the public international law framework, on its own, should not be followed for all the reasons given in Ch. 4: the Convention does not primarily operate at the inter-state level, as it grants remedies to individuals; effective protection demands that the Convention control private actors; the Convention takes effect in the national order of the Contracting Parties and constitutes a kind of European *ordre public*; a public/private dichotomy is arbitrary, unreasonably discriminatory, and perpetrates the exclusion of certain kinds of violations of rights which are then 'forgotten' (domestic violence, child abuse, discrimination against women in employment). For the possible convergence of traditional state responsibility with the application of human rights in the private sphere see Ch. 4.3.1.1.1. But one should bear in mind that the threshold must be different, as a finding of a violation of the ECHR does not have the same consequences as incurring state responsibility under public international law. Where there is state responsibility for an internationally wrongful act another State will be entitled to take countermeasures. No such reciprocity exists within the Convention system.

acts of individuals unconnected with the State has been Professor Sperduti, a Commissioner and former Vice-President of the European Commission of Human Rights. In a submission to the European Court of Human Rights in the *Young, James and Webster* case he stated that:

La théorie dite de la *Drittwirkung*, vue sous l'angle d'une théorie pouvant porter dans le domaine des droits fondamentaux aussi sur des répercussions d'ordre interne de certains traités internationaux, trouve un fondement rationnel du point de vue de droit international dans la doctrine d'origine grotienne de la responsabilité internationale des États à la suite d'atteintes portées par des particuliers à des droits reconnus au niveau international.[30]

Sperduti's arguments from international law rely not only on Grotius' concepts of 'receptus' and 'patientia' but also on the duty of due diligence towards foreigners. He points out that Contracting States under the Convention have duties to all persons under their jurisdiction.

The pleadings by Sperduti are perhaps the most vigorous defence of the *Drittwirkung* of the Convention so far. Sperduti goes beyond a comparison with international law and appeals to logic. He suggests that logic requires that no line can be drawn between active and permissive legislation. He gives the example of a State which allows private groups to endanger the liberty and security of individuals, and asks rhetorically if this is an example of a violation of Article 5 ECHR.[31] He further appeals to the Court to follow its own case-law, which demands that interpretations of the Convention should be aimed at achieving the goals of the Convention rather than limiting the responsibilities of the Contracting Parties.[32] The resulting judgment of the Court in this case opened the way for the application of the Convention in the private sphere, as it bases responsibility on the existence of legislation rather than on any state link with the action complained of.

Several Articles are of interest under this heading. Particularly interesting is Article 3 and the emerging idea that States may be responsible for the actions of autonomous groups of terrorists, or even for the actions of other non-contracting States. From a procedural point of view a non-contracting State is in the same juridical position as a private body. It may not be a respondent before the Convention machinery.

7.3.1 Article 3: Threats abroad, at home, and at school

Article 3 reads: 'No one shall be subjected to torture or to inhuman or degrading treatment or punishment.' There is a principle that extradition

---

[30] *Young, James and Webster* v. *UK* (1984) Series B, vol. 39 209–15 at 213.
[31] At 212.
[32] At 211, citing the *Wemhoff* case (1968) Series A, vol. 7, p. 23, para. 8.

or refusal of admission which results in an individual going to a country where he or she will suffer inhuman or degrading treatment by another State activates the responsibility of the extraditing State.[33] This has now been applied by the Court in the case of extradition to a non-contracting State, the United States.

7.3.1.1 The *Soering* case[34]

This important judgment by the Court establishes that Contracting States have a responsibility regarding torture or inhuman or degrading treatment or punishment inflicted on individuals outside their jurisdiction. Such responsibility arises should the Contracting State extradite a fugitive when there is a real risk of treatment contrary to Article 3 in the receiving State. This extension of responsibility to extra-jurisdictional acts was contested by the respondent Government in this case, but the Court's judgment finally confirms the Commission's earlier case-law.[35]

It is therefore now beyond doubt that States can be held responsible under the Convention even where the action which is proscribed by the Convention is not carried out by that State's own agents. However, two ambiguities remain: first, which Articles does this new doctrine cover? And second, is the State responsible for the acts of private groups or individuals operating in the other (non-contracting) State?

Before addressing these questions we should briefly outline the details of the *Soering* case in order to be able fully to appreciate the extraordinary factual circumstances of the case and the exceptional nature of the Court's judgment. Mr Soering, a German national, was detained in prison in the United Kingdom awaiting extradition to the United States to stand trial for murder committed in Virginia. Mr Soering, together with his girlfriend, had planned to kill the latter's parents and, following a row with the parents, inflicted stab and slash wounds on them with a knife. The parents both died, and Soering and his girlfriend were indicted on charges of murder. Soering was 18 at the time of the killings, and psychiatric evidence was presented on his behalf which pointed to his suggestibility at the time of the offence, as well as the overbearing influence which his girlfriend had had on him. Soering's girlfriend Ms Haysom was extradited to the United States and, after pleading guilty as an accessory to the murder of her parents, was sentenced to ninety years' imprisonment.

---

[33] *Applic 1802/63* v. *FRG* (1963) 6 Yearbook 462.

[34] Judgment of 19 July 1989, Series A, vol. 161.

[35] Applic. 10308/83, *Altun* v. *FRG*, decision of 3 May 1983, 36 D. & R. 209–35; Applic. 10078/82, *M.* v. *France*, decision of 13 Dec. 1984, 41 D. & R. 103; Applic. 10479/83, *Kirkwood* v. *UK*, decision of 12 Mar. 1984, 37 D. & R. 158–91; as well as the Commission's report in the *Soering* case, annexed to the Court's judgment, Series A, vol. 161.

The United States' request for the extradition of Soering was met with a request by the British authorities that the United States give an assurance, or, if this were not possible, recommend, that the death penalty would not be carried out. This request was answered with an affidavit, sworn by the Attorney for Bedford County, that should Soering be convicted of capital murder, a representation would be made in the name of the United Kingdom to the trial judge that the death penalty should not be imposed or carried out.

The British Secretary of State signed the warrant ordering Soering's surrender to the United States' authorities, but Soering was not transferred, as he had applied to the European Commission of Human Rights and interim measures had been ordered by the Commission under Rule 36 of its Rules of Procedure.[36] Soering alleged that the 'death row phenomenon' which he might be exposed to in the State of Virginia amounted to inhuman and degrading treatment. The United Kingdom contended that Article 3 should not be interpreted to impose responsibility for acts which occur outside its jurisdiction. They stated that surrendering a fugitive could not come within the wording of Article 3, which prohibits 'subjecting' anyone to torture or to inhuman or degrading treatment or punishment.

The Court rejected the United Kingdom's argument. However, one should note that the United Kingdom's responsibility in this case stems from the special nature of Article 3. First, the Court stressed the importance of interpreting the Convention so as to ensure its safeguards are 'practical and effective',[37] and that any interpretation has to be consistent with 'the general spirit of the Convention, an instrument designed to maintain and promote the ideals and values of a democratic society'.[38] The Court then explained the special nature of Article 3: no derogation is allowed under Article 15; similar provisions are to be found in the International Covenant on Civil and Political Rights (1966) and the American Convention on Human Rights (1969). Abhorrence of torture in the context of extradition is reflected in the UN Convention against Torture and Other Cruel, Inhuman, or Degrading Treatment or Punishment (Article 3 of this Convention prohibits extradition where there are substantial grounds for believing the person would be subjected to torture). The Court referred to the preamble to the European Convention on Human Rights, where it mentions the governments of European countries' 'common heritage of political traditions, ideals, freedom and the rule of law'. The Court concluded that there was an inherent right in the European Convention

---

[36] See Ch. 2.1 for details concerning this rule. The Court similarly ordered interim measures under Rule 36 of its own Rules of Procedure.

[37] Para. 87 of the judgment.

[38] At para. 87 of the judgment, which quotes from the *Kjeldsen, Busk Madsen and Pedersen* judgment of 7 Dec. 1976, Series A, vol. 23, p. 27.

on Human Rights not to be extradited where there were substantial grounds for believing that the person would be in danger of being subjected to torture. The Court continued: 'This inherent obligation not to extradite also extends to cases in which the fugitive would be faced in the receiving state by a real risk of exposure to inhuman or degrading treatment or punishment proscribed by [Article 3 ECHR].'[39]

The judgment then went on to consider whether there was a real risk of a death sentence, and whether the death row phenomenon would make extradition a breach of Article 3 in the specific circumstances of the applicant. The Court concluded that such a risk existed, and that the conditions of the applicant's eventual detention on death row could go beyond the threshold set by Article 3. The Court's judgment therefore held that the United Kingdom would be responsible for a violation of Article 3 should Soering be extradited to the United States.

Soering also complained about the absence of legal aid for his trial in Virginia. He relied on Article 6(3)(c) of the Convention. The Commission's report rejected the applicability of Article 6(3)(c) in such circumstances:

The Commission recalls that it can only examine complaints directed against one of the States Parties to the Convention. In this respect, the Commission points out that the respondent Government could not be held directly responsible under the Convention for the absence of legal aid under Virginia law, a matter entirely within the responsibility of the United States of America. Nor could the proposed extradition of the applicant give rise to the responsibility of the respondent Government under Article 6(3)(c) of the Convention.[40]

Nevertheless the Court did not follow this reasoning and held:

The Court does not exclude that an issue might exceptionally be raised under Article 6 by an extradition decision in circumstances where the fugitive has suffered or risks suffering a flagrant denial of a fair trial in the requesting country.[41]

In the instant case the Court found there was no such risk.

It is worth mentioning that Soering was eventually extradited to the United States. An exchange of diplomatic notes between the United Kingdom and the United States established that United States law would prohibit Soering's prosecution for capital murder and hence the imposition of the death penalty.[42]

---

[39] At para. 88 of the judgment.
[40] At para. 156 of the Commission's report.
[41] At para. 113 of the judgment.
[42] See Breitenmoser and Wilms (1990: 872). The Committee of Ministers in its supervisory role under Art. 54 ECHR was satisfied that the UK had had regard to its obligation to abide by the Court's judgment under Art. 53 ECHR. See Res. DH (90)8 of 12 Mar. 1990, reproduced in *Information Sheet No. 26* (Strasbourg: Council of Europe) at 115. Details of the diplomatic notes are to be found in an appendix to the Resolution.

In answering the first of the questions posed at the beginning of this section, we have to conclude that States may be held responsible if extradition means a risk of Article 3 being violated; in special circumstances Article 6 may be breached by an extradition, and the Court did not limit the application of the doctrine of extra-territorial responsibility to these two Articles. It is suggested that the Court's approach to this question is the more coherent one. If a State can be responsible for a non-contracting Party's action in violation of Article 3 then, theoretically, it may be responsible for violations of another Article, notwithstanding the special nature of Article 3. One can easily imagine extradition leading to risks to life, liberty, privacy, and property, to list but a few of the major rights protected under the Convention.

Turning to our second question concerning the threats from private individuals, the response is less clear. Soering had complained not only that the delays in the procedures were traumatic, but also that he expected to be the victim of violence and sexual abuse because of his age, colour, and nationality.[43] In fact, according to the psychiatric report of Dr D. Somekh: 'the applicant's dread of extreme physical violence and homosexual abuse from other inmates in death row in Virginia is in particular having a profound psychological effect on him.'[44]

The Court did not find it necessary to determine the reliability of Soering's evidence concerning homosexual abuse and physical attack on death row. From this one could extrapolate that such attacks by private persons are not automatically considered outside the scope of a judgment on the applicability of Article 3, although, in the end, one should admit that the issue would probably have turned on whether the state authorities contributed to this violence by failing to prevent inter-inmate attacks.[45]

It is suggested that, even though the Court started with the prohibition on extradition where there is a risk of *torture*,[46] the fact that it referred to the dynamics of the Convention to include a prohibition in these circumstances on other inhuman treatment negates the chances of a restrictive interpretation by the Court which would limit Article 3 to the acts of state agents. Although this issue has not been expressly dealt with by the Court several applications to the Commission[47] suggest that Article 3

[43] At paras. 64 and 105 of the judgment.

[44] At para. 25 of the judgment.

[45] See para. 63 of the judgment: 'when not in their cells, death row inmates are housed in a common area called "the pod". The guards are not within this area and remain in a box outside. In the event of disturbance or inter-inmate assault, the guards are not allowed to intervene until instructed to do so by the ranking officer present.'

[46] The Court referred to Art. 3 of the Convention against Torture and Other Cruel, Inhuman or Degrading Treatment or Punishment; this Article is limited to torture and torture is defined in Art. 1, which limits it to acts 'inflicted at the instigation of, or with the acquiescence of, a public official or person acting in an official capacity'.

[47] *X* v. *FRG*, Applic. 7216/75, 5 D. & R. 137; *X* v. *UK*, Applic. 8581/79, 29 D. & R. 48; *Altun* v. *FRG*, Applic. 10308/83, 36 D. & R. 209.

can be extended to cover the situation where, even if the receiving State pledges humane treatment for the extradited person, there is a risk that a private/non-state terrorist organization will seek out and assassinate or torture the individual. (A similar situation is that of a police informer who is extradited to the country where he or she did their informing and is therefore at grave risk from those who were punished as a result of the information given to the police.)

The summary of the Commission's decision in the *Altun* v. *Federal Republic of Germany* application states:

A person's extradition may, in certain exceptional circumstances, be contrary to the Convention, notably Article 3, where there are serious reasons to believe that the individual will be subjected, in the receiving State, to treatment proscribed by this Article. This may be so even if the danger does not emanate from public authorities for whom the receiving State is responsible.[48]

In this case the applicant was a Turkish national in detention pending extradition to Turkey. The applicant had been involved in politics in Turkey and had founded the Ankara Liseli Devrimci Genclik Dernegi (Association of Revolutionary Secondary Students) in 1978. He had also been a member of the outlawed DEV-GENC federation since 1970. In 1980 proceedings were issued against the applicant concerning the founding of the Association of Revolutionary Secondary Students, and he left Turkey. In 1982 the Ankara Interpol requested that the German authorities detain the applicant pending his extradition. He was at the time wanted for instigating the murder of the Customs Minister. The applicant requested political asylum but the German courts found no obstacles to extradition. The important factor to bear in mind in this case is that the extradition would have been to another Contracting Party and that the situation was covered by another Council of Europe Convention— the European Convention on Extradition. In the decision on admissibility the Commission states:

The Commission recalls firstly that extradition as such is not one of the matters covered by the Convention (cf. Application No. 7256/75, DR 8, p. 161). The High Contracting Parties remain as a rule free to conclude and apply extradition agreements and conventions. Increased co-operation as regards mutual assistance in legal matters is an area where Council of Europe activity has been fruitful.[49]

It is in this context that the Commission goes on to state that a finding of admissibility does not imply that the Commission implicitly condemns Turkey (another Council of Europe Member State) for political persecution or threatening torture or other inhuman or degrading treatment:

---

[48] *Altun* v. *FRG*, Applic. 10308/83, 36 D. & R. 209.
[49] At para. 3 of the decision on admissibility, annexed to the Commission's report of 7 Mar. 1984.

In this respect the Commission emphasises that only the existence of an objective danger to the person extradited may be considered. The finding that such a danger exists does not necessarily involve the liability of the Government of the State requesting extradition. The Commission moreover has taken account, in cases of expulsion, of a danger not arising out of the authorities of the State receiving the person concerned.[50]

If we examine this idea without the extradition factor, it could be concluded that States may be responsible for violations of Convention guarantees by terrorist organizations in their own country. In this way a State could be called on to protect, say, a socialist politician from the attacks of a right-wing terrorist organization. To what extent States actually condone or support terrorism is very difficult to determine.[51] Even more difficult is to try to determine how culpable States are for their internal terrorism, by virtue of their economic or political policies. It would be a brave court which tried to determine whether the British Government, through its policies, is indirectly responsible for the IRA.

It may be that it is not that States are 'responsible' for the activities of terrorist groups either at home or abroad, but that Article 3 grants to some extent a very limited 'right of asylum'.[52] The current methodology of the Commission and Court seems to be to fix state responsibility through the actual decision concerning *refoulement* rather than to condemn States for failing to prevent or control the activities of dangerous private groups. However, when we move away from the context of extradition and asylum seekers it may be that there could be state responsibility for dangers posed by private groups or individuals, and in some circumstances States may even be liable for failing to prevent violent attacks by private

---

[50] At para. 5 of the decision on admissibility. Note, the Commission refers to two of its own earlier decisions where the point had been raised although not decided: *Applic. 7216/75 v. FRG*, 20 May 1976, 5 D. & R. 137 (the applicant alleged plots by Palestinian commandos in Lebanon; however, the Commission simply states: 'It is not necessary to decide here whether the Commission, when examining a case of this kind from the standpoint of Article 3, may take into account an alleged danger arising not from public authorities but from autonomous groups' (at 143)); and *Applic. 8581/79 v. UK*, 6 Mar. 1980, 29 D. & R. 48, again concerning extradition to Turkey of a political activist; in this case, however, the applicant had been a member of the MHP (Milliyetei Haraket Partisi), an extreme right-wing party which had been feuding with an extreme left-wing party, the THKO (Turk Halk Kurtukus Ordusu). The applicant's main involvement had been as an informer, and according to the Commission's decision: 'the applicant fears for his safety if he is returned to Turkey as he is not confident in view of the many sectarian murders which have already occurred that the Turkish authorities can adequately protect him.' No conclusion was reached on the question: 'Does [Art. 3] also apply when the danger does not arise from the public authorities but from an autonomous group against which the authorities allegedly do not protect the individual concerned?' (summary of the Commission's decision).

[51] See Cassese (1984: 475–98).

[52] Nevertheless, the Court has stressed that the 'right to political asylum is not contained in either the Convention or its Protocols'. See *Case of Vilvarajah and Others v. UK*, judgment of 30 Oct. 1991, Series A, vol. 215, paras. 102–3.

bodies or individuals. There may nevertheless be an important difference between responsibility for *refoulement* and liability following a private violation. As the Dutch Government argued in the *X and Y* case, in the case of *refoulement* the prohibited treatment can only take place because of the *refoulement*, whereas in the case of an individual violation one cannot say that the attack or violation would definitely not have taken place had the proposed governmental preventive measures been in place.[53] So far the Commission and Court have not directly addressed such arguments concerning causation. However, the logic of this argument permeates the decisions, and applicants have only succeeded where preventive measures would have been very likely to have had an effect.[54] One could formulate this thesis as a 'but for' test: States will be liable under the Convention where, 'but for' the absence of legislation prohibiting the behaviour complained of, the violation of human rights would probably not have occurred. Of course this thesis does not solve the problem, but it does inch us nearer to understanding the limits of the application of the European Convention on Human Rights to the private sphere at the international level.

7.3.1.2 Transsexuals

The case of transsexuals is another area which raises questions under Article 3. Transsexuals may allege that they suffer degrading treatment due to the behaviour of private persons. They may encounter problems in daily life when trying to use a cheque book or other documents which show their original sex or forenames. This has been claimed to violate the Convention at the international level as a result of the State's refusal to recognize their actual sexual identity.[55] This issue has now been decided

---

[53] Pleading of Mr Korthals Altes, Series B, p. 91.

[54] In *X and Y* v. *The Netherlands*, Series A, vol. 91, it was stressed by the applicants' representatives that: 'It is, alas, well known to certain men, that they will go unpunished if they abuse such women' (Professor Alkema (representative of the applicants) at 85 of the Series B publication of the proceedings). The case is dealt with in more detail below. Similarly in the *Young, James and Webster* case, one can assume that had the appropriate legislation been in place the violation of the applicants' rights would have been prevented or compensated (either by the union and employers declining to insist on union membership, or through an action in the domestic courts).

[55] See Applic. 6699/74, *X* v. *FRG*, 11 D. & R. 16. This case resulted in a friendly settlement and so the matter was never finally decided. The case is cited by Warbrick (1983: 109), who continues: 'just as it was for the right to life, the question will be whether the State has taken effective action to prevent the torture or inhuman or degrading treatment and, possibly, whether it has taken sufficiently vigorous steps to enforce its law, a breach of the law having occurred.' See also the report of the Commission in *Van Oosterwijk* v. *Belgium*, report of 1 Mar. 1979, Series B, which suggests that an issue could arise under Arts. 3 in a situation where a transsexual is denied legal recognition of a change of sex. The Court found that domestic remedies had not been exhausted.

in favour of one individual by the Court in *B.* v. *France*.[56] But the Court limited its judgment to Article 8 and the specific situation in France. It held that there was as yet no consensus between the Member States of the Council of Europe to persuade the Court to reach opposite conclusions to those it had reached in the two previous cases against the United Kingdom.[57] Nevertheless, the case represents an important recognition by the Court that inaction on the part of the State can violate one's right to respect for private and family life.[58]

The Court did not address the question under Article 3 because the applicant did not raise it. However, we should note that the complaint was declared admissible under Article 3 even though the Commission found by fifteen votes to three that the situation did not attain the requisite minimum degree of severity for an infringement of Article 3. Nevertheless they did take into account that the 'situation thus creates embarrassment for her in respect of third persons to whom she is constantly forced to reveal her particular situation'. The evocation of 'third persons' is reminiscent of the *Drittwirkung* concept with which we opened this chapter.

A finding of a violation in the above case would have been consistent with the 'but for' thesis outlined above: 'but for' the decision not to change the applicant's documents, the applicant would not be humiliated and degraded by private individuals. The fact that this was in the end categorized as violating the applicant's right to respect for private life does not affect the theoretical underpinnings of the result.

7.3.1.3 The *X and Y* case

The issue of human rights in the private sphere arose again in *X and Y* v. *The Netherlands*. (This case is dealt with in detail in the section on Article 8 as the actual judgment only concerned this Article rather than Article 3.) The discussion concerning the applicability of Article 3 to the actions of private individuals is however of some interest here. The Commission's report in this case gives a rather cryptic response on the applicability of Article 3. (As will be seen later the case concerned the lack of criminal sanctions for sexual abuse of mentally retarded girls over the age of 16.) The Commission states:

However, the Commission does not consider it necessary to establish whether the mental suffering inflicted on the second applicant was of such a nature and had

---

[56] Judgment of 25 Mar. 1992.

[57] *Rees*, Series A, vol. 106; *Cossey*, Series A, vol. 184.

[58] Where the positive obligations actually have implications for resources, or the decisions are more complex than merely altering the sex entry on someone's papers, then judges may be more reluctant to find a violation of the Convention. Compare Ch. 6.1.3 above.

reached such a degree of intensity as to bring it within the scope of the above provision, since in any event the preliminary question whether the Netherlands Government could be held responsible for such treatment must be answered in the negative.

In reaching this conclusion, the Commission found it necessary in the present case to distinguish the issue under Article 3 clearly from the issue under Article 8. In the latter, it has held that the failure by the Netherlands legislator to include a particular category of especially vulnerable persons in an otherwise comprehensive system of criminal protection of the sexual integrity of vulnerable persons constituted a violation of the Convention. However, sexual abuse and inhuman or degrading treatment—even though they may overlap in individual cases—are by no means congruent concepts. The 'gap' in the law relating to the protection of the sexual integrity of vulnerable persons cannot therefore be assimilated to a 'gap' in the protection of persons against inhuman or degrading treatment.

In the absence of a close and direct link between the above mentioned failure by the Netherlands legislator with regard to the protection of the sexual integrity of vulnerable persons on the one hand and the field of protection covered by Article 3 of the Convention on the other, the Commission concludes, by fifteen votes against one, that Article 3 has not been violated in the present case.[59]

These paragraphs introduce a number of new factors which operate in a rather confusing way.[60] First one addresses the 'preliminary question' of the responsibility of the Netherlands Government and one finds that it is not responsible for the treatment in question, but we are not told why. Then we are told that sexual abuse and inhuman treatment are overlapping but not congruent concepts, and so the finding that the Government is responsible for the violation of the applicant's privacy cannot be likened to a gap in the State's protection from inhuman treatment, even though the Commission has refused to consider whether the treatment is inhuman or degrading. Finally, we are told that for Article 3 to be operative one needs a 'close and direct link' between the failure of the legislator regarding the protection of the sexual integrity of vulnerable persons and the 'field of protection covered by Article 3'. It is not clear what a 'close and direct link' might be, but it would seem that the link needs to be less 'close and direct' in the case of Article 8. What the Commission means by the 'field of protection covered by Article 3' is equally cryptic. Some clues can be gleaned from the submissions of the Commission's delegate before the Court.

Professor Trechsel, as the Commission's delegate, admits at the beginning of his submissions that: 'It may also be assumed that this interference

[59] Paras. 94–6 of the Commission's report.
[60] See also the dissenting opinion on this question by Mr Tenekides, who sees no reason to distinguish Art. 3 from Art. 8 in this way; indeed he suggests that 'the reasoning adopted by the Court in the *Marckx* case in regard to Article 8 is all the more valid in regard to Article 3'.

caused severe mental suffering and amounted to treatment contrary to Article 3 of the Convention.'[61] Therefore private action is not *per se* outside the scope of Article 3. What the Commission seems to suggest is that the finding of a violation relates not to the actual physical violation inflicted on the victim but to the omission of the legislator. The omission in this case related to a failure to protect private and family life (Article 8) rather than a failure to prevent torture and inhuman or degrading treatment (Article 3). As Professor Trechsel points out: 'Nor has it been alleged that Netherlands law provides insufficient protection against Article 3 as such.'[62]

One might conclude that the 'close and direct link' requirement is similar to the 'but for' test. In other words, although it is conceded that the actual behaviour complained of is a breach of the standard outlined in Article 3, it cannot be concluded that, *but for* the omission of the government in the field of application of Article 3, the attack would not have happened. It is the government's *omission* which falls more squarely within the scope of Article 8 than within the field of protection of Article 3.[63]

Professor Trechsel outlines another difference between protection under Article 8 and under Article 3. He suggests that 'the notion of torture as well as that of inhuman or degrading treatment implies an element of intent'.[64] He accepts that there could be debate whether intent is needed at the governmental level or merely at the level of the actual treatment, but concludes: 'It is conceivable in my submission that a violation of Article 3 is found in a case where private persons commit torture and no remedy at all is provided for the victim.'[65] He continues that in the present case there was no evidence of intent to humiliate either on the part of the attacker or on the part of the government.[66]

---

[61] At 67 of the Series B publication of the proceedings.

[62] At 72 of the Series B publication of the proceedings.

[63] Even though governmental omissions might be held to invoke reponsibility under Art. 3 in different circumstances (*Ireland* v. *UK*); see Trechsel at 71 of the Series B publication of the proceedings.

[64] At 72 of the Series B publication of the proceedings.

[65] Ibid.

[66] It may be this sort of approach which influenced the Commission's Committee (established under Art. 20 ECHR) in Applic. 14641/89, *Van Volsem* v. *Belgium*, 9 May 1990, reported in RUDH (1990) 384. This application concerned a claim that action by an electricity company in the form of reducing the power and cutting off the supply as a reaction to the applicant's arrears had led to a violation of the applicant's rights under Arts. 3, 8, and 6(1). As regards the imputation of the acts of the company ('une "intercommunale mixte" regroupant des personnes de droit public et de droit privé') the Commission found it did not have to consider this matter as the application would be dismissed for different reasons. Concerning Article 3 the Commission stated that 'la suspension ou les menaces de suspension des fournitures d'électricité n'atteignaient pas le niveau d'humiliation ou d'avilissement requis pour qu'il y ait un traitement inhumain ou dégradant'. One might ask whether the Committee would have reacted differently had the *Government* cut off the electricity as a reaction to the applicant's *behaviour*. The material conditions of the applicant

It is respectfully suggested that this reasoning cannot now be followed for two reasons. First, the *Soering* case would now seem to suggest that intent is irrelevant. The Article 3 threshold may be reached even where no intent is present but the victim's subjective fears mean that the particular circumstances give rise to a violation of Article 3. Second, this approach contradicts the Commission's earlier submissions concerning governmental responsibility, where Professor Trechsel states:

> I wish to stress that this is an issue of objective responsibility and even if the Court were to conclude, as the Commission has done in its report under Article 31, that the Government must indeed be held responsible, this does not mean that anyone is to blame. In applying the Convention, the emphasis is not on anybody's culpability but *on* the position of the individual in need of protection. As the Court has pointed out in the judgments *Zimmermann and Steiner* and *Foti and Others*, failure to protect individual rights does not have to be imputed to any specific authority but is a matter of the international responsibility of the State.

If the Convention system is really orientated towards taking such a 'victim perspective' it would seem incongruous to suggest that for Article 3, the Article which protects the victim from the most profound and lasting effects, the concern shifts from the victim's fears to the attacker's intentions. If the Convention is really concerned to protect the victim the supervisory organs should not start to question whether a rapist was driven by a desire to humiliate the victim, or whether the motive was purely sexual gratification. The effect on the victim will not necessarily be greater in one case than in the other.

The concern with intent under Article 3 would seem to be influenced by notions from criminal law. Violation of the norms of Article 3 have been equated with the crime of torture, and therfore it becomes necessary to look for the *mens rea* element of the crime and overcome a high burden of proof—to prove beyond reasonable doubt that the accused was guilty of the crime. Such an analogy is misplaced. In the operation of the Convention system in Strasbourg there is no danger of committing an innocent individual to a long prison sentence for a crime which that individual did not actually commit. In the Convention system the choice is between condemning or absolving a *State*. There is no risk that the State will be incarcerated; the worst fate that could befall it in the present

would have been the same. Although the fact that the actor was a commercial operator enforcing its contract rights was not tackled head on it may have had some influence. This decision has been seized on by commentators. Professor Antonio Cassese (1991) upbraids the Committee for not putting such an important question, the applicability of Article 3 to socio-economic conditions, before the full plenary Commission. He also asks us to consider whether the ethos behind the Convention may be emerging as neo-liberal rather than Welfare State orientated. Professor Fédéric Sudre laments the lost opportunity of dealing with the challenge of poverty. In addition he finds the Commission's failure to recognize that there might be positive obligations for the State under Art. 8 'scandalous' (1990).

case would be the embarrassment of a condemnation for an omission or gap in the legislative protection which it offers.

It is suggested that the better approach is consistently to take a 'victim's perspective', to decide if the act complained of comes within the aim of the Article in question, and then decide whether 'but for' the omission of the State the act would probably not have occurred.

7.3.1.4 Corporal punishment in private schools

Following the Court's finding of a violation by the United Kingdom in the *Campbell and Cosans* case the United Kingdom Government has only amended the relevant legislation to outlaw corporal punishment in state schools.[67] Arguing against the applicability of the Convention to corporal punishment in private schools Forde has pointed to the following passage in the Court's judgment in *Campbell and Cosans*:

the state has assumed responsibility for forming general [educational] policy and the schools attended by the applicant's children were state schools. Discipline is an integral, even indispensable part of any educational system, with the result that the functions assumed by the state in Scotland must be taken to extend to questions of discipline in general.[68]

The Court observes that when a teacher 'administers corporal punishment he is exercising not a power delegated to him by the State but a power vested in him by the Common Law by virtue of his status as a teacher'. According to Forde this last passage suggests that 'corporal punishment in private schools would not fall foul of the Convention's provisions' (1985: 274). On the contrary, it would seem to suggest the opposite. The Court would seem to be saying that state responsibility has not been triggered by the teacher acting as a state agent (as the teacher's authority derives from the Common Law) but by an educational policy on discipline which is ultimately the responsibility of the State. The reference to the fact that the applicant's children were in state schools does not exclude the possibility that in a case involving private schools the court would conclude (as it did in the *Young, James and Webster* case) that 'it was the domestic law in force at the relevant time that made lawful the treatment of which the applicants complained. The responsibility of the respondent State for any breach of the Convention is thus engaged on this basis.'[69]

---

[67] Judgment of 25 Feb. 1982, Series A, vol. 48. The new UK Education Act (No. 2) 1986 outlaws corporal punishment only in the state sector and in some cases for those pupils on assisted places in the private sector.

[68] Para. 34 of the Court's judgment, cited by Forde (1985: 274).

[69] European Court of Human Rights, judgment of 26 June 1981, Series A, vol. 44, para. 49.

It might also be suggested that the case-law on corporal punishment in schools cannot be applied to the private sector as parents consented to the beating or use of the tawse when they chose the school. Although this argument may be relevant in addressing Article 2 of the First Protocol, which deals with parents' philosophical convictions, it is hard to see how it could justify treatment which affronted an individual's dignity to such an extent that there was a violation of Article 3. In *Warwick* v. *United Kingdom* the Commission found that corporal punishment, in the form of a ruler being used by the headmaster to hit the girl on the hand in front of another male teacher, was held to have reached the level of seriousness prohibited by Article 3,[70] but the case was referred to the Committee of Ministers rather than the Court, and on the question of a violation of Article 3 the requisite two-thirds majority was not reached, so there was no finding of a violation.[71]

The question of corporal punishment in private schools in the United Kingdom has now been decided by the Commission and Court to come within the Convention.[72] In *Y* v. *United Kingdom* the applicant, a 15-year-old, was knocked over by another pupil who was chasing a younger boy. The next day the applicant scratched the file cover of the boy who had knocked him over. This was reported to the headmaster, who punished the applicant because he apparently had a history of bullying the other boy. The applicant was given four strokes of the cane with his trousers on. The applicant's parents put the matter in the hands of the police, who later decided not to bring a prosecution for assault. The parents then unsuccessfully claimed damages in civil proceedings.

Before the Commission the applicant was able to point to the *Tyrer* case and the Commission's conclusion in the *Warwick* application to argue that his punishment constituted institutionalized violence so as to violate Article 3. Claims have always been assessed on an individual basis. In this case 'The applicant was hit with such force with the cane that four weals appeared on his buttocks, with swelling and bruising, causing considerable pain for some time after the act itself.' The Commission avoids any purported link to the State, simply stating: 'such an injury to a teenage boy is unacceptable whoever were to inflict the punishment, be it parent or teacher. The Commission sees no justification for treating the applicant in this way.'[73] Therefore, despite the Commission's observations on the function of the State in the education sector, the Commission relates the violation to the punishment not the

[70] Report of 18 July 1986, para. 88.

[71] Res. DH (89)5 of 2 Mar. 1989.

[72] Applic. 13134/87, *Wendy and Jeremy Costello-Roberts* v. *UK*, report of 8 Oct. 1991, judgment of 25 March 1993; Applic. 14229/88, *Y* v. *UK*, report of 8 Oct. 1991, Res. DH (92)63. The judgment of the Court came too late to be discussed in detail here.

[73] At para. 44 of the report.

punisher. The state responsibility was due to the fact that the 'English legal system authorized [the ill treatment] and provided no effective redress'.[74] The case ended in a friendly settlement.

It is suggested that where a beating by a teacher has actually taken place Article 3 is applicable, even in the case of private schools, as preventive legislation would almost certainly have persuaded teachers against making such an attack on the dignity of the child.

7.3.2 Article 2

The cases on Article 2 which the Commission has dealt with are usually dismissed *ratione personae* where the killing resulted from terrorist activity. Nevertheless in several cases the Commission has admitted that the Convention requires positive preventive measures in order that the State 'shall secure' (Article 1 ECHR) the rights in the Convention. In a case involving an assassination by private individuals—*Mrs W.* v. *Ireland*—the Commission mentions the responsibility of the State for the acts or omissions of its agents in the event of a violation of the right to life even where this authority is exercised abroad;[75] and in *Mrs W.* v. *United Kingdom* the Commission states that the State's obligations under Article 1 mean that there is a positive duty to secure the rights guaranteed in Section I of the Convention, whether that infringement be by the State itself or by others within the State.[76]

According to Professor Frowein (the First Vice-President of the European Commission of Human Rights) this last decision 'seems to assume that a certain right to be protected against terrorism can indeed be seen as forming part of the Convention guarantees. This is not astonishing since Article 2, paragraph 1, states expressly: "everyone's right to life shall be protected by law".'[77]

The summary of the Commission's decision under the heading 'Competence ratione personae of the Commission' reads: 'The fact that an individual is killed by terrorists does not exclude the Commission's competence since the High Contracting Parties have a duty to protect the right to life.'[78] The Commission's actual decision on the law reads:

---

[74] At para. 45 of the report. The Commission found that the Art. 8 issue was absorbed by the Art. 3 finding. It also found a violation of Art. 13 (no effective remedy). The report of the commission in the other case (13134/87) found no violation under Art. 3 but did find a violation under Art. 8 and is dealt with below. £8000 were to be paid to the applicant under the friendly settlement.

[75] Applic. 9360/81, 32 D. & R. 211; the part of the decision which concerns *ratione loci* is an important extension of the concept of responsibility under the Convention: 'The High Contracting Parties are bound to secure the said rights and freedoms to all persons under their actual authority and responsibility, not only when the authority is exercised within their own territory but also when it is exercised abroad' (at para. 14 of the decision).

[76] Applic. 9348/81, 32 D. & R. 190.

[77] Frowein (1988: 87); and see J. A. Carrillo Salcedo at 46 of the same volume.

[78] 32 D. & R. 190, and repeated in *W.* v. *Ireland*, Applic. 9360/81, 32 D. & R. 211.

The Commission also finds that the applicant's complaint, concerning the killing of her husband by terrorists, raises the question of State responsibility for the protection of the right to life in accordance with Article 2 of the Convention. It follows that this complaint cannot be declared inadmissible, under Article 27, paragraph 2, as being incompatible with the Convention *ratione personae*, on the ground that it is directed against acts of private persons.[79]

The relevant part of the application concerned a complaint about the protection offered to the applicant's brother (who was murdered in Northern Ireland by the IRA) and her family's future protection. In dismissing the application as manifestly unfounded the Commission directly examines the adequacy of the positive obligations undertaken by the United Kingdom:

The Commission is of the opinion that Article 2, which states that 'the right to life shall be protected by law' may, as other Convention articles (cf. ECHR Marckx judgment of 13 June 1979, para. 31) indeed give rise to positive obligations on the part of the State. That, however, does not mean that a positive obligation to exclude any possible violence could be deduced from this article.

The Commission recalls that, in a previous application against the Republic of Ireland (No. 6040/73), it considered the case of a person who stated that, following an attempt on his life by the IRA, he had for several years been under police protection in the Republic of Ireland. His claim under Article 2 of the Convention for continued protection of a personal bodyguard was declared inadmissible by the Commission on the ground 'that Article 2 can not be interpreted as imposing a duty on a state to give protection of this nature, at least not for an indefinite period of time' (Collection 44, p. 121 (122)).

The Commission does not find that it can be its task, in the examination of the present applicant's complaint under Article 2, to consider in detail, as she appears to suggest, the appropriateness and efficiency of the measures taken by the United Kingdom to combat terrorism in Northern Ireland.

The Commission cannot find that the United Kingdom was required under the Convention to protect the applicant's brother by measures going beyond those actually taken by the authorities to shield life and limb of the inhabitants of Northern Ireland against attacks from terrorists.

Nor can it find that the applicant can under Article 2 require such further measures as regards her own protection. In this connection the Commission notes from the applicant's submissions that, while the peace-time army strength in Northern Ireland was 4,000 men, it currently stands at about 10,500 and that, between August 1969 and December 1981, several hundred members of the armed and security forces lost their lives there combatting terrorism.[80]

It is clearly inappropriate that the European Commission on Human Rights should have to determine whether an increase or a decrease in the

---

[79] At para. 4 of the decision on admissibility.
[80] Paras. 13–16 of the decision on admissibility. See also *X* v. *UK and Ireland*, Applic. 10018/82, decision of 7 Mar. 1985, unpublished, which similarly concludes that there cannot be an obligation 'to exclude any possible violence'.

armed forces in Northern Ireland would lead to fewer terrorist attacks. Nevertheless Contracting Parties may, in theory, be held responsible for threats to life from private persons.

It has also been confirmed that the State has positive duties to protect life even where death was not the result of an intentional killing. In *X* v. *United Kingdom* the applicant association complained that the vaccination programme organized by the Government had caused severe damage to some babies and had sometimes even resulted in death.[81] In its decision on admissibility the Commission states: 'The concept that "everyone's life shall be protected by law" enjoins the State not only to refrain from taking life *"intentionally"* but, further, to take appropriate steps to safeguard life.'[82] The Commission went on to find that in this case it could not be said that the State had not taken adequate and appropriate measures to protect life. Nevertheless the theoretical responsibility to take appropriate steps remains. One could imagine a State being found in violation of Article 2 should it fail to have adequately controlled the release of lethal medicine on to the market by private pharmaceutical companies.

There may be factual circumstances which lead to a more restrictive interpretation of Article 3 than of Article 2, but, in principle, the Commission would seem to admit that States have a responsibility with positive obligations where the loss of life is directly inflicted by private persons. The real difference must be at the national level. Whilst it is submitted that Article 3 gives rise to rights and obligations between private parties at the level of domestic law, and that States are obliged to provide for an effective remedy to those complaining of breaches of these rights (under Article 13 ECHR), the special nature of the positive obligations on the State under Article 2 cannot simply be transferred to private individuals at the national level. Private bodies are not obliged to provide the sort of protection and preventive measures which the State can be called on to implement. In other words private persons are prohibited from torturing under Article 3 but are not obliged to provide armed protection or health care to secure the right to life. The issues emerge obliquely in the admissibility decision *Hughes* v. *United Kingdom*.[83]

In this case the applicant's husband had been employed at Manchester High School (a private school); he had taken time off work as he was suffering from chest pains but returned to the school to collect his wages. At 16.10 he was discovered to have collapsed. According to the Commission's report, 'Several people, including teachers with some first aid training, saw him and decided he was dead. The school called an ambulance at 17.25 hrs and it took the applicant's husband to the hospital

---

[81] Applic. 7154/75, 14 D. & R. 31.   [82] At para. 2 of the decision.
[83] Applic. 11590/85, decision of 18 July 1986, 48 D. & R. 258.

nearby where he was pronounced dead by doctors at 18.05 hrs. A post mortem conducted revealed that her husband had died of a coronary occlusion.'

The applicant first complained that not all necessary measures which might have saved her husband's life were taken, and secondly that British law 'appears to condone such negligence by not imposing a specific obligation to take prompt emergency steps in such circumstances and by not awarding compensation to the victims or their families'. The Commission dismissed the first part of the claim, stating that they could not accept complaints against private individuals.[84] Whilst this is an obvious way to dismiss part of the claim, it is suggested that the public/private dichotomy should not be used in this way. First, although the school was private, education is usually considered a function of the State and private schools are covered by a state regulatory framework, second, all private schools are to some extent subsidized by the State whether through grants, scholarships, or tax relief, and third, the implication is that the Commission might impose a duty to rescue on state teachers whilst private teachers are bound by no such 'good Samaritan' principle.

The applicant complained in the second part of her claim that British law seemed to condone the negligence of the teachers by not imposing an obligation to take prompt action in such circumstances. If we follow the causation approach suggested above, we should first decide whether the right in question is operative as between the individuals (irrespective of their state/private employment) in the context of the application and with regard to the aim of the right in question. The relevant part of Article 2 reads: 'Everyone's right to life shall be protected by law.'

This phrase would not seem to impose positive obligations or responsibility for omissions on private individuals. However, even if we grant that Article 2 implies that everyone is bound to take positive measures to guarantee other people's right to life, and that in these circumstances the teachers owed the deceased such a duty, we still have to show that *but for* the government's lack of legislation this particular injury probably would have been avoided. It is unlikely, with regard to the facts as they emerge from the decision, that legislation or other administrative measures would have had the effect of preventing the loss of life. Therefore in these circumstances the State would not seem to be in breach of its obligation to ensure an effective and practical guarantee of this right. The Commission took causation as the key and dismissed the application, stating: 'the existence of any express obligation to take prompt emergency action would not have been of any avail to the applicant's husband.'

---

[84] They refer to their 'constant jurisprudence', Applic. 172/56, decision of 20 Dec. 1957, 1 Yearbook 211, 215, and Applic. 3925/69, decision of 2 Jan. 1970, 32 Collection 56, 58.

7.4 ARTICLE 2 OF PROTOCOL 1

Article 2 reads:

No person shall be denied the right to education. In the exercise of any functions which it assumes in relation to education and to teaching, the State shall respect the right of parents to ensure such education and teaching in conformity with their own religious and philosophical convictions.

According to the Court the second sentence of this Article 'aims in short at safeguarding the possibility of pluralism in education, which possibility is essential for the preservation of the "democratic society" as conceived by the Convention . . . in view of the power of the modern State, it is above all through State teaching that this aim must be realized'.[85] Van Dijk and van Hoof cite this passage and continue: 'From the formulation of the aim itself ("essential") and from the general wording of the second sentence it follows that the pluralism referred to must also be ensured in private education, at least in so far as the government is concerned with it in one way or another via subsidies, inspection of schools, instructions with regard to the curriculum, and the like.'[86] They then point out that parents may keep their children away from religious instruction and the school must be organized in such a way that they are enabled to do so. They suggest that where the religious education is integrated into the curriculum as a whole, children whose parents object are entitled to an alternative which receives the same state aid.[87]

This reasoning is only partially harmonious with the approach we proposed in Chapter 5. There it was suggested that the first step was to discern the aim of the right in question (here the protection of democratic society through pluralism); next one should determine if the operation of the right in the particular context of the application involves the sphere of the public or the intimate sphere, (in this case we have already seen that education is vital for determining the future of the sphere of the public and is not primarily intimate). Therefore according to our thesis the right in question is applicable to the actions of private bodies operating in the sphere of the public. Where our thesis parts company with the analysis by van Dijk and van Hoof is that it makes no reference to the state aid which any one school may or may not receive and excludes this as irrelevant. In fact including the state aid factor leads to insoluble situations: the State could not always be obliged to provide private Catholic or non-

---

[85] *Kjeldsen, Busk Madsen and Pedersen* case, judgment of 7 Dec. 1976, Series A, vol. 23, p. 25.
[86] Van Dijk and van Hoof (1990: 473).
[87] Van Dijk and van Hoof cite the friendly settlement in Applic. 4733/71, *X* v. *Sweden* (1971) 14 Yearbook 664 at 676 for this proposition.

denominational schools with a 50 per cent subsidy within reasonable distance from a Protestant school with a 50 per cent subsidy. When one considers that many private schools will have charitable status, and thus could be said to receive state aid in the form of tax relief, it is obvious that attempts to calculate the extent of the State's involvement in this sphere will be completely arbitrary.

7.5 ARTICLE 6(1) AND THE MEANING OF 'CIVIL RIGHTS AND OBLIGATIONS'

Article 6(1) straddles the public/private law distinction in a paradoxical way. It reads in part: '(1) In the determination of his civil rights and obligations or of any criminal charge against him, everyone is entitled to a fair and public hearing within a reasonable time by an independent and impartial tribunal established by law.' If we examine the extent to which Article 6 has been held relevant regarding employment disputes we find that public employment involving teachers, policemen, and clergymen does not give rise to 'civil rights', but the right to practise medicine or law leads to a private employment situation and the 'civil rights' of doctors and barristers are covered by Article 6![88] In other words public employees are often outside the scope of this Article of the Convention whereas those in private practice are entitled to protection!

It is not the nature of the tribunal (administrative or judicial) which gives rise to a 'civil right', but the right in dispute before the tribunal. Therefore if a 'civil right' is determined by a 'private' tribunal—such as a disciplinary board—Article 6 may be relevant. It is not that the tribunal itself has to conform to Article 6, but there must be the possibility of an appeal from the original decision and the procedure at appeal will then have to conform with Article 6. This was clearly stated by the Court in *Albert and Le Compte*:

Nonetheless, in such circumstances the Convention calls for at least one of the following systems: either the jurisdictional organs themselves comply with the

---

[88] It seems that the original exclusion of public rights from Art. 6(1) by the Court of Human Rights is giving way to a more flexible approach. The new approach is to balance the public and private rights involved in, say, proceedings concerning a widow's supplementary pension under industrial accident insurance, and if the private rights predominate then Art. 6(1) is applicable. See *Deumland* v. *FRG*, 26 May 1986, Series A, vol. 100, and *Feldebrugge* v. *The Netherlands*, 29 May 1986, Series A, vol. 99 (health insurance allowance —predominantly private rights). For comment see Sperduti (1986: 814). A review of this complex issue is outside the scope of the present work; for detailed analysis see M.-A. Eissen, *Case-Law on Article 6 of the Convention* (Strasbourg: Council of Europe, 1985); Boyle (1984: 89–111); van Dijk and van Hoof (1990: 294–358); van Dijk (1988: 131–43; 1987: 5–24).

requirements of Article 6(1), or they do not comply but are subject to subsequent control by a judicial body that has full jurisdiction and does provide the guarantees of Article 6(1).[89]

However, disciplinary proceedings on their own do not amount to a 'dispute about civil rights'. The issue determined has directly to affect those rights. This was the case where the right to practise medicine was determined by the Ordre des Médecins in the *Albert and Le Compte* case.

Although the tribunal in this case was established by law, Article 6 could come to cover autonomous disciplinary tribunals in other areas. If a trade union disciplines someone in a 'closed shop' situation, the right to practise that trade or profession may be lost. However, this situation is not exactly the same as the one covering doctors, as the link is indirect, the decision to dismiss being taken by the employers and not by the union.

So, in *X* v. *The Netherlands*[90] the applicant complained that the procedure before the director of the Regional Labour Office was in breach of Article 6. Under Dutch law Buitengenwoon Besluit Arbeidsverhoundingen Article 6 (special decree on labour relations) it was declared that neither the employer nor the employee may terminate a contract of employment without the authorization of the director of the Regional Labour Office. The application to the European Commission of Human Rights was dismissed as:

It is incontestable that the decision on dismissal rests ultimately with the employer himself.

The Commission considers therefore that, even if it is admitted that the procedure in question may have affected rights and obligations deriving from the relations between the applicant and his employer, it cannot be considered in any way to have decisively determined civil rights and obligations within the meaning of Article 6(1) of the Convention.[91]

As will be seen in the section on Article 11, the Commission has reserved the right to find a violation of Article 11 where an unreasonable expulsion from the union results in loss of livelihood. Only one tiny aspect of Article 6 has been touched on here but it has demonstrated that in some ways the norms of the Convention may have significant consequences for the ordering of private decisions and action when they touch on 'civil rights'.

Several commentators have criticized the Court's exclusion of public law situations from the ambit of Article 6(1), and most of the research into the *travaux préparatoires* of Article 14 of the Civil and Political

---

[89] *Albert and Le Compte* v. *Belgium* (1983) Series A, vol. 58, at 16.
[90] Applic. 8974/80, 24 D. & R. 187.
[91] At 191.

Rights Covenant, on which Article 6 was based, demonstrates that the phrase 'civil rights and obligations' was meant to cover all litigation of a non-criminal nature.[92] According to van Dijk:

In the French text of Article 6, in fact, the formula [from the Covenant] was adopted without any change. In the English text 'rights and obligations at a suit at law' was altered, at the very last stage of the drafting, into 'civil rights and obligations.' The reason for this is not traceable, but one may assume that 'suit at law' was not the obvious equivalent of '*de caractère civil*' in the eyes of the continental lawyers (and of the linguists involved).[93]

Van Dijk recognizes that the problems for the Court arise from its far-reaching decision in the *Golder* case,[94] where the Court found that Article 6 created a right to a court. Once one acknowledges this guarantee any extension of Article 6 to administrative decisions has enormous implications for the internal public law of the Contracting States. The dissent in the *Feldebrugge* case neatly expresses the concerns of the Member States: '[I]n the administrative sphere . . . organisational, social and economic considerations may legitimately warrant dispute procedures of a less judicial and formal kind.'[95] The response of the Member States to the Court's case-law (which has gradually come to include more and more administrative-type decisions) has been to draft a Protocol to the Convention which would grant special judicial guarantees in relation to administrative procedures. This draft Protocol was examined by the Steering Committee for Human Rights in 1989 but the draft has progressed no further.[96]

It is suggested that the Continental distinction between public and private law is unworkable at the supranational level of the Strasbourg organs. Indeed the results themselves could well be in breach of the Convention. Why should state officials (whose employment, health in-

---

[92] See van Dijk (1988) and the references therein.
[93] Van Dijk (1988: 138).
[94] Judgment of 21 Feb. 1975, Series A, vol. 18.
[95] Judgment of 29 May 1986, Series A, vol. 99, para. 15 of the dissenting opinion.
[96] *Information Sheet No. 25* (Strasbourg: Council of Europe), 61. For examples of the Austrian Constitutional Court's rejection of the European Court's jurisprudence see M. Nowak, 'The Implementation of the European Convention on Human Rights in Austria', in *The Implementation in National Law of the European Convention on Human Rights*, Proceedings of the Fourth Copenhagen Conference on Human Rights, 28–9 Oct. 1988 (Copenhagen: Danish Centre of Human Rights, 1989), 32–9 at 38. According to Nowak the Constitutional Court rejected the European Court's tendency to bring traditional administrative law within Art. 6 and stated that such changes in 'the traditional Roman law distinction between private and public law could only be achieved by a constitutional amendment passed by Parliament, but not by way of a dynamic interpretation by the European Court'. See also the proceedings of a colloquy organized by the Austrian Human Rights Institute, *Judicial Safeguards in Administrative Proceedings* (Kehl am Rhein: Engel, 1989).

surance, or pension schemes do not include a predominance of private law elements) be denied the protection of Article 6(1)? If they have an alternative system why should that system be immune from the safeguards which the Convention imposes on the private sector? New methods of regulation render any distinction based on the presence of private rights unworkable. How are we to decide the case of a National Health doctor who has some private patients? Are government counsel covered by private law? in which countries?

The problems surrounding the Court's development of Article 6(1) and the scope of 'civil rights and obligations' mainly concern the extent to which the Court is prepared to oblige Member States to amend their administrative proceedings. Both the Court and the Commission are split,[97] and the final determination of this question will depend on the make-up of the Commission and Court at the relevant time.

The Court has not yet reacted to the request of the Commission as formulated in the Commission's report in the *Benthem* case,[98] where the Commission states: 'there is still a great deal of uncertainty as to how far the applicability of Article 6(1) extends, and the Contracting States are clearly in need of further guidance on this matter which for many of them has a considerable impact on their legal systems.'[99] Although there is no doubt that Article 6(1) applies to disputes between private parties, the erection of a public/private boundary in order to exclude the operation of administrative law rights from the scope of Article 6 has led to the same confusion as was detected in cases where courts have attempted to exclude private action from the field of protection of human rights norms.

7.6 ARTICLE 8 AND THE PRIVATE SPHERE

Article 8 reads:

1. Everyone has the right to respect for his private and family life, his home and his correspondence.

2. There shall be no interference by a public authority with the exercise of this right except as is in accordance with the law and is necessary in a democratic

---

[97] For example the Court was split nine votes to eight in the *Deumland* case in favour of finding that procedures whereby a decision is taken on claims to a retirement pension through a compulsory accident insurance scheme fell within Art. 6(1); in *Feldebrugge* the majority was ten votes to seven concerning the application of Art. 6(1) to health insurance benefits; in *Benthem* v. *The Netherlands* the Commission concluded by nine votes to eight that Art. 6(1) was not applicable to the refusal of a licence for the operation of an installation for the delivery of liquefied petroleum gas. The opinion of the Commission is published as an annex to the Court's judgment Series A, vol. 97. The Court went on to find that Art. 6(1) was applicable by eleven votes to six.

[98] See n. 97.   [99] At para. 91.

society in the interests of national security, public safety or the economic well being of the country, for the prevention of disorder or crime, for the protection of health or morals, or for the protection of the rights and freedoms of others.

If this Article is interpreted to include violations by private individuals two consequences follow:

1. At the *international level* in Strasbourg, States become obliged not only to abstain from interference with the privacy of individuals, but also to ensure a practical and effective[100] system (legislative, administrative, or judicial) for the protection of privacy from other individuals.

2. At the *national level*, Article 8 can be used directly against private bodies in the national courts of those countries where the Convention has domestic status and Article 8 has been incorporated or is considered 'self-executing'. Even without incorporation of the Convention, as we saw in Part I, the Convention may still be relevant in a number of different contexts; Article 8 will fall to be considered even where the litigation involved two private parties.

7.6.1 The case-law of the European Commission and Court of Human Rights

In *Airey* v. *Ireland* Mrs Airey alleged that her husband was an alcoholic and that he frequently threatened her with violence. He had been convicted of assaulting her and fined. She complained that the State had failed, under Article 8, to ensure her an accessible legal procedure which would determine her rights. Because of the prohibitive cost of legal representation she could not obtain a judicial separation, there being no legal aid available for such proceedings.

Article 8 grants a right to respect for private and family life. In the *Airey* case this right was directly interfered with, not by Ireland but by Mr Airey. Nevertheless the European Court of Human Rights found that Ireland was bound to make the right to respect for private life effective.

The Court does not consider that Ireland can be said to have 'interfered' with Mrs. Airey's private or family life: the substance of her complaint is not that the State has acted but that it has failed to act. However, although the object of Article 8 is essentially that of protecting the individual against arbitrary interference by the public authorities, it does not merely compel the State to abstain from such interference: in addition to this primarily negative undertaking, there may be positive obligations inherent in an effective respect for private or family life (see the above mentioned Marckx judgment, p. 15, para. 31).

---

[100] The phrase is taken from the *Artico* case: 'The Convention is intended to guarantee not rights that are theoretical or illusory but rights that are practical and effective' (Series A, vol. 37, p. 16).

In Ireland, many aspects of private and family life are regulated by law. As regards marriage, husband and wife are in principle under a duty to cohabit but are entitled in certain cases, to a petition for a decree of judicial separation; this amounts to recognition of the fact that the protection of their private or family life may sometimes necessitate their being relieved from the duty to live together.

Effective respect for private or family life obliges Ireland to make this means of protection effectively accessible, when appropriate, to anyone who may wish to have recourse thereto. However, it was not effectively accessible to the applicant: not having been put in a position in which she could apply to the High Court (see paragraphs 20 to 28 above), she was unable to seek recognition in law of her *de facto* separation from her husband. She has therefore been a victim of a violation of Article 8.[101]

If the State is responsible for realistic 'access to justice'[102] in this way, then many other areas of private interference with 'rights' come to be covered. One might imagine positive obligations on the State to ensure effective injunctions following domestic violence and real practical support for the victims of this abuse of the right to respect for private and family life.

One of the most important cases on the application of Article 8 to the acts of private individuals is *X and Y* v. *The Netherlands*.[103] This case involved a 16-year-old mentally handicapped girl who was sexually assaulted by the son-in-law of the director of a private nursing home. There existed a gap in Dutch law, so that an effective criminal prosecution could not be brought by the father of the girl (Mr X) nor could Miss Y (the victim of the assault) file a complaint which could lead to a criminal prosecution. Civil remedies were available, but it was claimed that the procedure was lengthy, traumatic for the victim, and not sufficiently preventive to constitute adequate protection.

The European Court of Human Rights repeated the *Airey* formula: that in addition to the primarily negative undertaking demanded by Article 8, 'there may be positive obligations inherent in an effective respect for private or family life'. However, it then went on to state: 'These obligations may involve the adoption of measures designed to secure respect for private life *even in the sphere of the relations of individuals between themselves.*'[104]

This is the strongest indication so far that the European Court of Human Rights will intervene and hold States responsible for violations

---

[101] Series A, vol. 32, paras. 31–2.

[102] For a world-wide view of the 'access to justice' phenomenon, see the comprehensive 'Access to Justice' series, general ed. M. Cappelletti, 1978–9, 4 vols. 6 books (Milan: Guiffrè). For the implications of the *Airey* judgment and the subsequent *Artico* v. *Italy* (1980) Series A, vol. 37, judgment see Cappelletti, Garth, and Trocker (1982: 677).

[103] (1985) Series A, vol. 91.

[104] At para. 23 of the judgment (emphasis added).

of rights where the actor involved was a private individual. The full implications of this development are not yet clear. To what extent States will be obliged to take positive action to prevent individuals being humiliated by other individuals is difficult to determine. However, the decision has consequences not only in the context of legislation concerning the disabled and domestic violence but also for a number of marginalized groups: transsexuals, gay men, lesbians, Black people, drug abusers, immigrants, refugees, and ex-prisoners. These and other stigmatized groups are often faced with private discrimination and intolerance. It was suggested in Section 7.3.1.2 that, although the State cannot be internationally responsible for every private humiliation, a 'but for' test could be utilized to fix responsibility where there was a high probability that the private violation could have been prevented by state action.

Both *Airey* v. *Ireland* and *X and Y* v. *The Netherlands* involved positive obligations on the State in situations where the direct violator was a private individual. They confirm that such private behaviour is not outside the scope of Article 8. Article 8 can now be said to have been interpreted so that the reference to 'public' in paragraph (2) does not prevent the application of paragraph (1) to both public and private actions;[105] therefore one may infer that legally enforceable rights arise directly against private groups at the national level where national law allows this. Furthermore enforceable rights arise directly against States at the international level where there exist gaps in the legal framework providing protection from the behaviour of private actors. The implications of this development are important when one considers some of the private abuses currently facing individuals.

It is quite plain that private data banks and the sale of personal data have grave consequences for personal liberty. The Council of Europe's concern on this matter is evidenced by the Convention for the Protection of Individuals with Regard to Automatic Processing of Personal Data.[106] Similarly, bugging devices are, for example, available not only to the 'organs of the State' but also to private individuals. A 'tap' by the police and a 'bug' by a private detective result in equivalent violations of rights as far as the victim is concerned. Similarly, employers can be just as invasive as public officials. In the United States a recent survey revealed that companies regularly search cars, lockers, handbags, desks, etc., claiming that the economic risks of high medical costs and suits for

---

[105] For some time there was debate in the doctrine concerning the text of Art. 8 and whether it applied exclusively to public acts, or also to private acts, or to private acts with no permissible restrictions. See de Meyer (1973: 262–3 and the references therein), and Partsch (1973: 275). See also Jeammaud (1981: 71).

[106] This Convention has been partly 'incorporated' into UK law by the Data Protection Act 1984.

'negligent hiring' necessitate such action to guard against possible alcoholics and drug abusers.[107] It is only from the perspective of the State that one violation is preventable whilst the other is uncontrollable. Nevertheless, the State may be held responsible for either violation before the Strasbourg organs where the necessary measures have not been taken at the national level. In both *Airey* and *X and Y* v. *The Netherlands* the violation by the State resulted from inadequate protection for the victim within the national legal order. It is not that the State Party will be held responsible and required to pay compensation for every private attack on the dignity of any citizen. The state responsibility arises when the State has not fulfilled its positive obligation to secure the rights in the Convention to everyone within its jurisdiction. Even so, the Court ordered compensation of 3,000 florins ($1,800) to be paid to Miss Y (in the *X and Y* case) by way of just satisfaction in respect of non-pecuniary damage. It is also worth mentioning, parenthetically, that in the *Velásquez Rodríguez* case, discussed in Chapter 4, the Inter-American Court of Human Rights, whilst admitting that the disappearances were carried out by 'private' persons, not only awarded compensation but also stated that the Government must prevent any practice of disappearances in the future, must investigate the disappearances until there is certitude about what happened to Mr Velásquez, and must punish those found to have caused the disappearances.[108]

The approach of the European Court of Human Rights in the *Case of Powell and Rayner*[109] is instructive as to how this Court deals with harder questions. In this case the complaints under Article 8 concerned noise from Heathrow Airport. The United Kingdom Government attempted to rely on the private nature of the ownership of the aircraft. According to the judgment the Government submitted that:

the facts disclosed no 'interference by a public authority' with the applicants' right under Article 8, Heathrow Airport and the aircraft using it not being and never having been owned, controlled or operated by the Government or any agency of the Government. It was, [the Government] contended, not the negative but the positive obligations of the State under Article 8 which were in reality in issue; and there was no arguable ground for establishing any failure on the part of the Government to secure the right of either applicant to respect for his private life and his home.[110]

The Court avoided deciding whether the case raises the positive duties of the State under paragraph 8(1) or negative obligations stemming from the

[107] 'Don't Pry Companies', *The Economist* (6 Oct. 1990), 20.

[108] See C. Medina, 'Further Developments in the .Velásquez Rodrigues and Gondirez Cases before the Inter-American Court of Human Rights', 3 *NQHR* (1989), 377.

[109] Judgment of 21 Feb. 1990, Series A, vol. 172.

[110] Para. 39 of the judgment.

terms of paragraph 8(2) and the reference in that paragraph to 'interference by a public authority'. The Court stated that the applicable principles are 'broadly similar', as in both cases 'regard has to be had to the fair balance that has to be struck between the competing interests of the individual and the community as a whole; and in both contexts the State enjoys a certain margin of appreciation in determining the steps to be taken to ensure compliance with the Convention'.[111] The Court adds that 'even in relation to the positive obligations flowing from the first paragraph of Article 8, "in striking [the required] balance the aims mentioned in the second paragraph may be of a certain relevance" '.[112] This formula first appeared in the *Rees* case, but takes on a special significance in the present context as it gives a clue to the limits of the obligations on the State to regulate the private sphere. The Court picks up the Commission's point that 'the increasing use of jet aircraft have without question become necessary in the interests of a country's economic well-being'—thus incorporating Article 8(2) as a limitation on the positive obligations of the State.

The implications of this development in the case-law of the Court are quite important. One could deduce that, according to the Court, although Article 8(1) operates between individuals, there are restrictions on the operation of this right at the inter-individual level along the lines of those enumerated in Article 8(2). This approach has been questioned in the past, with some commentators suggesting that Article 8(2) is irrelevant to the application of Article 8 in cases involving two private parties.

---

[111] At para. 41 of the judgment. No examination of the evolution of the 'margin of appreciation' doctrine will be undertaken here. The issue as it relates to the privatization of human rights is briefly dealt with at the end of this section and at the beginning of the Conclusions to this work. For the details of the history of the doctrine see Macdonald (1987: 187–208). For present purposes it is interesting that Macdonald (a judge in the Court) highlights that the Court is 'concerned to strike a fair balance . . . between the demands of the general interest of the community and the requirements of the protection of an individual's fundamental rights', citing from the *Sporrong and Lönnroth* case, which concerned planning permission and permits. The Court continues: 'in an area as complex and difficult as that of development of large cities, the Contracting States should enjoy a wide margin of appreciation in order to implement their own town planning policy' (at para. 69). Macdonald adds that these may therefore be 'questions of evaluation to which different people might, quite properly, give different answers, and from which it is best for the Court to remain aloof' (1987: 194). The conclusion one might draw from Macdonald's review of the case-law is that where the community/public interest is to be weighed rather than the State's interest, then the margin of appreciation is wider. The operation of human rights in the private sphere raises complex questions in the former situation rather than the latter and so we can expect the Court to choose to 'remain aloof'. One can also conclude that where the right is an essential foundation of democracy then the margin diminishes, and where there is consensus in the Member States that certain action should be prohibited the margin is again reduced. See also R. St J. Macdonald, 'The Margin of Appreciation in the Jurisprudence of the European Court of Human Rights', in *Collected Courses in European Law*, vol. i, book 2 (Dordrecht: Martinus Nijhoff, 1990), 95–161; and O'Donnell (1982: 474–96).

[112] At para. 41 of the judgment.

Alternatively, one might adduce that the Court is only talking about the international supervision of the positive obligations arising for the State under Article 8(1) and not the operation of the Article in a purely private context at the national level. This second alternative is preferred, as it is suggested that there are good reasons for allowing the State greater powers of intrusion than individuals under Article 8(2).

One does not have to restrict the discussion of the application of Article 8 in the private sphere to new threats to human rights from emerging powerful private bodies. Apart from what might be considered as privatized 'threats' such as Heathrow Airport Limited in the *Case of Powell and Rayner* and the *Baggs* case,[113] 'forgotten' questions such as marital rape[114] and the prevention of child abuse could come to be considered.[115] The continuing legality of marital rape in The Netherlands was referred to in the *X and Y* case, and insufficient protection in cases of domestic violence could also be covered. In one of the private corporal punishment cases brought against the United Kingdom a 7-year-old boy was beaten on his buttocks with a gymshoe for talking in the corridor. Although the Commission's opinion stated that the punishment had not reached the level of severe ill treatment proscribed by Article 3, it did hold that there had been a violation of Article 8 (private life). The Commission referred to the *X and Y* case and recalled that Article 8 may impose certain 'positive obligations upon the state', and that 'the protection afforded by Article 8 to an individual's physical integrity may be wider than that contemplated by Article 3 of the Convention depending on the facts of the case'.[116]

---

[113] See report of the Commission, 8 July 1987. The case ended in a 'friendly settlement' and it is worth noting that Heathrow Airport was actually a nationalized body at the start of the proceedings and privatized by the time of the 'friendly settlement'.

[114] The question of the legality of marital rape is not purely a symbolic issue. Some judges in the UK insisted that the Common Law includes a marital exception to the law of rape. This was not merely a curious quirk of the 17th-century English Common Law but actually led to acquittals. See 'Marital Rape Case Acquittal', *NLJ* (1990), 1410. See also *R. v. Kowalski* [1988] 86 Court of Appeal Reports 399, and compare the statement of Owen, J., in an unnamed case at Leicester Crown Court, 30 July 1990, reported in The Times 31 July 1990. See also I. D. Brownlie, 'Marital Rape: Lessons from Scotland', *NLJ* (1989), 1275–6. Most recently see *R. v. C.*, Crown Court at Sheffield, Simon Brown, J., 5 Oct. 1990 *NLJ* (1990), 1497, where Brown, J., found that there was no marital exemption to the law of rape and brought English law into line with Scottish law (*R. v. Stallard* [1989] SLT 469). See also Law Commission Working Paper No. 116, *Rape within Marriage* (London: HMSO, 1990). The marital exception has now been overruled (*R. v. R. (Rape: Marital Exception)* [1991] 2 All ER 257 (Court of Appeal), 4 All ER 481 (House of Lords)).

[115] For the Strasbourg case-law which affirms that private beating can lead to a violation of Art. 3 see ss. 7.3.1.3 and 7.3.1.4. For a case under the US Constitution concerning domestic violence see Ch. 6.1.3.

[116] *Jeremy Costello-Roberts v. UK*, report of the Commission, 8 Oct. 1991, para. 49. See also the dissenting opinion of Professor Schermers on the appropriateness of using Art. 8 when Art. 3 exists as a 'clear lex specialis'. Interestingly, even if Art. 8 were held applicable

7.6.2 *The privatization of human rights and the sanctity of the private sphere*

It is proposed to return to the cases of *X and Y* v. *The Netherlands* and *Powell and Rayner* in order to examine in detail the philosophical and political kernel of the privatization of human rights *problématique*. It is not possible fully to detail here the different philosophies surrounding the public/private dichotomy; to some extent we have already hinted at this debate in Chapters 4 and 6. What we shall do is examine some of the arguments put forward by States and others concerning the inviolability of the private sphere, and attempt to illustrate the ideology inherent in arguments phrased in terms of state responsibility, private law, and the private sphere.

The protection of privacy through Article 8 ECHR arose in the wake of horrendous abuses of power by authoritarian States in the first part of the twentieth century. The origins of Article 8 are situated in the context of a classical liberal conception of a private sphere free from state interference. The concern to protect people from tyranny through the use of rights is Lockian in origin; but it has recently been pointed out:

We commonly think of boundaries as protecting society from government, forgetting that they were intended to work both ways. Erecting an independent public sphere was as important as protecting private liberty. Secular and later democratic authority was possible because religious faith had been expelled from the realm of government and religious establishments relegated to private life. The designation of a distinctive private sphere was intended to control the influence of private associations, making impartiality or at least the regular adjustment of interests possible. In addition, Locke and Madison insisted that the public sphere should limit not only the public power of religious groups but also the power private groups exercised over their own members. (Rosenblum 1987: 60)

A second tradition focuses more on the importance of intimacy and is traced by Hanna Arendt to Jean Jacques Rousseau:

The first articulate explorer and to an extent even theorist of intimacy was Jean-Jacques Rousseau who, characteristically enough, is the only great author still frequently cited by his first name alone. He arrived at his discovery through a rebellion not against oppression of the state but against society's unbearable perversion of the human heart, its intrusion upon an innermost region in man which until then had needed no special protection. The intimacy of the heart,

Professor Schermers's opinion states that the infringement of private life through the Government's failure to interfere with private school policies has to be balanced against the legitimate interests of those private schools and parents who consider discipline with corporal punishment important and acceptable. He adds that 'the conclusion may well be that there was no obligation to interfere in the present case'. But see now the 'judgment of the Court of 25 March 1993 paras. 34–6.

unlike the private household, has no objective tangible place in the world, nor can the society against which it protects and asserts itself be localized to the same certainty as the public space.[117]

Professor Nancy Rosenblum explains these different emphases: 'Pure romanticism and conventional liberalism are separated not only by their notions of private life, but also by their motivations for designating a privileged private sphere. The fear of political authority and official coercion that motivates liberals to limit government is plainly secondary to romantics, for whom privatization is a condition for individuality and self expression.'[118]

It is suggested that, so far, the tendency has been to adopt the methods of liberalism to ensure the aims of romanticism. Deep concern to preserve an intimate private world from within which one can realize full development of one's personality has led to the demarcation of the public and the private spheres—with the boundaries being determined under the influence of liberalism so that the private becomes equated with that area which is not covered by the State. The confusion has been further compounded by neo-liberals relying on the sanctity of the private sphere to equate the development of the personality with the functioning of the free market. Antipathy to regulation in the private world of business builds on the already established public/private boundaries and claims that private enterprise is suffocated and stifled when the Government enters its domain. The danger is that in accepting the inviolability of a private sphere (defined by what is not directly connected to Government), important areas of human rights violations come to be 'forgotten'. As we indicated in Chapter 4, Carole Pateman reminds us of Locke and Rousseau's exclusion of women from the public sphere and that 'the separation and opposition of the public and private spheres is an unequal opposition between women and men' (1983: 283). Locke's assertion that the domestic sphere has to be separated from the political because in the former

---

[117] *The Human Condition* (Chicago: University of Chicago Press, 1958), 38–9.

[118] Rosenblum (1987: 59). As suggested in Ch. 5 the rights in the Convention can be perceived as instruments for achieving Lockian and Rousseauan goals. Art. 8 and its guarantee for respect for privacy, correspondence, etc. can be used to prevent officials abusing power and to ensure that the democratic process is not compromised by restrictions on communication between individuals, but in other circumstances it protects the individual from any attack which threatens his or her personality and self-development. The first case can properly be confined to matters which concern the sphere of the public, whereas in the second case dignity has to be protected from every potential threat. One might illustrate this by taking the example of a mother's interception of her children's letters as not being equivalent to interference with a politician's mail by the secret service. Protection of correspondence having, as it does, its rationale in the protection of democracy can be limited to the sphere of the public. On the other hand, protection of dignity through privacy must extend to all potential violators. Being publicly strip-searched by a policeman can be equated with sexual assault in a private institution or in the home.

case man's rule falls 'naturally' on him 'as the abler and stronger'[119] is compounded by contemporary discussion of the public sphere which systematically excludes the domestic sphere.

The dilemma of the European Court of Human Rights, of whether to interfere in the private sphere, is doubly hard to resolve because not only does that Court have to decide whether to penetrate the hallowed private sphere, regarded as sacred by private individuals, it is also reacting from a position one step removed, and could be seen to be violating what the State perceives to be its own private sphere. The State may perceive that *its* private law, private ordering, and regulations concerning private enterprise are something to be closely guarded, over which it alone has sovereignty.[120]

The challenge would seem to be to discover how to dissolve traditional concepts of the hermetically sealed 'untouchable', 'forgotten' nature of the private sphere without abandoning the possibility of protecting that private activity which is best carried out without interference from the State. The problem is that in privatizing human rights we may end up with a 'publicization of the private' and renewed demands to be defended *from* the State.[121]

The Commission and Court faced this challenge in the *X and Y* case head on, and the two dilemmas 'to regulate or not to regulate?' and 'European standard or local autonomy?' emerge in the Commission's report: 'In this area [protection of those with insufficient ability of self-determination in respect of sexual advances] it is more difficult for the legislator to set rules in order to safeguard the physical integrity of the persons concerned since it carries with it the *risk of unacceptable interference by the State* in the right of the individual to respect for his sexual private life under Article 8 of the Convention.'[122]

The Commission goes on to make the link with the second dilemma: 'The above raise the question whether Article 8 is applicable amongst third parties (*Drittwirkung*). However, for a Convention right to be applicable amongst third parties it is necessary that its contents are unequivocal and not subject to a divergence of opinion in the different

---

[119] J. Locke, *The Second Treatise of Government*, ed. T. P. Peardon (New York: Macmillan, 1986), ch. 7 para. 82.

[120] This tension may now be heightened by changing social and scientific developments that throw up new situations which do not easily lend themselves to Europe-wide consensus. Obvious examples include questions of genetic engineering, surrogacy, sterilization of mentally handicapped individuals, transsexuality, pornography, and the regulation of the right to strike and the 'closed shop'. For the federal–State dynamic of the Convention see Warbrick (1989: 698–724).

[121] For a feminist approach which retains the desirability of a sphere of privacy where there is some protection from intrusion and control see S. M. Okin, 'Gender, the Public and the Private', in Held (1991: 67–90).

[122] At para. 55 of the report (emphasis added).

Member States.'[123] The Commission does not directly answer either of these questions but goes on to find that the Netherlands criminal legislation was inadequate in the context of Article 8.[124]

In the applicant's pleadings before the Court the first dilemma is expressed in a slightly different way:

On the one hand, it follows from Article 8 of the Convention that the recognition of what is acknowledged by the authorities on principle as the citizens' inalienable private sphere means that actions which come within the individual's personal sex life should not be a matter for the State or its bodies. On the other hand, the Convention implies that in a democratic society restrictions must be placed in principle on the tendency of individuals to express themselves in respect of other persons. The freedom of the individual must not restrict that of others. *Legislation serves to protect freedom of will from encroachments by third parties.*[125]

Lastly, we should consider the Government's approach:

Provisions forbidding in absolute terms sexual relations with certain categories of individuals who, for reasons of lack of maturity, mental disability or state of dependence, are insufficiently able to self-determination in the field of sexual relations with others, will—in so far as the law is respected—deprive these categories of individuals of all sexual contact, which might be at variance with their right to a private life under Article 8(1) of the Convention.[126]

The Government then refers to a Ministry of Justice Advisory Committee report which stated that 'it was utterly unacceptable to make this group of persons completely "untouchable" by means of an absolute prohibition supported by heavy sanctions. This would give them in theory an absolute protection but would in practice have the effect of emphasising their social disability.'[127]

The different approaches have been quoted in detail to demonstrate that the private sphere to be protected is moulded according to the interests and concerns of those advocating its protection. For the individual in this case, privacy means preventing sexual attacks. In the hypothetical case of an individual who has been prosecuted for unlawful sexual intercourse with a handicapped person, privacy would mean keeping Government out of sexual relations. For the Commission, protecting privacy runs the risk of unjustified state interference in the private sphere; it will only contemplate such a foray into the private sphere where

---

[123] Para. 56 of the Commission's report. (Note, the French version gives a preferable explanation of the *Drittwirkung* question: 'savoir si l'article 8 est opposable aux tiers.')

[124] The Commission's delegate Professor Trechsel, in his submission to the Court, does in fact engage in a comparative analysis of criminal legislation in this field (at 69 of the Series B publication).

[125] At 75 of the Series B publication (emphasis added).

[126] At 51 of the Series B publication.

[127] Ibid.

other States Parties have demonstrated their willingness to give such a *Drittwirkung* effect to the right in question. For the Government, the question is a delicate balance between protection and paternalism. The Government has two sets of positive obligations. One set involves protecting potential victims from unwanted sexual abuse, the other consists in ensuring normal sexual opportunities for the same group.

The Court is in the difficult position of having to respond to the actual cases and controversies which come before it. It cannot legislate but merely rules on the existence of a violation. In the private sphere it is less easy to lay down hard-and-fast standards. The Court has been wise both to confine its judgments to the actual facts of the case and also to avoid delimiting the public from the private. There will, however, be differences in the Court's treatment of cases involving an individual–State conflict over privacy, and an application of Article 8 in the private sphere. In the former case the Court will usually allow the State a margin of appreciation to the extent that the State's interests are proportionately served by the restrictions on freedom it is imposing. In the latter case a margin of appreciation is permitted in order to allow the State to protect (through law or the absence of law) the human rights of other private individuals. In some of these latter cases it will be legitimate to allow a wider margin of appreciation, as its function is the protection of human rights rather than deference to state sovereignty.

7.7 ARTICLE 10

Article 10 reads:

1. Everyone has the right to freedom of expression. This right shall include freedom to hold opinions and to receive and impart information and ideas without interference by public authority and regardless of frontiers. This article shall not prevent States from requiring the licensing of broadcasting, television or cinema enterprises.
2. The exercise of these freedoms, since it carries with it duties and responsibilities, may be subject to such formalities, conditions, restrictions or penalties as are prescribed by law and are necessary in a democratic society, in the interests of national security, territorial integrity or public safety, for the prevention of disorder or crime, for the protection of health or morals, for the protection of the reputation or rights of others, for preventing the disclosure of information received in confidence, or for maintaining the authority and impartiality of the judiciary.

In the same way that hard cases under Article 8 raise hard questions about whose privacy we rate higher (the head of the household or the victim of abuse? the economic actor or the victim of pollution?) Article

10 gives rise to obstacles which prevent its simple application across the spectrum of private relationships. The importance of information is beyond question. Patrick Birkenshaw has put it as follows: 'Information is necessary to make sensible choice or wise judgment. Moral and ethical evaluation depends on information acquired through our own and our predecessors' experience. Information in the form of facts constitutes the basis of order in our lives, of community, regularity and knowledge' (1988: 11). Birkenshaw stresses Habermas's suggestion that the conditions must be created to ensure the 'ideal speech situation', and the importance of finding procedures which ensure that consensus is achieved through a discourse where the better argument triumphs. Nevertheless Birkenshaw points us to the converse side of freedom of information:

there are spheres of our personal and private lives that are a legitimate object of secrecy. Without adequate protection for justifiable secrets our integrity can be compromised, our identity shaken, our security shattered. Details of legitimate, intimate relationships, medical facts, of prolonged sensitive negotiations, investigations in the public interest, development of strategic or commercial plans, often require secrecy, likewise the long-term development of products requiring constant experimentation and creative thought or the protection of ideas. (1988: 12–13)

Clearly the defences which an individual has when faced with a claim by another individual for information are different from those which the State may resort to. The State has no 'intimate relationships', no 'medical history', etc. Nevertheless there will be cases where it is important to enforce a right to information against a private body. '[W]ith information comes power, and with exclusive control and use of information power is augmented. The problem then becomes one of establishing when secrecy operates not only to protect or advance the interests of those possessing or sharing secrets, but to subvert the interests of those not privy to such secrets' (Birkenshaw 1988: 13). Subversion through information can threaten not only the stability of the state apparatus but also the economic interests of private actors. In an application which reached the European Court of Human Rights, the *Case of Markt Intern*,[128] the applicants produced a sort of newsletter 'to defend the interests of small and medium sized retail businesses against the competition of large-scale distribution companies such as supermarkets and mail-order firms'. When the applicants reported an incident whereby a mail order firm had failed to reimburse a customer as promised, the mail order firm instituted proceedings against the applicants and were successful under the German Unfair Competition Act of 1909.[129]

---

[128] Judgment of the European Court of Human Rights, 20 Nov. 1989, Series A, vol. 165.
[129] For another application currently before the European Commission of Human Rights see Applic. 15088/89, *Manfred Jaubowski v. FRG*, declared admissible 3 Dec. 1991 (not yet

The European Court of Human Rights was divided nine votes to nine and the casting vote of the President resulted in the majority preferring to leave a margin of appreciation to the national authorities and not substitute their own view for that of the national courts. The majority, while admitting that this sort of speech enjoyed the protection offered by Article 10, noted that the article was written in a commercial context and that, as journalists, the applicants had special 'duties and responsibilities'.[130] In the commercial context this meant that the producers of the journal had obligations to respect the rights of others and a duty to respect the confidentiality of certain commercial information. Because even a correct statement can insinuate a false impression, in the commercial context this type of expression was said to deserve special scrutiny and the Court felt that this task was 'primarily for the national courts'.[131] The majority judgment again illustrates how the margin of appreciation widens when the Court has to review state practice concerning the operation of private law or human rights in the private sphere. It is not surprising that the Court did not wish to substitute its view for that of the national court. By doing so it would have essentially been operating as a court of final appeal for private disputes. Whilst a judgment by the European Court of Human Rights in a case involving a state prosecution against a newspaper may be resolved so that the State ceases to act in contravention to the Convention in the future, a judgment by the same Court concerning the operation of human rights in the private sphere, such as the one it gave in *Markt Intern*, will have only a minimal effect on future private litigants even if eventually the approach to the question is taken up by national courts.

For the nine judges in the minority, freedom of expression was the overriding value to be protected. According to the minority, the majority of

---

reported). In this case a journalist was prevented from circulating letters about his former employers with adverse implications for those employers. The journalist was found to have acted with competitive intent and in breach of the Unfair Competition Act.

[130] See Art. 10(2). The Commission's opinion developed some of its previous case-law and held in this case that commercial speech constitutes expression, but that in the instant case the article was of an editorial nature and could not be assimilated to an advertisement to promote specific sales; in this case the test of necessity found in 10(2), which may be less strict in the case of advertising, was to be applied in the normal way. Report of 18 Dec. 1987, para. 231. See Krüger and Buquiccio-de Boer (1990: 100); see also M.-A. Eissen, 'La Liberté d'expression dans la jurisprudence de la Cour Européenne des Droits de l'Homme', in Cassese and Clapham (1990: 113–36). The decisions, reports, and judgments of the Strasbourg organs, although concerned with international responsibility, in fact provide a certain amount of guidance for the consideration of Art. 10 by national courts in the cases which arise in the private sphere. Whilst the Strasbourg organs will not actually judge the compatibility of private action with Art. 10, their approach to the weight to be given to editorial content, criticism of public officials, advertising a trade or profession, etc. is highly relevant for the use of the Convention at the national level against private bodies.

[131] At para. 35 of the judgment.

the Court had erred in showing such deference to the national authorities.[132] The theoretical question arises: is there a right to expression? or does the Convention merely construe a liberty, a liberty not to have one's freedom of expression interfered with by the State?[133] The case-law of the European Court of Human Rights leans in favour of recognizing a right. In particular the *Lingens* judgment clearly states that the Court considers that freedom of expression has a dual role. Not only is it an essential foundation of a democratic society and its progress, but it is also an essential condition for 'each individual's self-fulfilment'.[134] In the area of freedom of expression it may be that the threat to freedom of speech comes from private monopolies of newspapers or television stations. Because the Court sees the importance of freedom of expression in terms of self-development, and not only in terms of the protection of democratic procedures, it would seem to admit the importance of controlling the private sphere and not only supervising actions by state agents. If the State is obliged to ensure an effective system to protect the right to free speech from private violation, the European Court of Human Rights could oblige a State to control private press monopolies.[135] Indeed, such an obligation was hinted at by the European Commission of Human Rights in the *Guillustreerde* case.[136] The Commission stated that a State may breach the Convention should it fail 'in its duty to protect [newspapers and the public] against excessive press concentrations'.[137]

---

[132] The question really is: does the Court 'remain aloof' (Macdonald 1987: 194) in order not to take on complex matters which it is not in a position fully to investigate or is this an abrogation of its supervisory function? It is disagreement about this which would seem to be at the heart of the split in the Court in the *Markt Intern* case.

[133] Note Art. 13(3) of the American Convention on Human Rights and the *Rubin* v. *Paraguay* case discussed in Ch. 4.3.1.3.

[134] Series A, vol. 103, para. 41, and see Ch. 5.2.3. The Court similarly stresses the dual nature of freedom of expression in the *Barthold* case, where freedom of expression is 'one of the essential foundations of a democratic society and one of the basic conditions for its progress and for the development of every man and every woman' (Series A, vol. 90, para. 58). This analysis of the right to freedom of expression follows the German Constitutional Court in the *Luth* case (1958) 7 B. Verf. GE 198, where that Court stressed the two aspects of freedom of expression as, on the one hand, contributing to the individual's intellectual and spiritual dimension and, on the other hand, underpinning the social dimension of speech as an essential element in democracy. See Kommers (1989: 368). This case together with the *Schmid–Spiegel* case (1961) 12 B. Verf. GE 113 are given as examples of *Drittwirkung* in operation, as they involved private disputes yet the constitutional values were held applicable to private law.

[135] Cf. Art. 13(3) of the American Convention on Human Rights, which reads: 'The right of expression may not be restricted by indirect methods or means, such as the abuse of . . . private controls over newsprint, radio broadcasting frequencies, or in the equipment used in the dissemination of information.'

[136] *Guillustreerde Pers NV* v. *The Netherlands*, Applic. 5178/71, report of 6 July 1976, 8 D. & R. 5 at para. 88.

[137] For an analysis of some of the measures which a State may have to take to ensure freedom of expression not only for those with resources and access to the public broadcasting

In this way there is a move which can be expressed as a move from the idea of 'protection *against* the State' to 'protection *by* the State'. In other contexts this corresponds to the difference traditionally drawn between civil/political rights and social/economic rights. In the French literature the difference is expressed as the difference between 'droit de' and 'droit à'.

The extent to which the broadcasting regulations of any one State ensure pluralism is not an easy question for the Court to review. There is no agreement about whether reliance on advertising revenue increases or decreases the ease of access to the media. No one is sure whether quotas, of whatever nature, actually protect or suffocate creativity. What is clear is that it will be very difficult to lay down human rights norms which are applicable for the twenty-six signatories to the Convention. Some of the regulation has already been attempted at the supranational level in the form of the European Convention on Transfrontier Television (1989) and the Court is unlikely to demand that States implement regulations which go beyond the minimum guarantees contained therein.

A myriad of questions arise once we admit that freedom of expression has to be protected in the sphere of relations between individuals. For example, do editors have a duty to respect the right of expression of journalists on their payroll? Although some States already protect journalists from editorial interference, it is unlikely that the Court would find the necessary consensus at the European level to find a State in violation of the Convention for failing to offer this sort of protection in the private sphere. Similarly, the Commission has left open to what extent a denial of broadcasting time to an individual or group raises an issue under Article 10. The most that can be said is that the Commission has stated that, although Article 10 does not grant an 'unfettered right' to broadcasting time on television or radio, there may be an issue under Article 10 alone or in conjunction with Article 14 where, say, 'one political party was excluded from broadcasting facilities at election time while other parties were given broadcasting time'.[138]

facilities, but also for foreigners, minorities, and those with unpopular views, see M. Bullinger, 'Report on "Freedom of Expression and Information: An Essential Element of Democracy"', in *Proceedings of the Sixth International Colloquy about the European Convention on Human Rights* (Dordrecht: Martinus Nijhoff, 1988), 44–139.

[138] *X and the Assoc. of Z* v. *UK*, Applic. 4515/70, (1971) 14 Yearbook 538 at 546 (the Commission did not find it necessary to determine whether the Government could be responsible for the BBC, 544); see also *X* v. *Sweden*, Applic. 9297/81, 28 D. & R. 204, access to Swedish radio and television controlled exclusively by the Swedish Radio Corporation, no appearance of violation of Art. 10; interestingly the applicant's complaint concerning lack of an effective remedy was dismissed, as the Commission held that it was the effect of the (delegated) legislation which was the main object of the complaint, and Art. 13 does not guarantee the right to control legislation for conformity with the Convention. Should the Strasbourg organs have to tackle this question head on, the difficulties of finding

It may be worth outlining some of the duties to respect the rights of others which have been placed on individuals claiming their right to freedom of expression. These represent the application of the Convention against private bodies in the way outlined in Section 7.1, point (1). The Commission and Court's decisions on this point do not actually create enforceable duties on private bodies but they conclusively show that private individuals will lose their right to protection under the Convention should they fail to respect the rights of others in this sphere. It may even be suggested that some of the duties enunciated by the Commission could become directly enforceable at the national level.

In *Kuhnen* v. *Federal Republic of Germany* the applicant complained about penal measures taken to curb his neo-Nazi activities. The Commission noted that the law was 'aimed at protecting the basic order of freedom and democracy and the notion of understanding amongst peoples'. The aim was therefore legitimate under Article 10(2) as being established 'in the interests of national security [and] public safety [and] for the protection of the rights of others'.[139] Reference was also made to the preamble of the Convention, which mentions the importance of democracy, and to the fact that the applicant's policy contained elements of racial and religious discrimination. In another application a prisoner was denied access to a magazine which the authorities claimed was anti-Semitic. The Commission found this denial of the right to receive information justified, as the prison authorities had struck the necessary balance between the individual's freedom of expression and the legitimate interests of others, or the prevention of disorder or crime.[140]

In *X* v. *United Kingdom*, Applic. 8010/77, a teacher was dismissed following his insistence on advertising the anti-abortion movement with stickers and posters containing anti-abortion slogans. It was held that his freedom of expression should be limited in order to ensure the protection of the rights of others—in this case the rights of the parents to respect for

---

a minimal level of protection at the European level will be considerable. No progress was made at the inter-governmental level following the Parliamentary Assembly's Rec. 1077 (1988) on Access to Transfrontier Audio-Visual Media during Election Campaigns. The problem remains a real one, with the possibility that parties may avoid national legislation by broadcasting across frontiers. The Report of the Committee on Parliamentary and Public Relations of the Parliamentary Assembly includes a study of the situation in fifteen Member States; see doc. 5766, 8 July 1987.

On the question of public access to information about major events and the regulation of exclusivity for the media to certain events see Committee of Ministers Rec. R(91)5. The question of access to broadcasting facilities has been dealt with in the context of the UN Committee of Human Rights; see Communication 14/61, *Seta* v. *Finland*, mentioned in Ch. 4.3.1.1.2.

[139] Applic. 12194/86, decision of 12 May 1988, unreported; the citation is from p. 5 of the transcript.

[140] *Applic. 13214/87* v. *UK*, reported in the Law Society Gazette (26 Apr. 1989), 45.

their religious and philosophical convictions concerning the education of their children.[141]

In *X Ltd. and Y* v. *United Kingdom*[142] a gay magazine was subjected to a private prosecution after it had published a poem ascribing homosexual practices to Christ. According to the headnote from the House of Lords report the poem 'purported to describe in explicit detail acts of sodomy and fellatio with the body of Christ immediately after His death and ascribe to Him during His lifetime promiscuous homosexual practices with the Apostles and other men'.

The private prosecution by Mrs Whitehouse resulted in conviction and a fine of £1,000. In dismissing the application the Commission pointed to the rights of the private prosecutor, and concluded that the restriction of freedom of expression was covered by a legitimate purpose recognized in the Convention, namely the protection of the rights of others—in this case 'the right of citizens not to be offended in their religious feeling by publications'.[143] This was essentially the approach taken by Lord Scarman in the House of Lords.[144]

In *X* v. *Belgium* a teacher was interviewed on a television programme about lesbians and stated that she had been passed over for a promotion at her school, as it was said that it would be inappropriate for her to be in charge of 2,000 girls. She suggested that the fact that the school currently had two male directors posed a significant danger and she was eventually dismissed. The Commission rejected her application, stating that, as a teacher, she had special 'duties and responsibilities' and the dismissal had been necessary for the protection of the rights and reputation of others.[145]

Therefore it is to some extent recognized that individuals have duties under the Convention and a breach of those duties will deprive them of the ability to claim the right to freedom of expression. It is not inconceivable that, in a country where the Convention was directly effective in the private sphere, Article 10 could actually create enforceable duties on individuals, not only giving rise to private suits for blasphemy, libel, racial propaganda, and obscenity, but also grounding claims for access to information, which is also included in Article 10(1). This being said, the case-law is less developed as concerns the operation of the right in the private sphere.

The questions which arise under what were called type (3) situations at

---

[141] Applic. 8010/77, 16 D. & R. 101. One might ask if the teacher would have been obliged to recognize the rights of the parents to respect for their convictions concerning education if the First Protocol had not entered into force, or if the teacher came from a country which had not ratified it?
[142] Applic. 8710/79, 28 D. & R. 77.
[143] 28 D. & R. 77.
[144] [1979] 1 All ER 898 at 927; see Ch. 10.3.
[145] Applic. 11389/85, decision of 3 May 1988 (unreported).

the beginning of this chapter (public/private boundaries) have also been posed in the context of Article 10. However, the Commission avoided having to decide whether the United Kingdom was responsible for the BBC under the Convention.[146] This illustrates again the dangerous nature of the public/private distinction in this context. Although the Government has minimal control over the BBC (which was set up under Royal Charter), it has statutory control over the independent television companies. If the Commission were to decide that the BBC is not a state body due to the degree of independence under which it operates and the lack of a statutory basis for its powers, we could end up with the paradoxical result that the independent television companies would be obliged to respect individual rights under the Convention, yet the public service broadcaster, the BBC, would not.[147]

Two especially problematic questions concerning the application of Article 10 in the private sphere have been highlighted by van Dijk and van Hoof. First, to what extent does Article 10 imply rights to rectification and reply with respect to information incorrectly diffused by private bodies? The answer at the national level may have to wait for a suitable case in Strasbourg. Of course, in Strasbourg it would be the State that would be held responsible for a failure to implement appropriate remedies. But the scope of the Strasbourg judgment would give a lead as to the impact of Article 10 in this area. The issue has not yet been determined by the Commission,[148] and as van Dijk and van Hoof point out, any state restrictions in this field would be fully justified under Article 10(2), as they would be aimed at the 'protection of the rights of others'.[149]

Second, to what extent does Article 10 include a duty on private bodies to impart information? Van Dijk and van Hoof agree with Professor

---

[146] *X and the Assoc. of Z* v. *UK*, Applic. 4515/70, (1971) 14 Yearbook 538: 'In the present case the question arises whether the respondent Government could be held responsible under the Convention for any acts of the BBC (cf. Applic. No. 3059/67 *Collection of Decision* 28, p. 89). However, the Commission does not find it necessary to determine this issue in the circumstances of the present application as, even assuming that the allegations made by the applicants could involve such responsibility, this part of the application is, in any event, inadmissible on other grounds' (544).

[147] See Ch. 4.3.3; broadcasting law in the UK is currently in a state of flux. For details of the Broadcasting Bill 1990 and the statutory and non-statutory bodies which it creates see Robertson and Nicol (1990: 464). The Act will not fully enter into force until 1994.

[148] Applic. 1906/63, *X* v. *Belgium*, unpublished.

[149] 1990: 413. The right to reply was recently studied in the UK by the Calcutt Committee, who concluded that legislation to provide such a right was impractical. *Report of the Committee on Privacy and Related Matters*, Cmn. 1102 (London: HMSO, 1990). It is difficult to see how a right to reply could be made effective without unjustifiably restricting freedom of expression. Colin Munro has pointed to a Supreme Court decision in the USA which struck down a right of reply law as an interference with editors' right to publish what they wish: *Miami Herald Publishing Co.* v. *Tornillo* 418 US 241 (1974). See Munro (1991: 106).

Alkema that the phrase 'without interference by public authority' which follows the guarantee of freedom of information implies that 'the drafters would seem to have had in mind an authority which refrains from interfering rather than an authority which actively imparts information' (van Dijk and van Hoof 1990: 418); and they further note that the Civil and Political Rights Covenant includes the additional words 'to seek' whilst Article 10(1) does not, thus concluding that the *Drittwirkung* of the Convention does not impose on States obligations actively to impart information or to oblige private bodies to do so.

This reasoning is taken up again by van Dijk and van Hoof when they point out that the absence of the phrase 'without interference by public authority' in the Covenant's Article 19 'eliminates the strongest possible argument against the view that this provision may also have some *Drittwirkung*' (1990: 428). It is suggested that one should not rely on textual differences between the two texts to interpret the Convention restrictively. More importantly, one should not conclude that the omission of a phrase in one text implies that the drafters of the first text deliberately put it in for the same reasons that the drafters of the second text left it out.

The question of the inclusion of the phrase 'without interference by public authority' is documented in the *travaux préparatoires* of the Covenant, Article 19(1) (freedom to hold opinions; cf. Article 9 ECHR). According to the records: 'there were two views regarding this point. One was that the article was intended to protect the individual only against governmental interference. . . . The other view was that the article should protect the individual against all kinds of interference.'[150]

When the issue arose in the context of Article 19(2) (freedom of expression) insertion of the phrase 'without governmental interference, save as provided in paragraph 3' was opposed as 'private financial interests and monopoly control of media of information could be as harmful to the free flow of information as governmental intereference, and . . . the latter should not be singled out to the exclusion of the former'.[151] While the drafters of the Covenant made an explicit choice to allow the *Drittwirkung* of Article 19, it does not seem that the drafters of the Convention chose to limit the ambit of Article 10 to the public sphere by the insertion of the phrase 'without governmental interference'. In fact, at one point the

---

[150] Commission on Human Rights, 6th Session (1950), A/2929 ch. VI para. 122, reproduced in Bossuyt (1987: 379). The first view is recorded as being supported by the British, Americans, Australians, Indians, Chinese, and Belgians, whilst the second view is attributed to the French, Danish, and Chileans. The final suggestion, 'Everyone shall have the right to hold opinions without interference', was a British suggestion and was adopted unanimously.

[151] 3rd Committee, 16th Session (1961), A/5000 para. 24; Bossuyt (1987: 385).

phrase was inserted twice in Article 10(1) following the United Kingdom's general proposals for *definitions* of rights rather than the Consultative Assembly's *formulation/enumeration* of rights based on the Universal Declaration, which does not include such a phrase in its Article 19.[152] When the Italian delegate compared the two texts no difference was discerned as regards freedom of expression, and the United Kingdom's delegate claimed that the provisions on freedom of association and information in the proposed *definition* of human rights covered the rights *enumerated* in the Assembly's proposal.[153]

We may therefore conclude that, in the absence of any evidence that the drafters of the Convention intended to exclude private violations of freedom of expression, an evolutive, dynamic interpretation of the Convention requires that it be interpreted in accordance with changing international standards, and the deliberate exclusion of the phrase 'interference by public authority' by the drafters of the Covenant suggests that Article 10 may be interpreted so as to apply to the actions of private bodies. Indeed, following the hypotheses put forward in Chapter 4, we would go further and add that the inclusion of the phrase 'interference by public authority' was only intended to reinforce the State's willingness to hold public officials accountable rather than grant them immunity as state agents. The opposite interpretation is not justified on a plain reading of the text, nor with reference to the intention of the drafters. As the object of the Convention is an evolving standard of human rights protection, and the text of the Covenant is evidence of evolving standards,[154] there is no reason to restrict Article 10 by reference to the phrase 'interference by a public authority'. Article 10 can be said to imply *Drittwirkung* in the following ways. First, individuals owe other individuals a duty to respect their freedom of expression. Second, individuals have an obligation to other individuals to impart information. Third, the State has obligations to ensure that individuals can effectively exercise the former two rights. Of course, all these rights will be hedged with restrictions found in Article 10(2) and with regard to other human rights, but they should not be denied through a restrictive, textual, legalistic interpretation.

---

[152] Doc. CM/WP I (50)15 app.: CM/WP I (50)14 revised, A 925 of 16 Mar. 1950. Art. 10(1) read: 'Everyone shall have the right to freedom of expression without governmental interference; this right shall include freedom to hold opinions and to receive and impart information without governmental interference, regardless of frontiers, either orally, in writing or in print, in the form of art or by duly licenced visual or auditory devices' (See *Travaux préparatoires*, iv (Dordrecht: Martinus Nijhoff, 1977), 62).

[153] *Travaux préparatoires*, iv. 110.

[154] For a reference by the Commission to the text of the Covenant in the context of Art. 11 ECHR see below s. 7.8 (*X* v. *Ireland*, decision of 1 Feb. 1971 (1971) 14 Yearbook 198.

7.8 ARTICLE 11

Article 11 reads:

(1) Everyone has the right to freedom of peaceful assembly and freedom of association with others, including the right to form and join trade unions for the protection of his interests.

(2) No restrictions shall be placed on the exercise of these rights other than such as are prescribed by law and are necessary in a democratic society in the interests of national security or public safety, for the prevention of crime, for the protection of health or morals or for the protection of the rights and freedoms of others. This Article shall not prevent the imposition of lawful restrictions on the exercise of these rights by members of the armed forces, of the police or of the administration of the State.

This Article, if applied to relations in the private sphere, presents many opportunities for use and abuse.

The Article immediately throws up the problem of the public/private divide concerning nationalized bodies and the State's responsibility *qua* employer. In an early case *X* v. *Ireland*[155] the Commission found it unnecessary to decide whether the Irish Electricity Supply Board was controlled by the State. The Irish Government had invited the Commission to dismiss the application *ratione personae* as, although the Board was established by statute and financed by public funds, the Government considered that the Board was solely responsible for its functions and could not incur direct responsibility for the Government regarding Mr X's allegations. The Commission's decision contains an interesting remark which may one day be picked up, should similar cases come to Strasbourg involving nationalized bodies. The decision states:

whereas for the present purposes it is sufficient to note that, while the Government exercises, at least, general supervision over the policy of the Board, the day to day administration is solely in the hands of the Board; whereas the Commission considers that the acts alleged by the applicant clearly fall within the domain of such day to day administration for which the Government is not directly responsible.[156]

The Commission was however prepared to hold that anti-trade union activities in the form of dismissing a shop steward could amount to a breach of Article 11, and incur the responsibility of the State for failure to ensure the effective enjoyment of Article 11 (the right to form trade unions).[157] This was an important extension of the rights explicitly protected

---

[155] Applic. 4125/69, decision of 1 Feb. 1971 (1971) 14 Yearbook 198.
[156] At 218.
[157] See below the report of the Commission in the *Young, James and Webster* case, para. 169, for confirmation that Art. 11 applies to anti-union activities. For a purely private

by Article 11, namely the rights to join or form trade unions. The Irish Government had argued that on its face Article 11 does not protect individuals, such as Mr X, from pressure to relinquish the office of shop steward or dismissal for trade union activities. In giving this wide interpretation, the Commission relied on the International Labour Organization Convention of 1948 (no. 87) ratified (then) by all Members of the Council of Europe with the exception of Turkey, and Article 22 of the Covenant on Civil and Political Rights (not then in force). The main question then for the Commission was: 'whether the respondent Government had discharged its obligation under the Convention to ensure that the domestic law offers a remedy for the alleged violation of Article 11 of the Convention.'[158]

The Commission was satisfied that the applicant could have brought an action against the board and that there was 'no failure on the part of the respondent Government to ensure that there was an effective remedy for the violation of Article 11 alleged by the applicant'.[159] This last sentence is important as it implies and confirms that the rights guaranteed by Article 11 should be protected at the national level, so that an individual has an effective remedy for a breach of that Article by his employer, regardless of the public or private nature of the employer.

This would now seem to be confirmed by the Court in the *Young, James and Webster* v. *United Kingdom* case. It was the legislative provisions which allowed a violation of Article 11 in the case of the British Rail workers. But the actual violation resulted from the private closed shop agreement between British Rail and the unions involved. As the Court found it unnecessary to decide whether the Government was responsible for British Rail as a nationalized industry, it can be assumed that the same conclusions would have been drawn had British Rail been a completely private company. The Commission's report in this case was clearly in favour of the operation of Article 11 in the private sphere: 'It is well established by now that apart from protecting the individual against state action, there are Articles of the Convention which oblige the State to

---

employment situation which involved anti-union activities see *X* v. *Spain*, Applic. 10182/82, decision of 14 July 1983, unreported, where the Commission accepted that some Articles protected the individual not only against the State but also against other individuals. 'D'autre part, la Commission rappelle la jurisprudence selon laquelle il est bien établi que la Convention contient des articles qui, non seulement protègent l'individu contre l'État, mais encore obligent l'État à protéger les droits de l'individu même contre les agissements d'autrui (Commission eur. D.H., Affaire Young, James et Webster, Rapport du 14 décembre 1979; Cour eur. D.H., Affaire Marckx, arrêt du 13 juin 1979; Affaire Young, James et Webster, arrêt du 13 août 1981)', at 4 of the unpublished report. However the case was dismissed for non-exhaustion of domestic remedies.

[158] At 222.
[159] At 224.

protect individual rights even against the action of others.[160] . . . The Commission is of the opinion that Article 11 is such a provision as far as dismissal on the basis of union activity or as a sanction for not joining a specific union is concerned.'[161]

A subsequent case involved a purely private employment relationship between Mr Conroy and his employers Cunliffe Engravers. He was dismissed following his expulsion from his union as there was a union–management agreement. The case resulted in a 'friendly settlement' and the report of the Commission reveals that Mr Conroy was offered compensation by the United Kingdom Government of £37,600 for loss of earnings and £550 for non-pecuniary losses (anxiety and stress).[162] Although we cannot consider such a 'friendly settlement' case-law, it suggests that Article 11 is fully operative in the private sphere.

As is well known the Court left open the question as to whether the State was responsible for British Rail in the *Young, James and Webster* case and therefore directly responsible for the violations of Article 11. The arguments presented by the parties are long and complicated, and although the Commission had found that British Rail was a state body in their decision on admissibility, they revised this in their report and found it was unnecessary to determine the issue either way. None of the arguments which purport to declare the public/private nature of British Rail is particularly conclusive. The applicants referred to the fact that responsibility to Parliament is enforced through a Minister of the Crown.[163] The applicants then asserted that a 'fundamental matter [such as] making a "closed shop" agreement falls within the field of general policy rather than the day-to-day administration and accordingly engages the responsibility of the Minister concerned and, through him, of the Government'.[164]

At the admissibility stage the Commission had found that the Government was the employer of the applicants. The Government responded to this finding by submitting a detailed appendix arguing that (1) British Rail

---

[160] The Commission cites the European Court of Human Rights in the *Marckx* case, judgment of 13 June 1979, Series A, vol. 31, p. 15, para. 31.

[161] At para. 168 of the report, note that the Commission has reaffirmed, this time in the context of a report, that anti-union activity, even by private employers, comes within the scope of Art. 11.

[162] Applic. 10061/82, *Conroy* v. *UK*, report adopted 15 May 1986, 46 D. & R. 66; other friendly settlements concerning the 'closed shop' include *Reed* v. *UK*, Applic. 9520/81, 34 D. & R. 107, and *Eaton et al.* v. *UK*, Applics. 8476/79–8481/79, 39 D. & R. 11.

[163] They cited a passage by Professor Hood Philips, who in his *Constitutional and Administrative Law* textbook wrote: 'An important constitutional problem that has not yet been completely solved is how to secure adequate parliamentary supervision of public corporations in the interests of the consumer and taxpayer, while pursuing the policy of de-centralisation and freedom from detailed control. As far as industrial corporations are concerned, experience shows that it is extremely difficult to draw the line between general policy and day-to-day administration' (cited at 136 of the Series B report of the hearings).

[164] Ibid.

is not a part or an organ of the State, (2) British Rail is not, whether as employer or otherwise, under the control of the State, and (3) the State is not the 'employer' within the principle established by the *Swedish Engine Drivers'* case.[165] Without going into the detail of the Government's submissions, it is worth noting that the Government attached considerable importance to the fact that British Rail would not be granted immunity as an agent of the Crown in the United Kingdom courts nor would the Government seek to claim immunity for this body in foreign courts. However, a functional approach to the question would show that the reason for denying immunity to British Rail is to grant redress to those individuals affected by its actions and that Crown immunities and privileges have to be restrictively construed. But in the context of protection of human rights, the public nature of the body ought to be widely construed if a narrow construction would result in immunity for the same said body.

The *Memorial of the Trades Union Congress* (TUC) adopted the submissions of the United Kingdom Government and asserted that 'It is manifestly incorrect in law and in fact to regard British Rail as a body subject to the State as the hidden real employer.'[166] This assertion is understandable in the context of the defence of the 'closed shop'. But one might be tempted to ask: would the TUC have denied the link between the public corporation and the Government had the case been about anti-union practices? As we shall see in Chapter 8, in Community law the existence of the corporation–State nexus is vital to establishing individual rights to protection from sex discrimination under Community directives. In these cases unions will be called on by their members to intervene and argue that the requisite nexus exists. The public/private boundary is often merely a smokescreen which obscures the real clash of interests involved. Attempts to define the boundary simply hide the nature of the conflict.

The question of the direct applicability of Article 11 between private individuals or non-state actors has not actually been answered by the Court. It was expressly left open in the *Swedish Engine Drivers'* case,[167] even if it is now clear, following the *Young, James and Webster* case, that the State has positive obligations in the field of trade union activities. It is suggested that Article 11 is directly applicable between private actors at the national level. The Court's and Commission's case-law leads to the

---

[165] At 103 of the Series B publication.

[166] At 193 of the Series B publication.

[167] Judgment of 6 Feb. 1976, Series A, vol. 20, p. 14: 'Article 11 is accordingly binding upon the "State as employer", whether the latter's relations with its employees are governed by public or private law. Consequently, the Court does not feel constrained to take into account the circumstance that in any event certain of the applicant's complaints appear to be directed against both the Office and the Swedish State as holder of public power. Neither does the Court consider that it has to rule on the applicability, whether direct or indirect, of Article 11 to relations between individuals *stricto sensu*.'

conclusion that the direct *Drittwirkung* of this Article is now confirmed. Cases have already come before the Commission which involve a determination by national courts of the applicability of Article 11 between private bodies. Although the Commission rejects the application *ratione personae*, in so far as it is addressed to the acts of the union or employer involved, the Commission has not excluded the operation of Article 11 in private relations. Industrial relations in the private sector are covered by Article 11. Professor Frowein's submission to the Court in the *Young, James and Webster* case is perhaps indicative of the Commission's refusal to create a no-go area in this context. Frowein stated:

But recognising that the trade unions may be seen as privileged because they are expressly mentioned in Article 11 is one thing. It is something quite different, I would suggest, to say that regulations concerning the trade unions may be immune from the Convention system in general. I suggest that we must be very careful before admitting that in practice the trade union system is more or less an area which is free from the basic guarantees of our Convention.[168]

Although in *Cheall* v. *United Kingdom* the Commission dismissed Mr Cheall's application *ratione personae*, as it was effectively a complaint about action taken by his union, it admitted that exclusion or expulsion from a union may breach the right to join a union and, for this right to be effective,

the State must protect the individual aginst any abuse of a dominant position by trade unions. . . . Such abuse might occur, for example, where exclusion or expulsion was not in accordance with union rules or where the rules were wholly unreasonable or arbitrary or where the consequences of exclusion or expulsion resulted in exceptional hardship such as job losses because of a closed shop.[169]

The Commission did not find the rules in question unreasonable and noted that the decision did not involve job loss through operation of the 'closed shop'. The Commission had also noted earlier in its decision that 'The protection afforded by the provision is primarily against interference by the state.'[170] However, a recent application concerned the resignation of a lorry driver due to his employer's refusal to allow him to join the union of his choice (the URTU) rather than the TGWU. Although the United Kingdom Government argued that the applicant's employer was a private body and not the responsibility of the Government, the Commission declared the application admissible. The fact that the employers were a private company and the complaint was essentially against the trade union was not determinative for the Commission's eventual report. The

---

[168] At 199 of the Series B publication.
[169] Applic. 10550/83, 42 D. & R. 178 at 186.
[170] At 185.

Commission noted 'that actions leading to the dismissal of the applicant were primarily the responsibility of the applicant's employer and trade union. Where, however, the domestic law makes lawful the treatment complained of, the Commission finds that the responsibility of the respondent State may be engaged in particular cases.'[171] The Commission recalled the Court's jurisprudence that 'compulsion to join a trade union may not always be contrary to the Convention' and went on to state that 'Abuse might, in the Commission's opinion occur, for example, where the consequences of failure to join a trade union resulted in exceptional hardship such as dismissal.' However, in this case the Commission found that the applicant had failed to avail himself of some of the remdies available and therefore it could not be said that the Government had failed to provide protection for him. The Commission expressed the opinion by eight votes to six that there had been no violation of Article 11.[172]

Another example of the Commission deciding an application concerning the operation of Article 11 in the private sphere is *Van der Heijden* v. *The Netherlands*.[173] This application involved an employee who had been dismissed for membership of a political party whose objectives were opposed to those of his employer (a foundation concerned with the welfare of immigrants governed by private law). The case arose out of a court decision which upheld the termination of the employee's contract. The case was not dismissed *ratione personae*. The public/private status of the employer was not crucial. The Commission held that the domestic court decision constituted action by the State and so there was jurisdiction under Article 19. However, the Commission found that the interference was justified for the protection of the rights of others. The private nature of the dispute can no longer bar the application of Article 11 either at the international or national level.[174]

Leaving the area of industrial relations we must consider the Court's judgment in the *Plattform Ärzte* case.[175] The applicants were an association of doctors opposed to abortion. The complaint arose out the disruption of their meeting by counter-demonstrators. Before the Court the Austrian Government argued that 'Article 11 did not create any positive obligation

---

[171] *Sibson* v. *UK*, report of 10 Dec. 1991, para. 28.

[172] *Sibson* v. *UK*, Applic. 14327/88, report of 10 Dec. 1991. The dissenting opinion of Mr Loucaides *et al.* looked at the result of the applicant's wish not to join a trade union—his dismissal—and found that the State had an obligation to ensure by its legislation that individuals are not penalized in this way. The dissenting opinion of Mr Busuttil makes clear that Art. 11 applies as between the employers and the applicant: 'There was no pressing social need justifying the interference by the employers with the applicant's negative right to freedom of association for any of the purposes enumerated in Article 11 para 2.'

[173] Applic. 11002/84, 41 D. & R. 264.

[174] The use of Art. 11 directly against private bodies is dealt with in Ch. 10.

[175] Judgment of 21 June 1988, Series A, vol. 139.

to protect demonstrations . . . freedom of assembly was mainly designed to protect the individual from direct interferences by the State. Unlike some other provisions in the Convention and the Austrian Constitution, Article 11 did not apply to relations between individuals.'[176] The Court, following the Commission, rejected this completely:

A demonstration may annoy or give offence to persons opposed to the ideas or claims that it is seeking to promote. The participants must, however, be able to hold the demonstration without having to fear that they will be subjected to physical violence by their opponents; such a fear would be liable to deter associations or other groups supporting common ideas or interests from openly expressing their opinions on highly controversial issues affecting the community. In a democracy the right to counter-demonstrate cannot extend to inhibiting the exercise of the right to demonstrate.

Genuine effective freedom of peaceful assembly cannot, therefore, be reduced to a mere duty on the part of the State not to interfere: a purely negative conception would not be compatible with the object and purpose of Article 11. Like Article 8, Article 11 sometimes requires positive measures to be taken, even in the sphere of relations between individuals, if need be (see *mutatis mutandi*, the X and Y v the Netherlands judgment . . .).[177]

This approach emphasizes the importance of free speech in the public domain and that it may be threatened by private actors. The approach fits neatly in the framework suggested in Chapter 5. The right in question has as its aim the protection of democracy, and so in order for it to be applicable in the private sphere it must involve the sphere of the public. In this case it did so operate and the Court asserted the applicability of Article 11. However, had the right to assemble been invoked in the sphere of the private (say by the pro-abortion group in a church), then Article 11 might not have offered protection.

The Court went on to grant the authorities a wide discretion in the choice of means to be used to guarantee the right to assembly. The Court further stated that 'In this area the obligation they [the Contracting States] enter into under Article 11 of the Convention is an obligation as to measures to be taken and not as to results to be achieved.'[178] In the actual case the Court was only concerned to determine 'whether there is an arguable claim that the appropriate authorities failed to take the necessary measures'.[179] After an examination of the measures taken, the Court found no arguable claim that there had been a breach of Article 11 and so Article 13 did not apply.

Summarizing, we can conclude that Article 11 is seen as applicable in

---

[176] At para. 29 of the Court's judgment.
[177] At para. 32 of the judgment.
[178] At para. 34 of the judgment.
[179] At para. 36 of the judgment.

the private sector. In the area of labour relations the absence or presence of legislation is enough to engage the responsibility of the State, and even court decisions in private disputes may give rise to questions under Article 11. As long as the rules of unions are not unreasonable, individuals may not challenge expulsions or exclusion from the union. But in special circumstances, in particular where the existence of the 'closed shop' means that the individual will be dismissed, Article 11 may be applicable even at the international level. Anti-union practices in the private sphere would seem to be a violation of Article 11 and the State may have positive obligations to prevent this or at least ensure an effective remedy in such a situation. As far as concerns the right to assembly, Article 11 extends even into the sphere of relations between individuals. This Article may require positive measures to be taken by the State to protect individuals from other individuals. This is especially important where an assembly is formed in order to express ideas.

The issue at the international level involves the State as respondent, but invoking Article 11 at the national level means deciding exactly what duties employers, unions, professional associations, etc. have. The clear danger is that individuals may ensnare the operation of the organizations designed to protect their interests through vexatious legal action. The clash between the individual and the collective interest is not identical to the individual–State relationship. Continued legal attacks by individuals or dissenting minorities within an association could cripple the operation of that association. There is no such risk for the State. Furthermore there is an element of consent in the member–association relationship which is absent in the State–individual situation.

The Canadian experience is relevant at this point. Even though the Canadian Charter of Rights and Freedoms[180] has been held not to bind private bodies, it was applied to the collection of union dues and the way they were spent. In *Re Lavigne and Ontario Public Service Employees Union et al.*[181] Mr Lavigne challenged the use of $2 of $338 paid by him to the union. Although the political donations were consistent with the union's constitution and were supported by the majority of its members, the court of first instance found that Mr Lavigne's freedom of association had been violated. The procedure which unions were subsequently forced to set up by the courts were complex, potentially expensive, and time consuming. The implications of the *Lavigne* decisions are dramatically illustrated by Professor Mandel in his book *The Charter of Rights and the Legalization of Politics* (1989: 209–17). Mandel cites the vice-president of the National Citizens' Coalition (the right-wing pressure group that had backed Mr Lavigne) as saying that he hoped the Court's decision would

---

[180] Schedule B to Canada Act 1982 (UK).   [181] See Ch. 6.2.1.3.

cut $70 million from union budgets. We should be wary of allowing respect for fundamental principles to be exploited for motives which go way beyond concern for the individual's human rights.[182]

This brief review of some of the Strasbourg case-law surrounding the question of violations of human rights by private bodies has been designed to show that it is valid to examine the question Article by Article, as the policy questions regarding violations by private individuals have been developed in the context of specific Articles. We have, so far, concentrated on Articles 2, 3, 6(1), 8, 10, 11, and 17, as well as Article 2 of Protocol 1. Other Articles, such as Articles 4, 9, and 14, were also found potentially to touch the private sphere.[183] Issues arise under nearly all the other Articles but there has been little opportunity for the Commission and Court to examine them. In particular *Drittwirkung* has been suggested by commentators for Article 1 of Protocol 1,[184] for Article 5 of Protocol 7,[185] and for Article 12.[186]

However, it is suggested that where we are faced with difficult cases of applying human rights in the private sphere the approach detailed in Chapter 5 can still be taken: examine the aim of the right in question; if in the circumstances of the case it is supposed to protect dignity and the victim's dignity has been violated, then the State may have a duty to act, where, but for the State's omission, the violation might have been prevented or remedied. If, on the other hand, the overriding aim of the right in question is the protection of democracy, then for a violation to be relevant the actor should be acting in the sphere of the public; if democracy is thwarted or threatened by failure to recognize the right the Commission or Court can find the State has failed in its duty to secure the rights in the Convention.

7.9 STATE RESPONSIBILITY AS A CONSEQUENCE OF NATIONAL JUDICIAL DECISIONS AND THE QUESTION OF ARTICLE 13

Another way in which the Convention is pertinent in Strasbourg in the private sphere is when the State is held responsible for the acts of its

---

[182] The extent to which Art. 11 has already been directly applied in the private sphere against unions in the UK courts was dealt with in Ch. 1.2. The issue is re-examined in Ch. 10 in the light of the European and Canadian developments.

[183] The question of the applicability of Art. 14 (non-discrimination) presents a vast and important new field of possibilities. However, the jurisprudence is rather underdeveloped.

[184] Raymond (1988: 531–8).

[185] S. Trechsel, 'Das Verflixte Siebente? Bemerkungen zum 7. Zusatzprotokoll zur EMRK', in M. Nowak, D. Steurer, and H. Tretter (eds.), *Progress in the Spirit of Human Rights* (Kehl am Rhein: Engel, 1988), 195–211.

[186] See van Dijk and van Hoof (1990: 446), who raise the question of private employers discriminating against employees on grounds of their married status.

courts in denying or violating an applicant's rights under the Convention. The case-law of the Commission and Court of Human Rights is rather undeveloped in the field of reviewing national courts' decisions in essentially private disputes. This may be partly explained by the fact that the traditional conception of human rights suggests that they only protect citizens from abuses of power by the State, and so parties to a private law dispute would not think of taking their case on to Strasbourg subsequent to the decision of the national court. One case was mentioned in the section on Article 11, *Van der Heijden* v. *The Netherlands*, where the Commission found that the decision of a court in a private labour law dispute incurred the responsibility of the State.[187] An example of a private dispute which was dealt with by the European Court of Human Rights is the *Markt Intern* case, dealt with in the section on Article 10. In that case the Court states:

In the Court's view, the applicants clearly suffered an 'interference by public authority' in the exercise of the right protected under Article 10, in the form of the injunction issued by the Federal Court of Justice restraining them from repeating the statements appearing in the information bulletin of 20 November 1975. Such interference infringes the Convention if it does not satisfy the requirements of paragraph 2 of Article 10.[188]

One of the areas of contention in the case was whether the interference was 'prescribed by law', as required by Article 10(2). The European Court of Human Rights had to examine whether the law fulfilled the requirements of foreseeability and accessibility as developed in its own case-law. At this point the law which the Court examined was not the German legislation on unfair competition but the case-law of the German courts in this (private) sphere. The Court concluded on this point that consistent case-law from the Federal Court of Justice existed, and that 'This case-law, which was clear and abundant and had been the subject of extensive commentary, was such as to enable commercial operators and their advisers to regulate their conduct in the relevant sphere.'[189] As explained above, the case was decided on the question as to whether the injunction was necessary in a democratic society, and the Court's majority judgment held that the final decision of the Federal Court of Justice did not go beyond the 'margin of appreciation left to the national authorities'.[190]

We have seen that the margin of appreciation widens when the Court of Human Rights has to determine the positive obligations of the State in the private sphere cases. In the same way the decisions of national courts involving an essentially private dispute will not be second-guessed in Strasbourg. The European Court will 'not substitute its own evaluation

---

[187] Applic. 11002/84, 41 D. & R. 264.
[188] Judgment of 20 Nov. 1989, Series A, vol. 165 at para. 27.
[189] At para. 30.   [190] At para. 37.

for that of national courts . . . where those courts, on reasonable grounds, had considered the restrictions to be necessary'.[191]

It may be worth noting that in the *Markt Intern* case the Commission was prepared to find a violation by twelve votes to one.[192] However, the vote in the Court was so close (nine votes to nine, with the President's casting vote leading to a majority finding of no violation) that it would be rash to conclude that the Court shows more reverence to national courts than the Commission does. In fact, in the *Sunday Times* case[193] the Court had a slim majority in favour of finding that the House of Lords' injunction violated Article 10 (eleven votes against nine) and the Commission were split eight votes to five, again in favour of finding a violation. In that case the Court's majority judgment states that, even where 'the respondent State has exercised its discretion reasonably, carefully, and in good faith', the State remains subject to the control of the Court 'as regards the compatibility of its conduct with the engagements it has under the Convention'.

It is in this area of control by the Strasbourg organs of national courts' decisions in private law matters that the Commission and Court of Human Rights are most likely to influence the privatization of human rights at the national level. In *Hoffmann* v. *Austria*[194] the applicant had joined the Jehovah's Witnesses and had applied to the courts for custody of her children while her divorce proceedings were still pending. The Supreme Court awarded custody to the applicant's ex-husband. Custody was awarded on the grounds *inter alia* that this was for the best interests of the children, due to the influence that the applicant's religion might have on their future development. The Austrian Government claimed that there had been no interference with the applicant's rights under Articles 8, 9, and 14, as she had not been prevented from practising her religion, and the dispute over custody arose out of a private law dispute between the applicant and her husband. The Commission has declared the application admissible. In the opinions of the Commission in the two private corporal punishment applications (discussed above) the Commission found that there had been a violation of Article 13 in each case. In both cases it was the *civil* law in action in the County Court for assault which was held to be ineffective.[195]

---

[191] At para. 37.

[192] Report of 18 Dec. 1987. The Commission found that the domestic courts had 'failed to distinguish between the freedom of the business-orientated press to impart specialist information on the one hand and a competitor's advertising interests on the other' (*Stock-Taking on the European Convention on Human Rights* (Supplement 1987), 75).

[193] Judgment of 26 Apr. 1979, Series A, vol. 30.

[194] Applic. 12875/87, decision of 10 July 1990, not yet reported but see 1(4) *Human Rights Case Digest*, 132.

[195] See *Jeremy Costello-Roberts* v. *UK* and *Y* v. *UK*, opinions adopted 8 Oct. 1991. Cf. the most recent judgment in the former of 25 March 1993.

The above-mentioned case-law implies that the Convention obliges national courts to apply the principles in the Convention in a private law dispute. Of course, some national courts have already taken into account the rights in the Convention in private law disputes, but the manner in which this is done may ultimately depend on the lead given by Strasbourg.[196] For the moment the Strasbourg Court has noted that the Belgian courts have already applied Articles 6 and 8 of the Convention in 'private legal relationships' in the context of the 'right to a court'.[197]

It is suggested that the Court and Commission's case-law tends to suggest that national courts are obliged to ensure respect for the guarantees in the Convention when deciding private law disputes. This duty should not only arise once the case is before the national court but should actually involve ensuring access to an effective remedy under Article 13 of the European Convention on Human Rights.[198] A distinction whereby

---

[196] For examples see Velu (1990); Drzemczewski (1983: 119–218); P. Waquet, 'Perspectives ouvertes par la Convention', in *Convention européenne des droits de l'homme et droit communautaire* (Paris: La Documentation Française, 1987), 63–77 at 68–71, who refers to several cases, including a case decided by a German tribunal at Mannheim whereby an individual was granted the right to reply to allegations made by a newspaper under the terms of Art. 10 ECHR even though there was a lacuna in the German law. This example of the privatization of human rights is pertinent, as it goes beyond the established case-law of the Commission and Court of Human Rights, who have not yet granted rights to reply or rectification under Art. 10. See van Dijk and van Hoof (1990: 413). As is well known, the Strasbourg organs may be influenced in some cases by the decisions of national courts in their development of the Convention, so we can expect the privatization process to become increasingly well known as the Courts make more and more references to each other.

[197] *Deweer* case, judgment of 27 Feb. 1980, Series A, vol. 35, para. 49.

[198] Where the Convention right can be considered a 'civil right' for the purposes of Art. 6(1) ECHR then there will also exist a right to a court. However, where the right in question does not come within this autonomous concept then Art. 13 will be the more suitable provision and the guarantee will be for access to an effective remedy before a national authority. It should be stressed that I am suggesting that lack of such a remedy may give rise to a violation at the international level in Strasbourg under Art. 13 and not that Art. 13 creates directly effective rights at the national level. Even if there is evidence that Art. 6(1) can create directly effective rights at the national level in private law situations this is not necessarily the case for Art. 13. The *Drittwirkung* of Art. 13 was discussed in Ch. 4.3.2, point (1). See also van Dijk and van Hoof (1990: 15–16) for further references. However, these discussions concern the use of the wording of Art. 13 as *evidence* of the *Drittwirkung effect* of the Convention. What is being currently suggested is that, *given the Drittwirkung* effect of the Convention, failure by the State to guarantee this effect may result in a breach *by the State* of Art. 13. This was expressly denied by Raymond (1980: 161–75): 'However the following obstacle arises when it is alleged that a Contracting State has failed to provide a remedy against a violation of Convention rights by a private individual: Because of the limits of their competence ratione personae, the Commission and the Court are prevented from establishing whether or not the acts committed by the said private individual are within the scope of Articles 2 to 12 (and the Protocols). They cannot therefore decide whether Article 13 is applicable and a fortiori whether it has been violated. It must therefore be admitted that in such a case the obligation assumed by States under Article 13 has no sanction on the international plane' (at 170). It is suggested that because the Court and Commission are now prepared to admit that the Convention covers the private sphere they consequently rule on the scope of the rights in the Convention as

the Convention is not operational until someone else has started proceedings against you would seem to deny the right to an effective remedy before a national authority and favour the status quo. Of course the actual operation of directly effective Convention rights in national law will depend on that State's reception of the Convention into national law by whatever means its legal system provides for. But the lack of an effective remedy before a national authority to ensure respect by a private person of a Convention right would seem to be a violation of Article 13 and could be sanctioned at the international level.

regards the acts of private persons. Because Art. 13 demands access to a national authority rather than protection of the actual right, the Strasbourg organs' inability to judge the private act for conformity with the Convention should not prevent them from demanding that there be access to a national authority for violations committed by private persons. Raymond cites Hahne, Castberg, Eissen, Rolin, and Vasak as supporters of the view that the French text suggests a remedy against violations by private persons. Raymond himself suggests that 'the States Party are obliged by Article 13 to provide a remedy in domestic law against violations committed by private persons or by public authorities'; I am merely further suggesting that failure to fulfil this obligation is subject to sanction by the Commission and Court of Human Rights.

8

The European Community Legal Order

This chapter explores the operation of human rights in the private sphere within the Community legal order. There are two dimensions to rights in the private sphere within the Community legal order. The first involves what may be called 'fundamental Community rights' which individuals have under Community law and which may, or may not, be enforced against other private or non-state bodies (that is to say bodies such as employers, professional associations, corporations, etc.), or even used to invalidate the rules and regulations of such private organizations.

The second involves rights which one holds against the Community as such. As briefly mentioned in Chapter 1, for most purposes, under the Convention machinery in Strasbourg, the Community is a non-state or private body. An examination of the application of European human rights against non-state bodies should include an analysis of human rights against international organizations, and in the present context the most significant organization is the European Community.

8.1 FUNDAMENTAL RIGHTS APPLICABLE AGAINST PRIVATE BODIES IN THE COMMUNITY LEGAL ORDER

Although the ECJ stated in 1969 that 'the fundamental human rights are enshrined in the general principles of Community law and protected by the Court',[1] and the Commission, Parliament, and Council of Ministers have all signed the Joint Declaration on Human Rights of 5 April 1977,[2] and more recently the European Convention was specifically referred to in the Preamble of the Single European Act 1986, the status of fundamental rights in the Community legal order is rather complex.

Nevertheless it is worth analysing the jurisprudence of this Court and its approach to human rights questions. In particular we shall examine the case-law concerning the application of human rights in the private sphere. This may be useful as the policy questions which face this court are similar to those which face the European Court of Human Rights. More-

[1] *Stauder* v. *City of Ulm*, Case 29/69 [1969] ECR 419 at 425.
[2] *OJ* (1977), no. C 103/1.

over the Community Court has already had to decide that some rights are directly applicable against private bodies and that others bind only 'state authorities'; the Court has even given guidance to national courts on the scope of the notion of public authorities and its applicability to nationalized industries. Although such interpretations are not, in any way, binding on the European Court of Human Rights, the tensions and options facing such a supranational court clearly emerge from the judgments of the ECJ, as well as from the opinions of the Advocates-General and the parties' submissions. In addition there is evidence that Community law influences the development of the European Convention on Human Rights, and judgments of the ECJ have even been cited by the European Court of Human Rights.[3]

8.1.1 Rights outside the scope of Community law

Before starting on our analysis of human rights in the private sphere in the Community legal order we should briefly mention that there is a significant area which is 'out of bounds' for the ECJ. The Court will not review national provisions for conformity with fundamental human rights where this legislation is outside the scope of Community law. In such cases the victims of human rights abuses may have recourse to domestic courts under national legislation and, as we saw in the last chapter, eventually to the Strasbourg Commission and Court of Human Rights. The ECJ at Luxembourg has no competence to decide such matters. It has stated as much in the following way:

As to the point whether Article 8 of the European Convention on Human Rights has any bearing on the answer to that question, it must be observed that, as the Court ruled in its judgment of 11 July 1985 in Joined Cases 60 and 61/84 (*Cinéthèque v Fédération Nationale des Cinémas Français* [1985] ECR 2605), although it is the duty of the Court to ensure observance of fundamental rights in the field of Community law, *it has no power to examine the compatibility with the European Convention on Human Rights of national legislation lying outside the scope of Community law.*[4]

Whether a human rights situation falls inside or outside the scope of Community law is not self-evident.

---

[3] See Mendelson (1983: 99), who gives two examples of the European Court and Commission of Human Rights considering references to the case-law of the ECJ: *Marckx* case, Series A, vol. 31, reference to *Defrenne* v. *Sabena* (II) [1976] ECR 455; and *Vosper PLC* v. *UK*, Applic. 9262/81 [1983] 5 EHRR 465, where arguments were put forward concerning the development of indirect discrimination by the ECJ.

[4] *Association Agreement between the EEC and Turkey: Freedom of Movement for Workers*, Case 12/86, judgment of 30 Sept. 1987 [1987] ECR 3719 at para. 28 (emphasis added). See also *SPUC* v. *Grogan*, Case C-159/90, judgment of 4 Oct. 1991, para. 30 [1991] 3 CMLR 849.

The recent Irish cases concerning abortion services in Britain illustrate this point. In the first case, *Attorney-General (Society for the Protection of Unborn Children (SPUC) Ltd.) v. Open Door Counselling Ltd. and the Dublin Wellwoman Centre Ltd.*,[5] an order had been made by the High Court[6] restraining the defendants from counselling or assisting pregnant women to obtain further advice on abortion or an abortion itself. On appeal, the Supreme Court refused to make a reference to the ECJ, stating that no claim had been made that assistance of this sort was a corollary right to rights which women may have under the EEC Treaty—therefore no question of interpretation of Community law arose.

In the second case, *SPUC v. Grogan et al.*,[7] the defendants had produced and distributed the 'Welfare Guide UCD 1988/1989', which contained information about the location of abortion clinics in Britain. In this case there was no overt counselling, merely information. In contrast to the previous case, the judge Miss Justice Mella Carroll decided to refer the case to the ECJ for a preliminary ruling.[8] The Community freedom is the right to receive services in another Member State, and the question arises whether the corollary right to receive information about those services includes a right to give information; if it does, it will then have to be decided whether the Community freedoms to provide or to receive information can be legitimately restricted under the EEC Treaty on grounds of public policy (Article 56 EEC). The ECJ held that the medical interruption of pregnancy is a service within the scope of Article 60 EEC. But they also held that, because the students were not co-operating with the hospitals and the information was not distributed for profit, the exercise of freedom of expression and information was independent of the hospitals' economic activity in the other Member State. In response to an argument that the European Convention on Human Rights prohibited the injunction which had been issued against the defendants, the ECJ held that in this case the relevant national regulation lay outside the scope of Community law.[9]

It is worth noting that this case involves two private parties. The

---

[5] [1988] ILRM 19 Supreme Court, and see the opinion of the European Commission of Human Rights, Applics. 14234/88, 14235/88, opinion of 7 Mar. 1991, which found a violation of Art. 10 as the applicant could not have foreseen that the Irish Constitution contained a prohibition on informing women about abortion services abroad. The Court held that there had been a violation of Article 10 due to the lack of proportionality in the Supreme Court injunction. *Open Door and Dublin Well Woman v. Ireland*, Series A, vol. 246.

[6] [1987] ILRM 477 High Court.

[7] 11 Oct. 1989, unreported, but see articles in *Irish Times* (12 Oct. 1989), 1, 9, 11. The Supreme Court later granted an interlocutory injunction against the students who produced the 'Welfare Guide' but authorized the High Court to modify the injunction should this be necessary in the light of the ECJ ruling [1990] 57 CMLR 684.

[8] *SPUC v. Grogan*, Case C-159/90, judgment of 4 Oct. 1991, [1991] 3 CMLR 849.

[9] Compare the Advocate-General's opinion in this case.

plaintiffs, SPUC, are a pressure group arguing that the defendants' freedom of expression should be restricted. In a related action the Supreme Court held that this was not a matter which could be brought to Court exclusively by the Attorney-General (*Attorney-General (SPUC)* v. *Coogan*).[10]

These two Irish abortion cases clearly illustrate that different judges will have different opinions on whether issues are outside the scope of Community law. Bearing in mind that cases of this kind mostly depend on preliminary ruling references from judges in twelve different countries, it is clear that what comes within the category 'outside the scope of Community law' is far from obvious.

This first area is defined by what it does not contain—Community law. Where demands and claims arise within this area, the Community will either have no competence to act or will have to draft a new provision.

8.1.2 Rights arising in the field of Community law

This category includes rights in the field of Community law which arise at the national level within the framework of Community law. These rights are found in hundreds of Community provisions. Provisions in the EEC Treaty alone cover areas such as the free movement of workers,[11] rights of establishment,[12] freedom to provide services,[13] non-discrimination on grounds of nationality,[14] and the principle that men and women should receive equal pay for equal work.[15] Secondary Community legislation may often relate to human rights in the private sphere and the obvious examples are the directives on sex discrimination.[16] However, it is worth pointing out that these rights should be considered 'fundamental Community rights' rather than 'universal human rights'. This is because their enforcement may depend on being a Community national or on the Community transnational context in which they operate.[17] Human rights such as those found in the European Convention on Human Rights are universal and granted to anyone within the jurisdiction of the Contracting Parties regardless of nationality.

We will now examine the ECJ's case-law in some detail to determine to what extent these Community rights have been declared applicable against private parties and their rules of organization. From early in the Court's case-law it has been clear that Community law gives rise to enforceable

---

[10] [1990] IRLM 70.   [11] Art. 48.   [12] Art. 52.
[13] Art. 59.   [14] Art. 7.   [15] Art. 119.
[16] Directive 75/117 (equal pay), Directive 76/207 (equal treatment), Directive 79/7 (equal treatment in social security matters), Directive 86/378 (equal treatment in occupational pension schemes), Directive 86/613 (equal treatment in self-employment).
[17] The most important exception is protection in the area of sex discrimination, which operates regardless of nationality or the transnational context.

rights and duties for individuals. It is sufficient to refer to the often quoted paragraph from the ECJ's judgment in *Van Gend en Loos*: 'Independently of the legislation of Member States, Community law therefore not only *imposes obligations on individuals* but is also intended to confer upon them rights which become part of their legal heritage.'[18] These rights and obligations are constantly evolving with the evolution of the Community, and in the same case the Court went on to state: 'These rights arise not only where they are expressly granted by the Treaty, but also by reason of *obligations which the Treaty imposes in a clearly defined way upon individuals* as well as upon the Member States and upon the institutions of the Community.'[19] The Court was here actually referring to rights arising out of the Treaty of Rome in the context of the elimination of customs duties.

The analysis which follows concentrates on areas which are relevant to the rights protected under the European Convention on Human Rights. The first case which should be considered is *Walrave and Koch* v. *Association Union Cycliste Internationale*,[20] where the Treaty of Rome's prohibition of discrimination based on nationality was held by the ECJ to extend to the rules of an international cycling organization. The rule in question provided that for a world championship race the pacemaker (motorcyclist) must be the same nationality as the stayer (cyclist). The decision was based on the applicability of Articles 7, 48, and 59 of the Treaty of Rome (EEC). To the extent that sport is an economic activity within Article 2 EEC it is subject to Community law, and when such activity is gainful employment, or remunerated service, it comes within the protection of the Community freedoms (freedom of movement of workers, Articles 48–51; and freedom of establishment of services, Articles 59–66). These rules were said to give effect to the general rule found in Article 7 EEC which prohibits any discrimination on grounds of nationality in the field of application of the Treaty.

The Court then tackles the question of the application of these freedoms to the private sphere: 'It has been alleged that the prohibitions in these Articles refer only to restrictions which have their origin in acts of an authority and not to those resulting from legal acts of persons or associations who do not come under public law.'[21] The Court then states in general terms that: 'Articles 7, 48, [and] 59 have in common the prohibition, in their respective spheres of application, of any discrimination on grounds of nationality.'[22] The judgment then directly addresses the particular circumstances of the case at issue and states: 'Prohibition on such

---

[18] *Van Gend en Loos* v. *Netherlandse Administratie der Belastingen* [1963] ECR 1 at 12 (emphasis added).
[19] [1963] ECR 1 at 12 (emphasis added).
[20] [1974] ECR 1405.   [21] At para. 15.   [22] At para. 16.

discrimination does not only apply to the action of public authorities but extends likewise to the rules of any other nature aimed at regulating in a collective manner gainful employment and the provision of services.'[23] The Court then continues, stating that any interpretation which permitted private organizations to construct obstacles to free movement for persons and freedom to provide services would compromise the fundamental objectives of the Community (as defined in Article 3(c) EEC). (Such reasoning finds a parallel in the 'effectiveness' doctrine developed by the European Court of Human Rights.)

The ECJ adds a further reason why 'associations and organizations which do not come under public law' are covered by the prohibitions in question: any solution which limited these prohibitions to the rules of public authorities would 'risk creating inequality in their application'.[24] One can imagine two kinds of inequality that would arise from a restrictive interpretation which imposed duties only on public authorities. First, there would be a certain inequality between workers in the public and private sectors, and second, there would be inequality between workers in one Member State and those in another as the sphere which was defined as belonging to public authorities would vary from State to State.

To summarize, it can be stated that the prohibition on discrimination based on nationality extends to agreements and rules which do not emanate from public authorities—concerning both gainful employment (Article 48 EEC) and the provision of services (Article 59 EEC). This prohibition is enforceable before national courts.

Less than two years later the Court gave its judgment in the *Defrenne* case.[25] The case raised similar questions to those raised in *Walrave*, but this time we are concerned with the field of equal pay for men and women for equal work (Article 119 EEC). It was argued before the Court, in particular by Ireland, that a distinction should be drawn between the 'fundamental freedoms' provided for in the Treaty of Rome (free movement of goods, persons, and services), which have the objective of realizing the basic tasks and activities of the Community as defined by Articles 2 and 3 of the Treaty, and the principle of equal pay for equal work (Article 119), which is limited to a specific class of persons (women workers). The Court was asked to draw the conclusion that Article 119 could not create individual rights enforceable before national tribunals. Furthermore, because Article 119 specifically refers to Member States,[26] it was argued that this demonstrated that the 'authors of the Treaty' did not intend this Article to create rights and obligations between employers

---

[23] At para. 17.   [24] At para. 19.

[25] Case 43/75 [1976] ECR 455.

[26] 'Each Member State shall during the first stage ensure and subsequently maintain the application of the principle that men and women should receive equal pay for equal work.'

and employees. Lastly, we should mention that it was suggested by the United Kingdom that, should the Court decide that Article 119 did create individual rights, this would create new forms of discrimination across the public/private divide, and that therefore no such individual right should be created at all.

The Court, following the opinion of the Advocate-General, rejected all these arguments and opted for a teleological interpretation which recognizes both the importance of fundamental rights in the Community legal order and the need to make Community law effective. The Court stated:

Article 119 pursues a double aim.

First, in the light of the different stages of the development of social legislation in the various Member States, the aim of Article 119 is to avoid a situation in which undertakings established in States which have actually implemented the principle of equal pay suffer a competitive disadvantage in intra-Community competition as compared with undertakings established in States which have not yet eliminated discrimination against women workers as regards pay.

Secondly, this provision forms part of the social objectives of the Community, which is not merely an economic union, but is at the same time intended, by common action, to ensure social progress and seek the constant improvement of the living and working conditions of their peoples, as is emphasized in the Preamble to the Treaty.[27]

These passages are cited in full in order to give an insight into the remarkable dynamics of the Court of Justice's approach to interpretation. The logic of the judgment is supranational—the Court insists on inter-state competition as well as fundamental values for a union which transcends economic integration. It is obvious why the European Court of Human Rights has not exhibited such a 'federal' attitude to questions brought before it. The legal order and political objectives are quite different. Although the Preamble to the European Convention on Human Rights states that the 'aim of the Council of Europe is greater unity between its Members' and that one way to achieve this is through the 'further realization of human rights and fundamental freedoms' the European Court of Human Rights does not have the mandate or opportunity to achieve this aim.

It is against this background that one can appreciate the Court's decision that this right to equal pay has to be protected 'in particular in the case of those forms of discrimination which have their origin in legislative provisions or collective labour agreements, as well as where men and women receive unequal pay for equal work which is carried out in the same establishment or service, *whether private or public*'.[28] The Court dismissed

---

[27] Paras. 8–10.
[28] Para. 1 of the ruling at p. 482 of the judgment (emphasis added).

objections that the application of equal pay for equal work would 'amount to modifying independent agreements concluded privately or in the sphere of industrial relations such as individual contracts and collective labour agreements'. The private sphere was not considered impermeable in this context.

The Court then had to deal with the objections of the United Kingdom that such a ruling 'could throw the social and economic situation in the United Kingdom into confusion' as 'certain relationships of longstanding would have to be readjusted'. For Ireland direct applicability of Article 119 'would certainly involve for Ireland a financial burden which many employers would be unable to bear'. The Court dealt with this concern by simply outlawing any retroactive effect and ruled: 'Except as regards those workers who have already brought legal proceedings or made an equivalent claim, the direct effect of Article 119 cannot be relied on in order to support claims concerning pay periods prior to the date of this judgment.'[29]

The Treaty right of men and women to equal pay for equal work was therefore stated to create directly enforceable individual rights before national courts against both public and private employers or against the operation of collective agreements. From *Walrave* and *Defrenne* it is now clear that Articles 7, 48, 59, and 119 of the Treaty of Rome create legal duties for private individuals. The list is not closed,[30] but consideration of the other Articles would be outside the scope of the present work, which concentrates on human rights rather than rights in general.

Although Articles in the Treaty of Rome may be enforced against private individuals, the Court has ruled that those rights contained in directives which are enforceable against emanations of the State are not to be enforceable against private bodies. This is the consequence of the judgment in *Marshall* v. *Southampton and SW Hampshire Area Health Authority*,[31] where the equal treatment directive was held only to bind 'organs of the State' when relied on at the national level. For some time there had been speculation concerning the applicability of directives in

---

[29] Para. 5 of the Court's ruling at p. 482 of the judgment.

[30] For consideration of the appropriateness of adding Art. 30 to this list see M. Quinn and N. MacGowan, 'Could Article 30 Impose Obligations on Individuals', *ELR* (1987), 163–78, who conclude that there are 'compelling policy considerations which should make the European Court extremely reluctant to interpret Article 30 as imposing obligations on private parties' (at 178).

[31] Case 152/84 [1986] ECR 723; briefly, Mrs Marshall had been employed by the authority as a senior dietician, and she was dismissed at the age of 62, whereas had she been a man she would have been entitled to continue working until at least 65. She could not rely on the Sex Discrimination Act 1975 as s. 6(4) provided that sex discrimination by employers is not prohibited in relation to death or retirement. She relied on Art. 5 of Directive 76/207 as the date for implementation of the directive had expired and the terms of the Article were clear, precise, and unconditional. Cf. *Becker* v. *Finanzamt Munster-Innenstadt* [1982] ECR 53.

the private sphere, and the policy implications of such an application would have been considerable.[32] In fact, bearing in mind that some jurisdictions were refusing to comply with the Court's jurisprudence on the direct effect of directives in the public sector, it might even be suggested that application in the private sphere might have precipitated a crisis in some Member States,[33] although, on the other hand, the Court's earlier development of the doctrines of direct effect, supremacy, and exclusive competence did not actually jeopardize obedience to Community law.[34]

Before considering the policy factors and practical implications of this judgment we will turn to the Court's abstract legal reasoning. The Court took a literal approach to Article 189 EEC. It stated:

With regard to the argument that a directive may not be relied on against an individual, it must be emphasised that according to Article 189 of the EEC Treaty the binding nature of a directive, which constitutes the basis for the possibility of relying on the directive before a national court, exists only in relation to 'each Member State to which it is addressed'. It follows that a directive may not of itself impose obligations on an individual and that a provision of a directive may not be relied on as such against such a person. It must therefore be examined whether, in this case, the respondent must be regarded as having acted as an individual.[35]

This seems a rather different approach from the *Defrenne* judgment, cited above, where, although Article 119 commences 'Each Member State shall during the first stage ensure and subsequently maintain the application of the principle that men and women should receive equal pay for equal work', the Court referred to 'competitive disadvantage' and the 'social objectives' of the Community. Mrs Marshall like Ms Defrenne was claiming to have been discriminated against on ground of sex. Furthermore, the literal interpretation of Article 189 is difficult to reconcile with the Court's earlier cases on the direct effect of directives, where the 'effectiveness' of Community law required that individuals have, in certain circum-

---

[32] For a speculative article predating the judgment see Easson (1979).

[33] The French Conseil d'État and the German Bundesfinzhof were refusing to recognize the direct effect of directives: *Minister of the Interior* v. *Daniel Cohn-Bendit* [1980] 1 CMLR 543, *Re Value Added Tax Directives* [1982] 1 CMLR 527, and see T. C. Hartley, *The Foundations of European Community Law* (2nd edn. Oxford: Clarendon Press, 1988), 209, 225–7, 230–5.

[34] See Cappelletti (1987: 10).

[35] At para. 48. Art. 189 reads as follows: 'In order to carry out their task the Council and the Commission shall, in accordance with the provisions of this Treaty, make regulations, issue directives, take decisions, make recommendations or deliver opinions. A regulation shall have general application. It shall be binding in its entirety and directly applicable in all Member States. A directive shall be binding, as to the result to be achieved, upon each Member State to which it is addressed, but shall leave to the national authorities the choice of aims and methods. A decision shall be binding in its entirety upon those to whom it is addressed. Recommendations and opinions shall have no binding force.'

stances, enforceable, and sometimes 'identical', rights before national courts.[36] Lastly, the judgment flies in the face of the 'equality' principle which is central to Community law. It discriminates between workers employed in the private sector (who have no rights under the directives) and those employed in the public sector. The United Kingdom had argued (as it had done in the *Defrenne* case) that such a result is unfair (the United Kingdom was suggesting that there should be no rights either in the public or private sector). In reply the Court stated:

> The argument submitted by the United Kingdom that the possibility of relying on a provision of the Directive against the respondent *qua* organ of the State would give rise to an arbitrary and unfair distinction between the rights of State employees and those of private employees does not justify any other conclusion. Such a distinction may easily be avoided if the Member State concerned has correctly implemented the Directive in national law.[37]

We must also mention the Court's second rationale for directly applying the obligations under the directive exclusively to organs of the State; the Court stated:

> [I]t must be pointed out that where a person involved in legal proceedings is able to rely on a directive as against the State he may do so regardless of the capacity in which the latter is acting, whether employer or public authority. In either case it is necessary to prevent the State from taking advantage of its own failure to comply with Community law.[38]

This is known as the 'estoppel' principle,[39] and it is this argumentation which is relied on in subsequent cases concerning the scope of the application of directives to 'emanations of the State'.[40]

According to the remarks of one judge, speaking informally at a seminar at the European University Institute, it would be unreasonable to expect private businesses to keep abreast of the plethora of directives which are issued and the varying states of the implementation (or non-implementation) at the national level.[41] This argumentation may be considered valid

---

[36] See: Case 9/70, *Grad* [1970] ECR 825; Case 33/70, *SACE* [1970] ECR 1213; Case 41/74, *Van Duyn* [1974] ECR 1337; Case 51/76, *Verbond* [1977] ECR 113; Case 38/77, *Enka* [1977] ECR 2203.

[37] At para. 51. As is well known the record of Member States is not particularly good either as regards implementation or as regards correct implementation.

[38] At para. 49, and see para. 47 and Case 8/81, *Becker v. Finanzamt Münster-Innenstadt* [1982] ECR 53.

[39] For a judicial reference to this label see Donaldson, MR, in *Foster v. British Gas* [1988] 2 CMLR 697 at 699: 'However, the European Court of Justice has developed a doctrine which is akin to estoppel.'

[40] See Case 222/84, *Johnston v. Chief Constable of the Royal Ulster Constabulary* [1986] 3 CMLR 240 para. 56.

[41] 'Rapports entre droit communautaire et droits nationaux, aspects récents de la jurisprudence de la Cour de Justice', seminar given by Professor Gil Carlos Rodríguez Iglesias, 26 May 1987, European University Institute, Florence.

in the context of some of the more technical areas of Community law, and indeed can even be legally justified, bearing in mind that under Article 191 EEC publication of directives is not mandatory, as is the case for regulations.

Whilst lack of publicity may justify exempting private bodies from some duties contained in Community directives, it is suggested that no such exemption is justified under the European Convention on Human Rights. The duties contained in directives evolve on an almost daily basis, whereas the principles contained in the Convention are well known, reproduced in many other international treaties, and are hardly altered at all by the Additional Protocols, which rarely affect the duties of private individuals as they are mostly concerned with procedural matters or state duties. The suggestion by Dr Hermod Lannung that no duties for individuals arise under the Convention because individuals have no obligation to familiarize themselves with the Convention in countries where it has not been incorporated into domestic law[42] should be rejected. As was demonstrated in Part I, the Convention's rights and duties may be just as relevant in the legal orders of States which have not incorporated as in States which have done so.

Without going into a detailed analysis of the periods of judicial activism and self-restraint of the ECJ it can be fairly said that the decision to limit the direct effect of directives so that they are merely applicable against state bodies cannot be easily divorced from the reality of the unease which had been expressed in some quarters with the Court's activist, integrationist, teleological methods of interpretation.[43] Professor Pescatore, speaking in his professorial capacity after he had left the Court, described the situation as coming at a time when the Court was looking to enter a different phase. The Court had been driving for some time in top gear (he said) and it was time to shift down, or even put it into reverse.[44]

---

[42] See *The Implementation in National Law of the European Convention on Human Rights*, Proceedings of the Fourth Copenhagen Conference on Human Rights, 28–9 Oct. 1988 (Copenhagen: Danish Centre for Human Rights, 1989), at 103.

[43] For different views on the activist nature of the Court and the usefulness of a policy input study which would provide the 'basic data to be used as a measuring rod for identifying the limits to activism' see H. Rasmussen, 'Between Self-Restraint and Activism: A Judicial Policy for the European Court', *ELR* (1988), 28–38; see also the objections to Rasmussen's approach and factual bases made by Cappelletti (1987: 1–17 esp. at 10), where he points out that 'most of the highest national courts, too, have tended to accept the most important doctrines established by the activist European Court' (book review of Rasmussen (1986)). See also J. H. H. Weiler, 'The Court of Justice on Trial; A Review Essay', 24 *CML Rev.* (1987), 555. Deirdre Curtin, Legal Secretary at the Court, writing in her personal capacity, actually cites the *Marshall* judgment as an example of a recent case where the Court's 'dynamic interpretative approach has been assigned to the closet and a more modest mantle donned' (see Curtin 1990: 196).

[44] 'The Role of the European Court of Justice', 23 Oct. 1987, seminar at the European University Institute, Florence.

This cautious federalism is the key to understanding the difficulties which surround the extension of the European Convention on Human Rights into the private sphere. Almost exactly the same obstacles face the Luxembourg Court of Justice as face the Strasbourg machinery responsible for the implementation of the Convention: the application of the supranational norm to the private law sphere in the Member/Contracting States means interfering in a delicate social order and causing considerable difficulties for States which may go way beyond mere obligations to change state practice. The way the economic and social spheres are regulated is still an ideological question to which governments consider it is their privilege to provide the answer. Interference in areas such as the duty of an employer to consult a union, the regulation of advertising in the professions, freedom of expression in the broadcasting sphere, and the regulation of working time may be seen as overstepping the boundaries of what States have agreed to, especially where the Court's interference will create directly enforceable new duties on private actors. Restrictions on the state apparatus are not usually perceived as unwarranted by private citizens, especially where the State's measures are unpopular. Restrictions on private interests would lead to enormous pressure on governments to protect citizens' 'liberty' from outside oppression. Furthermore, in the particular field under discussion the economic consequences of a finding that private actors have to compensate employees, both past and present, for illegal discrimination concerning their pension, redundancy, or other payments will be considerable. In fact with one judgment the European Court of Justice could cripple hundreds, if not thousands, of businesses across Europe. Pension and redundancy schemes have been carefully calculated over decades on the assumption that different age limits could be imposed for men and women. These practical constraints on the full implementation of equality between men and women are what initiated the Court's proactive ruling in *Defrenne*. In that case the Court's final ruling limited the direct effect of Article 119 to claims which had already been brought concerning periods prior to the date of the judgment. Similarly in *Barber* v. *Guardian Royal Exchange*,[45] whilst holding that pensions are pay for the purposes of Article 119, the ECJ limited relevant sex discrimination claims in respect of pensions to claims in being or arising at the time of the judgment.[46] Such restrictions do not yet apply to cases involving claims for redundancy payments where there has been discrimination contrary to Article 119 EEC. Bearing in mind that there are no time limits on the bringing of claims under Community law, employers may yet face expensive claims based on discrimination in redundancy both past and present.[47]

---

[45] [1990] IRLR 258. [46] Judgment of 17 May 1990.
[47] For the details of how this question arises in the UK see Bourne (1990: 1240).

Despite these difficulties three factors have contributed to a widening of the scope of the *Marshall* judgment. First, a number of recent cases have given a broad interpretation to the meaning of pay in Article 119 (which as a result of *Defrenne* has horizontal effect). *Bilka-Kaufhaus* added statutory pension schemes to the ambit of 'pay' in Article 119,[48] *Worrington* v. *Lloyds Bank* added other benefits calculated according to gross salary,[49] *Barber* ruled that pensions are pay for the purposes of Article 119 (see above), *Kowalska* assimilated severance payments to deferred remuneration and hence 'pay' within the scope of Article 119,[50] *Rinner-Kuhn* held that statutory sick pay may be 'pay',[51] and that legislative provisions which limit access to benefits in a discriminatory way have to be justified in accordance with proportionality (therefore the exclusion of part-timers will have to be shown to be objectively justified).[52] In the *Danfoss* case pay systems which give rise to discrimination against women were brought within the scope of Article 119 so that employers bear the burden of proof and have to show that their pay system is not discriminatory.[53] In effect, whilst private employers have been spared enforceable duties under directives, similar obligations have been imposed on them through a series of broad interpretations of the scope of Article 119 EEC.

Second, we should mention what has been labelled 'The Von Colson principle'[54] or 'The Interpretive "Solution" to the Horizontal Direct Effect Problem'.[55] In *Von Colson*[56] the Court stated:

[I]n applying the national law and in particular the provisions of a national law specifically introduced in order to implement Directive 76/207, national courts are required to interpret their national law in the light of the wording and the purpose of the directive in order to achieve the result referred to in the third paragraph of Article 189.[57]

---

[48] Case 170/84 [1986] 2 CMLR 701.

[49] Case 69/80 [1981] ECR 767.

[50] Case 33/89, *Kowalska* v. *Freie und Hansestadt Hambourg*, judgment of 27 June 1990, not yet reported.

[51] *Rinner-Kuhn* v. *Fww Spezial-Gebaudereinigung* [1989] IRLR 493.

[52] For the effects of this development and the possibilities which it opens up concerning challenges to minimum hours and service requirements for all sorts of benefits see Bourne (1990: 1284).

[53] [1989] IRLR 532. See Bourne (1990: 1286) for comments on the Court's treatment of the terms 'transparency' and 'flexibility'.

[54] Arnull (1987: 391).

[55] Morris and David (1987: 116); Prechal (1990: 451–73); note Prechal's suggestion concerning the application by national judges of international human rights with 'horizontal direct effect', such as those found in the ECHR and the International Covenant on Civil and Political Rights as a substitute for the defective implementing measure (at 464).

[56] Case 14/83, *Von Colson and Kamann* v. *Land Nordrhein-Westfalen* [1984] ECR 1891, and *Harz* v. *Deutsche Tradex GmbH* [1984] ECR 1921. Note, in the latter case both parties were non-state actors.

[57] At para. 26.

Nevertheless, although this principle applies to claims brought in the private sector, it has been given a restrictive interpretation, at least in the British courts. In *Duke* v. *Reliance Systems Ltd.*[58] the Court of Appeal and the House of Lords dismissed the use of the principle in the instant case and relied on Sir Gordon Slynn's interpretation of the scope of this principle in the *Marshall* case. In *Marshall* Sir Gordon Slynn's opinion as Advocate-General had limited the principle to legislation 'adopted specifically with a proposed directive in mind'.[59] This interpretation by the Advocate-General has been vigorously criticized,[60] and now in the *Mareleasing* case the European Court of Justice has ruled that national courts have to interpret national law so as to conform with the wording and text of Council Directive 68/151/EC of 9 March 1968;[61] the Court made no mention of national laws specifically introduced to implement the Community law in question.

The third factor is the open notion of the State given by the European Court of Justice in *Marshall* and the subsequent judgment of the Court in the *Foster* v. *British Gas* case.[62] As stated above, the House of Lords had already held in *Duke* that it was impossible, in an action between workers and a private employer, to interpret the Sex Discrimination Act 1975 in such a way as to make it consistent with Directive 76/207.[63] In the *Foster* case the question put to the ECJ was whether the British Gas Corporation (at the material time a nationalized industry) was 'a body of such a type that the appellants are entitled in English Courts to rely directly upon Directive 76/207'. In this case the argument is no longer about whether directives apply to private bodies but about what constitutes a public body, that is, which bodies are bound by the equality provisions in Directive 76/207. We will briefly review some of the legal arguments, but it is only after an analysis of the other arguments put forward by the various parties that it emerges that values, interests, practicality, and certainty are also at stake. It is proposed to examine the positions of the various parties separately.

Mrs Foster and the other appellants argued that the 'State' must be considered as including all organs of the State, including those engaged in

---

[58] [1987] 2 All ER 858 (Court of Appeal), [1988] 1 All ER 626 (House of Lords).

[59] [1986] ECR 723 at 732.

[60] See Arnull (1987: 395) and M. Akehurst, 'Decisions of the European Court of Justice of the European Communities during 1985–6', *BYIL* (1987), 477 at 481.

[61] Case C-106/89, judgment of 13 Nov. 1990, not yet reported.

[62] Case 188/89, judgment of 12 July 1990, not yet reported. Applied by the House of Lords in *Foster and Others* v. *British Gas* 19 Apr. 1991 The Times 30.

[63] *Duke* v. *Reliance Ltd.* [1988] AC 618; G. G. Howells, 'European Directives: The Emerging Dilemmas,' 54 *MLR* (1991), 456–63. See also *Webb* v. *EMO Air Cargo (UK) Ltd.* [1992] 1 CMLR 793; pregnancy could not *per se* be considered impermissible as a ground for dismissal in any circumstances.

commercial and similar activities. They relied on the ECJ's judgment in *Fratelli Costanzo SpA* v. *Comune di Milano*,[64] together with the opinion of Advocate-General Sir Gordon Slynn in the *Marshall* case. In the *Costanzo* case the Court had held that a local authority was obliged to apply the provisions of a directive over national rules when examining tenders for public works contracts. The Court's judgment pointed to a wide definition of the State.[65] Similarly, the Advocate-General had urged that

the 'State' must be taken broadly, as including all the organs of the State. In matters of employment, which is what Directive 76/207 is concerned with, this means all the employees of such organs and not just the central civil service. I would, thus, reject the argument put to the Court that a distinction should be drawn between the State as employer and the State in some other capacity.[66]

Mrs Foster and the other appellants also suggested that the Court's judgment in the *Johnston* case had introduced a dichotomy which divided respondents into private individuals and public authorities. No third category of public authorities which should not be considered state authorities was present in any of the Court's judgments. Mrs Foster and the other appellants then outlined three main practical difficulties which militate against limiting the direct effect of directives to the classical duties of the State (which is what the Court of Appeal had done in the instant case[67]).

First, the classic duties of the State may vary over time and to restrict the application of the directive to this field would jeopardize the uniform application of Community law and the principle of legal certainty. Second, limiting the direct effect of directives to bodies exercising the powers of the Crown (which is what the industrial tribunal had done in the instant case[68]) would not be workable in other Community countries, nor would it be satisfactory in the British context as it 'would enable the State to evade the consequences of direct effect by not giving certain bodies the status of Crown bodies'.[69] Third, excluding authorities of a commercial character was illogical as the rationale for applying the directive was that a Member State should not benefit from its failure to implement the directive, and anyway it would be difficult to decide what was a commercial activity. For example, hospitals charge for some services but provide a nationalized service financed by the State.

The respondents, British Gas PLC, argued that the principle which

---

[64] Case 103/88, judgment of 22 June 1989.
[65] '[A]ll organs of the administration, including decentralized authorities such as municipalities, are obliged to apply those provisions' (at para. 31).
[66] [1986] ECR 735.
[67] *Foster and Others* v. *British Gas* [1988] 2 CMLR 697.
[68] *Foster* v. *British Gas PLC* [1987] ICR 52.
[69] At 8 of the unpublished report of the ECJ.

enabled individuals to rely on directives was that the State cannot take advantage of its own failure to implement the directive and that this failure to fulfil its responsibility could only bind the executive, legislature, and courts.[70] British Gas also argued that the degree of control was irrelevant. They argued that a constitutionally independent body (such as the Chief Constable in *Johnston*) may be an organ of the State, whilst a body subject to a substantial degree of state control through the appointment of administrators (which was the situation for British Gas) is not necessarily an organ of the State (relying on the definition of an 'organ' of the High Authority in *Worms* v. *High Authority of the ECSC*[71]). British Gas stressed that their power to legislate was only as great as that of a public limited company and that they were not 'part of the State in the sense of the Crown'. Finally, British Gas pleaded that, in the event that the Court should hold that individuals may rely upon a directive as against them, it should limit the effects of the ruling *ratione temporis* so as to minimize the financial consequences of the decision. British Gas claimed this would be necessary 'in view of the serious financial consequences the judgment of the Court would have and on grounds of legal certainty'.[72]

The United Kingdom relied on the passages in *Marshall* which stated that it was for the national courts to decide what constitutes a part of the State in the circumstances of each case. It also pointed to other areas of Community law where a distinction is made between 'public authorities' and 'public undertakings',[73] where the concept 'a body covered by public law' is defined as any body 'established for the specific purpose of meeting needs in the general interest, not having an industrial or commercial

---

[70] British Gas cited the Court's judgment in *Von Colson and Kamann*, but one might observe: if the courts are bound by this principle then they themselves should give effect to the rights contained in the directive, even where the interpretation principle does not allow them to bend national law into conformity with Community law; if they are really bound as the third component of what constitutes the State then are they not bound to invent (at least in Common Law countries) new remedies? In *Duke* the House of Lords could not invent a new tort of sexual discrimination on grounds of retirement age because such behaviour was specifically permitted by the Sex Discrimination Act 1975 s. 6(4) and s. 6(1A)(b) of the Equal Pay Act 1970. The Act which outlawed such discrimination was the Sex Discrimination Act 1986, which did not operate with retroactive effect so as to avail a remedy to Mrs Duke. But if the argument that the courts are bound as classic entities of the State is upheld then one might imagine new areas where the courts could find themselves bound by Community law to give effect to provisions of directives in the private sphere. This would not seem to follow from the Court's judgment in *Foster* but the operative part of the judgment is limited to Art. 5(1) of Directive 76/207/EEC.

[71] [1962] ECR 195.

[72] At 11 of the unpublished judgment.

[73] Art. 2 of Directive 80/723/EEC of 25 June 1980 on the transparency of financial relations between Member States and public undertakings (*OJ* (1980), no. L 195, p. 35). 'Public undertakings' are defined as 'any undertaking over which the public authorities may exercise directly or indirectly a dominant influence by virtue of their ownership of it, their financial participation therein, or the rules which govern it'.

character'. The relevant directive included an annex which omitted the British Gas Corporation.[74] Finally, the United Kingdom pointed to the exception to the Community freedom of movement for workers found in Article 48(4) EEC, which permits nationality restrictions on workers 'employed in the public service'. According to the Court's jurisprudence this exception is to be construed restrictively and does not cover authorities with economic or commercial functions.[75] (Of course, this jurisprudence, by restricting the scope of the notion of the State, gives maximum effect to Community law, as in this case the Community obligation attaches only to the private sphere. The goal of the free movement of workers requires a restrictive interpretation of public service. On the other hand the goals of the fundamental principle of prohibiting sex discrimination require a broad interpretation of 'organ of the State'.) The United Kingdom advocated a functional approach whereby bodies which carry out the functions of the State have directly enforceable duties before national courts. They argued that this best corresponded with the principle that the State may not take advantage of its failure to implement the directive.

Yet it is not that self-evident that the obligation which arises from the estoppel principle only attaches to authorities carrying out the classic functions of the State. The estoppel principle presumably arises in order to achieve a sense of fairness in the operation of the law. Unlike the various doctrines of estoppel which are to be found in English law, the estoppel principle found in *Marshall* and the subsequent cases does not require that one party act in reliance on the estopped party's promises or conduct. No one suggested that Mrs Marshall or Mrs Foster had rearranged their careers when the Council directive was published and that the United Kingdom had implicitly promised them protection against discrimination and should therefore now be obliged to recognize their rights. If any promise can be extracted it is a promise to protect against discrimination in both sectors as the directive covers private employment as well. Mrs Marshall and Mrs Foster would have been entitled to rely on this promise whether or not they thought they were working in the state sector. The problem arises because individuals cannot claim that their employers made such a promise. The State made it; and so it seems fair that only the State should be bound by it. Fairness demands that what seems to be the State be seen to act consistently. The rationale for

[74] Council Directive 71/305/EEC of 26 July 1971, *OJ* English Special Edition (1971) (II), p. 682, as amended by Council Directive 89/440/EEC of 18 July 1989, *OJ* (1989), no. L 210, p. 1.
[75] The UK cites *Commission* v. *Belgium* [1980] ECR 3881, and Commission Communication 'Freedom of Movement of Workers and Access to Employment in Respect of the Application of Article 48(4) of the EEC Treaty', *OJ* (1988), no. C 72, p. 2.

excluding private employers would seem to have more to do with fairness and duties to the Community and less to do with the central/classical/authoritarian functions of the State. It seems unfair to bind private employers with obligations undertaken by the Government. The direct effect of directives reminds States of their duties to the Community where they have failed to implement a directive. It is not supposed to render redundant the national implementation of directives through legislation. Nevertheless the United Kingdom insisted on drawing the boundary between central and peripheral functions of the State.

According to the report of the judgment, the United Kingdom refers to British Gas as having a commercial character and not performing any of the central functions of the State, such as legislative, judicial, or law and order functions.[76] The implication of this is that the United Kingdom is suggesting that the *Marshall* judgment is an aberration to the rules concerning public authorities. In fact the Court of Appeal in *Foster* accused the ECJ of committing a 'terminological error' in *Marshall*, when it stated that the English courts had held that the health authority was a 'public authority'. According to Lord Donaldson, MR: 'In fact [the Court of Appeal] had held no such thing.'[77] Indeed, the question was at the heart of the debate in the *Marshall* case, as, far from conceding that the health authority should be bound, the United Kingdom and the health authority argued that a distinction should be drawn between the State *qua* employer and the State *qua* public authority, and that the health authority fell into the former category and should not be bound by this directive.

Finally, the United Kingdom rejected the power of control as a decisive criterion. It points out that 'For reasons of public policy, a wide variety of bodies, such as banks, insurance companies, independent schools, are regulated, to various degrees and in various ways, by the State, without those bodies thereby becoming part of the State.'[78]

The Commission's preoccupations were of a different nature. They stressed that this case was not an isolated one, and that the Court has to

[76] Compare Lord Donaldson in the Court of Appeal: 'In my judgment these two decisions [*Marshall* and *Johnston*] establish that, as a matter of European law, the directive gives rise to legal rights in employees of the State itself and of any organ or emanation of the State, an emanation of the State being understood to include an independent public authority charged by the State with the performance of any of the classic duties of the state, such as the defence of the realm or the maintenance of law and order within the realm' (*Foster* v. *British Gas* [1988] 2 CMLR 697 at 701).

[77] [1988] 2 CMLR 697 at 700; the Court of Appeal had stated that the authority was an 'emanation of the state', but obviously they were not declaring that the authority fell on the public side of the public/private boundary as developed by the ECJ in *Marshall*, because that dichotomy had not been invented at the time. The Court of Appeal's questions had related to (1) whether there had been discrimination prohibited by the directive and (2) whether the appellant can rely on the directive in national courts notwithstanding the inconsistency with the Sex Discrimination Act 1975.

[78] At 13–14 of the Court's judgment.

address the issue head on in order to give some guidance to courts across the Community. It cited two cases decided by the United Kingdom's courts. The first was *Turpie* v. *University of Glasgow*,[79] where the industrial tribunal held that the University was not an organ of the State even though the University received 80 per cent of its funding from the State. The decision was based on a consideration of the freedom enjoyed by universities in their organization and their 'long tradition of independent thought'. The result was that Mrs Turpie could not rely on Article 5(1) of the equal treatment directive (76/207/EEC). The fact that she had been forced to retire at 60 (instead of 65 had she been a man) did not constitute unfair dismissal.

The other case involved Rolls-Royce at a time when the State owned 100 per cent of its shares.[80] The Employment Appeal Tribunal refused to lift the corporate veil and emphasized that Rolls-Royce was not carrying out a state function. The Commission voiced its fears that leaving the question of what constitutes an organ of the State to national courts would obviously lead to divergent and contradictory results and such a use of national law should be avoided where it would impair the unity and efficacy of Community law. The Commission stressed that a directive cannot be pleaded against individuals, as those individuals had no responsibility with regard to national legislation. (The rationale behind the estoppel principle would here seem to be that the State is being punished for its failure to implement the directive properly.) For the Commission it was enough that the courts had already acknowledged the public character of British Gas and that the corporation's status led to the conclusion that it was carrying out state policy. The Commission felt that this case could be disposed of on its facts with an answer which would cover similar bodies to British Gas and hold that directives may be pleaded against such bodies. However, the Commission urged the Court to go beyond the facts of this case and lay down general criteria for determining the bodies which may be liable to claims arising from rights contained in this equality directive. The Commission's reasoning at this point exposes the values and practicalities which the Court is obliged to accommodate whatever choice it makes.

The Commission first reminds the Court that the principle of equal treatment for men and women is one of the fundamental principles of Community law and that it would therefore be inappropriate to give the concept of 'state authority' an over-restrictive meaning. The Commission then reviews Community law for the ambit of the concept of state authority in different Community contexts. Bodies which carry out a public function on behalf of the State are said to fall within the concept of state

[79] Unreported.　　[80] *Rolls-Royce* v. *Doughty* [1987] ICR 932, [1987] IRLR 447.

authorities (following *Marshall* and *Auer*[81]). When it comes to ensuring that the boundaries of the concept would include commercial companies controlled, in reality, by the State, the Commission makes an allusion to the approach taken in the field of state aids, which is based on the existence of control, but then concludes that there would be evidential difficulties and that the issue could not be decided outside the context of Article 5(1) of Directive 76/207/EEC and that that Article 'may be relied upon against any body exercising a public function on behalf of the State'. In the end, the Commission wisely refrains from suggesting any criteria which will define the 'State' for a variety of Community purposes. The Commission's duty lies in ensuring the effectiveness of Community law, and as we saw above a wide definition of the State does not imply greater effectiveness for Community law in areas such as permissible derogations from Community freedoms in the context of work for non-nationals in the public service. The Commission pressed the Court for an answer which would be limited to Article 5(1) of Directive 76/207. The Court did so limit its decision.

The operative part of the Court's judgment is complex and owes much to the different positions outlined above. It reads as follows:

Article 5(1) of Council Directive 76/207/EEC of 9 February 1976 on the implementation of the principle of equal treatment for men and women as regards access to employment, vocational training and promotion, and working conditions may be relied upon in a claim for damages against a body, whatever its legal form, which has been made responsible, pursuant to a measure adopted by the State, for providing a public service under the control of the State and has for that purpose special powers beyond those which result from the normal rules applicable in relations between individuals.

It is suggested that there are six elements to this ruling.

1. *It refers only to sex discrimination and to conditions of employment and dismissal* (Article 5 of Directive 76/207). The Court has repeatedly affirmed the fundamental importance of the principle of equality of treatment and the importance of interpreting exceptions to this principle strictly.[82] This assertion finds its most far-reaching application in *Razzouk and Beydoun* v. *Commission*.[83] In that case the Commission's decision not to grant a

---

[81] *Auer* v. *Ministère Public* [1983] ECR 2727 defined professional societies as 'bodies entrusted with public duties', and so they were obliged to recognize a professional qualification where this was provided for by the directive.

[82] e.g. the judgment in *Marshall*, where the Court stresses this principle of interpretation with regard to Art. 1(2) of Directive 76/207, which excludes social security matters from the scope of the directive. See also Case 262/84, *Beets-Proper* v. *Van Lanschot Bankiers* [1986] ECR 773, which applies this principle to Art. 7(1) (*a*) of Directive 79/7, so that the directive's restrictions on rights to sex equality apply only to the determination of pensionable age for the purposes of the granting of pensions and other social security benefits and not in the context of dismissal (paras. 38–40 of the judgment).

[83] Cases 75 and 117/82 [1984] ECR 1509 paras. 16–19.

widower's pension was annulled. The Staff Regulations discriminated against men and were contrary to a fundamental right. It was for the Community legislature to take the necessary measures to alter the Community pension scheme so as to establish equality between the sexes. The judgment is far-reaching in that it goes beyond the protection of Article 119 of the EEC Treaty and the directives adopted in the field. It incorporates sex equality in the Community legal order at the level of the highest law. But this incorporation is limited to cases involving Community employees.[84] One could characterize the European Court of Justice's jurisprudence concerning sex discrimination as offering protection on a sliding scale depending on who one's employer is. Top protection goes to Community employees and their dependants. Second-best protection goes to those employed by public bodies as defined by *Foster*. And third-best protection goes to employees in the private sector (the only Community provision they can rely on is Article 119 EEC). Behind the legal justifications for this hierarchy of protection lies a pragmatism and respect for the autonomy of the Member States which is best revealed in the opinion of the Advocate-General Sir Gordon Slynn in the *Marshall* case:

The State can legislate but a private employer cannot. It is precisely because the State can legislate that it can remedy its failure to implement the directive concerned. This consideration puts it in a fundamentally different position from a private employer, and justifies it being treated differently as regards the right of a person to rely on the provisions of a directive. The Court has already accepted that in the Community's relations with its officials fundamental principles may be relied on which are not necessarily applicable to other employees (*Razzouk*). I see no reason why Member States in default in implementing Community rules should not be in an analogous position to that of the Community. If this means that employees of private employers are at a disadvantage compared with state employees, it is for the State, as its duty is to do, to remedy the position by conferring the same advantages upon other employees.[85]

When the *Foster* case was decided four years later Sir Gordon Slynn was the acting President of the Court and the importance of the legislative capacities of the public bodies is reflected in the fifth element of the definition of those bodies (dealt with below).

2. *The body must be made responsible for providing a public service under the control of the State.* The concept of responsibility is referred to in the judgment in the context of independent authorities responsible for the maintenance of public order and safety (the *Johnston*-type situation). Where a body has not been made responsible for a public service but has voluntarily decided to act for this public purpose it would not seem to

---

[84] For other staff cases see Case 20/71, *Sabbatini, née Bertoni* v. *European Parliament* [1972] ECR 345, and Case 21/41, *Airola* v. *Commission* [1975] ECR 221.
[85] [1986] ECR 723 at 735.

satisfy this element of the definition. Therefore a private hospital or school, albeit acting for public purpose under the control of the State, would not be caught by the *Foster* definition. This would seem to respond to the United Kingdom's argument that the existence of a power of control is not the determining factor as to whether a body is part of the State. As explained above, the United Kingdom cited bodies such as banks, insurance companies, and independent schools as examples of bodies which, though regulated by the State, do not become part of the State. The Court would not seem to have incorporated a notion of delegation but more the sense of accountability. The notion of delegation was rejected by the Advocate-General, who mentions that even so-called classical functions of the State such as public security 'can be "privatized" by contracting out to approved security services'.[86] He further states that, although health authority employees in the *Marshall* case were Crown servants, 'in some Member States health care is "privatized" to a large extent'.[87] Perhaps it is respect for the incidence of privatization and the diversity of practice in the Member States which has led to the inclusion of this element of responsibility in the Court's definition of a public body. The definition allows States to divest themselves of responsibility and deregulate certain activities, leaving the privatized bodies free from obligations under Community law arising from unimplemented directives.

3. *The body must be made responsible pursuant to a measure adopted by the State.* This condition is not complicated. We can nevertheless imagine that it could possibly pose problems where authorities are responsible for providing a public service but do not derive their authority from any measure which emanated from the State. One might imagine professional organizations, trade unions, schools and colleges, kindergartens, museums, and so on. Again this would seem to reinforce the possibility of retaining control over bodies yet excluding them from obligations under unimplemented directives.

4. *The body is responsible for providing a public service.* This condition would also seem to be unambiguous. The Court is likely to construe this criterion widely and follow its case-law in *Auer* v. *Ministère Public*,[88] where it held that professional associations were 'bodies entrusted with a

---

[86] At para. 19 of the Advocate-General's opinion of 8 May 1990.

[87] Ibid. The Advocate-General's suggested reply to the House of Lords is rather different in its use of the notion of responsibility. He would impose obligations under directives on undertakings in respect of which the State has assumed responsibilities which put the State in a position decisively to influence the conduct of that undertaking with regard to the matter contained in the relevant directive (at para. 24). The Advocate-General makes the duty dependent on the retention of a power to influence. The result would mean that privatized or self-regulated bodies, where the State has retained no power in the matter concerned, would have no obligations under the directive.

[88] [1983] ECR 2727.

public duty' and therefore required to recognize a professional qualification as demanded by the directive in question. Of course the matter there was particular as the directive related to professional qualifications. The ruling in *Foster* is limited to sex discrimination. One might ask whether a directive on worker participation would bind unions and employers' organizations.

5. *The body is under the control of the State*. We have already alluded to this condition when discussing the dual requirements that the body be made *responsible* by a *state measure*. The key to understanding this fifth condition is to be found in the opinion of the Advocate-General. For the Advocate-General, the *Auer, Marshall, Johnston*, and *Costanzo* judgments were situations where the respondents all fell under the concept of the State as they exercised authority over individuals. He felt there was no need for criteria of control or delegation in these cases. What he goes on to examine is 'how much further the application of those judgments can extend, in particular with regard to undertakings, in this case public undertakings, which as such exercise *no authority* in the strict sense over individuals'. The Advocate-General answers himself by stating that it should extend as far as the State (or any body with public authority) 'has given itself powers which place it in a position to decisively influence the conduct of persons—whatever their nature, public or private, or their sphere of activity—with regard to the subject matter of the directive'. He goes on to state that it is immaterial whether the State influences this conduct *de jure* or *de facto*. It may be enough that the influence is as a shareholder or through the possibility of appointing or dismissing the majority of the directors, or even through an interruption of its funding so as to threaten its existence. The influence must however stem from something more than general legislative power.

This is a very wide definition of control. Although it was obviously intended to cover undertakings such as British Gas in the instant case, the Advocate-General's final opinion is phrased in general terms citing Article 5 of Directive 76/207 as an example.[89] Such a wide definition seems justified. If the State is to be liable for failure to grant Community rights to those who come into direct contact with it, it should also be liable for failing to ensure that those bodies over which it has control grant individuals those same rights.

[89] 'Individuals may rely on an unconditional and sufficiently precise provision *such as* Article 5(1) of Directive 76/207/EEC against an undertaking in respect of which the State (understood as any body endowed with public authority, regardless of its relationship with other public bodies or the nature of the duties entrusted to it) has assumed responsibilities which put it in a position to decisively influence the conduct of that undertaking in any manner whatsoever (other than by means of general legislation) with regard to the matter in respect of which the relevant provision of a directive imposes an obligation which the Member State has failed to implement in national law' (emphasis added).

The control criterion will always necessitate a complex and searching examination of the State's influence over the body in question. However, control *per se* is not enough. There is one more condition.

6. *The body has special powers relating to its purpose of providing a public service which go beyond those which result from the normal rules applicable in relations between individuals.* In the Court's judgment this last condition was mentioned as an alternative to state control.[90] However, the operative part of the judgment substitutes 'and' for 'or' and so we must presume that this is an additional condition. The operative part also includes the condition that the powers are specific to the purpose of providing a public service. This is not the condition which the Advocate-General suggested, namely that the State should have influence in connection with the matter to which the provision in the directive is addressed. It is enough for the Court that the undertaking can exercise authority greater than that which is available to bodies under the general law. The condition is not defined in functional or practical terms. For instance a professional association or union may have the right to refuse membership to someone without relying on special powers; however, the consequences of such a refusal may mean that that individual is denied a livelihood. The effective or practical power is greater than that pertaining between individuals yet the Court's formal test will exclude these sorts of organizations from the scope of the obligations which arise under unimplemented directives.

Several commentators, whilst recognizing the arbitrariness of denying horizontal effect to directives, suggested in the wake of the *Marshall* decision that there are 'sound reasons' for such a public/private distinction.[91] In the light of the *Foster* case the distinction is beginning to look less and less workable. It is also evident that what is considered public and what is considered private depends on what one's interests are. The public/private distinction now runs like a battleline through Community law. Victory is assured to those who convince the courts to draw it in their favour. In the last part of this chapter suggestions are made as to how the complex and arbitrary nature of this distinction could be

---

[90] 'The Court has held in a series of cases that unconditional and sufficiently precise provisions of a directive could be relied on against organizations or bodies which were subject to the authority or control of the State *or* had special powers beyond those which result from the normal rules applicable to relations between individuals' (para. 18; emphasis added).

[91] Morris (1987: 343); see also Greenwood (1987: 9–12), who suggests that denying horizontal effect may encourage national courts to accept earlier judgments of the ECJ concerning the direct effect of directives, and that any other result would have assimilated directives to regulations, thus removing the necessity of implementing legislation which is, in the end, the most effective way to implement the relevant Community law. See also Easson (1979: 70–3).

ameliorated. It is to be hoped that the European Court of Human Rights manages to avoid similar complexities.

To conclude this section, the present situation in Community law means that vital social and economic rights enshrined in directives may be useless against 'private' social and economic forces where a directive remains unimplemented at the national level. Recent cases in the United Kingdom have shown how arbitrary this distinction is, and tribunals have even denied the applicability of the sex discrimination directives against nationalized industries and universities.[92] The situation is now that a woman working in a state hospital may benefit from a Community directive whereas her sister working in a private hospital will not. A third woman working in a state clinic on a private ward would have to go to court to discover whether she is covered or not. Not only does this development hinder the effectiveness of Community law but it also contradicts two Community legal principles, 'equality of treatment' and 'legal certainty'.

For completeness it should be stated that regulations (which may be very similar in form to directives) may be directly effective against both state and private bodies and decisions are similarly enforceable against both state and private bodies (where the decision has been addressed to that body).

So treaty provisions, regulations, directives, and decisions are all capable of granting individual rights. Some fundamental Community rights (notably Articles 7 and 119 EEC), certain provisions of regulations with direct effect, and decisions addressed to actual bodies will also give rise to enforceable duties for private bodies. But what happens when Community provisions such as these conflict with human rights contained in international treaties such as the Convention and enshrined in the constitutions of some Member States? What if a private body, faced with a Community obligation, or even a duty to respect a fundamental Community right, counter-claimed that the duty conflicted with its human rights as guaranteed by international or constitutional law? Furthermore, can the ECJ impose obligations on private bodies so that those bodies have to observe the European Convention?

8.1.2.1 National legislation operating in the field of Community law

These legislative provisions are not at present judged by the Court for compliance with the European Convention on Human Rights (and presumably other non-EC human rights). This is clearly stated by the Court in the *Cinéthèque* case:

[92] *Foster* v. *British Gas PLC* [1987] ICR 52 (pre-privatization) and *Rolls-Royce* v. *Doughty* [1987] IRLR 447 (pre-privatization), *Turpie* v. *University of Glasgow*, unreported.

Although it is true that it is the duty of this Court to ensure observance of fundamental rights in the field of Community law, it has no power to examine the compatibility with the European Convention of national legislation which concerns, as in this case, an area which falls within the jurisdiction of the national legislator.[93]

The implications of this and subsequent judgments of the ECJ have been dealt with elsewhere.[94] However, we should mention the latest statement by the ECJ in *SPUC* v. *Grogan*, that the 'Court, when required to give a preliminary ruling, must provide the national court with all the elements of interpretation which are necessary in order to enable it to assess the compatibility of that legislation with fundamental rights—as laid down in particular in the European Convention—the observance of which the Court ensures.'[95]

Similarly in the *Kabelregeling* case[96] the national court asked:

can the generally accepted principles of Community law (in particular the principle of proportionality) and the fundamental rights enshrined in Community law (in particular the freedom of expression and freedom to receive information) impose directly applicable obligations on Member States in the light of which national rules such as those concerned here must be assessed, regardless of whether or not any written provisions of Community law are applicable thereto?[97]

As regards the first part of the question conerning proportionality, Advocate-General Mancini referred to the *Coener* v. *Sociaal-Economische Road* case[98] and stated that Member States that wish to restrict the exercise of certain activities in the public interest may only take those measures which are strictly necessary for the protection of that interest.[99]

As regards the question of fundamental rights, the situation is different. Having referred to the *Cinéthèque* case (quoted above) the Advocate-General refers to a section written by Professor Frowein in the *Integration through Law* project. It is worth quoting the passage by Frowein in full:

[I]t is possible to foresee a dialectical development by which the legal order of a Member State will be influenced by the jurisprudence of the Court of the Communities. Since Community law is directly applicable in the domestic sphere

---

[93] *Cinéthèque SA* v. *Fédération Nationale des Cinémas Français*, Cases 60, 61/84 [1985] ECR 2605, para. 25.

[94] See A. Clapham, *European Union: The Human Rights Challenge*, i: *Human Rights and the European Community: A Critical Overview* (Baden-Baden: Nomos, 1991). For another analysis see Weiler (1991: 555–642).

[95] C-159/90, judgment of 4 Oct. 1991, para. 30. The paragraph continues: 'However the Court has no such jurisdiction with regard to national legislation lying outside the scope of Community law.' See s. 8.1.1 above.

[96] *L'Association Bond Van Adverteerders* v. *The Netherlands*, Case 352/85, 26 Apr. 1988 [1988] 2085.

[97] Para. 10, subpara. 9 of judgment.

[98] Case 39/75 ECR [1975] 1547, paras. 11 and 12.

[99] At para. 12 of the Advocate-General's opinion.

it is rather unlikely that national courts will fall behind established Community standards when applying domestic fundamental rights even in matters which have nothing to do with Community law. To this extent there may be indirect integration through the jurisprudence of the European Court of Justice concerning fundamental rights and freedoms. (1986: 302)

The Advocate-General stated that he felt we had to wait for this 'dialectical development' and the Court did not address the question.

One might offer the conclusion that when the action complained of does not depend on a Community provision yet may be covered by the general field of Community law, free movement of people, services, etc., then national courts are not ready to judge that action against a list of Community fundamental rights and freedoms, nor will the Court of Justice judge national legislation against human rights standards.

More recently it has been suggested that this 'dialectical development' now has a stronger legal base to spring from. In a short article published in the *European Law Review*,[100] A. J. Riley argues that the reference in the third preambular paragraph of the Single European Act (1986) to the Council of Europe's European Social Charter (1961) means that the Charter is now 'part of Community law', and some provisions therefore have direct effect against both national and private bodies. This thesis finds a little support in a judgment of the ECJ in the *Blaizot* case,[101] where the Court briefly referred to the Charter to find that university education may be a form of vocational training. In this case, it was not a question of national legislation implementing a Community provision but of national legislation operating in the field of Community law. Interestingly, the Social Charter was used as an aid to interpretation even though the case was against Belgium, which has not yet ratified the Charter. If the Charter is to be eventually incorporated in this way, then the case is just as strong for the European Convention on Human Rights, which has for some time been ratified by all the Community Member States.[102] Furthermore, the ECJ has now made an express reference to the preamble of the Single European Act (which mentions both the Charter and the Convention) in deciding a case involving human rights. In *Commission* v. *Federal Republic of Germany*[103] the Court affirmed that Regulation 1612/68 has to be interpreted with respect to the demands of Article 8 ECHR. This is demanded by Community law's commitment to ensuring respect for fundamental rights as defined by the jurisprudence

---

[100] Riley (1989: 80–6). And see the criticism by Gould (1989: 223–6).
[101] Case 24/86, *Vincent Blaizot and the University of Liège and Others* v. *Belgium* ECR [1988] 379.
[102] Belgium, Denmark, France, Germany, Greece, Ireland, Italy, Luxembourg, The Netherlands, Portugal, Spain, UK.
[103] Case 249/86, judgment of 18 May 1989 [1989] ECR 1263.

of the Court and now reaffirmed by the preamble of the Single European Act.[104]

It is suggested that this incorporation of the human rights treaties of the Council of Europe through the Court's reference to the preamble does not give rise to enforceable rights with direct effect at the national level. First, the reference in the preamble is merely evidence of the Member States' intention to work towards greater protection for human rights. It is not a clear and unambiguous affirmation which could give rise to new rights and obligations at the national level. Secondly, in the relevant cases (*Blaizot, Commission* v. *Federal Republic of Germany*) the Court used the treaties as an *aid to interpretation*, it did not grant enforceable rights or duties with direct effect (as it did in *Van Gend en Loos* for Article 12 EEC, and in *Van Duyn* for a provision in a directive).

The Maastricht Treaty has reinforced the status of the Convention by including a paragraph in Article F stating:

2. The Union shall respect Fundamental rights as guaranteed by the European Convention for the Protection of Human Rights and Fundamental Freedoms and as they result from the constitutional traditions common to the Member States as general principles of law.

The effect of this affirmation would seem to be limited to acts of the Union rather than the validity of national legislation or acts of state or private bodies. But this provision can only reinforce the jurisprudence of the Court of Justice as developed in the *ERT* case. This case suggests that fundamental rights, and the Convention in particular, have to be considered by national courts not only when interpreting Community provisions and the national implementation of Community law, but also when weighing the proportionality and legitimacy of derogations from Community freedoms. In the *ERT* case the Court stated that the permissible restrictions under Article 56 EEC (public policy, public security, or public health) had to be looked at in the light of the general principle of freedom of expression. The Community could not allow measures which were incompatible with human rights.[105] Therefore national consideration of Community law will have to take the Convention fully into account. The extent to which national courts do this may in some cases be reviewed by the ECJ through the preliminary ruling procedure.

---

[104] See para. 10 of the judgment: 'Regulation No 1612/68 must also be interpreted in the light of the requirements of respect for family life set out in Article 8 of the European Convention for the Protection of Fundamental Rights and Freedoms. That requirement is one of the fundamental rights which according to the Court's settled case-law, restated in the preamble to the Single European Act, are recognized by Community law.'

[105] *Elliniki Radiophonia Tiléorani-Anonimi Etairia* v. *Dimotiki Etairia Pliroforissis*, C-260/89, judgment of 18 June 1991, para. 41 (not yet reported).

8.1.2.1.1 Full incorporation of the Convention by the European Court of Justice

Should the Court go further and review all national legislation (or even the acts of private bodies) within the field of Community law for conformity with the Convention or the Social Charter (1961) such a development would be similar to the nationalization of the American Bill of Rights by the Supreme Court. This was however a slow gradual process, and the application of the Bill of Rights to state as well as federal action came about in the wake of a civil war and in the face of fierce opposition. It is worth opening a parenthesis and noting that much of the impetus behind the move towards incorporation came from pressure groups such as the American Civil Liberties Union, the International Labor Defense, the American Newspaper Publishers' Association, and the Industrial Workers of the World.[106] These groups targeted cases so that they could force changes in all the States by relying on the federal Bill of Rights rather than state constitutions.[107] Although there exist hundreds of interest groups at the European level, few of these, if any, are primarily concerned with civil rights. Perhaps as European supranational pressure groups emerge the 'dialectical development' will take place and the Convention will become incorporated in this way.[108]

8.1.2.2 National authorities implementing Community provisions

8.1.2.2.1 Judicial review by the European Court of Justice

The history of the Court's jurisprudence on this question has been analysed in great detail,[109] and the background is well known. Even though proposals for insertion of a provision guaranteeing political and fundamental rights were rejected when the Community Treaties were drafted,[110] the Court has gradually incorporated the protection of fundamental rights as a general principle of Community law. This came about against a background of discontent in the Constitutional Courts of Italy and Germany, which

---

[106] See generally Cortner (1981).

[107] Of course much will depend on the enthusiasm of the judges: 'Thus not only the push of litigation, but also the pull of their own commitments either to rights, or to integration, or both, may move the judges of high courts to the pronouncement of trans-state or transnational standards of rights. It then follows that the tempo of integration will be determined by the accident of which judges, with what kinds of human rights temperaments and views on legal integration, are appointed to these high courts' (Frowein, Schulhofer, and Shapiro 1986: 341–2).

[108] The role of interest groups in the 'privatization of human rights' is dealt with in detail in Ch. 9.

[109] Gaja (1988: 574–89); Foster (1987: 245); Weiler (1986: 1103–42); Mendelson (1981: 121).

[110] See Betten (1985: 4).

had suggested that they might one day have to review Community provisions for compatibility with basic human rights.[111] The ECJ, having rejected arguments based on human rights principles found in national law in an early case,[112] later stated in the *Stauder* case[113] that 'the provision at issue contains nothing capable of prejudicing *the fundamental human rights enshrined in the general principles of Community law and protected by the Court'*. However, this was merely *obiter* and hardly a very concrete assertion of the rights which merit protection. In the *Second Nold* case[114] the Court went further and explained that:

In safeguarding these rights, the Court is bound to draw inspiration from constitutional traditions common to the Member States, and it cannot therefore uphold measures which are incompatible with fundamental rights recognized and protected by the constitutions of those States. Similarly, international treaties for the protection of human rights on which the Member States have collaborated or of which they are signatories,[115] can supply guidelines which should be followed within the framework of Community law.[116]

After these cases, the Court had to deal with the right to property in the *Hauer* case,[117] where it stated that such a right is guaranteed in the Community legal order. The Court referred to Article 1 of the First Protocol to the European Convention on Human Rights and 'ideas common to the Constitutions of the Member States'. Similarly in other cases concerning the right to an effective judicial remedy[118] the Court has also referred to the European Convention and constitutional traditions common to the Member States.

However, we cannot forget that the ECJ is the guardian of the EC Treaties and that it has stated categorically that 'The protection of such rights, whilst inspired by the constitutional traditions common to the Member States must be ensured *within the framework of the structure and*

---

[111] *Frontini* case (no. 183), Corte Costitutionale 27 Dec. 1973 [1974] 2 CMLR 386 (in fact the Italian court stated it would have to review the constitutionality of the ratification of the Treaty of Rome); and *German Handelsgesellschaft* case Bundesverfassungsgericht 29 May 1974 [1974] 2 CMLR 551. But at least in Germany this threat has now abated; see the *Solange II* decision of 22 Oct. 1986 *Re Wünsche Handelsgesellschaft* [1987] 3 CMLR 225, where the Constitutional Court stated that so long as the level of protection of human rights under Community law remained adequate by German standards the Court would not review secondary Community legislation for compatibility with the human rights provisions of the *Grundgesetz* (para. 48).

[112] *Stork* case, Case 1/58 [1959] ECR 17.

[113] *Stauder* v. *City of Ulm*, Case 29/69 [1969] ECR 419 at 425.

[114] *J. Nold* v. *Commission*, Case 4/73 [1974] ECR 491.

[115] The only EC Member State which had merely signed the ECHR was France, which ratified during the course of the judgment.

[116] At p. 507.

[117] *Hauer* v. *Land Rheinland-Pfalz*, Case 44/79 [1979] ECR 3727.

[118] Case 222/84, *Johnston* v. *Chief Constable of the Royal Ulster Constabulary* [1986] ECR 1651.

objectives of the Community.[119] This means that human rights values will have to be interpreted in the light of the demands of European integration. They are not considered the highest law.

In two recent cases the Court repeated its promise to ensure the protection of fundamental rights and its intention to draw inspiration both from the 'constitutional traditions common to the Member States', and from 'international instruments concerning human rights on which the Member States have collaborated or of which they are signatories'. But it continued:

The fundamental rights recognised by the Court are not absolute, however, but must be considered in relation to their social function. Consequently, restrictions may be imposed on the exercise of those rights, in particular in the context of the common organization of a market, provided that those restrictions in fact correspond to the objectives of general interest pursued by the Community, and do not constitute, with regard to the aim pursued, a disproportionate and intolerable interference, impairing the very substance of these rights.[120]

The Court then stated that when implementing the Community regulation at issue Member States are obliged to ensure that the result is not incompatible with the protection of fundamental rights in the Community legal order.[121] The Court concluded that the regulation in question leaves the competent national authorities a large margin of appreciation in the application of the regulation so that the result conforms with the protection of fundamental rights.[122]

Whilst the ECJ remains cautious about imposing Convention-type duties on Member States where they are implementing Community provisions it is unlikely that it will impose Convention duties on private bodies in a review of their implementation of a Community provision. However, this is not an impossible scenario. The ECJ is not bound by Article 25 of the

---

[119] *International Handelsgesellschaft*, Case 11/70 [1970] ECR 1125 at 1134 (emphasis added), quoted and relied on in *Hauer*, and more recently in *Staatsanwalt Freiburg* v. *Keller*, Case 239/85 [1987] CMLR 875. It has been suggested that some human rights may take legal priority even over primary Community law (the objectives of the Community); see Dauses (1985: 412): 'It would seem appropriate to make a distinction between the substratum of supra-positive principles of law incorporated in the Convention and their substantive legal form. Whilst the former, as general principles deriving from a source of law independent of the Treaties, no doubt takes precedence even over primary Community law, the latter is superior to secondary Community law but takes second place to the Treaties.' Although it was for some time suggested that Art. 234 EEC meant that the ECHR (1950) took priority over the subsequent EEC provisions, this doctrine has never been taken up by the Court, and Gaja (1988: 584) suggests that it was implicitly rejected by the Court in Cases 50–8/82 [1982] ECR 3949 at 3959, para. 13.

[120] *Hubert Wachauf* v. *FRG*, Case 5/88, judgment of 13 July 1989, para. 18 [1989] ECR 2609. The other case is *Hermann Schräder HS Kraftfutter GmbH and Co. KG* v. *Hauptzullamt Gronau*, Case 265/87, judgment of 11 July 1989, para. 15 [1989] ECR 2237.

[121] At para. 19.   [122] At para. 22.

Convention, and following the case-law of the European Court of Human Rights, which asserts that the Convention applies in relations between individuals, we can see that, for example, an employer who implements a migrant workers' regulation so as to deny the right to family life could have his or her action reviewed for conformity with the Convention with a final interpretation given by the ECJ by means of a preliminary ruling.

8.2 THE PROTECTION OF ENFORCEABLE RIGHTS FOR VICTIMS OF VIOLATIONS BY COMMUNITY INSTITUTIONS OR AGENTS: THE COMMUNITY AS A NON-STATE ACTOR IN THE PRIVATE SPHERE

Whereas the measures discussed above can be scrutinized for human rights compliance either at the national level or at Strasbourg under the Convention machinery, action taken by Community organs can only be reviewed by the ECJ. The European Commission of Human Rights has rejected applications against Community bodies, simply stating that the Community is not a party to the Convention.[123] Claims directed against the Member States jointly[124] and the individual Member States were also dismissed.[125] One could attempt to distinguish these cases as involving acts which take effect within the framework of the European Communities. Should a Community act have effects reaching beyond a strict Community context it may one day be held to invoke the responsibility of all the Member States under Article 1 of the Convention. Indeed in an application[126] brought by an ex-employee of the European Parliament complaining about the procedure before the ECJ, the European Commission of Human Rights has hinted that it may entertain applications against Community organs where this could be said to invoke the responsibility of each of the twelve Member States. In any event this case was declared inadmissible for non-exhaustion of domestic remedies, and it is interesting that the Commission considered that the Community Court should be

---

[123] *Re the European School in Brussels: D. v. Belgium and the European Communities* [1986] 2 CMLR 57; and see also *Confédération Française Démocratique du Travail v. The European Communities*, Applic. 8030/77 [1979] 2 CMLR 229.

[124] See M. Mendelson, who has criticized this result in the *CFDT* case: 'As a matter of principle, it is surely undesirable, notwithstanding the separate legal personality of the Community, for some of the States parties to the Convention to be able to acquire "immunity and impunity" under it merely by delegating some of their powers to an organization which they control collectively (and to some extent individually, by means of the veto power)' (1983: 116).

[125] In the *CFDT* case, the main State involved had not yet accepted the individual right of petition, Art. 25 ECHR.

[126] *Christine Dufay v. Les Communautés Européennes, subsidiairement, la collectivité de leurs États membres et leurs États membres pris individuellement*, Applic. 13539/88, 19 Jan. 1989 (unpublished). See also *C. Dufay v. European Parliament* [1987] ECR 1561.

considered a domestic remedy. However this last question has not been finally settled, and there is some disagreement as to whether references under Article 177 EEC count as domestic remedies.[127]

In speculating on when cases against the Community may be brought in Strasbourg, it is worth noting that the First Vice-President of the Human Rights Commission, writing in his professorial capacity, has stated:

One may conclude that the European Community is, at present, not subject to the control of the supervisory organs set up by the European Convention on Human Rights. The responsibility of individual Member States under the Convention for acts of the European Community could be engaged only in rather exceptional cases. It does not seem likely that this gap could be bridged by the jurisprudence of the European Commission of Human Rights. (Frowein 1986: 335)

This means that the only protection available to victims of abuses by the Community is to be found at the ECJ. This Court has examined the action of Community organs for compliance with the rights contained in the European Convention and the staff regulations.[128] We should recall in this context the importance of the Joint Declaration of the European Parliament, the Council, and the Commission, made on 5 April 1977, which stresses the importance which these institutions attach to fundamental rights, as derived in particular from the Constitutions of the Member States and the European Convention on Human Rights, and pledges to respect these rights in the exercise of their powers.[129]

Questions of religious discrimination,[130] invasion of privacy,[131] and due process under Article 6[132] have all been considered by the ECJ. The Community was found to be justified in all these cases. Two cases deserve particular examination. In the *Fedetab* case[133] it was claimed that the EC Commission had violated Article 6(1) ECHR. This Article protects the right to a tribunal for the determination of one's civil rights and obligations. The Court rejected the claim, stating that the Commission was not a

---

[127] Ghandi (1981: 23), and see also Mendelson (1983: 109), who also raises the question of Art. 27(1) ECHR and the ECJ, and concludes that the ECJ should not be regarded as a domestic remedy under Art. 26 ECHR.

[128] The Staff Regulations contain a number of provisions which touch on human rights: Art. 12 contains details of permissible restrictions on Community employees' freedom of expression, Art. 24 refers to the rights to association and to join a trade union, Art. 27(2) states that officials shall be selected without reference to race, creed, or sex, and Art. 86(3) outlines the *Non bis in idem* rule.

[129] *OJ* (1977), C 103/1, 27 Apr. 1977.

[130] *Prais v. Council*, Case 130/75 [1976] ECR 1185.

[131] *National Panasonic* case, Case 136/79 [1980] ECR 2033.

[132] *Landewyck et al.*, Cases 209–15 and 218/78 [1980] ECR 3125; and *Musique Diffusion Française v. Commission*, Cases 100–3/80 [1983] ECR 1825. *Dufay v. European Parliament* [1987] ECR 1561.

[133] Cases 209–15 and 218/75 [1980] ECR 3125.

tribunal.[134] However, closer examination of the case-law of the Court of Human Rights would have revealed that, if the right in question is a 'civil right', then the Member State is obliged to ensure that recourse can be had to a tribunal; whether the body already carrying out that role is or is not a tribunal is irrelevant.[135] The second case is *Hoechst AG* v. *Commission*,[136] where the plaintiff company complained that the search of its premises carried out by the Commission's agents was an invasion of privacy and in violation of Article 8 of the Convention. The ECJ noted that there were divergencies in the Member States concerning human rights protection *vis-à-vis* commercial premises,[137] and denied the protection of Article 8 of the Convention to Hoechst AG. They also remarked that 'il y a lieu de constater l'absence d'une jurisprudence de la Cour européenne des droits de l'homme'.[138] This last remark is open to criticism, as six months earlier the European Court of Human Rights handed down a judgment in the *Chappell* case[139] which concerned a search and seizure of video cassettes and documents from premises comprising one floor with offices, another floor with a bedroom, an office, and a room for processing videos, and a third floor with three offices. Although the Court did not discuss whether strictly commercial premises were covered by Article 8, the fact that they held that the case fell within Article 8 was of some relevance. Furthermore, in the report of the Commission of Human Rights adopted in October 1987 there are passages suggesting that respect for the private sphere is not a question of the type of premises, but of the kind of documents which are interfered with.[140]

In this field, which is concerned with offering protection to Community citizens from the actions of the Community's own agents and institutions, the Court can afford to go beyond the common constitutional traditions

---

[134] See also *Musique Diffusion Française*, Cases 100–3/80 [1983] ECR 1825: 'As the Court held in . . . *Van Landewyck* . . . the Commission cannot be described as a "tribunal" within the meaning of Article 6 of the European Convention for the Protection of Human Rights' (at 1880 para. 8).

[135] For a more detailed criticism see Ghandi (1981: 11).

[136] Cases 46/87 and 227/88, judgment of 21 Sept. 1989 [1989] ECR 2859.

[137] At para. 17.

[138] At para. 18.

[139] Judgment of 30 Mar. 1989, Series A, vol. 152.

[140] See para. 96 of *Chappell* v. *UK*, Applic. 10461/83. Report of the Commission (adopted 14 Oct. 1987): 'In sum, therefore, although directed against the applicant's, and his company's, business activities, the search under the Order impinged directly on the applicant's private life and the private sphere of items and associations which are the attributes of a home. This sphere clearly includes the applicant's private papers whether in the form of letters or other material.' Some of the material seized was correspondence between Mr Chappell and his girlfriends as well as a 'leaflet showing that he was using contact magazines to meet men and women for sexual relations' (para. 53). It would seem to be the documents which make up 'the private sphere of items' rather than the designation of premises as commercial or domestic.

of the Member States and offer the highest protection. As we saw above, the Court did this in the *Razzouk* case, when it struck down the Commission's provisions on widowers' pensions, which were discriminatory as they offered women greater advantages than men. At least in the field of protection against the Community the ECJ has the potential to become one of the most progressive human rights' courts in the world—offering protection which goes beyond the guarantees contained in international treaties and common constitutional provisions.

8.3 SOME TENTATIVE SUGGESTIONS

Despite substantial case-law from the ECJ on the question of the protection of human rights and the application of directives to bodies which straddle the public/private divide, a number of questions still need clarification. Which bodies have directly enforceable duties under unimplemented directives? Does this vary depending on the right at issue? Is sex discrimination a special case in the Community legal order? What exactly constitutes 'control' by the State according to the Court in *Foster*? Can national courts judge Community provisions for conformity with human rights? Which rights are applicable? Only those which appear in every Member State constitution? Or a maximum standard designed to ensure the objectives of the Community? Will obligations under the Convention be imposed directly on individuals?

As explained above these questions relate to the privatization of human rights on two planes. First we have the issue of protection from private actors in the sphere of Community law, and second we have the issue of protection from the Community (which under the Convention system is equated with private or non-state bodies, or even occasionally given a sort of immunity). Each issue demands a separate solution.

8.3.1 Horizontal effect for directives dealing with human rights

It was explained above that in a situation where an individual seeks to rely on a right contained in a directive which has not been implemented by the national authority then the right is not enforceable against private bodies. It was suggested that where the rights were of a fundamental nature this led to unacceptable discrimination and unfair treatment as well as a lacuna in the protection of human rights. One solution would involve appropriate directives explicitly stating that they were intended to bind private actors. In some cases it may be enough that only some Articles of the directive are stated to bind private actors.

8.3.2 Accession by the Community to the European Convention on Human Rights

The issue of accession by the Community to the European Convention on Human Rights is not new and the problems have been extensively discussed in the literature on the subject. The following discussion addresses the accession issue from the perspective of some of the issues raised in this chapter. Accession is not a panacea which can solve all the problems dealt with earlier. Nevertheless there is renewed interest in this from the Commission and on 19 November 1990 it approved a proposal for accession to be transmitted to the Committee of Ministers.[141] With the eventual entry into force of any future Protocol to the Convention, the Community and its institutions will no longer be treated as private/non-state bodies under the Convention system. Individuals and groups will be able to bring applications against the Community institutions in the same way that they would bring an application against any other Contracting Party.

Accession to the Convention may have a number of major advantages. As the Commission points out in its 1979 memorandum:

However satisfactory and worthy of approval the method developed by the Court may be, it cannot rectify at least one of the shortcomings affecting the legal order of the Communities through the lack of a written catalogue of fundamental rights: the impossibility of knowing in advance which are the liberties which may not be infringed by the Community under any circumstances. The European Citizen has a legitimate interest in having his rights *vis-à-vis* the Community laid down in advance. He must be able to assess the prospects of any possible legal dispute from the outset and therefore have at his disposal clearly defined criteria.[142]

Accession would give citizens not only a clearly defined list, but also the benefit of a large amount of case-law as developed by the Strasbourg organs.

In addition, the invisible effects of accession should not be underestimated. Accession could mean that national judges would have to consider the Convention (and its case-law) when deciding matters covered by Community law. Although the Commission states that 'Additional obligations would arise only with regard to the freedom of action of the Community institutions and their legislative and administrative functions' (para. 41), it is quite likely that accession would mean the Convention exerting a creeping influence on Community law generally. Furthermore, following the decision by the European Commission of Human Rights in the *M*. v. *Federal Republic of Germany* application,[143] accession would

---

[141] *Bull. EC* 1990/11 para. 1.3.203; SEC(90)2087 final.
[142] Adopted by the Commission, 4 Apr. 1979, *Bull. EC* Supplement 2/79 para. 5.
[143] Applic. 13258/87, decision of 9 Feb. 1990, and see Schermers (1990: 249–58).

now cover such a situation. In other words, where a Member State has no discretion in the implementation or execution of a Community decision or provision, the actual national behaviour could be overtly scrutinized by the European Commission of Human Rights and the Community would be the respondent. The procedure for electing the respondents in such cases is not yet even in draft form, but it would surely be preferable if the Community itself elected to be the respondent in such cases, even where the application had originally been lodged against another Contracting Party. In this way the Community could present its defence of the Community provisions or their implementation, and explain their necessity in a democratic society, or why they are proportionate to the aim which the Community is pursuing.

It is only fair to state that Member States have shown little enthusiasm for accession in the past. There has been very little national debate on this question but when the matter comes to be debated at the national level one can foresee misgivings about such a step. It could be seen as a first step towards block voting in the Commission or Court of Human Rights. Although the present composition of these two bodies would indicate independence from government pressure there is some concern that the twelve Member States of the Community already confer before decisions taken by the Committee of Ministers of the Council of Europe when exercising their quasi-judicial jurisdiction under the Convention. Some quarters have even foreseen the Community judge gradually taking over from the twelve Member State judges and being eventually given an extra twelve votes as the other judges become redundant. As European Political Union becomes a reality it is already being suggested that the Community should have a permanent seat in the Security Council of the UN. At the moment it seems very unlikely that a Community judge would replace the twelve Member State judges; however, another problem may also worry States Parties. If the Protocol allows for the Community to bring inter-state cases this may cause resentment by States who do not wish to be 'policed' by the Community in human rights matters such as conditions in prisons and rules of military discipline, where the Community has no equivalent duties or experience of the problems involved. In short, the debate at the national level and especially in non-Community States has yet to begin.[144]

At the Community level, it boils down to a difficult question of tactics: accession would be of some symbolic importance (as well as filling certain legal gaps), but it would take the wind out of the sails of those who desire

---

[144] The debate in the UK at the end of the 1970s did actually reach the House of Lords, which voted against accession. In 1992 the matter was again examined by the Select Committee on the European Communities of the House of Lords. The Committee did not favour accession *Human Rights Re-examined*, HL paper 10 (London: HMSO, 1992).

a modern, specially adapted Community catalogue or Bill of Rights.[145] In the light of the new Parliamentary Declaration of Fundamental Rights and Freedoms (12 April 1989),[146] it is hard to imagine the European Parliament showing much enthusiasm for accession. Although Parliament has in the past tabled and passed resolutions pronouncing itself in favour of accession, the mood may now be rather different.[147]

In conclusion it can be said that accession would bring with it a number of benefits for the victims of human rights abuses by the Community. Instead of having to rely on cases brought before the ECJ individuals could petition the Commission of Human Rights complaining about the acts of what is now considered a non-state body—the Community

8.4 SUMMARY CONCERNING COMMUNITY LAW

1. Directives do not impose direct legal obligations on private bodies even though some Treaty Articles, regulations, and decisions do. The *Foster* judgment provides the criteria by which one judges whether a body is private or public and hence has enforceable duties under Article 5(1) of Directive 76/207. It should be possible expressly to state that appropriate provisions in directives be directly applicable against private bodies. This could be written into directives.

---

[145] Dr Ehlermann has suggested accession followed by a catalogue; see *The European Convention on Human Rights: Two New Directions, EEC: UK* (London: British Institute of Human Rights, 1980), 7–14 at 9. Although Ehlermann states that accession would be relevant only to the control of Community acts (at 13) McBride and Brown suggest it would be relevant for national provisions which implement Community obligations (1981: 167). This question is most important for the three countries which have not incorporated the Convention (UK, Ireland, and Denmark). For a more recent statement by Ehlermann see the 'Public hearing on fundamental rights in the European Union' meeting of the Committee on Institutional Affairs held at the European University Institute, Florence, 25–7 May 1988 (PE 124.155 at 26–7), where he casts some doubt on the political expediency of either accession or a catalogue.

[146] *OJ* (1989), no. C 120/50.

[147] See the intervention by Mr Rothley, MEP, at the Conference on 'Human Rights and the European Community: Towards 1992 and Beyond' (Strasbourg, 20–1 Nov. 1989), who comes out strongly against accession. The proceedings are available in the original language from the Commission. In 1987 a motion for a Resolution tabled by Mr Rothley proposed a regulation incorporating the ECHR so that it bound the Community institutions (doc. B2-494/87, 17 June 1987 (Session Documents)). Resolutions were passed by the Parliament calling for accession in 1979 (*OJ*, no. C 127/69) and in 1982 (*OJ*, no. C 304/253). The Parliamentary Resolution on the Inter-Governmental Conference (1990) proposes accession alongside incorporation in the Treaty of the Parliament's Declaration of Fundamental Rights and Freedoms (1989). Most recently see the lukewarm enthusiasm for accession expressed by Lord Inglewood, MEP, Spokesman for the European Democratic Group (Conservatives) on the Legal Affairs Committee, written evidence submitted to the House of Lords Select Committee on the European Communities, *Human Rights Re-Examined* (London: HMSO, 1992), 46.

2. Cases cannot be brought against the Community as such before the European Commission of Human Rights; the Community is considered a private body for which Member States cannot be held responsible. A possible solution would be accession to the Convention by the Community.

3. Private bodies operating in the sphere of Community law have not yet been restricted by human rights norms found in the Convention when relying on Community freedoms. However, in the light of the judgment in the *ERT* case, national courts have to consider the Convention when looking at the legitimacy of restrictions on Community freedoms.

4. National legislation in the sphere of Community law will only be judged against the Convention where it is actually implementing a Community provision. However, in the *Grogan* case the ECJ said that it must provide national courts with all the elements of interpretation necessary for them to assess the compatibility of that legislation with fundamental rights.

5. Where national legislation implements a directive so that individuals have rights against private bodies, that legislation has to be interpreted in accordance with the directive even where it imposes duties on private bodies (the *Von Colson* principle).

6. The history of the ECJ's case-law concerning fundamental rights illustrates the dynamics of the privatization of human rights and the choices facing any supranational or quasi-federal court. The Court has interpreted the law so as to create a sliding scale of judicial interference. Fundamental rights will sometimes be upheld *against the Community* even beyond the strict limits of the Treaty. Lower down the scale of protection, fundamental and other rights contained in unimplemented directives are enforceable against *emanations of the State*. Yet these same obligations are not directly imposed on private bodies. Although the legal framework is very different from that of the Convention, the cautious federalism of the Court in extending the protection of fundamental rights into the private sphere will be partly a result of the opposition of Member States and private economic actors. The fears of loss of autonomy, reregulation, and economic disaster emerge from the reports of the cases. The same considerations face the European Court of Human Rights when it deals with human rights in the private sphere.

9

A 'Private Police' for Human Rights
in the Private Sphere

9.1 INTRODUCTION

A recurring theme in this study has been the suggestion that the current and future success of the European Convention on Human Rights owes a great deal to a number of pressure and interest groups. These groups have seized the opportunities which the Convention offers and have often exploited its potential through a number of applications.

Furthermore, these applications have often been fought over fundamental principles; victory for the applicants has meant fundamental changes in the law affecting whole classes of people. Examples include the campaign by STOPP (Society of Teachers Opposed to Physical Punishment) which, following the *Campbell and Cosans* case, resulted in the legislation which abolished corporal punishment in state schools, and the campaign by NIGRA (Northern Ireland Gay Rights Association) which, following the *Dudgeon* case, resulted in the repeal of the law which criminalized homosexual relations in Northern Ireland. In addition to the technical changes in the law, a considerable educational effect transcends the immediate results. In the private sphere this is ultimately the most important consequence. The proscriptions on the beating of schoolchildren and intolerance towards gay men have their greatest effect when private individuals start to question their own morality and behaviour.

Three other areas merit particular mention. Prisoners' rights, mental health patients' rights, and immigrants' rights are all areas which have benefited from the support and expertise of non-governmental organizations in applications under the Convention: the NCCL (the National Council for Civil Liberties, now known as 'Liberty'), MIND (National Association of Mental Health), and JCWI (Joint Council for the Welfare of Immigrants) have all been particularly active and successful.[1]

Even where non-governmental organizations are not acting on behalf

---

[1] For further details of the decisions, reports, and judgments concerning these areas and the role which these non-governmental organizations have played see Grosz and Hulton (1986: 138–57).

of the applicant they have been instrumental in bringing extra information to the attention to the Court in the form of third-party submissions.[2] This activity is of increasing importance and a number of the most recent cases have clearly been influenced by the information submitted by these organizations. This chapter seeks to demonstrate the special importance of fully accommodating these groups where cases involve the operation of the Convention in the private sphere. It may be helpful to distinguish between third-party submissions and support by non-state organizations.

9.2 THIRD-PARTY SUBMISSIONS

In the *Malone* case the Commission had been forced, due to lack of evidence, to conclude that there was no violation of Article 8 as concerns the practice of 'metering' (Post Office metering enabled the police to know the destination, duration, and timing of an individual's telephone calls). This Post Office Engineering Union, with the assistance of Interights and Justice, prepared a submission for the European Court of Human Rights with detailed evidence of how the police obtained information (without a warrant) through metering. In reply to the Government's contention that metering only involved recording the fact of a conversation and therefore did not constitute a violation of the Convention, as it involves only signals sent to the Post Office, the Union's submission stated: 'The recorded fact of conversations with a trade union, a political body, a betting organization or a known prostitute is not merely a record of "signals sent only to [the Post Office] itself", but information on a conversation about which both parties should be able to entertain a reasonable expectation of privacy. Knowledge of such calls by third

---

[2] The term 'interventions' has been avoided as intervening parties may in some legal systems have similar or identical rights to the original party. Furthermore, the rationale for intervention in a system such as the Community legal order is that persons having an interest in the result of the Court of Justice's judgment should be prevented from asserting this interest after the judgment has been made (Cases 9 and 12/60, *Belgium* v. *Société Commerciale Antoine Vloebergs Sa and High Authority* [1961] ECR 197). Rights to intervene were granted under the Community Treaties and Rules of Procedure but it should be noted that these rights mostly concern Member States and Community institutions. Under the EEC and Euratom Statutes of the Court of Justice other persons must have an interest in the outcome of the case and may only intervene where the case concerns Community institutions on the one hand and private bodies on the other hand. The case is different under the ECSC Statute, where the person has merely to establish an interest in the result of the case before the Court. A number of national and international non-governmental organizations have intervened in Community law cases before the ECJ. These include the Bureau Européen des Unions de Consommateurs, the European Council of Chemical Manufacturers' Federation, and the Consultative Committee of the Bars and Law Societies of the European Communities. In order to distinguish this right to intervene from the options under the Convention the term 'intervention' has been avoided in the context of the Convention.

parties in an obvious invasion of privacy.'[3] The Court found (unanimously) that the practice of metering was a breach of the Convention even though Malone was only *potentially* likely to be affected by this practice. No legislation made it unlawful for the Post Office to pass on this information to the police (which the submission showed they were in the practice of doing in response to requests by the police). Despite the fact that the practice was not in breach of any domestic law the Court held that it could not be said to be 'in accordance with the law' for the purposes of Article 8(2). We should note that it was the release of the information without the subscriber's consent which amounted to an interference with Malone's right under Article 8. This release was executed by Post Office workers. After 1981 this sector of the Post Office was privatized and became British Telecom, the employees no longer being employed by the State. The Court does not suggest that the practice of metering would fall outside the scope of Article 8 after privatization. In accordance with what was said in Chapters 5 and 7 it is suggested that the harm to the victim in this case concerns a threat to his or her dignity and that privacy ought to be protected from telephone operators whether they are working in the public or the private sector. The practice of metering clearly demonstrates how inappropriate a 'state agent' test may be.

Two other cases where submissions of this kind have had an impact are particularly important in the context of the application of human rights in the private sphere. The first concerns the evidence of the Trades Union Congress (TUC) in the *Young, James and Webster* case. It should be remembered that the applicants were complaining about the fact that they had to become members of a union in order to retain their jobs with British Rail. This practice was sanctioned under labour legislation endorsed by the Labour Government. Yet, by the time the case came before the European Court of Human Rights, the 1979 general election had returned a Conservative Government, which expressly refused to argue that the treatment of the applicants, and the operation of the closed shop in general, could be 'necessary in a democratic society . . . for the protection of the rights and freedoms of others'. Nevertheless, the Court did consider this point and the lengthy submissions of Lord Wedderburn (on behalf of the TUC) explaining factual details about the 'closed shop'. In this way the wider social and economic implications of any decision played an important part in the overall procedure and hearings.[4] The Court's judgment in this case did not outlaw the 'closed shop', or even create the right not to associate; the question was decided on proportionality in the specific circumstances of the case.

---

[3] At para. 89 of the submission. The full text is available from Interights, London.
[4] See the Series B publication of the Proceedings pp. 161–93 and 283–97.

The second case is the *Soering* case, which, it will be recalled, involved an extradition to the United States, where the applicant was likely to remain on death row for some time. Amnesty International presented written comments concerning the death penalty in general. One can only speculate as to the influence Amnesty International's brief had on the Court, but it should be pointed out that the Court specifically mentions Amnesty International's conclusions in its judgment on the law. Having referred to the fact that the applicant did not suggest that the death penalty *per se* violated Article 3, it stated: 'On the other hand, Amnesty International in their written comments . . . argued that the evolving standards in Western Europe regarding the existence and use of the death penalty required that the death penalty should now be considered as an inhuman and degrading punishment within the meaning of Article 3.'[5] The Court's judgment goes on to quote from the Amnesty International submission, which stated that there is 'virtual consensus in Western European legal systems that the death penalty is, under current circumstances, no longer consistent with regional standards of justice'.[6] Judge de Meyer's concurring opinion refers to this evidence on the death penalty: 'Such punishment is not consistent with the present state of European civilization,' and he concludes that extradition would violate the applicant's right to life. The Court's judgment does not deal with the right to life (there was no complaint under Article 2), and although the actual judgment did not hold that Article 3 can be interpreted as generally prohibiting the death penalty, the Court's judgment did state that 'Present-day attitudes in the Contracting States to capital punishment are relevant for the assessment whether the acceptable threshold of suffering or degradation has been exceeded.'[7] The Court unanimously found that the implementation of a decision to extradite would violate Article 3. This has to be compared to the Commission's opinion which concluded, by six votes to five, that extradition would not constitute a violation of Article 3. The different conclusions of the Commission and Court cannot simply be attributed to the submission presented by Amnesty International to the Court. Nevertheless, the Court was apparently better informed than the Commission on the legal evolution in Europe concerning the death penalty. In fact, the United Kingdom argued before the Court that extending responsibility for extraditing States to treatment which might be suffered outside the jurisdiction of that State 'entails grave difficulties of evaluation and proof in requiring the examination of alien systems of law and of conditions in foreign states'.[8] It appears that international non-governmental organizations may well have a special role to play in gathering information in

---

[5] At para. 101 of the judgment. [6] At para. 102 of the judgment.
[7] At para. 104 of the judgment. [8] At para. 83 of the judgment.

similar situations, now that the Court has held that such responsibility does extend outside the jurisdiction of Contracting States.

These three cases are all very important in the present context. All concern the application or potential application of the Convention to abuses or threatened abuses of human rights emanating from non-state or private bodies. In the first case the complaint concerned the activities of telephone workers; in the second the applications were essentially about the actions of employers (British Rail) and the trade unions involved. The third case turns on the behaviour of the State of Virginia (for present purposes a 'non-state body' as it is not a Contracting State and so not bound by the Convention).[9] In all these cases the actions of the 'private' bodies concerned were more easily assessed through the help of 'third-party' submissions. In all such cases concerning the Strasbourg supervision of the protection of human rights in the private sphere, private defendants will never actually be parties before the Court. Therefore the operation of the system for third-party submissions is—in this situation—crucial. In two of the cases mentioned it was especially important. In the *Young, James and Webster* case the Government had ideological objections to putting forward the 'third-party' (non-state party) point of view; and in *Soering* the Government not only had a number of diplomatic features to consider (risk of offending either or both of the friendly States requesting extradition, the United States and the Federal Republic of Germany[10]), but was also understandably unfamiliar with the actual 'non-state party' action complained of, namely, death row in the State of Virginia. Both these cases also illustrate that, where the complaint is not directly aimed at Member State action, the respondent government in Strasbourg may not be able to step directly into the shoes of the third (non-state) party whose behaviour is the real cause of the complaint. The governmental defence may be determined by ignorance, ideology, or even diplomatic considerations. Any of these factors may hinder or distract from a thorough debate of the issues, facts, and law involved and therefore make it impossible for the European Court of Human Rights to consider the full social and economic implications of their judgment.[11]

[9] Compare C. van den Wyngaert, 'Applying the European Convention on Human Rights to Extradition: Opening Pandora's Box', 39 *ICLQ* (1990), 757–79 at 759–61.

[10] Mr Soering was a German national and the case had been brought to the Court under Art. 48 of the Convention by the Commission, the UK, and the FRG. This action by the FRG was the first of its kind before the Court and meant that the FRG was a party to the case. Germany had requested extradition from the UK but the UK Government gave priority to the USA's earlier request supported by prima-facie evidence. The possibility of extraditing Mr Soering to the FRG without breaching the Convention was at the heart of Professor Frowein's dissenting opinion to the report of the Commission and was included as relevant in the Court's 'proportionality' test, which led to an eventual finding of a violation. For criticism of the Court's failure properly to address the issue of extradition to the Federal Republic see Breitenmoser and Wilms (1990: 872–9).

[11] For a discussion of some of the advantages and disadvantages of the *amicus curiae* system see Re (1984: 522–33); Ennis (1984: 603–7).

9.3 SUPPORT BY NON-STATE ORGANIZATIONS[12]

As stated in the introduction to this chapter, it is not only the role of private organizations as *amicus curiae* that needs to be highlighted. Their role in the support of applications, and in particular group applications, may be of considerable importance. This is due to the fact that the actions of private groups may affect individuals in diffuse and fragmented ways, so that an individual application would stand little chance of success; a co-ordinated group application could not only bear the expenses of the application but also better explain the extent of the violation.

Private groups could be said to be more likely to violate social rights rather than political rights. The response at the European Court of Human Rights may be to impose positive obligations on the Contracting State where the applicant's freedom has not been fully ensured (*Marckx, Airey, Young, James and Webster, X and Y* v. *The Netherlands*). In such cases the State is obliged to act or even introduce legislation where none existed previously. The State is not obliged merely to refrain from doing something. Individual applicants will not possess the information concerning possible alternative policies and so are unlikely to be in a position to present to the Court a full picture of the practicable options available to a government. Non-state organizations may be in a good position to give this sort of input and their role in these sorts of cases is therefore especially relevant for 'the privatization of human rights'. Indeed one might almost say that the privatization of human rights (namely the application of human rights protection to the actions to private bodies) means that the procedure may also need to be privatized. The Strasbourg Court may have to look to private organizations for details on the factual and legal implications of the actions of private bodies. We should also expect to see an even greater role played by private organizations in the preparation and execution of applications brought under the Convention. A good example of the sort of important role which may be played by such organizations can be found in the *Baggs* v. *United Kingdom* application.[13]

In *Baggs* the Federation of Heathrow Anti-Noise Groups (FHANG) had initially registered an application before the Commission and it was FHANG which submitted the statements on behalf of Mr Baggs and

---

[12] The expression 'non-state organizaiton' is used here in a order to include associations which are not normally perceived as non-governmental organizaitons (NGOs). For example professional associations for lawyers, doctors, etc. may have statutory powers or even quasi-governmental status. Similarly, a trade union is not always perceived as an NGO and may even be cast in the role of human rights violator rather than as a supporter for an individual's claim.

[13] Applic. 9310/81, *Baggs* v. *UK*: the decision is partially reproduced in 44 D. & R. 13; the report of the Commission of 8 July 1987 (friendly settlement) is unpublished at the time of writing.

represented him during his application. The complaint concerned aircaft noise. The Government's response illustrates the traditional approach to human rights in the private sphere:

while the scope of Art 8 is wide, the Article could not on its proper construction be extended to provide guarantees against any act which directly or indirectly affects a person's comfort or enjoyment of his private or home life. Still less could the Article be interpreted as requiring a State to take positive steps to prevent or control the activities of non-governmental bodies or private individuals which incidently have, or may have, this effect.[14]

The complaints concerning Article 8, Article 1 of Protocol 1, and Article 13 were declared admissible and the case finished as a friendly settlement with the Government offering an *ex gratia* settlement of £24,000, the Commission noting that a scheme had been drawn up 'for the purchase of noise blighted properties close to Heathrow Airport', and that a formal offer had been made under the scheme for the purchase of Mr Baggs's property.[15] It is worth mentioning that by the time of the friendly settlement the British Airports Authority had been dissolved by the Airports Act 1986, and that by then it was the privatized Heathrow Airport Limited which administered the scheme.[16]

9.4 THE ROLE OF INTERNATIONAL NON-GOVERNMENTAL ORGANIZATIONS

In an article on 'third-party' submissions before the European Court of Human Rights, Anthony Lester, QC, has highlighted the importance of *international* non-governmental organizations in the context of 'third-party' submissions (1988: 341–50). Lester explains that, in the *Glasenapp*[17] and *Kosiek*[18] cases, the Prison Officers' Association in the United Kingdom requested leave under Rule 37(2) to present written submissions on the scope of freedom of expression for civil servants in the United Kingdom.

---

[14] Decision on the admissibility, 16 Oct. 1985, at 9 of the transcript of the decision.

[15] See report of the Commission, adopted 8 July 1987; for the case-law on Art. 13 in these circumstances see F. J. Hampson, 'The Concept of an "Arguable Claim" under Article 13 of the European Convention on Human Rights', 39 *ICLQ* (1990), 891–9.

[16] The Commission's decision on the law explains the grounds of its jurisdiction: 'The Commission has already held in the Arondelle case (Dec. No. 7889/77, 15.7.80 , DR 19, p. 186) that the United Kingdom is answerable under the Convention with regard to a complaint on aircraft noise in the vicinity of British airports because it is a State body, namely the British Aviation Authority (BAA) which is responsible for the planning and construction of civil airports. In addition air traffic is regulated by legislation, the Civil Aviation Act (CAA) 1982' (at para. 2 of 'the law').

[17] Judgment of 28 Aug. 1986, Series A, vol. 104.

[18] Judgment of 28 Aug. 1986, Series A, vol. 105.

Leave was refused by the Court on the grounds that the submissions did not have 'a sufficiently proximate connection' to the cases before the Court. Mrs Glasenapp was dismissed from her post as a secondary school teacher for refusing to dissociate herself from the Communist Party of Germany; Mr Kosiek was similarly dismissed from his post as lecturer for support for the National Democratic Party of Germany. Both complained of breaches of their right to freedom of expression under Article 10 of the Convention. The Court never addressed the issue of freedom of expression in the civil service but dismissed the cases, stating that the Convention did not grant a right to access to the civil service. Lester asks whether 'a body representative of the civil service in Europe might have been granted leave to submit written comments, and, if so, whether the Court might have been more ready to address the issues of principle raised by the cases' (1988: 346). Lester illustrates the success which such international bodies can have as *amici curiae* before the European Court of Human Rights by referring to the *Lingens* case.[19] This case concerned the Austrian law of defamation and resulted from an article criticizing the Federal Chancellor Bruno Kriesky for his attitude towards the leader of a political party who had formerly been a member of an SS Brigade during the Second World War. The article appeared in the magazine *Profil* and the Chancellor had brought a private prosecution against Mr Lingens which resulted in a fine of 15,000 Austrian schillings for the latter. The case raised fundamental questions concerning the freedom of the press, and the International Press Institute through Interights were granted leave to submit written comments on the law and practice in ten Contracting States and the United States. Two issues were singled out as relevant to the alleged violation before the European Court of Human Rights. The first was how far the protection afforded to public officials under the law of defamation differs from that afforded to private individuals; and the second was how far a distinction is drawn between expressions of fact and expressions of opinion.[20] The summary of comparative law reveals that, in Europe, although public officials enjoy greater or equal statutory protection, in practice public officials receive less protection under the statutory law of defamation.[21] It also demonstrated that in the United States the Supreme Court's case-law demands a higher burden of proof for public officials bringing defamation cases than it does for private individuals.[22] Although the immediate issue was criminal law, the case

[19] Judgment of 8 July 1986, Series A, vol. 103.
[20] See the third-party intervention of the International Press Institute (available from Interights, London), 1–20.
[21] At 2 of the intervention.
[22] See 10–11 of the intervention. The relevant cases are *New York Times* v. *Sullivan* 376 US 254 (1964) and *Gertz* v. *Robert Welch Inc.* 418 US 323 (1974).

actually involved a private prosecution and the comparative analysis submitted by the International Press Institute ranges over private law and Common Law as there is no uniform European practice in this area.

This is a useful illustration of the role which supranational or European organizations can play in the privatization of human rights. Even if the case against Austria concerned a public official and his use of criminal law the implications of the Court's judgment go beyond Austria and its public law and may come to affect many other European civil, private, or Common Law jurisdictions. In order that the European Court of Human Rights should fully appreciate the implications that its judgments may have in the private sphere European interest groups should be encouraged to file third-party submissions in Strasbourg and the *locus standi* requirement for such groups should be generously interpreted.[23]

9.5 THE COMMISSION'S RULES OF PROCEDURE

The cases dealt with above mostly concerned actions brought before the Court. Submissions by third parties are not possible before the Commission of Human Rights. There is no equivalent to the Court's Rule 37(2).[24] This rule entitles the President of the Court to grant Contracting States or persons concerned, other than the applicant, leave to submit written comments on any issues which the President shall specify. Furthermore any 'third-party' granted such leave is entitled to request the Court to obtain 'any evidence which it [the Court] considers capable of Providing clarification of the facts of the case' (Rule 40(1)). Neither of these rules finds its counterpart in the Rules of Procedure of the European Commission of Human Rights.[25]

It is suggested that the Commission should institute a similar rule so that maximum information might be available to it. This aspect of the Commission's activities will be of increasing importance should the privatization of human rights become a significant dimension in the Convention.

---

[23] This may involve no more than the Court inviting the relevant organizations to submit the relevant information or granting leave when such organizations request it. Art. 37(2) of the Court's Rules of Procedure reads: 'The President may, in the interest of the proper administration of justice, invite or grant leave to any Contracting State which is not a Party to the proceedings to submit written comments within a time-limit and on issues which he shall specify. He may extend such an invitation or grant such leave to any person concerned other than the applicant.'

[24] See n. 23.

[25] The current rules were adopted by the Commission on 4 Sept. 1990 and entered into force on 1 Oct. 1990.

9.6 PROCEDURE BEFORE THE COMMITTEE OF MINISTERS

It is also worth recalling that if the Commission's report is not referred to the Court under Article 48 it will be decided on by the Committee of Ministers under Article 32. In such cases, under the present rules of Procedure, there will have been no opportunity for third-party submissions and the matter will be decided without regard to the further perspective which such briefs can offer.[26] It would be unrealistic to call for the implementation of a third-party submission procedure before the Committee of Ministers. There are no adversarial proceedings such as one finds before the Commission and Court. The respondent Member State, although represented through its delegate in the Committee of Ministers itself, does not actually present its case in detail. It is the Directorate of Human Rights which presents all aspects of the case and, in a way, acts as *amicus curiae*.[27] Although the Directorate could theoretically consider the third-party brief of a non-governmental organization as relevant, it would not be able to present the entire brief before the Committee of Ministers in order to help that body come to a decision. The Directorate could not therefore attach any real weight to the brief, as neither the State nor the applicant would have had a chance to refute it. In addition the Commission would not have had the opportunity to consider it. Allowing such a brief to influence the Directorate would therefore contravene the right to due process.

It is suggested that the appropriate solution is that the Commission adopts clear and generous rules concerning third-party submissions. Not only would this enhance the quality of the Commission's decision and eventual report and thus help the Court, which would still be able to request and receive relevant third-party interventions, but it would also ensure that decisions before the Committee of Ministers were taken in cognizance of all the implications of such a decision.

By the end of May 1991 a total of 194 cases had been referred to the Committee of Ministers for a decision to be taken on the merits.[28] Although all States Parties to the Convention have now accepted the Court's jurisdiction under Article 46, the applicant still has no right to

---

[26] The rules were last amended in Jan. 1991 at the 451st meeting of the Committee of Ministers. Under Rule 4 the Committee may decide to take evidence although the procedure to be followed will be decided on an *ad hoc* basis. See the appendix to the Rules para. 2.

[27] See F. W. Hondius, 'The Other Forum', in Matscher and Petzold (1988: 245–58); Drzemczewski (1990: 89–117).

[28] *The Council of Europe and Human Rights* (Strasbourg: Council of Europe, 1991), 7. See C. Ravaud, 'Vademecum de la procédure suivie par le Comité des Ministres pour l'application de l'article 32 de la Convention européenne des droits de l'homme', *Rivista internazionale dei diritti del'uomo* (1991, forthcoming).

seise the Court and it remains within the discretion of the Commission or relevant Member State[29] to refer the case to the Court. The Ninth Protocol was signed by fifteen states on 6 November 1990 but is not yet in force. This Protocol amends the Convention so as to allow for the applicant(s) to submit the case to a panel composed of three members of the Court. As long as the panel does not unanimously consider that the case 'does not raise a serious question affecting the interpretation or application of the Convention and does not for any other reason warrant consideration by the Court' the case proceeds to the Court.[30] But until this Protocol enters into force the Committee of Ministers will continue to play an important role in the implementation of the Convention.[31] According to Peter Leuprecht, the Director of Human Rights, the Commission is inclined not to refer the case in three situations: first where it has concluded that there was no violation and no fundamental legal issue is raised; secondly, where a violation has been found but the legal issue has already been settled by the Court; and thirdly, 'where it has found a violation, but the respondent Government has given to understand that it accepts the Commission's findings and that it is willing to take the necessary consequential measures' (1988: 100). In this last situation a case involving a human rights question in the private sphere could, in theory, be decided without discussion of the wider interests involved.

9.7 A LEAD FROM THE COMMISSION?

Should the Rules of Procedure of the Commission come to be adapted to facilitate third-party intervention this would also be a valuable lead for other international or regional decision-making bodies. Although the African Commission of Human and Peoples' Rights has not had to grapple with this problem yet, the Inter-American Court of Human Rights has received *amici curiae* briefs from interested private parties in non-contentious cases, and the ICJ granted an application by the International League for the Rights of Man in the *South West Africa* case

---

[29] Under Art. 48 the following States may bring a case before the Court: the State whose national is alleged to be victim, the State which referred the case to the Commission, and the State against which the complaint has been lodged. In 252 cases before the Court only five have been solely referred by a State; it is the Commission which refers cases to the Court. In only one case has a non-respondent State referred the case to the Court on the ground that the applicant was one of its nationals under Art. 48(*b*) ECHR (see the *Soering* case above).

[30] See Art. 5 of the Ninth Protocol, signed in Rome 6 Nov. 1990, Council of Europe doc. H(90)9.

[31] For a recent review of the Committee's work concerning the Convention see Leuprecht (1988: 95–108).

under Article 66(2) of the Statute of the International Court of Justice.[32] However, no rules exist under the Inter-American system for *amicus* briefs and the rules of the International Court are rather restrictive. Similarly there is no provision for *amicus* briefs before the Human Rights Committee responsible for the Optional Protocol to the International Civil and Political Rights Covenant. These meetings are held in camera, thus further hindering the possibility of fully understanding the Committee's appreciation of the implications of decisions affecting the private sphere.[33]

9.8 THE PARLIAMENTARY ASSEMBLY (COUNCIL OF EUROPE) AND THE EUROPEAN PARLIAMENT (EUROPEAN COMMUNITY)

The role that these bodies have played in the shaping of the case-law of the European Court of Human Rights was alluded to in Chapter 4.3.1. There is clearly a legitimate and essential role for these bodies to give context to the problems which come before the two European supranational Courts. The search for a European consensus on the morality of certain types of sexual activity or the morality of allowing illegitimate children equal rights cannot be determined by a supranational court simply through an excursus into comparative law. Nor can these courts seriously hope to reflect what constitutes a 'pressing social need', or the least intrusive measures 'necessary in a democratic society', without some representation from civil society. Of course the Courts should not be enslaved by the Assembly and Parliament. But a healthy dialogue between the European Courts and the respective assemblies of representatives could do much to inform the judges of society's expectations and actually reinforce the respect and authority of the supranational judiciary.

---

[32] See Lester (1988: 343).

[33] So far it would not seem that the Committee has had to deal with communications invoking the Covenant in the sphere of relations between individuals. For a communication which potentially raised the 'horizontal effect' of the Covenant but which was dismissed for other reasons see Communication 209/1986, *FGG* v. *The Netherlands*, which concerned a claim by a Spanish seaman who had been dismissed together with 222 other foreign sailors by a private Dutch shipping company on the grounds that their Dutch was not sufficient and that the company had been forced to reduce its workforce due to economic difficulties. The complainant pointed out that most of the foreign sailors had been employed for fifteen years and that no Netherlands nationals had been dismissed. The claim was essentially concerned with the procedure before the state body the Arbeidsburo, but The Netherlands argued that the case fell outside the Covenant as it was primarily concerned with economic and social rights. The complaint was found inadmissible due to failure to exhaust domestic remedies. See *Selected Decisions of the Human Rights Committee under the Optional Protocol*, ii. 68–72, declared inadmissible 25 Mar. 1987.

Without suggesting that these parliamentary bodies should drive the Courts there is some scope for a more reflexive relationship between these different arms of European integration. In the same way that national courts consider the reports of special commissions or even sometimes parliamentary debates so too could the European Courts—especially when they are presenting their jurisprudence as the result of a 'European consensus inquiry'.[34] The future of this relationship will depend as much on advocates familiarizing themselves with the work of these European assemblies as on those assemblies preparing serious studies and reports on pertinent topics.

9.9 SUMMARY CONCERNING 'PRIVATE POLICE FOR PRIVATIZED RIGHTS'

1. The success of the Convention in certain areas is partly due to the activities of a number of non-state organizations. The role which these groups can play in the process before the Strasbourg bodies may be particularly important in a situation where the acts complained of are directly attributable to private actors and the State is required to take positive measures under the Convention. This is for two reasons.

First, the damage complained of may be relatively minor when viewed from the point of view of any one individual and so the option of an application under the Convention will be inappropriate. Taken collectively, the overall damage to sectors of society can be presented. This may be best co-ordinated by appropriate non-state bodies. Second, the required governmental response (probably in the form of new legislation to cover this area of private activity) may be best assessed by organizations with considerable experience in the relevant sphere and with an overall picture of the operation of the private law involved. A human rights claim in the private sphere raises issues and dilemmas which by definition are not the direct concern of governments; they may therefore need the assistance of this type of private human rights policing.[35] Non-state bodies will not

---

[34] For a critique of the Commission and Court's methods see L. R. Helfer, 'Finding a Consensus on Equality: The Homosexual Age of Consent and the European Convention on Human Rights', 65 *New York University Law Review* (1990), 1044–100, and 'Lesbian and Gay Rights as Human Rights: Strategies for a United Europe', 32 *Virginia Journal of International Law* (1991), 157–212.

[35] According to E. Alkema there is another reason why non-governmental organizations may play a particularly important role in cases involving the third-party applicability of the Convention: 'if recognised, the *Drittwirkung* will have effect only *pro futuro*. The legal position of the private party, the wrongdoer, is not affected; he is neither forced to repair the wrong nor is he punished. For that matter, punishment would probably be contrary to Article 7: *nulla poena sine lege previa*. Therefore, an interest group may be more inclined to apply to the European Commission claiming *Drittwirkung* than an aggrieved individual

necessarily always intervene on behalf of the applicants. In some cases they may wish to argue for the status quo by presenting arguments to counter the claims of the applicants.[36]

2. In cases where the State (Government) has specific reasons for fully arguing or presenting the facts of a case, third-party interventions may well have a vital role to play. These *amici curiae* briefs are particularly important in the context of the privatization of human rights, as the State may be reluctant to present the point of view of other parties where these conflict with the ideology of a particular government. Moreover States may simply not have the information concerning the situation of the third party whose actions have led to the allegations of an abuse of human rights.

3. The development of new or existing pan-European interest groups would enhance the possibility of bringing actions which aim to protect fragmented interests. Most importantly such pan-European interest groups could play a vital role as *amici curiae* informing the Court (and perhaps also the Commission) of the legal situation in other jurisdictions. Given that a judgment by the European Court may have *de facto*, if not *de jure*, repercussions in the private sphere across Europe, it seems evident that information on such consequences should be made available by those with the best knowledge of the relevant private law. This type of group has yet to emerge, even though some sectoral interests are already represented at the European level. A clear advantage of forming these types of non-state bodies would be that they would enjoy standing before the European Courts where standing might be denied to less 'federal' groups.

---

seeking to end a conflict with his fellow citizen' (1988: 38). This suggestion should be considered in the light of the fact that any such interest group would have to show that it was in some way the victim of a violation under the Convention. This has not always proved an easy burden to discharge for groups acting in the collective interest.

[36] e.g. where individuals complain about the operation of the 'closed shop', unions may desire to present the case that the restrictions are necessary for the protection of the rights of others.

10

The Application of Human Rights in the Private Sphere in the United Kingdom

10.1 INTRODUCTION

Part II has so far demonstrated three things. First, that international treaties can create duties for individuals to respect the rights of others. (The most relevant example is the Treaty establishing the European Economic Community, but mention was also made of duties in the context of war crimes, genocide, and apartheid.)

Secondly, it has been shown that, although the European Commission of Human Rights rejects applications against non-state bodies (including the European Community) as inadmissible *ratione personae*, the Strasbourg Court's interpretation of the European Convention authoritatively states that the Convention is relevant 'even in the sphere of relations between individuals'.[1] However, the exact way in which duties arise under national law cannot be decreed by the European Court of Human Rights (in the way that the ECJ created Community duties for individuals under Community law). Everything depends on the rules and remedies which apply in national law. In some countries rights under the Convention will be self-executing and are directly enforceable even against private bodies.

Thirdly, it was suggested that one cannot simply declare that rights which one has against the State are equally enforceable against private bodies. This is because the respondent private body may have rights of its own, whereas the State has no *human* rights, it merely has a claim legitimately to restrict human rights.[2] In order to overcome the difficulties

---

[1] This is the phrase used in the judgment of the Court in the *Case of Plattform 'Ärzte für das Leben'*, judgment of 21 June 1988, Series A, vol. 139, para. 32. The Court specifically refers to Arts. 8 and 11, but other Articles are not excluded.

[2] One of the most thoughtful 'adversaries of the *Drittwirkung* of the Convention' is K. J. Partsch (1973: 282): 'Relations between individuals are far more complex and versatile [than relations between the individual and the state]. It is not only a problem of power; the more differentiated problems of love and hatred, of affection and dislike, of envy and competition, of neighbourhood and living side by side, of common interest and diversity are involved, not to mention the particular situations of personal care, guardianship, educational influence, and all other influences connected with the different forms of dependency. Adequate care

involved it was suggested that one solution might be a method of enforcement which, on the one hand, protects *dignity* from every type of actor; but where rights were aimed at the protection of *democracy* then protection may be appropriate only where the action takes place in the sphere of the public.

This final chapter synthesizes these results into the United Kingdom legal order and anticipates how development at the European level may affect the application of the Convention in that legal order. The structure developed in Part I will be revisited, but with the emphasis not on the legal status of the Convention, but on its possible application to the actions of non-state bodies.

10.2 STATUTORY INTERPRETATION

In *Charter* v. *Race Relations Board*[3] the House of Lords considered the case of Mr Amarjit Singh Shah, who had joined the local Conservative association in 1966 and had applied in 1969 to join the East Ham South Conservative Club. His application was considered by the committee, whose decision depended on the president's casting vote. The chairman indicated that the colour of Mr Shah's skin was relevant, and his application was rejected. The case turned on the applicability of Section 2(1) of the Race Relations Act 1968, which outlawed discrimination by persons 'concerned with the provision to the public or a section of the public (whether by payment or otherwise) of any goods, facilities or services'. The majority of the House of Lords (four to one) found for the club, holding that club members were not a 'section of the public'. We will come back to the reasoning in this case later, but the result should be compared with that in *Applin* v. *Race Relations Board*.[4]

In *Applin* the same section of the Race Relations Act 1968 was considered. The opinions of their Lordships are revealing, as they oscillate between examples of discrimination in the public and intimate spheres in order to demonstrate the limits to the application of the discrimination laws. Mr Applin, the appellant, was the branch organizer of the South Hertfordshire Branch of the National Front. He had written a letter to a couple who ran a foster home, Mr and Mrs Watson, inciting them to accept only white children as boarders. The letter had been circulated to local residents. The question for the House of Lords was whether, if Mr and Mrs Watson had refused to accept 'coloured' children, they would

should be taken of all these elements of a common life in a social community if the idea of transferring fundamental rights and freedoms from the public to the social sphere is to be realized.'

[3] [1973] AC 868.   [4] [1975] AC 258.

have committed an act of unlawful discrimination. Only if this behaviour would have constituted an offence could Mr Applin come within the scope of the Act for having 'incited' an unlawful act. The House of Lords decided (by four votes to one) that the children could be considered a section of the public and so the behaviour of Mr Applin and his associate was prohibited by the Act.

For present purposes it is proposed to highlight the different terminology and hypothetical cases which their Lordships developed. It is suggested that this language gives us pertinent clues as to the limits of the application of human rights in the private sphere. Lord Wilberforce (dissenting) did not agree that the Act:

> can ever have been intended to apply to a situation so essentially *private, domestic and familial* as this. To say otherwise means that a woman maintaining a household, with perhaps her own children and others taken in from care, may not say: 'I am very sorry, I have nothing against coloured children, or white children, or children from far off countries about which I know nothing, but I cannot take the responsibility of caring for them as my own.' To say this, represents an *undesirable* and *impractical* intrusion into the *spheres of private decision* and one which is not likely to advance the cause of improving race relations.[5]

For Lord Wilberforce 'the separation is between acts in the public sphere, to which the statute is to apply, and acts in the private sphere, which are to be exempted'.[6]

However, the judges in the majority were prepared to draw a line which distinguished between 'treating a child as if he were a member of the family and in fact making him a member of the family'.[7] It seemed clear that 'Parliament had refrained from carrying its sanctions into the family circle',[8] and Lord Simon continued: 'For example, it would not be unlawful for a stepfather to discriminate on the ground of colour in favour of a white stepson and against a coloured stepson.'[9] But Lord Simon points out that the appellants were not inciting discrimination within the family circle; they were inciting the Watsons 'to *deny entry* to coloured children'.[10] Thus this could not be said to be a situation of a 'purely private character' as the 'incited action was to prevent the coloured children's very entry into the Watsons' household so that they would remain outside, in the public domain'.[11] Lord Simon's division between the family circle and the public domain draws the boundaries differently from Lord Wilberforce's division between public and private spheres. Their concern is however the same: to protect an intimate sphere of decision-making.

---

[5] At 282 (emphasis added).　　　[6] At 277.　　　[7] Lord Reid at 272.
[8] Lord Simon of Glaisdale at 287.
[9] Ibid.　　　[10] Ibid. (emphasis added).　　　[11] At 289.

Lord Salmon, too, was prepared to offer hypothetical examples to illustrate the boundaries of the 'private or domestic sphere'.[12]

Suppose A has a large number of acquaintances, black and white, and he gives a party to which he invites only those who are white, or for that matter, only those who are black, he would not be infringing the Act. He would be concerned in providing facilities only to his invited guests who cannot, in my view, sensibly be regarded as a 'section of the public'. Suppose, however, that A throws his stately home open to the public and excludes those who are black, he would clearly be infringing the Act for, in such a case, he would be concerned with the provision of facilities or services to the public.[13]

The crucial factors which determine the applicability of the Act seem to concern the intimacy of the relationship, and access by the public to the private sphere. What is clearly irrelevant is the legal, financial, or organizational link to the State or any 'public' body. Their Lordships were not concerned with finding a state nexus or omission on the part of the public authorities. What concerned them was that there were clearly limits to the application of these rights in the private sphere and they had to decide whether this case fell within an inviolable, private, domestic, familial, intimate sphere.

The European Convention on Human Rights was not raised in argument or mentioned in their Lordships' opinions. Following the Commission's report in the *East African Asians'* application it would seem that Article 3 may apply to cases of racial discrimination.[14] As we saw in Chapter 7, there are strong arguments in favour of applying the Convention in circumstances such as the *Applin* case. One's immediate reaction might be: 'but the Convention is hardly an aid to interpretation in such a situation as the Convention is primarily addressed to States, provides only minimum protection, and does not resolve the ambiguity in the statute concerning what is meant by "a section of the public".' In the absence of relevant case-law from the Strasbourg organs, the Convention may indeed be of minimal assistance in such a situation. But once a court has decided that the statute does not apply it may be a vital factor in the ensuing vacuum. Once it has been decided that the statute does not apply the judges are forced to resort to the Common Law, and as Lord Simon stated in *Applin*: 'The common law before the making of the first Race Relations Act (1965) was that people could discriminate against others on the ground of colour etc., to their hearts' content. The unbridled capacity

---

[12] At 292.
[13] At 293.
[14] See Res. DH (77)2 of the Committee of Ministers of 21 Oct. 1977. The Committee failed to reach the requisite two-thirds majority concerning Art. 3 in three cases and so it cannot be concluded that Art. 3 has no application regarding racial discrimination.

to discriminate was the mischief and defect for which common law did not provide.'[15]

10.3 COMMON LAW

As explained in Chapter 4, Dicey's legacy concerning the 'rule of law' has resulted in rejection of any public/private law divisions in the Common Law. Although Dicey's concern was the accountability of public officials, the absence of parallel public/private jurisdictions has meant that, traditionally, Common Law remedies for violations of fundamental rights, such as habeas corpus, are available to individuals for them to protect themselves against other private parties.[16] Early cases include *Somersett's Case*,[17] where the habeas corpus application concerned a slave imprisoned by a captain of a ship, and *R. v. Jackson*,[18] where a wife was granted her application, having been imprisoned by her husband.

10.3.1 The national courts' application of the Convention when developing the Common Law

10.3.1.1 Discrimination

In *Blathwayt* v. *Baron Cawley* the House of Lords had to consider a will which contained a prohibition on being or becoming a Roman Catholic. One of the beneficiaries was received into the Roman Catholic Church and the validity of the forfeiture clause came to be determined by the House of Lords. The argument that the clause was void on grounds of public policy failed. Nevertheless Lord Wilberforce admitted the potential relevance of the Convention in such cases:

> It was said that the law of England was not set against discrimination on a number of grounds including religious grounds and appeal was made to the Race Relations Act 1968, which does not refer to freedom of religion, and to the European Convention of Human Rights of 1950, which refers to freedom of religion and to enjoyment of that freedom and other freedoms without discrimination on grounds of religion. My Lords, I do not doubt that conceptions of public policy should

---

[15] At 286.

[16] I am grateful to Monica Seccombe for the references to private actions for habeas corpus as well as several of the other references used in this chapter concerning cases and parliamentary debates. See 'Human Rights Seminar: Point 8, England: Consequences for Relations between Parties: Extent to which Fundamental Rights Affect Relations between Private Persons', 23 Jan. 1978, unpublished paper prepared for EUI seminar.

[17] (1772) 20 St. Tr. 1.

[18] (1891) 1 QB 671.

move with the times and that widely accepted treaties and statutes may point the direction in which such conceptions, as applied by the courts ought to move. It may well be that conditions such as these are, or at least are becoming, inconsistent with standards now widely accepted. But acceptance of this does not persuade me that we are justified, particularly in relation to a will which came into effect as long ago as 1936 and which has twice been the subject of judicial consideration, in introducing for the first time a rule of law which would go far beyond the mere avoidance of discrimination on religious grounds. To do so would bring about a substantial reduction of another freedom, firmly rooted in our law, namely that of testamentary disposition. Discrimination is not the same thing as choice, it operates over a larger and less personal area, and neither by express provision nor by implication has private selection yet become a matter of public policy.[19]

According to Drzemczewski this case is evidence that: 'Unfortunately in so far as the Convention has been invoked in relations between private persons, its impact (legal weight) seems not to have been adequately appreciated' (1983: 217). On the other hand, P. J. Duffy suggests that this decision illustrates 'a judicial reference to the Convention in circumstances beyond its strict application' (1980: 606–7), as he thinks 'it is clear that the European Commission of Human Rights would have rejected as inadmissible an application brought on the *Blathwayt* case'. Considering the recent developments at the European Commission and Court of Human Rights which we examined in Chapter 7, this last assertion may need to be revised as the necessary state (in)action will be provided by the judgment of the national court.[20] However, Duffy continues: 'the Convention should be given more weight as a source of public policy in those circumstances where there are positive obligations incumbent on States Parties to the Convention and when therefore the UK may be under some duty to ensure that private individuals do not interfere with the rights of others under the Convention' (1980: 607). It is suggested that one can go further than Duffy and suggest that national courts should give the Convention more weight, even where the United Kingdom is not necessarily under an enforceable international duty to ensure that private individuals do not interfere with Convention rights. Several distinguished authors have suggested that the Convention can create rights and duties which go beyond those which are justiciable in Strasbourg, and that

---

[19] [1976] AC 397 at 426.
[20] See *Van der Heijden* v. *The Netherlands*, Applic. 11002/84, 41 D. & R. 264, for a decision of the Commission finding the necessary state action due to a decision by a national court in a private labour dispute, and *Markt Intern*, judgment of 20 Nov. 1989, Series A, vol. 165, for a judgment of the Court of Human Rights which reviewed an injunction issued by a civil court in a fair trading case. There is no reason to believe that the Commission of Human Rights will develop a jurisprudence whereby state responsibility is only triggered when the Court actually brings the full force of the State into play by issuing an injunction and that no state action can be deduced from a refusal by the Court, as in the case of *Blathwayt*, to intervene.

Article 13 guarantees a remedy for individuals at the national level for violations committed by private persons.[21] It suffices to cite a passage by Professor de Meyer, written before he became a judge at the European Court of Human Rights:

The fact that there exist no direct remedies against parties bound by the Convention, other than States, at the international or supranational level, does not mean that such parties have no duties binding on them. It is quite conceivable that only the judicial organs of contracting parties should be competent to consider complaints alleging violation of fundamental rights by parties bound by the Convention other than the States themselves: an instrument such as the European Convention on Human Rights may quite well have established rights and duties which cannot be upheld before the international or supranational bodies created or referred to by that instrument, but only before the courts of the contracting parties (1973: 257).

As stated at the beginning of this study, comparative exercises in this field are not that helpful, as most, if not all, courts in other European States would refer to their constitutions rather than the Convention in circumstances such as those which arose in the *Blathwayt* case. It may be worth referring to one French case, cited by Rivero,[22] which raised the same problem. Whereas in *Blathwayt* the testator had discriminated against Roman Catholics in his will, in this French case a clause in the will stipulated that the beneficiary could not inherit should he marry an Israeli (*Israélite*). The Tribunal de la Seine held the clause void and referred to the prohibition of discrimination contained in the preamble of the 1946 Constitution. This broad brush approach contrasts to the methods of the English judges, who have tended to give restrictive interpretations to anti-discrimination provisions, even when they appear in legislation. For example, in *Ealing London Borough Council* v. *Race Relations Board*[23] the House of Lords decided that 'national origins' in the Race Relations Act 1968 could not be read to mean 'nationality' and so a Council rule which extended its housing lists only to applications from British nationals was valid. English judges seem unwilling to grant new emerging rights to non-discrimination, preferring instead the ancient 'right to discriminate against the stranger'.[24] In *Dockers' Labour Club* v. *Race Relations Board* Lord Diplock described the Race Relations Act in the following terms:

---

[21] See Raymond (1980: 170) and the references therein. As was stressed in Ch. 7, we do not share Raymond's final conclusion that: 'given the limits of their competence ratione personae, the Convention organs are not in a position to examine whether there is a basis on which to apply Article 13 when it is alleged that a private person was responsible for infringing a fundamental right' (at 172).

[22] Rivero (1971: 218): Tribunal de la Seine, 22 Jan. 1947, D. 1947, p. 126.

[23] [1972] AC 342.

[24] In the *Dockers' Labour Club* case (below).

[It] is a statute which, however admirable its motives, restricts the liberty which the citizen has previously enjoyed at common law to differentiate between one person and another in entering or declining to enter into transactions with them. It falls to be construed within the framework of the general law relating to transactions between private citizens. Unless he follows the calling of common carrier or common innkeeper, a private citizen providing goods, facilities or services to others for any purpose that is not unlawful, has at common law freedom of choice as to whom and on what terms he will provide them. He may treat one person less favourably than another, however unreasonable or discreditable his reasons for doing so may be.[25]

Lord Diplock then pointed out that the Common Law exceptions of common carriers had their origin in medieval England, where there was a need to facilitate trade between self-contained communities in which the traveller was a stranger. He declared that these exceptions had been obsolete for some time. His opinion continues:

The arrival in this country within recent years of many immigrants from disparate and distant lands has brought a new dimension to the problem of the legal right to discriminate against the stranger. If everyone were rational and humane—or for that matter Christian—no legal sanctions would be needed to prevent one man being treated by his fellow men less favourably than another *simply on grounds of his colour, race or ethnic or national origins*. But in the field of domestic or social intercourse differentiation in treatment of individuals is unavoidable. No one has room to invite everyone to dinner. The law cannot dictate one's choice of friends. The legal process is not adequate to analyse the multifarious and inscrutable reasons why a Dr Fell remains unloved.

Thus, in discouraging the intrusion of coercion by legal process in the fields of domestic or social intercourse, the principle of effectiveness joins force with the broader principle of freedom to order one's private life as one chooses.

This case is especially relevant as it was explicitly concerned with the public/private divide. The facts were that a Mr Sherrington had been taken by a member of the Dockers' Club in Preston to the club, where Mr Sherrington had been told 'we do not serve coloured people' by the secretary of the club and subsequently told to leave. Mr Sherrington was a member of another club in Preston, which did not have a colour bar, and all the clubs were connected as a union so that members of one club were associate members of all the other clubs in the union. As we have already seen, the Race Relations Act covered the provision of services 'to the public or a section of the public'. The House of Lords gave the phrase 'a section of the public' a restrictive meaning and found the Act inapplicable. Lord Diplock later 'ventures' an effective test with which to delineate the public from the private:

[25] [1974] 3 All ER 592 at 598.

The Race Relations Act 1968 does not operate in some esoteric field of law. It provides for the enforcement by legal sanctions of a code of conduct to be followed in day-to-day transactions between ordinary citizens. The test as to whether a particular transaction is one to which the code applies ought to be simple and readily comprehensible by ordinary men and women. I venture to suggest that the test could be put in a way which everyone could understand by putting the question: would a notice 'Public Not Admitted', exhibited on the premises on which the goods, facilities or services were provided, be true?

　　If such a notice had been exhibited on the premises of the Dockers' Labour Club and Institute at Preston, I believe the ordinary man or woman would have said it was true.[26]

Lord Reid also envisages a membrane separating the public and private spheres. *Charter* v. *Race Relations Board*[27] was the case concerning the East Ham South Conservative Club. Lord Reid stressed in the *Dockers' Labour Club* case that the *Charter* decision had decided that the words 'the public or section of the public' must be regarded as words of limitation. And that:

It was there admitted by the Board and it has, so far as I am aware, never been in doubt that the Act does not apply to discrimination in the domestic sphere: it is no offence to discriminate between persons in a private household. The reason for that can only be that members of a private household are not, within the meaning of this section, a section of the public. But in *Charter's* case it was held that the sphere excluded by those words was wider than the purely domestic sphere. The true antithesis of public is not domestic but private. Then it had to be determined whether clubs fell within the private or public sphere.[28]

In *Charter* 'it was held that an appropriate test was to see whether there was any genuine selection on personal grounds in electing candidates for membership'.[29] 'In that case there was a system of selection so that it was no offence against the Act to discriminate against a candidate on grounds of colour.'[30] But Lord Reid found this test inappropriate for 'guests, temporary members under reciprocal arrangements with other clubs, or associates of this union—persons selected by some person or body other than the club or its committee'. Lord Reid then turns to the 'obvious exclusion from the 1968 Act—the private household'.[31] He starts with this 'because it shows that selection is not the only basis for holding that one is in the private and not the public sphere'.[32]

　　Lord Reid's solution is intriguing because it works from the intimate sphere through the private sphere into the public sphere and gives us indicators as to when these boundaries are transgressed. He outlined his approach in the following way:

[26] At 599.　　[27] [1973] AC 868.　　[28] At 594.
[29] Per Lord Reid in *Dockers' Labour Club* at 595.
[30] Ibid.　　[31] Ibid.　　[32] Ibid.

Here I think it best to go back to the central and most obvious exclusion from the 1968 Act—the private household—because it shows that selection is not the only basis for holding that one is in the private and not the public sphere. A father does not select his children. He selects his own guests and may select his servants. But he need not select his children's guests whom they bring to the house. Yet I do not think that it could possibly be argued that he commits an offence if he discriminates against a guest brought to his house by his child on ground of colour, race or ethnic origin. Or suppose that a friend asks him to give hospitality to someone whom he recommends and when that person arrives the householder refuses to receive him on one of these grounds. That would be utterly deplorable but it would not be an offence against the Act.[33]

Lord Reid thought that similar considerations applied to the club. He assimilated the guests of the householder's children to the guests of club members. He also explained at what point he thought such behaviour would spill over into the public sphere:

On the other hand, the head, of the household can go outside the private sphere. If he opens his house to the public on certain occasions I have no doubt that he would commit an offence if he refused admission to anyone on any grounds stated in the Act. And I think the same would apply if he opened his house to a section of the public, e.g. members of a particular profession.[34]

He was also prepared to hypothesize as to when the club might be close to operating in the public sphere:

So I think that the question here is whether a working men's club which belongs to the union goes out of the private into the public sphere in offering admission to associates of the union. I would reserve my opinion about a case when so many non-members habitually attend that the club loses its character of a private meeting place. Here there is nothing of the kind.[35]

In Chapters 5 and 7 we suggested that the exclusion of certain private spheres from interferences by public authorities was often premissed on an expressed desire to protect the intimate sphere, but that these two spheres are not coextensive. Nor should they be treated as analogous. If we premiss the right to privacy on the need to protect dignity and self-realization then protecting the right to choose who is invited into one's own house in order to respect private life cannot be assimilated to protecting the right to affront someone's dignity on account of the colour of their skin. It is possible to imagine clubs which could legitimately exclude someone on grounds of sex, race, colour, religion, etc., and declare that the legislation was not intended to cover certain private meetings, but such justifications would not seem to be present in the instant case. The case is discussed in this section on the Common Law as once the statute

---

[33] At 595.   [34] Ibid.   [35] Ibid.

had been declared inapplicable as an 'intrusion of coercion by legal process in the fields of domestic or social intercourse' then the relations between individuals came to be governed by the Common Law. Under the Common Law 'the principle of effectiveness joins force with the broader principle of freedom to order one's private life as one chooses' and trumps the right not to be discriminated against on grounds of race.

The Convention may have a new role to play in such cases. As we saw in Chapter 1.2, substantive rights under the Convention may be 'subsumed in our domestic law'.[36] As the case-law of the Commission and Court comes to cover more and more cases concerning the obligations of States 'in the sphere of relations between individuals' the Common Law right to discriminate on grounds of race will be overtaken by rights which protect individuals from different sorts of discrimination and other abuses of human rights in respect to privacy, assembly, forced labour, inhuman treatment, etc.

10.3.1.2 Industrial relations

In Chapter 1 several instances were mentioned where judges had had recourse to the Convention in labour law cases. The *Cheall* case will now be revisited but examined only from the perspective of the application of the Convention in the private sphere. In *Cheall* v. *APEX*[37] the European Convention was relied on by Lord Denning, MR, in the Court of Appeal, and its usefulness was rejected by Donaldson, LJ (as he then was), in his dissenting judgment in the same case. In the High Court Mr Cheall claimed that Rule 14, 'taken in conjunction with the Bridlington Principles, constituted a restriction on the individual's right to belong to a union of his choice. As such it was contrary to British public policy and so void.'[38] He relied *inter alia* on the Convention and the judgment of the European Court of Human Rights in the *Young, James and Webster* case. In particular Mr Cheall relied on passages from the judgment and from the separate concurring opinion of seven judges in the majority. These passages stressed the importance of choice as regards unions. Mr Cheall submitted that these showed the direction of British public policy. APEX countered by relying on the separate concurring opinion of one judge in the majority. This opinion stated that the wording of Article 11 and the case-law of the Court demonstrate that trade union freedom has the character of a collective right and that 'account has to be taken of the welfare of the public and of the collective interests of the trade union organisation that

---

[36] Donaldson, MR, in *A.-G.* v. *Guardian (No. 2)* [1988] 3 All ER 594 at 596.
[37] [1982] 3 WLR 685.
[38] [1982] 3 All ER 855 at 871.

are at stake'.[39] In addition it was asserted: first, that the right to join APEX was not for the protection of Mr Cheall's interests as they would be protected by ACTSS; second, the restriction contended by APEX was necessary in a democratic society for the protection of the rights of others; third, the decision in the *Young, James and Webster* case was wrong; and fourth, the Convention was not directly applicable.

The judge, Mr Justice Bingham, accepted that 'where the court is presented with alternative formulations of legal principle regard may be paid to the fact that one or other of them may be more consistent with international treaty obligations undertaken by Her Majesty'. However, he qualified this: 'but I must bear in mind that the obligations assumed and the rights conferred by the European convention are not justiciable in our municipal courts.'[40]

Bingham, J., then proceeded to 'look for more specific indications of public policy'. He examined changes in legislation, case-law, and the report of the Royal Commission on Trade Unions and Employers' Associations 1965–8. These sources gave no guidance as to the policy of the law towards the rule in question and the judge turned to the Convention. He concluded:

I do not find that the European Convention gives a clear lead on this question. The language of art. 11 permits of arguments on which it would be idle for me to speculate and wrong for me to express views. Some passages from the judgments, which I have quoted, read helpfully to Mr Cheall, but arose in a case where the facts were quite different from the present and where the injustice to the individuals involved was much more pronounced than anything Mr Cheall can complain of.[41]

This cautious approach to the case-law of the European Court of Human Rights would seem to be appropriate. The case in Strasbourg did not decide that lack of choice of union led to a violation of Article 11. The Court decided the case on the *proportionality principle*, finding that the measures taken against the applicants went further than was necessary to achieve the aims of protecting the rights of others.[42]

---

[39] At 872 of the judgment quoting the separate concurring opinion of Judge Evrigenis.

[40] At 873.

[41] At 876.

[42] *Young, James and Webster* v. *UK*, Series A, vol. 44, para. 65. Although the Labour Government had argued the necessity of the measures before the Commission, the Conservative Government expressly stated to the Court that they would not seek to argue that the interference was justified under para. 2. Nevertheless, the Court went on to assume that the interference had the aim of protecting the 'rights and freedoms of others' as there were a number of advantages which could be said to flow from the closed shop system. The whole case turned on the 'necessity' of the actual measures taken. This case dramatically illustrates the dangers of using the case-law of the Strasbourg organs in order to define public policy. Should the Government of the day concede part of a case in Strasbourg, this may not accord with the development of public policy, especially where the political party in Government has changed and the issue was an ideological one.

Mr Cheall appealed to the Court of Appeal.[43] Lord Denning, MR (in the majority), found that the right to join a union of one's choice was part of the Common Law and that this was buttressed by Article 11. Moreover he stated that Mr Cheall should not have to go to Strasbourg to get redress. In the words of Lord Denning, MR:

The European Court of Human Rights directed that the United Kingdom Government should pay compensation to the three railwaymen. That was on August 13, 1981, in *Young v United Kingdom*. By being vindicated in this way, we reach the conclusion that Article 11(1) of the Convention is part of the law of England or at any rate the same as the law of England. The Courts of England should themselves give effect to it rather than put a citizen to all the trouble and expense of going to the European Court at Strasbourg. Our courts should themselves uphold the right of everyman to join a trade union of his choice for the protection of his interests.[44]

The judgment of Lord Denning has already been criticized in Chapter 1. In the context of the operation of the Convention in the sphere of relations between individuals we should state that it is just possible that, had a 'closed shop' been in operation, then the European Court of Human Rights might have held that by failing to legislate, the United Kingdom Government was responsible for a violation of Mr Cheall's rights.[45] However, for the actual law of the United Kingdom to change, legislation would have to be debated and passed by Parliament.[46] The most the European Court could have done would have been to order compensation to be paid by the Government (it cannot order the unions to change their rules, readmit members, or pay compensation).[47] Apart from the 'closed shop' case the area in which the European Court of Human Rights has held Governments liable for failure to legislate in the

[43] [1982] 3 All ER 875.

[44] At 879.

[45] The Commission dismissed Mr Cheall's application as inadmissible: 'In these circumstances the expulsion of the applicant from A.P.E.X. must be seen as the act of a private body in the exercise of its Convention rights under Article 11. As such it can not engage the responsibility of the respondent Government' (Applic. 10550/83 42, D. & R. 178 at 186). But earlier in its decision the Commission had made the following reservation: 'Nonetheless for the right to join a trade union to be effective the State must protect the individual against any abuse of a dominant position by trade unions (see Eur. Court H. R., Young, James and Webster judgment of 13 August 1981, Series A no. 44 p. 25 para. 63). Such abuse might occur, for example, where exclusion or expulsion was not in accordance with union rules or where the rules were wholly unreasonable or arbitrary or where the consequences of exclusion or expulsion resulted in exceptional hardship such as job loss because of a closed shop. . . . The Commission does not consider that either rule 14 or principle 2 can be regarded as unreasonable. Moreover it notes that the applicant's expulsion from A.P.E.X. did not involve loss of his job because of a closed shop' (at 186).

[46] The House of Lords, in reversing the Court of Appeal, held that there was no contravention of the European Convention on Human Rights and that any limitation of the Bridlington Principles on the grounds of public policy was a matter for Parliament and not for the courts.

[47] Art. 50.

sphere of relations between individuals has so far usually been related to violent threats to privacy by a private individual where no effective remedy was available.[48] The Court has been much more reticent when it comes to interfering with how States structure their industrial relations legislation.[49] Moreover, the Strasbourg reports and judgments often stress that the right to choose a union in the European context may arise in the situation where the unions are divided along religious, linguistic, or ideological lines.[50] Lastly, the *Cheall* case in the Court of Appeal illustrates that judges often exhibit a preference for individual rights over collective rights. At first instance Bingham, J., in seeking to find the formulation of legal principle most consistent with international obligations under the Convention, stated:

Mr Cheall starts with this advantage, that the policy of English law is in general, where possible and appropriate, to lean in favour of the liberty of the individual; but the advantage is whittled down somewhat by the countervailing consideration that the law also, in general, leans in favour of upholding contracts, and Mr Cheall became a member of APEX on terms which included r 14 (even if he was unaware of it).[51]

In the same way Lord Denning gravitates to the individual right. When confronted with the argument that the rule in question was necessary for the proper functioning of industrial relations Lord Denning replied:

I take my stand on something more fundamental. It is the freedom of the individual to join a trade union of his choice. He is not to be treated as a pawn on the chessboard. He is not to be moved across it against his will by one or other of the conflicting parties, or by their disputes committee. It might result, when there is a 'closed shop', in his being deprived of his livelihood. He would be crushed between the upper and nether millstones. Even though it should result in industrial chaos, nevertheless the freedom of each man should prevail over it.[52]

The collective rights of unions and their members under Article 11 are absent from the opinions of nearly all the English judges in this case.[53]

---

[48] e.g. *X and Y v. The Netherlands*, Series A, vol. 91, and *Airey v. Ireland*, Series A, vol. 32.

[49] National Union of Belgian Police case, Series A, vol. 19; *Swedish Engine Drivers' Union* case, Series A, vol. 20; *Schmidt and Dahlstrom* case, Series A, vol. 21.

[50] e.g. in *X v. Belgium*, Applic. 4072/69 (1970) 13 Yearbook 708, the applicant was faced with the choice between a socialist or a Catholic union.

[51] At 873.

[52] At 881.

[53] Slade, LJ (did not rely on the Convention); Donaldson, LJ, found that the degree of freedom of choice which was necessary under the Convention had not been spelt out in the *Young, James and Webster* case and declined to apply 'considerations of political rather than public policy' (at 886–7). In the House of Lords Lord Diplock, who gave the sole opinion, recognized the collective character of the right to associate and stated: 'freedom of association can only be mutual; there can be no right of an individual to associate with other individuals

The language of rights leads inevitably to concern for 'the liberty of the individual' and the right to join the union of one's choice. It is only in Strasbourg that reference is made to the fact that the union was 'in the exercise of its Convention rights under Article 11'.[54]

There may develop a hiatus between the Strasbourg decisions, where applications against employers[55] and trade unions[56] are dismissed *ratione personae* on the grounds of lack of jurisdiction, and the national decisions, where the Articles of the Convention may be used against private bodies. This means that the situation may arise whereby no clear lead is given by Strasbourg as to the limits of the Convention in the private sphere.

Therefore one can see that using the Strasbourg decisions concerning the Convention directly in private litigation at the national level may be undesirable in some circumstances. First, because they bypass the democratic process, Strasbourg decisions do not become binding law in the United Kingdom legal order. They are taken in the knowledge that the Government or Parliament will introduce the appropriate legal measures. In the same way that a Community directive only exceptionally creates directly applicable rights and leaves the task of law-making to the national authorities, so the Strasbourg decision requires national implementation. Secondly, because the decisions in Strasbourg often revolve around the particular facts of the case, they do not really create *precedents* in the English Common Law sense. Because they apply the alien concept of 'proportionality' they actually decide whether the particular facts disclose that the measures taken were disproportionate to the aim to be achieved. If an applicant is successful in Strasbourg the Court can award compensation, and the State may be required to furnish an explanation of the manner in which its internal law ensures the effective implementation of any of the provisions of the Convention.[57] The risk is that, by applying the Convention and its case-law in the private sphere, national judges could fundamentally change the social and economic balance of power in certain sectors. Doing this under the heading of 'fundamental freedom' or

---

who are not willing to associate with him,' ([1983] 2 AC 180 at 191). But he suggests that if the facts were different individual rights would 'trump' the collective rights: 'Different considerations might apply if the effect of Cheall's expulsion from A.P.E.X. were to have put his job in jeopardy, either because of a closed shop or for some other reason' (at 191).

[54] 42 D. & R. 178 at 186.

[55] *X* v. *Belgium*, Applic. 4072/69 (1970) 13 Yearbook 708.

[56] But see the comments of Commissioner Fawcett when pleading as delegate for the Commission before the European Court of Human Rights: 'Coming to Article 11, it would seem to me beyond argument that if a trade union denied admission to any workers in its area on grounds of race, Article 14 would immediately come into issue; and if the State allowed this situation to continue, there would be a breach of the Convention' (*Swedish Engine Drivers' Union* case, Series B, vol. 18, p. 199); similarly in *Cheall* v. *UK*, Applic. 10550/83, 13 May 1985, 42 D. & R. 178, although the issue was dismissed *ratione personae*, it would have been admissible if there had been a closed shop in operation.

[57] Art. 57 ECHR.

'human rights' means that the situation becomes fossilized, and the possibilities for democratic change through political processes are diminished. Where the Convention has constitutional status such an interpretation may be extremely difficult to reverse. Whilst part of the rationale of human rights rests on their ability to protect a minority from legislation introduced by a majority, once we move away from rights which protect against gross violations of human dignity and confront rights which are also designed to reinforce democracy, then their application in the sphere of relations between private parties may have to be circumscribed. For example, as we shall see below, we may have to admit that there is a difference between political speech which offends the State and speech which offends individuals. The case-law cannot be transposed. The big difference is that the State possesses no human rights to dignity whereas individuals do.

10.3.1.3 Blasphemy

In Chapter 7 the Commission's decision in the *Gay News* application was briefly examined. When this case was before the House of Lords as *Whitehouse* v. *Lemon*, only one of their Lordships relied on the Convention. Lord Scarman (in the majority) was prepared to uphold the usefulness of the offence of blasphemy as well as strict liability for the publishers. Lord Scarman saw the offence in the context of laws designed to 'safeguard the internal tranquillity of the kingdom'.[58] He considered a number of recent statutes concerning obscene publications, public order, and race relations which did not require intention for the commission of an offence. He divined a private duty from Article 9 of the Convention:

Article 9 provides that everyone has the right to freedom of religion, and the right to manifest his religion in worship, teaching, practice and observance. By necessary implication the article imposes a duty on all of us to refrain from insulting or outraging the religious feeling of others. Article 10 provides that everyone shall have the right to freedom of expression. The exercise of this freedom 'carries with it duties and responsibilities' and may be subject to such restrictions as are prescribed by law and are necessary 'for the prevention of disorder or crime, for the protection of health or morals, for the protection of the reputation or rights of others . . .' It would be intolerable if by allowing an author or publisher to plead the excellence of his motives and the right of free speech he could evade the penalties of the law even though his words were blasphemous in the sense of constituting an outrage upon the religious feelings of his fellow citizens. This is no way forward for a successful plural society.[59]

---

[58] *Whitehouse* v. *Lemon* [1979] AC 617 at 657. Note, this was a 'private' prosecution which had resulted in a jury trial and conviction. The appeal to the House of Lords concerned the necessity of intention for the crime of blasphemous libel.

[59] At 665.

Although the case concerns criminal law it was a private prosecution and the clear logic of Lord Scarman's opinion is that the Convention should be seen to impose duties on private individuals.

It is worth dwelling on what might be called a 'third-party effect' of this clash of rights between two private parties. In Rushdie's case, dealt with below, the 'third party' is a group which is not represented in the litigation process.[60] The third party is the group of intolerant readers who may be provoked to persecute members of the group whose religion has been 'scurrilously' attacked. In the case of the poem in *Gay News* such behaviour may seem rather far-fetched, but in the case of pornography which degrades women, the behaviour which legislation may seek to prevent will be the reaction of readers who are incited to assault and rape as well as to various forms of discrimination against women.[61] The same approach could be taken to other forms of expression, so that ridiculing a religious group could be said to lead to racial discrimination by the readers of the material, even where the readers themselves are not offended. Such a broad policy approach may sometimes be more appropriate than a human rights 'balancing exercise' between the parties to the litigation.

The recent case of *R. v. Bow St. Ct., ex parte Choudhury*[62] combines questions concerning discrimination on grounds of religion with the Common Law of blasphemy. The case illustrates the application of the European Convention on Human Rights in the private sphere in a particularly concrete way as both sides (both private parties) relied on different substantive provisions of the Convention. The case therefore involves the clash of rights rather than the proportionality of derogating measures.

The case concerned judicial review of a magistrate's refusal to grant an application for a summons by Abdul Hussain Choudhury against Salman Rushdie and Viking Penguin Publishing Co. Ltd. (Penguin) alleging the commission of the offences of blasphemous libel[63] and seditious libel at Common Law. The applicant sought summonses alleging that the author

---

[60] This reference to a 'third party' should not be confused with the third party in the *Drittwirkung* doctrine, which is the private individual involved in the litigation. In *Drittwirkung* one party is the State, the second is the right-bearer, and the third is held to have a duty to obey the constitutional right. I am, in fact, introducing a fourth party to this scenario.

[61] For details of the attempts in the USA to move towards anti-pornography measures which are concerned with the female victims of pornography see C. MacKinnon, 'Pornography, Civil Rights and Speech', 20 *Harv. CR-CLL Rev.* (1985), 1–70. See also C. R. Sunstein, 'Pornography, Sex Discrimination, and Free Speech', in Gostin (1988: 152–69); compare B. Lynn, 'Pornography and Free Speech: The Civil Rights Approach', in the same vol., 170–84. More recently, see R. Langton, 'Whose Right: Ronald Dworkin, Women and Pornographers', 19 *Philosophy and Public Affairs* (1990), 311–59; A. Dworkin (1989); MacKinnon (1989: 195).

[62] [1990] 3 WLR 986. For a critical appraisal of the judgment see Tregilgas-Davey (1991: 294–9).

[63] For an up-to-date commentary on the law of blasphemy see Robertson and Nicol (1990: 124).

and publishers of *The Satanic Verses* had unlawfully and wickedly published or caused to be published 'a blasphemous libel concerning Almighty God (Allah), the Supreme Deity common to all the major religions of the world, the Prophet Abraham and his son Ishmael, Muhammad (Pbuh) the Holy Prophet of Islam, his wives and companions and the religion of Islam and Christianity, contrary to common law'.[64]

The Chief Metropolitan Magistrate had refused to grant the summons. The Divisional Court decided that it had jurisdiction to review the refusal on the grounds that the magistrate had misdirected himself in law or that his findings were perverse. Counsel's proposition that the court had no power to grant judicial review of the magistrate's decision where it was a lawful, albeit erroneous, exercise of his judgment and discretion was explicitly rejected.[65] Therefore we are not dealing with the reasonableness of a decision but with an authoritative interpretation of the law.

The main question for the court was whether the offence of blasphemy was restricted to the Christian religion. After an extensive review of the authorities the court stated: 'We have no doubt that as the law now stands it does not extend to religions other than Christianity.'[66] Nevertheless the applicant suggested that the courts should extend it to cover other religions. The court stated that if the law is uncertain then 'in interpreting and declaring the law the judges will do so in accordance with justice and to avoid anomaly or discrimination against certain classes of citizens'. Despite the certainty of the law the court considered the policy arguments against extending it. First, such action would create a criminal offence retroactively. Second, attempts in Parliament to extend the law to religious feeling generally had failed. Third, the Law Commission had recommended abolition of the offence of blasphemy. Fourth, it was deemed 'virtually impossible' to set limits to the offence.[67] Defining religion is difficult and to expect juries or even authors to decide whether 'material scandalised one sect and not another' was too demanding.

At this point the applicant raised the European Convention on Human Rights. The Convention and the case-law of the Strasbourg organs are considered for the next three and a half pages of the judgment. This must be one of the most detailed considerations of the Convention by the British courts. Three admissibility decisions of the Commission and one judgment of the European Court of Human Rights were referred to by

---

[64] From the judgment at 989; the details of the allegations concerning seditious libel will not be dealt with.

[65] At 991; the court noted that Anthony Lester had put forward this proposition 'without much apparent enthusiasm'.

[66] At 999.

[67] Robertson and Nicol (1990: 125) note that the Law Commission 'despaired of any definition which could draw workable distinctions between Baptists, Scientologists, Rastafarians, Anglicans and Moonies'.

the court. It is interesting that this examination occurred in the sphere of relations between individuals and in the context of developing the Common Law. It is proposed to examine the court's approach to the Convention in some detail.

It was Choudhury who raised the Convention. He relied on Articles 9, 10, and 14. He claimed that the courts' failure to recognize that the Common Law of blasphemy comprehended an offence not only against Christianity but also against Islam 'might well bring the United Kingdom into conflict with the Convention'.[68] As evidence of the European Commission of Human Rights' approach he cites the following passage from the Commission's decision in *Ahmed v. United Kingdom*:[69]

[The Commission] noted that, during the relevant period, the United Kingdom society was with its increasing Muslim community in a period of transition. New and complex problems arose, *inter alia*, in the field of education, both as regards teachers and students. The parties agree that the applicant's case is not an isolated one and that it raises questions of general importance.[70]

The court then cites Article 9 of the Convention in full and draws attention to the existence of limitations in Article 9(2). But the court does not go on to explain which limitations are relevant (presumably because there was no examination of Article 9(2) by the Commission in the *Ahmed* decision). The court's judgment continues as follows:

Mr Lester [counsel for Penguin] responded impressively to Mr Azhar's [counsel for Choudhury] attempt to show that the absence of a domestic law of blasphemy relating to Islam would or might be in breach of the Convention.

He accepted that the obligations imposed on the United Kingdom by the Convention are relevant sources of public policy where the common law is uncertain. But, he maintained, the common law of blasphemy is, without doubt, certain. Accordingly, it is not necessary to pay any regard to the convention.[71]

In Chapter 1 it was stressed that ambiguity is a subjective notion which may arise because of the guarantees in the Convention rather than as a pre-condition to using the Convention.[72]

Despite the apparent legitimacy of eschewing the Convention the court accepted that Mr Lester 'thought it necessary, and we agree, in the context of this case, to attempt to satisfy us that the United Kingdom is

[68] At 1001.
[69] At 1000 of the judgment; *Ahmed* is reported in (1981) 4 EHRR 126, and 22 D. & R. 27. This was the case discussed in detail in Ch. 1.1.
[70] At para. 17 of the decision.
[71] At 1001.
[72] It was suggested that examination of the direction in which the Common Law should develop may legitimately consider the development of the UK's international obligations. The ambiguity would seem to arise because of these evolving obligations (Ch. 1.3.1, summary para. (2), and see Dworkin (1986: 350–4)).

not in any event in breach of the Convention'.[73] It follows that the arguments which were presented are not subjective pleadings concerning the public policy arguments for extending or restricting the Common Law. What the parties are arguing is the hypothetical outcome should the case go to Strasbourg. Because the case involves two private parties it would not be the same case before the Strasbourg organs. It would be the loser who would file an application against the United Kingdom. The case differs from the classic State–individual case because both parties are claiming that the courts' rejection of their case would result in a violation of their human rights, and that both could obtain victory in Strasbourg as a *victim* of a human rights violation.

Mr Lester asserted that if the application before the national court resulted in an eventual, successful prosecution, Mr Rushdie and Penguin would be protected by Articles 7 and 10 of the Convention. The court's judgment cites the two Articles in full and continues:

The exceptions in paragraph 2 of Article 10 are, of course, important. But, Mr Lester contended, neither Mr Rushdie nor Viking Penguin had come within any one of those exceptions especially in the light of the fact that the law of blasphemy in the United Kingdom applies to Christianity alone and there is no warrant for its extension at common law to any other religion.

What the applicant seems to do, Mr Lester said, is to interfere with a well founded right to freedom of expression, a kind of interference never at any time foreshadowed by the common law of this country. Moreover, it would be an interference such as would contravene article 7 by creating ex post facto a criminal offence: see *Gay News Ltd v United Kingdom* (1982) 5 E.H.R.R. 123. Nothing in Mr Azhar's argument could possibly, he repeated, bring either Mr Rushdie or "Gay News" within one of the exceptions in article 10(2).[74]

Unfortunately, the court does not offer its own evaluation of this analysis of the Commission's case-law. As we saw in Chapter 7 the Commission did in fact deny *Gay News* the protection of Article 10 as their publication came within one of the exceptions in Article 10(2). To quote the Commission:

As regards the applicants' further allegation that the restriction of their freedom of expression did not pursue a legitimate purpose covered by Article 10(2) of the Convention, the Commission notes that the Government has invoked three grounds of restriction included in this provision, namely prevention of disorder, protection of morals, and protection of the rights of others.

All these grounds may be pertinent.[75]

The Commission continued in terms which are particularly relevant in the context of the Choudhury application before the Divisional Court. The

[73] At 1001.
[74] At 1002.
[75] *Gay News* v. *UK* (1982) 5 EHRR 123 at 129–30.

passage related directly to private prosecutions for blasphemy and is so important for the present analysis of the use of the Convention in the sphere of relations between individuals that it will be quoted in full:

but the Commission nevertheless finds it appropriate to observe that in this case the public authorities themselves did not consider it necessary to institute criminal proceedings against the applicants either for blasphemous libel or obscenity. The case was therefore brought only on the basis of a private prosecution, and although this procedure required the consent of a public authority, namely leave by a single judge, it cannot be said that the public interest (prevention of disorder and protection of morals) was so preponderant that it provided the real basis for the interference with the applicants' right to freedom of expression. In the circumstances, the justifying ground for the restriction must therefore *primarily be sought in the protection of the rights of the private prosecutor*. The Commission considers that the offence of blasphemous libel as it is construed under the applicable common law in fact has the main *purpose to protect the right of citizens not to be offended in their religious feeling by publications*. This was the thrust of the arguments put before the jury by the trial judge, arguments which were subsequently confirmed by the higher courts in this case. *The Commission therefore concludes that the restriction was indeed covered by a legitimate purpose recognised by the Convention, namely the protection of the rights of others.*[76]

The Commission also considered the applicants' rights under Article 9 and concluded:

Even assuming that there had in fact been an interference with the applicant's rights under Article 9, it would have been justified under Article 9(2) on the same grounds as the restriction of the applicants' freedom of expression under Article 10(2). It follows that this part of the application is also manifestly ill-founded.[77]

Clearly, according to the case-law of the Commission, Article 10(2) may allow the Common Law to protect the rights of the private prosecutor not to be offended in his or her religious feelings by publications.

In reply to Mr Choudhury's claim concerning Article 9, Anthony Lester, QC, suggested that the limitations in Artice 9(2) included the denial of

---

[76] Emphasis added, (1982) 5 EHRR 123 at 130. For the approach in the higher courts see in particular Lord Scarman in *R. v. Lemon* [1979] AC 617 (the *Gay News* case in the House of Lords) at 665, who justifies strict liability for the offence of blasphemous libel by reference to 'the rights of others' examined in detail above. For the Government's submission on the meaning of the 'rights of others' see the transcript of the Commission's decision at 10: 'The exercise of the freedom of expression by its nature affects the rights of others, and those who sincerely hold religious beliefs have a legitimate right not to be shocked or outraged by scurrilous and obscene material which goes to the root of their beliefs. Religious beliefs are far more deep rooted than e.g. political convictions, and that is why they have been given special protection in the law of England. Also the Law Commission has said that the strongest argument in favour of a law of blasphemy is that insulting attacks upon matters held sacred by religious believers causes injury to their feelings of a unique kind against which the law should provide protection.'

[77] At 131.

'the right to bring proceedings for blasphemy where it can not be shown that a domestic law has been offended against'.[78] But if the question had really gone to Strasbourg the answer would have turned not on the legitimacy of restricting the applicant's rights by denying a right to bring private prosecutions, but on the positive obligations of the State to make the right 'real and effective'. In addition the Convention will be interpreted as a 'living instrument' in 'the light of present day conditions'.[79] The question in Strasbourg would turn on the gap in the State's legal protection offered to Muslims. In the same may that the Netherlands legislation was found to contain a lacuna barring a certain class of persons from the courts,[80] so too the United Kingdom's law might have been found to offer insufficient protection in this field. In addition Article 14 would be relevant even if a violation of Article 9 had not been found by the Commission.

Mr Azhar relied on Article 14 before the English Court. In the judgment of the Court: 'Mr Lester dealt at length with that contention.'[81] According to Mr Lester, Article 14 read alongside Article 9 clearly indicated that there was no discrimination. The judgment mentions two admissibility decisions of the Commission and adds that 'the Commission decided that it is inadmissible to complain of discrimination in breach of article 14, read with article 9, on the ground that the law of blasphemy protects only the Christian but no other religion'. A careful reading of the two decisions in question reveals that the first was concerned with a refusal by the immigration authorities to admit members of a sect to the United Kingdom.[82] Blasphemy was not mentioned in the decision. The second case was the *Gay News* case, where the allegations of discrimination were made *by the publishers* on the grounds that 'they were singled out for restriction on account of their *homosexual* views'.[83] The Commission rejected this, stating that there were no indications in the facts to support this allegation. In addition the applicants submitted 'that the law of blasphemy protects only the Christian religion, in particular the doctrines of the Church of England, and that it is discriminatory in a multi-religious and to a considerable extent non-religious society to judge the applicants by standards of practicing [*sic*] Christians'.[84] The Commission expressly rejected this in the following

---

[78] At 1002.

[79] See generally *Tyrer* v. *UK*, Series A, vol. 26, para. 24; *Marckx* v. *Belgium*, Series A, vol. 31, para. 41; *Dudgeon* v. *UK*, Series A, vol. 45, para. 60; *Inze* v. *Austria*, Series A, vol. 126, para. 41.

[80] See *X and Y* v. *The Netherlands*, Series A, vol. 91, where the legislative framework did not allow for a mentally handicapped minor over 16 to institute criminal proceedings against an alleged sexual attacker.

[81] At 1003.

[82] *Church of X* v. *UK*, Applic. 3798/68, decision of 17 Dec. 1968, 29 Collection 70.

[83] At para. 14, emphasis added.

[84] At 13 of the transcript of the decision.

terms: 'the applicants cannot complain of discrimination because the law of blasphemy protects only the Christian but no other religion. The distinction in fact relates to the object of legal protection, but not the personal status of the offender.'[85] In other words the applicants were not the victims of the discriminatory law. Had they been Jews or Muslims and published the same poem they would still have been prosecuted. The objects of the discrimination are presumably those citizens who are 'offended in their religious feelings by the publications',[86] yet are unable to prosecute the offenders due to discrimination in the law.

Mr Lester's further arguments concerning Article 14 are set out in the court's judgment 'as stated by him in his skeleton argument'. Briefly, he argued that such discrimination had an objective and reasonable justification. This justification was based on the idea that if the offence were to be extended this would encourage 'intolerance, divisiveness and unreasonable interference and interferences with freedom of expression'. It was suggested that an extended law of blasphemy would be used as a weapon between different religions. The court was convinced that extending the law of blasphemy 'would be likely to do more harm than good',[87] and that the 'makers of the Convention could not have had in mind such an extension of the law in this country'.

This case has been examined in considerable detail because it represents the archetypal case at the heart of this study. It involves the application of the Convention to the sphere of relations between individuals; the parties to the case are private individuals; and the judgment illustrates the way the English courts currently use the Convention.

Instead of merely pointing to the case as an illustration of the courts applying the Convention and its case-law, we have dissected it in order to offer an insight into the real effect of applying the Convention in the British courts. It would be rash to draw too many conclusions from one decision but a number of salient points emerge.

First, when the British courts are faced with the Convention they are forced to rely heavily on the submissions of counsel due to the court's lack of experience with the Strasbourg case-law. Second, in anticipating the Strasbourg decision they inevitably mimic the Strasbourg organs rather than securing the guarantees at the national level. This is carried out with little sensibility for the dynamics of the Convention or its methods of interpretation. Taken to extremes this could lead to a downward spiral in the protection of human rights under the Convention. If the English courts guess what would happen in Strasbourg, where the Convention organs already allow a margin of appreciation, then, when the Strasbourg

---

[85] At para. 14 of 'the law'.
[86] At para. 11 of 'the law'.
[87] At 1003.

organs come to consider the same case, they may feel constrained again to allow a margin to the national authorities (especially where the Convention's provisions have been explicitly examined).

It is suggested that in order to escape this vicious circle the Convention should be given a stronger legal basis in the United Kingdom legal order. In this way the Bench and the Bar could develop a familiarity with the Convention and its application at the national level. Under the present situation the Convention risks hindering rather than helping judicial articulation of the conflicts which arise in the sphere of relations between individuals. This brings us back to the thorny question of incorporation of the Convention.

Of course, as we have seen, some quarters will argue that incorporation will have an adverse rather than beneficial effect. Even if judges become more familiar with its terms, incorporation creates the risk that judges will decide matters more properly left to politicians. Professor Mandel takes the extreme view that the first experiences of litigation under the Canadian Charter of Rights and Freedoms lead to the conclusion that 'Despite the heavenly exaltation, the Charter has merely handed over the custody of our politics to the legal profession.'[88] But the *Choudhury* case also demonstrates that the British courts already have custody of controversial matters. What the case illustrates is that there is a risk that, instead of addressing the national debate, the courts may rely on admissibility decisions of the European Commission of Human Rights. This supranational body has to take its decisions under conditions which rely on the continuing goodwill of Member States with very different legal systems.[89] On the other hand, the Commission has become more and

---

[88] Mandel continues: 'The defence of the status quo has followed from that as naturally as night follows day. The Charter would be a mute oracle without the legal priesthood to give it life. And the legal profession has shown itself more than willing to play the lead part in this hoax. Canadian lawyers and judges have, for the most part, gleefully and greedily undertaken a job—deciding the important political questions of the day—for which they lack all training and competence. And they have been more than willing to adopt the necessary pretexts to disguise their political, and politically conscious, interventions as *a*political interpretations of a document so vague as to be meaningless. For this they deserve a far rougher ride than they have been given here' (1989: 309); for a comment on the possible politicization of law following incorporation of the Convention in the UK see F. G. Jacobs, 'The Convention and the English Judge', in Matscher and Petzold (1988: 273–9); for suggestions concerning judicial appointments in the context of incorporation see P. Cumper, 'A Path to a Bill of Rights', *NLJ* (1991), 100–6; for a 'deflation' of the incorporation issue see Smith (1991: 120). The whole issue of incorporation was dealt with in Ch. 3.

[89] For a frank admission concerning the timidity of the Commission when faced with opposition by the Member States see the following passage concerning the scope of Art. 6(1) by Professor Schermers, a serving member of the Commission: 'Apart from the fear that too wide a scope of the Article would affect the impact of the Treaty provision, there also was the fear that the member states might not be willing to follow the Commission as they did not want administrative law to be included in the Article. The Commission and the Court have no real executive power of any kind; we need to build on the goodwill of public

more confident over the last forty years and some older decisions could now be seen to be very conservative and unlikely to be dealt with in the same way if brought again today.[90] Attention by the British courts to the Strasbourg case-law is a double-edged sword. Whilst ensuring that the Convention develops in a coherent way in accordance with minimum standards it simultaneously threatens to undercut any dynamic use of the Convention as a national Bill of Rights.

10.3.1.4 Wardship and custody

Disputes involving children present an obvious example of a clash of rights. The rights of parents, foster parents, and children all have to be accommodated. Although the State controls this area through the actions of local authorities, the courts, and legislation, cases may involve mother, father, and local authority. The same principles permeate the different conflicts and are sometimes presented as a clash of human rights. Only recently has this been articulated in the English courts with respect to the European Convention on Human Rights and the case-law of the European Court.

In *Re K.D.*[91] the House of Lords had to consider an appeal by the natural mother of a minor against an order that the minor should remain a ward of court and that access by the mother would be terminated. The mother argued that the Convention and its case-law meant she had an enforceable human right to access to her child.

Lord Templeman commenced his speech by comparing the situation under English Common Law and statute with the Convention. He explains that under English law 'in all matters concerning the upbringing of an infant the welfare of the child shall be the first and paramount consideration'.[92] He then quotes part of Article 8, and continues:

The English rule was evolved against an historical background of conflicts between parents over the upbringing of their children. The convention rule was evolved against an historical background of claims by the state to control the private lives of individuals. Since the 1939–45 war interference by public authorities with families for the protection of children has greatly increased in this country. In my opinion there is no inconsistency of principle or application between the English rule and the Convention rule. The best person to bring up the child is the natural

opinion and of the member states. If we antagonise them too much that might in the long run have a detrimental effect on the application of the decisions of the Court and Commission' ('The Right to a Fair Trial under the European Convention on Human Rights', in Blackburn and Taylor (1991: 60).

[90] e.g. *Kommunistische Partei Deutschland* v. *FRG* (1955–7) 1 Yearbook 223.
[91] [1988] 1 All ER 577.
[92] At 578.

parent. It matters not whether the parent is wise or foolish, rich or poor, educated or illiterate, provided the child's moral and physical health are not endangered. Public authorities cannot improve on nature. Public authorities exercise a supervisory role and interfere to rescue a child when the parental tie is broken by abuse or separation. In terms of the English rule the court decides whether and to what extent the welfare of the child requires that the child shall be protected against harm caused by the parent, including harm which could be caused by the resumption of parental care after separation has broken the parental tie. In terms of the convention rule the court decides whether and to what extent the child's health or morals require protection from the parent and whether and to what extent the family life of parent and child has been supplanted by some other relationship which has become the essential family life of the child.[93]

Lord Templeman concluded that in this case the welfare of the child required that he should no longer see his mother, as he had been with his foster mother for over two years and 'at the age of three years he could not cope with two competing mothers'. Lord Templeman did not address those rights under the Convention which relate to the rights of the parent. This task was undertaken by Lord Oliver.

Lord Oliver's speech illustrates the difficulties inherent in applying international human rights to cases in the sphere of relations between individuals. The mother relied on Article 8 as interpreted by the European Court of Human Rights to reinforce her claim to a right to access to her child.[94] The House of Lords was asked to reconsider its own judgment in *J. v. C.*[95] which had elaborated the rule that the first and paramount consideration is the welfare of the child, and that the parent's rights to access are subservient to the child's welfare. Lord Oliver examined in detail the judgment of the European Court of Human Rights in *R. v. United Kingdom* and found that no conflict existed between the 'propositions' of the House of Lords in *J. v. C.* and the 'pronouncements' of the European Court of Human Rights in *R. v. United Kingdom*:

Such conflict as exists is, I think, semantic only and lies only in different ways of giving expression to the single common concept that the natural bond and relationship between parent and child gives rise to universally recognized norms which ought not to be gratuitously interfered with and which, if interfered with at all, ought to be so only if the welfare of the child dictates it. The word 'right' is used in a variety of different senses, both popular and jurisprudential. It may be used as importing a positive duty on some other individual for the non-performance of which the law will provide an appropriate remedy, as in the case of a right to the performance of a contract. It may signify merely a privilege conferring no corresponding duty on any one save that of non-interference, such as the right to

[93] Ibid.
[94] See Cases *W., B., and R. v. UK*, Series A, vol. 136.
[95] [1969] 1 All ER 788.

walk on the public highway. It may signify no more than the hope or aspiration to a social order which will permit the exercise of that which is perceived as an essential liberty, such as for instance, the so-called 'right to work' or a 'right' of personal privacy. Parenthood, in most civilised societies, is generally conceived of as conferring on parents the exclusive privilege of ordering, within the family, the upbringing of children of tender age, with all that that entails. That is a privilege which, if interfered with without authority, would be protected by the courts, but it is a privilege circumscribed by many limitations imposed both by the general law and, where the circumstances demand, by the courts or by the authorities on whom the legislature has imposed the duty of supervising the welfare of children and young persons. When the jurisdiction of the court is invoked for the protection of the child the parental privileges do not terminate. They do, however, become immediately subservient to the paramount consideration which the court has always in mind. That is to say the welfare of the child. That is the basis of the decision of your Lordships' House in *J v C* and I see nothing in *R v UK* which contradicts or casts any doubt on that decision or which now calls for any reappraisal of it by your Lordships. In particular, the description of those familial rights and privileges enjoyed by parents in relations to their children as 'fundamental' or 'basic' does nothing, in my judgment, to clarify either the nature or the extent of the concept which is sought to describe.[96]

The speech of Lord Oliver has been cited at length because it gives us a useful insight into the English judicial approach to 'rights'. One might be tempted to conclude that the Convention rights are more confusing than useful when national courts have to deal with conflicts of rights in the sphere of relations between individuals. An individual 'victory' in Strasbourg cannot always be translated to the national level because the State is no longer the respondent. Different considerations apply. In *Cheall* the defendant at the national level was the union whilst at Strasbourg the respondent was the United Kingdom. When the Strasbourg Court considered the *R. v. United Kingdom* case it was not being asked to reverse its own case-law and elevate parental access to the status of a right equivalent to the rights of the child to paramount concern for its welfare. The Strasbourg Court is in the unique position of being able to review the whole situation in the United Kingdom. It was being asked to determine whether the parents' rights under Articles 8 and 6 had been violated by virtue of the *process* adopted by English law. They were not asked to decide whether a mother should have access to her children or not. The Strasbourg cases in question concerned what could be termed 'due process rights' and not the substantive rights of the parents to access. For the English courts to review the conformity of the legal process with the Convention the case would have to have been formulated as a request for judicial review of the local authority's decision rather than an appeal

---

[96] At 588.

against the order of the judge. In the terminology which was developed in Chapter 5, the Strasbourg Court was concerned with safeguarding dignity through democracy. The Strasbourg judgment relates to participation, representation, and accountability rather than a violent interference with the applicant's dignity. The relevant passage from the Strasbourg Court's judgment reads:

what therefore has to be determined is whether, having regard to the particular circumstances of the case and notably the serious nature of the decisions to be taken, the parents have been involved in the decision-making process, seen as a whole, to a degree sufficient to provide them with the requisite protection of their interests. If they have not, there will have been a failure to respect their family life and the interference resulting from the decision will not be capable of being regarded as 'necessary' within the meaning of Article 8.[97]

The Strasbourg Court found a violation of Article 8 due to the lack of participation in the decision-making process of the local authority. This part of the judgment was not quoted by the House of Lords, presumably because their Lordships were concerned with wardship and not participation rights in decisions of the local authority.[98] But the case is another illustration of the English courts claiming to apply the Convention in the same manner as the Strasbourg Court yet failing to admit that the international obligations of the United Kingdom are determined under a completely different approach.

On the other hand, where the judges consider that the words of the statute are 'unambiguous' they will reaffirm that in this situation the statute has to be applied in preference to the Convention rights. Five months after the *K. D.* case the issue of parental access was again before the House of Lords. This time it was not a question of deciding whether parental rights to access are equivalent to the child's right to consideration for its welfare under the wardship jurisdiction, but a question of statutory interpretation and review of the discretionary decision of the local authority. In *Re M. and H.* the local authority terminated access for the father with a view to fostering and adoption. According to the speech of Lord Brandon the amendments to the Child Care Act 1980 had been undertaken in anticipation of the judgment of the European Court of Human Rights in the above-mentioned *R. v. United Kingdom* case. These amendments

---

[97] *W., B., and R.* v. *UK*, Series A, vol. 136, pp. 28, 73–4, and 119 respectively.

[98] For a general comment on the 'distressing' nature of the case see David Pearl, 'Parental Access to Children in Care', *CLJ* (1988), 182–5, who reminds us that by the time one of the parties takes court action it is too late for any significant intervention. Pearl concludes: 'What *Re K.D.* illustrates all too clearly is that decisions about children, which we should really describe as decisions for children, should be taken after full consultation with parents and professionals working as a team for the welfare of the child. Is this such a difficult concept?' (at 185).

allowed for parents and guardians of children to apply to a court to challenge the effect of the local authority's resolution. Because the children were born out of wedlock the father could not challenge the decision of the local authority as he was not a 'parent' or a 'guardian' as defined in Section 87 of the Act.

The father was being denied the sort of remedy which would seem to be required by Articles 6 and 8 of the Convention. The House of Lords dealt with the Convention by asserting that 'English courts are under no duty to apply its provisions directly', and where statutes are unambiguous English courts have to give effect to those statutes rather than the Convention, 'even if those statutes may be in conflict with the Convention'.[99]

10.4 JUDICIAL REVIEW OF DISCRETIONARY DECISIONS BY NON-STATE BODIES

We saw in Part I that the United Kingdom courts excluded the Convention as a ground for judicial review of ministerial discretion in certain circumstances. The procedural law regarding what constitutes a 'public' body for the purposes of jurisdiction by the courts for judicial review is complex. It would be outside the scope of this study to offer an analysis of the English case-law on what is 'public' and what is 'private' for the purposes of administrative law.[100] Nevertheless the fact that a dichotomy between public and private law has emerged in English law means that the ground has been laid for an application of the Convention which relates only to bodies which would be susceptible to judicial review under the Order 53 procedure.[101] Moreover the developing divide has been reinforced by the ECJ's demands that national courts determine the 'publicness' of defendant bodies in the context of the direct applicability of rights in directives.[102]

So far, this public/private distinction has not been applied to the application of the Convention when courts have applied administrative law principles. The 'publicness' of a primarily private body may justify public law privileges such as the right to withhold confidential information in the public interest, and public law duties may be imposed on technically 'private' bodies which are obviously not state bodies.[103]

---

[99] [1988] 3 WLR 485 at 498; see Ch. 1.1.2, where the paragraph is quoted in full.

[100] For an examination of this question and the implications of the emerging dichotomy in English law see Beatson (1987: 34–65); another excellent article on the theme of the public/private distinction in English administrative law is Cane (1987: 57).

[101] See Order 53 of the Rules of the Supreme Court and s. 31 of the Supreme Court Act 1981.

[102] See Ch. 8.

[103] e.g. *D.* v. *NSPCC* [1978] AC 171; *Swain* v. *Law Society* [1983] 1 AC 598; *Law* v. *National Greyhound Racing Club Ltd.* [1983] 3 All ER 300; *R.* v. *Panel on Take-Overs and Mergers, ex p. Datafin PLC and Another* [1987] 1 QB 815.

An interesting case is the *Panel on Take-Overs and Mergers* case.[104] This was an application for judicial review of a decision of the Panel. The judge refused leave on the grounds that the decision was not susceptible to judicial review. On appeal the Court of Appeal decided that the High Court had jurisdiction over such a body which was performing public law duties. The court came to this decision even though the Panel is an 'unincorporated association without legal personality', was specifically set up to be 'self-regulating', and has no 'visible means of legal support'.[105] The court noted that the Panel had public duties, was supported by public law sanctions, had an obligation to act judicially, and was operating as an integral part of the regulation by the Government of the financial activity of the City of London. The conclusion is that the source of a body's powers is not the determining factor as to whether it comes within public law for the purposes of judicial review.[106] Whether or not such a body would be considered a 'state organ' by the European Commission of Human Rights, and whether such a body would qualify as an 'emanation of the State' under Community law are questions which will probably remain academic, and will not be entered into here.

A case which did raise the question in the context of judicial review of a non-state body was *Colman* v. *General Medical Council*.[107] In addition it was claimed that this case fell in the field of Community law. The case concerned an application by a doctor (in private practice) for judicial review of a decision of the General Medical Council (GMC) concerning restriction on press advertising. In the Divisional Court it was stated that the GMC is susceptible to judicial review as it is a public body established by statute and exercising a statutory power. Auld, J., considered the arguments under 'European law'[108] presented by Anthony Lester, QC, and decided that the principles of proportionality and equality were but aspects of the rationality or reasonableness test. As regards the issues under Articles 85(1), 59, and 60 EEC, Auld, J., found that the court was not equipped to deal with issues under Article 85, and 'even if it were, the validity of the guidance [issued by the GMC] falls to be decided under domestic law.' Articles 59 and 60 were dismissed as it was determined that Community law allows for professional codes of conduct which may be in restraint of trade.

---

[104] See n. 103.

[105] Per Lord Donaldson, MR, at 824–5.

[106] The test to be applied is not yet clear; see C. F. Forsyth, 'The Scope of Judicial Review: "Public Duty" not "Source of Power"', *PL* (1987), 356–67; see also Beatson (1987).

[107] [1989] 1 Medical Law Reports 23 (QBD); *R.* v. *General Medical Council, ex p. Colman* [1990] 1 All ER 489 (CA).

[108] The case-law of both the ECJ and the European Court of Human Rights was used in argument.

As regards the European Convention, Anthony Lester, QC, submitted that the guidance against advertising was contrary to Article 10 of the Convention. The Court of Appeal disagreed with the Divisional Court on the relevance of the Convention in this context and ruled that:

it is not possible for this argument to be accepted and applied by this court because it would be in breach of the law of this country to do so. I refer again to the judgment of Lord Donaldson MR in *Ex p. Brind*. I agree that to apply the argument of counsel for Mr Colman to s 35 of the 1983 Act would be to impute to Parliament an intention to import the convention into domestic law by the back door when it has quite clearly refrained from doing so by the front door.[109]

Despite this rejection of the use of the Convention in this context it is quite clear that in different circumstances (for example where the empowering statute is ambiguous or there is no statute) it will be quite legitimate to use the Convention in cases of judicial review of the decisions of non-state bodies. Certain remarks made in the Divisional Court give us clues as to how the Convention might be applied in such circumstances. The Divisional Court referred to the *Barthold* case decided by the European Court of Human Rights. That case concerned advertising by a vet and a breach of the rules of professional conduct. The Divisional Court made the interesting observation that:

it is by no means clear that the ECHR jurisprudence would go so far as to require a professional body like the GMC to demonstrate a pressing social need for its guidance against advertising in order to justify it as a protection of health or morals or for the protection of the rights of other doctors and patients under Article 10(2). The European Court of Human Rights said in paragraph 59 of its majority judgment in the *Barthold* case that the initial responsibility for securing compliance with the Convention lies with the individual contracting States, and that article 10(2) leaves each of them with a margin of discretion, albeit not an unlimited margin.[110]

Without reading too much into this remark, it could be suggested that national courts are ready to apply the margin of appreciation doctrine so that non-government bodies are given similar, if not wider, margins of discretion to state bodies. This is likely to be the case where the State has deliberately left non-state bodies (such as the GMC and the Panel) a significant amount of discretionary power.

---

[109] [1990] 1 All ER 489 at 505 per Ralph Gibson, LJ.
[110] [1989] 1 Medical Law Reports 23 at 35.

10.5 CONCLUSIONS CONCERNING THE USE OF THE CONVENTION IN THE SPHERE OF RELATIONS BETWEEN INDIVIDUALS IN CASES CONCERNING STATUTORY INTERPRETATION, THE COMMON LAW, AND JUDICIAL REVIEW

One can conclude that there is House of Lords authority that it is the duty of the judge to interpret the law in accordance with the obligations of the Crown under the Convention (where the judge is free to do so),[111] and that this duty applies even when the parties are private or non-state bodies. In the *Spycatcher* and *Blathwayt* cases the law to be considered was the Common Law of confidentiality and succession respectively. *R.* v. *Lemon* and *Choudhury* both concerned 'private' prosecutions and the Common Law of blasphemy, whilst *Gleaves* v. *Deakin* concerned a 'private' prosecution for the ancient offence of defamatory libel.[112] The absence of 'public law' or a state actor does not preclude the application of the Convention.[113]

This conclusion was explicitly affirmed by Lord Denning in *Associated Newspapers Group* v. *Wade*, where he stressed the importance of a free press in a dispute involving a trade union in the printing sector. He quoted Article 10(1) of the Convention and continued: 'If there is to be no interference by public authority, *all the more so there should be no interference by private individuals.*'[114]

---

[111] Per Lord Goff in *A.-G.* v. *Guardian Newspapers (No. 2)* [1990] 1 AC 109 at 283 (the second *Spycatcher* case): 'I conceive it to be my duty, when I am free to do so, to interpret the law in accordance with the obligations of the Crown under this treaty. The exercise of the right to freedom of expression under article 10 may be subject to restrictions (as are prescribed by law and are necessary in a democratic society), in relation to certain prescribed matters, which include "the interests of national security" and "preventing disclosure of information received in confidence." It is established in the jurisprudence of the European Court of Human Rights that the word "necessary" in this context implies the existence of a pressing social need, and that interference with freedom of expression should be no more than is proportionate to the legitimate aim pursued. I have no reason to believe that English law, as applied in the courts, leads to any different conclusion.' For a Scottish dictum see *Lord Advocate* v. *Scotsman Publications Ltd. and Others* [1989] 2 All ER 852 at 863, where the Convention seems to be used as an aid to interpretation.

[112] [1979] 2 All ER 497. In this case Lord Diplock suggested that the scope of this offence contravenes Art. 10 of the Convention as the publisher of the offence must be convicted unless the publisher can prove to the satisfaction of a jury that the publication was for the public benefit. As Lord Diplock put it: 'This is to turn Art. 10 of the Convention on its head' (at 499). The Law Commission has recommended the abolition of this offence; see Law Commission Working Paper no. 84 (London: HMSO).

[113] See *Derbyshire CC* v. *Times Newspapers* [1992] 3 All ER 65 at 79 for the suggestion by Balcombe, LJ, that, in the context of Art. 10 ECHR, 'In the normal case the interfering public authority is the court which entertains the suit for defamation.' And see Ch. 10.7.6 for a fuller citation.

[114] [1979] 1 WLR 697 at 709 (emphasis added).

10.6 EEC LAW

Chapter 8 covered the application of the human rights contained in the Convention against private bodies through Community law. At present the House of Lords continues to give precedence to statutory provisions over Community directives, even where the statutory provisions were enacted after the relevant directive.[115] In 'borderline' cases turning on the 'publicness' of the respondent body the Employment Appeal Tribunal has given a restrictive interpretation to 'emanations of the state'. So, only where the respondent is 'an organ or agent of the State carrying out a State function' can individuals actually rely on directly effective Articles in Community directives.[116] This has meant that universities, nationalized industries, and companies where the State holds 100 per cent of the shares have all been held to be 'private' bodies and outside the reach of the equal treatment directive.[117] Nevertheless the influence of Community law on 'the privatization of human rights' should not be underestimated. In *Shields* v. *E. Coomes* the Court of Appeal considered a claim by a woman who worked in a betting shop, who complained that her employers had discriminated against her as male workers were paid more due to their duties concerning awkward customers. Lord Denning, MR, confessed to having some difficulty in overcoming the finding that the differences merited an additional bonus. But he did overcome these difficulties by 'giving supremacy to Community law'.[118] He reviewed the relevant Community law and stated:

All this shows that the flowing tide of Community law is coming in fast. It has not stopped at high-water mark. It has broken the dykes and the banks. It has submerged the surrounding land. So much so that we have to learn to become amphibious if we wish to keep our heads above water.[119]

10.7 INCORPORATION OF THE CONVENTION AND ITS POSSIBLE USE AGAINST PRIVATE BODIES

This section addresses the question: should incorporation of the Convention into United Kingdom law be effected so that the Convention is relevant

---

[115] *Finnegan* v. *Clowney Youth Training Programme Ltd.* [1990] 2 WLR 1305; the case concerned sex discrimination under the equal treatment directive in Northern Ireland.

[116] *Doughty* v. *Rolls-Royce* [1988] CMLR 569.

[117] Curtin has noted that in Common Law countries the growth of bodies with executive functions has happened 'in a haphazard fashion', and so a Community test which is linked to the formation of the body by the State (seemingly a component of the *Foster* test; see Ch. 8) means that Rolls-Royce Ltd. or British Petroleum Ltd. are beyond the reach of the directives, whereas the same directives could be relied on in court against British Telecom, the BBC, or British Airways (Curtin 1990: 217).

[118] [1979] 1 All ER 456 at 465.

[119] At 462.

in the sphere of relations between non-state bodies? The answer to this question may eventually determine:

1. the likelihood of consensus for incorporation of the Convention;
2. the likely impact of incorporation;
3. the dominant philosophy to be used in interpreting the Convention; that is, will the courts recognize the inherent dignity of human beings and protect their individual autonomy against *any* invasion, or is it an institutional device to check the abuse of governmental power?

It would be outside the scope of this study to tackle the question of a possible Bill of Rights which went beyond incorporation of the Convention. Presumably the same questions concerning the 'horizontal effect' or the 'privatization of rights' will have to be faced in the discussion concerning any eventual constitutional settlement concerning a Bill of Rights. But the debate will be different as the 'Strasbourg factor' will be less pronounced. This study has been concerned to show the scope of the Convention in relations between individuals as developed in the Strasbourg case-law. The broad question of a Bill of Rights need not be shackled with the limits of the Convention. Indeed three important recent initiatives, the Labour Party's *Charter of Rights* (1990), the Institute of Public Policy Research's *A British Bill of Rights* (Constitutional Paper no. 25), and Liberty's *A People's Charter* are not formulas for incorporation.[120]

Having said this, the only time the matter was studied by a Select Committee the conclusions were clear. The House of Lords Select Committee on a Bill of Rights, established in 1977, did not reach agreement on the desirability of a Bill of Rights: six members were in favour, five against. But on the question of the form such a Bill of Rights should take the Committee was unanimous that 'if there were to be such a Bill of Rights, it should be a Bill based on the European Convention on Human Rights'.[121] Since the publication of this report it would be fair to say that most of the debates about a Bill of Rights have centred on the Con-

---

[120] On the desirability of incorporation first and serious debate on a Bill of Rights second see Smith (1991: 120). Other recent literature includes Holme and Elliott (1988), and esp. Lord Scarman at 103–11, 'Bill of Rights and Law Reform'; R. Blackburn, 'Legal and Political Arguments for a United Kingdom Bill of Rights', in Blackburn and Taylor (1991: 109–30); Graham and Prosser (1988); Ewing and Gearty (1990). A fuller bibliography on this question is contained in the footnotes to Ch. 3; see also the bibliography attached to the end of this study.

[121] *Report of the Select Committee on a Bill of Rights*, HL paper 176 (London: HMSO, 1978); see also *Minutes of Evidence taken before the Select Committee on a Bill of Rights*, House of Lords (1977); Zander (1985). At a meeting on the larger question of the need for a written constitution, chaired by Dr David Butler at Nuffield College, Oxford, the unofficial record of the proceedings states that there was almost unanimous agreement that the Convention should be incorporated; see 'The Preconditions for a Written Constitution', Nuffield College, Oxford, 31 Jan. 1986.

vention.[122] The following analysis concentrates only on those discussions where the potential application of the Convention against private bodies was considered.

10.7.1 The Protection of Human Rights Bill (1971)

It is worth examining this initiative by Sam Silkin (Labour) in the House of Commons because the Bill specifically accommodated threats to human rights from private bodies. The purpose of the Bill was explained by Silkin as follows:

The Bill would enable the humblest of our citizens and those who visit our shores to complain to a new tribunal, the National Tribunal of Human Rights, of the violation, whether by public authority *or by private organisation*, of those rights and freedoms which society believes should be protected but which remain, for the time being, outside the protection of the law.[123]

Interestingly, the purpose of the Bill was expressly stated to be to bring the United Kingdom into line with international obligations under Article 13 of the Convention, and to do in Britain what is already done in Strasbourg. The 'Tribunal' was to have almost identical functions to those of the European Commission of Human Rights. This 'United Kingdom Commission of Human Rights . . . would investigate, report and recommend but would have no power to enforce.'[124]

It is tempting to dismiss the Bill as legally toothless and mere window dressing. But such an initiative could fulfil many of the aims of incorporation without creating some of the drawbacks. Applicants would have an opportunity to have their cases heard quickly and cheaply; there is no reason to believe that administrative practices would not be changed following an adverse decision of the United Kingdom Commission (Tribunal); and Parliament would remain free to legislate in any field.

What the brief debate actually illustrates is that one of the main aims of the Bill seems to have been to curb private power. This may have been partly in order to score political points in an ideological battle— Conservative support for the introduction of a Bill of Rights at this time seems to have been aimed at the programme of the Labour Party in Government. Parliament was considered by some Conservatives to be 'virtually an elective dictatorship'.[125] On the other hand Sam Silkin and

[122] See the parliamentary debates cited in Ch. 3 and the bibliographical references in the first footnotes to that chapter. But see also the three initiatives referred to above.

[123] 2 Apr. 1971, HC Debs., col. 1854, emphasis added.

[124] At col. 1858, S. Silkin.

[125] Q. Hogg, MP (later Lord Chancellor, Lord Hailsham), *New Charter*, Conservative Political Centre, no. 430, p. 7; Lord Hailsham returned to this line of approach after Labour had been returned to power in 1974, again claiming that the executive had too much power within Parliament; see Zander (1985: 11).

Peter Archer (both Labour, and at the time in Opposition[126]) were seeking to control the press, advertisers, employers, neighbours, landlords, property companies, and the people who control individuals' lives in a technological age. Peter Archer's speech makes this quite clear, even if the images are more evocative of a 1920s silent film than the dawning of the computer age.

> There are times when we all have the feeling of being lashed to a railway track in the path of an on-rushing train. As my hon. and learned Friend said, it may be that this is one of the prices that we have to pay for the privilege of living in a technological age. It is undoubtedly a privilege, because few people would want to put the clock back to the simpler days before the age of technology. . . .
>
> We on this side of the House take the view that there are other relationships, not only relationships between the individual and Government, which can also blight lives, and which, for many individuals can result in tragedy. Very serious distress can be caused by an employer, by a landlord, or by a neighbour. Not all wrecked lives are wrecked by Governments. Sometimes to safeguard individuals from this kind of danger may entail giving more power to governmental officials. . . .
>
> [W]ith modern communications, people are governed and dealt with and related [to] in much larger units than previously. So it is inevitable that their lives are governed by decisions taken by people whose faces they do not know and often whose very names and identities are unknown to them . . .
>
> This becomes more frightening for individuals. The wicked landlord of Victorian melodrama was a frightening enough individual, but at least the heroine could talk to him, and, in the last resort, could appeal to his better nature. These days the tenant who seeks to obtain the reversal of a decision from his landlord will be lucky indeed if he can find anyone who admits to having the power to alter such a decision, because usually it is a big property company.[127]

In the 1990s there is similar anxiety. In particular the legal frameworks for the control of the newly privatized monopolies would not seem to offer the same accountability as the regime which operated when they were 'public' bodies.[128] Where electricity, gas, or water companies take action against individuals the results can be dramatic. In fact, following a recent admissibility decision by the European Commission of Human Rights, Professors Antonio Cassese and Fédéric Sudre have individually suggested that, in some circumstances, cutting off the power supply to someone's residence could lead to a violation of Article 3 of the Convention

---

[126] They went on to become Attorney-General and Solicitor-General respectively.

[127] Cols. 1861–2. The debate was curtailed due to there being less than forty members present and the Bill was never resurrected. I hope the reader will forgive the licence which has been taken in splicing these passages together.

[128] See J. F. Garner, 'After Privatisation: Quis Custodiet Ipsos Custodes?', *PL* (1990), 329–37; T. Prosser, 'Constitutions and Political Economy: The Privatisation of Public Enterprises in France and Great Britain', *MLR* (1990), 304–20.

(inhuman and degrading treatment).[129] The 'private world of commerce' cannot be easily divorced from the 'public world of human rights'.

10.7.2 The Labour Party Discussion Document (1976)

This document, entitled *United Kingdom Charter of Rights*, was drawn up by the Subcommittee of the Home Policy Committee of the National Executive. The paper starts by stressing the changes in society which have taken place since the War and points to 'the growth in the number, size and power of large organisations in both the private and the public sectors, which increasingly affect our lives'.[130] The introduction continues by drawing attention to Labour's commitment to a system of 'watchdogs' to protect 'rights and liberties against the abuse of power in the private as well as the public sector'.[131] The proposal for a *Charter of Human Rights* was said to respond to the 'need to tip the scales away from public and private concentrations of power back in favour of the individual'.[132] The paper finishes with a proposal to incorporate the European Convention on Human Rights. It is not clear whether incorporation was intended to offer protection against private power. The paper mentions 'the big battalions' at one point but the emphasis in the paper is often on protecting against public officials. Considering that Mr Silkin and Mr Archer were members of the Subcommittee it is likely that the Charter was supposed to operate in both the public and the private sphere.

10.7.3 The Home Office Discussion Document (1976)[133]

This report presented a thorough examination of the advantages and disadvantages of incorporation of the Convention or a Bill of Rights. The conclusions of the working group concerning 'rights against individuals' are summarized in their report in the following way:

On the one hand:

   a. Our legal system makes no distinction between public and private law. Any attempt to introduce such a distinction might have anomalous and artificial consequences.

   b. A limitation to public or quasi-public authorities might be difficult to defend, especially in modern conditions where people feel no less threatened by powerful private organisations.

---

[129] See Cassese (1991); Sudre (1990: 349–53); the decision of the Commission with which these two articles are concerned is reported in *RUDH* (1990) at 384, Applic. 14641/89, *Van Volsem* v. *Belgium*, declared inadmissible 9 May 1990. These two articles were dealt with in more detail in Ch. 7.3.1.2.

[130] Labour Party (1976: 3). (The document was not published as official Labour Party policy following decisions of the Home Policy Committee and the National Executive.)

[131] Ibid.   [132] Ibid.   [133] Home Office (1976).

On the other hand

    a. Constitutional guarantees of fundamental rights are usually regarded as protecting the individual against public authorities rather than other individuals or private bodies.

    b. Making the guaranteed rights avail against private persons and organisations would greatly extend the likely area of controversy.

In the main body of the report the working group conclude that either approach 'would inevitably seem to lead to controversy'.[134] They also state that if the incorporating legislation limited the rights, so that they were applicable only against public authorities, defining 'public authority' would not be easy. The report put forward the suggestion that the Bill of Rights could be drafted so that it applied to 'State action'. In this way it could be applied to 'non-governmental bodies of a quasi public character'. The report also suggests that the concept of 'State action' would allow courts to 'hold the State responsible for not ensuring (by legislation or otherwise) that a citizen's rights were adequately protected from infringement by anybody, whether by a public authority or by another citizen or by private organisation'.[135] The working group also foresaw that the 'general evolutionary approach in Strasbourg' could mean that the Commission and Court might come to adopt 'a wider interpretation' than the original intention of the framers of the Treaty.

This far-sighted approach to the problem has the merit that it would replicate in the United Kingdom's courts what is currently done in Strasbourg. It also openly admits the existence of a grey zone of quasi-governmental activity. Nevertheless the working group recognized the dangers of allowing the courts 'room for manœuvre'. They foresaw that the problem would not disappear, and that it would have to be tackled head on as 'there would be objections to leaving the effect of the Bill imprecise, particularly about its application to politically controversial areas'.[136]

10.7.4 The Northern Ireland Standing Advisory Committee on Human Rights (1977)

When the Northern Ireland Standing Advisory Commission on Human Rights investigated the question of incorporation of the Convention, they addressed the particular question: 'should the European Convention be applicable against private bodies?'[137] They concluded that incorporation

---

[134] At para. 2.18. [135] Para. 2.19. [136] Para. 2.19.
[137] *The Protection of Human Rights by Law in Northern Ireland*, Northern Ireland Standing Advisory Commission on Human Rights, Cmnd. 7009 (London: HMSO, 1977), para. 7.11 and p. 78 para. 6.

ought to exclude the creation of new rights and remedies between private individuals and private organizations:

The confrontation between the Industrial Relations Court and the trades union movement over the Industrial Relations Act 1971 indicates the need to approach the private field with particular care so as to ensure that there is a wide public support for control by the judges of this field before it is entrusted to them. Public confidence needs to be won and maintained.[138]

A Bill of Rights which limits not only the power of government but also the 'freedom' of trade unions, mass media, and private corporations may have difficulty gaining broad support either for its implementation or for its operation.

As we have seen, the European Convention itself has been used to question the practice of the 'closed shop' and the operation of the TUC's Bridlington Principles (which regulate inter-union disputes over members).[139] There is even now a fear that, should the European Convention be incorporated into the law of the United Kingdom, 'The protection of freedom in the Convention may yet give the English courts another stick with which to beat workers' organisations.'[140]

10.7.5 The Human Rights Bill (1986) and the continuing debate

Clauses 1, 2, and 3 of the 1986 Human Rights Bill[141] imply that the 'Bill of Rights' is to be used only against the organs of the State. Liability is imposed on 'the Crown', 'Ministers of the Crown', 'a person holding statutory office', 'a public body', and 'a person holding public office'. However, 'public body' is defined as 'a body of persons, whether corporate or unincorporate, carrying on a service or undertaking of a public nature'.[142]

This formulation, if adopted, could create the dichotomy which the present study has warned against at such length. Such a public/private distinction allows the Convention to be disregarded in those cases where it may be especially relevant. Arguably it is also a retrograde step in that it would remove consideration of the Convention from certain types of cases where it is currently considered to be relevant. Is *Gay News* a public body under this definition? Lord Scarman held that it had duties under the Convention. Is Salman Rushdie a public body? Are trade unions public bodies? Do they become more public when they operate a 'closed shop' or 'unreasonable rules'? It was suggested by the Commission, and

---

[138] *The Protection of Human Rights*, para. 7.11.
[139] See Chs. 1.2 and 10.3.
[140] Ewing (1987: 23). For a fuller account of Ewing's approach to the dangers of incorporation of the Convention see Ewing and Gearty (1990: 275).
[141] Bill 19, 10 Dec. 1986 (House of Commons).
[142] Ibid. Clause 1.

hinted at in the House of Lords, that the Convention comes into play at this point. Are foster parents offering a public service? Are adoptive parents a public body? Are the privatized electricity, gas, and water boards obliged to act so that Convention rights are respected?

Furthermore, the Bill does not seem to allow for courts to 'hold the State responsible for not ensuring (by legislation or otherwise) that a citizen's rights were adequately protected from infringement by anybody, whether a public authority or by another citizen or by a private organization'.[143] The Bill prohibits 'acts' which infringe fundamental rights and freedoms and defines an 'act' as including a deliberate omission.[144] It is unlikely that a United Kingdom court would find a failure to legislate to close a loophole in the law (such as the one in *X and Y* v. *The Netherlands*) a deliberate omission by a Minister, public body, etc.

The debates in 1986 and 1987 concerning these attempts to incorporate the Convention did not address the public/private dichotomy, nor did the House of Lords debates on incorporation in 1990.[145] More and more the issue of incorporation has been presented as a question of 'repatriating' or 'domesticating' the Convention.[146] In December 1990, when the question of incorporation was last debated in Parliament, the idea of incorporation was 'simply to take the European convention and make it part of British law so that British citizens in British courts may have access to the rights for which at present they have to travel a long, expensive and weary road to Strasbourg'.[147]

---

[143] Home Office (1976: para. 2.19), the 'state action' approach.

[144] Clause 1(2).

[145] Debate of the Human Rights and Fundamental Freedoms Bill, 9 Apr. 1986, HL Debs., vol. 109, no. 47, col. 267; debate on the Human Rights Bill, 6 Feb. 1987, HC Debs., vol. 109, no. 47, col. 1223 (Sir Ian Percival seems to have foreseen that in a rerun of the *Young, James and Webster* case it would be for the courts to decide in a case of judicial review whether the legislation was necessary in a democratic society: 'The Bill does not give everybody the right to take proceedings against everybody else who is thought to be in breach of its terms. It gives the right to take proceedings against public authorities' (at col. 1235)); debate to call attention to the state of civil liberties under this Administration, 23 May 1990, HL Debs., col. 904; Early Day Motion to call attention to the case for the incorporation of the European Convention on Human Rights into UK law as a Bill of Rights, 5 Dec. 1990, HL Debs., vol. 524, no. 16, col. 185.

[146] See e.g. R. Holme (later Lord Holme and mover of the motion on incorporation in the House of Lords on 5 Dec. 1990), 'How to Keep out of Strasbourg', *The Times* (12 Aug. 1988), and 'Put Britain on the Rights Road', *The Times* (8 Jan. 1985); Lord Broxbourne (sponsor of the 1986 Bill), 'Bringing our Rights Home', *Sunday Times* (8 Dec. 1985); 'An Imported Magna Carta: Britain's Citizens should not Need to Go to Strasbourg to Protect their Human Rights', *The Economist* (editorial) (29 June 1985); G. Robertson, 'Repatriating a Bill of Rights', *New Statesman* (6 Dec. 1985); R. Alexander (now Lord Alexander), 'Bringing Strasbourg Home', *Counsel: The Journal of the Bar of England and Wales* (Hilary 1987), 40, and 'Human Rights: Trust our Judges', *The Times* (10 Dec. 1985).

[147] Lord Holme of Cheltenham, author of the motion calling for attention to be paid to the case for incorporation of the European Convention on Human Rights (5 Dec. 1990, HL Debs., vol. 524, no. 16, col. 187).

But, as we have seen, the sphere of relations between individuals may be considered in Strasbourg. It is possible that the Commission may find the rules of a trade union unreasonable and hence a violation of the Convention.[148] Questions of sexual assault, terrorist threats, private corporal punishment, media concentrations, offensive publications, and discriminatory dismissal have all been considered justiciable in Strasbourg even though all the action at the national level took place between private actors (in the private sphere). If incorporation is designed to save victims the 'the long five year trek to Strasbourg, supported by lawyers who largely take no fee',[149] then it ought to cover cases in the private sphere.

It is difficult to imagine that the present proposals for incorporation of the Convention would allow individuals to bring a case against the United Kingdom (as they do in Strasbourg) alleging that the State had failed to legislate in the private sphere. Even if this possibility were permitted it is unlikely that the courts would provide the sort of 'instant justice' which incorporation is designed to create. In any case, we have seen that this type of case turns more on the facts than anything else. The test applied by Strasbourg is the proportionality principle and relates to the effect on the victim rather than the state inaction. (See, for example, *X and Y v. The Netherlands, Young, James and Webster, Cheall.*) Considering the number of ways in which the Convention can effectively be used to complain about action by private bodies it would seem that, in order to do in the Strand what is being done in Strasbourg, one has to import its application of human rights in the private sphere.

One of the arguments used for demanding incorporation of the European Convention is that incorporation would fulfil an outstanding international obligation on the United Kingdom. It has been suggested that an obligation arises by virtue of Article 13 of the Convention.[150] As we have seen, there is no clear interpretation of this Article. According to the Registrar of the Strasbourg Court, the word 'notwithstanding' 'admits implicitly, but inevitably that breaches of the Convention may be committed by private individuals' (Eissen 1967: 237). In the opinion of the Deputy Secretary of the European Commission of Human Rights, 'State parties are obliged by article 13 to provide a remedy in domestic law against violations committed by private persons or by private authorities' (Raymond 1980: 170).

To what extent Article 13 creates an obligation on Member States to

---

[148] See *Cheall* v. *UK* (above).

[149] Lord Hutchinson, 5 Dec. 1990, HL Debs., vol. 524, no. 16, col. 197.

[150] Art. 13 reads: 'Everyone whose rights and freedoms as set forth in this Convention are violated shall have an effective remedy before a national authority notwithstanding that the violation has been committed by persons acting in an official capacity.'

incorporate the European Convention has been a matter of some debate.[151] It is a question which the European Court of Human Rights has so far avoided.[152] This question was examined fully in Chapter 7, where we concluded that (even if incorporation *per se* is not required by Article 13) where no domestic remedy exists there may be a sanctionable violation of that Article. Article 13 does not require a judicial remedy and so is unlikely to come actually to create new judicial remedies in the United Kingdom.[153] Under the current proposals for a Bill of Rights it is a question which will not be decided in the United Kingdom courts, as Article 13 has not been included in the Schedule to the Human Rights Bill 1986.[154]

10.7.6 Conclusions on incorporation of the Convention and the question of rights against private power

It would be presumptuous to suggest a formula to address the public/private question for incorporation in any future Bill of Rights. What is suggested is that formulas which allow for cases to be declared outside the scope of the Bill due to the 'private' nature of the respondent will mean

---

[151] Drzemczewski (1983: 40–53: 'Divergent Legal Opinions'). Drzemczewski concludes that there is no obligation on States under Art. 13 to incorporate the Convention. For the opposite conclusion see Buergenthal (1965: 79); also Black (1973: 173); P. Wallington, 'The European Convention on Human Rights and English Law', *Cambridge Law Journal* (1975), 9; Mann (1978: 512); Jaconelli (1976: 226).

[152] The Court has not found it necessary to decide this issue with regard to the UK. It usually asserts that no separate issue arises under Art. 13: *Case of Fox, Campbell and Hartley* v. *UK*, Series A, vol. 182; *Case of Brogan and Others* v. *UK*, Series A, vol. 145-B; *Case of Boyle and Rice* v. *UK*, Series A, vol. 131; *Case of Powell and Rayner*, Series A, vol. 172; *Soering* v. *UK*, Series A, vol. 161; note, the Commission unanimously found a breach of Art. 13 in its opinion in *Boyle and Rice* and the majority (seven votes to four) of the Commission found a violation of Art. 13 in *Soering*. It may be that the Court has exercised greater self-restraint on this issue than the Commission has.

[153] For the 'situation as seen from Strasbourg' see Drzemczewski (1989: 25). Drzemczewski relies on a paragraph in the *Ireland* v. *UK* case: 'By substituting the words "shall secure" for the words "undertake to secure" in the text of Article 1, the drafters of the Convention also intended to make it clear that the rights and freedoms set out in Section I would be directly secured to anyone within the jurisdiction of the Contracting States (document H(61)4, pp. 664, 703, 733 and 927). That intention finds a particularly faithful reflection in those instances where the Convention has been incorporated into domestic law (De Wilde, Ooms and Versyp judgment of 18 June 1971, Series A, no. 12, p. 43, para. 82; Swedish Engine Drivers' Union judgment of 6 Feb. 1976, Series A no. 20, p. 18, para. 50). The Convention does not merely oblige the higher authorities of the Contracting States to respect for their own part the rights and freedoms it embodies; as is shown by Article 14 and the English text of Article 1 ("shall secure"), the Convention also has the consequence that, in order to secure the enjoyment of those rights and freedoms, those authorities must prevent or remedy any breach at subordinate levels' (Series A, vol. 25, para. 239).

[154] Human Rights Bill 1986 (Bill 19); the Bill attaches Arts. 2–12 and 14 as well as Protocol no. 1 in Schedule 1. Schedule 2 includes the UK's reservation to Art. 2 of Protocol 1. The paper produced by the Institute for Public Policy Research, *A British Bill of Rights* (London, 1990), does not contain an equivalent to Art. 13 ECHR.

that courts may transform substantive questions into jurisdictional questions about the boundaries of the public and private sectors. As we have seen, judicial appreciation of a concept such as 'a service or undertaking of a public nature' varies considerably from judge to judge and attempts to guess the legislature's intention may fail completely. (In both *Dockers' Labour Club* and *Applin* Parliament intervened to reverse the House of Lords' decision so that clubs became covered by the race relations legislation and foster parents were removed from its scope.) The great risk is that the whole issue is presented as merely a decision on the public/private nature of the respondent whilst the actual conflict is never explicitly resolved.

We have seen that the labels 'public' and 'private' are more like tactical weapons than descriptive labels. This is not surprising because in the human rights context 'private' quickly becomes 'privacy' and hence inviolable. For example, in the 1970s, when the issue of racial discrimination in working men's clubs arose, the Labour Party argued that these clubs should be covered by the law on discrimination because of their public nature; in the 1990s the Labour Party protested about legislation allowing police to enter these same clubs and argued that such clubs were private places. There is no contradiction in such statements.[155] They only go to show that the choice of label 'public' or 'private' may depend on the harm you wish to avoid.

One solution may be to leave any incorporation Bill silent on the application of rights against private parties. This is the solution adopted in the new Dutch Constitution and it was advocated in the context of proposals for a Bill of Rights in New Zealand.[156] However, the New

---

[155] Cf. Lord Hutchinson of Lullington: 'It was amusing to hear the vehemence with which noble Lords on the Labour Benches opposed that part of the Law Reform (Miscellaneous Provisions) (Scotland) Bill giving police the right of almost unfettered entry to clubs, arguing as they did that clubs, particularly working men's clubs, were essentially private places. As the noble and learned Lord, Lord Hailsham, will remember, that is almost precisely the opposite of the stance that Labour took when in power. In 1976 the Labour Government took precisely the opposite line, arguing that clubs, and in particular working men's clubs, were essentially public places and must therefore be subject to the restrictions and obligations of race relations legislation' (Debate on Civil Liberties, 23 May 1990, HL Debs., col. 917).

[156] See Elkind and Shaw (1986). Note, the draft 'Basic Law' for Hong Kong specifically allowed for protection from private abuses including individuals' interferences with privacy. However the Hong Kong Bill of Rights Ordinance 1991, enacted 8 June 1991, contains a new formula in its s. 7: '(1) This Ordinance binds only—(a) the Government and all public authorities; and (b) any person acting on behalf of the Government or a public authority.' This Bill of Rights incorporates rights from the Civil and Political Rights Covenant, and, as we saw in Ch. 4, there is considerable authority to suggest that some of the rights in the Covenant should be interpreted to cover private activity. Other Articles do not exclude private actors from their scope. Comparisons with other European jurisdictions where the Convention has the status of domestic law are not particularly helpful. This is because the Convention will nearly always take second place to an examination of the domestic constitution. Even where the Convention has been specifically incorporated through a separate

Zealand Bill of Rights as adopted in September 1990 included the following section:

3. Application—This Bill of Rights applies only to acts done—

(*a*) By the legislative, executive, or judicial branches of the government of New Zealand; or

(*b*) By any person or body in the performance of any public function, power, or duty conferred or imposed on that person or body pursuant to law.

At first glance this would seem to limit the scope of application to the public sphere. But the section specifically mentions the judiciary and therefore seems to bind them in their determination of disputes concerning private actors. In this way human rights principles become relevant for the determination of conflicts in the private sphere. Human rights need not be relegated to an exclusive zone on the public side of the public/private divide. What the New Zealand formula does not permit is for one party to bring the case before the courts by claiming a remedy against a non-governmental body solely basing the case on the rights contained in the Bill of Rights. The Bill of Rights only comes into play once the case is before the judge.[157]

Considering that incorporation of the European Convention into UK law would be in order to reinforce its role as an aid to interpretation, and considering that British judges already defer to the Convention in 'private law' cases, the New Zealand formula would seem relatively appropriate. One can even cite the approach in *Derbyshire County Council* v. *Times Newspapers*.[158] In this case the Council sought to sue the *Sunday Times* for libel. Balcombe, LJ, relied heavily on the Convention but clearly implies that he would have done so even if both parties had been private actors:

Article 10(1) in terms expresses an absolute right, that of freedom of expression. That right of freedom of expression includes freedom to impart information and ideas without interference by public authority. Prima facie that right will be interfered with by a public authority if the maker of the statement is sued for defamation. In the normal case the interfering public authority is the court which entertains the suit for defamation. (Here the interference is twofold since the council, which has initiated the suit, is itself a public authority.)[159]

Act of Parliament such as the European Convention Act (Act No. XIV of 1987) in Malta, a case concerning private individuals came to be determined by an application of the constitutional right prohibiting inhuman and degrading treatment and not the Convention right, which was held not to give rise to a remedy in national law; see *Buttigiey* v. *Air Malta*, 9 Oct. 1989, Constitutional Court of Malta.

[157] This is not dissimilar to the *Von Colson* principle explained in Ch. 8.1.2 in the context of national judges being 'required to interpret their national law in the light of the wording and purpose of the directive' in a dispute between two private parties, even though the Community directive cannot actually found an action against a private party.

[158] [1992] 3 All ER 65; see Ch. 1.2.1.

[159] At 79.

This solution recognizes the applicability of the Convention between private parties. The reference to public authority is not determinative and only relates to the legitimacy of restrictions on the right and not the existence of a right operating in the private sphere. Even if the New Zealand formula were adopted so that only when a case was before the court would the Bill of Rights come into play, this is not necessarily that disadvantageous. Most situations will be covered by some sort of domestic legislation and the Convention would be of interpretative value. Those situations where plaintiffs cannot put their complaints before the courts may constitute a violation of the 'right to a remedy' under Article 13 ECHR and can be dealt with by the European Commission and Court of Human Rights as a failure by the State to provide domestic legislation in this field. The actual legislation to be enacted is then debated in Parliament and in civil society. This diffuses two of the most powerful arguments against human rights in the private sphere: first, that allowing everyone to claim violations of human rights against everyone else would clog up the courts and dilute the notion of human rights; and second, that complex conflicts of interests between different sectors of civil society are better dealt with by democratically enacted legislation than by recourse to abstract conflicting principles such as 'freedom of expression' or 'privacy'.

Moreover, it ensures that human rights principles are applied by judges in all cases and that certain spheres are not excluded arbitrarily from the public world of the Bill of Rights. If a Bill of Rights is to have a really educative and preventive function then everyone should feel bound by its norms—whether or not they perceive themselves as carrying out a public function. To create a culture of human rights means going beyond instructing officials that there are annoying limits on government action. The challenge must be to allow everyone to feel that such principles and rules contribute to greater respect for people's dignity, and that it is respect for these rights which enables one's own better participation in civil society and decision-making in the public domain.

Either leaving the question out of any future Bill or adopting the New Zealand approach would have the advantage that developments in Strasbourg could be easily accommodated in the United Kingdom. In addition the Strasbourg bodies could consider national cases which had already addressed the application of the Convention in the sphere of relations between individuals. This sort of 'dialectical development' could eventually lead to a constructive evolution in the application of human rights in the private sphere.

Conclusions

The thesis presented in this study is that the European Convention on Human Rights ought to be interpreted so that it is applicable where victims face *abuses from private actors*. Two approaches were said to justify such a conclusion. First, international human rights law is moving towards the recognition and prohibition of private action which violates human rights; as the European Court of Human Rights has affirmed that the European Convention has to be interpreted in the context of other developments, this means that the Convention ought to apply as far as possible to protect victims from private action (this is a legal argument).

Secondly, the consequences of failing to protect against private violations are undesirable; not only does such a failure leave vulnerable groups and individuals unprotected, but it also creates a false public/private dichotomy capable of functioning as a tool arbitrarily to weed out applicants and potential applicants and deny them access to justice. (This is a policy argument.) Furthermore, once the falsity of the dichotomy has been exposed the functions (intended or unintended) that such a dichotomy serves are revealed: to hide the extent of state intervention in society, to reinforce existing power relationships, to annul welfare legislation while rejuvenating ancient Common Law privileges, to frustrate attempts by private actors to enter the debate on public matters, and to deny women and children freedom from oppression in the forgotten domestic sphere. (This is a political/ideological argument.)

Whilst these last two arguments do not deny that there might be an intimate sphere which ought to be protected from unnecessary state interference, they do suggest that this sphere should not be considered coexistent with the whole of the non-state sector.

The reasons why such a thesis has not been embraced with any enthusiasm at the federal or supranational level emerge from the analysis of 'the practice' in Part II. The federal and supranational courts examined were clearly under both legal and political restrictions. Not only are they bound to find links to state action in order to have any jurisdiction in a case, but they were often experiencing periods of 'cautious federalism', when rulings which interfered with the private or civil law of States would not necessarily have been welcomed by the state governments concerned.

The perceived problematic of *Drittwirkung*, as it affects the European Convention on Human Rights, owes more to this 'cautious federalism' and certain legal restrictions found in the Convention itself than to any inherent value to be found in the public/private distinction. The supranational–Contracting State tension emerges neatly from an analysis of the case-law of the European Court of Justice. That Court is prepared to offer the highest protection to Community employees, and a reduced level of protection to Member State employees, with a further reduced level of protection granted to employees in the private sector. Setting aside the legal reasons for this division (which are nevertheless very important), we have to acknowledge that that Court is operating within a supranational legal order which relies heavily on national implementing measures (which usually take the form of legislation). The supranational Court cannot diminish the importance of this process by giving judgments which, in effect, actually usurp the legislative process. Therefore, whilst this Court can strike down Community legislation for non-conformity with fundamental rights, it must respect the fact that in this field the Member States' primary obligation may be to implement directives. Therefore, any legal duties which the Court wishes to impose flow from this obligation. In this way directly enforceable duties are placed on the State where it has failed to implement a directive. Private bodies, while owing some duties under Community law, are not obliged to introduce implementing legislation. In most fields private bodies cannot simply introduce the implementing measures on their own. Saddling private bodies with obligations contained in those directives would seem to pre-empt the discretion allowed to States in the choice of manner of implementation.

This area of discretion finds its counterpart, if not its equivalent, in the 'margin of appreciation' doctrine developed by the European Commission and Court of Human Rights. This doctrine reminds us that supranational supervision of the Convention is limited, to the extent that the European Court of Human Rights is not prepared to legislate for the Contracting States. Although the European Court of Human Rights is not constrained by the need to respect the normal process of implementing Community directives through national measures, it is instead likely to be confronted by Contracting States who claim the need to protect such values as morals and the rights of others. The European Court of Human Rights is sensitive to these claims. Finding a uniform European standard (in the twenty-six Member States of the Council of Europe) in matters such as obscenity, illegitimacy, homosexuality, compensation for the nationalization of property, and the rights of transsexuals is not always obvious or easy. The European Court of Human Rights does not deal with harmonized provisions such as those which are actually agreed to by the Member States themselves under the Community legislative process. Furthermore,

Member States often claim to be in a better position than international judges to assess the national reality of a 'pressing social need' for the national measures which are claimed to violate the Convention.

Similarly, the European Court of Human Rights is hesitant about second-guessing a decision of a national court. As most applications of human rights in the private sphere in Strasbourg will involve reviewing a national court's decision in a private law matter, it is unlikely that the Commission and Court will 'privatize' human rights so that every dispute between individuals becomes a potential case at the international level. Nevertheless, in the *Markt Intern* case the Court was split down the middle on the necessity of the national court's injunction preventing publication of the consumer complaints. This was essentially a private law dispute between two private parties.

Both European Courts therefore allow States a margin of discretion and it is suggested that this margin will certainly be wider when we are dealing with situations involving human rights in the private sphere. For the European Court of Human Rights these situations arise principally in two ways: first, when the Court decides whether a State has violated the Convention through its failure to fulfil its positive obligations to take the necessary measures to guarantee that Convention rights are enjoyed in the private sphere, and second, where the Court reviews the decision of a national court in a private dispute or examines the lack of a recourse to a national authority in a matter concerning the protection of Convention rights or their equivalent against abuse by private individuals.

As regards the first category of situations, there is now no doubt that, according to the European Court of Human Rights, the Convention creates obligations for States which may involve the adoption of measures 'even in the sphere of the relations of individuals between themselves' (*X and Y* v. *The Netherlands*, para. 23). These measures have to go beyond the mere availability of a remedy, and, in the context of Article 8, they must be 'designed to secure respect for private life' (*X and Y* v. *The Netherlands*, para. 23). In the context of Article 11 the Convention may require 'positive measures to be taken, even in the sphere of relations between individuals, if need be' (*Plattform Ärzte*, para. 32). Close examination of these phrases suggests that the state obligation is more than a duty to provide a forum for the resolution of the dispute. The obligation extends to taking preventive action. The obligation to 'secure respect' goes beyond providing reparation for damage suffered. And the obligation to take 'positive measures' may mean actual expenditure and the deployment of resources to ensure that the right can be freely exercised without interference from private individuals.

As regards the second category, the Court's decision in the *Markt Intern* case shows that, although private law decisions can be reviewed in

Strasbourg, the Court's members are divided as to the appropriateness of reviewing discretionary decisions taken by national authorities. If and when the minority in the *Markt Intern* case becomes the majority, we may expect to start getting authoritative statements about the way Convention rights operate in the private sphere. For the moment, the reports of the Commission provide the only guidance.

Where there is no national authority competent to grant an effective remedy for a breach of a Convention right by a private individual it is suggested that this may give rise to a violation of Article 13 at the international level in Strasbourg.[1]

Where human rights operate at the national level and free from what Mr Raymond (Deputy Secretary of the European Commission of Human Rights) calls 'des raisons techniques de compétence'[2] such as those found in Articles 19 and 25 ECHR, all the arguments put forward in this book point towards applying human rights in the private sphere. At the national level we find none of the restrictions or difficulties mentioned above. Unfortunately, it is likely that the rulings of the supranational courts will have most influence in this area; human rights norms will continue to be traditionally perceived as usually only applicable against state entities. We noted that the European Court of Human Rights has explicitly referred to the application by national courts of the Convention in relations between individuals, but this European Court is unlikely to be greatly influenced by national theories concerning the application of human/ constitutional rights as it has to consider the Contracting States' obligations rather than an individual's constitutional duties. The success of the privatization of human rights through the European Convention will primarily depend on the particular national legal order. This study has examined in some detail the United Kingdom's legal order. In the United Kingdom the lack of a Bill of Rights means that the Convention is of particular relevance, as an aid to interpretation when courts consider statutes or the Common Law. Bearing in mind that there is an under-developed division between public and private law in the United Kingdom, the path is open for an application of the Convention in both the private and public spheres. In addition, the incorporation of Community law through legislation, together with the case-law of the ECJ, means that the Convention has to be taken into consideration by the United Kingdom courts, at least when a case concerns the direct effect of Community

---

[1] Although the Court has assimilated an 'unarguable claim' under Art. 13 to a 'manifestly inadmissible' application, the two terms are not congruent and there is still room for Art. 13 violations where the claim concerning the substantive right may be declared inadmissible. See *Powell and Rayner*, Series A, vol. 172, para. 33.

[2] Raymond (1988: 533); see also Raymond (1980: 170).

provisions or their implementation through national legislation or other measures. Again the sphere of Community law cuts through classic public/private boundaries.

Even if the civil law distinction between public and private law is still firmly established on the Continent, at both the theoretical and procedural levels, this does not mean that human rights, or the Convention, have been confined to the field of public law. The Continental division between public and private law can be traced to a number of factors including Justinian's separation of the *Institutes* from the *Corpus iuris*, a mistrust by the French revolutionaries of the *parlements*, and a timidity on the part of jurists about challenging the authority of the State.[3] However, it was never intended to remove the sphere of private law from the rule of law; rather the intention was to remove the sphere of public law from the judges. There is no reason to believe that the Convention need be imprisoned in the field of public law or that the newly emerging field of British administrative law provides a watertight receptacle into which the Convention can be conveniently poured and stored away. The public/private law distinction need have no relevance for the operation of the Convention, and national courts are more and more likely to find it invoked in private litigation.

To adopt the phraseology of Professor Frowein (1986: 302), we can expect a 'dialectical development' whereby the national courts adjudicate private disputes so as to conform with the States' international obligations as interpreted by Strasbourg, and the Strasbourg organs in turn take these developments as evidence of an evolving European interpretation of the rights under the Convention, thereby reinforcing their own case-law concerning the applicability of the Convention to relations between individuals. This self-referential process illustrates the symbiotic nature of the Convention, which is both its strength and its weakness. The Convention's zenith will come when human rights violations are prevented through potential violators fearing immediate sanctions by the national courts. The risk in the present context is that with national courts following Strasbourg following national developments, we finish with a dog chasing its tail and no explanation as to how the Convention can be used to solve private disputes.

Throughout this study various legal systems have been mined in the search for the building blocks with which to lay the foundations for a Convention which protects the victims of all human rights abuses and not only those emanating from state organs. The proposed ground plan ignores

---

[3] See A. Watson, *The Making of the Civil Law* (Cambridge, Mass.: Harvard University Press, 1981), 144; R. David and J. E. C. Brierley, *Major Legal Systems of the World Today* (London: Stevens, 1985), 60–1.

the boundaries between public and private law. Perhaps we can now sketch in the outer limits of the Convention's territory and some of the new areas which might fall within them.

Returning to the importance which Community law gives to imposing duties on transnational actors we might foresee new uses for the Convention without straying outside the established case-law. Synthesizing the Commission's reasoning *ratione loci* in the *W.* v. *Ireland* decision (Applic. 9360/81) and the Court's reasoning concerning jurisdiction in *Soering*, together with the developments concerning positive obligations to legislate/ regulate as stated in *X and Y* v. *The Netherlands* and *Powell and Rayner*, one can imagine that an application could be brought under the Convention for the consequences of a company's actions in State A due to a failure by State B to legislate. In this way a Bhopal-type situation, with the polluter essentially under the control of a State which is not the one where the violation occurred, could be covered by the Convention.[4] Such cases are of more than merely theoretical interest. The elimination of barriers to transfrontier trade in Europe will mean that national authorities will be less able to control activities on their territory where the actors are non-nationals from companies incorporated in a different State.[5] The human rights questions go beyond environmental pollution and potentially extend to broadcasting, data protection, and trade union rights, to name but a few areas.[6]

Second, the flexible approach towards bodies with a public function exhibited by the English courts suggests that formalistic distinctions need play no part at the jurisdictional stage in Strasbourg. Applications need not be dismissed *ratione personae* where the violation can be directly attributed to a 'private person'. Once we admit the 'ecological liability' of the State for all human rights violations, the questions which remain are: could action by the State have reasonably prevented this violation? and has the State implemented a remedy so that such violations can be compensated? This suggested shift in emphasis takes place in the context of the privatizing of what were once considered the functions of the State. This means that remedies which attached to the execution of those functions may have to be carried over to the private sphere. In the United Kingdom not only have we witnessed the privatization of essential services such as water, gas, and electricity, but the Administration has deregulated and reregulated various sectors so that, for example, immigration is to

---

[4] According to D. H. Ott such responsibility does not arise under the current state of international law, which would impose no responsibility on the USA for having failed to regulate the parent company in the Bhopal context (1987: 175).

[5] It is clear that the harmonization of European company law or the inplementation of the European Company Statute are long-term projects which are riddled with difficulties.

[6] See generally the series *European Union: The Human Rights Challenge* (Baden-Baden: Nomos, 1991) and esp. Cassese, Clapham, and Weiler (1991: 1–75).

some extent now the responsibility of the airlines,[7] the stock market is supervised by a non-statutory body (the Panel for Take-Overs and Mergers),[8] and the privatization of punishment is quite feasible.[9]

Third, bearing in mind the success of some of the interest groups and the civil rights tradition in America we might revisit a new use for the Convention which was suggested in 1977. Anne Williams, in an article published in that year, drew inspiration from the strategies of groups of lawyers, such as the Lawyers' Committee for Civil Rights under Law, which had co-ordinated cases designed to force the United States and its citizens to curtail support for South Africa.[10] In a number of cases brought in domestic courts the Committee used various laws (state, federal, international) to attack the actions of private actors which, directly or indirectly, supported South Africa. Williams suggests that, by analogy, the Convention can be used to counter apartheid where it is reliant on advertising in the European media, as well as challenging 'attempts by Arab nations to exlude Jews from European organizations and corporations'.[11] South African adverts for tourism and employment meant 'no blacks need apply'.[12]

According to Williams, 'such advertisements published under the rights accorded by Article 10, constitute violations of Articles 3, 10, 11 and 14 of the Convention. Under such conditions, articles 1 and 17 may obligate States bound by the Convention to eliminate South African advertising.' The legal basis for this conclusion is the assertion that Article 17 read together with Article 1 implies that Article 17 not only furnishes States with a defence against applications, but it also leads to positive obligations on States. These positive obligations include introducing domestic legislation and active prosecution under existing domestic laws. In addition Williams concludes that under the Convention there exists the possibility of 'direct domestic action' against private bodies in breach of their duties under the Convention.

Williams's conclusion that both the domestic and international fora are

---

[7] See D. Burgess, 'Asylum by Ordeal', *NLJ* (1991), 52–4, where the author asks, 'With Government having so successfully contracted out immigration control to the airlines, what if any is the role of the European Human Rights Convention?' (at 52).

[8] For other examples see Lewis (1989: 219–45): 'My conclusions can be stated quite briefly. The first is that there is no clear divide between the public and private spheres. The public interest in the general governance of the nation is extensive, in fact unlimited. We should not, in particular, be confused by the labels ordinarily attached to functions as being distinctly private or public' (at 244–5).

[9] See M. Ryan and T. Ward, 'Privatising Punishment', *Parliamentary Quarterly* (1988), 86–9. The first private prison opened in the UK in Apr. 1992.

[10] 1977: 279–92; see also R. B. Lillich, 'The Role of Domestic Courts in Promoting International Human Rights Norms', *New York Law School Law Review* (1978), 153–77.

[11] At 280.

[12] Although the apartheid laws are gradually being dismantled apartheid-type discrimination is still applicable to many spheres inside South Africa.

open 'to those who wish to prevent individuals from destroying the human rights under the Convention' is unobjectionable. Nevertheless, thirteen years on, her reliance on Article 17 would not seem to be a useful approach. Furthermore, we are now in a position to point to a number of political and legal factors which weigh against such a creative suggestion that human rights abroad can be enhanced through the Convention at the national and international levels.

First, judges in the Council of Europe Member States are traditionally unenthusiastic about actively interfering in policy decisions of national government. Indeed, as was seen in Chapter 1, the United Kingdom's courts currently do not even require Ministers to have regard to the Convention when exercising discretion in individual cases. To expect that they would enforce a positive obligation on the Government to enhance human rights abroad by bringing prosecutions against companies which aggravate the continued breaches of such rights is not yet realistic.

Nevertheless, Williams's thesis is useful as it could provide extra arguments for an organization (private or public) which seeks to restrict freedom of expression in its contribution to the fight against apartheid. An obvious example would be a newspaper refusing to publish adverts connected with South Africa.[13]

At the international level the prospects are even less promising. First, the European Court of Human Rights, although ready in the *Soering* case to intervene in a foreign policy decision, is unlikely actually to demand that governments act *vis-à-vis* human rights violations where the victims are outside the jurisdiction of the Member States. Admittedly offensive employment advertisements which were indeed closed to Blacks or other protected classes could constitute inhuman or degrading treatment for those within the jurisdiction of the Member State which permitted such advertising. But the better strategy would be to claim that this was a breach of the guarantee in Article 3, in those cases where the State had

---

[13] An interesting case cited by Drzemczewski (1983: 212) is a decision of the Amsterdam Court of Appeal of 30 Oct. 1980. He explains it as follows: 'In this case the *Reclame Code Commissie (RCC)* (created by the private sector to control and evaluate commercial advertisements, the decisions of which bind all contracting parties) considered an advertisement requesting readers not to buy oranges from South Africa to be in breach of its "Commercial Code." This decision, in effect, prevented a private group, the *Boycot Outspan Aktie*, from placing the same advertisements in about 90 per cent of Dutch newspapers and periodicals. . . . the Court of Appeal . . . ordered that the *RCC* decision be ignored by the press as it infringed the right of free speech which is protected by, among other sources, Article 10 of the European Convention.' Although this case does not touch on Williams's point, her argument could be used to differentiate this case from one where advertisers were banned because of their South African sympathies rather than their antagonism. Compare the distinction made by J. E. S. Fawcett concerning the difference between Christians against Racism and Fascism and the National Front. Fawcett, relying on Art. 17, stated that the National Front alone would be denied the protection of the Convention (Fawcett 1987: 267).

refused to act, and that this constituted a violation by the State of Articles 1 and 3, and 13 if necessary. It is suggested that reliance on Article 17 would be misplaced and one cannot rely on this Article to bolster the positive obligations of the State. First, the obligations of the State arise through Article 1, which specifically refers to the rights contained in Articles 2–14. Second, the historical context of Article 17 was a fear of totalitarian political parties which would abuse the Convention to escape governmental control. Although the *Glimmerveen* application confirms that Article 17 covers racist behaviour, it remains within the context of a governmental defence rather than a fundamental positive obligation.

Questions of positive obligations are not as easily justiciable as questions of governmental restrictions on freedom of expression, the use of torture, etc., and there is ample evidence that the European Court of Human Rights would invoke the 'margin of appreciation' doctrine when faced with claims which demand governmental policy changes which *promote* the enjoyment of Convention rights in the private sphere, rather than merely ensuring that the protected rights are practical and effective. (See the *Case of Powell and Rayner* and the *Rees* and *Cossey* cases.) This reticence concerning active promotion of the enjoyment of rights such as the right to private and family life should be contrasted with the Court's willingness to intervene to oblige States to fill gaps in their legislation where an individual's private life has been violently attacked and the State has failed to provide the necessary preventive or reparatory legislation (*X and Y v. The Netherlands*).

The case-law suggests, then, that the Convention has a potential use in cases where the human rights abuse takes place in countries outside the Council of Europe. Where individual victims are threatened in a concrete way the Convention may intervene but its scope as an instrument of foreign commercial policy is less certain. Nevertheless there is room for such a development.

These suggestions inevitably lead to the outer limits of the privatization of human rights. It is clear that such developments create an extra strain on the role of the judge. Although admitting the application of human rights in the private sphere greatly increases the number of theoretical possibilities for rights claims, the political reality is that the judges cannot simply replace the legislators and policy-makers through invoking the duty to secure rights to everyone. A second limitation stems from the ideological and political resistance we encountered in Part II. One has to admit that the application of human rights in the private sphere not only means interference in the private, domestic, intimate, and economic spheres and therefore advances rather than rolls back the frontiers of the State, but it also takes one into conflicts where both sides are relying on fundamental, basic, natural rights which protect human dignity. The judicial choice becomes contentious rather than simply a question of defining the acceptability of state limitations on personal freedom.

But this difficulty may be more apparent than real. When examining the position of the State the court will often really be examining the human rights of other individuals in the collective. Cases where the State does not appear simply expose the conflict in clear terms. Nevertheless there are limits. Private bodies do not have the same duties as the State to protect life. Private associations may limit dissent in order to operate effectively. Private persons may withhold information from others. Private bodies may sometimes legitimately discriminate in order to achieve legitimate ends.

But these are the exceptions. The case-law of the two European Courts suggests that there is a trend towards recognizing the applicability of fundamental rights in the private sphere. We have seen that this application is not unproblematic as a publicization of the private may threaten freedom rather than enhance it. In Chapter 5 it was suggested that one solution might be to consider each rights claim in terms of the protection of dignity and democracy. The conclusion reached was that the enforcement of human rights is an attempt to protect *dignity* and *democracy*. It was suggested that by using these analytical tools we may discover the limits and extent to which the human rights norms contained in the European Convention can be applied to the private sphere; dignity has to be protected against everyone, yet where a right is being claimed in the context of the protection of democracy, a public element is needed. 'Public element' does not mean a nexus with the State, but an element of community or collective good.

In this reconstruction of the Convention from the bottom up a number of abstract theories have been applied in the design. But the furnishings will inevitably be provided by the applicants through the ever-increasing cases and controversies fought under the Convention. Claims that rights are violated in the private sphere are increasingly made, and the importance of recognizing these claims is now clearer than ever. Just as over 200 years ago various declarations of the Rights of Man were framed to meet the demands of the people, so the construction of today's human rights protection must adapt to include new demands.

It is suggested that judicial bodies dealing with allegations of human rights violations should discard the public/private distinction and examine the *harm to the victim*. Only then should they decide whether this sort of harm is covered by the European Convention on Human Rights. This would represent a shift in emphasis away from 'policing' state institutions and the search for 'guilty state actors' towards protection and reparation for those who suffer violations of their human rights as such. Evidence that this type of shift is already taking place elsewhere was present in the judgment of the Inter-American Court of Human Rights in the *Velásquez Rodríguez* v. *Honduras* case,[14] where the Court was faced with the difficulty of proving that the disappearance of Rodríguez had been carried out by state agents: 'The objective of international human rights law is not to punish those individuals who are guilty of violations, but rather to protect the victims and to provide for the reparation of damages resulting from the acts of the States responsible' (para. 134).

Finally, we might also put forward some more general conclusions:

1. The application of human rights in the private sphere squarely addresses the effectiveness of human rights protection and so goes some way to answering those critics who point to the empty formal nature of rights. The criticism is often based on the failure of a rights discourse to address *all* forms of oppression and suffering. This is particularly important in an era of powerful corporations, ambiguous state intervention, increasing privatization, and racial and sexual violence.

2. By suggesting that the State may violate human rights norms by its failure to tackle a situation involving 'private' interference with human rights, the application of human rights in the private sphere admits the importance of 'positive' liberty and not just the 'negative' liberty of freedom from state interference.

3. By jettisoning the state-nexus test as a jurisprudential trigger, the application of human rights in the private sphere demands a concentration on victims rather than on state actors. It is suggested that up till now the weakness of the Strasbourg machinery has been its over-concentration on the State's role at the expense of the victim. Although the Ninth Protocol (when it enters into force) will allow individuals to seise the Court under certain conditions, at present only the Commission or the relevant Contracting Party may do so (Article 48). Furthermore, the responsibility for all improvements to the Convention system rests with the Steering Committee for Human Rights, which is mostly composed of government agents whose experience of the Convention is often gained through defending their Government before the Commission and Court.

Of course it is inevitable that the Convention system should emphasize the role of governments, founded as it was by the Member States of the Council of Europe. However, it is hoped that this examination of the public/private distinction in the European Convention on Human Rights has demonstrated the need for a more victim-orientated approach at both the substantive and procedural levels. This is particularly evident in the present context, where the victim may not be able to pinpoint a responsible state actor, or the suffering may arise from the State being a *non-*

---

[14] Judgment of 29 July 1988 (emphasis added); for the text of the judgment see 28 *ILM* (1989) 291.

actor, that is, failing to act. The difficulty which the applicant may have in formulating the exact basis of state responsibility should not deprive a victim of protection under the Convention. The concept of 'ecological liability', which was referred to at the beginning of Chapter 7, and which presumes a responsibility on the part of the State for all abuses within its jurisdiction, would seem a good starting-point. Commencing with such liability is a way of shifting the burden of proof so that it is then for the State to show that the appropriate measures have already been taken to ensure respect for the Convention's rights in the private sphere.

4. The application of human rights in the private sphere suggests the need to address a number of procedural changes where rights are determined in a judicial forum. First, the role of interest groups may have to be facilitated by alleviating the requirement that applicants be victims of human rights violations.[15] Interest groups need to be able not only to support the rights of disparate individuals, but also to bring cases aimed at lacunae in the legislative framework of any one state. More generally, at the end of the twentieth century some of the main issues on the public agenda have been put there and articulated primarily by social movements. Questions relating to sexual politics, the environment, religious intolerance, humanitarian aid, and disarmament have originated in the private sphere yet require both a public and private response.

Secondly, procedural measures may have to be taken so that *amici curiae* briefs can be submitted both on the law and facts of the instant case, and on comparative law studies which encompass the law and practice in other jurisdictions. This last role is vital where the 'third-party' defendant is not actually represented before any of the adjudicating bodies (see Chapter 9).

5. The vocabulary of human rights has been dominated this century by the rhetoric and posturing of diplomats and state officials denigrating each others' systems in international fora such as the UN. However, the winds of change are quite detectable and more and more ordinary people now word their claims in terms of rights. Many demonstrations now rally around a rights banner. Although States still rely on human rights as a weapon with which to question each other's legitimacy, they are increasingly faced with a barrage of rights claims. If the emphasis shifts towards the victims' use of human rights the role of the State in this context may start to change. It will no longer be the State which positions itself at the centre of the rights discourse. In other words it is suggested that the State

---

[15] See *Klass* case: 'In principle it does not suffice for an individual applicant to claim that the mere existence of a law violates his rights under the Convention, it is necessary that the law should have been applied to his detriment' (judgment of 6 Sept. 1978, Series A, vol. 28, para. 33). This restriction has been interpreted fairly widely in subsequent cases and it is enough if the victim runs the risk of being subsequently affected by the law in question. See *Norris* case, judgment of 26 Oct. 1988, Series A, vol. 142, para. 33.

is losing its monopoly over the language of human rights—we may be witnessing a sort of 'privatization of human rights'.

Rather than diminishing the role of the State this process ought to highlight the fact that an important function of it ought to be the creation of the conditions in which each group and individual can achieve their own self-fulfilment. Because the obstacles to such autonomy often come from individuals and structures in the private sphere the State has to address these threats and create a climate which facilitates the attainment of such well-being.

On the other hand we should not focus too narrowly on the State as we risk missing some of the most pervasive threats to human dignity and possible ways to address them. Similarly the long-term solution may not always lie in state institutions but in group and individual self-reflection. When addressing human rights in the private sphere we have to consider the private morality of the indignities we subject others to as well as the public consequences of our private acts. Our private acts must respect each other's dignity; and our public decisions must consider our collective goals.

6. Running counter to these trends we have discovered the restraint of supranational judicial bodies in relation to interference with state 'autonomy'. This is particularly acute in the context of applying human rights in the private sphere, as it means attempting to 'harmonize' or 'unify' the private/civil/labour law of very diverse countries. However, it is suggested that this problem has been overstated in the past. The European Convention on Human Rights does not attempt to rewrite the laws of murder, rape, theft, industrial relations, divorce, child care, privacy, etc.; what it does is guarantee a *minimum degree of protection*. There would only be real cause for concern should States become prohibited from taking steps to ensure greater protection than that enunciated by the Strasbourg organs.

7. A further danger which arises from the application of human rights to the private sphere is that human rights come to be seen by some as tools of oppression rather than as instruments of liberation. This is especially so in the context of the changes in Central and Eastern Europe. Hungary, Poland, and Bulgaria are now all parties to the Convention. States such as Romania have had constitutionally protected rights for years, but the people came to equate rights such as the 'right to work' with 'the duty to work anywhere the State decided to send you'. Duties under the Romanian Constitution included the duty of every citizen to obey the Constitution, 'to defend Socialist Property', and to 'contribute towards strengthening and developing the Socialist system'.

One could merely suggest that it is too early for some countries to accept human rights duties in the 'private sphere', but the economic programmes in the ex-Communist States currently favour privatization over social protection, and, considering some of the racial and sexual prejudice which is currently resurfacing in Europe, and especially in the 'new democracies', the privatization of human rights may serve a useful role by filling the legislative vacuum left when the deregulation programmes are completed.

The dangers of the privatization of human rights are particularly acute where human rights norms are invoked against associations. Should associations which form in order to provide a collective defence for their members' interests be prevented from operating effectively by the unnecessary application of human rights regulation, then we will be faced with the re-emergence of the abuse of the human rights discourse. It is suggested that as long as the application of human rights in the private sphere is limited to the protection of dignity and democracy then we can avoid unduly over-regulating that area. Of course, trade unions are not permitted to discriminate on grounds of race or sex, but they may not be under the same obligations as government to supply information about their activities to others. On balance, the educational advantages of demanding that everyone seek to respect the rights in the Convention outweigh the disadvantages that such an extension of duties might suggest. Several commentators complain that continually proclaiming new rights and duties 'dilutes' their effectiveness. It is said that too much rights talk diminishes the essential message. The thesis here is not that we should add more rights to the list, but that the rights that are protected in the European Convention on Human Rights should be enforceable in such a way as to ensure their real and effective protection. Rights should not operate in the arbitrary, discriminatory way which has traditionally meant that they may only operate against the State and its organs. The challenge will be to ensure that human rights are enforced in order to protect the values of dignity and democracy, and that no flexible public/private distinction is introduced in order to carve out privileges and immunities for anyone.

8. Lastly, an examination of the public/private issue in the application of the European Convention on Human Rights demonstrates how much the emphasis in international law is geared to actors, in particular state actors, at the expense of concern for victims. This is a particularly difficult *problématique* to escape from, as those who fashion and shape international law are the States themselves. As the European Convention on Human Rights operates at both the national and international level, there is a chance that a shift towards 'victim concern' could in some way come to influence international law generally. Only as the international community becomes more concerned about the victims of oppression will headway be made towards a just and peaceful community of mankind.

Select Bibliography

BOOKS AND ARTICLES

ABERNATHY, M. (1977), *Civil Liberties under the Constitution* (3rd edn. New York: Harper & Row).

—— (1983), 'Should the United Kingdom Adopt a Bill of Rights?', *AJCL* 431.

ALDER, J. (1986), 'Public and Private Law Remedies against the Crown and its Servants: The Question of Interim Relief', *CJQ* 218.

ALKEMA, E. A. (1978), *Studies over Europese Grondrechten* (Deventer: Kluwer).

—— (1988), 'The Third-Party Applicability or "Drittwirkung" of the European Convention on Human Rights', in Matscher and Petzold (1988: 33).

ARNOLD, C. (1984), 'Analyses of Right', in Kamenka & Tay (1984: 74).

ARNULL, A. (1985), 'Making the European Convention Work', *PL* 376.

—— (1987), 'The Incoming Tide: Responding to Marshall', *PL* 383.

BARBOZA, J. (1984), 'The International Personality of the Individual', in *Studi in onore di Giuseppe Sperduti* (Milan: Giuffrè), 375.

BARENDT, E. (1987), 'Free Speech in the Universities', *PL* 344.

BARSOTTI, R. (1984), 'Per una protezione più efficace dei diritti e delle libertà fondamentali: La tutela dalla offese provenienti da persone private,' in *Studi in onore di Giuseppe Sperduti* (Milan: Giuffrè), 395.

BAYEFSKY, A. F., and EBERTS, M. (1985), *Equality Rights and the Canadian Charter of Rights and Freedoms* (Toronto: Carswell).

BEATSON, J. (1987), ' "Public" and "Private" in English Administrative Law', *LQR* 34.

BEDAU, H. A. (1984), 'Why do we Have the Rights we do?', 1(2) *SP & P.* 56.

BENN, S. I. (1988), *A Theory of Freedom* (Cambridge: Cambridge University Press).

—— and GAUS, G. F. (1983) (eds.), *Public and Private in Social Life* (London: Croom Helm).

BERAUD, J. M. (1986), 'Aspects de la liberté syndicale au sens de la Convention européenne des droits de l'homme', *Droit social*, 384.

BERCUSSON, B. (1988), 'Economic Policy: State and Private Ordering', in Daintith (1988: 359).

BERENSTEIN, A. (1981), 'Economic and Social Rights: Their Inclusion in the European Convention on Human Rights: Problems of Formulation and Interpretation', *HRLJ* 257.

BERGER, V. (1989), *The Case Law of the European Court of Human Rights*, i: *1960–1987* (Dublin: Round Hall Press).

BERNHARDT, R., and JOLOWICZ, J. A. (1987) (eds.), *International Enforcement of Human Rights* (Berlin: Springer-Verlag).

BETTEN, L. (1985), *The Right to Strike in Community Law* (Amsterdam: Elsevier Science Publishing).

—— and KORTE, J. (1987), 'A Procedure for Preliminary Rulings in the Context of Merger', *HRLJ* 75.

BIRKENSHAW, P. (1988), *Freedom of Information: The Law, the Practice and the Ideal* (London: Weidenfeld and Nicolson).

BISCOTTINI, G. (1981), *La Convenzione europea de diritti dell'uomo nell'applicazione giurisprudenziale in Italia* (Milan: Giuffrè).

BLACK, C. (1973), 'Is there already a British Bill of Rights?', 89 *LQR* 173.

BLACKBURN, R. W. (1984), 'F. A. Hayek and British Constitutionalism', *PL* 410.

—— and TAYLOR, J. (1991) (eds.), *Human Rights for the 1990's* (London: Mansell).

BLOM COOPER, L. (1986), 'The Role of the Judge in Modern Society', *PQ* 144.

BOSSUYT, M. J. (1987), *Guide to the 'Travaux préparatoires' of the International Covenant on Civil and Political Rights* (Dordrecht: Martinus Nijhoff).

BOUCAUD, P. (1989), *The Council of Europe and Child Welfare: The Need for a European Convention on Children's Rights*, Human Rights File no. 10 (Strasbourg: Council of Europe).

BOURNE, C. (1990), 'Equal Pay: I and II', *NLJ* 1240, 1286.

BOYLE, A. (1984), 'Administrative Justice, Judicial Review and the Right to a Fair Hearing under the European Convention on Human Rights', *PL* 89.

BREITENMOSER, S., and WILMS, G. E. (1990), 'Human Rights v. Extradition: The *Soering* Case', 11 *Michigan Journal of International Law*, 845.

BRIDGE, Lord (1984), 'Attempts towards a European Constitution in the Light of the British Legal System', in J. Schwarze and R. Bieber (eds.), *Eine Verfassung für Europa* (Baden-Baden: Nomos), 115.

BROWNLIE, I. (1979), *Principles of Public International Law* (3rd edn. Oxford: Clarendon Press).

—— (1981), *Basic Documents on Human Rights* (2nd edn. Oxford: Clarendon Press).

—— (1983a), *Basic Documents in International Law* (3rd edn. Oxford: Clarendon Press).

—— (1983b), *State Responsibility*, part 1 (Oxford: Clarendon Press).

BRUDER, A. (1985), 'The Domestic Enforcement of International Covenants on Human Rights: A Theoretical Framework', *University of Toronto Law Journal*, 215.

BRUNER, A. (1985), 'Sexual Orientation and Equality Rights', in Bayefski and Eberts (1985: 457).

BUERGENTHAL, T. (1964), 'The Domestic Status of the European Convention on Human Rights', 13 *Buffalo Law Review*, 354.

—— (1965), 'The Effect of the European Convention on Human Rights on the Internal Law of the Member States', *ICLQ* supp. 11: 79.

—— (1981), 'To Respect and Ensure: State Obligations and Permissible Derogations', in L. Henkin (ed.), *The International Bill of Rights* (New York: Columbia UP), 72.

BULLINGER, M. (1985), 'Freedom of Expression and Information an Essential Element of Democracy', *GYIL* 88.

BUQUICCHIO-DE BOER, M. (1988), 'Children and the European Convention on Human Rights', in Matscher and Petzold (1988: 73).

BURKENS, M. C. B. (1982), 'The Complete Revision of the Dutch Constitution', 29 *NILR* 323.

BURNS, J. H. (1972), 'The Rights of Man since the Reformation', in Vallet (1972: 16).

BYRNE, A. (1988), *Human Rights at the Workplace* (Longmead: Blackmore Press).

CAMPBELL, T. (1983), *The Left and Rights: A Conceptual Analysis of the Idea of Socialist Rights* (London: Routledge & Kegan Paul).

—— (1986) (ed.), *Human Rights: From Rhetoric to Reality* (Oxford: Basil Blackwell).

CANE, P. (1987), 'Public and Private Law: A Study of the Analysis and Use of a Legal Concept', in Eekelaar and Bell (1987: 57).

CAPPELLETTI, M. (1971), *Judicial Review in the Contemporary World*, (Indianapolis: Bobbs-Merrill).

—— (1978) (ed.), *Access-to-Justice* Project, 4 vols., 6 books (Milan: Guiffrè & Sijthoff and Noordhoff).

—— (1981) (ed.), *Access to Justice and the Welfare State* (Alphen aan den Rijn: Sijthoff and Noordhoff & Bruylant).

—— (1985), 'Repudiating Montesquieu? The Expansion and Legitimacy of "Constitutional Justice"', *Catholic University Law Review*, 1.

—— (1987), 'Is the European Court of Justice "Running Wild"?', *ELR* 1.

—— (1989), *Judicial Process in Comparative Perspective* (Oxford: Clarendon Press).

—— and GARTH, B. (1985), 'Finding an Appropriate Compromise: A Comparative Study of Individualistic Models and Group Rights in Civil Procedure', *CJQ* 111.

—— —— and TROCKER, N. (1982), 'Access to Justice: Variations and Continuity of a World Movement', *Rabels Zeitschrift*, 677.

—— and GOLAY, D. (1986), 'The Judicial Branch in the Federal and Transnational Union: Its Impact on Integration', in Cappelletti, Seccombe, and Weiler (1986: vol. i, book 2, p. 261).

—— SECCOMBE, M., and WEILER, J. H. H. (1986) (eds.), *Integration through Law: Europe and the American Federal Experience* (Berlin: Walter de Gruyter).

CARTY, H. (1984), 'The Legality of Peaceful Picketing on the Highway', *PL* 600.

CASSESE, A. (1979, 1980) (ed.), *The New Humanitarian Law of Armed Conflict* (2 vols. Naples: Scientifica).

—— (1984), 'The International Community, Terrorism and Human Rights', in *Studi in onore di Giuseppe Sperduti* (Milan: Giuffrè), 475.

—— (1986), *International Law in a Divided World* (Oxford: Clarendon Press).

—— (1987*a*), *Il caso 'Achille Lauro'* (Rome: Riuniti).

—— (1987*b*), *Violence and Law in the Modern Age* (Cambridge: Polity Press).

—— (1989), 'A New Approach to Human Rights: The European Convention for the Prevention of Torture', 83 *AJIL* 128.

—— (1990), *Human Rights in a Changing World* (Cambridge: Polity Press).

—— (1991), 'Can the Notion of Inhuman and Degrading Treatment Apply to Socio Economic Conditions?, *European Journal of International Law* (forthcoming).

—— and CLAPHAM, A. (1990) (eds.), *Transfrontier Television in Europe: The*

Human Rights Dimension (Baden-Baden: Nomos).

CASSESE, A., CLAPHAM, A., and WEILER, J. (1991), '1992: What Are our Rights?', in A. Cassese, A. Clapham, and J. Weiler (eds.), *European Union: The Human Rights Challenge*, ii: *Human Rights and the European Community: Methods of Protection* (Baden-Baden, Nomos), 1.

CASSIN, R. (1951), 'La Déclaration universelle at la mise en œuvre des droits de l'homme', 2 *RCDI* 241.

CHRISTIAN, T. J., and EWING, K. D. (1987), 'Labouring under the Canadian Constitution', *CLJ* 195.

CHURCHILL, R., and FOSTER, N. (1987), 'Double Standards in Human Rights? The Treatment of Spanish Fishermen by the European Community', *ELR* 430.

CLIFFORD, K. A., and INCULANO, R. P. (1987), 'Aids and Insurance: The Rationale for Aids-Related Testing', 100 *Harvard Law Rev.* 1806.

COHEN-JONATHAN, G. (1991), 'Responsabilité pour atteinte aux droits de l'homme', in *La Responsabilité dans le système international*, Société Française pour le Droit International (Paris: Pédone), 101.

—— and EISSEN, M.-A. (1985), *Droits de l'homme en France: Dix ans d'application de la Convention européenne des droits de l'homme devant les juridictions judiciaires françaises* (Kehl am Rhein: N. P. Engel).

COHN, H. H. (1983), 'On the Meaning of Human Dignity', *Israel Yearbook of Human Rights* 228.

Committee on the Administration of Justice (1984), 'A Bill of Rights for Northern Ireland' (available from the CAJ, Belfast).

—— (1985), 'Ways of Protecting Minority Rights in Northern Ireland' (available from the CAJ, Belfast).

CONDORELLI, L. (1988), 'L'Imputation à l'État d'un fait internationalement illicite: Solutions classiques et nouvelles tendances', 189(6) *RCDI* 9.

CONKLIN, W. E. (1979), *In Defence of Fundamental Rights* (Alphen aan den Rijn: Sijthoff and Noordhoff).

COOPER, J. (1986), 'Public Interest Lawyers', in Cooper and Dhavan (1986: 161).

—— and DHAVAN, R. (1986) (eds.), *Public Interest Law* (Oxford: Basil Blackwell).

CORTNER, R. (1981), *The Supreme Court and the Second Bill of Rights* (Madison, Wis.: University of Wisconsin Press).

CRANSTON, M. (1973), *What Are Human Rights?* (London: Bodley Head).

CROSSICK, S., and KARPENSTEIN, P. (1981), 'Pleading Human Rights in the British Courts: The Impact of EEC Law', *Law Society Gazette* (28 Jan. 1981), 90.

CUMMINS, R. (1985), 'Constitutional Protection of Civil Liberties in France', *AJCL* 721.

—— (1986), 'The General Principles of Law, Separation of Powers and Theories of Judicial Decisions in France', *ICLQ* 594.

CURTIN, D. (1990), 'The Province of Government: Delimiting the Direct Effect of Directives in the Common Law Context', *ELR* 195.

CVETIC, G. (1987), 'Immigration Cases in Strasbourg: The Right to Family Life under Article 8 of the European Convention', *ICLQ* 647.

DAES, E.-I. A. (1983), *The Individual's Duties to the Community and the Limitations on Human Rights and Freedoms under Article 29 of the Universal Declaration of Human Rights* (New York: United Nations), E/CN.4/Sub.2/432/Rev.2.

DAINTITH, T. C. (1985), 'The Executive Power Today', in Jowell and Oliver (1985: 174).

—— (1988) (ed.), *Law as an Instrument of Economic Policy: Comparative and Critical Approaches* (Berlin: Walter de Gruyter).

DAUSES, M. (1985), 'The Protection of Fundamental Rights in the Community Legal Order', *ELR* 398.

DE MEYER, J. (1973), 'The Right to Respect for Family Life, Home and Communications in Relations between Individuals and the Resulting Obligations for States Parties to the Convention', in Robertson (1973*b*: 255).

DE MONTIGNY, Y. (1985), 'Section 23 and Equality Rights', in Bayefski and Eberts (1985: 565).

DENNING, A. (1980), *The Due Process of Law* (London: Butterworths).

DE SALVIA, M. (1979), 'La protezione dei diritti dell'uomo nel quadro della Convenzione europea e seconda il diritto Comunitario: Interferenze e problemi di coordinamento', *Diritto Comunitario e degli scambi internazionali*, 489.

DHAVAN, R., and PARTINGTON, M. (1986), 'Co-optation or Independent Strategy? The Role of Social Action Groups', in Cooper and Dhavan (1986: 236).

DICEY, V. A. (1889), *The Law of the Constitution* (5th edn. London: Macmillan).

DONNELLY, J. (1985), *The Concept of Human Rights* (London: Croom Helm).

DOURAKI, T. (1986), *La Convention européenne des droits de l'homme et le droit à la liberté de certains malades et marginaux* (Paris: Librairie Générale de Droit et de Jurisprudence).

DRZEMCZEWSKI, A. (1979), 'The European Human Rights Convention and Relations between Private Parties', 26 *NILR* 163.

—— (1980), 'The Sui Generis Nature of the European Convention on Human Rights', *ICLQ* 54.

—— (1981), 'The Domestic Application of the European Convention as European Community Law', *ICLQ* 118.

—— (1983), *European Human Rights Convention in Domestic Law* (Oxford: Clarendon Press).

—— (1987), 'The Growing Impact of the European Human Rights Convention upon National Case Law', *Law Society Gazette* (25 Feb 1987), 561.

—— (1988), 'Un État en violation de la Convention européenne des droits de l'homme: L'Exécution interne des décisions des institutions de Strasbourg', in Matscher and Petzold (1988: 149).

—— (1989), 'The Council of Europe's Position', in *The Implementation in National Law of the European Convention on Human Rights* (Copenhagen: Danish Centre for Human Rights), 22.

—— (1990), 'The Work of the Council of Europe's Directorate of Human Rights', *HRLJ* 89.

DUFFY, P. (1980), 'English Law and the European Convention on Human Rights', *ICLQ* 585.

—— (1983), 'Article 3 of the European Convention on Human Rights', *ICLQ* 316.

DURKHEIM, E. (1964), *The Division of Labour in Society*, tr. George Simpson (New York: Free Press of Glencoe).

DWORKIN, A. (1989), *Letters from a War Zone* (New York: E. P. Dutton).

362 Select Bibliography

Dworkin, G. (1988), *The Theory and Practice of Autonomy* (Cambridge: Cambridge University Press).

Dworkin, R. (1977), *Taking Rights Seriously* (London: Duckworth).

—— (1978), 'Liberalism', in Hampshire (1978: 113).

—— (1984), 'Rights as Trumps', in Waldron (1984).

—— (1985a), *A Matter of Principle* (Cambridge, Mass.: Harvard University Press).

—— (1985b), 'Do we have a Right to Pornography?', in Dworkin (1985a: 335).

—— (1986), *Law's Empire* (London: Fontana).

Easson, A. J. (1979), 'Can Directives Impose Obligations on Individuals?', *ELR* 67.

Eekelaar, J., and Bell, J. (1987), *Oxford Essays in Jurisprudence* (Oxford: Clarendon Press).

Eissen, M.-A. (1961), 'La Convention et les devoirs de l'individu', in *La Protection des droits de l'homme dans le cadre européen*, Travaux du colloque de Strasbourg de novembre 1960 (Paris: Pédone), 167.

—— (1962), 'The European Convention on Human Rights and the Duties of the Individual', 32 *Nordisk Tidsskrift for International Ret*, 229.

—— (1971), 'La Convention européenne des droits de l'homme et les obligations de l'individu: Une mise à jour', in *René Cassin*, iii. 151.

—— (1982), *La Convention européenne des droits de l'homme dans la jurisprudence française* (Bordeaux: Association d'Études et de Recherches de l'école Nationale).

Elkind, J. A., and Shaw, A. (1986), *A Standard for Justice: A Critical Commentary on the Proposed Bill of Rights for New Zealand* (Auckland: Oxford University Press).

Ely, J. H. (1980), *Democracy and Distrust* (Cambridge, Mass.: Harvard University Press).

Ennis, B. J. (1984), 'Effective Amicus Briefs', *Catholic University Law Review*, 603.

Evans, Sir Vincent (1979), 'The Practice of European Countries where Direct Effect is Given to the European Convention on Human Rights in Internal Law', in *Colloquy about the European Convention on Human Rights in Relation to Other International Instruments for the Protection of Human Rights*, Athens, 21–2 Sept. 1978 (Strasbourg: Council of Europe), 109.

Evrigenis, D. (1982), 'Recent Case-Law of the European Court of Human Rights on Articles 8 and 10 of the European Convention on Human Rights', *HRLJ* 121.

Ewing, K. D. (1987), 'Strike Snare', *Guardian* (30 Jan. 1987), 23.

—— (1988), 'Trade Unions and the Constitution: The Impact of the New Conservatives', in Graham and Prosser (1987: 135).

—— and Finnie, W. (1982), *Civil Liberties in Scotland* (Edinburgh: V. Green & Son).

—— and Gearty, C. A. (1990), *Freedom under Thatcher: Civil Liberties in Modern Britain* (Oxford: Clarendon Press).

—— and Napier, B. (1986), 'The Wapping Dispute and Labour Law', *CLJ* 285.

Favoreu, L., and Jolowicz, J. A. (1986) (eds.), *Contrôle juridictionnel des lois* (Paris: Economica et Presses Universitaires d'Aix-Marseille).

FAWCETT, Sir JAMES (1987), *The Application of the European Convention on Human Rights* (2nd edn. Oxford: Clarendon Press).

FINNIS, J. M. (1985), 'A Bill of Rights for Britain? The Moral of Contemporary Jurisprudence', 71 *Proceedings of the British Academy*, 303.

FITZGERALD, P., and LEOPOLD, M. (1987), *Stranger on the Line: The Secret History of 'Phone Tapping* (London: Bodley Head).

FLAUSS, J. F. (1983), 'Le Juge administrative français et la Convention européenne de droits de l'homme', *Actualité juridique: Droit administratif*, 389.

FORDE, M. (1982), 'The "Closed Shop" Case', *ILJ* 1.

—— (1984), 'European Convention on Human Rights and Labor Law', *AJCL* 301.

—— (1985), 'Non Governmental Interferences with Human Rights', 56 *BYIL* 253.

FOSTER, N. (1987), 'The European Court of Justice and the European Convention for the Protection of Human Rights', *HRLJ* 245.

FRIENDLY, H. (1982), 'The Public–Private Penumbra: Fourteen Years Later', 130 *University of Pennsylvania Law Review*, 1289.

FRITZ, C. J. (1981), 'An Entrenched Bill of Rights for the United Kingdom: The Constitutional Dilemma', *Anglo-American Law Review*, 105.

FROWEIN, J. A. (1986), 'Fundamental Human Rights as a Vehicle of Legal Integration in Europe', in Cappelletti, Seccombe, and Weiler (1986: vol. i, book 3, p. 300).

—— (1988), *The Legal Aspects of International Terrorism* (Dordrecht: Martinus Nijhoff).

—— SCHULHOFER, S., and SHAPIRO, M. (1986), 'The Protection of Fundamental Human Rights as a Vehicle of Integration', in Cappelletti, Seccombe, and Weiler (1986: vol. i, book 3, p. 231).

FUDGE, J. (1987), 'The Public/Private Distinction: The Possibilities of and the Limits to the Use of Charter Litigation to Further Feminist Struggles', *Osgoode Hall Law Journal*, 485.

FURMSTON, M. P., KERRIDGE, R., and SURFIN, B. (1983) (eds.), *The Effect on English Domestic Law of Membership of the European Communities and of Ratification of the European Convention of Human Rights* (The Hague: Martinus Nijhoff).

GAJA, G. (1988), 'Aspetti problematici della tutela dei diritti fondamentali nell'-ordinamento comunitario', 71 *Rivista di diritto internazionale*, 574.

GANSHOF DER MERSCH, W. J. (1983), 'Le Respect des droits fondamentaux de l'homme: Condition exigée du droit des États européens', *Revue de droit international et de droit comparé*, 9.

GEDDES, A. C. (1990), '*Foster v. British Gas*: Widening the Field of Direct Effect', *NLJ* 1611.

GEORGE, R. P. (1989), 'Individual Rights, Collective Interests, Public Law and American Policy', 8 *Law and Philosophy*, 254.

GEWIRTH, A. (1981), 'The Basis and Content of Human Rights', in Pennock and Chapman (1981: 119).

—— (1982), *Human Rights: Essays on Justification and Applications* (Chicago: University of Chicago Press).

GEWIRTH, A. (1984*a*), 'Are there any Absolute Rights?', in Waldron (1984: 91).
—— (1984*b*), 'The Epistemology of Human Rights', 1(2) *SP & P.* 1.
GHANDI, S. (1981), 'Interaction between the Protection of Fundamental Rights in the EEC and under the European Convention on Human Rights', *LIEI* 1.
GIBSON, D. (1982), 'The Charter of Rights and the Private Sector', 12 *Manitoba LR* 213.
GIFFORD, T. (1986), *Where's the Justice? A Manifesto for Law Reform* (Harmondsworth: Penguin).
GOODMAN, F. I. (1982), 'Professor Brest on State Action and Liberal Theory and a Postscript to Professor Stone', 130 *University of Pennsylvania Law Review*, 1331.
GOSTIN, L. (1988) (ed.), *Civil Liberties in Conflict* (London: Routledge).
GOULD, M. (1989), 'The European Social Charter and Community Law: A Comment', *ELR* 223.
GOULD, W. B. (1986), 'The Idea of the Job as Property in Contemporary America: The Legal and Collective Bargaining Framework', *Brigham Young University Law Review*, 885.
GRAHAM, C., and PROSSER, T. (1988), *Waiving the Rules: The Constitution under Thatcherism* (Milton Keynes: Open University Press).
GREENWOOD, C. (1987), 'Directives: Time to Retire', *CLJ* 9.
GRIFFITH, J. A. G. (1979), 'The Political Constitution', *MLR* 17.
—— (1985*a*), 'Judicial Decision Making in Public Law', *PL* 565.
—— (1985*b*), *The Politics of the Judiciary* (3rd edn. London: Fontana Press).
GROSZ, S., and HULTON, S. (1986), 'Using the European Convention on Human Rights', in Cooper and Dhavan (1986: 138).
GULLEFORD, K. (1986), *Data Protection in Practice* (London: Butterworths).
HAMPSHIRE, S. (1978) (ed.), *Public and Private Morality* (Cambridge: Cambridge University Press).
HARDEN, I., and LEWIS, N. (1986), *The Noble Lie* (London: Hutchinson).
HARLOW, C. (1980), ' "Public" and "Private" Law: Definition without Distinction', *MLR* 241.
HELD, D. (1991), *Political Theory Today* (Stanford, Calif.: Stanford University Press).
HENKIN, L. (1979), *The Rights of Man Today* (London: Stevens & Sons).
—— (1987), 'The International Bill of Rights', in Bernhardt and Jolowicz (1987: 1).
HEPPLE, B. (1987), 'The Crisis in EEC Labour Law', *Industrial Law Journal*, 77.
HEWITT, P. (1982), *The Abuse of Power* (Oxford: Martin Robertson).
HIRST, P. Q. (1986), *Law, Socialism and Democracy* (London: Allen & Unwin).
HIXSON, R. F. (1987), *Privacy in a Public Society* (New York: Oxford University Press).
HOGG, P. W. (1985), *The Constitutional Law of Canada* (Toronto: Carswell).
HOGWOOD, B. (1987), *From Crisis to Complacency* (Oxford: Oxford University Press).
HOLME, R., and ELLIOT, M. (1988) (eds.), *1688–1988: Time for a New Constitution* (Basingstoke: Macmillan).

Home Office (1976), *Legislation on Human Rights with Particular Reference to the European Convention: A Discussion Document* (London: HMSO).

HONORE, A. (1987), *Making Law Bind* (Oxford: Clarendon Press).

HORAN, M. J. (1976), 'Contemporary Constitutionalism and Legal Relationships between Individuals', 25 *ICLQ* 848.

HOVIUS, B. (1985), 'The Limitation Clauses of the European Convention on Human Rights: A Guide for the Application of Section 1 of the Charter', *Ontario Law Review*, 213.

International Institute of Human Rights (1969–72), *Amicorum discipulorumque liber* (4 vols. Paris: Pédone) (cited as *René Cassin*).

JACKSON, J. H. (1992), 'Status of Treaties in Domestic Legal Systems: A Policy Analysis', 86 *AJIL* 310.

JACKSON, P. (1979), *Natural Justice* (London: Sweet & Maxwell).

JACOBS, F. G. (1975), *The European Convention on Human Rights* (Oxford: Clarendon Press).

—— (1978), 'The Extension of the European Convention on Human Rights to Include Economic, Social and Cultural Rights', *HRR* 166.

—— and KARST, K. L. (1986), 'The "Federal" Legal Order: The U.S.A. and Europe Compared: A Juridical Perspective', in Cappelletti, Seccombe, and Weiler (1986: vol. i, book 1, p. 169).

JACONELLI, J. (1976), 'The European Convention on Human Rights: The Text of a British Bill of Rights', *PL* 226.

—— (1980), *Enacting a Bill of Rights* (Oxford: Clarendon Press).

JAKOSA, J. Y. (1984), 'Parsing Public from Private: The Failure of Differential State Action Analysis', 19 *Harv. CR-CLLR* 193.

JEAMMAUD, A. (1981), 'Convention européenne des droits de l'homme: Les Relations de travail et droit français', *Annales de l'Université Jean Moulin XVIII*, 71.

JONES, G. (1988), 'Government: Business Relations: A Large Gap in Constitutional Thinking', 3(1) *Constitutional Reform Centre Review*, 4.

JOWELL, J., and LESTER, A. (1987), 'Beyond *Wednesbury*: Substantive Principles of Administrative Law', *PL* 368.

—— and MCAUSLAN, M. (1984), *Lord Denning, the Judge and the Law* (London: Sweet & Maxwell).

—— and OLIVER, D. (1985) (eds.), *The Changing Constitution* (Oxford: Clarendon Press).

KAIRYS, D. (1982) (ed.), *The Politics of Law* (New York: Pantheon Books).

KAMENKA, E., and TAY, A. E.-S. (1984) (eds.), *Human Rights* (London: Edward Arnold).

KAMMINGA, M. (1990), 'Inter-State Accountability for Violations of Human Rights' (doctoral thesis, Erasmus University, Amsterdam; to be published by: University of Pennsylvania Press).

KENNEDY, D. (1982a), 'Legal Education as Training for Hierarchy', in Kairys (1982: 40).

—— (1982b), 'The Status of the Decline of the Public/Private Distinction', 130 *University of Pennsylvania Law Review*, 1349.

KERRIDGE, K. (1983), 'Incorporation of the European Convention on Human Rights into the United Kingdom Law', in Furmston, Kerridge, and Surfin (1983).

KHOL, A. (1971), 'The Protection of Human Rights in Relationships between Private Individuals: The Austrian Situation', in *René Cassin*, iii. 195.

KIDD, J. (1983), ' 'Twas Easier Said than Done: Britain and the European Convention on Human Rights', *Melbourne University Law Review*, 104.

KISS, A. C. (1971), 'La Protection des droits de l'homme dans les rapports entre personnes privées en droit international public', in *René Cassin*, iii. 215.

KLARE, K. E. (1982), 'The Public/Private Distinction in Labor Law', *University of Pennsylvania Law Review*, 1358.

KOMMERS, D. P. (1989), *The Constitutional Jurisprudence of the Federal Republic of Germany* (Durham, NC: Duke University Press).

KORTE, J. (1989), 'Towards a Citizens' Europe', 1 *Netherlands Quarterly of Human Rights*, 57.

KRÜGER, H.-C. (1980), 'The European Commission of Human Rights', *HRLJ* 66.

—— and BUQUICCIO-DE BOER, M. (1990), 'The Case-Law of the European Commission of Human Rights Concerning the Application of Article 10 ECHR', in Cassese and Clapham (1990: 97).

Labour Party (1976), *United Kingdom Charter of Human Rights: A Discussion Document* (London: Labour Party).

—— (1990), *The Charter of Rights: Guaranteeing Individual Liberty in a Free Society* (London: Labour Party).

LAUTERPACHT, H. (1950), *International Law and Human Rights* (London: Stevens & Sons).

LESTER, A. (1968), *Democracy and Individual Rights*, Fabian Tract no. 390 (London: Fabian Society).

—— (1984), 'Fundamental Rights: The United Kingdom Isolated?', 46 *PL* 56.

—— (1985), 'The Constitution, Decline and Renewal', in Jowell and Oliver (1985: 273).

—— (1988), 'Amici curiae: Third-Party Interventions before the European Court of Human Rights', in Matscher and Petzold (1988: 341).

—— CORNFIELD, J., DWORKIN, R., GOODHART, W., HEWITT, P., JOWELL, J., LACEY, N., PATCHETT, K., and SPENCER, S. (1990), *A British Bill of Rights* (London: Institute for Public Policy Research).

LEUPRECHT, P. (1988), 'The Protection of Human Rights by Political Bodies: The Example of the Committee of Ministers of the Council of Europe', in M. Nowak, D. Steurer, and H. Tretter (eds.), *Festschrift für F. Ermacora* (Kehl am Rhein: Engel), 95.

LEWAN, K. M. (1968), 'The Significance of Constitutional Rights for Private Law: Theory and Practice in West Germany', 17 *ICLQ* 571.

LEWIS, N. (1985), 'Who Controls Quangos and the Nationalized Industries?', in Jowell and Oliver (1985: 198).

—— (1989), 'Regulating Non-Government Bodies: Privatization, Accountability, and the Public–Private Divide', in J. Jowell and D. Oliver (eds.), *The Changing Constitution* (2nd edn. Oxford: Clarendon Press), 219.

LISTENER (1987), 'Would a Bill of Rights Politicise British Judges?' (17 Feb. 1987), 16.

LLOYD, Lord (1976), 'Do we Need a Bill of Rights?', *MLR* 121.

LOWE, N. V. (1983), 'The English Law of Contempt of Court and Article 10 of the European Convention on Human Rights', in Furmston, Kerridge, and Surfin (1984).

LUKES, S. (1985), *Marxism and Morality* (Oxford: Clarendon Press).

MCBRIDE, J., and NEVILLE BROWN, L. (1981), 'The United Kingdom, the European Community and the European Convention on Human Rights', *YEL* 167.

MCCLUSKEY, Lord (1987), *Law, Justice and Democracy* (London: BBC Publications).

MACDONALD, R. St J. (1987), 'The Margin of Appreciation in the Jurisprudence of the European Court of Human Rights', in *International Law at the Time of its Codification: Essays in Honour of Roberto Ago*, iii (Milan: Giuffrè), 187.

MCFARLANE, G. (1990), 'Indecency and Obscenity: The View from Europe', *NLJ* 50.

MACGOWAN, N., and QUINN, M. (1987), 'Could Article 30 Impose Obligations on Individuals?', *ELR* 163.

MACKIE, J. L. (1984), 'Can there be a Right-Based Moral Theory?', in Waldron (1984: 168).

MACKINNON, C. A. (1989), *Towards a Feminist Theory of the State* (Cambridge, Mass.: Harvard University Press).

MANCINI, G. F. (1980), 'Politics and the Judges: The European Perspective', *MLR* 1.

MANDEL, M. (1989), *The Charter of Rights and the Legalization of Politics in Canada* (Toronto: Wall & Thompson).

MANN, F. A. (1978), 'Britain's Bill of Rights', 94 *LQR* 512.

—— (1986), *Foreign Affairs in English Courts* (Oxford: Clarendon Press).

MARIE, J.-B. (1985), *Human Rights or a Way of Life in a Democracy* (Strasbourg: Council of Europe).

MATSCHER, F., and PETZOLD, H. (1988) (eds.), *Protecting Human Rights: The European Dimension (Studies in Honour of Gérard J. Wiarda)* (Cologne: Carl Heymanns Verlag KG).

MENDELSON, M. (1981), 'The European Court of Justice and Human Rights', *YEL* 121.

—— (1983), 'The Impact of European Community Law on the Implementation of the European Convention on Human Rights', *YEL* 99.

MERON, T. (1985), 'The Meaning and Reach of the International Convention on the Elimination of All Forms of Racial Discrimination', *AJIL* 283.

—— (1989), *Human Rights and Humanitarian Norms as Customary Law* (Oxford: Oxford University Press).

MERRILLS, J. G. (1988), *The Development of International Law by the European Court of Human Rights* (Manchester: Manchester University Press).

MIKAELSEN, L. (1980), *European Protection of Human Rights: The Practice and Procedure of the European Commission of Human Rights on the Admissibility of Applications from Individuals and States* (Alphen aan den Rijn: Sijtoff and Noordhoff).

MILLETT, T. (1987), 'European Community Law: Sex Equality and Retirement Age', *ICLQ* 616.

MILNE, A. J. M. (1977), 'Should we Have a Bill of Rights?', *MLR* 389.

—— (1986), *Human Rights and Human Diversity (An Essay in the Philosophy of Human Rights)* (Albany, NY: New York University Press).

MITCHELL, J. D. B. (1971), 'Some Aspects of the Protection of Individuals against Private Power in the United Kingdom', in *René Cassin*, iii. 234.

MORRIS, P. E. (1987), 'Sex Discrimination, Public Order and the European Court', *PL* 334.

—— and DAVID, P. W. (1987), 'Directives, Direct Effect and the European Court: The Triumph of Pragmatism—Pt II', *Business Law Review*, 116.

MORRISSON, C. C. (1981), *The Dynamics of Development in the European Convention on Human Rights Convention System* (The Hague: Martinus Nijhoff).

MUCHLINSKI, P. T. (1984), 'Improving the Protection of Human Rights' (book review), *MLR* 240.

—— (1985), 'The Status of the Individual under the European Covention on Human Rights and Contemporary International Law', *ICLQ* 376.

MUNRO, C. (1991), 'Press Freedom: How the Beast was Tamed', *MLR* 104.

NELSON, W. N. (1981), 'Human Rights and Human Obligations', in Pennock and Chapman (1981: 281).

NERKEN, I. (1977), 'A New Deal for the Protection of Fourteenth Amendment Rights: Challenging the Doctrinal Bases of the *Civil Rights Cases* and State Action Theory', 12 *Harv. CR-CLL Rev.* 297.

NEUBERGER, J. (1987) (ed.), *Freedom of Information . . . Freedom of the Individual* (London: Papermac).

NEVILLE BROWN, L. (1978), 'A Bill of Rights for the United Kingdom?', *Parliamentarian*, 79.

NICKEL-LANZ, C. (1978), 'Les Effets des droits fondamentaux dans les relations entre les personnes privées: Étude comparative' (on file at the European University Institute, Florence).

NISET, J. (1987), 'Droits de l'homme: Devoirs de l'homme', 40(2) *Studia diplomatica*, 123.

NORTON, P. (1982), *The Constitution in Flux* (Oxford: Martin Robertson).

O'DONNELL, T. A. (1982), 'The Margin of Appreciation Doctrine: Standards in the Jurisprudence of the European Court of Human Rights', *HRQ* 474.

O'HAGAN, T. (1984), *The End of Law?* (Oxford: Basil Blackwell).

OLIVER, D. (1986), 'Constitutional Reform: Means and Ends', *CLP* 131.

—— (1988), 'Politicians and the Courts', *Parliamentary Affairs*, 13.

O'MAHONY, P. J. (1980), *Multinationals and Human Rights* (Great Wakering: Mayhew McCrimmon Ltd.).

OTT, D. H. (1987), *Public International Law in the Modern World* (London: Pitman).

PALLISTER, A. (1971), *Magna Carta: The Heritage of Liberty* (Oxford: Clarendon Press).

PANNICK, D. (1987), *Judges* (Oxford: Clarendon Press).

PARTSCH, K. J. (1973), Written Communication, in Robertson (1973*b*: 275).

PATEMAN, C. (1983), 'Feminist Critiques of the Public/Private Dichotomy', in Benn and Gaus (1983: 281).

PENNOCK, J. R., and CHAPMAN, J. W. (1971) (eds.), *Nomos XIII: Privacy* (New York: Atherton Press).

—— —— (1973) (eds.), *Due Process* (New York: New York University Press).

—— —— (1981) (eds.), *Human Rights* (New York: New York University Press).

POULTER, S. M. (1986), *English Law and Ethnic Minority Customs* (London: Butterworths).

—— (1987), 'Ethnic Minority Customs, English Law and Human Rights', *ICLQ*.

PRECHAL, S. (1990), 'Remedies after *Marshall*', 27 *CML Rev.* 451.

RASMUSSEN, A. (1986), *On Law and Policy in the European Court of Justice: A Comparative Study in Judicial Policy Making* (Dordrecht: Martinus Nijhoff).

RAWLS, J. (1971), *A Theory of Justice* (Oxford: Oxford University Press).

RAYMOND, J. (1980), 'A Contribution to the Interpretation of Article 13 of the European Convention on Human Rights', 5 *HRR* 161.

—— (1988), 'L'Article 1 du Protocole additionnel et les rapports entre particuliers', in Matscher and Petzold (1988: 531).

RAZ, J. (1986), *The Morality of Freedom* (Oxford: Clarendon Press).

RE, L. (1984), 'The Amicus Curiae Brief: Access to the Courts for Public Interest Associations', *Melbourne University Law Review*, 522.

RIGAUX, F. (1990), *La Protection de la vie privée et des autres biens de la personalité* (Brussels: Bruylant).

RILEY, A. J. (1989), 'The European Social Charter and Community Law', *ELR* 80.

RIVERO, J. (1971), La Protection des droits de l'homme dans les rapports entre personnes privées', in *René Cassin*, iii. 311.

—— (1984), *Le Conseil Constitutionnel et les libertés* (Paris: Economica).

ROBERTSON, A. H. (1968a), *Human Rights in National and International Law*, 2nd International Colloquy about the European Convention on Human Rights, Vienna, 18–20 Oct. 1965 (Manchester: Manchester University Press).

—— (1968b), 'Some Reflexions on the History of Human Rights', in *Mélanges offerts à Polys Modinos: Problèmes des droits de l'homme et de l'unification européenne* (Paris: Pédone).

—— (1973a), *European Institutions* (London: Stevens & Sons).

—— (1973b), *Privacy and Human Rights*, 3rd International Colloquy about the European Convention on Human Rights, Brussels, 30 Sept.–3 Oct. 1970 (Manchester: Manchester University Press).

—— (1982), *Human Rights in the World* (2nd edn. Manchester: Manchester University Press).

—— and MERRILLS, J. G. (1990), *Human Rights in the World* (3rd edn. Manchester: Manchester University Press).

ROBERTSON, G. (1989), *Freedom, the Individual and the Law* (6th edn. London: Penguin).

—— and NICOL, A. G. L. (1990), *Media Law* (2nd edn. London: Longmans).

RÖLING, B. V. A. (1979), 'Aspects of the Criminal Responsibility for Violations of the Law of War', in Cassese (1979: 199).

ROSE, N. (1987), 'Beyond the Public/Private Division: Law, Power and the Family', in P. Fitzpatrick and A. Hunt (eds.), *Critical Legal Studies* (Oxford: Basil Blackwell), 61.

ROSENBLUM, N. L. (1988), *Another Liberalism: Romanticism and the Reconstruction of Liberal Thought* (Cambridge, Mass.: Harvard University Press).

SACHOV LANDAU, C. (1989), 'Reflections on the Two European Courts of Justice', in Y. Dinstein (ed.), *International Law at a Time of Perplexity* (Dordrecht: Kluwer), 772.

SAMUEL, G. (1987), ' "Le Droit subjectif" and English Law', *CLJ* 264.

SCANLON, T. M. (1973), 'Due Process', in Pennock and Chapman (1973: 93).

SCARMAN, Sir LESLIE (1974), *English Law: The New Dimension* (London: Stevens & Sons).

—— (1984), 'Britain and the Protection of Human Rights', *Cambrian Law Review*, 5.

—— (1987), 'Wright: How the Law Lords Got it Wrong', *The Times* (19 Aug. 1987), 10.

SCHACHTER, O. (1981), 'The Obligation to Implement the Covenant in Domestic Law', in L. Henkin (ed.), *The International Bill of Rights* (New York: Columbia UP), 311.

SCHERMERS, H. G. (1986), 'Human Rights in Europe', *LS* 170.

—— (1990), 'The European Communities Bound by Fundamental Human Rights', 27 *CML Rev.* 249.

SCHEUNER, U. (1971), 'Fundamental Rights and the Protection of the Individual against Social Groups and Powers in the Constitutional System of the Federal Republic of Germany', in *René Cassin*, iii. 253.

SCHWARTZ, I. E. (1990), 'La liberté d'expression (Art. 10 CEDH) et la libre prestation des services (Art. 59 Traité de CEE) dans le domaine de la radiodiffusion télévisuelle', in Cassese and Clapham (1990: 165).

SCHWARZE, J. (1986a) (ed.), *Perspectives for the Development of Judicial Protection in the European Community* (Baden-Baden: Nomos).

—— (1986b) 'The Administrative Law of the European Community and the Protection of Human Rights', *CML Rev.* 401.

SCHWELB, E. (1966), 'The International Convention on the Elimination of All Forms of Racial Discrimination', *ICLQ* 996.

SEDLEY, S. (1986), 'Where Next?', in Cooper and Dhavan (1986: 415).

SEIGHART, P. (1983), *The International Law of Human Rights* (Oxford: Clarendon Press).

SHATZ, B. (1987), 'The Aids Insurance Crisis: Underwriting or Overreaching?', 100 *Harvard Law Rev.* 1782.

SHEINGOLD, S. A. (1988), 'Radical Lawyers and Socialist Ideas', *Journal of Law and Society*, 122.

SHELTON, D. (1990), 'Private Violence, Public Wrongs, and the Responsibility of States', 13 *Fordham Journal of International Law*, 1.

SMITH, R. (1991), 'Where's the Beef?', *NLJ* 120.

SPARER, E. (1984), 'Fundamental Rights, Legal Entitlements, and the Social Struggle: A Friendly Critique of the Critical Legal Studies Movement', 36(1) *Stanford Law Review*, 509.

SPERDUTI, G. (1975), 'Osservazione sui ricorsi individuali alla Commissione europea dei diritti dell'uomo', in *Il processo internazionale: Studi in onore di Gaetano Morelli*, Comunicazione e studi dell'Istituto di Diritto Internazionale e Straniero dell'Università di Milano (Milan: Giuffrè), 818.

—— (1976), 'Nouvelles Perspectives des droits de l'homme', *RDH/HRJ* 575.

—— (1984), 'L'Article 6 de la Convention europèenne des droits de l'homme et les décisions administratives internes affectant des droits de caractère civil', in Swinarski (1984: 813).

—— (1986), 'Recenti sviluppi nella giurisprudenza della Commissione e della Corte Europea dei Diritti dell'Uomo', *Rivista di diritto internazionale*, 814.

SPIELMANN, D. F. (1990), 'The Potential Applicability between Non-State Persons of the Provisions of the European Convention on Human Rights', unpublished LLM thesis (Cambridge University) on file at the Human Rights Library, Council of Europe, Strasbourg.

STARCK, C. (1982), 'Europe's Fundamental Rights in their Newest Garb', *HRLJ* 103.

SUDRE, F. (1990), 'La Première Décision "quart-monde" de la Commission Européenne: Une "bavure" dans la jurisprudence dynamique/Affaire Van Volsen', *RUDH* 349.

SUPIOT, A. (1987), 'Actualité de Durkheim: Notes sur le néocorporatisme en France', *Droit et société*, 177.

SWINARSKI, C. (1984) (ed.), *Studies and Essays in International Humanitarian Law and Red Cross Principles: Essays in Honour of Jean Pictet* (The Hague: Martinus Nijhoff).

SWINTON, K. (1982), 'Application of the Canadian Charter of Rights and Freedoms', in Tarnopolski and Beaudoin (1982: 41).

SYMMONS, C. (1983), 'The Effect of the European Convention on Human Rights on the Preparation and Amendment of Legislation, Delegated Legislation and Administrative Rules in the United Kingdom', in Furmston, Kerridge, and Surfin (1983).

TARNOPOLSKI, W. S. (1983), 'The New Canadian Charter of Rights and Freedoms as Compared and Contrasted with the American Bill of Rights', *HRQ* 227.

—— and BEAUDOIN, G. (1982) (eds.), *The Canadian Charter of Rights and Freedoms* (Toronto: Carswell).

TAUB, N., and SCHNEIDER, E. M. (1982), 'Perspectives on Women's Subordination and the Role of Law', in Kairys (1982: 117).

TETTENBORN, A. M. (1987), 'Universities: A Boost for Free Speech?', *NLJ* 1021.

TEUBNER, G. (1987) (ed.), *Juridification of Social Spheres* (Berlin: Walter de Gruyter).

THOROLD, O. (1982), 'Britain: Facing another Caning from Europe', *The Times* (2 Mar. 1982).

TREGILGAS-DAVEY, M. (1991), '*Ex Parte Choudhury*: An Opportunity Missed', *MLR* 294.

TRIBE, L. H. (1978), *American Constitutional Law* (New York: Foundation Press).

—— (1985), *Constitutional Choices* (Cambridge, Mass.: Harvard University Press).

—— (1987), 'Contrasting Constitutional Visions', 22 *Harv. CR-CLL Rev.* 95.

TSAKIRIDIS, P. (1988), *Das Recht der Meinungsäußerungsfreiheit nach Artikel 10 der Europäischen Menschenrechtskonvention die Frage seiner Drittwirkung* (Frankfurt: Verlag Peter Lang).

VALLET, F. (1972) (ed.), *An Introduction to Human Rights* (London: Europa).

VAN BOVEN, T. (1982), 'Distinguishing Criteria of Human Rights', in K. Vasak (ed.), *The International Dimensions of Human Rights* (Westport, Conn.: Greenwood Press), 43.

―― (1989), 'The Future of Human Rights in Europe', 1 *Netherlands Quarterly of Human Rights*, 6.

VAN DIJK, P. (1987), 'The Benthem Case and its Aftermath in the Netherlands', *NILR* 5.

―― (1988), 'The Interpretation of "Civil Rights and Obligations" by the European Court of Human Rights: One More Step to Take', in Matscher and Petzold (1988: 134).

―― and VAN HOOF, G. J. H. (1984), *Theory and Practice of the European Convention on Human Rights* (Deventer: Kluwer Law and Taxation Publishers).

―― ―― (1990), *Theory and Practice of the European Convention on Human Rights* (2nd edn. Deventer: Kluwer Law and Taxation Publishers).

VELU, J. (1970), 'Article 6 of the European Convention on Human Rights in Belgian Law', *AJCL* 259.

―― (1981), 'Les Effets directs des instruments internationaux en matière des droits de l'homme', in *L'Effet direct en droit belge des traités internationaux en général et des instruments relatifs aux droits de l'homme en particulier*, Société Belge de Droit International, réunion d'études à Wilrijk, 7 Nov. 1980 (Brussels: Bruylant), 293.

―― (1986), 'Essential Elements for a Legal Regime Governing Public Liability for Judicial Acts', *Judicial Power and Public Liability*, 77.

―― (1990), 'Convention européenne des droits de l'homme', in *Répertoire pratigue du droit belge*, vii (Brussels: Bruylant), 138.

VINCENT, R. J. (1986) (ed.), *Foreign Policy and Human Rights* (Cambridge: Cambridge University Press).

WACKS, R. (1988), 'Controlling AIDS: Some Legal Issues―Part I', *NLJ* 254.

WALDRON, J. (1984) (ed.), *Theories of Rights* (Oxford: Oxford University Press).

WALLINGTON, P. (1984) (ed.), *Civil Liberties 1984* (Oxford: Martin Robertson).

―― and McBRIDE, J. (1976), *Civil Liberties and a Bill of Rights* (London: Cobden Trust).

WARBRICK, C. (1980), 'European Convention of Human Rights and English Law', *NLJ* 852.

―― (1983), 'The European Convention on Human Rights and the Prevention of Terrorism', *ICLQ* 82.

―― (1989), ' "Federal" Aspects of the European Convention on Human Rights', 10 *Michigan Journal of International Law*, 698.

WARNOCK, M. (1985), *A Question of Life* (Oxford: Basil Blackwell).

WEDDERBURN, Lord (1986), *The Worker and the Law* (3rd edn. London: Sweet & Maxwell).

――(1987), 'Labour Law from here to Autonomy?', *ILJ* 1.

WEILER, J. H. H. (1986), 'Eurocracy and Distrust: Some Questions Concerning the Role of the European Court of Justice in the Protection of Fundamental Human Rights within the Legal Order of the European Communities', 61 *Washington Law Review*, 1103.

—— (1991), 'Methods of Protection: Towards a Second and Third Generation of Protection', in A. Cassese, A. Clapham, and J. H. H. Weiler (eds.), *European Union: The Human Rights Challenge*, ii: *Human Rights and the European Community: Methods of Protection* (Baden-Baden: Nomos), 555.

WILLIAMS, A. (1977), 'The European Convention on Human Rights: A New Use', 12 *Texas International Law Journal*, 279.

WRIGHT, A. (1986), 'The Politics of Constitutional Reform', *PQ* 414.

ZANDER, M. (1985), *A Bill of Rights?* (3rd edn. London: Sweet & Maxwell).

ZANGHI, G. (1971), 'La Protection des droits de l'homme dans les rapports entre personnes privées (Italie)', in *René Cassin*, iii. 269.

CONFERENCES AND COLLOQUIA

'Aspects of Incorporation of the European Convention on Human Rights into Domestic Law', conference organized by the British Institute of Human Rights and the British Institute of International and Comparative Law, 11–12 May 1991 (unpublished at the time of writing).

'A Bill of Rights for the U.K.?', conference on the Incorporation of the European Convention on Human Rights (29 Jan. 1987), organized by the NCCL, the Cobden Trust, and the Rights Campaign, held at the City Conference Centre, London (unpublished at the time of writing).

Colloquy about the European Convention on Human Rights in Relation to Other International Instruments for the Protection of Human Rights, Athens, 21–2 Sept. 1978 (Strasbourg: Council of Europe, 1979).

The European Convention on Human Rights: Two New Directions, EEC:UK, conference, King's College, London, 15 Feb. 1980 (mimeograph available from British Institute of Human Rights, 1980).

The Implementation in National Law of the European Convention on Human Rights, Proceedings of the Fourth Copenhagen Conference on Human Rights, 28–9 Oct. 1988 (Copenhagen: Danish Centre for Human Rights, 1989).

Judicial Power and Public Liability, Fifteenth Colloquy on European Law, held Bordeaux, 17–19 June 1985 (Strasbourg: Council of Europe, 1986).

La Protection internationale des droits de l'homme dans le cadre européen (Travaux du Colloque de Strasbourg de november 1960) (Paris: Dalloz, 1961).

Les Devoirs de l'homme: Les Actes du Vème coloque interdisciplinaire de Freibourg, 1987 (Freibourg: Éditions Universitaires, 1989).

Les Droits de l'homme et les personnes morales: Premier colloque du Département des Droits de l'Homme, Université Catholique de Louvain, 24 Oct. 1969 (Brussels: Bruylant, 1970).

Parliamentary Conference on Human Rights, Vienna, 18–20 Oct. 1971 (Strasbourg: Council of Europe, 1972).

Perspectives for the Development of Judicial Protection in the European Community, conference held at the EUI, 30–1 Oct. 1986; see Schwarze (1986a).

WAALDIJK, K., and CLAPHAM, A. (eds.) *Homosexuality: A European Community Law* (Dordrecht, Nijhoff, 1993).

Index